CHRISTIAN PUBLICATIONS, INC.
CAMP HILL, PENNSYLVANIA

CHRISTIAN PUBLICATIONS, INC.
3825 Hartzdale Drive, Camp Hill, PA 17011
www.christianpublications.com

Faithful, biblical publishing since 1883

Voices in Worship: Hymns of the Christian Life
PEW EDITION
ISBN: 0-87509-981-5

Printed in the United States of America

05 06 07 08 6 5 4 3

Pew Edition: 0-87509-981-5
Accompanist Edition: 0-87509-982-3
Worship Team Edition: 0-87509-983-1
Software Edition: 0-87509-996-3

Foreword

God loves music—all kinds of music. He's not partial to a particular style any more than He is partial to a particular culture or ethnic group. He created variety!

The Israelites enjoyed singing hymns of praise to Yahweh to commemorate significant events, special days and the remarkable acts of their Creator. The psalmist filled a book with songs of devotion and adoration to the Lord. First-century cities like Jerusalem, Antioch and Ephesus were filled with the songs of the early Church Christians. The people of God always have been a singing community.

Alliance Christians have been part of this living tradition of the Church. From the days when Dr. A.B. Simpson's hymns were sung for the first time, through the 1950s and 1960s when the Council Preacher's Chorus was at its height, and up to present times when worship bands and vocalists line the platforms of most C&MA churches, music continues to be an integral part of our worship experience.

Voices in Worship has been prepared with God's glory in view. It is intended to help sincere worshipers to *enter His gates with thanksgiving and His courts with praise.* Acknowledging the creative nature of God, this collection of songs focuses on a variety of styles and rhythms. People of all ages and cultures are encouraged to lift their voices in praise to the Savior in ways that express their deep and fervent love for Him.

After all, this is why we sing. It's not for our own pleasure or enjoyment. We sing to God—for He alone is worthy of our praise.

May this new hymnal be used by God to release an explosion of worship in honor of King Jesus as we joyfully anticipate His soon return.

Dr. Peter Nanfelt, president
The Christian and Missionary Alliance
Colorado Springs, Colorado

Preface

In 1891 A.B. Simpson compiled the very first hymnal for The Christian and Missionary Alliance. He opened the preface with these sentences: "The musical taste of our day is in a state of transition. Beyond controversy, the people *will* have new tunes and hymns that move in a more spirited time than those our fathers sang." More than a century and seven hymnals later, this statement is still remarkably true. Significant changes have taken place in Christian worship since the 1978 *Hymns of the Christian Life* was published. Many fresh, new songs have been written, worship leadership styles and instrumental accompaniments have changed and electronic projection has been added to the printed page as a means of providing lyrics for the congregation. Indeed, the musical taste of the twenty-first-century Church is still "in a state of transition."

Many churches now use both traditional and contemporary music in their services, a blend that best serves their diverse congregations. *Voices in Worship* was designed to meet the needs of these blended churches, helping worshipers to glorify God with both time-tested hymns and Scripturally faithful songs from today's generation.

We believe the twenty-first-century Church still needs a collection of hymns and songs that are both carefully compiled and theologically sound. As Christ-followers we "sing our theology," and so it is essential that a good modern hymnal express our Christian faith in all its truth and breadth, using "psalms, hymns and spiritual songs" (Colossians 3:16). Further, a good modern hymnal should be faithful to the distinctives of the church family it serves, and so *Voices in Worship* emphasizes Alliance themes of the deeper life, missions and the fourfold gospel of Jesus Christ as Savior, Sanctifier, Healer and Coming King. It has been prepared for use in the U.S., Canada and other English-speaking countries by Christian Publications, Inc., the publishing arm of The Christian and Missionary Alliance.

It is the prayer of the hymnal revision team that this new worship resource in its four editions (pew, accompanist, worship team and software) will be a valuable asset for church services, events and small groups in both the Alliance and the wider Church family. It is our further prayer that individual believers will use it in their homes to enhance their personal worship of God. We humbly present *Voices in Worship: Hymns of the Christian Life* for His greater honor and glory.

Dr. Gene Rivard, executive director
Hymnal Executive Committee

Speak to one another with psalms, hymns and spiritual songs.
Sing and make music in your heart to the Lord. Ephesians 5:19

Acknowledgments

Hymnal Executive Committee
Richard Brust, chairman
Dr. Gene Rivard, executive director
Linda Rivard, administrative assistant
Helen Young
Scott Simpson
David E. Kucharsky
Rev. George McPeek

New Materials Committee
Scott Simpson, chairman
Rev. Doug Anthony
Jennifer Bliss-Huston
Diane Bowker
Dan Dinkler
Rev. Jim Jensen
Rev. Gene Vincent
Rev. Kelvin Walker
Steve Yost

Music
Richard Brust

Medley Transition Composers
Scott Simpson
Rev. Bill Fasig†

Arrangers
David Hahn
Eldon McBride
Tim Shuey
Scott Simpson
Rev. Bill Fasig†

Guitar Chords
David Hahn

Scripture Readings
Rev. George McPeek

Inspirational Readings
David E. Kucharsky

Theology Committee
Rev. Paul Hazlett
Dr. Rexford Boda
Rev. Gordon Cathey
Dr. K. Neill Foster

Psalms Consultant
Dr. Mark Boda

Typesetting/Engraving
Kyle Hill, Music Production Services

Layout
Linda Rivard
Dr. Gene Rivard
Laurie Gustafson

Proofreading
Helen Young, music
Rev. James Meadows, texts
Gretchen Nesbit
Joan Brust
Richard Brust
Scott Simpson
Tim Shuey
Laurie Gustafson

Board of Directors, Christian Publications, Inc.
Rev. Terry Truffin, chairman
Dennis Bayes
Richard Bond
Larry Brown
Rev. Randy Corbin
Ray Kincaid
Rev. Joseph Kong
David E. Kucharsky
Rev. Angel Ortiz
Rev. David Presher
Dr. Melvin Vance
Elizabeth White

Presidents, Christian Publications, Inc.
Rev. Ken Paton
Dr. K. Neill Foster, past president

The publisher is grateful for the many people who participated in the surveys and seminars, and who submitted materials for this hymnal.

† *deceased*

New Features

Contents

Voices in Worship is an extensive revision of the 1978 Christian and Missionary Alliance hymnal, *Hymns of the Christian Life*. From this source 359 selections were chosen, while 255 new songs and hymns were added.

In 2001 and 2002 members of the Alliance family were asked for suggestions and submissions, and many were made. The New Materials Committee, comprised of church musicians from the U.S. and Canada, brought other suggestions from a variety of contemporary sources. From this wide base of both new and familiar congregational music, the Hymnal Executive Committee attempted to glean worthy expressions of worship which demonstrate that rare quality of endurance and which are widely used in churches today. In addition, the committee is pleased to introduce eleven new songs that appear for the first time in *Voices in Worship*, written especially for this collection.

Fifty-nine Scripture readings are now interspersed throughout the hymnal and have been reformatted to assist in congregational response. Sixty-five scripted Psalms now appear in a topically arranged index as well.

New to this hymnal are inspirational readings and prayers from many classic sources as well as the writings of A.B. Simpson and A.W. Tozer.

Revisions

Updated Texts

Many words that are no longer in modern usage have been updated. For some hymns this affected few words, while others needed more careful reworking. Some were not changed at all if it meant a total rewriting of the poetry. The intent was to make these hymns more accessible to this generation's worshiper without affecting their meaning. For hymns that are widely known and loved in their present form no changes were made.

Footnotes

Archaic words, terms or difficult phrases are now footnoted to assist singing with understanding.

Lowered Keys

Many keys have been lowered to aid congregational singing. Some key changes took into consideration the instruments used in today's worship teams.

Medleys and Segues

To assist those who use "free-flowing style," many medleys were constructed with newly written transitions. *Voices in Worship* also includes many *segues*, or songs which can be played smoothly in succession with no need for a transition.

A.B. Simpson Hymn Revisions

Many people asked for musical revisions to the hymns of A.B. Simpson, founder of The Christian and Missionary Alliance. His songs have always been appreciated for their deeply spiritual texts, and many now have newly written melodies. Some have new arrangements, while others are now paired with easy-to-sing or familiar tunes.

Guitar Chords for the Accompanist and Worship Team Editions

A professional guitarist constructed chord symbols for *every* hymn and song in the hymnal, with capo suggestions for flat keys. There is a tablature chart index in both the accompanist and worship team editions.

Format Features

In songs with five or more verses, the middle verse appears in *italics* to help the singers keep their places. Suggested instrumental introductions are clearly marked.

Four Editions

Voices in Worship is now available in pew, accompanist, worship team and software editions.

Table of Contents

God, The Holy Trinity 1-19

God, The Father
His Nature 20-27
His Creation, Providence and Redemption 28-44
His Praise 45-71

God, The Son
His Advent 72-80
His Nativity 81-108
His Epiphany 109-112
His Life and Ministry 113-124
Palm Sunday 125-130
His Sufferings and Death 131-154
His Resurrection and Exaltation 155-180
His Coming in Glory 181-198
His Praise 199-236

God, The Holy Spirit 237-253

The Life in Christ
Confession and Repentance 254-261
Redemption and Salvation 262-275
Faith, Peace and Joy 276-288
Sanctification, Consecration and the Deeper Life 289-338
Trust and Submission 339-364
Pilgrimage, Protection and Guidance 365-391
Spiritual Conflict and Victory 392-406
Divine Healing 407-419
Death, Resurrection and Life Everlasting 420-435
Prayer 436-447
Love and Gratitude 448-472

The Body of Christ
The Church 473-482
Fellowship of Believers 483-487
The Word of God 488-496
Stewardship 497-500
Ministry and Service 501-515
Missions 516-559
Testimony 560-594
Evangelism and Invitation 595-615
Gathering and Dismissal 616-627
The Lord's Supper 628-639
Baptism 640-644

Dedication of Children 645-650
Family Life and Relationships 651-656

Special Times and Seasons
Thanksgiving 657-664
God and Country 665-673

Psalms 674-734

Pages

Worship Helps
Calls to Worship 769
Invocations 769
Offertory Sentences 770
Benedictions 770
Words of Pardon 771
The Apostles' Creed 771
The Nicene Creed 772
The Ten Commandments 772

Indexes
Copyright Owners and Administrators 773
Responsive Scripture Readings
Titles 775
Scripture References 775
Inspirational Readings and Prayers 776
Medleys 777
Segues 778
Alphabetical Index of Tunes 779
Metrical Index of Tunes 782
Authors, Translators, Composers, Arrangers and Sources 784
Scriptural Allusions 791
Topical Index 794
Titles and First Lines 803

Glory Be to God the Father 1

. . . the Father, the Word, and the Holy Spirit; and these three are one. 1 John 5:7, NKJV

1. Glo - ry be to God the Fa - ther, Glo - ry be to
2. Glo - ry be to Him who loved us, Washed us from each
3. Glo - ry to the King of an - gels, Glo - ry to the
4. "Glo - ry, bless - ing, praise e - ter - nal!" Thus the choir of

God the Son, Glo - ry be to God the Spir - it,
spot and stain! Glo - ry be to Him who bought us,
Church's King, Glo - ry to the King of na - tions!
an - gels sings; "Ho - nor, rich - es, power, do - min - ion!"

Great Je - ho - vah, Three - in - One! Glo - ry, glo - ry,
Made us kings with Him to reign! Glo - ry, glo - ry,
Heaven and earth, your prais - es bring; Glo - ry, glo - ry,
Thus its praise cre - a - tion brings; Glo - ry, glo - ry,

glo - ry, glo - ry, While e - ter - nal a - ges run!
glo - ry, glo - ry, To the Lamb that once was slain!
glo - ry, glo - ry, To the King of glo - ry bring!
glo - ry, glo - ry, Glo - ry to the King of kings!

WORDS: Horatius Bonar, 1808-1889
MUSIC: Henry T. Smart, 1813-1879

REGENT SQUARE
8.7.8.7.8.7.

OUR GOD IS HOLY

MEDLEY

Holy, Holy, Holy, Lord God Almighty
Hide Me in Your Holiness

2 Holy, Holy, Holy, Lord God Almighty

. . . who was, and is, and is to come. Revelation 4:8

1. Ho-ly, ho-ly, ho - ly! Lord God Al - might - y!
2. Ho-ly, ho-ly, ho - ly! all the saints a - dore Thee,
3. Ho-ly, ho-ly, ho - ly! though the dark-ness hide Thee,
4. Ho-ly, ho-ly, ho - ly! Lord God Al - might - y!
Ear - ly in the morn - ing our song shall rise to Thee;
Cast - ing down their gold - en crowns a - round the glass - y sea;
Though the eye of sin - ful man Thy glo - ry may not see.
All Thy works shall praise Thy name in earth, and sky, and sea;
Ho - ly, ho - ly, ho - ly, mer - ci - ful and might - y!
Cher - u - bim and ser - a - phim1 fall - ing down be - fore Thee,
On - ly Thou art ho - ly, there is none be - side Thee,
Ho - ly, ho - ly, ho - ly, mer - ci - ful and might - y!
God in three Per - sons, bless - ed Trin - i - ty!
Which wert, and art, and ev - er - more shalt be.
Per - fect in power, in love and pur - i - ty.
God in three Per - sons, bless - ed Trin - i - ty!

WORDS: Reginald Heber, 1783-1826
MUSIC: John B. Dykes, 1823-1876

NICAEA
11.12.12.10.

1. cherubim and seraphim: angelic beings surrounding the throne of God

Optional modulation
Optional stanza 4
4. Ho - ly, ho - ly, ho - ly! Lord God Al -
might - y! All Thy works shall praise Thy name in earth, and sky, and
sea; Ho - ly, ho - ly, ho - ly, mer - ci - ful and
might - y! God in three Per - sons, bless - ed Trin - i -
ty!
Optional transition to "Hide Me in Your Holiness"
rit.

3 Hide Me in Your Holiness

Hide me in the shadow of your wings. Psalm 17:8

Hide me, Lord, in Your ho - li - ness,
Ev - ery sin I now con - fess.
Praise to You, for - giv - ing Lord,
Hide me in Your ho - li - ness,
Hide me in Your ho - li - ness.

WORDS: Steve Ragsdale, 20th century
MUSIC: Steve Ragsdale, 20th century

HIDE ME
Irregular

Come, Thou Almighty King 4

The LORD is the great God, the great King. Psalm 95:3

1. Come, Thou Al - might - y King, Help us Thy name to sing, Help us to praise. Fa - ther, all - glo - ri - ous, O'er all vic - to - ri - ous, Come, and reign o - ver us, An - cient of Days.[1]
2. Come, Thou In - car - nate Word, Gird on Thy might - y sword, Our prayer at - tend: Come, and Thy peo - ple bless, And give Thy Word suc - cess. Spir - it of ho - li - ness, On us de - scend.
3. Come, Ho - ly Com - for - ter, Thy sa - cred wit - ness bear In this glad hour: Thou, who al - might - y art, Now rule in ev - ery heart, And ne'er from us de - part, Spir - it of power.
4. To Thee, great One - in - Three, E - ter - nal prais - es be Hence ev - er - more. Thy sov - ereign ma - jes - ty May we in glo - ry see, And to e - ter - ni - ty Love and a - dore.

WORDS: Anonymous, circa 1757
MUSIC: Felice de Giardini, 1716-1796

ITALIAN HYMN
6.6.4.6.6.6.4.

1. *Ancient of Days: a name for God in Daniel 7:9*

TRINITY AS FAMILY

There is in the divine Trinity a personality corresponding to human relationships. Human fatherhood expresses a need which is met in God the Father. Human motherhood has its origin in the Holy Spirit. Human brotherhood, and the higher, closer fellowship of the husband and the bridegroom are met in Christ, the Son of God, our Brother and our Bridegroom. We cannot reason out the divine Trinity, but God can make it real to our spiritual instincts.

A.B. Simpson (1843-1919), *The Holy Spirit*

5 Holy God, We Praise Your Name

And they were calling to one another: "Holy, holy, holy is the LORD Almighty; the whole earth is full of his glory." Isaiah 6:3

1. Ho - ly God, we praise Your name; Lord of all, we
2. Hark, the loud ce - les - tial[2] hymn An - gel choirs a -
3. Lo! the ap - os - tol - ic train[4] Join Your sa - cred
4. Ho - ly Fa - ther, Ho - ly Son, Ho - ly Spir - it—
bow be - fore You; All on earth Your scep - ter[1] claim,
bove are rais - ing; Cher - u - bim and ser - a - phim[3]
name to hal - low; Proph - ets swell the glad re - frain,
Three we name You; Though in es - sence on - ly one,
All in heav-en a - bove a - dore You. In - fi - nite Your
In un - ceas - ing cho - rus prais - ing, Fill the heavens with
And the white - robed mar - tyrs fol - low; And from morn to
Un - di - vid - ed God we claim You, And a - dor - ing
vast do - main, Ev - er - last - ing is Your reign.
sweet ac - cord: Ho - ly, ho - ly, ho - ly Lord.
set of sun, Through the church the song goes on.
bend the knee While we own the mys - ter - y.

WORDS: Attrib. Ignace Franz, 1719-1790
tr. Clarence A. Walworth, 1820-1900, alt.; para. *Te Deum*, 4th century
MUSIC: From *Katholisches Gesangbuch*, 1774

GROSSER GOTT, WIR LOBEN DICH
7.8.7.8.7.7.

1. *scepter: ceremonial rod or staff of royalty*
2. *celestial: heavenly*
3. *cherubim and serephim: angelic beings surrounding the throne of God*
4. *apostolic train: procession of saints, elders, apostles*

Doxology 6

For since the creation of the world [God's] invisible attributes are clearly seen . . . even His eternal power and Godhead. Romans 1:20, NKJV

Praise God from whom all bless-ings flow; Praise Him, all crea-tures here be-low;
Praise Him a-bove, ye heaven-ly host; Praise Fa-ther, Son and Ho-ly Ghost. A-men.

WORDS: Thomas Ken, 1637-1711
MUSIC: *Geneva Psalter,* 1551, attrib. Louis Bourgeois, 1510-1561

OLD HUNDREDTH
L.M.

Father, Son and Holy Spirit 7

Then Jesus came from Galilee to the Jordan to be baptized by John. But John tried to deter him, saying, "I need to be baptized by you, and do you come to me?" Jesus replied, "Let it be so now; it is proper for us to do this to fulfill all righteousness." Then John consented. As soon as Jesus was baptized, he went up out of the water. At that moment heaven was opened, and he saw the Spirit of God descending like a dove and lighting on him. And a voice from heaven said, "This is my Son, whom I love; with him I am well pleased."

Matthew 3:13-17

[Jesus said:]"All this I have spoken while still with you. But the Counselor, the Holy Spirit, whom the Father will send in my name, will teach you all things and will remind you of everything I have said to you." *John 14:25-26*

Then the eleven disciples went to Galilee, to the mountain where Jesus had told them to go. When they saw him, they worshiped him; but some doubted. Then Jesus came to them and said, "All authority in heaven and on earth has been given to me. Therefore go and make disciples of all nations, baptizing them in the name of the Father and of the Son and of the Holy Spirit, and teaching them to obey everything I have commanded you. And surely I am with you always, to the very end of the age." *Matthew 28:16-20*

8 Praise Ye the Triune God

Praise your name for your love and your faithfulness. Psalm 138:2

1. Praise ye the Fa - ther for His lov - ing kind - ness, Ten - der - ly
2. Praise ye the Sav - ior– great is His com - pas - sion, Gra - cious - ly
3. Praise ye the Spir - it, Com - fort - er of Is - rael, Sent of the

cares He for His err - ing chil - dren; Praise Him, ye an - gels,
cares He for His cho - sen peo - ple; Young men and maid - ens,
Fa - ther and the Son to bless us; Praise ye the Fa - ther,

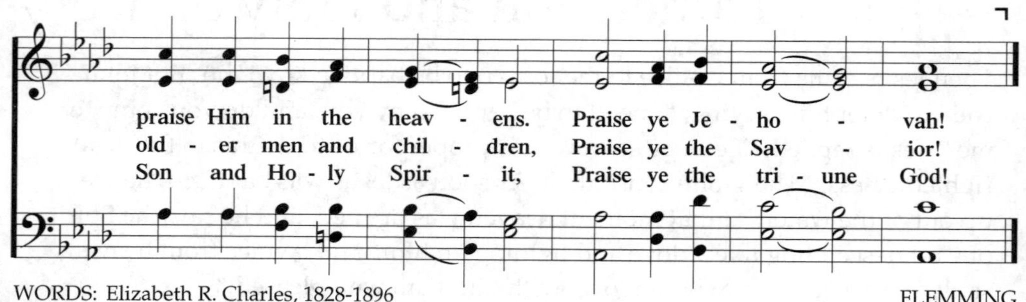
praise Him in the heav - ens. Praise ye Je - ho - vah!
old - er men and chil - dren, Praise ye the Sav - ior!
Son and Ho - ly Spir - it, Praise ye the tri - une God!

WORDS: Elizabeth R. Charles, 1828-1896
MUSIC: Friedrich F. Flemming, 1778-1813

FLEMMING
11.11.11.5.

WE LIVE AND MOVE IN GOD

Almighty God in whom we live and move and have our being,
You have made us for Yourself, so that our hearts are restless until they rest in You;
grant us purity of heart and strength of purpose, that no selfish passion may hinder us
from knowing Your will, no weakness from doing it; but that in Your light we may see
light clearly, and in Your service find our perfect freedom; through Jesus Christ our Lord.

Augustine (345-430)

Glory Be to God the Father 9

My soul glorifies the Lord and my spirit rejoices in God my Savior. Luke 1:46-47

1. Glo-ry be to God, the Fa-ther; Yah-weh's ho-ly name we bless;
2. Glo-ry be to God, the Son, Our great Re-deem-er, Sav-ior, Friend;
3. Glo-ry be to God, the Spir-it, To our Com-fort-er and Guide;
Sov-ereign o-ver all cre-a-tion, Full of grace and right-eous-ness.
Though in es-sence with the Fa-ther, To our like-ness did de-scend.
Breath of Life, the Liv-ing Wa-ter, Ev-er with us to a-bide.
Who to God His might has giv-en? Who has been His coun-sel-lor?
Made Him-self to be our ser-vant, Died for our un-right-eous-ness;
We may share His joy and full-ness, Bap-tized with the Ho-ly Ghost;
None can know His wealth of wis-dom. Praise His name for-ev-er-more.
Now as Lord in heaven ex-alt-ed, So shall ev-ery tongue con-fess.
Freed from sin to life vic-tor-ious By the power of Pen-te-cost.

WORDS: T. Lynn Sloan, b. 1966
MUSIC: T. Lynn Sloan, b. 1966

GLORY TO GOD
8.7.8.7.D.

10 Glory Be to the Father

Ascribe to the LORD the glory due his name. Psalm 96:8

Glo - ry be to the Fa - ther, And to the Son, and to the Ho - ly Ghost; As it was in the be - gin - ning, Is now and ev - er shall be, World with - out end, A - men, A - men.

WORDS: Latin, 2nd century
MUSIC: Henry W. Greatorex, 1813-1858

GLORIA PATRI
Irregular

11 Be Thou Exalted

O LORD . . . we will sing and praise your might. Psalm 21:13

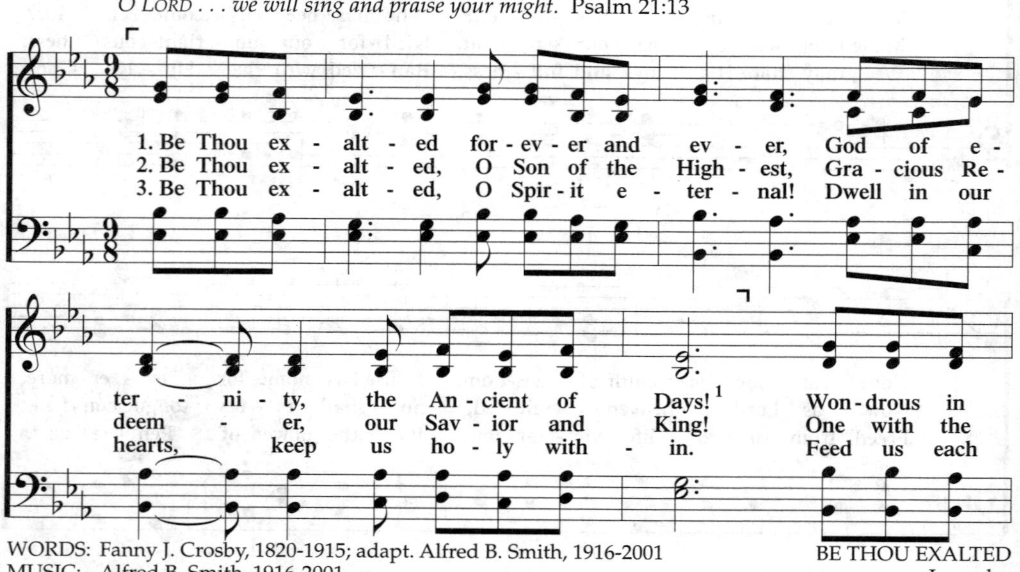
1. Be Thou ex - alt - ed for - ev - er and ev - er, God of e - ter - ni - ty, the An - cient of Days![1] Won - drous in
2. Be Thou ex - alt - ed, O Son of the High - est, Gra - cious Re - deem - er, our Sav - ior and King! One with the
3. Be Thou ex - alt - ed, O Spir - it e - ter - nal! Dwell in our hearts, keep us ho - ly with - in. Feed us each

WORDS: Fanny J. Crosby, 1820-1915; adapt. Alfred B. Smith, 1916-2001
MUSIC: Alfred B. Smith, 1916-2001

BE THOU EXALTED
Irregular

1. *Ancient of Days: name of God in Daniel 7:9*

maj - es - ty, so might - y in wis - dom, Per - fect in
Fa - ther, co - e - qual in glo - ry, Here at Thy
day with Thy heav - en - ly man - na. Heal - er of
ho - li - ness and worth - y of praise.
foot - stool our hom - age we bring.
wound - ed hearts, Thy prais - es we sing.
Refrain
Be Thou ex -
alt - ed by ser - aphs2 and an - gels, Be Thou ex -
alt - ed with harp and with song. Saints in their
an - thems3 of rap - ture a - dore Thee, Thine be the
glo - ry for - ev - er, A - men.

2. *seraphs: angelic beings surrounding the throne of God*
3. *anthems: songs*

12 Holy, Holy, Holy Is the Lord of Hosts

Holy, holy, holy is the LORD Almighty; the whole earth is full of his glory. Isaiah 6:3

Ho - ly, ho - ly, ho - ly is the Lord of hosts.
Ho - ly, ho - ly, ho - ly is the Lord of hosts. The
whole earth is full of His glo - ry, The whole earth is full of His glo - ry, The
whole earth is full of His glo - ry. Ho - ly is the Lord.

Optional segue to "Glory Be to God, Creator." No transition required.

WORDS: Nolene Prince, 20th century
MUSIC: Nolene Prince, 20th century

PRINCE
Irregular

Glory Be to God, Creator 13

The heavens declare the glory of God; the skies proclaim the work of his hands. Psalm 19:1

1. Glo - ry be to God, Cre - a - tor, Glo - ry be to God the Son, Glo - ry be to God the Spir - it, Known as Three, yet God the One.
2. As it was in the be - gin - ning, It is now and so shall be In a world with - out an end - ing, Glo - ry through e - ter - ni - ty.
3. Ho - ly, ho - ly God Al - might - y, Ho - ly, ho - ly Prince of Peace, Ho - ly, ho - ly Wind of Pres - ence, Ho - ly, ho - ly, ho - ly. A - men.
1, 2.
3.

WORDS: Richard K. Carlson, b. 1956
MUSIC: Richard K. Carlson, b. 1956

RENEWED
8.7.8.7.

THE TRINITY

The Father was neither made nor created nor begotten from anyone. The Son was neither made nor created; He was begotten from the Father alone. The Holy Spirit was neither made nor created nor begotten; He proceeds from the Father and the Son. . . . Nothing in this trinity is before or after, nothing is greater or smaller; in their entirety the three persons are coeternal and coequal with each other. So in everything, we must worship their trinity in their unity and their unity in their trinity.

From the *Athanasian Creed*

14 Holy, Holy

You alone are holy. All nations will come and worship before you. Revelation 15:4

1. Ho - ly, ho - ly, ho - ly, ho - ly, Ho - ly, ho - ly Lord God Al - might - y; And we lift our hearts be - fore You as a to - ken of our love, Ho - ly, ho - ly, ho - ly, ho - ly.
2. Gra - cious Fa - ther, gra - cious Fa - ther, We're so blest to be Your chil - dren, gra - cious Fa - ther; And we lift our heads be - fore You as a to - ken of our love, Gra - cious Fa - ther, gra - cious Fa - ther.
3. Pre - cious Je - sus, pre - cious Je - sus, We're so glad that You've re - deemed us, pre - cious Je - sus; And we lift our hands be - fore You as a to - ken of our love, Pre - cious Je - sus, pre - cious Je - sus.
4. Ho - ly Spir - it, Ho - ly Spir - it, Come and fill our hearts a - new, Ho - ly Spir - it; And we lift our voice be - fore You as a to - ken of our love, Ho - ly Spir - it, Ho - ly Spir - it.
5. Hal - le - lu - jah, hal - le - lu - jah, Hal - le - lu - jah, hal - le - lu - jah; And we lift our hearts be - fore You as a to - ken of our love, Hal - le - lu - jah, hal - le - lu - jah.

WORDS: Jimmy Owens, b. 1930
MUSIC: Jimmy Owens, b. 1930

HOLY, HOLY
Irregular

O Splendor of God's Glory Bright 15

The true light that gives light to every man was coming into the world. John 1:9

1. O splen - dor of God's glo - ry bright From light e - ter - nal bring - ing light; O Light of light, the foun - tain spring, O Day, all days il - lu - min - ing.
2. O come, true Sun[1] of heav - en's love, In last - ing ra - diance from a - bove, And pour the Ho - ly Spir - it's ray On all we think or do to - day.
3. Con - firm our will to do the right, And keep our hearts from en - vy's blight; Let faith her ea - ger fires re - new, And hate the false, and love the true.
4. All praise to God the Fa - ther be, All praise the Son e - ter - nal - ly, Whom with the Spir - it we a - dore For - ev - er and for - ev - er - more.

WORDS: Ambrose of Milan, ca. 339-397; tr. composite, alt.
MUSIC: Trier manuscript, 15th century; adapt. Michael Praetorius, 1571-1621

PUER NOBIS
L.M.

1. *Sun: play on the word "Son," also found in Malachi 4:2*

O TRINITY OF BLESSED LIGHT

O Trinity of blessed light, O unity of princely might,
The fiery sun now goes his way; shed Thou within our hearts a ray.

To Thee our morning song of praise, to Thee our evening prayer we raise;
O grant us with Thy saints on high to praise Thee through eternity.

Let God the Father be adored, and God the son, the only Lord,
And God the Holy Spirit be adored throughout eternity!

Attributed to Ambrose of Milan, 4th Century
Translation composite

16 Doxology

Praise be to the God and Father of our Lord Jesus Christ, who has blessed us. Ephesians 1:3

Praise God from whom all bless - ings flow, Praise Him all
crea - tures here be - low. Praise Him a - bove, you heav - en - ly host, Praise
Fa - ther, Son and Ho - ly Ghost. A - men.

WORDS: Thomas Ken, 1637-1711, adapt. Jimmy Owens, b. 1930 FAIRHILL
MUSIC: Jimmy Owens, b. 1930 L.M.

17 Holy, God Almighty

Yours, O LORD, is the greatness and the power and the glory and the majesty. 1 Chronicles 29:11

1. Ho - ly, God Al - might - y.
2. Wor - thy, Lord, You are wor - thy.
3. Gra - cious, Ho - ly Spir - it.

WORDS: Scott A. Simpson, b. 1966 BOSTDORFF
MUSIC: Scott A. Simpson, b. 1966 Irregular

3
Ho - ly, Lord of
Wor - thy, the Lamb that was
Cleanse us. Pur - i -
3
Hosts. Ho - ly,
slain. Wor - thy,
fy. Gra - cious,
God Al - might - y. As we
Lord, You are wor - thy. As a -
Ho - ly Spir - it, As You
bow be - fore Your throne, to
round Your throne we sing praise to
burn a - way our sin, come and
wor - ship You a - lone, we cry Ho - ly.
You our Ris - en King, we cry Wor - thy.
fill us once a - gain, Ho - ly Spir - it.

18 Glorify Thy Name

Father, glorify your name! John 12:28

1. Fa - ther, we love You, we wor - ship and a - dore You.
2. Je - sus, we love You, we wor - ship and a - dore You.
3. Spir - it, we love You, we wor - ship and a - dore You.

Glo - ri - fy Thy name in all the earth. Glo - ri - fy Thy name,

Glo - ri - fy Thy name, Glo - ri - fy Thy name in all the earth.

WORDS: Donna Adkins, b. 1940
MUSIC: Donna Adkins, b. 1940

GLORIFY THY NAME
Irregular

19 Holy Is the Lord

Exalt the LORD our God and worship at his footstool; he is holy. Psalm 99:5

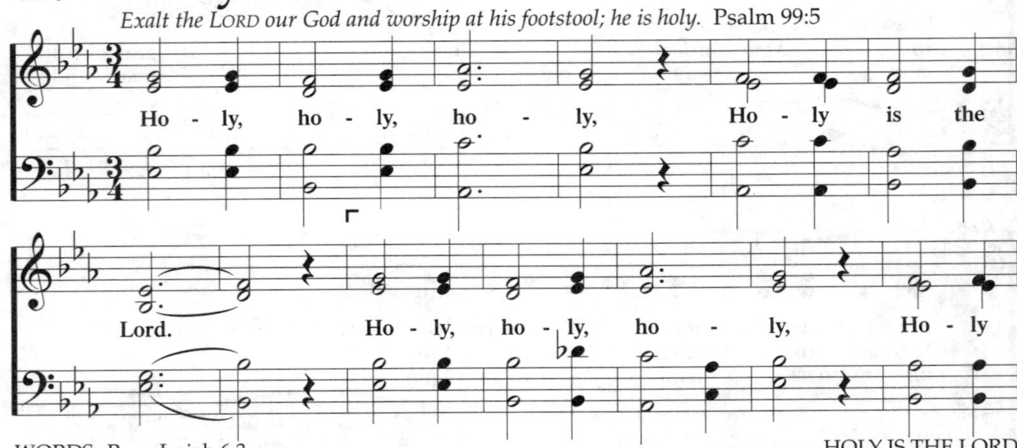
Ho - ly, ho - ly, ho - ly, Ho - ly is the
Lord. Ho - ly, ho - ly, ho - ly, Ho - ly

WORDS: Para. Isaiah 6:3
MUSIC: Franz Schubert, 1797-1828

HOLY IS THE LORD
6.5.6.5.D.

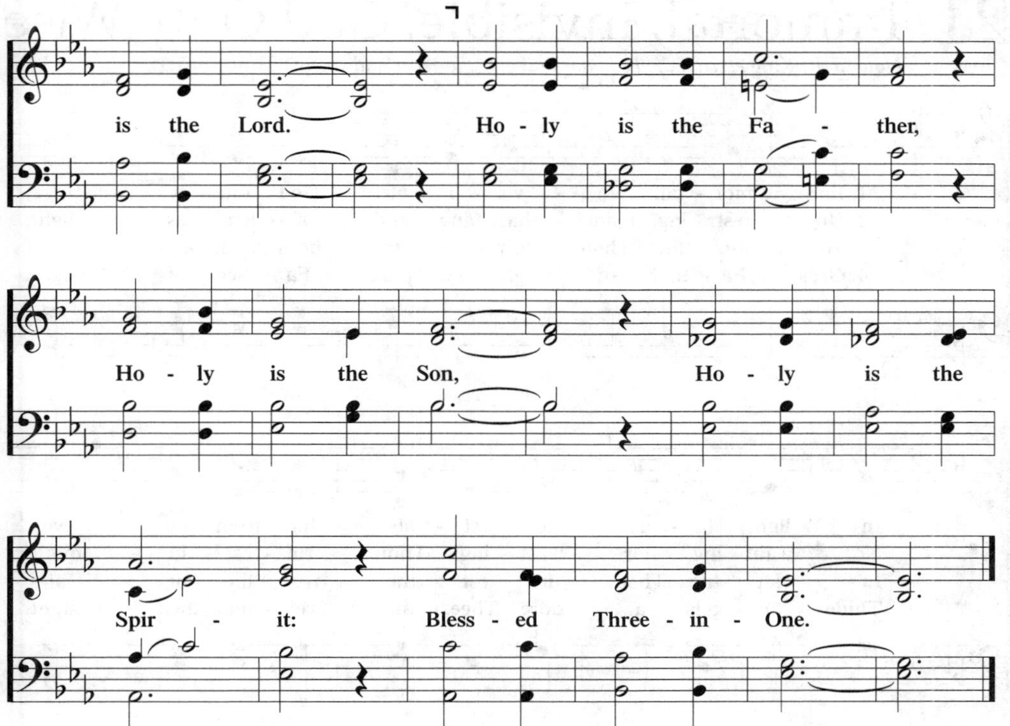
is the Lord. Ho - ly is the Fa - ther,
Ho - ly is the Son, Ho - ly is the
Spir - it: Bless - ed Three - in - One.

The Nature of the Lord 20

The LORD is gracious and full of compassion, slow to anger and great in mercy.
The LORD *is* good to all, and His tender mercies *are* over all His works.
All Your works shall praise You, O LORD, and Your saints shall bless You.
They shall speak of the glory of Your kingdom, and talk of Your power,
To make known to the sons of men His mighty acts, and the glorious majesty of His kingdom.
Your kingdom is an everlasting kingdom, and Your dominion endures throughout all generations.
The LORD upholds all who fall, and raises up all who are bowed down.
The eyes of all look expectantly to You, and You give them their food in due season.
You open Your hand and satisfy the desire of every living thing.
The LORD is righteous in all His ways, gracious in all His works.
The LORD is near to all who call upon Him, to all who call upon Him in truth.
He will fulfill the desire of those who fear Him; He also will hear their cry and save them.
The LORD preserves all who love Him, but all the wicked He will destroy.
My mouth shall speak the praise of the LORD, and all flesh shall bless His holy name forever and ever. *Psalm 145:8-21, NKJV*

21 Immortal, Invisible, God Only Wise

Now to the King eternal . . . be honor and glory for ever and ever. 1 Timothy 1:17

1. Im - mor - tal, in - vis - i - ble, God on - ly wise,
2. Un - rest - ing, un - hast - ing, and si - lent as light,
3. To all, life Thou giv - est, to both great and small;
4. Great Fa - ther of glo - ry, pure Fa - ther of light,
In light in - ac - ces - si - ble hid from our eyes,[1]
Nor want - ing, nor wast - ing, Thou rul - est in might;
In all life Thou liv - est, the true life of all.
Thine an - gels a - dore Thee, all veil - ing their sight.
Most bless - ed, most glo - rious, the An - cient of Days,[2]
Thy jus - tice like moun - tains high soar - ing a - bove
We blos - som and flour - ish as leaves on the tree,
All praise we would ren - der; O, help us to see
Al - might - y, vic - to - rious, Thy great name we praise.
Thy clouds, which are foun - tains of good - ness and love.
And with - er and per - ish— but naught chang - eth Thee.
'Tis on - ly the splen - dor of light hid - eth Thee.

WORDS: Walter C. Smith, 1824-1908
MUSIC: Welsh melody, from John Roberts' *Caniadau y Cyssegr*, 1839

ST. DENIO
11.11.11.11.

1. *In light inaccessible hid from our eyes: just as the sun is "hidden" because we cannot look directly at it*
2. *Ancient of Days: a name for God in Daniel 7:9*

Faithful One 22

The L*ORD, the compassionate and gracious God, slow to anger, abounding in love and faithfulness . . .* Exodus 34:6

Faith - ful
One, so un - chang - ing,
Age - less
One, You're my rock of peace.
Lord of all, I de - pend on You,

WORDS: Brian Doerksen, b. 1965
MUSIC: Brian Doerksen, b. 1965

FAITHFUL ONE
Irregular

I call out to You again and a - gain.
I call out to You a - gain and a -
gain. You are my rock in
times of trou - ble. You lift me

up when I fall down.
All through the storm Your love
is the an - chor, My hope is
in You a - lone.

23 God Moves in a Mysterious Way

You do not realize now what I am doing, but later you will understand. John 13:7

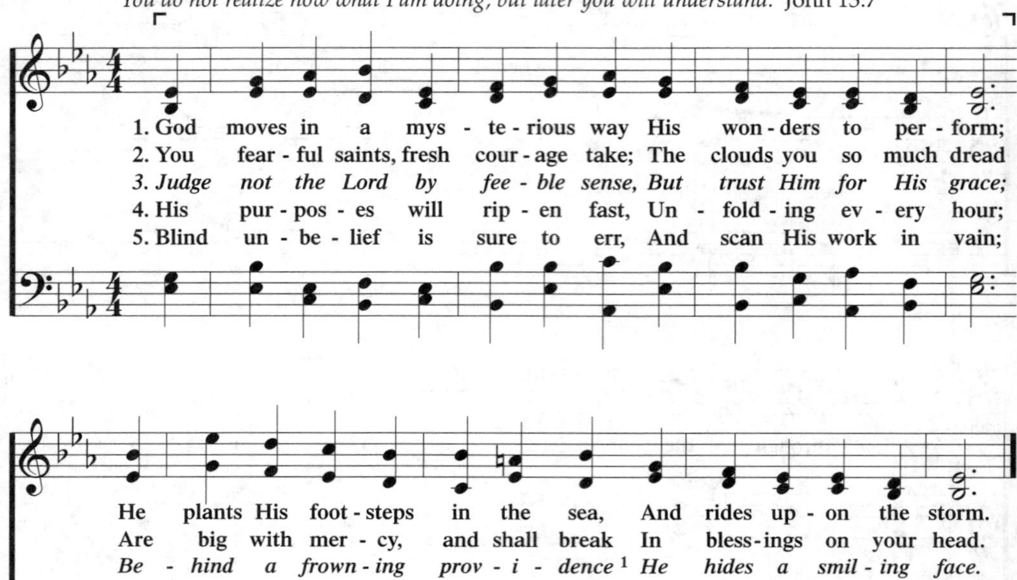

1. God moves in a mys - te - rious way His won - ders to per - form;
2. You fear - ful saints, fresh cour - age take; The clouds you so much dread
3. Judge not the Lord by fee - ble sense, But trust Him for His grace;
4. His pur - pos - es will rip - en fast, Un - fold - ing ev - ery hour;
5. Blind un - be - lief is sure to err, And scan His work in vain;
He plants His foot - steps in the sea, And rides up - on the storm.
Are big with mer - cy, and shall break In bless - ings on your head.
Be - hind a frown - ing prov - i - dence 1 He hides a smil - ing face.
The bud may have a bit - ter taste, But sweet will be the flower.
God is His own in - ter - pre - ter, And He will make it plain.

WORDS: William Cowper, 1731-1800, alt.
MUSIC: From *Scottish Psalter*, 1615

DUNDEE
C.M.

1. *providence: appearance of Divine care or direction*

THE UNIVERSAL PRESENCE

God and Father, I repent of my sinful preoccupation with visible things.
The world has been too much with me.
You have been here and I knew it not.
I have been blind to Your presence.
Open my eyes that I may behold You in and around me.
For Christ's sake. Amen

A.W. Tozer (1897-1963), *The Pursuit of God*

The Steadfast Love of the Lord 24

Because of the LORD'S *great love we are not consumed.* Lamentations 3:22

The stead - fast love of the Lord nev - er ceas - es; His
mer - cies nev - er come to an end. They are new ev - ery
morn - ing, new ev - ery morn - ing, Great is Thy faith - ful -
ness, O Lord, Great is Thy faith - ful - ness.

Optional segue to "Great Is Thy Faithfulness." No transition required.

WORDS: Edith McNeill, b. 1920
MUSIC: Edith McNeill, b. 1920

STEADFAST LOVE
Irregular

25 Great Is Thy Faithfulness

His compassions never fail. They are new every morning. Lamentations 3:22-23

1. Great is Thy faith - ful - ness, O God my Fa - ther. There is no
2. Sum - mer and win - ter, and spring - time and har - vest, Sun, moon and
3. Par - don for sin and a peace that en - dur - eth, Thy own dear
shad - ow of turn - ing with Thee. Thou chang - est not, Thy com -
stars in their cours - es a - bove Join with all na - ture in
pres - ence to cheer and to guide, Strength for to - day and bright
pas - sions they fail not; As Thou hast been Thou for - ev - er wilt be.
man - i - fold[1] wit - ness To Thy great faith - ful - ness, mer - cy and love.
hope for to - mor-row— Bless-ings all mine, with ten thou-sand be - side!
Refrain
Great is Thy faith - ful - ness! Great is Thy faith - ful - ness! Morn - ing by

WORDS: Thomas O. Chisholm, 1866-1960
MUSIC: William M. Runyan, 1870-1957

FAITHFULNESS
11.10.11.10. with Refrain

1. *manifold: numerous and varied*

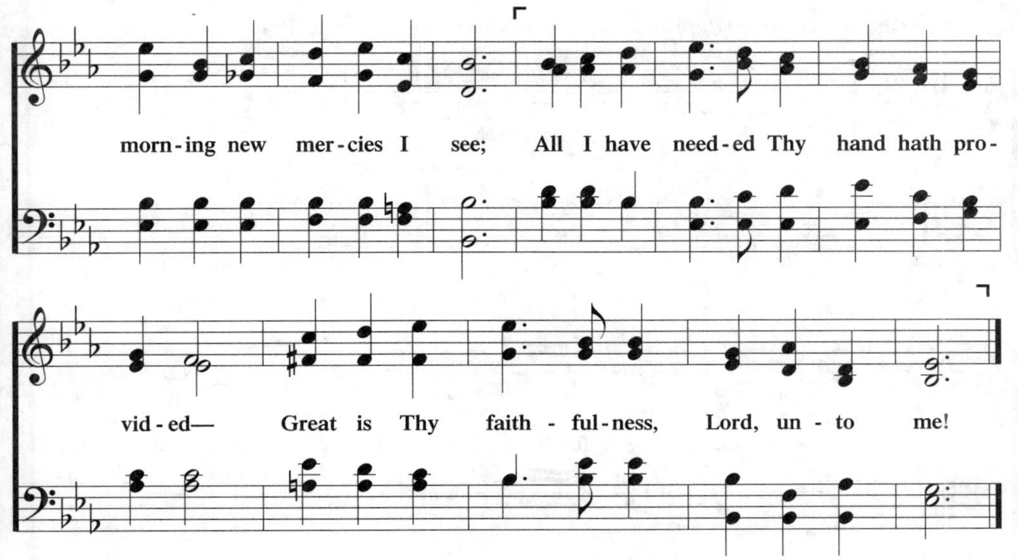
morn-ing new mer-cies I see; All I have need-ed Thy hand hath pro-
vid-ed— Great is Thy faith-ful-ness, Lord, un-to me!

God's Goodness 26

Give thanks to the LORD, for he is good;
his love endures forever.
Let the redeemed of the LORD say this—
those he redeemed from the hand of the foe,
those he gathered from the lands,
from east and west, from north and south.
Let them give thanks to the LORD for his unfailing love
and his wonderful deeds for men,
for he satisfies the thirsty
and fills the hungry with good things.
Let them give thanks to the LORD for his unfailing love
and his wonderful deeds for men.
Let them sacrifice thank offerings
and tell of his works with songs of joy.
Let them exalt him in the assembly of the people
and praise him in the council of the elders.
The upright see and rejoice,
but all the wicked shut their mouths.
Whoever is wise, let him heed these things
and consider the great love of the LORD.

Psalm 107:1-3, 8-9, 15, 22, 32, 42-43

27 Good to Me

Give thanks to the LORD, *for he is good. His love endures forever.* Psalm 136:1

I cry out for Your hand of mer-cy to heal me.
I am weak. I need Your love to free me. O Lord, my
rock, my strength in weak-ness, Come res - cue me, O
Lord.
1.
2.
You are my hope; Your

WORDS: Craig Musseau, b. 1965
MUSIC: Craig Musseau, b. 1965

GOOD TO ME
Irregular

pro - mise nev - er fails me. And my de - sire is to
fol - low You for - ev - er. For You are good, for You are
good, For You are good to me. For You are
D.S. al Coda
2nd time to Coda
good, for You are good, For You are good to me.
CODA
repeat ad lib
last time fine
me. For You are good, for You are good, For You are good to me. For You are

28 All Creatures of Our God and King

Let them praise the name of the LORD. Psalm 148:5

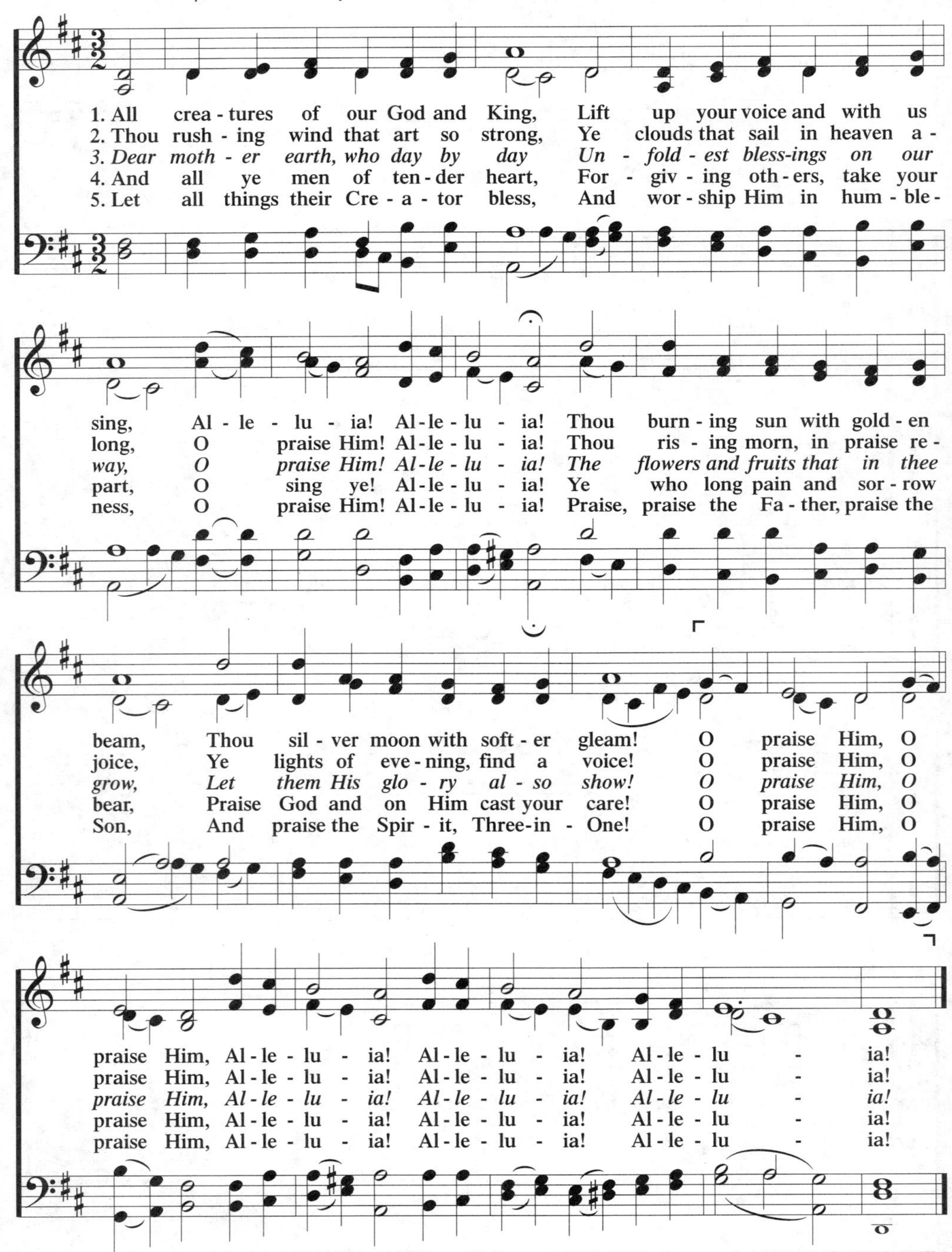
1. All creatures of our God and King, Lift up your voice and with us sing, Alleluia! Alleluia! Thou burning sun with golden beam, Thou silver moon with softer gleam! O praise Him, O praise Him, Alleluia! Alleluia! Alleluia!
2. Thou rushing wind that art so strong, Ye clouds that sail in heaven along, O praise Him! Alleluia! Thou rising morn, in praise rejoice, Ye lights of evening, find a voice! O praise Him, O praise Him, Alleluia! Alleluia! Alleluia!
3. Dear mother earth, who day by day Unfoldest blessings on our way, O praise Him! Alleluia! The flowers and fruits that in thee grow, Let them His glory also show! O praise Him, O praise Him, Alleluia! Alleluia! Alleluia!
4. And all ye men of tender heart, Forgiving others, take your part, O sing ye! Alleluia! Ye who long pain and sorrow bear, Praise God and on Him cast your care! O praise Him, O praise Him, Alleluia! Alleluia! Alleluia!
5. Let all things their Creator bless, And worship Him in humbleness, O praise Him! Alleluia! Praise, praise the Father, praise the Son, And praise the Spirit, Three-in-One! O praise Him, O praise Him, Alleluia! Alleluia! Alleluia!

WORDS: St. Francis of Assisi, 1182-1226; tr. William H. Draper, 1855-1933, alt.
MUSIC: From *Geistliche Kirchengesäng*, 1623,
harm. Ralph Vaughan Williams, 1872-1958

LASST UNS ERFREUEN
L.M. with Alleluias

(For different harmony, see No. 79)

The Heavens Declare His Glory 29

The heavens declare the glory of God;
the skies proclaim the work of his hands.
Day after day they pour forth speech;
night after night they display knowledge.
There is no speech or language
where their voice is not heard.
Their voice goes out into all the earth,
their words to the ends of the world.

Psalm 19:1-4

For the Beauty of the Earth 30

He has made everything beautiful in its time. Ecclesiastes 3:11

1. For the beau - ty of the earth, For the glo - ry of the skies,
2. For the won - der of each hour Of the day and of the night.
3. For the joy of hu - man love, Broth-er, sis - ter, par - ent, child;
4. For Thy Church that ev - er - more Lifts her ho - ly hands a - bove,
For the love which from our birth O - ver and a - round us lies;
Hill and vale, and tree and flower, Sun and moon, and stars of light;
Friends on earth, and friends a - bove; For all gen - tle thoughts and mild;
Of - fering up on ev - ery shore Her pure sac - ri - fice of love;
Lord of all, to Thee we raise This our hymn of grate - ful praise.
Lord of all, to Thee we raise This our hymn of grate - ful praise.
Lord of all, to Thee we raise This our hymn of grate - ful praise.
Lord of all, to Thee we raise This our hymn of grate - ful praise.

WORDS: Folliott S. Pierpoint, 1835-1917, alt.
MUSIC: Conrad Kocher, 1786-1872; arr. William H. Monk, 1823-1889

DIX
7.7.7.7.7.7.

31 This Is My Father's World

The earth is the LORD's and everything in it. Psalm 24:1

1. This is my Fa-ther's world, And to my lis-tening ears All na-ture sings, and round me rings The mu-sic of the spheres. This is my Fa-ther's world; I rest me in the thought Of rocks and trees, of skies and seas— His hand the won-ders wrought.
2. This is my Fa-ther's world, The birds their car-ols raise, The morn-ing light, the lil-y white, De-clare their Mak-er's praise. This is my Fa-ther's world; He shines in all that's fair; In the rus-tling grass I hear Him pass, He speaks to me ev-ery-where.
3. This is my Fa-ther's world, O let me ne'er for-get That though the wrong seems oft so strong, God is the Rul-er yet. This is my Fa-ther's world; Why should my heart be sad? The Lord is King; let the heav-ens ring! God reigns; let earth be glad!

WORDS: Maltbie D. Babcock, 1858-1901, alt.
MUSIC: English melody; adapt. Franklin L. Sheppard, 1852-1930

TERRA BEATA
S.M.D.

Morning Has Broken 32

In the morning you will see the glory of the LORD. Exodus16:7

1. Morn - ing has bro - ken Like the first morn - ing, Black-bird has spo - ken Like the first bird. Praise for the sing - ing! Praise for the morn - ing! Praise for them, spring - ing Fresh from the Word!
2. Sweet the rain's new fall Sun - lit from heav - en, Like the first dew - fall On the first grass. Praise for the sweet - ness Of the wet gar - den, Sprung in com - plete - ness Where His feet pass.
3. Mine is the sun - light! Mine is the morn - ing Born of the one light E - den saw play![1] Praise with e - la - tion, Praise ev - ery morn - ing, God's re - cre - a - tion Of the new day!

WORDS: Eleanor Farjeon, 1881-1965
MUSIC: Traditional Gaelic melody; arr. Mark Hayes, b. 1953

BUNESSAN
5.5.5.4.D.

1. *Refers to the creation of light in Genesis 1*

OUR GOD IS MIGHTY

MEDLEY
I Sing the Mighty Power of God
Great and Mighty

33 I Sing the Mighty Power of God

The LORD made the heavens and the earth, the sea, and all that is in them. Exodus 20:11

1. I sing the might - y power of God, That made the moun - tains rise;
2. I sing the good - ness of the Lord, That filled the earth with food;
3. There's not a plant or flower be - low, But makes Your glo - ries known;
That spread the flow - ing seas a - broad, And built the loft - y skies.
He formed the crea - tures with His word, And then pro - nounced them good.
And clouds a - rise, and tem - pests blow, By or - der from Your throne;
I sing the wis - dom that or - dained The sun to rule the day;
Lord, how Your won - ders are dis - played, Wher - e'er I turn my eye:
While all that bor - rows life from You Is ev - er in Your care,
The moon shines full at His com - mand, And all the stars o - bey.
If I sur - vey the ground I tread, Or gaze up - on the sky!
And ev - ery - where that I may be, God, You are pre - sent there.

(For lower key, see No. 476)

WORDS: Isaac Watts, 1674-1748, alt.
MUSIC: From *Gesangbuch der Herzogl*, Württemberg, 1784

ELLACOMBE
C.M.D.

Great and Mighty 34

For the LORD your God is God of gods and Lord of lords, the great God, mighty and awesome.
Deuteronomy 10:17

Optional transition to "Great and Mighty."
lively
accel.
Great and might - y is the Lord our God,
Great and might - y is He.
Great and might - y is the Lord our God,
Great and might - y is He.
Lift up your ban - ner, let the an - thems ring prais - es to our King;
Great and might - y is the Lord our God,
Great and might - y is He.

WORDS: Marlene Bigley, b. 1952
MUSIC: Marlene Bigley, b. 1952

GREAT AND MIGHTY
Irregular

35 A Mighty Fortress Is Our God

God is our refuge and strength. Psalm 46:1

1. A might - y for - tress is our God, A bul - wark[1] nev - er fail - ing;
2. Did we in our own strength con - fide Our striv - ing would be los - ing;
3. And though this world, with dev - ils filled, Should threat - en to un - do us,
4. That Word a - bove all earth - ly powers, No thanks to them, a - bid - eth;
Our help - er He, a - mid the flood Of mor - tal ills pre - vail - ing.
Were not the right Man on our side, The Man of God's own choos - ing.
We will not fear, for God hath willed His truth to tri - umph through us.
The Spir - it and the gifts are ours Through Him who with us sid - eth.
For still our an - cient foe Doth seek to work us woe; His craft and power are
Dost ask who that may be? Christ Je - sus, it is He; Lord Sa - ba - oth,[2] His
The Prince of Dark - ness grim— We trem - ble not for him; His rage we can en -
Let goods and kin - dred go, This mor - tal life al - so; The bod - y they may
great, And armed with cru - el hate, On earth is not his e - qual.
name, From age to age the same, And He must win the bat - tle.
dure, For lo, his doom is sure, One lit - tle word shall fell him.
kill; God's truth a - bid - eth still; His kingdom is for - ev - er.

WORDS: Martin Luther, 1483-1546; tr. Frederick H. Hedge, 1805-1890
MUSIC: Martin Luther, 1483-1546

EIN' FESTE BURG
8.7.8.7.6.6.6.6.7.

1. bulwark: a defensive wall
2. Lord Sabaoth: supreme commander of the armies

O God, Our Help in Ages Past 36

Lord, you have been our dwelling place throughout all generations. Ps. 90:1

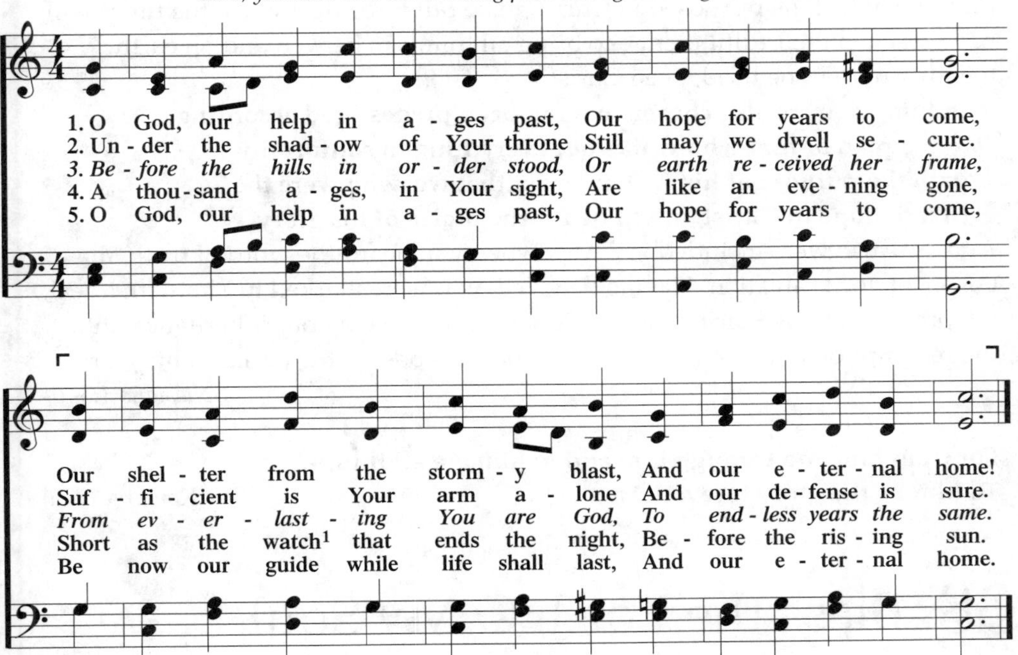
1. O God, our help in a - ges past, Our hope for years to come,
2. Un - der the shad - ow of Your throne Still may we dwell se - cure.
3. Be - fore the hills in or - der stood, Or earth re - ceived her frame,
4. A thou - sand a - ges, in Your sight, Are like an eve - ning gone,
5. O God, our help in a - ges past, Our hope for years to come,
Our shel - ter from the storm - y blast, And our e - ter - nal home!
Suf - fi - cient is Your arm a - lone And our de - fense is sure.
From ev - er - last - ing You are God, To end - less years the same.
Short as the watch1 that ends the night, Be - fore the ris - ing sun.
Be now our guide while life shall last, And our e - ter - nal home.

WORDS: Isaac Watts, 1674-1748, alt.
MUSIC: Attrib. William Croft, 1678-1727

ST. ANNE
C.M.

1. *watch: night shift for a guard*

He Has Blessed Us 37

Praise be to the God and Father of our Lord Jesus Christ, who has blessed us in the heavenly realms with every spiritual blessing in Christ.

For he chose us in him before the creation of the world to be holy and blameless in his sight.

In love he predestined us to be adopted as his sons through Jesus Christ, in accordance with his pleasure and will—to the praise of his glorious grace, which he has freely given us in the One he loves.

In him we have redemption through his blood, the forgiveness of sins, in accordance with the riches of God's grace that he lavished on us with all wisdom and understanding.

And he made known to us the mystery of his will according to his good pleasure, which he purposed in Christ, to be put into effect when the times will have reached their fulfillment—to bring all things in heaven and on earth together under one head, even Christ.

In him we were also chosen, having been predestined according to the plan of him who works out everything in conformity with the purpose of his will, in order that we, who were the first to hope in Christ, might be for the praise of his glory.

And you also were included in Christ when you heard the word of truth, the gospel of your salvation. Having believed, you were marked in him with a seal, the promised Holy Spirit, who is a deposit guaranteeing our inheritance until the redemption of those who are God's possession—to the praise of his glory.

Ephesians 1:3-14

For from him and through him and to him are all things.
To him be the glory forever! Amen.

Romans 11:36

38 Bless the Lord, O My Soul

All my inmost being, praise his holy name. Psalm 103:1

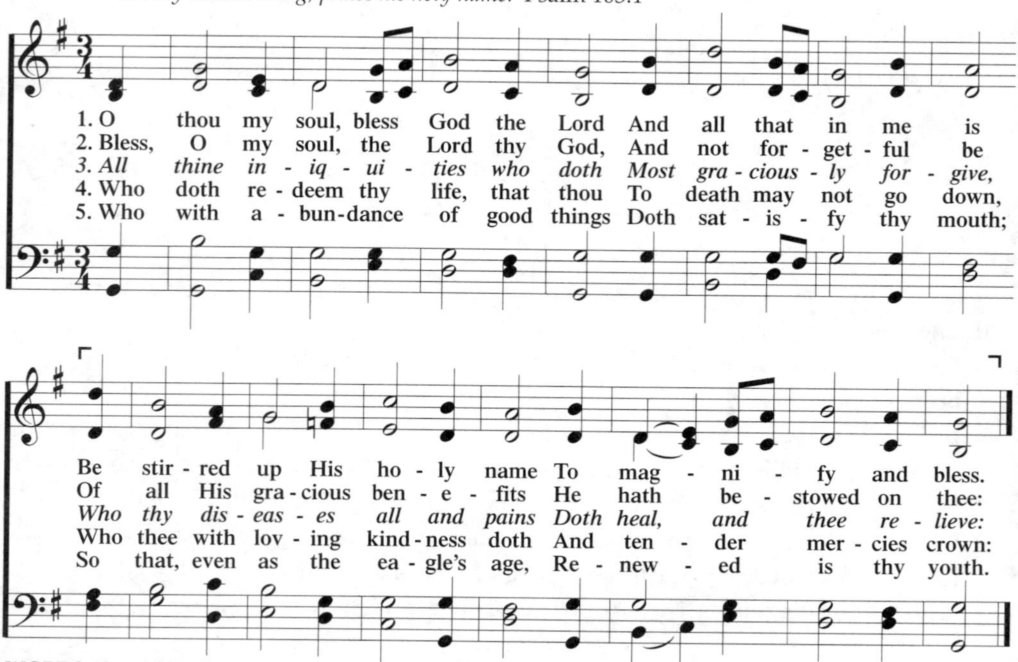
1. O thou my soul, bless God the Lord And all that in me is
Be stirred up His holy name To magnify and bless.
2. Bless, O my soul, the Lord thy God, And not forgetful be
Of all His gracious benefits He hath bestowed on thee:
3. All thine iniquities who doth Most graciously forgive,
Who thy diseases all and pains Doth heal, and thee relieve:
4. Who doth redeem thy life, that thou To death may not go down,
Who thee with loving kindness doth And tender mercies crown:
5. Who with abundance of good things Doth satisfy thy mouth;
So that, even as the eagle's age, Renewed is thy youth.

WORDS: *Scottish Psalter*, 1650
MUSIC: Hugh Wilson, 1764-1824

MARTYRDOM
C.M.

By Gracious Powers 39

You are my L*ORD; apart from you I have no good thing.* Psalm 16:2

1. By gracious powers so wonderfully sheltered,
And confidently waiting come what may.
We know that God is with us night and morning,
And never fails to greet us each new day.

2. Yet is this heart by its old foe tormented,
Still evil days bring burdens hard to bear;
O, give our frightened souls the sure salvation,
For which, O Lord, You taught us to prepare.

3. And when this cup You give is filled to brimming
With bitter suffering, hard to understand,
We take it thankfully and without trembling
Out of so good and so beloved a hand.

4. Yet when again in this same world You give us
The joy we had, the brightness of Your sun,
We shall remember all the days we lived through
And our whole life shall then be Yours alone.

5. By gracious powers so faithfully protected,
So quietly, so wonderfully near,
I'll live each day in hope, with You beside me,
And go with You through every coming year.

May be sung to No. 656 (O PERFECT LOVE) or No. 363 (FINLANDIA, abbreviated.)

WORDS: Dietrich Bonhöffer, 1906-1945; tr. Fred Pratt Green, 1903-2000 11.10.11.10.

GOD'S CREATION, PRAISE HIM!

May none of God's wonderful works keep silence, night or morning.
Bright stars, high mountains, the depths of the seas, sources of rushing rivers:
may all of these break into song as we sing to Father, Son and Holy Spirit.
May all the angels in the heavens reply: "Amen, Amen, Amen.
Power, praise, honor, eternal glory to God, the only Giver of grace,
Amen, Amen, Amen!"

Anonymous, ca. 4th century

40 Children of the Heavenly Father

As a father has compassion on his children, so the LORD *has compassion on those who fear him.*
Psalm 103:13

1. Children of the heavenly Father
Safely in His bosom gather.
Nestling bird nor star in heaven
Such a refuge e'er was given.

2. God His own doth tend and nourish,
In His holy courts they flourish.
From all evil things He spares them,
In His mighty arms He bears them.

3. Neither life nor death shall ever
From the Lord His children sever.
Unto them His grace He showeth,
And their sorrows all He knoweth.

4. Though He giveth or He taketh,
God His children ne'er forsaketh.
His the loving purpose solely
To preserve them pure and holy.

WORDS: Carolina V.S. Berg, 1832-1903; tr. Ernest W. Olson, 1870-1958
MUSIC: Swedish melody

TRYGGARE KAN INGEN VARA
L.M.

41 He's Got the Whole World in His Hands

In his hand is the life of every creature. Job 12:10

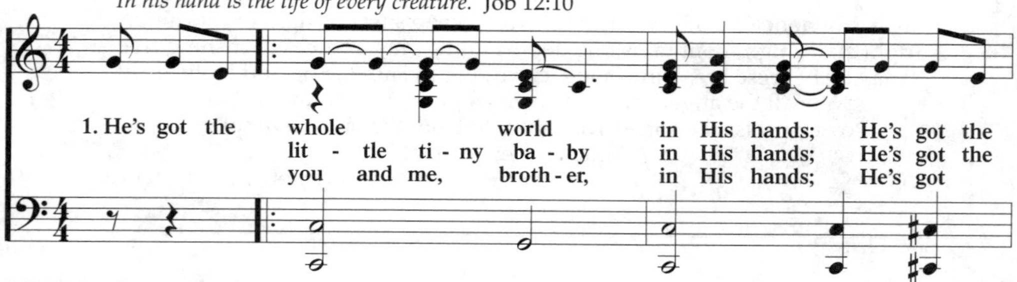
1. He's got the whole world in His hands; He's got the
little tiny baby in His hands; He's got the
you and me, brother, in His hands; He's got

WORDS: African-American spiritual
MUSIC: African-American spiritual; arr. Scott A. Simpson, b. 1966

WHOLE WORLD
Irregular

whole world in His hands; He's got the whole world
lit - tle ti - ny ba - by in His hands; He's got the lit - tle ti - ny ba - by
you and me, broth - er, in His hands; He's got you and me, broth - er,
in His hands; He's got the whole world in His hands.
in His hands; He's got the whole world in His hands.
in His hands; He's got the whold world in His hands.
1, 2.
2. He's got the
3. He's got
3.
He's got the whole world in His hands; He's got the
whole world in His hands; He's got the whole world
in His hands; He's got the whole world in His hands.
He's got the
whole world in His hands.

42 God Will Take Care of You

Cast your cares on the LORD and he will sustain you. Psalm 55:22

1. Be not dis - mayed what - e'er be - tide, God will take care of you.
2. Through days of toil when heart doth fail, God will take care of you.
3. All you may need He will pro - vide, God will take care of you.
4. No mat - ter what may be the test, God will take care of you.
Be - neath His wings of love a - bide, God will take care of you.
When dan - gers fierce your path as - sail, God will take care of you.
Noth - ing you ask will be de - nied, God will take care of you.
Lean, wea - ry one, up - on His breast, God will take care of you.
Refrain
God will take care of you Through ev - ery day, O'er all the way.
He will take care of you. God will take care of you.

WORDS: Civilla D. Martin, 1869-1948
MUSIC: Walter S. Martin, 1862-1935

GOD CARES
C.M. with Refrain

He Leadeth Me 43

He guides me in paths of righteousness. Psalm 23:3

1. He lead - eth me— O bless - ed thought! O words with heaven - ly com - fort fraught! What - e'er I do, where - e'er I be, Still 'tis God's hand that lead - eth me.
2. Some-times 'mid scenes of deep - est gloom, Some - times where E - den's flow - ers bloom, By wa - ters calm, o'er trou - bled sea, Still 'tis His hand that lead - eth me.
3. Lord, I would clasp Thy hand in mine, Nor ev - er mur - mur nor re - pine;[1] Con - tent, what - ev - er lot I see, Since 'tis my God that lead - eth me.
4. And when my task on earth is done, When, by Thy grace, the vic - tory's won, E'en death's cold wave I will not flee, Since God through Jor - dan lead - eth me.
Refrain
He lead - eth me, He lead - eth me, By His own hand He lead - eth me. His faith - ful fol - lower I would be, For by His hand He lead - eth me.

WORDS: Joseph H. Gilmore, 1834-1918, alt.
MUSIC: William B. Bradbury, 1816-1868

HE LEADETH ME
L.M. with Refrain

1. *repine: complain*

44 To God Be the Glory

Ascribe to the LORD the glory due his name. Psalm 29:2

1. To God be the glo - ry, great things He has done. So loved He the
2. O per - fect re - demp - tion, the pur - chase of blood, To ev - ery be -
3. Great things He has taught us, great things He has done, And great our re -
world that He gave us His Son, Who yield - ed His life an a -
liev - er the prom - ise of God. The vil - est of - fen - der who
joic - ing through Je - sus the Son, But pur - er, and high - er, and
tone - ment for sin, And o - pened the life - gate that all may go
tru - ly be - lieves, That mo - ment from Je - sus a par - don re -
great - er will be Our won - der, our trans - port,[1] when Je - sus we
Refrain
in.
ceives. Praise the Lord, praise the Lord, Let the earth hear His voice! Praise the Lord, praise the
see.

WORDS: Fanny J. Crosby, 1820-1915, alt.
MUSIC: William H. Doane, 1832-1915

TO GOD BE THE GLORY
11.11.11.11. with Refrain

1. *transport: rapture, ecstasy*

Lord, Let the peo - ple re - joice! O come to the Fa - ther through
Je - sus the Son, And give Him the glo - ry; great things He has done.

Praise the Almighty King 45

Yours, O LORD, is the greatness and the power
and the glory and the majesty and the splendor,
for everything in heaven and earth is yours.
Yours, O LORD, is the kingdom;
you are exalted as head over all.
Wealth and honor come from you;
you are the ruler of all things.
In your hands are strength and power
to exalt and give strength to all.
Now, our God, we give you thanks,
and praise your glorious name.

1 Chronicles 29:11-13

46 How Majestic Is Your Name

O LORD, our Lord, how majestic is your name in all the earth! Psalm 8:1

O Lord, our Lord, how ma - jes - tic is your name in all the earth. O earth. O Lord, we praise Your name. O Lord, we mag - ni - fy Your name: Prince of Peace, might - y God, O Lord God Al - might - y. O y.

1. D.S. 2. Final ending

WORDS: Michael W. Smith, b. 1957
MUSIC: Michael W. Smith, b. 1957

HOW MAJESTIC
Irregular

Praise to the Lord, the Almighty 47

Surely then you will find delight in the Almighty. Job 22:26

1. Praise to the Lord, the Al - might - y, the King of cre - a - tion!
2. Praise to the Lord, who o'er all things so won-drous - ly reign - eth,
3. Praise to the Lord, who with mar - vel - ous wis - dom hath made thee!
4. Praise to the Lord! O, let all that is in me a - dore Him!
O my soul, praise Him, for He is thy health and sal - va - tion!
Shel - ters thee un - der His wings, yea, so gent - ly sus - tain - eth!
Decked thee with health, and with lov - ing hand guid - ed and stayed thee.
All that hath life and breath, come now with prais - es be - fore Him!
All ye who hear, Now to His tem - ple draw near;
Hast thou not seen How thy de - sires e'er have been
How oft in grief Hath not He brought thee re - lief,
Let the A - men Sound from His peo - ple a - gain;
Join me in glad ad - o - ra - tion!
Grant - ed in what He or - dain - eth?
Spread - ing His wings for to shade thee!
Glad - ly for - ev - er a - dore Him.

(For lower key, see No. 529)

Optional segue to "O Worship the King." No transition required.

WORDS: Joachim Neander, 1650-1680; tr. Catherine Winkworth, 1827-1878, alt.
MUSIC: From *Stralsund Gesangbuch*, 1665

LOBE DEN HERREN
14.14.4.7.8.

48 O Worship the King

I will sing praise to my God. Psalm 104:33

1. O wor - ship the King, all glo - rious a - bove;
2. O, tell of His might, O, sing of His grace,
3. Your boun - ti - ful care, what tongue can re - cite?
4. Frail chil - dren of dust, and fee - ble as frail,

O, grate - ful - ly sing His power and His love;
Whose robe is the light, whose can - o - py space;
It breathes in the air; it shines in the light;
In You do we trust, nor find You to fail;

Our Shield and De - fend - er, the An - cient of Days,[1]
His char - iots of wrath the deep thun - der - clouds form,
It streams from the hills; it de - scends to the plain,
Your mer - cies how ten - der, how firm to the end,

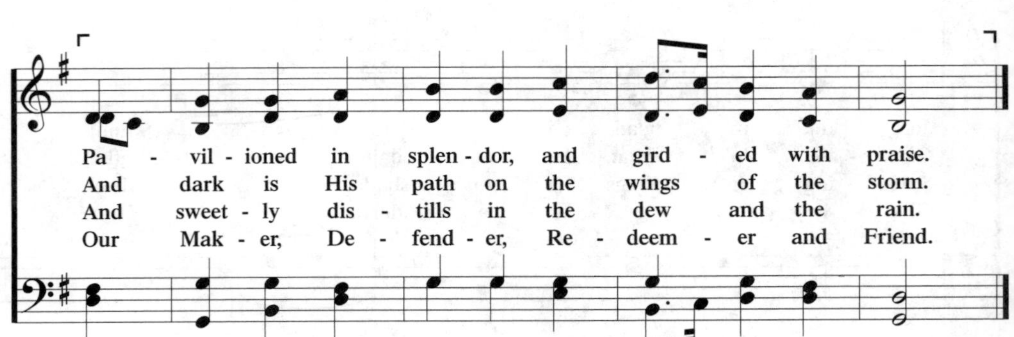
Pa - vil - ioned in splen - dor, and gird - ed with praise.
And dark is His path on the wings of the storm.
And sweet - ly dis - tills in the dew and the rain.
Our Mak - er, De - fend - er, Re - deem - er and Friend.

WORDS: Robert Grant, 1779-1838, alt.
MUSIC: Adapt. from Johann M. Haydn, 1737-1806

LYONS
10.10.11.11.

1. *Ancient of Days: a name for God in Daniel 7:9*

Optional last stanza setting
rit.
4. Frail chil - dren of dust, and
fee - ble as frail, In You do we trust, nor find You to
fail; Your mer - cies how ten - der, how firm to the end, Our
Mak - er, De - fend - er, Re - deem - er and Friend.

APPREHENDING GOD

O God, quicken to life every power within me, that I may lay hold on eternal things. Open my eyes that I may see; give me acute spiritual perception; enable me to taste You and know that You are good. Make heaven more real to me than any earthly thing has ever been. Amen.

A.W. Tozer (1897-1963), *The Pursuit of God*

49 We Bow Down

Come, let us bow down in worship, let us kneel before the LORD our Maker. Psalm 95:6

1. You are Lord of cre - a - tion and Lord of my life,
2. You are King of cre - a - tion and King of my life,
Lord of the land and the sea. You were Lord of the heav -
King of the land and the sea. You were King of the heav -
ens be - fore there was time, And Lord of all lords You will be!
ens be - fore there was time, And King of all kings You will be!
Refrain
We bow down (bow down) and we wor - ship You,
We bow down (bow down) and we crown You the
Lord. We bow down (bow down) and we wor - ship You,
King. We bow down (bow down) and we crown You the

WORDS: Twila Paris, b. 1958
MUSIC: Twila Paris, b. 1958

WE BOW DOWN
Irregular

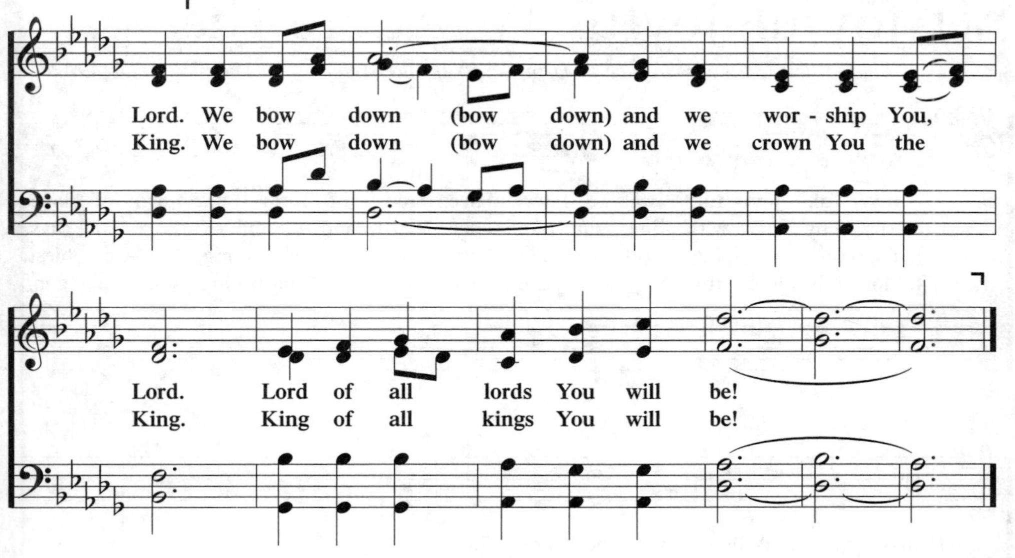
Lord. We bow down (bow down) and we wor - ship You,
King. We bow down (bow down) and we crown You the
Lord. Lord of all lords You will be!
King. King of all kings You will be!

PRAYER OF PRAISE TO GOD

We praise You, O God.
We acclaim You as Lord;
All creation worships You, Father everlasting
To You all angels, all the powers of heaven,
Cherubim and seraphim, sing in endless praise,
"Holy, holy, holy Lord, God of power and might!
Heaven and earth are full of Your glory!"
The glorious company of the apostles praise You.
The noble fellowship of prophets praise You.
The white-robed army of martyrs praise You.
Throughout the world the holy Church acclaims You:
Father, of majesty unbounded,
Your glorious, true, and only Son,
And the Holy Spirit, Advocate and Guide
You, Christ, are the King of Glory,
The eternal Son of the Father.
When You became incarnate to set us free
You humbly accepted the Virgin's womb.
You overcame the sting of death,
And opened the kingdom of heaven to all believers.
You are seated at God's right hand in glory.
We believe that You will come to be our judge.
Come then, Lord, and help Your people,
Bought with the price of Your own blood,
And bring us with Your saints to glory everlasting.

Te Deum Laudamus
(Traditional prayer from the 4th Century)

50 Joyful, Joyful, We Adore Thee

Shout for joy, O heavens; rejoice, O earth, . . . for the LORD *comforts his people.* Isaiah 49:13

1. Joy - ful, joy - ful, we a - dore Thee, God of glo - ry, Lord of love;
2. All Thy works with joy sur-round Thee, Earth and heaven re - flect Thy rays,
3. Thou art giv - ing and for - giv - ing, Ev - er bless - ing, ev - er blest,
4. Mor - tals, join the might - y cho - rus Which the morn - ing stars be - gan.
Hearts un - fold like flowers be - fore Thee, Open - ing to the sun a - bove.
Stars and an - gels sing a - round Thee, Cen - ter of un - bro - ken praise.
Well - spring of the joy of liv - ing, O - cean depth of hap - py rest!
God's great love is reign - ing o'er us, Join - ing us with - in its span.
Melt the clouds of sin and sad - ness, Drive the dark of doubt a - way;
Field and for - est, vale and moun - tain, Flow - ery mead - ow, flash - ing sea,
Thou our Fa - ther, Christ our Sav - ior, Let Your light up - on us shine.
Ev - er sing - ing, march we on - ward, Vic - tors in the midst of strife,
Giv - er of im - mor - tal glad - ness, Fill us with the light of day!
Chant - ing bird and flow - ing foun - tain, Call us to re - joice in Thee!
Teach us how to love each oth - er, Lift us to the Joy di - vine!
Joy - ful mu - sic leads us Sun - ward In the tri - umph song of life!

(For different harmony and lower key, see No. 543)

WORDS: Henry Van Dyke, 1852-1933, alt.
MUSIC: Melody by Ludwig van Beethoven, 1770-1827; arr. Edward Hodges, 1796-1867

HYMN TO JOY
8.7.8.7.D.

Praise, My Soul, the King of Heaven 51

Praise the LORD, O my soul, and forget not all his benefits. Psalm 103:2

1. Praise, my soul, the King of heav - en, To His feet your trib - ute bring. Ran - somed, healed, re - stored, for - giv - en, Who, like me, His praise should sing? Al - le - lu - ia! Al - le - lu - ia! Praise the ev - er - last - ing King!
2. Praise Him for His grace and fa - vor To our fa - thers in dis - tress; Praise Him, still the same for - ev - er, Slow to chide and swift to bless. Al - le - lu - ia! Al - le - lu - ia! Glo - rious in His faith - ful - ness!
3. Fa - ther - like, He tends and spares us. Well our fee - ble frame He knows. In His hands He gent - ly bears us, Res - cues us from all our foes. Al - le - lu - ia! Al - le - lu - ia! Wide - ly as His mer - cy flows!
4. An - gels, help us to a - dore Him— You be - hold Him face to face. Sun and moon, bow down be - fore Him, Dwell - ers all in time and space. Al - le - lu - ia! Al - le - lu - ia! Praise with us the God of grace!

(For alternate tune, see No. 474)

WORDS: Henry F. Lyte, 1793-1847, alt.
MUSIC: Mark Andrews, 1875-1939

ANDREWS
8.7.8.7.8.7.

52 Great Is the Lord

I will extol You, my God, O King;
And I will bless Your name forever and ever.
Every day I will bless You,
And I will praise Your name forever and ever.
Great is the LORD, and greatly to be praised;
And His greatness is unsearchable.
One generation shall praise Your works to another,
And shall declare Your mighty acts.
I will meditate on the glorious splendor of Your majesty,
And on Your wondrous works.
Men shall speak of the might of Your awesome acts,
And I will declare Your greatness.
They shall utter the memory of Your great goodness,
And shall sing of Your righteousness. *Psalm 145:1-7, NKJV*

OUR GOD IS EXALTED

MEDLEY
Great Is the Lord
He Is Exalted

53 Great Is the Lord

Great is the LORD and most worthy of praise; his greatness no one can fathom. Psalm 145:3

Great is the Lord, He is ho - ly and just, by His pow - er we trust in His
love. Great is the Lord, He is faith - ful and true, by His

WORDS: Michael W. Smith, b. 1957; Deborah D. Smith, b. 1958
MUSIC: Michael W. Smith, b. 1957; Deborah D. Smith, b. 1958

GREAT IS THE LORD
Irregular

Refrain
mer-cy He proves He is love.
Great is the Lord and wor-thy of glo-ry,
Great is the Lord and wor-thy of praise.
Great is the Lord, now
lift up your voice, now lift up your voice:
Great is the
Lord! Great is the Lord!
1.
2.
D.S.
3. Final ending
Lord!
Lord!
3. Final ending with optional transition to "He Is Exalted"
Lord!

54 He Is Exalted

Yours, O LORD, is the kingdom; you are exalted as head over all. 1 Chronicles 29:11

He is ex-alt-ed, the King is ex-alt-ed on high; I will praise Him.
He is ex-alt-ed, for-ev-er ex-alt-ed And I will praise His name!
He is the Lord, for-ev-er His truth shall reign;
Heav - en and earth re-joice in His ho - ly name.
He is ex - alt - ed, the King is ex - alt - ed on high.

WORDS: Twila Paris, b. 1958
MUSIC: Twila Paris, b. 1958

HE IS EXALTED
Irregular

I Exalt Thee 55

You are exalted far above all gods. Psalm 97:9

For Thou, O Lord, art high a - bove all the earth.
Thou art ex - alt - ed far a - bove all gods.
For Thou, O bove all gods. I ex -
alt Thee, I ex - alt Thee, I ex - alt Thee,
O Lord. I ex - O Lord.
1.
2.
3

WORDS: Pete Sanchez, Jr., b. 1948; based on Psalm 97:9
MUSIC: Pete Sanchez, Jr., b. 1948

I EXALT THEE
Irregular

OUR GOD IS WORTHY OF PRAISE

MEDLEY

Blessed Be the Name of the Lord
I Sing Praises

56 Blessed Be the Name of the Lord

Praise be to his glorious name forever. Psalm 72:19

Bless-ed be the name of the Lord, He is wor-thy to be praised and a-
dored; So we lift up ho-ly hands in one ac-cord, Sing-ing,
"Bless-ed be the name, bless-ed be the name,
Bless-ed be the name of the Lord!"
Song ending
Optional transition to "I Sing Praises"
Lord!"

WORDS: Don Moen, b. 1950
MUSIC: Don Moen, b. 1950

BLESSED
Irregular

I Sing Praises 57

I will praise you among the nations, O LORD; I will sing praises to your name. Psalm 18:49

1. I sing prais-es to Your name, O Lord, prais-es to Your name, O Lord, For Your name is great and great-ly to be praised. I sing prais-es to Your name, O Lord, prais-es to Your name, O Lord, For Your name is great and great-ly to be praised.

2. I give glo-ry to Your name, O Lord, glo-ry to Your name, O Lord, For Your name is great and great-ly to be praised. I give glo-ry to Your name, O Lord, glo-ry to Your name, O Lord, For Your name is great and great-ly to be praised.

WORDS: Terry MacAlmon, b. 1955
MUSIC: Terry MacAlmon, b. 1955

I SING PRAISES
Irregular

58 We Praise You, O God, Our Redeemer

You, O LORD, are our Father, our Redeemer from of old. Isaiah 63:16

1. We praise You, O God, our Re - deem - er, Cre - a - tor; In
2. We wor - ship You, God of our fa - thers, we bless You; Through
3. With voic - es u - nit - ed our prais - es we of - fer, And
grate - ful de - vo - tion our trib - ute we bring. We
life's storm and tem - pest our guide You have been. When
glad - ly our songs of true wor - ship we raise. Your
lay it be - fore You; we kneel and a - dore You; We
per - ils o'er - take us, You will not for - sake us, And
strong arm will guide us; our God is be - side us. To
bless Your ho - ly name, glad prais - es we sing.
with Your help, O Lord, life's bat - tles we win.
You, our great Re - deem - er, for - ev - er be praise.

WORDS: Julia Cady Cory, 1882-1963, alt.
MUSIC: Netherlands folk song; arr. Edward Kremser, 1838-1914

KREMSER
12.11.12.11.

The God of Abraham Praise 59

God said to Moses, "I AM WHO I AM." Exodus 3:14

1. The God of A - braham praise, Who reigns en - throned a - bove;
2. Your Spir - it still flows free, High surg - ing where it will;
3. You have e - ter - nal life Im - plant - ed in the soul;
The an - cient of e - ter - nal days And God of love.
In pro - phet's words You spoke of old And You speak still.
Your love shall be our strength and stay, While a - ges roll.
The Lord, the great I AM, By earth and heaven con - fessed;
Es - tab - lished is Your law, And change - less it shall stand,
We praise You, liv - ing God! We praise Your ho - ly name;
We bow be - fore Your ho - ly name, For - ev - er blest.
Deep writ - ten on the hu - man heart, On sea or land.
Who was, and is, and is to be, For - e'er the same!

WORDS: Newton Mann, 1836-1926; Max Landsberg, 1845-1928; based on the *Yigdal* of Daniel ben Judah, ca. 1400, alt.
MUSIC: Hebrew melody; adapt. Thomas Olivers, 1725-1799; Meyer Lyon, 1751-1797

LEONI
6.6.8.4.D.

60 Ancient of Days

Thrones were set in place, and the Ancient of Days took his seat. Daniel 7:9

Bless - ing and hon - or, glo - ry and pow - er
be un-to the An-cient of Days; From ev - ery na - tion,
all of cre-a - tion bow be-fore the An-cient of Days.
Ev - ery tongue in heav-en and earth shall de-clare Your glo - ry,
Ev - ery knee shall bow at Your throne in wor - ship;

WORDS: Gary Sadler, b. 1954; Jamie Harvill, 20th century
MUSIC: Gary Sadler, b. 1954; Jamie Harvill, 20th century

ANCIENT OF DAYS
Irregular

You will be ex-alt-ed, O God, and Your king-dom shall not pass a-way,
O An-cient of Days.
1.
2.
Your king-dom shall reign o-ver all the earth;
sing un-to the An-cient of Days; For none can com-pare to Your
match-less worth; sing un-to the An-cient of Days.
D.S.
3.

61 O, for a Heart to Praise My God

I will praise you, O LORD, with all my heart. Psalm 9:1

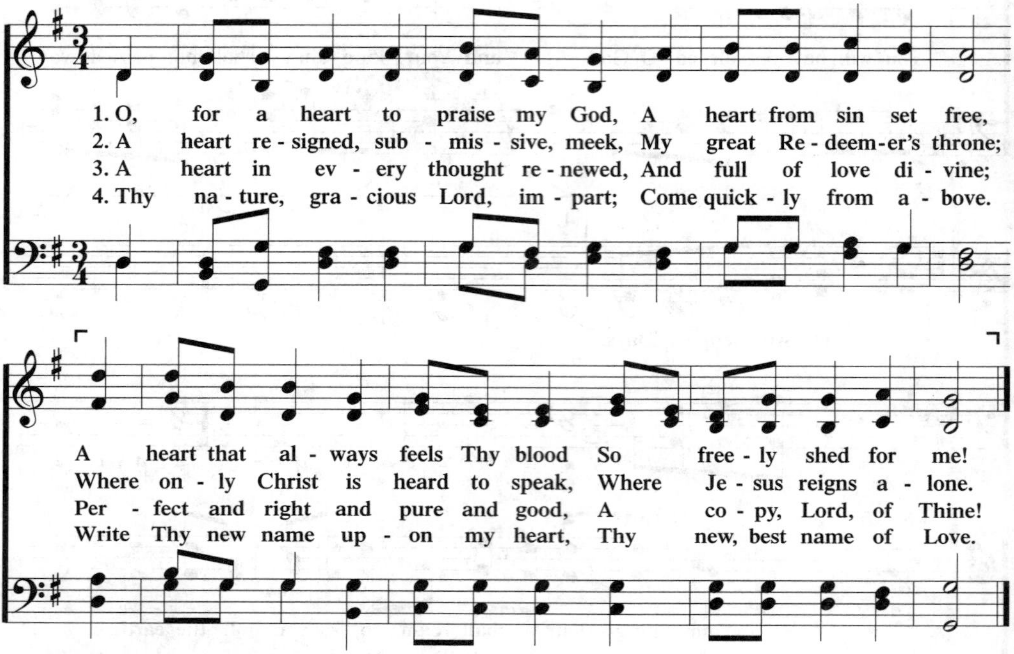

1. O, for a heart to praise my God, A heart from sin set free,
A heart that always feels Thy blood So freely shed for me!

2. A heart resigned, submissive, meek, My great Redeemer's throne;
Where only Christ is heard to speak, Where Jesus reigns alone.

3. A heart in every thought renewed, And full of love divine;
Perfect and right and pure and good, A copy, Lord, of Thine!

4. Thy nature, gracious Lord, impart; Come quickly from above.
Write Thy new name upon my heart, Thy new, best name of Love.

WORDS: Charles Wesley, 1707-1788, alt.
MUSIC: Carl G. Gläser, 1784-1829; adapt. Lowell Mason, 1792-1872

AZMON
C.M.

62 Awesome God

The LORD your God . . . is a great and awesome God. Deuteronomy 7:21

Our God is an awe - some God; He reigns from heav - en a - bove With
wis - dom, power and love; Our God is an awe - some God! Our God!
1.
2.

WORDS: Rich Mullins, 20th century
MUSIC: Rich Mullins, 20th century

AWESOME GOD
Irregular

Psalm 146 63

I will sing praise to my God as long as I live. Psalm 146:2

I will sing praise to the Lord With ev-ery part of my life.
My hope is in You, the Mak-er of heav-en and
earth, The Lord who reigns for-ev-er and ev-er. ev-er and ev-er-more.
1.
2, 3.
fine
1. You bring sight to the blind, grace to the low-ly,
2. You give hope to the poor, food to the hun-gry,
You watch o-ver the weak, You set the pris-oner free!
You are faith-ful to those who call up-on Your Name!
D.C. al fine

WORDS: Tom Jennings, b. 1966; based on Psalm 146
MUSIC: Tom Jennings, b. 1966

JENNINGS
Irregular

64 In the Name of the Lord

The name of the LORD is a strong tower. Proverbs 18:10

There is strength in the name of the Lord; There is
power in the name of the Lord; There is
hope in the name of the Lord! Bless-ed is he who
comes in the name of the Lord!
3

WORDS: Phill McHugh, b. 1951; Gloria Gaither, b. 1942; Sandi Patty, b. 1956
MUSIC: Phill McHugh, b. 1951; Gloria Gaither, b. 1942; Sandi Patty, b. 1956

IN THE NAME OF THE LORD
Irregular

OUR GOD IS MIGHTY

MEDLEY
Mighty Is Our God
How Great Thou Art

Mighty Is Our God 65

You are worthy, O Lord, to receive glory and honor and power; for You created all things.
Revelation 4:11, NKJV

1., 3. Might-y is our God, might-y is our King;
2., 4. Glo - ry to our God, glo-ry to our King;
last time to Coda
Might-y is our Lord, Rul-er of ev - ery-thing.
Glo - ry to our Lord, Rul-er of ev - ery-thing.
1, 3.
2.
His name is high - er, high-er than an - y oth - er name; His power is
great - er, for He has cre-at - ed ev - ery-thing.
D.C. al Coda
CODA
Song Ending
Optional Segue to 𝄋 of "How Great Thou Art"
Rul-er of ev - ery - thing.
rit.
Then sings my

WORDS: Don Moen, b. 1950; Eugene Greco, b. 1960; Gerrit Gustafson, b. 1948
MUSIC: Don Moen, b. 1950; Eugene Greco, b. 1960; Gerrit Gustafson, b. 1948

MIGHTY IS OUR GOD
Irregular

66 How Great Thou Art

Great is the L*ORD, and most worthy of praise.* Psalm 48:1

1. O Lord, my God! When I in awe - some won - der Con - sid - er
2. When through the woods and for - est glades I wan - der And hear the
3. And when I think that God, His Son not spar - ing, Sent Him to
4. When Christ shall come with shout of ac - cla - ma - tion And take me
all the worlds* Thy hands have made, I see the
birds sing sweet - ly in the trees, When I look
die, I scarce can take it in; That on the
home, what joys shall fill my heart! Then I shall
stars, I hear the roll - ing* thun - der, Thy power through -
down from loft - y moun - tain gran - deur And hear the
cross, my bur - den glad - ly bear - ing, He bled and
bow in hum - ble ad - o - ra - tion And there pro -
Refrain
out the u - ni - verse dis - played.
brook and feel the gen - tle breeze.
died to take a - way my sin.
claim, my God, how great Thou art!
Then sings my

WORDS: Stuart K. Hine, 1899-1989
MUSIC: Stuart K. Hine, 1899-1989

O STORE GUD
11.10.11.10. with Refrain

**Author's original words are "works" and "mighty."*

soul, my Sav - ior God, to Thee. How great Thou art, how great Thou
art! Then sings my soul, my Sav - ior God, to
Thee. How great Thou art, how great Thou art!

The Lord Is Robed in Majesty 67

The LORD reigns, he is robed in majesty;
the LORD is robed in majesty
and is armed with strength.
The world is firmly established;
it cannot be moved.
Your throne was established long ago
you are from all eternity.
The seas have lifted up, O LORD,
the seas have lifted up their voice;
the seas have lifted up their pounding waves.
Mightier than the thunder of the great waters,
mightier than the breakers of the sea—
the LORD on high is mighty.
Your statutes stand firm;
holiness adorns your house
for endless days, O LORD. *Psalm 93*

68 I Will Call upon the Lord

I will call upon the LORD, who is worthy of praise. Psalm 18:3

I will call up-on the Lord
I will call up-on the Lord
Who is wor-thy to be
Who is wor-thy to be praised.
So shall I be
praised.
So shall I be saved from my en-e-mies.
saved from my en-e-mies.
I will call up-on the Lord.
1.
2.
Lord. The
I will call up-on the Lord.
Lord. The

WORDS: Michael O'Shields, b. 1948; based on Psalm 18:3 and 2 Samuel 22:47
MUSIC: Michael O'Shields, b. 1948

O'SHIELDS
Irregular

Lord liv-eth, and bless-ed be the Rock, And let the God of my sal-va-tion be ex-
alt - ed. The Lord liv-eth, and bless-ed be the Rock, And let the God
of my sal-va-tion be ex-alt - ed. The ed.
1.
2.

THE GAZE OF THE SOUL

Lord, I have heard a good word inviting me to look away to You and be satisfied. My heart longs to respond, but sin has clouded my vision till I see You but dimly. Be pleased to cleanse me in Your own precious blood, and make me inwardly pure, so that I may with unveiled eyes gaze upon You all the days of my earthly pilgrimage. Then shall I be prepared to behold You in full splendor in the day when You shall appear to be glorified in Your saints and admired in all them that believe. Amen.

A.W. Tozer (1897-1963), *The Pursuit of God*

69 All People That on Earth Do Dwell

Worship the LORD with gladness; come before him with joyful songs. Psalm 100:2

1. All people that on earth do dwell, Sing to the Lord with cheerful voice. Him serve with mirth, His praise forth tell; Come ye before Him and rejoice.
2. Know that the Lord is God indeed; Without our aid He did us make. We are His flock; He doth us feed, And for His sheep He doth us take.
3. O, enter then His gates with praise, Approach with joy His courts unto; Praise, laud and bless His name always, For it is seemly so to do.
4. For why the Lord our God is good; His mercy is forever sure. His truth at all times firmly stood, And shall from age to age endure.

WORDS: From *Scottish Psalter*, 1650; attrib. William Kethe, 1510-1594
MUSIC: From *Geneva Psalter*, 1551; attrib. Louis Bourgeois, circa 1510-1561

OLD HUNDREDTH
L.M.

PRAISE

We shall never know the full joy of salvation until we begin to praise. This is the first evidence of faith, real faith, and is ever the support and inspiration of faith.

A.B. Simpson (1843-1919), *The Christ in the Bible Commentary*

Thou Art Worthy 70

You are worthy, O Lord, to receive glory and honor and power. Revelation 4:11, NKJV

Thou art wor-thy, Thou art wor-thy, Thou art wor-thy, O Lord,
To re-ceive glo-ry, glo - ry and hon-or, Glo - ry and
hon-or and power. For Thou hast cre - at - ed, hast all things cre-
at-ed; Thou hast cre - at - ed all things. And for Thy plea-sure
they are cre - at - ed, For Thou art wor-thy, O Lord.

WORDS: Pauline M. Mills, 1898-1995; based on Revelation 4:11
MUSIC: Pauline M. Mills, 1898-1995

THOU ART WORTHY
Irregular

71 Be Exalted, O God

Great is your love . . . Be exalted, O God, above the heavens. Psalm 57:10-11

I will give thanks to Thee, O Lord, a - mong the peo - ple. I will
sing prais - es to Thee a - mong the na - tions. For Thy
stead - fast love is great, is great to the heav - ens, And Thy
faith - ful - ness, Thy faith - ful - ness to the clouds. Be ex -

WORDS: Brent Chambers, b. 1948; based on Psalm 57:9-11
MUSIC: Brent Chambers, b. 1948

BE EXALTED
Irregular

alt - ed, O God, a - bove the heav - ens; Let Thy glo - ry be
o - ver all the earth. Be ex - alt - ed, O God, a - bove the
heav - ens; Let Thy glo - ry be o - ver all the earth.

Prince of Peace 72

For to us a child is born,
to us a son is given,
and the government will be on his shoulders.
And he will be called
Wonderful Counselor, Mighty God,
Everlasting Father, Prince of Peace.
Of the increase of his government and peace
there will be no end.
He will reign on David's throne
and over his kingdom,
establishing and upholding it
with justice and righteousness
from that time on and forever.
The zeal of the LORD Almighty
will accomplish this.

Isaiah 9:6-7

73 O Come, O Come, Emmanuel

The virgin will be with child and will give birth to a son, and will call him Immanuel. Isaiah 7:14

1. O come, O come, Em - man - u - el, And ran - som cap - tive
2. O come, Thou Rod of Jes - se, free Thine own from Sa - tan's
3. O come, Thou Day - spring, come and cheer Our spir - its by Thine
4. O come, Thou Key of Da - vid, come, And o - pen wide our
Is - ra - el, That mourns in lone - ly ex - ile here Un -
tyr - an - ny; From depths of hell Thy peo - ple save And
ad - vent here. And drive a - way the shades of night, And
heaven - ly home; Make safe the way that leads on high, And
til the Son of God ap - pear. Re - joice! Re - joice! Em -
give them vic - tory o'er the grave. Re - joice! Re - joice! Em -
pierce the clouds and bring us light! Re - joice! Re - joice! Em -
close the path to mis - er - y. Re - joice! Re - joice! Em -
man - u - el Shall come to thee, O Is - ra - el!
man - u - el Shall come to thee, O Is - ra - el!
man - u - el Shall come to thee, O Is - ra - el!
man - u - el Shall come to thee, O Is - ra - el!

WORDS: Latin, 12th century; stanzas 1 and 2 tr. John M. Neale, 1818-1866, alt.; stanzas 3 and 4 tr. Henry S. Coffin, 1877-1954, alt.
MUSIC: Plainsong; adapt. Thomas Helmore, 1811-1890

VENI EMMANUEL
L.M. with Refrain

Let All Mortal Flesh Keep Silence 74

The LORD is in his holy temple; let all the earth be silent before him. Habakkuk 2:20

1. Let all mor - tal flesh keep si - lence, And with fear and
2. King of kings, yet born of Ma - ry, As of old on
3. Rank on rank the host of heav - en Spreads its van - guard[3]
4. At His feet the six - winged ser - aph, Cher - u - bim,[4] with
trem - bling stand; Pon - der noth - ing earth - ly mind - ed,
earth He stood, Lord of lords, in hu - man ves - ture,[2]
on the way, As the Light of light de - scend - eth
sleep - less eye, Veil their fac - es in God's pres - ence,
For with bless - ing in His hand Christ our God to earth de -
In the bod - y and the blood, He will give to all the
From the realms of end - less day, That the powers of hell may
As with cease - less voice they cry, "Al - le - lu - ia, Al - le -
scend - eth, Our full hom - age[1] to de - mand.
faith - ful His own self for heaven - ly food.
van - ish As the dark - ness clears a - way.
lu - ia, Al - le - lu - ia, Lord Most High!"

WORDS: *Liturgy of St. James*, 4th century; tr. Gerard Moultrie, 1829-1885
MUSIC: French melody, 17th century; harm. Ralph Vaughan Williams (1872-1958)

PICARDY
8.7.8.7.8.7.

1. *homage: adoration*
2. *human vesture: body*
3. *vanguard: the troops moving at the head of an army*
4. *seraph, cherubim: angelic beings around the throne of God*

75 Come, Thou Long-Expected Jesus

I will shake all nations, and the desired of all nations will come. Haggai 2:7

1. Come, Thou long - ex - pect - ed Je - sus, Born to set Thy peo - ple free.
2. Born Thy peo - ple to de - liv - er, Born a Child and yet a King,
From our fears and sins re - lease us; Let us find our rest in Thee.
Born to reign in us for - ev - er, Now Thy gra - cious king - dom bring.
Is - rael's Strength and Con - so - la - tion, Hope of all the earth Thou art;
By Thine own e - ter - nal Spir - it, Rule in all our hearts a - lone;
Dear De - sire of ev - ery na - tion, Joy of ev - ery long-ing heart.
By Thine all - suf - fi - cient mer - it, Raise us to Thy glo-rious throne.

Optional segue to "Jesus, Name Above All Names." No transition required.

WORDS: Charles Wesley, 1707-1788
MUSIC: Rowland H. Prichard, 1811-1887; arr. Robert Harkness, 1880-1961

HYFRYDOL
8.7.8.7.D.

Jesus, Name Above All Names 76

God exalted him to the highest place and gave him the name that is above every name.
Philippians 2:9

Je - sus, name a - bove all names, beau - ti - ful
Sav - ior, glo - ri - ous Lord. Em -
man - u - el, God is with us, bles-sed Re -
Optional Repeat
Final Ending
deem - er, Liv - ing Word. Word.

WORDS: Naida Hearn, b. 1944
MUSIC: Naida Hearn, b. 1944

HEARN
Irregular

77 Of the Father's Love Begotten

I am the Alpha and Omega . . . the Beginning and the End. Revelation 22:13

1. Of the Fa - ther's love be - got - ten, Ere the worlds be - gan to be,
2. O that birth for - ev - er bless - ed, When the Vir - gin, full of grace,
3. O ye heights of heaven, a - dore Him; An - gel hosts, His prais - es sing;
4. Christ, to Thee, with God the Fa - ther, And, O Ho - ly Ghost, to Thee,
He is Al - pha and O - me - ga, He the Source, the End - ing He,
By the Ho - ly Ghost con - ceiv - ing, Bore the Sav - ior of our race;
Powers, do - min - ions, bow be - fore Him, And ex - tol our God and King.
Hymn and chant and high thanks - giv - ing And un - wea - ried prais - es be:
Of the things that are, that have been,
And the Babe, the world's Re - deem - er,
Let no tongue on earth be si - lent,
Hon - or, glo - ry and do - min - ion,
And that fu - ture years shall see, Ev - er - more and ev - er - more!
First re - vealed His sa - cred face, Ev - er - more and ev - er - more!
Ev - ery voice in con - cert ring, Ev - er - more and ev - er - more!
And e - ter - nal vic - to - ry, Ev - er - more and ev - er - more!

WORDS: Marcus Aurelius C. Prudentius, 348-413;
tr. John M. Neale, 1818-1866 and Henry W. Baker, 1821-1877, alt.
MUSIC: Plainsong, 13th century

DIVINUM MYSTERIUM
8.7.8.7.8.7.7.

Lo, How a Rose E'er Blooming 78

A shoot will come up from the stump of Jesse. Isaiah 11:1

1. Lo, how a Rose e'er bloom - ing From ten - der stem hath sprung! Of Jes - se's lin - eage com - ing As men of old have sung. It came, a flow - er bright, A - mid the cold of win - ter, When half - gone was the night.
2. I - sa - iah 'twas fore - told it, The Rose I have in mind; With Ma - ry we be - hold it, The vir - gin moth - er kind. To show God's love a - right She bore to men a Sav - ior, When half - gone was the night.
3. This Flower, whose fra - grance ten - der With sweet - ness fills the air, Dis - pels with glo - rious splen - dor, The dark - ness ev - ery - where. True man, yet ver - y[1] God, From sin and death He saves us, And light - ens ev - ery load.

WORDS: 15th century German; stanzas 1, 2, tr. Theodore Baker, 1851-1934; stanza 3, tr. Harriet Krauth Spaeth, 1845-1925
MUSIC: *Geistliche Kirchengesäng*, 1599; harm. Michael Praetorius, 1571-1621

ES IST EIN ROS'
7.6.7.6.6.7.6.

1. *very: true*

OUR GOD IS WITH US

MEDLEY

God Is with Us! Alleluia!

Emmanuel

79 God Is with Us! Alleluia!

Surely I am with you always, to the very end of the age. Matthew 28:20

1. His name is called Em-man-u-el— More won-der-ful than words can tell. God is with us! Al-le-lu-ia! Born in our dark-ness, He is Light. Born in our weak-ness, He is might.
2. Re-joice and lay a-side your fear. Re-joice, the Ho-ly One is here. God is with us! Al-le-lu-ia! Lift up your voic-es, come and sing; Come wor-ship Christ, the new-born King. God is with us! Al-le-lu-ia! God is with us! Al-le-
3. Praise God, from whom all bless-ings flow. Praise Him, all crea-tures here be-low. God is with us! Al-le-lu-ia! Praise Him a-bove, ye heaven-ly host. Praise Fa-ther, Son and Ho-ly Ghost.

(For different harmony, see No. 28)

WORDS: Ken Bible, b. 1950; Tom Fettke, b. 1941; stanza 3, Thomas Ken, 1637-1711
MUSIC: *Geistliche Kirchengesäng*, 1623

LASST UNS ERFREUEN
L.M. with Alleluias

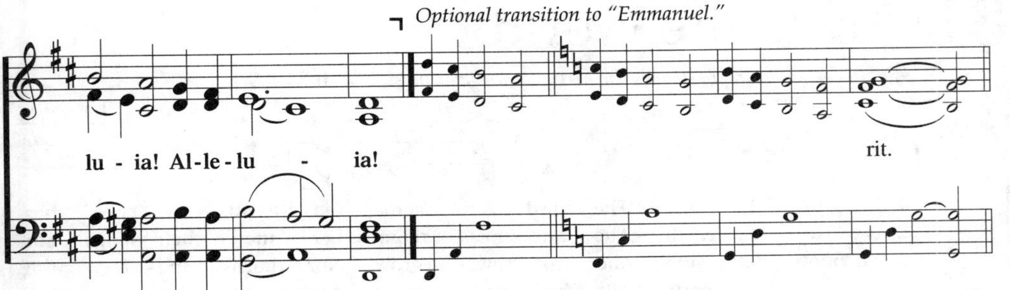
Optional transition to "Emmanuel."
lu - ia! Al-le-lu - ia!
rit.

Emmanuel 80

They will call him Immanuel—which means, "God with us." Matthew 1:23

Em-man - u - el, Em - man - u - el,

His name is called Em-man - u - el;

God with us, re - vealed in us;

His name is called Em-man - u - el.

WORDS: Bob McGee, b. 1944
MUSIC: Bob McGee, b. 1944

EMMANUEL
Irregular

81 Joy to the World!

Shout for joy to the LORD, *all the earth . . . for he comes.* Psalm 98:4, 9

1. Joy to the world! The Lord is come; Let earth re - ceive her
2. Joy to the earth! The Sav - ior reigns; Let men their songs em -
3. No more let sins and sor - rows grow, Nor thorns in - fest the
4. He rules the earth with truth and grace, And makes the na - tions
King. Let ev - ery heart pre - pare Him room, And
ploy, While fields and floods, rocks, hills and plains Re -
ground. He comes to make His bless - ings flow Far
prove The glo - ries of His right - eous - ness, And
heaven and na - ture sing, And heaven and na - ture
peat the sound - ing joy, Re - peat the sound - ing
as the curse is found, Far as the curse is
won - ders of His love, And won - ders of His
1. And heaven and na - ture sing,
1. And heaven and na - ture sing, And
sing, And heaven, and heaven and na - ture sing.
joy, Re - peat, re - peat the sound - ing joy.
found, Far as, far as the curse is found.
love, And won - ders, won - ders of His love.
heaven and na - ture sing,

WORDS: Isaac Watts, 1674-1748
MUSIC: G.F. Handel, 1685-1759; arr. Lowell Mason, 1792-1872

ANTIOCH
C.M. with repeats

Go, Tell It on the Mountain 82

When they had seen him, they spread the word . . . about this child. Luke 2:17

Refrain
Go, tell it on the moun - tain, O - ver the hills and ev - ery - where;
Go, tell it on the moun - tain That Je - sus Christ is born!
fine
1. While shep - herds kept their watch - ing O'er si - lent flocks by night, Be - hold through - out the heav - ens There shone a ho - ly light.
2. The shep - herds feared and trem - bled When, lo! a - bove the earth Rang out the an - gel cho - rus That hailed our Sav - ior's birth.
3. Down in a low - ly man - ger The hum - ble Christ was born, And God sent us sal - va - tion That bless - ed Christ - mas morn.
to Refrain

WORDS: John W. Work, 1872-1925
MUSIC: African-American spiritual

GO, TELL IT
Irregular

83 He Is Born

A Savior has been born to you. Luke 2:11

He is born, the holy Child; Play the oboe and bagpipes merrily!
He is born, the holy Child; Sing we all of the Savior mild.
fine
1. Through long ages of the past, Prophets have foretold His coming;
2. O, how lovely, O, how pure Is this perfect Child of heaven;
3. Jesus, Lord of all the world, Coming as a Child among us;
D.C. al fine
Through long ages of the past, Now the time has come at last!
O, how lovely, O, how pure, Gracious gift to humankind!
Jesus, Lord of all the world, Grant to us Thy heavenly peace.

WORDS: Traditional French carol, 19th century
MUSIC: French carol, 18th century; arr. Mark Blankenship, b. 1943

IL EST NÉ
Irregular

The Savior's Birth 84

In those days Caesar Augustus issued a decree that a census should be taken of the entire Roman world.

(This was the first census that took place while Quirinius was governor of Syria.)

And everyone went to his own town to register.

So Joseph also went up from the town of Nazareth in Galilee to Judea, to Bethlehem the town of David, because he belonged to the house and line of David.

He went there to register with Mary, who was pledged to be married to him and was expecting a child.

While they were there, the time came for the baby to be born,

and she gave birth to her firstborn, a son. She wrapped him in cloths and placed him in a manger, because there was no room for them in the inn.

And there were shepherds living out in the fields nearby, keeping watch over their flocks at night.

An angel of the Lord appeared to them, and the glory of the Lord shone around them, and they were terrified.

But the angel said to them, "Do not be afraid. I bring you good news of great joy that will be for all the people.

Today in the town of David a Savior has been born to you; he is Christ the Lord.

This will be a sign to you: You will find a baby wrapped in cloths and lying in a manger."

Suddenly a great company of the heavenly host appeared with the angel, praising God and saying,

"Glory to God in the highest,
and on earth peace to men on whom his favor rests."

When the angels had left them and gone into heaven, the shepherds said to one another, "Let's go to Bethlehem and see this thing that has happened, which the Lord has told us about."

So they hurried off and found Mary and Joseph, and the baby, who was lying in the manger.

When they had seen him, they spread the word concerning what had been told them about this child,

and all who heard it were amazed at what the shepherds said to them.

But Mary treasured up all these things and pondered them in her heart.

The shepherds returned, glorifying and praising God for all the things they had heard and seen, which were just as they had been told.

Luke 2:1-20

85 Away in a Manger

FIRST TUNE

She gave birth to her firstborn, a son . . . and placed him in a manger. Luke 2:7

1. A - way in a man - ger, no crib for a bed,
2. The cat - tle are low - ing; the Ba - by a - wakes,
3. Be near me, Lord Je - sus; I ask Thee to stay
The lit - tle Lord Je - sus laid down His sweet head.
But lit - tle Lord Je - sus, no cry - ing He makes.
Close by me for - ev - er, and love me, I pray.
The stars in the sky looked down where He lay;
I love Thee, Lord Je - sus; look down from the sky,
Bless all the dear chil - dren in Thy ten - der care,
The lit - tle Lord Je - sus a - sleep on the hay.
And stay by my cra - dle till morn - ing is nigh.
And fit us for heav - en to live with Thee there.

WORDS: Stanzas 1, 2 from *Little Children's Book*, 1885; stanza 3, John T. McFarland, 1851-1913
MUSIC: James R. Murray, 1841-1905

AWAY IN A MANGER
11.11.11.11.

Away in a Manger 86

SECOND TUNE

She gave birth to her firstborn, a son . . . and placed him in a manger. Luke 2:7

1. A - way in a man - ger, no crib for a bed,
2. The cat - tle are low - ing; the Ba - by a - wakes,
3. Be near me, Lord Je - sus; I ask Thee to stay
The lit - tle Lord Je - sus laid down His sweet head.
But lit - tle Lord Je - sus, no cry - ing He makes.
Close by me for - ev - er, and love me, I pray.
The stars in the bright sky looked down where He lay;
I love Thee, Lord Je - sus; look down from the sky,
Bless all the dear chil - dren in Thy ten - der care,
The lit - tle Lord Je - sus a - sleep on the hay.
And stay by my cra - dle till morn - ing is nigh.
And fit us for heav - en to live with Thee there.

WORDS: Stanzas 1, 2 from *Little Children's Book*, 1885; stanza 3, John T. McFarland, 1851-1913
MUSIC: William J. Kirkpatrick, 1838-1921

CRADLE SONG
11.11.11.11.

87 Infant Holy, Infant Lowly

He is Lord of lords and King of kings. Revelation 17:14

1. In - fant ho - ly, In - fant low - ly, For His bed a cat - tle
2. Flocks were sleep - ing, shep-herds keep - ing Vig - il till the morn-ing
stall; Ox - en low - ing, lit - tle know - ing Christ, the Babe, is Lord of
new Saw the glo - ry, heard the sto - ry, Tid - ings of a gos - pel
all. Swift are wing - ing an - gels sing - ing, No - els ring - ing, tid - ings
true. Thus re - joic - ing, free from sor - row, Prais - es voic - ing greet the
bring - ing: Christ, the Babe, is Lord of all! Christ, the Babe, is Lord of all!
mor - row: Christ, the Babe, was born for you! Christ, the Babe, was born for you!

WORDS: Polish carol; para. Edith M.G. Reed, 1885-1933
MUSIC: Traditional Polish melody

W ZLOBIE LEZY
8.7.8.7.8.8.7.7.

Good Christian Friends, Rejoice 88

My spirit rejoices in God my Savior. Luke 1:47

1. Good Chris-tian friends, re - joice, With heart and soul and voice!
2. Good Chris-tian friends, re - joice, With heart and soul and voice!
3. Good Chris-tian friends, re - joice, With heart and soul and voice!
Give you heed to what we say: News! News! Je - sus Christ is
Now you hear of end - less bliss: Joy! Joy! Je - sus Christ was
Now you need not fear the grave: Peace! Peace! Je - sus Christ was
born to - day! Ox and ass be - fore Him bow, And He is in the
born for this! O - pened He the heaven - ly door, And we are blest for -
born to save! Calls you one and calls you all To gain His ev - er -
man - ger now. Christ is born to - day! Christ is born to - day!
ev - er - more. Christ was born for this! Christ was born for this!
last - ing hall. Christ was born to save! Christ was born to save!

Optional segue to "Worship the King." No transition required.

WORDS: Latin carol, 14th century; tr. John M. Neale, 1818-1866, alt.
MUSIC: German melody, 14th century; harm. John Stainer, 1840-1901

IN DULCI JUBILO
Irregular

89 Worship the King

They saw the child with his mother Mary, and they bowed down and worshiped him.
Matthew 2:11

1. O, come to the place where the ho - ly Child is laid;
2. The Sav - ior has come, let all the na - tions sing;
O come, let us see the new - born King.
The moun - tains ring out with an - gel - ic praise.
For He is our God, and great - ly to be praised;
The heav - ens re - joice, for the earth re - ceives her King;
Come, let us wor - ship the King.

WORDS: Bill George, 20th century; Billy Smiley, 20th century
MUSIC: Bill George, 20th century; Billy Smiley, 20th century

WORSHIP THE KING
Irregular

1.
2.
Come let us wor-ship the King— Je-sus the Sav-ior is
born; For the Lord will reign o-ver all the earth.
Lord is great, and great-ly to be praised through all the
earth— Let us wor - ship the King. (wor-ship the King.)

90 The First Noel

They bowed down and worshiped him. Then they opened their treasures. Matthew 2:11

1. The first No - el, the an - gel did say, Was to cer - tain poor
2. They look - ed up and saw a star Shin - ing in the
3. And by the light of that same star, Three wise men
4. This star drew nigh to the north - west, O'er Beth - le -
5. Then en - tered in those wise men three Full rev - erent -
6. Then let us all with one ac - cord Sing prais - es
shep - herds in fields as they lay, In fields where they lay
east be - yond them far, And to the earth it
came from coun - try far; To seek for a king was
hem it took its rest, And there it did both
ly up - on their knee, And of - fered there in
to our heaven - ly Lord, That hath made heaven and
keep - ing their sheep, On a cold win - ter's night that was so deep.
gave great light, And so it con - tin - ued both day and night.
their in - tent, And to fol - low the star wher - ev - er it went.
stop and stay Right o - ver the place where Je - sus lay.
His pres - ence Their gold, and myrrh, and frank - in - cense.
earth of naught,1 And with His blood man - kind hath bought.

WORDS: Traditional English carol
MUSIC: From William Sandys' *Christmas Carols*, 1833; arr. John Stainer, 1840-1901

THE FIRST NOEL
Irregular with Refrain

1. naught: nothing

Refrain
No - el, No - el, No - el, No - el. Born is the King of Is - ra - el!

How Great Our Joy 91

I bring you good news of great joy. Luke 2:10

1. While by the sheep we watched at night, Glad tid - ings brought an an - gel bright.
2. There shall be born, so he did say, In Beth - le - hem a Child to - day.
3. There shall the Child lie in a stall, This Child who shall re - deem us all.
4. This gift of God we'll cher - ish well, That ev - er joy our hearts shall fill.

f How great our joy! *p* Great our joy! *f* Joy, joy, joy! *p* Joy, joy, joy! *f* Praise we the Lord in heaven on high! *p* Praise we the Lord in heaven on high!

* *May be sung alternating Men's and Women's voices.*

WORDS: Traditional German carol
MUSIC: Traditional German melody; arr. Hugo Jüngst, 1853-1923

JÜNGST
Irregular

92 While Shepherds Watched Their Flocks

There were shepherds living out in the fields nearby, keeping watch over their flocks at night.
Luke 2:8

1. While shep - herds watched their flocks by night, All seat - ed on the
2. "Fear not," said he, for might - y dread Had seized their trou - bled
3. "To you, in Da - vid's town this day Is born of Da - vid's
4. "The heaven - ly Babe you there shall find To hu - man view dis -
5. Thus spake the ser - aph,1 and forth - with Ap - peared a shin - ing
6. "All glo - ry be to God on high, And to the earth be
ground, The an - gel of the Lord came down, And
mind, "Glad tid - ings of great joy I bring To
line, A Sav - ior, who is Christ the Lord; And
played, All mean - ly wrapped in swad - dling clothes, And
throng Of an - gels prais - ing God, who thus Ad -
peace. Good will hence - forth, from heaven to men, Be -
glo - ry shone a - round, And glo - ry shone a - round.
you and all man - kind, To you and all man - kind.
this shall be the sign, And this shall be the sign:
in a man - ger laid, And in a man - ger laid."
dressed their joy - ful song, Ad - dressed their joy - ful song:
gin and nev - er cease! Be - gin and nev - er cease!"

WORDS: Nahum Tate, 1652-1715
MUSIC: Adapt. from G.F. Handel, 1685-1759; from Weyman's *Melodia Sacra*, 1815

CHRISTMAS
C.M. with repeat

1. seraph: angelic being

Sing We Now of Christmas 93

The heavenly host appeared . . . saying, "Glory to God in the highest." Luke 2:13-14

1. Sing we now of Christ - mas, No - el, sing we here!
2. An - gels called to shep - herds, "Leave your flocks at rest;
3. In the stall they found Him; Jo - seph and Ma - ry mild
4. From the east - ern coun - try came the kings a - far,
5. Gold and myrrh they took there, gifts of great - est price;
Hear our grate - ful prais - es to the Babe so dear.
Jour - ney forth to Beth - l'hem, find the Lamb - kin blest."
Seat - ed 'round the man - ger, watch - ing the ho - ly Child.
Bear - ing gifts to Beth - l'hem, guid - ed by a star.
There was ne'er a sta - ble so like par - a - dise.
Sing we No - el, the King is born, No - el!
Sing we now of Christ - mas, sing we now No - el!

WORDS: Traditional French carol
MUSIC: Traditional French carol; arr. Mark Blankenship, b. 1943

FRENCH CAROL
Irregular

94 Hark, the Herald Angels Sing

Glory to God in the highest, and on earth peace. Luke 2:14

1. Hark, the her - ald an - gels sing, "Glo - ry to the new-born King;
2. Christ, by high - est heaven a - dored; Christ, the ev - er - last - ing Lord!
3. Hail, the heaven-born Prince of Peace! Hail, the Sun of Right-eous-ness!
Peace on earth, and mer - cy mild, God and sin - ners rec - on - ciled!"
Late in time be - hold Him come, Off - spring of the Vir - gin's womb.
Light and life to all He brings, Risen with heal - ing in His wings.
Joy - ful, all ye na - tions, rise, Join the tri - umph of the skies;
Veiled in flesh the God - head see; Hail th'in - car - nate De - i - ty,
Mild He lays His glo - ry by, Born that man no more may die,
With th'an - gel - ic host pro - claim, "Christ is born in Beth - le - hem!"
Pleased as man with men to dwell, Je - sus, our Em - man - u - el!
Born to raise the sons of earth, Born to give them sec - ond birth.
Refrain
Hark, the her - ald an - gels sing, "Glo - ry to the new - born King."

WORDS: Charles Wesley, 1707-1788
MUSIC: Felix Mendelssohn, 1809-1847; adapt. William H. Cummings, 1831-1915

MENDELSSOHN
7.7.7.7.D. with Refrain

Angels We Have Heard on High 95

The heavenly host appeared with the angel, praising God. Luke 2:13

1. An - gels we have heard on high, Sweet - ly sing - ing o'er the plains,
2. Shep - herds, why this ju - bi - lee? Why your joy - ous strains pro - long?
3. Come to Beth - le - hem and see Him whose birth the an - gels sing;
4. See with - in a man - ger laid Je - sus, Lord of heaven and earth!
And the moun - tains in re - ply Ech - o back their joy - ous strains.
Say what may the tid - ings be Which in - spire your heaven - ly song?
Come, a - dore on bend - ed knee Christ the Lord, the new - born King.
Ma - ry, Jo - seph, lend your aid, With us sing our Sav - ior's birth.
Refrain
Glo - - ri - a
in ex - cel - sis De - o,
Glo - - - ri - a in ex - cel - sis De - o.

Optional segue to "Angels, from the Realms of Glory." No transition required.

WORDS: Traditional French carol
MUSIC: Traditional French carol

GLORIA
7.7.7.7. with Refrain

96 Angels, from the Realms of Glory

We saw his star in the east and have come to worship him. Matthew 2:2

1. An - gels, from the realms of glo - ry, Wing your flight o'er all the earth; Ye who sang cre - a - tion's sto - ry, Now pro - claim Mes - si - ah's birth: Come and wor - ship, come and wor - ship, Wor - ship Christ, the new - born King!
2. Shep - herds, in the fields a - bid - ing, Watch - ing o'er your flocks by night, God with man is now re - sid - ing, Yon - der shines the in - fant Light: Come and wor - ship, come and wor - ship, Wor - ship Christ, the new - born King!
3. Sa - ges, leave your con - tem - pla - tions, Bright - er vi - sions beam a - far; Seek the great De - sire of na - tions; Ye have seen His na - tal star: Come and wor - ship, come and wor - ship, Wor - ship Christ, the new - born King!
4. Saints, be - fore the al - tar bend - ing, Watch - ing long in hope and fear, Sud - den - ly the Lord, de - scend - ing, In His tem - ple shall ap - pear: Come and wor - ship, come and wor - ship, Wor - ship Christ, the new - born King!

WORDS: James Montgomery, 1771-1854
MUSIC: Henry T. Smart, 1813-1879

REGENT SQUARE
8.7.8.7.8.7.

O Little Town of Bethlehem 97

Bethlehem . . . out of you will come for me one who will be ruler over Israel. Micah 5:2

1. O lit - tle town of Beth - le - hem, How still we see thee lie;
2. For Christ is born of Ma - ry, And gath - ered all a - bove,
3. How si - lent - ly, how si - lent - ly The won - drous Gift is given!
4. O Ho - ly Child of Beth - le - hem! De - scend to us, we pray.
A - bove thy deep and dream - less sleep The si - lent stars go by.
While mor - tals sleep, the an - gels keep Their watch of won - dering love.
So God im - parts to hu - man hearts The bless - ings of His heaven.
Cast out our sin, and en - ter in; Be born in us to - day.
Yet in thy dark streets shin - eth The ev - er - last - ing Light;
O morn - ing stars, to - geth - er Pro - claim the ho - ly birth;
No ear may hear His com - ing, But in this world of sin,
We hear the Christ - mas an - gels The great glad ti - dings tell;
The hopes and fears of all the years Are met in thee to - night.
And prais - es sing to God the King, And peace to men on earth.
Where meek souls will re - ceive Him, still The dear Christ en - ters in.
O, come to us, a - bide with us, Our Lord Em - man - u - el.

WORDS: Phillips Brooks, 1835-1893
MUSIC: Lewis H. Redner, 1831-1908

ST. LOUIS
8.6.8.6.7.6.8.6.

98 A Christmas Hymn

I tell you . . . if they keep quiet, the stones will cry out. Luke 19:40

1. A sta - ble lamp is light - ed Whose glow shall wake the sky; The stars shall bend their voic - es, And ev - ery stone shall cry. And ev - ery stone shall cry, And straw like gold shall shine; A barn shall har - bor heav - en, A stall be - come a shrine.
2. This child through Da - vid's ci - ty Shall ride in tri - umph by; The palm shall strew its branch - es, And ev - ery stone shall cry. And ev - ery stone shall cry, Though heav - y, dull, and dumb, And lie with - in the road - way, To pave His king - dom come.
3. Yet He shall be for - sak - en And yield - ed up to die; The sky shall groan and dark - en, And ev - ery stone shall cry. And ev - ery stone shall cry For ston - y hearts of men: God's blood up - on the spear - head, God's love re - fused a - gain.
4. But now, as at the end - ing, The low is shift - ed high; The stars shall bend their voic - es, And ev - ery stone shall cry. And ev - ery stone shall cry In prais - es of the child By whose de - scent a - mong us The worlds are re - con - ciled.

WORDS: Richard Wilbur, b. 1921
MUSIC: Greg Martin, b. 1950

LIU
7.6.7.6.6.6.7.6.

I Heard the Bells on Christmas Day 99

And he will be their peace. Micah 5:5

1. I heard the bells on Christ - mas day Their old fa - mil - iar car - ols play, And wild and sweet the words re - peat Of peace on earth, good will to men.
2. I thought how, as the day had come, The bel - fries of all Chris - ten - dom Had rolled a - long th'un - bro - ken song Of peace on earth, good will to men.
3. And in de - spair I bowed my head: "There is no peace on earth," I said, "For hate is strong, and mocks the song Of peace on earth, good will to men."
4. Then pealed the bells more loud and deep: "God is not dead, nor doth He sleep; The wrong shall fail, the right pre - vail, With peace on earth, good will to men."
5. Till, ring - ing, sing - ing on its way, The world re - volved from night to day— A voice, a chime, a chant sub - lime, Of peace on earth, good will to men.

WORDS: Henry W. Longfellow, 1807-1882
MUSIC: John Calkin, 1827-1905

WALTHAM
L.M.

100 O Come, All Ye Faithful

Let's go to Bethlehem and see this thing that has happened. Luke 2:15

1. O come, all ye faith - ful, Joy - ful and tri - um - phant, O
2. Sing, choirs of an - gels, Sing in ex - ul - ta - tion, O
3. Yea, Lord, we greet Thee, Born this hap - py morn - ing; O
come ye, O come ye to Beth - le - hem; Come and be - hold Him
sing, all ye cit - i - zens of heaven a - bove: "Glo - ry to God
Je - sus, to Thee be all glo - ry given; Word of the Fa - ther,
Born the King of an - gels.
In the high - est!"
Now in flesh ap - pear - ing.
Refrain
O come! O come a - dore Him,
O come, let us a - dore Him, O come, let us a - dore Him, O come, let us a - dore Him, Christ the Lord.

WORDS: Attrib. John F. Wade, 1711-1786; tr. (Latin) Frederick Oakeley, 1802-1880
MUSIC: John F. Wade's *Cantus Diversi*, 1751

ADESTE FIDELES
Irregular with Refrain

There's a Song in the Air 101

Do not be afraid. I bring you good news of great joy. Luke 2:10

1. There's a song in the air! There's a star in the sky!
2. There's a tu - mult of joy O'er the won - der - ful birth,
3. In the light of that star Lie the a - ges im - pearled:
4. We re - joice in the light, And we ech - o the song
There's a moth - er's deep prayer And a ba - by's low cry!
For a Vir - gin's sweet Boy Is the Lord of the earth.
And that song from a - far Has swept o - ver the world.
That comes down through the night From the heav - en - ly throng;
And the star rains its fire while the beau - ti - ful sing,
And the star rains its fire while the beau - ti - ful sing,
Ev - ery hearth is a - flame, and the beau - ti - ful sing,
And we shout for the love - ly good news that they bring,
For the man - ger of Beth - le - hem cra - dles a King!
For the man - ger of Beth - le - hem cra - dles a King!
In the homes of the na - tions that Je - sus is King!
And we greet in His cra - dle our Sav - ior and King!

WORDS: Josiah G. Holland, 1819-1881, alt.
MUSIC: Karl P. Harrington, 1861-1953

CHRISTMAS SONG
6.6.6.6.12.12.

102 It Came upon the Midnight Clear

An angel of the Lord appeared to them, and the glory of the Lord shone around them. Luke 2:9

1. It came up - on the mid - night clear, That glo - rious song of old,
2. Still through the clo - ven skies they come, With peace - ful wings un - furled,
3. And ye, be - neath life's crush - ing load, Whose forms are bend - ing low,
4. For lo, the days are has - tening on, By proph - et bards fore - told,
From an - gels bend - ing near the earth, To touch their harps of gold:
And still their heaven - ly mu - sic floats O'er all the wea - ry world:
Who toil a - long the climb - ing way With pain - ful steps and slow,
When with the ev - er cir - cling years Comes round the age of gold;
"Peace on the earth, good will to men, From heaven's all - gra - cious King."
A - bove its sad and low - ly plains They bend on hov - ering wing,
Look now! For glad and gold - en hours Come swift - ly on the wing:
When peace shall o - ver all the earth Its an - cient splen - dors fling,
The world in sol - emn still - ness lay To hear the an - gels sing.
And ev - er o'er its Ba - bel sounds The bless - ed an - gels sing.
O, rest be - side the wea - ry road And hear the an - gels sing.
And the whole world give back the song Which now the an - gels sing.

WORDS: Edmund H. Sears, 1810-1876
MUSIC: Richard S. Willis, 1819-1900

CAROL
C.M.D.

In the Bleak Midwinter 103

When the time had fully come, God sent his Son, born of a woman. Galatians 4:4

1. In the bleak midwinter,
Frosty wind made moan,
Earth stood hard as iron,
Water like a stone;
Snow had fallen, snow on snow,
Snow on snow,
In the bleak midwinter,
Long ago.

2. Our God, heav'n cannot hold Him,
Nor earth sustain;
Heaven and earth shall flee away
When He comes to reign:
In the bleak midwinter
A stable-place sufficed
The Lord God incarnate,
Jesus Christ.

3. Angels and archangels
May have gathered there,
Cherubim and seraphim[1]
Thronged the air;
But His mother only,
In her maiden bliss,
Worshiped the beloved
With a kiss.

4. What can I give Him,
Poor as I am?
If I were a shepherd,
I would bring a lamb;
If I were a wise man,
I would do my part;
Yet what I can, I give Him:
Give my heart.

WORDS: Christina Rossetti, 1830-1894
MUSIC: Gustav T. Holst, 1874-1934

CRANHAM
Irregular

1. *Cherubim and seraphim: angelic beings*

CHRIST IS BORN

MEDLEY

Silent Night! Holy Night!
Child in the Manger

104 Silent Night! Holy Night!

So they hurried off and found Mary and Joseph, and the baby. Luke 2:16

1. Si - lent night! Ho - ly night! All is calm, all is bright,
2. Si - lent night! Ho - ly night! Shep - herds quake at the sight;
3. Si - lent night! Ho - ly night! Son of God, love's pure light,
Round yon vir - gin moth-er and Child. Ho - ly In - fant, so ten - der and mild,
Glo - ries stream from heav-en a - far, Heaven-ly hosts sing, "Al - le - lu - ia,
Ra - diant beams from Thy ho - ly face, With the dawn of re - deem - ing grace,
Sleep in heav - en - ly peace, Sleep in heav - en - ly peace.
Christ, the Sav - ior, is born! Christ, the Sav - ior, is born!"
Je - sus, Lord, at Thy birth, Je - sus, Lord, at Thy birth.
Song ending
Optional transition to "Child in the Manger."
birth.

WORDS: Joseph Mohr, 1792-1848; tr. John F. Young, 1820-1885
MUSIC: Franz Grüber, 1787-1863

STILLE NACHT
Irregular

Child in the Manger 105

You will find a baby wrapped in cloths and lying in a manger. Luke 2:12

1. Child in the man - ger, In - fant of Ma - ry; Out - cast and stran - ger, Lord of all; Child who in - her - its All our trans - gres - sions, All our de - mer - its On Him fall.
2. Once the most ho - ly Child of sal - va - tion Gent - ly and low - ly Lived be - low; Now as our glo - rious Might - y Re - deem - er, See Him vic - to - rious O'er each foe.
3. Proph - ets fore - told Him In - fant of won - der; An - gels be - hold Him On His throne; Wor - thy our Sav - ior Of all our prais - es; Hap - py for - ev - er Are His own.

WORDS: Mary MacDonald, 1789-1872; tr. Lachlan Macbean, 1853-1931
MUSIC: Traditional Gaelic melody; arr. Mark Hayes, b. 1953

BUNESSAN
5.5.5.3.D.

106 What Child Is This?

They spread the word concerning what had been told them about this child. Luke 2:17

1. What Child is this, who, laid to rest, On Ma-ry's lap is sleep-ing? Whom
2. Why lies He in such mean es-tate² Where ox and ass are feed-ing? Good
3. So bring Him in-cense, gold and myrrh, Come, peas-ant, king, to own Him. The
an-gels greet with an-thems sweet, While shep-herds watch are keep-ing?
Chris-tian, fear; for sin-ners here The si-lent Word is plead-ing.
King of kings sal-va-tion brings; Let lov-ing hearts en-throne Him.
This, this is Christ the King, Whom shep-herds guard and an-gels sing:
Nails, spear, shall pierce Him through, The cross be borne for me, for you:
Raise, raise the song on high, The Vir-gin sings her lul-la-by:
Haste, haste to bring Him laud,¹ The Babe, the Son of Ma-ry!
Hail, hail the Word made flesh, The Babe, the Son of Ma-ry!
Joy, joy, for Christ is born, The Babe, the Son of Ma-ry!

WORDS: William C. Dix, 1837-1898
MUSIC: Traditional English melody, 16th century; harm. John Stainer, 1840-1901

GREENSLEEVES
8.7.8.7.6.8.6.7.

1. *laud: praise*
2. *mean estate: poor conditions*

Once in Royal David's City 107

For there is born to you this day in the city of David a Savior, who is Christ the Lord.
Luke 2:11, NKJV

1. Once in roy - al Da - vid's cit - y Stood a low - ly cat - tle shed,
2. He came down to earth from heav - en Who is God and Lord of all,
3. And, through all His won - drous child - hood, He would hon - or and o - bey,
4. And our eyes at last shall see Him Through His own re - deem - ing love;
5. Not in that poor low - ly sta - ble, With the ox - en stand - ing by,
Where a moth - er laid her Ba - by In a man - ger for His bed.
And His shel - ter was a sta - ble, And His cra - dle was a stall.
Love, and watch the low - ly maid - en In whose gen - tle arms He lay.
For that Child so dear and gen - tle Is our Lord in heaven a - bove;
We shall see Him; but in heav - en Set at God's right hand on high;
Ma - ry was that moth - er mild, Je - sus Christ her lit - tle Child.
With the poor, and mean[1] and low - ly, Lived on earth our Sav - ior ho - ly.
Chris - tian chil - dren all must be Mild, o - be - dient, good as He.
And He leads His chil - dren on To the place where He has gone.
When like stars His chil - dren crowned, All in white shall wait a - round.

WORDS: Cecil F.H. Alexander, 1818-1895
MUSIC: Henry J. Gauntlett, 1805-1876

IRBY
8.7.8.7.7.7.

1. *mean: common*

108 Thou Didst Leave Thy Throne

He came to that which was his own, but his own did not receive him. John 1:11

1. Thou didst leave Thy throne and Thy king - ly crown When Thou cam - est to earth for me, But in Beth - le - hem's home there was found no room For Thy ho - ly na - tiv - i - ty.
2. Heav - en's arch - es rang when the an - gels sang, Pro - claim - ing Thy roy - al dec - ree; But in low - ly birth didst Thou come to earth, And in great hu - mil - i - ty.
3. The fox - es found rest, and the birds their nest In the shade of the for - est tree; But Thy couch was the sod, O Thou Son of God, In the des - erts of Gal - i - lee.
4. Thou cam - est, O Lord, with the liv - ing Word That should set Thy peo - ple free; But with mock - ing scorn and with crown of thorn They bore Thee to Cal - va - ry.
5. When the heav - ens shall ring and the an - gels sing At Thy com - ing to vic - to - ry, Let Thy voice call me home, say - ing, "Yet there is room, There is room at My side for thee."
1–4. O, come to my heart, Lord Jesus— There is room in my heart for Thee!
5. My heart shall re - joice, Lord Je - sus, When Thou com - est and call - est for me.

WORDS: Emily E.S. Elliott, 1836-1897, alt.
MUSIC: Timothy R. Matthews, 1826-1910

MARGARET
Irregular

We Three Kings 109

After Jesus was born in Bethlehem . . . Magi from the east came. Matthew 2:1

1. We three kings of Orient are; Bearing gifts we traverse afar—
2. Born a King on Bethlehem's plain; Gold I bring to crown Him again,
3. Frankincense to offer have I; Incense owns a Deity nigh.
4. Myrrh is mine: its bitter perfume Breathes a life of gathering gloom—
5. Glorious now behold Him arise, King and God and Sacrifice;
Field and fountain, moor and mountain— Following yonder star.
King forever, ceasing never Over us all to reign.
Prayer and praising, all men raising, Worship Him, God on high.
Sorrowing, sighing, bleeding, dying, Sealed in the stone-cold tomb.
Alleluia, alleluia! Earth to heaven replies.
Refrain
O star of wonder, star of night, Star with royal beauty bright,
Westward leading, still proceeding, Guide us to thy perfect light.

WORDS: John H. Hopkins, Jr., 1820-1891
MUSIC: John H. Hopkins, Jr., 1820-1891

KINGS OF ORIENT
8.8.4.4.6. with Refrain

110 We Have Come to Worship

After Jesus was born in Bethlehem in Judea, during the time of King Herod, Magi from the east came to Jerusalem and asked,

"Where is the one who has been born king of the Jews? We saw his star in the east and have come to worship him."

When King Herod heard this he was disturbed, and all Jerusalem with him. When he had called together all the people's chief priests and teachers of the law, he asked them where the Christ was to be born.

"In Bethlehem in Judea," they replied, "for this is what the prophet has written:

'But you, Bethlehem, in the land of Judah, are by no means least among the rulers of Judah; for out of you will come a ruler who will be the shepherd of my people Israel.'"

Then Herod called the Magi secretly and found out from them the exact time the star had appeared. He sent them to Bethlehem and said,

"Go and make a careful search for the child. As soon as you find him, report to me, so that I too may go and worship him."

After they had heard the king, they went on their way, and the star they had seen in the east went ahead of them until it stopped over the place where the child was. When they saw the star, they were overjoyed. On coming to the house, they saw the child with his mother Mary, and they bowed down and worshiped him.

Then they opened their treasures and presented him with gifts of gold and of incense and of myrrh. *Matthew 2:1-11*

111 Adoration

Worship the LORD in the splendor of his holiness. Psalm 96:9

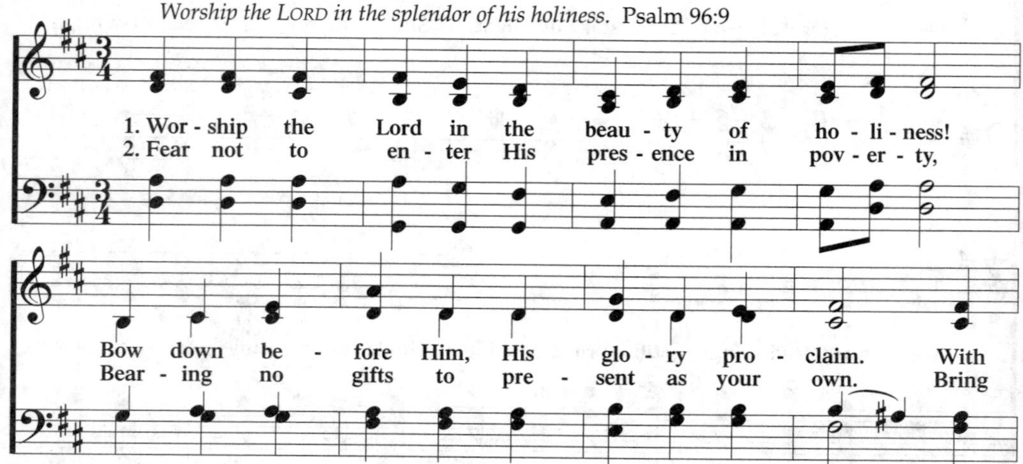
1. Wor - ship the Lord in the beau - ty of ho - li - ness!
2. Fear not to en - ter His pres - ence in pov - er - ty,
Bow down be - fore Him, His glo - ry pro - claim. With
Bear - ing no gifts to pre - sent as your own. Bring

WORDS: Stanza 1, John S. B. Monsell, 1811-1875; stanza 2, Ken Bible, b. 1950
MUSIC: Tom Fettke, b. 1941

JANICE
12.10.13.10.

gold of o - be - dience and in - cense of low - li - ness,
truth in its beau - ty, and love in its pu - ri - ty—
Kneel and a - dore Him— the Lord is His name!
These are the of - ferings to lay at His throne.
As with Gladness Men of Old 112
When they saw the star, they were overjoyed. Matthew 2:10
1. As with glad - ness men of old Did the guid - ing star be - hold;
2. As with joy - ful steps they sped To that low - ly man - ger bed,
3. As they of - fered gifts most rare At that man - ger rude and bare,
4. Ho - ly Je - sus, ev - ery day Keep us in the nar - row way;
As with joy they hailed its light, Lead - ing on - ward, beam - ing bright.
There to bend the knee be - fore Him whom heaven and earth a - dore.
So may we with ho - ly joy, Pure and free from sin's al - loy,
And, when earth - ly things are past, Bring our ran - somed souls at last
So, most gra - cious Lord, may we Ev - er - more be led to Thee.
So may we with will - ing feet Ev - er seek the mer - cy seat.
All our cost - liest treas - ures bring, Christ, to Thee, our heaven - ly King.
Where they need no star to guide, Where no clouds Thy glo - ry hide.

WORDS: William C. Dix, 1837-1898
MUSIC: Conrad Kocher, 1786-1872; arr. William H. Monk, 1823-1889

DIX
7.7.7.7.7.7.

113 O, Sing a Song of Bethlehem

He appeared in a body . . . was believed on in the world, was taken up in glory.
1 Timothy 3:16

1. O, sing a song of Beth-le-hem, of shep-herds watch-ing there,
2. O, sing a song of Naz-a-reth, of sun-ny days of joy,
3. O, sing a song of Gal-i-lee, of lake and woods and hill,
4. O, sing a song of Cal-va-ry, its glo-ry and dis-may;
And of the news that came to them from an-gels in the air:
O, sing of frag-rant flow-ers' breath, and of the sin-less Boy:
Of Him who walked up-on the sea and bade the waves be still:
Of Him who hung up-on the tree, and took our sins a-way:
The light that shone in Beth-le-hem fills all the world to-day;
For now the flowers of Naz-a-reth in ev-ery heart may grow;
For though, like waves on Gal-i-lee, dark seas of trou-ble roll,
For He who died on Cal-va-ry is ris-en from the grave,
Of Je-sus' birth and peace on earth the an-gels sing al-way.
Now spreads the fame of His dear name on all the winds that blow.
When faith has heard the Mas-ter's word, falls peace up-on the soul.
And Christ, our Lord, by heaven a-dored, is might-y now to save.

WORDS: Louis F. Benson, 1855-1930
MUSIC: English melody; arr. Ralph Vaughan Williams, 1872-1958

KINGSFOLD
C.M.D.

Who Is He in Yonder Stall? 114

The LORD *Almighty—he is the King of glory.* Psalm 24:10

1. Who is He in yon - der stall, at whose feet the shep-herds fall?
2. Who is He the peo - ple bless for His words of gen - tle - ness?
3. Who is He who stands and weeps at the grave where Laz - arus sleeps?
4. Lo! at mid-night, who is He prays in dark Geth-sem - a - ne?
5. Who is He who, from the grave, comes to heal and help and save?
Who is He in deep dis - tress, fast - ing in the wil - der - ness?
Who is He to whom they bring all the sick and sor - row - ing?
Who is He the gath - ering throng greet with loud, tri - um - phant song?
Who is He on yon - der tree dies in grief and ag - o - ny?
Who is He that, from His throne, rules through all the world a - lone?
Refrain
'Tis the Lord! O won-drous sto - ry! 'Tis the Lord! the King of glo - ry!
At His feet we hum-bly fall, Crown Him, crown Him Lord of all!

WORDS: Benjamin R. Hanby, 1833-1867
MUSIC: Benjamin R. Hanby, 1833-1867

LOWLINESS
7.7.7.7. with Refrain

115 One Day!

At just the right time, when we were still powerless, Christ died for the ungodly. Romans 5:6

1. One day when heav - en was filled with His prais - es, One day when sin was as black as could be, Je - sus came forth to be born of a vir - gin, Dwelt a - mong men, my ex - am - ple is He!
2. One day they led Him up Cal - va - ry's moun - tain, One day they nailed Him to die on the tree; Suf - fer - ing an - guish, de - spised and re - ject - ed, Bear - ing our sins, my Re - deem - er is He!
3. One day they left Him a - lone in the gar - den, One day He rest - ed, from suf - fer - ing free; An - gels came down o'er His tomb to keep vig - il; Hope of the hope - less, my Sav - ior is He!
4. One day the grave could con - ceal Him no long - er, One day the stone rolled a - way from the door; Then He a - rose, o - ver death He has con - quered, Now is as - cend - ed, my Lord ev - er - more!
5. One day the trum - pet will sound for His com - ing, One day the skies with His glo - ry will shine; Won - der - ful day, my be - lov - ed ones bring - ing; Glo - ri - ous Sav - ior, this Je - sus is mine!
Refrain
Liv - ing, He loved me; dy - ing He saved me; Bur - ied, He

WORDS: J. Wilbur Chapman, 1859-1918
MUSIC: Charles H. Marsh, 1886-1956

CHAPMAN
11.10.11.10. with Refrain

car - ried my sins far a - way; Ris - ing, He jus - ti - fied free - ly for -
e - ver; One day He's com - ing— O glo - ri - ous day!

The Word Became Flesh 116

In the beginning was the Word, and the Word was with God, and the Word was God.

He was with God in the beginning.

Through him all things were made; without him nothing was made that has been made.

In him was life, and that life was the light of men.

The light shines in the darkness, but the darkness has not understood it.

There came a man who was sent from God; his name was John.

He came as a witness to testify concerning that light, so that through him all men might believe.

He himself was not the light; he came only as a witness to the light.

The true light that gives light to every man was coming into the world.

He was in the world, and though the world was made through him, the world did not recognize him.

He came to that which was his own, but his own did not receive him.

Yet to all who received him, to those who believed in his name, he gave the right to become children of God—

children born not of natural descent, nor of human decision or a husband's will, but born of God.

The Word became flesh and made his dwelling among us. We have seen his glory, the glory of the One and Only, who came from the Father, full of grace and truth. *John 1:1-14*

117 Songs of Thankfulness and Praise

The Word became flesh and made his dwelling among us. John 1:14

1. Songs of thank-ful-ness and praise, Je-sus, Lord, to You we raise,
2. God re-vealed at Jor-dan's stream, Proph-et, Priest and King su-preme,
3. God re-vealed in val-iant fight, Con-quer-ing the dev-il's might,
4. Stars shall fall and heav-ens fade, Sun and moon shall dark be made;
Once re-vealed, when heav-en's star Brought the wise men from a-far:
Once re-vealed in power di-vine Chang-ing wa-ter in-to wine:
Sins for-giv-en, sick-ness healed, Life re-stored and God re-vealed:
Christ will then like light-ning shine, All will see the glo-rious sign:
Branch of roy-al Da-vid's stem In Your birth at Beth-le-hem,
Ca-na's ho-ly wed-ding Guest Keep-ing to the last the best,
Once re-vealed in gra-cious will Ev-er bring-ing good from ill,
All will then the trum-pet hear, All will see the Son ap-pear,
Word be-fore the world be-gan, God re-vealed to us in man.

WORDS: Christopher Wordsworth, 1807-1885;
rev. *Hymns for Today's Church*, 1982
MUSIC: George J. Elvey, 1816-1893

ST. GEORGE'S, WINDSOR
7.7.7.7.D.

That Beautiful Name 118

You are to give him the name Jesus. Matthew 1:21

1. I know of a Name, a beau - ti - ful Name, That an - gels brought
2. I know of a Name, a beau - ti - ful Name, That un - to a
3. The One of that Name, my Sav - ior be - came, My Sav - ior of
4. I love that blest Name, that won - der - ful Name, Made high - er than
down to earth; They whis - pered it low one night long a -
Babe was giv - en; The stars glit - tered bright through - out that glad
Cal - va - ry; My sins nailed Him there, my bur - dens to
all in heav - en; 'Twas whis - pered, I know, in my heart long a -
go To a maid - en of low - ly birth.
night, And an - gels praised God in heaven.
bear; He suf - fered all this for me.
go; To Je - sus my life I've given.
Refrain
That beau - ti - ful Name, that beau - ti - ful Name, From sin has pow - er to free us! That beau - ti - ful
Name, That won - der - ful Name, That match - less Name is Je - sus!

WORDS: Jean Perry, 1865-1935, alt.
MUSIC: Mabel J. Camp, 1871-1937

THAT BEAUTIFUL NAME
Irregular with Refrain

119 The Beatitudes

Now when he saw the crowds, he went up on a mountainside and sat down. His disciples came to him, and he began to teach them, saying:

"Blessed are the poor in spirit,
for theirs is the kingdom of heaven.
Blessed are those who mourn,
for they will be comforted.
Blessed are the meek,
for they will inherit the earth.
Blessed are those who hunger and thirst for righteousness,
for they will be filled.
Blessed are the merciful,
for they will be shown mercy.
Blessed are the pure in heart,
for they will see God.
Blessed are the peacemakers,
for they will be called sons of God.
Blessed are those who are persecuted because of righteousness,
for theirs is the kingdom of heaven.

Blessed are you when people insult you, persecute you and falsely say all kinds of evil against you because of me.
Rejoice and be glad, because great is your reward in heaven, for in the same way they persecuted the prophets who were before you."

Matthew 5:1-12

TO BE LIKE JESUS

Lord Jesus, by the indwelling of Your Holy Spirit,
purge our eyes to discern and contemplate You until
we see as You see,
judge as You judge,
choose as You choose;
and having sought and found You
to behold You forever and ever.
We ask this for Your name's sake. Amen.

Christina Rossetti (1830-1894)

Tell Me the Story of Jesus 120

Then Philip began with that very passage of Scripture and told him the good news about Jesus. Acts 8:35

1. Tell me the sto - ry of Je - sus; Write on my heart ev - ery word.
2. Fast - ing a - lone in the des - ert, Tell of the days that are past,
3. Tell of the cross where they nailed Him, Writh-ing in an - guish and pain;
Refrain: Tell me the sto - ry of Je - sus, Write on my heart ev - ery word;
Fine
Tell me the sto - ry most pre - cious, Sweet - est that ev - er was heard.
How for our sins He was tempt - ed, Yet was tri - um - phant at last.
Tell of the grave where they laid Him. Tell how He lives once a - gain.
Tell me the sto - ry most pre - cious, Sweet - est that ev - er was heard.
Tell how the an - gels, in cho - rus Sang as they wel - comed His birth:
Tell of the years of His la - bor; Tell of the sor - row He bore.
Love in that sto - ry so ten - der, Clear - er than ev - er I see;
D.C. for Refrain
"Glo - ry to God in the high - est! Peace and good tid - ings to earth."
He was de - spised and af - flict - ed, Home - less, re - ject - ed and poor.
Stay, let me weep while you whis - per, Love paid the ran - som for me.

WORDS: Fanny J. Crosby, 1820-1915, alt.
MUSIC: John R. Sweney, 1837-1899

STORY OF JESUS
8.7.8.7.D. with Refrain

121 Yesterday, Today, Forever

Jesus Christ is the same yesterday and today and forever. Heb. 13:8

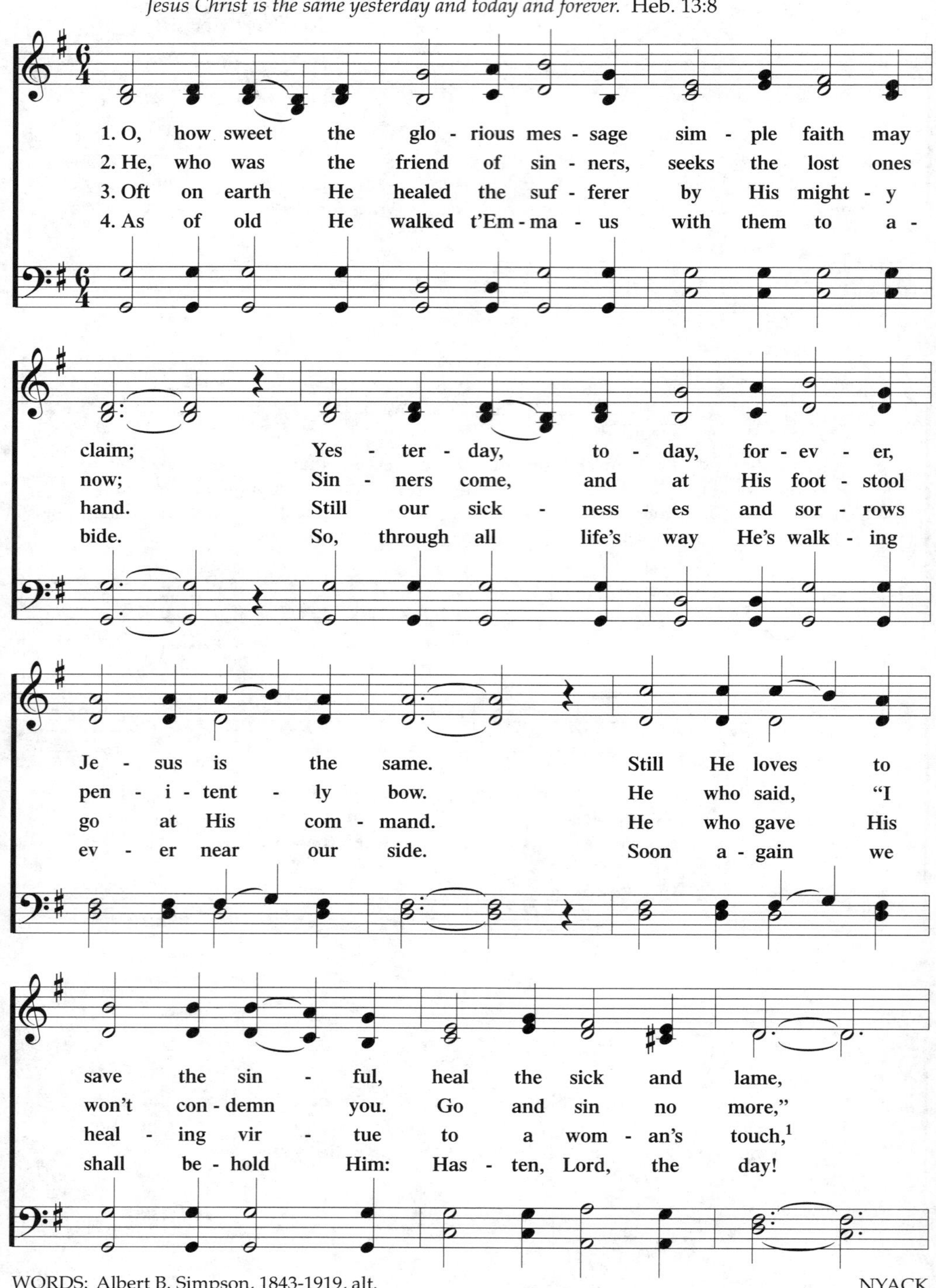
1. O, how sweet the glo - rious mes - sage sim - ple faith may claim; Yes - ter - day, to - day, for - ev - er, Je - sus is the same. Still He loves to save the sin - ful, heal the sick and lame,
2. He, who was the friend of sin - ners, seeks the lost ones now; Sin - ners come, and at His foot - stool pen - i - tent - ly bow. He who said, "I won't con - demn you. Go and sin no more,"
3. Oft on earth He healed the suf - ferer by His might - y hand. Still our sick - ness - es and sor - rows go at His com - mand. He who gave His heal - ing vir - tue to a wom - an's touch,[1]
4. As of old He walked t'Em - ma - us with them to a - bide. So, through all life's way He's walk - ing ev - er near our side. Soon a - gain we shall be - hold Him: Has - ten, Lord, the day!

WORDS: Albert B. Simpson, 1843-1919, alt.
MUSIC: J. H. Burke, 19th century

NYACK
8.5.8.5.D. with Refrain

1. *Refers to the woman in Luke 8:44 who was healed as she touched Jesus' robe.*

Cheer the mourn - er, still the temp - est: Glo - ry to His name!*
Speaks to us those words of par - don as in days be - fore.
To the faith that claims His full - ness still will give as much.
Still it will be "this same Je - sus," as He went a - way.*
Refrain
Yes - ter - day, to - day, for - ev - er, Je - sus is the same.
All may change, but Je - sus nev - er! Glo - ry to His name!
Glo - ry to His name, Glo - ry to His name;
All may change, but Je - sus nev - er! Glo - ry to His name.

*Option: the Refrain could be sung on these verses only.

122 Yesterday, Today, Forever

SECOND SETTING

Jesus Christ is the same yesterday and today and forever. Hebrews 13:8

1. O, how sweet the glo - rious mes - sage
2. He, who was the friend of sin - ners,
3. Oft on earth He healed the suf - ferer
4. As of old He walked t'Em - ma - us
sim - ple faith may claim. Yes - ter - day, to -
seeks the lost ones now; Sin - ners come, and
by His might - y hand. Still our sick - ness -
with them to a - bide. So, through all life's
day, for - ev - er, Je - sus is the same.
at His foot - stool pen - i - tent - ly bow.
es and sor - rows go at His com - mand.
way He's walk - ing ev - er near our side.

WORDS: Albert B. Simpson, 1843-1919, alt.
MUSIC: J. H. Burke, 19th century; arr. Don Marsh, b. 1943

NYACK
8.5.8.5.D. with Refrain

Still He loves to save the sin - ful, heal the sick and lame.
He who said, "I won't con-demn you. Go and sin no more,"
He who gave His heal - ing vir - tue to a wo - man's touch,1
Soon a - gain we shall be - hold Him: Has - ten, Lord, the day!
Cheer the mourn - er, still the temp - est: Glo - ry to His name!*
Speaks to us those words of par - don as in days be - fore.
To the faith that claims His full - ness still will give as much.
Still it will be "this same Je - sus," as He went a - way.*
Refrain **
Yes - ter - day, to - day, for - ev - er, Je - sus is the same.

1. *Refers to the woman in Luke 8:44 who was healed as she touched Jesus' robe.*
* *option: the Refrain could be sung on these verses only*
** *Refrain rhythm may also be played*

All may change, but Je - sus nev - er! Glo - ry to His
name!
Glo - ry to His name,
Glo - ry to His name;
All may change, but
Je - sus nev - er!
Glo - ry to His
name.
1, 2, 3.
4.

Ivory Palaces 123

From palaces adorned with ivory the music of the strings makes you glad. Psalm 45:8

1. My Lord has gar-ments so won-drous fine, And myrrh[1] their tex-ture fills;
2. His life had al-so its sor-rows sore, For al-oes[2] had a part;
3. His gar-ments too were in cas-sia[3] dipped, With heal-ing in a touch;
4. In gar-ments glo-ri-ous He will come To o-pen wide the door;
Its fra-grance reached to this heart of mine, With joy my be-ing thrills.
And when I think of the cross He bore, My eyes with tear-drops start.
Each time my feet in some sin have slipped, He took me from its clutch.
And I shall en-ter my heaven-ly home, To dwell for-ev-er-more.
Refrain
Out of the i-vo-ry pal-a-ces, In-to a world of woe,
On-ly His great, e-ter-nal love Made my Sav-ior go.

WORDS: Henry Barraclough, 1891-1983
MUSIC: Henry Barraclough, 1891-1983

MONTREAT
9.6.9.6. with Refrain

1. *myrrh: incense*
2. *aloes: medicinal plant used in salves*
3. *cassia: cinnamon-like medicinal plant*

124 Meekness and Majesty

(This Is Your God)

A bruised reed he will not break, and a smoldering wick he will not snuff out. Isaiah 42:3

1. Meek - ness and maj - es - ty, man - hood and De - i - ty,
2. Fa - ther's pure ra - di - ance, per - fect in in - no - cence;
3. Wis - dom un - search - a - ble, God, the in - vis - i - ble;

In per - fect har - mo - ny, the Man who is God;
Yet learns o - be - di - ence to death on a cross;
Love in - de - struct - i - ble in frail - ty ap - pears.

Lord of e - ter - ni - ty, dwells in hu - man - i - ty,
Suf - fering to give us life, con - quering through sac - ri - fice;
Lord of in - fin - i - ty, stoop - ing so ten - der - ly;

Kneels in hu - mil - i - ty and wash - es our feet.
And as they cru - ci - fy prays, "Fa - ther, for - give."
Lifts our hu - man - i - ty to the heights of His throne.

WORDS: Graham Kendrick, b. 1950
MUSIC: Graham Kendrick, b. 1950

MEEKNESS AND MAJESTY
Irregular with Refrain

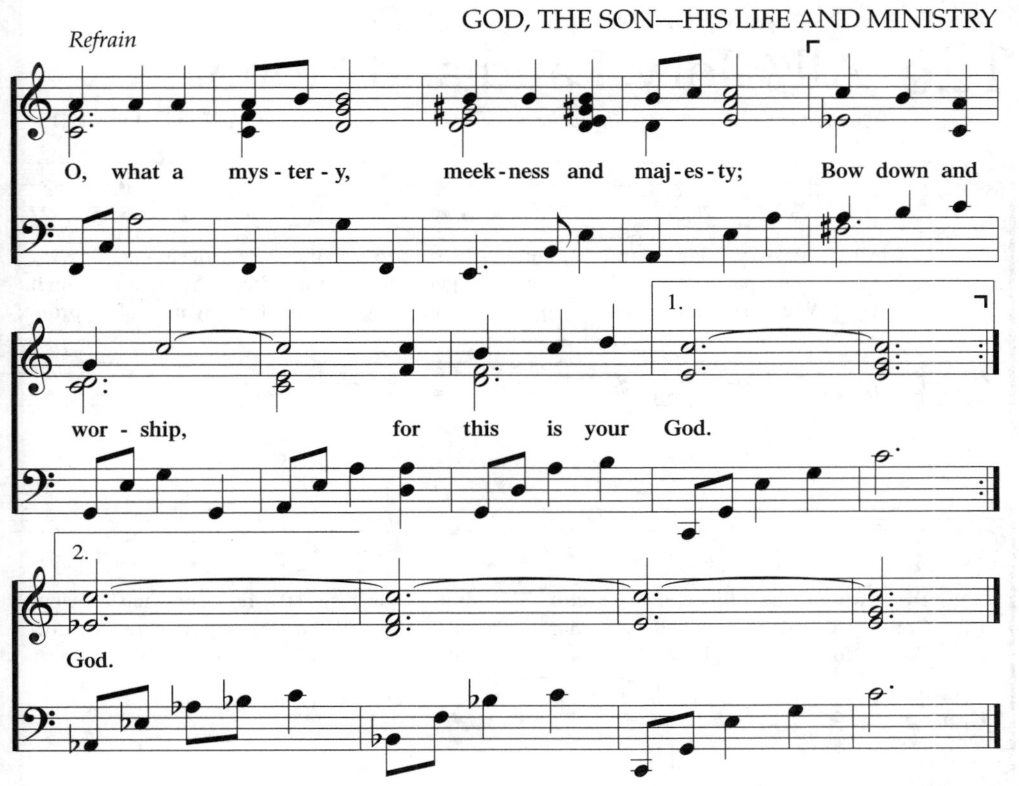
Refrain
O, what a mys - ter - y, meek - ness and maj - es - ty; Bow down and
wor - ship, for this is your God.
1.
2.
God.

The Triumphal Entry 125

As they approached Jerusalem and came to Bethphage and Bethany at the Mount of Olives, Jesus sent two of his disciples, saying to them,

"Go to the village ahead of you, and just as you enter it, you will find a colt tied there, which no one has ever ridden. Untie it and bring it here. If anyone asks you, 'Why are you doing this?' tell him, 'The Lord needs it and will send it back here shortly.'"

They went and found a colt outside in the street, tied at a doorway. As they untied it, some people standing there asked,

"What are you doing, untying that colt?"

They answered as Jesus had told them to, and the people let them go. When they brought the colt to Jesus and threw their cloaks over it, he sat on it. Many people spread their cloaks on the road, while others spread branches they had cut in the fields. Those who went ahead and those who followed shouted,

"Hosanna!"
"Blessed is he who comes in the name of the Lord!"
"Blessed is the coming kingdom of our father David!"
"Hosanna in the highest!"

Jesus entered Jerusalem and went to the temple. He looked around at everything, but since it was already late, he went out to Bethany with the Twelve. *Mark 11:1-11*

126 All Glory, Laud and Honor

Blessed is he who comes in the name of the Lord! Blessed is the King of Israel! John 12:13

1. All glo - ry, laud[1] and hon - or to You, Re - deem - er, King,
2. The com - pa - ny of an - gels are prais - ing You on high,
3. To You, be - fore Your pas - sion, they sang their hymns of praise;
To whom the lips of chil - dren made sweet ho - san - nas ring.
Cre - a - tion and all mor - tals in cho - rus make re - ply.
To You, now high ex - alt - ed, our mel - o - dy we raise.
You are the King of Is - ra - el and Da - vid's roy - al Son,
The peo - ple of the He - brews with palms be - fore You went;
As You re - ceived their prais - es, ac - cept the prayers we bring,
Now in the Lord's name com - ing, our King and bless - ed One!
Our praise and prayer and an - thems be - fore You we pre - sent.
For You de - light in good - ness, O good and gra - cious King!

WORDS: Theodulph of Orleans, c. 760-821; tr. John M. Neale, 1818-1866, alt.
MUSIC: Melchior Teschner, 1584-1635

ST. THEODULPH
7.6.7.6.D.

1. *laud: praise*

Hosanna, Loud Hosanna 127

The crowds . . . shouted, "Hosanna . . . in the highest!" Matthew 21:9

1. Ho - san - na, loud ho - san - na, The lit - tle chil - dren sang;
2. From Ol - i - vet they fol - lowed 'Mid an ex - ult - ant crowd,
3. "Ho - san - na in the high - est!" That an - cient song we sing,
Through pil - lared court and tem - ple The love - ly an - them rang.
The vic - tor palm branch wav - ing, And chant - ing clear and loud;
For Christ is our Re - deem - er, The Lord of heaven our King.
To Je - sus, who had blessed them Close fold - ed to His breast,
The Lord of earth and heav - en Rode on in low - ly state,
O, may we ev - er praise Him With heart and life and voice,
The chil - dren sang their prais - es, The sim - plest and the best.
Nor scorned that lit - tle chil - dren Should on His bid - ding wait.
And in His bliss - ful pres - ence E - ter - nal - ly re - joice!

WORDS: Jennette Threlfall, 1821-1880, alt.
MUSIC: Henry T. Smart, 1813-1879

LANCASHIRE
7.6.7.6.D.

128 Hosanna

Hosanna to the Son of David! . . . Hosanna in the highest! Matthew 21:9

1. Ho - san - na! Ho - san - na! Ho - san-na in the high - est! Ho-
2. Glo - ry! Glo - ry! Glo-ry to the King of kings!
san - na! Ho - san - na! Ho - san-na in the high - est!
Glo - ry! Glo - ry! Glo-ry to the King of kings!
Lord, we lift up Your name With hearts full of praise.
Lord, we lift up Your name With hearts full of praise.
Be ex-alt-ed, O Lord, my God, Ho - san-na in the high - est!
Be ex-alt-ed, O Lord, my God, Glo-ry to the King of kings!

Optional segue to "The King of Glory Comes." No transition required.

WORDS: Carl Tuttle, b. 1953
MUSIC: Carl Tuttle, b. 1953

HOSANNA
Irregular

The King of Glory Comes 129

Lift up your heads, O you gates . . . that the King of glory may come in. Psalm 24:7

Refrain

The King of glo - ry comes, the na - tion re - joic - es. O - pen the gates be - fore Him, lift up your voic - es. voic - es.

1 - 4. Final ending

1. Who is the King of glo - ry? What shall we call Him?
2. In all of Gal - i - lee, in cit - y or vil - lage,
3. He gave His life for us, the pledge of sal - va - tion;
4. He con - quered sin and death; He tru - ly has ris - en.

He is Em - man - u - el, the prom - ised of a - ges.
He goes a - mong His peo - ple, cur - ing their ill - ness.
He took up - on Him - self the sin of the na - tions.
And He will share with us His heav - en - ly vi - sion.

D.C.

WORDS: Willard F. Jabusch, b. 1930
MUSIC: Israeli folk song; arr. John Ferguson, b. 1941

PROMISED ONE
12.12. with Refrain

130 Ride On, Ride On in Majesty

See, your king comes to you . . . gentle and riding on a donkey. Zechariah 9:9

1. Ride on, ride on in maj - es - ty! Hark! All the
2. Ride on, ride on in maj - es - ty! In low - ly
3. Ride on, ride on in maj - es - ty! The host of
4. Ride on, ride on in maj - es - ty! In low - ly
tribes ho - san - na cry; O Sav - ior meek, pur -
pomp ride on to die. O Christ, Your tri - umphs
an - gels in the sky Look down with sad and
pomp ride on to die; Bow Your meek head to
sue Your road With palms and scat - tered gar - ments strowed.
now be - gin O'er cap - tive death and con - quered sin.
won - dering eyes To see th'ap - proach - ing sac - ri - fice.
mor - tal pain, Then take, O God, Your power and reign!
8

WORDS: Henry H. Milman, 1791-1868, alt.
MUSIC: Thomas Williams' *Psalmodia Evangelica*, 1789

TRURO
L.M.

CHRIST REVEALS THE FATHER

Apart from Christ, the world has no God. Man's conceptions of the Father are all distorted and false. Jesus alone has revealed Him.

Jesus is the revelation of God to the world and to the believer, and only as we receive him can we know God and enter into union with Him through Jesus Christ. When we receive His Son, we at once pass into direct and personal acquaintance with the Father.

A.B. Simpson (1843-1919), *The Christ in the Bible Commentary, Vol. 4*

The Crucifixion 131

Finally Pilate handed him over to them to be crucified. So the soldiers took charge of Jesus.

Carrying his own cross, he went out to the place of the Skull (which in Aramaic is called Golgotha).

Here they crucified him, and with him two others—one on each side and Jesus in the middle.

Pilate had a notice prepared and fastened to the cross. It read: JESUS OF NAZARETH, THE KING OF THE JEWS.

Many of the Jews read this sign, for the place where Jesus was crucified was near the city, and the sign was written in Aramaic, Latin and Greek.

The chief priests of the Jews protested to Pilate, "Do not write 'The King of the Jews,' but that this man claimed to be king of the Jews."

Pilate answered, "What I have written, I have written."

When the soldiers crucified Jesus, they took his clothes, dividing them into four shares, one for each of them, with the undergarment remaining. This garment was seamless, woven in one piece from top to bottom.

"Let's not tear it," they said to one another. "Let's decide by lot who will get it."
This happened that the scripture might be fulfilled which said,

"They divided my garments among them
and cast lots for my clothing."
So this is what the soldiers did.

Near the cross of Jesus stood his mother, his mother's sister, Mary the wife of Clopas, and Mary Magdalene.

When Jesus saw his mother there, and the disciple whom he loved standing nearby, he said to his mother, "Dear woman, here is your son,"

and to the disciple, "Here is your mother." From that time on, this disciple took her into his home.

Later, knowing that all was now completed, and so that the Scripture would be fulfilled, Jesus said, "I am thirsty."

A jar of wine vinegar was there, so they soaked a sponge in it, put the sponge on a stalk of the hyssop plant, and lifted it to Jesus' lips.

When he had received the drink, Jesus said, "It is finished." With that, he bowed his head and gave up his spirit.

John 19:16-30

132 O Sacred Head, Now Wounded

They . . . twisted together a crown of thorns and set it on him. Mark 15:17

1. O sa - cred Head, now wound - ed, With grief and shame weighed down;
2. O Lord of life and glo - ry, What bliss till now was Thine!
3. What lan - guage shall I bor - row To thank Thee, dear - est Friend,
Now scorn - ful - ly sur - round - ed With thorns, Thine on - ly crown.
I read the won - drous sto - ry; I joy to call Thee mine.
For this Thy dy - ing sor - row, Thy pit - y with - out end?
How pale Thou art with an - guish, With sore a - buse and scorn;
What Thou, my Lord, hast suf - fered Was all for sin - ners' gain;
O, make me Thine for - ev - er, And should I faint - ing3 be,
How does that vis - age1 lan - guish,2 Which once was bright as morn!
Mine, mine was the trans - gres - sion, But Thine the dead - ly pain.
Lord, let me nev - er, nev - er Out - live my love to Thee.

WORDS: Attr. Bernard of Clairvaux, 1091-1153; tr. (Ger.) Paul Gerhardt, 1607-1676; tr. (Eng.) James W. Alexander, 1804-1859
MUSIC: Hans L. Hassler, 1564-1612; harm. J.S. Bach, 1685-1750

PASSION CHORALE
7.6.7.6.D.

1. *visage: appearance*
2. *languish: fade, weaken*
3. *fainting: dying*

Lead Me to Calvary 133

I resolved to know nothing . . . except Jesus Christ and him crucified. 1 Corinthians 2:2

1. King of my life, I crown Thee now, Thine shall the glo - ry be;
2. Show me the tomb where Thou wast laid, Ten - der - ly mourned and wept;
3. Let me, like Ma - ry, through the gloom, Come with a gift to Thee;
4. May I be will - ing, Lord, to bear Dai - ly my cross for Thee;
Lest I for - get Thy thorn-crowned brow, Lead me to Cal - va - ry.
An - gels in robes of light ar - rayed Guard - ed Thee while Thou slept.
Show to me now the emp - ty tomb, Lead me to Cal - va - ry.
Ev - en Thy cup of grief to share, Thou hast borne all for me.
Refrain
Lest I for - get Geth - sem - a - ne, Lest I for - get Thine ag - o - ny,
Lest I for - get Thy love for me, Lead me to Cal - va - ry.

WORDS: Jennie E. Hussey, 1874-1958
MUSIC: William J. Kirkpatrick, 1838-1921

DUNCANNON
C.M. with Refrain

134 Hallelujah, What a Savior!

He was despised and rejected by men, a man of sorrows, and familiar with suffering.
Isaiah 53:3

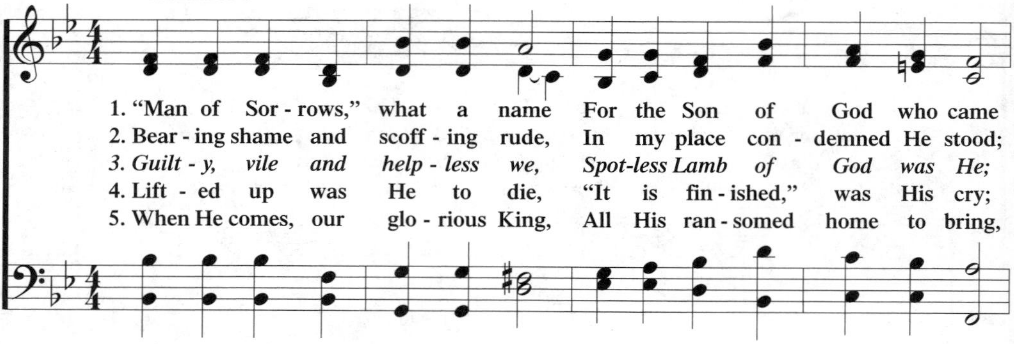

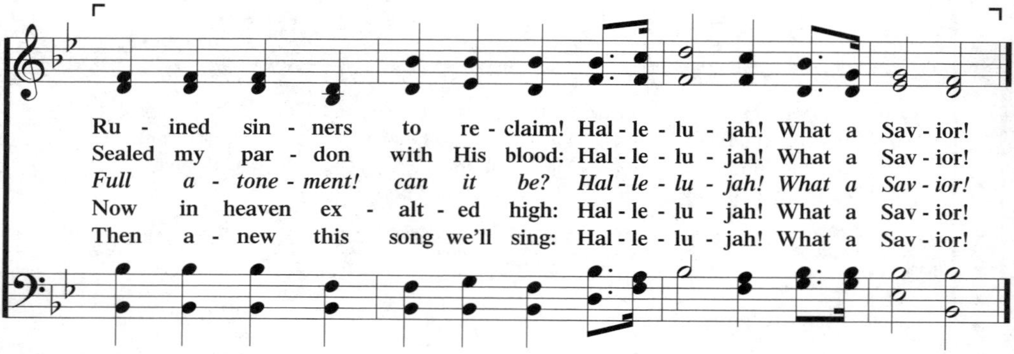

1. "Man of Sor - rows," what a name For the Son of God who came
Ru - ined sin - ners to re - claim! Hal - le - lu - jah! What a Sav - ior!

2. Bear - ing shame and scoff - ing rude, In my place con - demned He stood;
Sealed my par - don with His blood: Hal - le - lu - jah! What a Sav - ior!

3. Guilt - y, vile and help - less we, Spot-less Lamb of God was He;
Full a - tone - ment! can it be? Hal - le - lu - jah! What a Sav - ior!

4. Lift - ed up was He to die, "It is fin - ished," was His cry;
Now in heaven ex - alt - ed high: Hal - le - lu - jah! What a Sav - ior!

5. When He comes, our glo - rious King, All His ran - somed home to bring,
Then a - new this song we'll sing: Hal - le - lu - jah! What a Sav - ior!

WORDS: Philip P. Bliss, 1838-1876
MUSIC: Philip P. Bliss, 1838-1876

MAN OF SORROWS
7.7.7.8.

135 A Purple Robe

They put a purple robe on him, then twisted together a crown of thorns and set it on him.
Mark 15:17

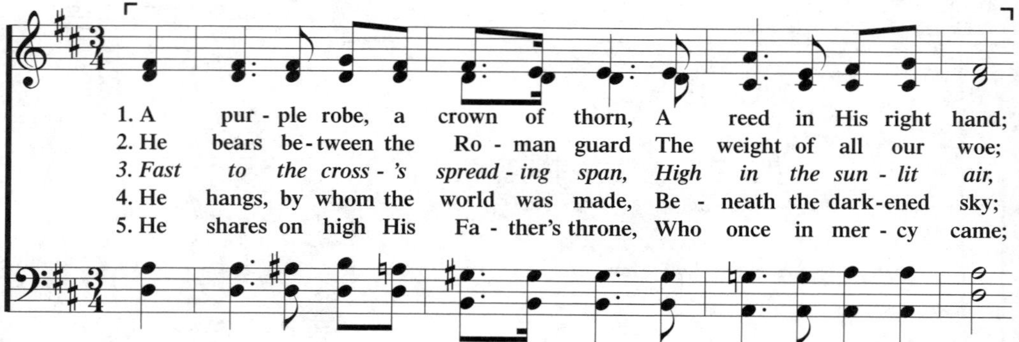
1. A pur - ple robe, a crown of thorn, A reed in His right hand;
2. He bears be - tween the Ro - man guard The weight of all our woe;
3. Fast to the cross - 's spread - ing span, High in the sun - lit air,
4. He hangs, by whom the world was made, Be - neath the dark - ened sky;
5. He shares on high His Fa - ther's throne, Who once in mer - cy came;

WORDS: Timothy Dudley-Smith, b. 1926
MUSIC: William V. Wallace, 1814-1865

SERENITY
C.M.

Be - fore the sol - diers' spite and scorn I see my Sav - ior stand.
A stum - bling fig - ure bowed and scarred I see my Sav - ior go.
All the un - num - bered sins of man I see my Sav - ior bear.
The ev - er - last - ing ran - som paid, I see my Sav - ior die.
For all His love to sin - ners shown I sing my Sav - ior's name.

Ah, Holy Jesus 136

He was despised, and we esteemed him not. Isaiah 53:3

1. Ah, ho - ly Je - sus, how have You of - fend - ed,
2. Who was the guilt - y? Who brought this up - on You?
3. For me, kind Je - sus, was Your in - car - na - tion,
4. There - fore, dear Je - sus, since I can - not pay You,

That mor - tal judg - ment has on You de - scend - ed? By foes de -
It is my trea - son, Lord, that has un - done You. 'Twas I, Lord
Your mor - tal sor - row, and Your life's ob - la - tion,[1] Your death of
I do a - dore You, and will ev - er pray You, Think on Your

rid - ed, by Your own re - ject - ed, O most af - flict - ed!
Je - sus, I it was de - nied You; I cru - ci - fied You.
an - guish, and Your bit - ter pas - sion, For my sal - va - tion.
pit - y and Your love un - swerv - ing, Not my de - serv - ing.

WORDS: Johann Heermann, 1585-1647, para. of Jean de Fécamp, 11th century; tr. Robert Bridges, 1844-1930, alt.
MUSIC: Johann Crüger, 1598-1662

HERZLIEBSTER JESU
11.11.11.5.

1. *oblation: offering*

137 Were You There

It was the third hour when they crucified him. Mark 15:25

1. Were you there when they cru - ci - fied my Lord? Were you there when they cru - ci - fied my Lord? Oh!
2. Were you there when they nailed Him to the tree? Were you there when they nailed Him to the tree? Oh!
3. Were you there when they laid Him in the tomb? Were you there when they laid Him in the tomb? Oh!
*4. Were you there when He rose up from the grave? Were you there when He rose up from the grave? Oh!
Some - times it caus - es me to trem - ble, trem - ble, trem - ble.
Some - times it caus - es me to trem - ble, trem - ble, trem - ble.
Some - times it caus - es me to trem - ble, trem - ble, trem - ble.
Some - times I feel like shout - ing, "Glo - ry, glo - ry, glo - ry!"
Were you there when they cru - ci - fied my Lord?
Were you there when they nailed Him to the tree?
Were you there when they laid Him in the tomb?
Were you there when He rose up from the grave?

Optional segue to "At the Cross." No transition required.

WORDS: African-American spiritual; stanza 4 from popular usage
MUSIC: African-American spiritual; adapt. John W. Work, Jr. 1872-1925 and Frederick J. Work, 1879-1942

WERE YOU THERE
Irregular

*optional stanza

At the Cross 138

. . . making peace through his blood, shed on the cross. Colossians 1:20

1. A - las! And did my Sav - ior bleed? And did my Sov-ereign die?
2. Was it for crimes that I have done He groaned up - on the tree?
3. Well might the sun in dark - ness hide And shut its glo - ries in
4. But drops of grief can ne'er re - pay The debt of love I owe:

Would He de - vote that sa - cred head *For such a worm as I?
A - maz - ing pit - y! grace un - known! And love be - yond de - gree!
When Christ, the might - y Mak - er, died To bear His crea - tures' sin.
Here, Lord, I give my - self to Thee. 'Tis all that I can do!

Refrain

At the cross, at the cross where I first saw the light, And the bur - den of my heart rolled a - way, It was there by faith I re - ceived my sight, And now I am **hap - py all the day!

WORDS: Isaac Watts, 1674-1748, alt.; refrain, Ralph E. Hudson, 1843-1901, alt.
MUSIC: Ralph E. Hudson, 1843-1901

HUDSON
C.M. with Refrain

** or: For sinners such as I*
*** or: joyful*

139 Near the Cross

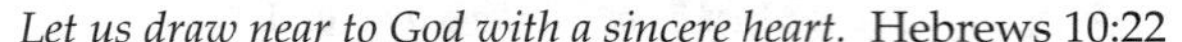
Let us draw near to God with a sincere heart. Hebrews 10:22

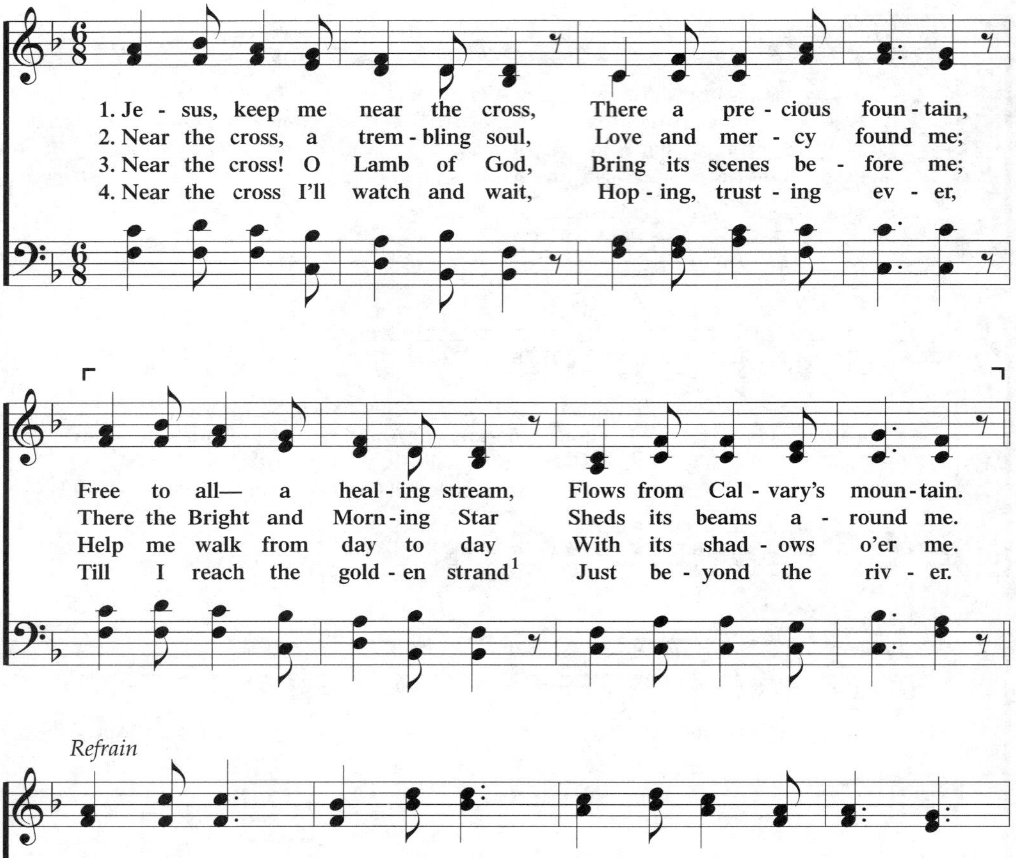

1. Je - sus, keep me near the cross, There a pre - cious foun - tain,
Free to all— a heal - ing stream, Flows from Cal - vary's moun - tain.

2. Near the cross, a trem - bling soul, Love and mer - cy found me;
There the Bright and Morn - ing Star Sheds its beams a - round me.

3. Near the cross! O Lamb of God, Bring its scenes be - fore me;
Help me walk from day to day With its shad - ows o'er me.

4. Near the cross I'll watch and wait, Hop - ing, trust - ing ev - er,
Till I reach the gold - en strand[1] Just be - yond the riv - er.

Refrain

In the cross, in the cross Be my glo - ry ev - er,
Till my rap - tured soul shall find Rest be - yond the riv - er.

WORDS: Fanny J. Crosby, 1820-1915
MUSIC: William H. Doane, 1832-1915

NEAR THE CROSS
7.6.7.6. with Refrain

1. *strand: shore*

Beneath the Cross of Jesus 140

. . . the shadow of a great rock in a thirsty land. Isaiah 32:2

1. Be - neath the cross of Je - sus I glad - ly take my stand—
2. Up - on that cross of Je - sus My eyes at times can see
3. I take, O cross, your shad - ow For my a - bid - ing place;
The shad - ow of a might - y Rock With - in a wea - ry land;
The ver - y dy - ing form of One Who suf - fered there for me;
I ask no oth - er sun - shine than The sun - shine of His face;
A home with - in the wil - der - ness, A rest up - on the way,
And from my strick - en heart with tears Two won - ders I con - fess:
Con - tent to let the world go by, To know no gain nor loss,
From the burn - ing of the noon - tide heat And the bur - den of the day.
The won - ders of re - deem - ing love And my un - wor - thi - ness.
My sin - ful self my on - ly shame, My glo - ry all the cross.

WORDS: Elizabeth C. Clephane, 1830-1869, alt.
MUSIC: Frederick C. Maker, 1844-1927

ST. CHRISTOPHER
7.6.8.6.8.6.8.6.

141 'Tis Midnight, and on Olive's Brow

Jesus went out as usual to the Mount of Olives, and his disciples followed him. Luke 22:39

1. 'Tis mid - night, and on Ol - ive's brow1 The
2. 'Tis mid - night, and from all re - moved, The
3. 'Tis mid - night, and for oth - ers' guilt The
4. 'Tis mid - night, and from heav - en's plains Is
star is dimmed that late - ly shone. 'Tis mid - night; in the
Sav - ior wres - tles lone with fears; E'en that dis - ci - ple
Man of Sor - rows weeps in blood; Yet He that has in
born the song that an - gels know; Un - heard by mor - tals
gar - den now The suf - fering Sav - ior prays a - lone.
whom He loved Heeds not his Mas - ter's grief and tears.
an - guish knelt Is not for - sak - en by His God.
are the strains That sweet - ly soothe the Sav - ior's woe.

WORDS: William B. Tappan, 1794-1849, alt.
MUSIC: William B. Bradbury, 1816-1868

OLIVE'S BROW
L.M.

1. *brow: hill (Mount Olivet)*

CHRIST, THE DIVIDING LINE

Human character and destiny are revealed by contact with Jesus Christ. Men are not saved or lost merely by moral character, but by their attitude toward the Son of God. As of old He hung on Calvary between two men that represented at once both heaven and hell, so still it is true that the cross of Jesus is the dividing line between lost and saved men.

A.B. Simpson (1843-1919), *The Christ in the Bible Commentary, Vol. 3*

'Tis Finished! The Messiah Dies 142

When he had received the drink, Jesus said, "It is finished." John 19:30

1. 'Tis finished! the Messiah dies, cut off for sins, but not His own.
Accomplished is the sacrifice, the great redeeming work is done.

2. The veil is rent[1]; in Christ alone the living way to heaven is seen;
The middle wall is broken down, and all the world may enter in.

3. 'Tis finished! All my guilt and pain, I want no sacrifice beside;
For me, for me the Lamb is slain; 'tis finished! I am justified.

4. The reign of sin and death is o'er, and all may live from sin set free;
Satan has lost his mortal power; 'tis swallowed up in victory.

WORDS: Charles Wesley, 1707-1788, alt. L.M.
(may be sung to OLIVE'S BROW, No. 141)
1. *veil is rent: refers to the tearing of the temple veil at Jesus' death and new access to God*

Alas, and Did My Savior Bleed 143

He was pierced for our transgressions. Isaiah 53:5

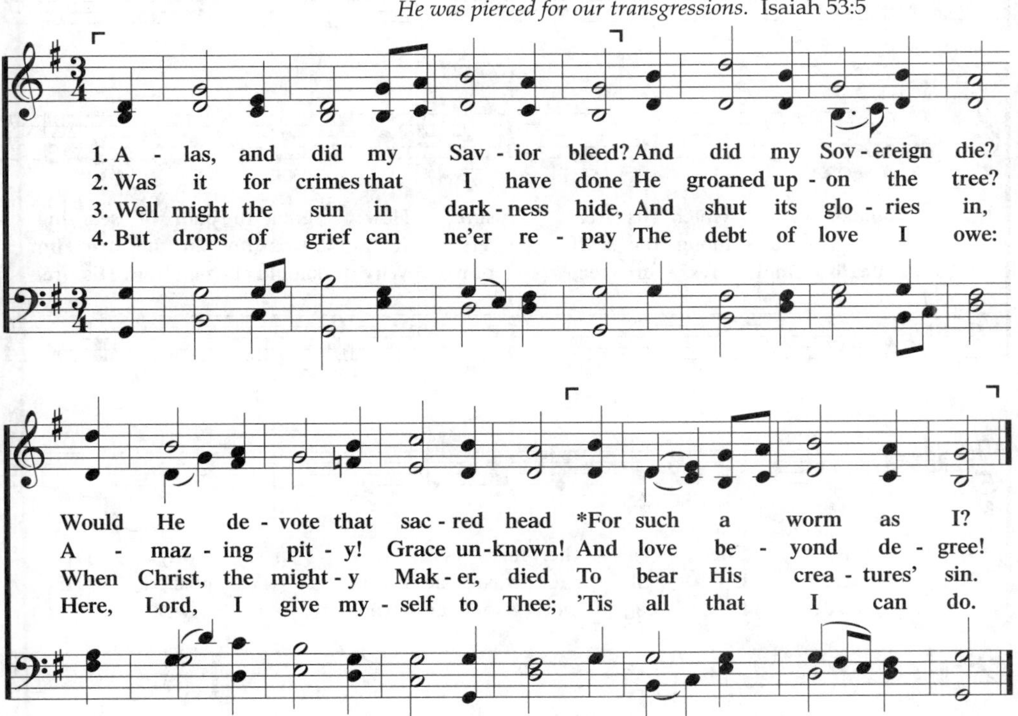

1. A - las, and did my Sav - ior bleed? And did my Sov - ereign die?
2. Was it for crimes that I have done He groaned up - on the tree?
3. Well might the sun in dark - ness hide, And shut its glo - ries in,
4. But drops of grief can ne'er re - pay The debt of love I owe:
Would He de - vote that sac - red head *For such a worm as I?
A - maz - ing pit - y! Grace un - known! And love be - yond de - gree!
When Christ, the might - y Mak - er, died To bear His crea - tures' sin.
Here, Lord, I give my - self to Thee; 'Tis all that I can do.

WORDS: Isaac Watts, 1674-1748, alt. MARTYRDOM
MUSIC: Hugh Wilson, 1764-1824 C.M.
* or: *For sinners such as I*

144 How Deep the Father's Love for Us

For God so loved the world that he gave his one and only Son. John 3:16

1. How deep the Fa - ther's love for us, How vast be - yond all mea - sure, That He should give His on - ly Son To make a wretch His trea - sure. How great the pain of sear - ing loss; The Fa - ther turns His face a - way, As
2. Be - hold the man up - on a cross, My sin up - on His shoul - ders; A - shamed, I hear my mock - ing voice Call out a - mong the scoff - ers. It was my sin that held Him there Un - til it was ac - com - plished; His
3. I will not boast in an - y - thing, No gifts, no power, no wis - dom; But I will boast in Je - sus Christ, His death and res - ur - rec - tion. Why should I gain from His re - ward? I can - not give an an - swer, But

WORDS: Stuart Townend, b. 1962
MUSIC: Stuart Townend, b. 1962

FATHER'S LOVE
Irregular

wounds which mar the Cho - sen One Bring
dy - ing breath has brought me life— I
this I know with all my heart: His
man - y sons to glo - ry.
know that it is fin - ished.
wounds have paid my ran - som.

WE GLORY IN YOUR CROSS, O LORD

We glory in Your cross, O Lord, and praise and glorify Your holy resurrection;
for by virtue of Your cross joy has come to the whole world.
May God be gracious to us and bless us and make His face shine upon us,
that Your ways may be known on earth, Your salvation among all nations.
May the peoples praise You, O God; may all the peoples praise You.
We glory in Your cross, O Lord, and praise and glorify Your holy resurrection;
for by virtue of Your cross joy has come to the whole world.

Ancient Prayer of the Church

145 When I Survey the Wondrous Cross

They will look on me, the one they have pierced. Zechariah 12:10

1. When I sur - vey the won - drous cross On which the
2. For - bid it, Lord, that I should boast, Save in the
3. See, from His head, His hands, His feet, Sor - row and
4. Were the whole realm of na - ture mine, That were a
Prince of glo - ry died, My rich - est gain I
death of Christ my God. All the vain things that
love flow min - gled down. Did e'er such love and
pres - ent far too small. Love so a - maz - ing,
count but loss, And pour con - tempt on all my pride.
charm me most, I sac - ri - fice them to His blood.
sor - row meet, Or thorns com - pose so rich a crown?
so di - vine, De - mands my soul, my life, my all!
Optional 3rd and 4th stanza setting
mp
3. See, from His head, His hands, His

WORDS: Isaac Watts, 1674-1748
MUSIC: From *Psalm Tone I*, adapt. Lowell Mason, 1792-1872; arr. Tom Fettke, b. 1941

HAMBURG
L.M.

feet, Sor - row and love flow min - gled
down. Did e'er such love and sor - row
meet, Or thorns com - pose so rich a
crown?
rit.
Broader
4. Were the whole realm of
8va
na - ture mine, That were a pres - ent far too

small.
Love so a - maz - ing, so di -
8va
vine, De - mands my soul, my life, my
1.
8va
all! life, my all!
2.
8va

146 Man of Sorrows

Who has believed our message
and to whom has the arm of the LORD been revealed?
He grew up before him like a tender shoot,
and like a root out of dry ground.
He had no beauty or majesty to attract us to him,
nothing in his appearance that we should desire him.
He was despised and rejected by men,
a man of sorrows, and familiar with suffering.
Like one from whom men hide their faces
he was despised, and we esteemed him not.

Surely he took up our infirmities
and carried our sorrows,
yet we considered him stricken by God,
smitten by him, and afflicted.
But he was pierced for our transgressions,
he was crushed for our iniquities;
the punishment that brought us peace was upon him,
and by his wounds we are healed.
We all, like sheep, have gone astray,
each of us has turned to his own way;
and the LORD has laid on him
the iniquity of us all.

Isaiah 53:1-6

In the Cross of Christ I Glory 147

May I never boast except in the cross of our Lord Jesus Christ. Galatians 6:14

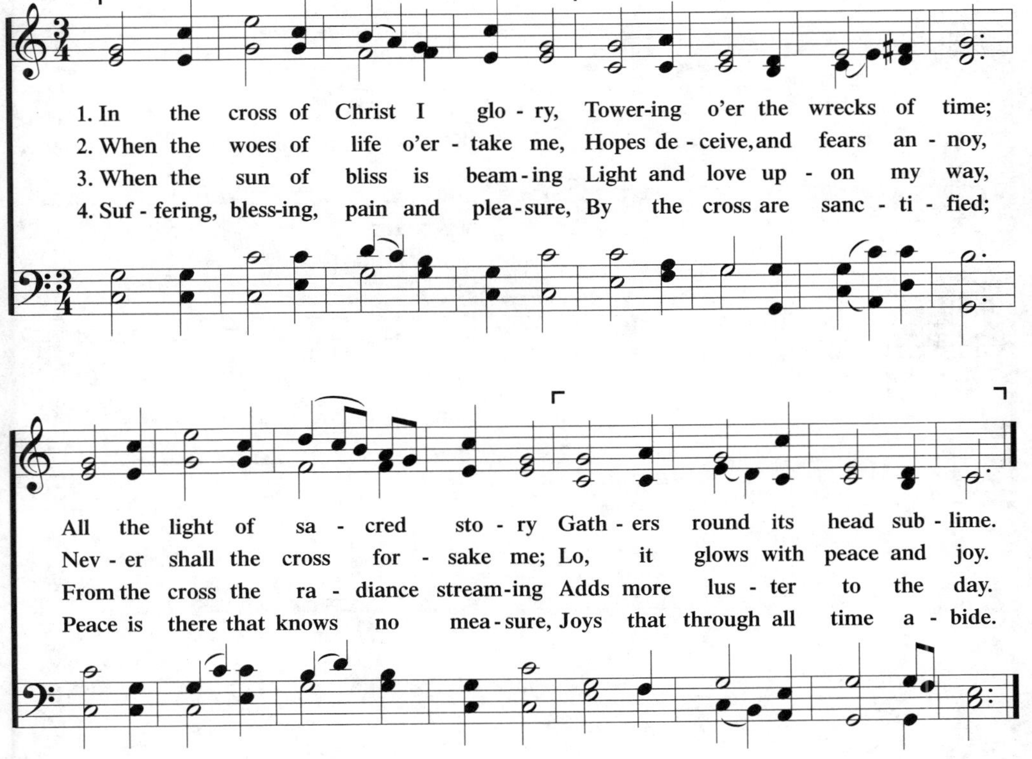
1. In the cross of Christ I glo - ry, Tower-ing o'er the wrecks of time;
2. When the woes of life o'er - take me, Hopes de - ceive, and fears an - noy,
3. When the sun of bliss is beam - ing Light and love up - on my way,
4. Suf - fering, bless-ing, pain and plea - sure, By the cross are sanc - ti - fied;
All the light of sa - cred sto - ry Gath - ers round its head sub - lime.
Nev - er shall the cross for - sake me; Lo, it glows with peace and joy.
From the cross the ra - diance stream-ing Adds more lus - ter to the day.
Peace is there that knows no mea - sure, Joys that through all time a - bide.

WORDS: John Bowring, 1792-1872, alt.
MUSIC: Ithamar Conkey, 1815-1867

RATHBUN
8.7.8.7.

148 Behold the Lamb

. . . that was slain from the creation of the world. Revelation 13:8

Be - hold the Lamb, be - hold the Lamb,
Slain from the foun - da - tion of the world. For sin - ners cru - ci - fied,
O ho - ly sac - ri - fice, Be - hold the Lamb of God, be - hold the
Lamb.
Fine
More movement
Crown Him, crown Him, Wor - thy
play cued notes
first time only
is the Lamb. Praise Him, praise Him,

WORDS: Dottie Rambo, b. 1934
MUSIC: Dottie Rambo, b. 1934

BEHOLD THE LAMB
Irregular

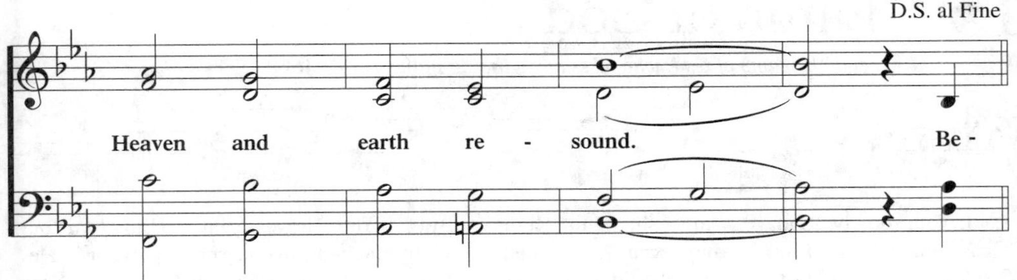
D.S. al Fine
Heaven and earth re - sound. Be -

The Suffering Lamb 149

He was oppressed and afflicted,
yet he did not open his mouth;
he was led like a lamb to the slaughter,
and as a sheep before her shearers is silent,
so he did not open his mouth.
By oppression and judgment he was taken away.
And who can speak of his descendants?
For he was cut off from the land of the living;
for the transgression of my people he was stricken.
He was assigned a grave with the wicked,
and with the rich in his death,
though he had done no violence,
nor was any deceit in his mouth.
Yet it was the LORD's will to crush him and cause him to suffer,
and though the LORD makes his life a guilt offering,
he will see his offspring and prolong his days,
and the will of the LORD will prosper in his hand.
After the suffering of his soul,
he will see the light of life and be satisfied;
by his knowledge my righteous servant will justify many,
and he will bear their iniquities.
Therefore I will give him a portion among the great,
and he will divide the spoils with the strong,
because he poured out his life unto death,
and was numbered with the transgressors.
For he bore the sin of many,
and made intercession for the transgressors.

Isaiah 53:7-12

150 Lamb of God

Look, the Lamb of God, who takes away the sin of the world! John 1:29

1. Your on - ly Son, no sin to hide; But You have sent Him from Your side To walk up - on this guilt - y sod And to be - come the Lamb of God.
2. Your gift of love they cru - ci - fied, They laughed and scorned Him as He died; The hum-ble King they named a fraud And sac-ri - ficed the Lamb of God.
3. I was so lost, I should have died, But You have brought me to Your side To be led by Your staff and rod And to be called a lamb of God.
Refrain
O Lamb of God, sweet Lamb of God; I love the ho - ly Lamb of God. O wash me in His pre-cious blood, 1,2. My Je-sus Christ, the Lamb of God.
3. 'Til I am just a lamb of God.
last time rit.

WORDS: Twila Paris, b. 1958
MUSIC: Twila Paris, b. 1958

LAMB OF GOD
L.M. with Refrain

There Is a Fountain 151

A fountain will be opened . . . to cleanse them from sin. Zechariah 13:1

1. There is a foun-tain filled with blood Drawn from Im - man - uel's veins,
2. The dy - ing thief re - joiced to see That foun-tain in his day,
3. Dear dy - ing Lamb, Thy pre - cious blood Shall nev - er lose its power,
4. E'er since, by faith, I saw the stream Thy flow-ing wounds sup - ply,
5. When this poor lisp - ing, stam - mering tongue Lies si - lent in the grave,
And sin - ners plunged be - neath that flood Lose all their guilt - y stains:
And there may I, though vile as he, Wash all my sins a - way:
Till all the ran - somed Church of God Be saved, to sin no more:
Re - deem - ing love has been my theme And shall be till I die:
Then in a no - bler, sweet - er song I'll sing Thy power to save:
Lose all their guilt - y stains, Lose all their guilt - y stains;
Wash all my sins a - way, Wash all my sins a - way;
Be saved, to sin no more, Be saved, to sin no more;
And shall be till I die, And shall be till I die;
I'll sing Thy power to save, I'll sing Thy power to save;
And sin - ners plunged be - neath that flood Lose all their guilt - y stains.
And there may I, though vile as he, Wash all my sins a - way.
Till all the ran - somed Church of God Be saved, to sin no more.
Re - deem - ing love has been my theme And shall be till I die.
Then in a no - bler, sweet - er song I'll sing Thy power to save.

WORDS: William Cowper, 1731-1800
MUSIC: American melody; arr. Lowell Mason, 1792-1872

CLEANSING FOUNTAIN
8.6.8.6.6.6.8.6.

152 My Savior's Love

The Son of God . . . loved me and gave himself for me. Galatians 2:20

1. I stand a - mazed in the pres - ence Of Je - sus, the Naz - a - rene,
2. For me it was in the gar - den He prayed, "Not My will, but Thine."
3. He took my sins and my sor - rows; He made them His ver - y own.
4. When with the ran - somed in glo - ry His face I at last shall see,
And won - der how He could love me, A sin - ner, con - demned, un - clean.
He had no tears for His own griefs, But sweat drops of blood for mine.
He bore the bur - den to Cal - vary, And suf - fered and died a - lone.
'Twill be my joy through the a - ges To sing of His love for me.
Refrain
How mar - vel - ous, How won - der - ful!
O, how mar - vel - ous, O, how won - der - ful!
And my song shall ev - er be:
How mar - vel - ous, How won - der - ful!
O, how mar - vel - ous, O, how won - der - ful!
Is my Sav - ior's love for me!

Optional segue to "O, How He Loves You and Me." No transition required.

WORDS: Charles H. Gabriel, 1856-1932
MUSIC: Charles H. Gabriel, 1856-1932

MY SAVIOR'S LOVE
8.7.8.7 with Refrain

O, How He Loves You and Me 153

Greater love has no one than this. John 15:13

1. O, how He loves you and me! O, how He loves you and me! He gave His life; what more could He give? O, how He loves you, O, how He loves me, O, how He loves you and me!
2. Je - sus to Cal - vary did go, His love for sin - ners to show. What He did there brought hope from de - spair. O, how He loves you, O, how He loves me, O, how He loves you and me!

WORDS: Kurt Kaiser, b. 1934
MUSIC: Kurt Kaiser, b. 1934

PATRICIA
Irregular

JESUS IS LOVE ITSELF

We are not love, and we never expect to love by our own impulses as God expects us to. But Jesus is the heart of love. Jesus is love itself, and Jesus is ours. His love is ours. We draw it in and give it out.

A.B. Simpson (1843-1919), *Christ in the Tabernacle*

154 He Died for Me

He himself bore our sins in his body on the tree. 1 Peter 2:24

1. I saw One hang-ing on a tree, In ag - o - ny and blood;
2. Sure, nev - er till my lat - est breath Can I for - get that look;
3. My con-science felt and owned the guilt, And plunged me in de - spair;
4. A sec - ond look He gave, which said, "I free - ly all for - give.
He fixed His lov - ing eyes on me, As near His cross I stood.
It seemed to charge me with His death, Though not a word He spoke.
I saw my sins His blood had spilt And helped to nail Him there.
This blood is for your ran - som paid. I die that you may live."
Refrain
O, can it be, up - on a tree The Sav - ior died for me?
My soul is thrilled, my heart is filled, To think He died for me!

WORDS: John Newton, 1725-1807
MUSIC: Edwin O. Excell, 1851-1921

EXCELL
C.M. with Refrain

CHRIST IS RISEN

MEDLEY

Christ the Lord Is Risen Today
Celebrate Jesus

Christ the Lord Is Risen Today 155

Christ has indeed been raised from the dead. 1 Corinthians 15:20

1. "Christ the Lord is risen to - day," Al - le - lu - ia!
2. Love's re - deem - ing work is done, Al - le - lu - ia!
3. Lives a - gain our glo - rious King; Al - le - lu - ia!
4. Soar we now where Christ has led, Al - le - lu - ia!
Sons of men and an - gels say, Al - le - lu - ia!
Fought the fight, the bat - tle won; Al - le - lu - ia!
Where, O death, is now thy sting? Al - le - lu - ia!
Fol - lowing our ex - alt - ed Head; Al - le - lu - ia!
Raise your joys and tri - umphs high; Al - le - lu - ia!
Death in vain for - bids Him rise, Al - le - lu - ia!
Dy - ing once, He all doth save; Al - le - lu - ia!
Made like Him, like Him we rise; Al - le - lu - ia!
Song Ending
Sing, ye heavens, and earth re - ply: Al - le - lu - ia!
Christ has o - pened Par - a - dise. Al - le - lu - ia!
Where's thy vic - to - ry, O grave? Al - le - lu - ia!
Ours the cross, the grave, the skies. Al - le - lu - ia!

WORDS: Charles Wesley, 1707-1788
MUSIC: *Lyra Davidica*, 1708

EASTER HYMN
7.4.7.4.D.

156 Celebrate Jesus

I am the Living One; I was dead, and behold I am alive for ever and ever! Revelation 1:18

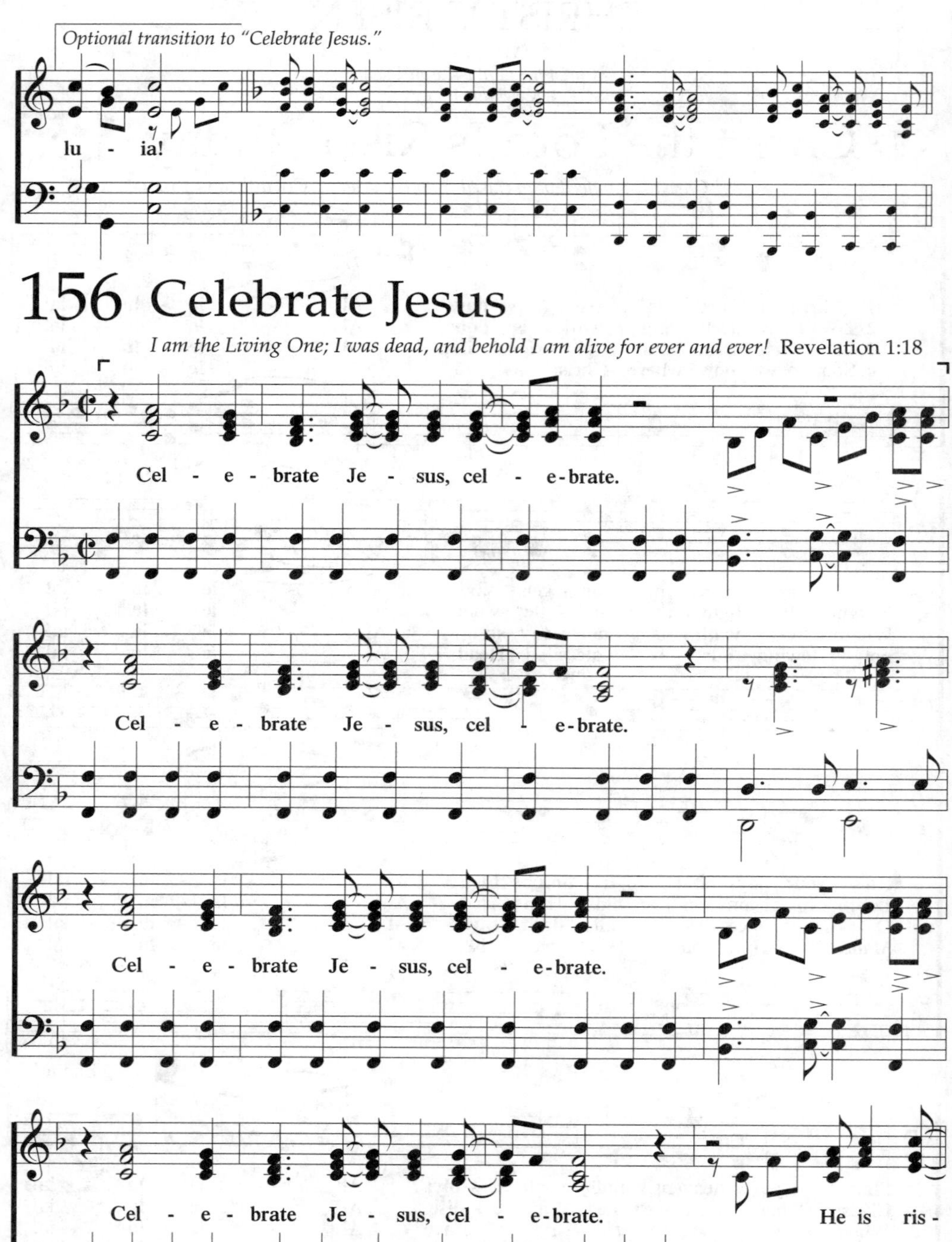
Optional transition to "Celebrate Jesus."
lu - ia!
Cel - e - brate Je - sus, cel - e - brate.
Cel - e - brate Je - sus, cel - e - brate.
Cel - e - brate Je - sus, cel - e - brate.
Cel - e - brate Je - sus, cel - e - brate. He is ris -

WORDS: Gary Oliver, b. 1956
MUSIC: Gary Oliver, b. 1956

CELEBRATE JESUS
Irregular

en, He is ris - en and He
lives for-ev-er-more. He is
ris - en, He is ris - en; Come on and cel-
e-brate the re-sur-rec - tion of our Lord.
1. Repeat optional
D.C.
2.

157 The Risen Savior

After the Sabbath, at dawn on the first day of the week, Mary Magdalene and the other Mary went to look at the tomb.

There was a violent earthquake, for an angel of the Lord came down from heaven and, going to the tomb, rolled back the stone and sat on it.

His appearance was like lightning, and his clothes were white as snow.

The guards were so afraid of him that they shook and became like dead men.

The angel said to the women, "Do not be afraid, for I know that you are looking for Jesus, who was crucified.

He is not here; he has risen, just as he said. Come and see the place where he lay.

Then go quickly and tell his disciples: 'He has risen from the dead and is going ahead of you into Galilee. There you will see him.' Now I have told you."

So the women hurried away from the tomb, afraid yet filled with joy, and ran to tell his disciples.

Suddenly Jesus met them. "Greetings," he said. They came to him, clasped his feet and worshiped him.

Then Jesus said to them, "Do not be afraid. Go and tell my brothers to go to Galilee; there they will see me." *Matthew 28:1-10*

On the evening of that first day of the week, when the disciples were together, with the doors locked for fear of the Jews, Jesus came and stood among them and said, "Peace be with you!"

After he said this, he showed them his hands and side. The disciples were overjoyed when they saw the Lord. . . .

A week later his disciples were in the house again, and Thomas was with them. Though the doors were locked, Jesus came and stood among them and said, "Peace be with you!"

Then he said to Thomas, "Put your finger here; see my hands. Reach out your hand and put it into my side. Stop doubting and believe."

Thomas said to him, "My Lord and my God!"

Then Jesus told him, "Because you have seen me, you have believed; blessed are those who have not seen and yet have believed."

John 20:19-20, 26-29

I am the Living One; I was dead, and behold I am alive for ever and ever! And I hold the keys of death and Hades. *Revelation 1:18*

Christ Is Alive! 158

He has risen! He is not here. Mark 16:6

1. Christ is a - live! Let Chris - tians sing. The cross stands emp - ty to the sky. Let streets and homes with prais - es ring. Love, drowned in death, shall nev - er die.
2. Christ is a - live! No long - er bound to dis - tant years in Pal - es - tine, but sav - ing, heal - ing, here and now, and touch - ing ev - ery place and time.
3. In ev - ery in - sult, rift and war, where col - or, scorn or wealth di - vide, Christ suf - fers still, yet loves the more, and lives, where e - ven hope has died.
4. Wom - en and men, in age and youth, can feel the Spir - it, hear the call, and find the way, the life, the truth, re - vealed in Je - sus, freed for all.
5. Christ is a - live, and comes to bring good news to this and ev - ery age, till earth and sky and o - cean ring with joy, with jus - tice, love and praise.
8

WORDS: Brian Wren, b. 1936
MUSIC: Thomas Williams' *Psalmodia Evangelica*, 1789

TRURO
L.M.

CHRIST IS OUR EXAMPLE

In His life, Christ is an example, showing us how to live;
In His death, He is a Sacrifice, satisfying for our sins;
In His resurrection, a Conqueror;
In His ascension, a King;
In His intercession, a High Priest.

Martin Luther (1483-1546)

---

159 Christ Is Risen! Shout Hosanna!

Why do you look for the living among the dead? He is not here; he has risen! Luke 24:5

1. Christ is ris - en! Shout Ho - san - na! Cel - e - brate this day of days.
2. Christ is ris - en! Raise your spir - its from the cav - erns of de - spair.
3. Christ is ris - en! Earth and heav - en nev - er - more shall be the same.
Christ is ris - en! Hush in won - der; all cre - a - tion is a - mazed.
Walk with glad - ness in the morn - ing. See what love can do and dare.
Break the bread of new cre - a - tion where the world is still in pain.
In the des - ert all - sur - round - ing, see, a spread - ing tree has grown.
Drink the wine of re - sur - rec - tion, not a ser - vant, but a friend;
Tell its grim, de - mon - ic cho - rus: "Christ is ris - en! Get you gone!"
Heal - ing leaves of grace a - bound - ing, bring a taste of love un - known.
Je - sus is our strong com - pan - ion. Joy and peace shall nev - er end.
God the First and Last is with us. Sing Ho - san - na ev - ery - one!

WORDS: Brian Wren, b. 1936
MUSIC: Melody by Ludwig van Beethoven, 1770-1827; arr. Edward Hodges, 1796-1867.

HYMN TO JOY
8.7.8.7.D.

Christ Arose 160

It was impossible for death to keep its hold on him. Acts 2:24

1. Low in the grave He lay— Je - sus, my Sav - ior! Wait - ing the coming day— Je - sus, my Lord!
2. Vain - ly they watch His bed— Je - sus, my Sav - ior! Vain - ly they seal the dead— Je - sus, my Lord!
3. Death can - not keep his prey— Je - sus my Sav - ior! He tore the bars a - way— Je - sus, my Lord!
Refrain
Up from the grave He a - rose, With a might - y tri - umph o'er His foes; He a - rose! He a - rose a vic - tor from the dark do - main, And He lives for - ev - er with His saints to reign. He a - rose! He a - rose! He a - rose! He a - rose! Hal - le - lu - jah! Christ a - rose!

WORDS: Robert Lowry, 1826-1899
MUSIC: Robert Lowry, 1826-1899

CHRIST AROSE
6.5.6.4. with Refrain

161 The Day of Resurrection!

Go and tell my brothers to go to Galilee; there they will see me. Matthew 28:10

1. The day of res - ur - rec - tion! Earth, tell it out a - broad;
2. Our hearts be pure from e - vil, That we may see a - right
3. Now let the heavens be joy - ful! Let earth its song be - gin!
The pass - o - ver of glad - ness, The pass - o - ver of God!
The Lord in rays e - ter - nal Of res - ur - rec - tion light;
The world re - sound in tri - umph And all that is there - in;
From death to life e - ter - nal, From sin's do - min - ion free,
Our ears at - tuned to lis - ten May hear, so calm and plain,
Let all things seen and un - seen, Their notes of glad - ness blend,
Our Christ has brought us o - ver With hymns of vic - to - ry!
His own "All Hail!" and, hear - ing, May raise the vic - tor strain.
For Christ the Lord has ris - en, Our Joy that has no end.

(For different tune, see No. 33)

WORDS: John of Damascus, ca. 700-754; tr. John M. Neale, 1818-1866, alt.
MUSIC: Henry T. Smart, 1813-1879

LANCASHIRE
7.6.7.6.D.

Alleluia, Sing to Jesus 162

Salvation belongs to our God, who sits on the throne, and to the Lamb. Revelation 7:10

1. Al - le - lu - ia, sing to Je - sus! His the scep - ter,1 His the throne:
2. Al - le - lu - ia! not as or - phans are we left in sor - row now;
3. Al - le - lu - ia! heav-enly High Priest, here on earth our help, our stay;
Al - le - lu - ia! His the tri - umph, His the vic - to - ry a - lone.
Al - le - lu - ia! He is near us; faith be - lieves nor ques - tions how.
Al - le - lu - ia! hear the sin - ful cry to You from day to day.
Hark! the songs of peace - ful Zi - on thun - der like a might - y flood.
Though the cloud from sight re - ceived Him when the for - ty days were o'er
In - ter - ces - sor, Friend of sin - ners, earth's Re - deem - er, hear our plea,
Je - sus, out of ev - ery na - tion, has re - deemed us by His blood.
Shall our hearts for - get His prom - ise, "I am with you ev - er - more"?
Where the songs of all the sin - less sweep a - cross the crys - tal sea.

WORDS: William C. Dix, 1837-1898, alt.
MUSIC: Rowland H. Prichard, 1811-1887; arr. Ralph Vaughan Williams, 1872-1958

HYFRYDOL
8.7.8.7.D.

1. *scepter: a staff which is an emblem of authority*

LIFT UP HIS NAME

MEDLEY

All Hail the Power of Jesus' Name
Lord, I Lift Your Name on High

163 All Hail the Power of Jesus' Name

FIRST TUNE

God exalted him . . . and gave him the name that is above every name. Philippians 2:9

1. All hail the power of Je - sus' name! Let an - gels pros - trate[1]
2. Ye cho - sen seed of Is - rael's race, Ye ran - somed from the
3. Let ev - ery kin - dred, ev - ery tribe, On this ter - res - trial
4. O, that with yon - der[4] sa - cred throng We at His feet may
fall. Bring forth the roy - al di - a - dem,[2] And crown Him
fall, Hail Him who saves you by His grace, And crown Him
ball,[3] To Him all maj - es - ty as - cribe, And crown Him
fall! We'll join the ev - er - last - ing song,[5] And crown Him
Lord of all; Bring forth the roy - al di - a - dem, And crown Him
Lord of all; Hail Him who saves you by His grace, And crown Him
Lord of all; To Him all maj - es - ty as - cribe, And crown Him
Lord of all! We'll join the ev - er - last - ing song, And crown Him

WORDS: Edward Perronet, 1726-1792; adapt. John Rippon, 1751-1836
MUSIC: Oliver Holden, 1765-1844

CORONATION
C.M. with Repeats

1. *prostrate: lying face down*
2. *diadem: crown*
3. *terrestrial ball: the planet Earth*
4. *yonder: heavenly afterlife*
5. *everlasting song: "Holy, holy, holy . . ." of Revelation 4:8*

Song ending
Optional transition to "Lord, I Lift Your Name on High."
Lord of all!
Lord of all!
Lord of all!
Lord of all!
all!

Lord, I Lift Your Name on High 164

Christ died for our sins according to the Scriptures . . . he was raised on the third day.
1 Corinthians 15:3-4

Lord, I lift Your name on high;
Lord, I love to sing Your

prais - es.
I'm so glad You're in my life;

I'm so glad You came to save us.

WORDS: Rick Founds, b. 1954
MUSIC: Rick Founds, b. 1954

LORD, I LIFT YOUR NAME
Irregular

You came from heav - en to earth to show the way,
From the earth to the cross my debt to pay;
From the cross to the grave, from the grave to the sky;
Lord I lift Your name on high.

Optional repeat of "All Hail the Power of Jesus' Name," No. 163

All Hail the Power of Jesus' Name 165

SECOND TUNE

At the name of Jesus every knee should bow, in heaven and on earth and under the earth.
Philippians 2:10

1. All hail the power of Je - sus' name! Let an - gels pros - trate[1] fall, Let an - gels pros-trate fall; Bring forth the roy - al di - a - dem,[2] And crown Him, crown Him, crown Him, crown Him, crown Him, crown Him, crown Him, And crown Him Lord of all!
2. Ye cho - sen seed of Is - rael's race, Ye ran-somed from the fall, Ye ran - somed from the fall; Hail Him who saves you by His grace,
3. Let ev - ery kin - dred, ev - ery tribe, On this ter - res - trial ball,[3] On this ter - res - trial ball; To Him all maj - es - ty as - cribe,
4. O that with yon - der[4] sa - cred throng We at His feet may fall, We at His feet may fall! We'll join the ev - er - last - ing song,[5]
crown

WORDS: Edward Perronet, 1726-1792; adapt. John Rippon, 1751-1836
MUSIC: James Ellor, 1819-1899

DIADEM
C.M. with Repeats

1. *prostrate: lying face down*
2. *diadem: crown*
3. *terrestrial ball: the planet earth*
4. *yonder: heavenly afterlife*
5. *everlasting song: "Holy, holy, holy..." of Revelation 4:8*

166 All Hail the Power of Jesus' Name

THIRD TUNE

And every tongue confess that Jesus Christ is Lord. Philippians 2:11

1. All hail the power of Je - sus' name! Let an - gels pros - trate[1] fall. Bring forth the roy - al di - a - dem,[2]
2. Ye cho - sen seed of Is - rael's race, Ye ran-somed from the fall, Hail Him who saves you by His grace,
3. Let ev - ery kin - dred, ev - ery tribe, On this ter - res - trial ball,[3] To Him all maj - es - ty as - cribe,
4. O that with yon - der[4] sa - cred throng We at His feet may fall, We'll join the ev - er - last - ing song,[5]
Refrain
And crown Him, crown Him, crown Him, Crown Him, Lord of all!

WORDS: Edward Perronet, 1726-1792; adapt. John Rippon, 1751-1836
MUSIC: William Shrubsole, 1760-1806

MILES LANE
8.6.8. with Refrain

1. *prostrate: lying face down*
2. *diadem: crown*
3. *terrestrial ball: the planet earth*
4. *yonder: heavenly afterlife*
5. *everlasting song: "Holy, holy, holy..." of Revelation 4:8*

The Ascension 167

While [the two Emmaus travelers] were still talking [to the disciples] about this, Jesus himself stood among them and said to them, "Peace be with you."

They were startled and frightened, thinking they saw a ghost.

He said to them, "Why are you troubled, and why do doubts rise in your minds?

"Look at my hands and my feet. It is I myself! Touch me and see; a ghost does not have flesh and bones, as you see I have."

When he had said this, he showed them his hands and feet.

And while they still did not believe it because of joy and amazement, he asked them, "Do you have anything here to eat?"

They gave him a piece of broiled fish,

and he took it and ate it in their presence.

He said to them, "This is what I told you while I was still with you: Everything must be fulfilled that is written about me in the Law of Moses, the Prophets and the Psalms."

Then he opened their minds so they could understand the Scriptures.

He told them, "This is what is written: The Christ will suffer and rise from the dead on the third day,

and repentance and forgiveness of sins will be preached in his name to all nations, beginning at Jerusalem.

You are witnesses of these things.

I am going to send you what my Father has promised; but stay in the city until you have been clothed with power from on high."

When he had led them out to the vicinity of Bethany, he lifted up his hands and blessed them.

While he was blessing them, he left them and was taken up into heaven.

Then they worshiped him and returned to Jerusalem with great joy.

And they stayed continually at the temple, praising God. *Luke 24:36-53*

The Exaltation of Christ 168

Then I looked and heard the voice of many angels, numbering thousands upon thousands, and ten thousand times ten thousand. They encircled the throne and the living creatures and the elders. In a loud voice they sang:

"Worthy is the Lamb, who was slain,
to receive power and wealth and wisdom and strength
and honor and glory and praise!"

Then I heard every creature in heaven and on earth and under the earth and on the sea, and all that is in them, singing:

"To him who sits on the throne and to the Lamb
be praise and honor and glory and power,
for ever and ever!"

Revelation 5:11-13

169 The Name of the Lord

The name of the LORD is a strong tower; the righteous run to it and are safe. Proverbs18:10

WORDS: Clinton Utterbach, 20th century
MUSIC: Clinton Utterbach, 20th century

UTTERBACH
Irregular

Refrain
Most High!
Most High!
Most High!
The name of the Lord is
a strong tow - er,
The right-eous run in - to it
and they are saved.
The name of the Lord
is a strong tow - er,
The right-eous run in-
to it and they are saved.

170 The Head That Once Was Crowned with Thorns

Death has been swallowed up in victory. 1 Corinthians 15:54

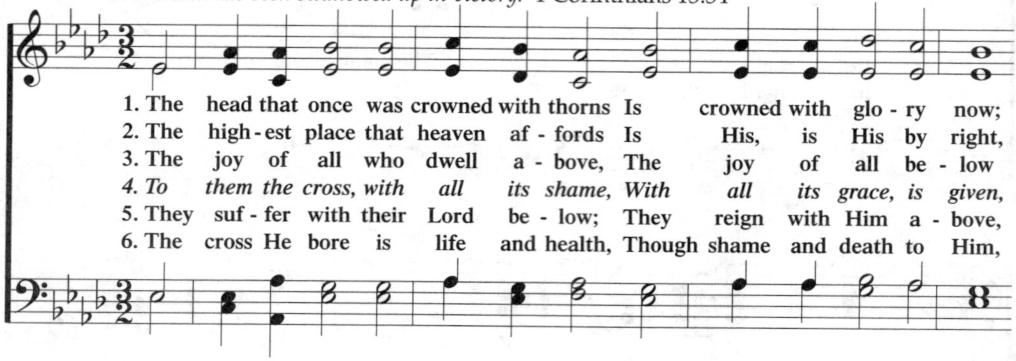

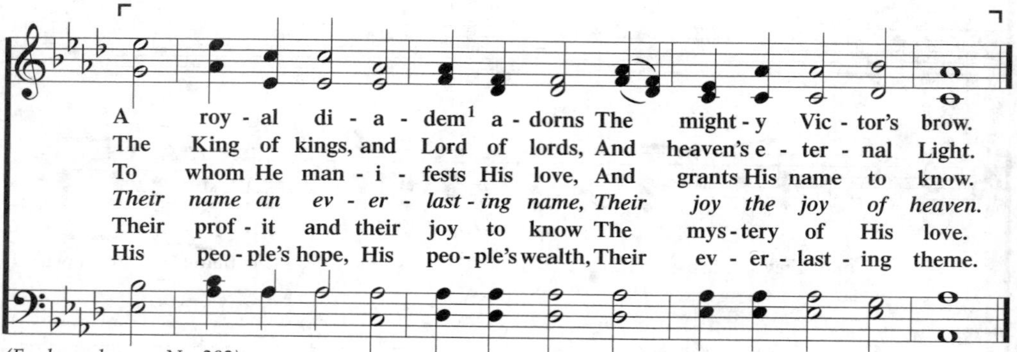

1. The head that once was crowned with thorns Is crowned with glo - ry now;
A roy - al di - a - dem[1] a - dorns The might - y Vic - tor's brow.

2. The high - est place that heaven af - fords Is His, is His by right,
The King of kings, and Lord of lords, And heaven's e - ter - nal Light.

3. The joy of all who dwell a - bove, The joy of all be - low
To whom He man - i - fests His love, And grants His name to know.

4. To them the cross, with all its shame, With all its grace, is given,
Their name an ev - er - last - ing name, Their joy the joy of heaven.

5. They suf - fer with their Lord be - low; They reign with Him a - bove,
Their prof - it and their joy to know The mys - tery of His love.

6. The cross He bore is life and health, Though shame and death to Him,
His peo - ple's hope, His peo - ple's wealth, Their ev - er - last - ing theme.

(For lower key, see No. 202)

WORDS: Thomas Kelly, 1769-1855
MUSIC: Carl G. Gläser, 1784-1829; adapt. Lowell Mason, 1792-1872

AZMON
C.M.

1. diadem: crown

171 I Know That My Redeemer Lives

I know that my Redeemer lives, and that in the end he will stand upon the earth. Job 19:25

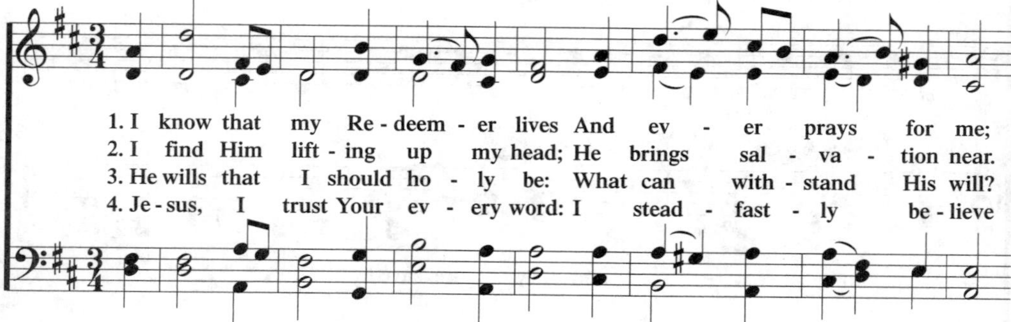
1. I know that my Re - deem - er lives And ev - er prays for me;
2. I find Him lift - ing up my head; He brings sal - va - tion near.
3. He wills that I should ho - ly be: What can with - stand His will?
4. Je - sus, I trust Your ev - ery word: I stead - fast - ly be - lieve

WORDS: Charles Wesley, 1707-1788, alt.
MUSIC: Arr. from *Messiah*, G.F. Handel, 1685-1759

MESSIAH
C.M.

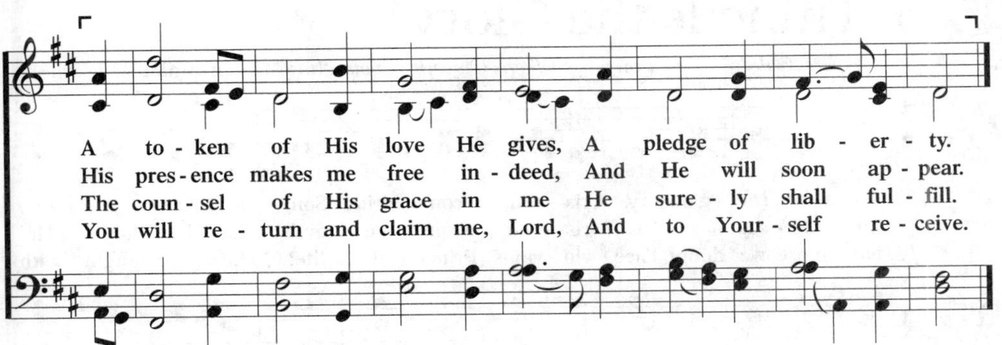
A to - ken of His love He gives, A pledge of lib - er - ty.
His pres - ence makes me free in - deed, And He will soon ap - pear.
The coun - sel of His grace in me He sure - ly shall ful - fill.
You will re - turn and claim me, Lord, And to Your - self re - ceive.

Rejoice, the Lord Is King! 172

After he had provided purification for sins, he sat down at the right hand of the Majesty in heaven. Hebrews 1:3

1. Re - joice, the Lord is King! Your Lord and King a - dore!
2. Our Sav - ior, Je - sus, reigns, The God of truth and love;
3. His king - dom can - not fail, He rules o'er earth and heaven;
4. Re - joice in glo - rious hope! Our Lord, the Judge, shall come,

Re - joice, give thanks, and sing, And tri - umph ev - er - more.
When He had purged our stains, He took His seat a - bove.
The keys of death and hell Are to our Je - sus given.
And take His ser - vants up To their e - ter - nal home.

Lift up your heart, lift up your voice! Re - joice, a - gain I say, re - joice!

WORDS: Charles Wesley, 1707-1788, alt.
MUSIC: John Darwall, 1731-1789

DARWALL
6.6.6.6.4.4.8.

173 Thine Is the Glory

Where, O death, is your victory? Where, O death, is your sting? 1 Corinthians 15:55

1. Thine is the glo - ry, ris - en, con-quering Son; End-less is the vic - tory Thou o'er death hast won. An - gels in bright rai - ment rolled the stone a - way, Kept the fold - ed grave-clothes where Thy bo - dy lay.
2. Lo! Je - sus meets us, ris - en from the tomb; Lov - ing - ly He greets us, scat - ters fear and gloom. Let His Church with glad - ness hymns of tri - umph sing, For her Lord now liv - eth; death hath lost its sting.
3. No more we doubt Thee, glo - rious Prince of life! Life is naught[1] with-out Thee; aid us in our strife. Make us more than con-querors, through Thy death - less love; Bring us safe through Jor - dan to Thy home a - bove.
Refrain
Thine is the glo - ry, ris - en, con-quering Son;

WORDS: Edmond L. Budry, 1854-1932; tr. Richard B. Hoyle, 1875-1939
MUSIC: G.F. Handel, 1685-1759

JUDAS MACCABEUS
10.11.11.11. with Refrain

1. *naught: nothing*

End - less is the vic - tory Thou o'er death hast won.

Majestic Sweetness Sits Enthroned 174

We see Jesus . . . now crowned with glory and honor. Hebrews 2:9

1. Majestic sweetness sits enthroned
Upon the Savior's brow;
His head with radiant glories crowned,
His lips with grace o'erflow,
His lips with grace o'erflow.

2. No mortal can with Him compare
Among the sons of men;
Fairer is He than all the fair
That fill the heavenly train,
That fill the heavenly train.

3. To Him I owe my life and breath,
And all the joys I have;
He makes me triumph over death,
And saves me from the grave,
And saves me from the grave.

4. To heaven, the place of His abode,
He brings my weary feet,
Shows me the glories of my God,
And makes my joys complete,
And makes my joys complete.

5. Since from His bounty I receive
Such proofs of love divine;
Had I a thousand hearts to give,
Lord, they should all be Thine,
Lord, they should all be Thine.

WORDS: Samuel Stennett, 1727-1795
MUSIC: Thomas Hastings, 1784-1872

ORTONVILLE
C.M. with repeat

CROWN HIM KING

MEDLEY

Crown Him with Many Crowns
All Hail, King Jesus

175 Crown Him with Many Crowns

His eyes are like blazing fire, and on His head are many crowns. Revelation 19:12

1. Crown Him with man - y crowns, The Lamb up - on His throne.
2. Crown Him the Lord of love! Be - hold His hands and side;
3. Crown Him the Lord of life! Who tri - umphed o'er the grave;
4. Crown Him the Lord of years, The Rul - er of all time,
Hark! how the heaven - ly an - them drowns All mu - sic but its own!
Those wounds yet vis - i - ble a - bove In beau - ty glo - ri - fied.
And rose vic - to - rious in the strife For those He came to save.
Cre - a - tor of the roll - ing spheres,1 Un - speak - a - bly sub - lime.
A - wake, my soul, and sing Of Him who died for thee, And hail Him as thy
No an - gels in the sky Can ful - ly bear that sight, But down-ward bend their
His glo - ries now we sing, Who died and rose on high, Who died e - ter - nal
All hail! Re-deem-er, hail! For Thou hast died for me; Thy praise shall nev - er,
Song ending
Optional transition to "All Hail, King Jesus."
match - less King Through all e - ter - ni - ty. ty.
burn - ing eyes At mys - ter - ies so bright.
life to bring And lives that death may die.
nev - er fail Through - out e - ter - ni - ty.
rit.

WORDS: Matthew Bridges, 1800-1894, alt.; stanza 3, Godfrey Thring, 1823-1903
MUSIC: George J. Elvey, 1816-1893

DIADEMATA
S.M.D.

1. *rolling spheres: planets*

All Hail, King Jesus 176

He has this name written: KING OF KINGS AND LORD OF LORDS. Revelation 19:16

All hail, King Je - sus! All hail Em - man - u - el,
King of kings, Lord of lords, Bright Morn - ing Star.
3
And through - out e - ter - ni - ty, I'll sing Your prais - es;
3
And I'll reign with You through - out e - ter - ni - ty.

WORDS: Dave Moody, b. 1948
MUSIC: Dave Moody, b. 1948

KING JESUS
Irregular

177 Arise, My Soul, Arise!

He is able to save completely . . . because he always lives to intercede for them. Hebrews 7:25

1. A - rise, my soul, a - rise! Shake off thy guilt - y fears.
2. He ev - er lives a - bove For me to in - ter - cede,
3. Five bleed - ing wounds He bears, Re - ceived on Cal - va - ry.
4. The Fa - ther hears Him pray, His dear A - noint - ed One;
5. My God is rec - on - ciled; His par - doning voice I hear.
The bleed - ing Sac - ri - fice In my be - half ap - pears.
His all - re - deem - ing love, His pre - cious blood to plead.
They pour ef - fec - tual prayers; They strong - ly plead for me.
He can - not turn a - way The pres - ence of His Son.
He owns me for His child; I can no long - er fear.
Be - fore the throne my Sure - ty[1] stands, Be - fore the throne my
His blood a - toned for all our race, His blood a - toned for
"For - give him, O, for - give," they cry, "For - give him, O, for -
His Spir - it an - swers to the blood, His Spir - it an - swers
With con - fi - dence I now draw nigh, With con - fi - dence I
Sure - ty stands; My name is writ - ten on His hands.
all our race, And sprin - kles now the throne of grace.
give," they cry, "Nor let that ran - somed sin - ner die!"
to the blood, And tells me I am born of God.
now draw nigh, And, "Fa - ther, Ab - ba, Fa - ther," cry.

WORDS: Charles Wesley, 1707-1788
MUSIC: Lewis Edson, 1748-1820

LENOX
6.6.6.6.8.8.8.

1. *surety: one who becomes legally liable for another's debt*

Lift Up, Lift Up Your Voices Now 178

He will swallow up death forever. Isaiah 25:8

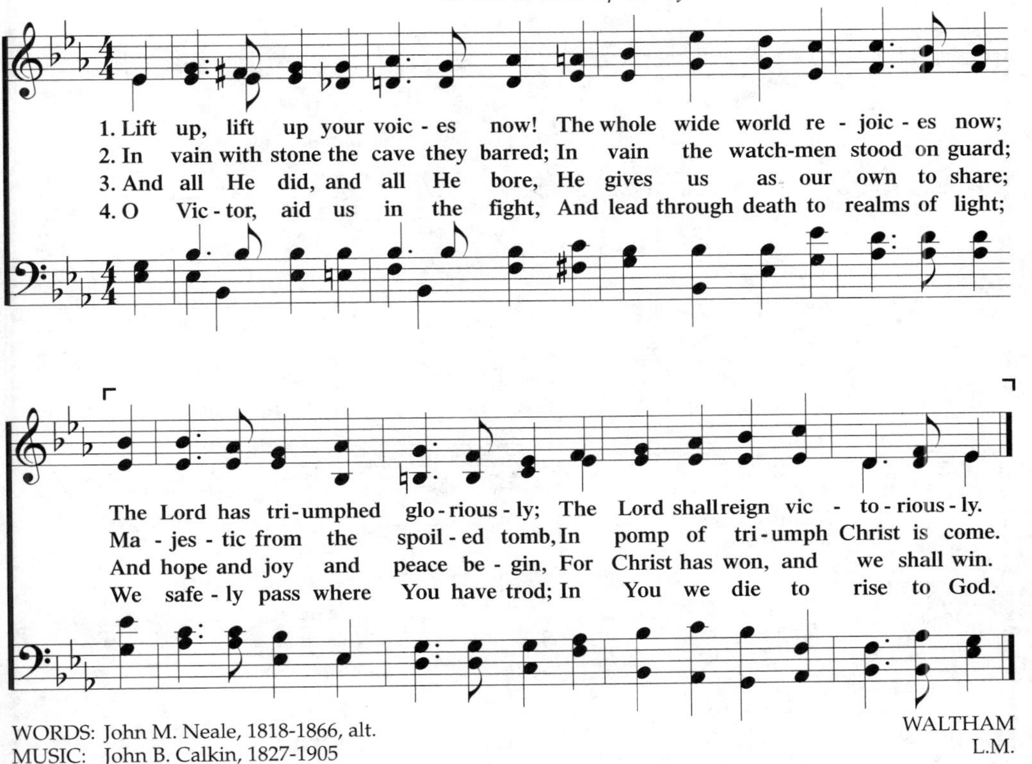
1. Lift up, lift up your voic - es now! The whole wide world re - joic - es now;
2. In vain with stone the cave they barred; In vain the watch-men stood on guard;
3. And all He did, and all He bore, He gives us as our own to share;
4. O Vic - tor, aid us in the fight, And lead through death to realms of light;
The Lord has tri - umphed glo - rious - ly; The Lord shall reign vic - to - rious - ly.
Ma - jes - tic from the spoil - ed tomb, In pomp of tri - umph Christ is come.
And hope and joy and peace be - gin, For Christ has won, and we shall win.
We safe - ly pass where You have trod; In You we die to rise to God.

WORDS: John M. Neale, 1818-1866, alt.
MUSIC: John B. Calkin, 1827-1905

WALTHAM
L.M.

Name Above All Names 179

Your attitude should be the same as that of Christ Jesus:
Who, being in very nature God,
did not consider equality with God something to be grasped,
but made himself nothing,
taking the very nature of a servant,
being made in human likeness.
And being found in appearance as a man,
he humbled himself and became obedient to death—
even death on a cross!
Therefore God exalted him to the highest place
and gave him the name that is above every name,
that at the name of Jesus every knee should bow,
in heaven and on earth and under the earth,
and every tongue confess that Jesus Christ is Lord,
to the glory of God the Father.

Philippians 2:5-11

180 At the Name of Jesus

Every knee should bow . . . and every tongue confess that Jesus Christ is Lord.
Philippians 2:10-11

At the name of Je - sus,
At the name of Je - sus,
Ev-ery knee shall bow in
heav-en and in earth.
1.
2.
earth.
That ev-ery
knee shall bow
And ev-ery tongue con - fess that
Je - sus Christ is Lord.
rit.
8va

WORDS: Cindy Berry, b. 1949; based on Philippians 2:10-11
MUSIC: Cindy Berry, b. 1949

BERRY
Irregular

The Lord's Return 181

[The disciples] were looking intently up into the sky as Jesus was going, when suddenly two men dressed in white stood beside them.

"Men of Galilee," they said, "why do you stand here looking into the sky? This same Jesus, who has been taken from you into heaven, will come back in the same way you have seen him go into heaven." *Acts 1:10-11*

According to the Lord's own word, we tell you that we who are still alive, who are left till the coming of the Lord, will certainly not precede those who have fallen asleep.

For the Lord himself will come down from heaven, with a loud command, with the voice of the archangel and with the trumpet call of God, and the dead in Christ will rise first.

After that, we who are still alive and are left will be caught up together with them in the clouds to meet the Lord in the air. And so we will be with the Lord forever.

Therefore encourage each other with these words. *1 Thessalonians 4:15-18*

"You also must be ready, because the Son of Man will come at an hour when you do not expect him." *Matthew 24:44*

Our citizenship is in heaven. And we eagerly await a Savior from there, the Lord Jesus Christ. *Philippians 3:20*

Since everything will be destroyed in this way, what kind of people ought you to be? You ought to live holy and godly lives

as you look forward to the day of God and speed its coming. That day will bring about the destruction of the heavens by fire, and the elements will melt in the heat.

But in keeping with his promise we are looking forward to a new heaven and a new earth, the home of righteousness.

So then, dear friends, since you are looking forward to this, make every effort to be found spotless, blameless and at peace with him.

2 Peter 3:11-14

CHRIST IS RETURNING

MEDLEY

Christ Is Coming Back Again
Lift Up Your Heads

182 Christ Is Coming Back Again

If I go and prepare a place for you, I will come back and take you to be with me. John 14:3

1. Star of hope for hearts for - lorn, Her - ald of the Ad - vent morn,
2. Christ is com - ing back the same, As of old to earth He came.
3. He is com - ing back a - gain; Christ the same, but not as then.
4. Christ is com - ing back a - gain; Ev - ery tongue shall praise His name.
Part - ing prom - ise of the Lord, Strong and sure pro - phet - ic word,
As He rose from Beth - a - ny, "This same Je - sus still He'll be."
Now He's com - ing to a throne, Heaven and earth His rule to own.
Let the might - y ech - o roll, 'Round the globe from pole to pole.
Sing a - loud the glad re - frain: "Christ is com - ing back a - gain!"
And the an - gels did pro - claim: "Christ is com - ing back a - gain!"
We will share His sec - ond reign; "Christ is com - ing back a - gain!"
'Til the world shall shout the strain: "Christ is com - ing back a - gain!"
Song Ending
Sing a - loud the glad re - frain: "Christ is com - ing back a - gain!"
And the an - gels did pro - claim: "Christ is com - ing back a - gain!"
We will share His sec - ond reign; "Christ is com - ing back a - gain!"
'Til the world shall shout the strain: "Christ is com - ing back a - gain!"

WORDS: Albert B. Simpson, 1843-1919; adapt. Gene Rivard, b. 1949
MUSIC: Gene Rivard, b. 1949; harm. Eldon McBride, b. 1962

STAR OF HOPE
Irregular

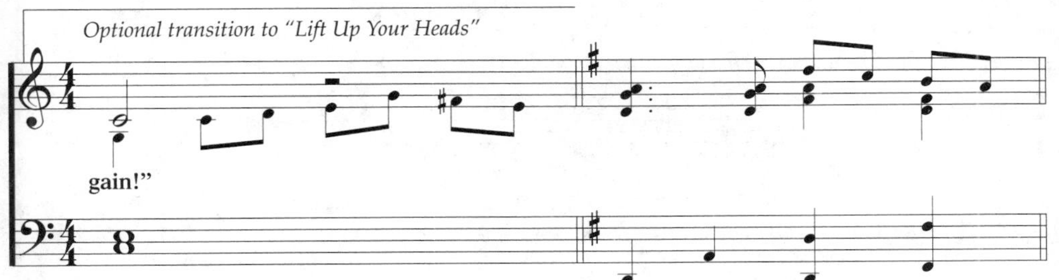
Optional transition to "Lift Up Your Heads"
gain!"

Lift Up Your Heads 183

. . . because your redemption is drawing near. Luke 21:28

Lift up your heads to the com-ing King.
Bow be-fore Him and a-dore Him, sing!
To His Maj-es-ty, let your prais-es be
Pure and ho-ly, giv-ing glo-ry to the King of kings.
1. kings. 2. kings.

WORDS: Steven L. Fry, b. 1954
MUSIC: Steven L. Fry, b. 1954

LIFT UP YOUR HEADS
Irregular

184 He Is Coming Again

See the Son of Man coming in a cloud with power and great glory. Luke 21:27

1. Lift up your heads, pil - grims a - wea - ry, See day's ap -
2. Dark was the night, sin warred a - gainst us. Heav - y the
3. O bless - ed hope! O bliss - ful prom - ise! Fill - ing our
4. E - ven so, come, pre - cious Lord Je - sus. Cre - a - tion
proach now crim - son the sky. Night shad - ows flee, and your Be -
load of sor - row we bore. But now we see signs of His
hearts with rap - ture di - vine. O day of days! Hail Your ap -
waits re - demp - tion to see. Caught up in clouds, soon we shall
lov - ed, A - wait - ed with long - ing, at last has drawn nigh.
com - ing. Our hearts glow with - in us, our cup's run - ning o'er!
pear - ing! Your tran - scend - ent glo - ry for - ev - er shall shine.
meet Thee. O bless - ed as - sur - ance, for - ev - er with Thee!
Refrain
He is com - ing a - gain, He is com - ing a - gain, The ver - y same
Je - sus, re - ject - ed of men. He is com - ing a - gain, He is com - ing a -

WORDS: Mabel J. Camp, 1871-1937, alt.
MUSIC: Mabel J. Camp, 1871-1937

CAMP
Irregular with Refrain

gain, With power and great glo - ry, He is com - ing a - gain!
is com - ing a - gain!

When He Shall Come 185

I will come back and take you to be with me. John 14:3

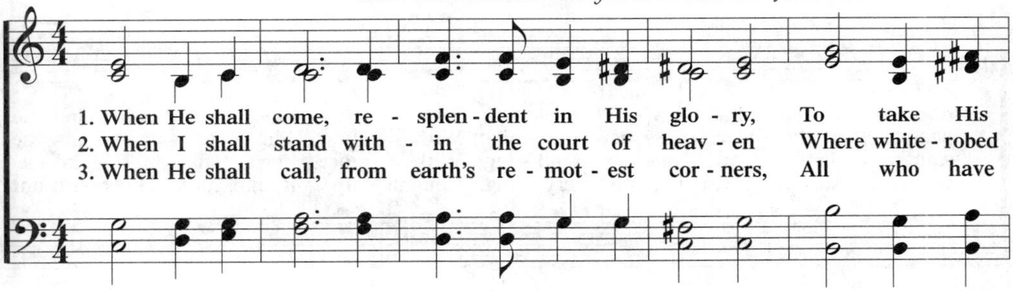

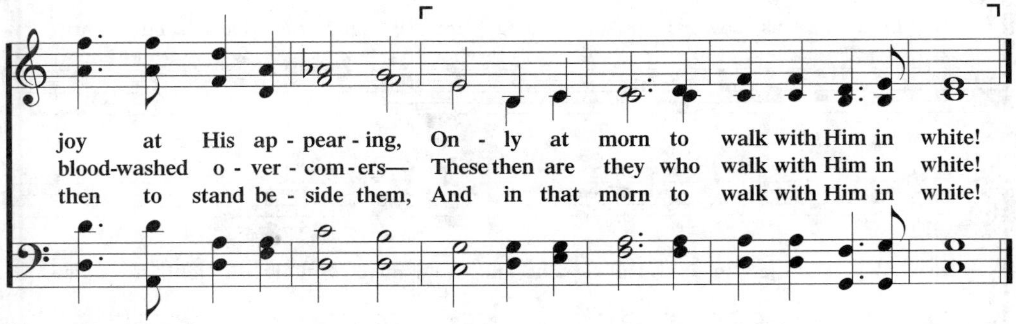

1. When He shall come, re - splen - dent in His glo - ry, To take His own from out this vale[1] of night, O, may I know the joy at His ap - pear - ing, On - ly at morn to walk with Him in white!

2. When I shall stand with - in the court of heav - en Where white - robed pil - grims pass be - fore my sight— Earth's mar - tyred saints and blood-washed o - ver - com - ers— These then are they who walk with Him in white!

3. When He shall call, from earth's re - mot - est cor - ners, All who have stood tri - umph - ant in His might, O, to be wor - thy then to stand be - side them, And in that morn to walk with Him in white!

WORDS: Almeda J. Pearce, 1893-1986
MUSIC: Almeda J. Pearce, 1893-1986

PEARCE
11.10.11.10.

1. *vale: valley*

186 Christ Returneth

You will see the Son of Man . . . coming on the clouds of heaven. Mark 14:62

1. It may be at morn, when the day is a - wak - ing, When sun-light through dark - ness and shad - ow is break - ing, That Je - sus will come in the full - ness of glo - ry To re - ceive from the world His own.
2. It may be at mid - day, it may be at twi - light, It may be, per - chance, that the black - ness of mid - night Will burst in - to light in the blaze of His glo - ry, When Je - sus re - ceives His own.
3. While its hosts cry "Ho - san - na," from heav - en de - scend - ing, With glo - ri - fied saints and the an - gels at - tend - ing, With grace on His brow, like a ha - lo of glo - ry, Will Je - sus re - ceive His own.
4. O joy, O de - light, should we go with-out dy - ing! No sick-ness, no sad - ness, no dread - ing, no cry - ing! Caught up through the clouds with our Lord in - to glo - ry, When Je - sus re - ceives His own.
Refrain
O Lord Je - sus, how long, how long Ere we shout the glad song? Christ re - turn - eth— Hal - le - lu - jah! Hal - le - lu - jah! A - men. Hal - le - lu - jah! A - men.

WORDS: H.L. Turner, 19th century, ca. 1878
MUSIC: James McGranahan, 1840-1907

CHRIST RETURNETH
Irregular with Refrain

Lo, Jesus Comes! 187

The day of the LORD is coming. It is close at hand. Joel 2:1

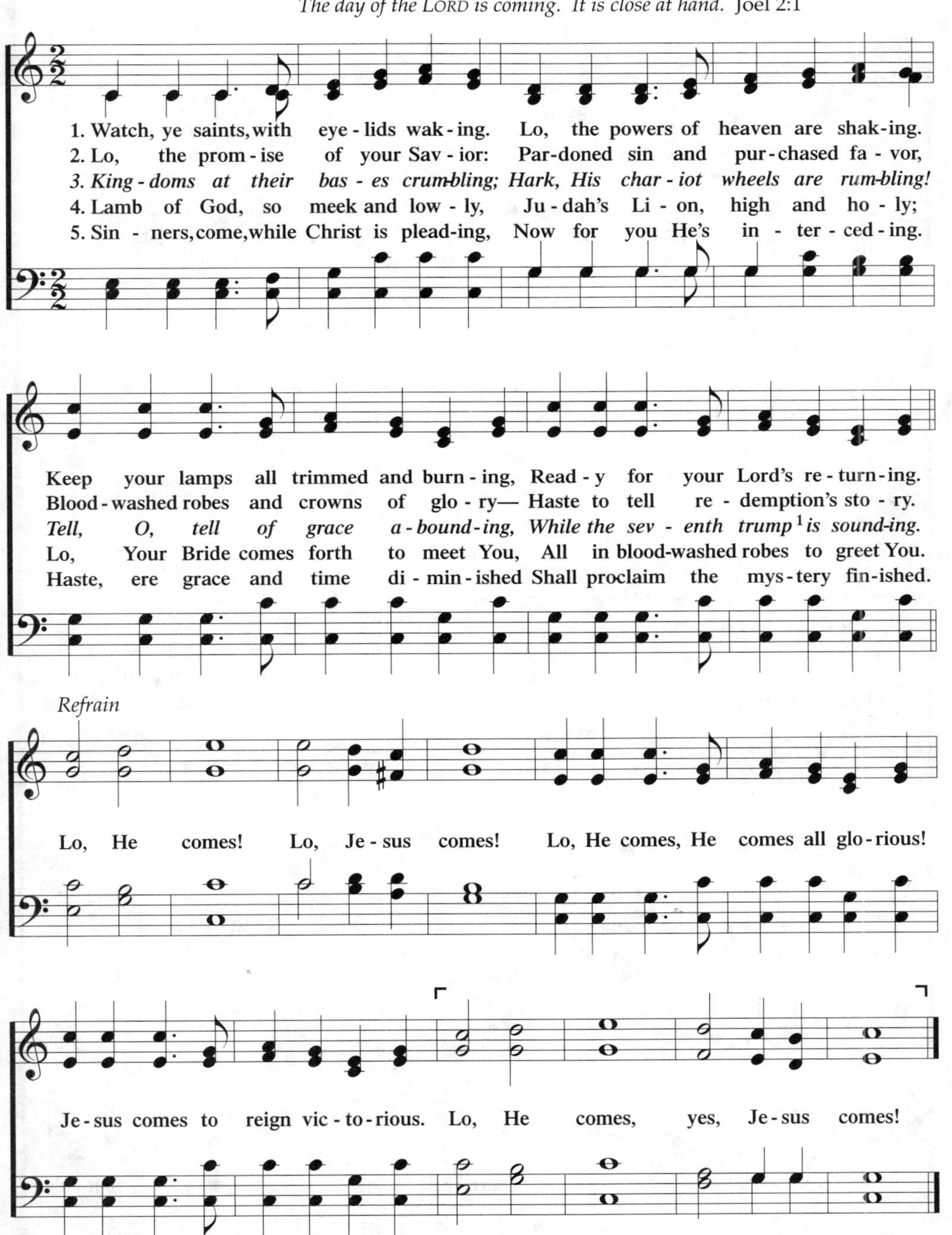
1. Watch, ye saints, with eye-lids wak-ing. Lo, the powers of heaven are shak-ing.
2. Lo, the prom-ise of your Sav-ior: Par-doned sin and pur-chased fa-vor,
3. King-doms at their bas-es crum-bling; Hark, His char-iot wheels are rum-bling!
4. Lamb of God, so meek and low-ly, Ju-dah's Li-on, high and ho-ly;
5. Sin-ners, come, while Christ is plead-ing, Now for you He's in-ter-ced-ing.
Keep your lamps all trimmed and burn-ing, Read-y for your Lord's re-turn-ing.
Blood-washed robes and crowns of glo-ry— Haste to tell re-demption's sto-ry.
Tell, O, tell of grace a-bound-ing, While the sev-enth trump[1] is sound-ing.
Lo, Your Bride comes forth to meet You, All in blood-washed robes to greet You.
Haste, ere grace and time di-min-ished Shall proclaim the mys-tery fin-ished.
Refrain
Lo, He comes! Lo, Je-sus comes! Lo, He comes, He comes all glo-rious!
Je-sus comes to reign vic-to-rious. Lo, He comes, yes, Je-sus comes!

WORDS: Phoebe P. Knapp, 1839-1908, alt.
MUSIC: William J. Kirkpatrick, 1838-1921

LO, JESUS COMES
L.M. with Refrain

1. *seventh trump: from Revelation 11:15, the final trumpet at the end times*

188 What If It Were Today?

The Lord himself will come down from heaven, with a loud command. 1 Thessalonians 4:16

1. Je - sus is com - ing to earth a - gain; What if it were to - day?
2. Sa - tan's do - min - ion will then be o'er. O, that it were to - day!
3. Faith - ful and true would He find us here, If He should come to - day?
Com - ing in pow - er and love to reign; What if it were to - day?
Sor - row and sigh - ing shall be no more. O, that it were to - day!
Watch - ing in glad - ness and not in fear, If He should come to - day?
Com - ing to claim His cho - sen Bride, All the re - deemed and pu - ri - fied,
Then shall the dead in Christ a - rise, Caught up to meet Him in the skies.
Signs of His com - ing mul - ti - ply; Morn - ing light breaks in east - ern sky;
O - ver this whole earth scat - tered wide. What if it were to - day?
When shall these glo - ries meet our eyes? What if it were to - day?
Watch, for the time is draw - ing nigh! What if it were to - day?
Refrain
Glo - ry! Glo - ry! Joy to my heart 'twill bring: Glo - ry! Glo - ry!

WORDS: Leila N. Morris, 1862-1929
MUSIC: Leila N. Morris, 1862-1929

SECOND COMING
Irregular with Refrain

When we shall crown Him King. Glo - ry! Glo - ry! Haste to pre-pare the
way! Glo - ry! Glo - ry! Je - sus will come some day!

The King Shall Come 189

"Yes, I am coming soon." Revelation 22:20

1. The King shall come when morn-ing dawns And light tri - um-phant breaks;
2. Not as of old, a lit - tle child, To bear, and fight, and die,
3. The King shall come when morn-ing dawns And earth's dark night is past.
4. Then let the end - less bliss be - gin, By wea - ry saints fore - told,
5. The King shall come when morn-ing dawns And light and beau - ty brings:
When beau - ty gilds the east - ern hills And life to joy a - wakes.
But crowned with glo - ry like the sun That lights the morn - ing sky.
O, haste the ris - ing of that morn, The day that e'er shall last.
When right shall tri - umph o - ver wrong, And trust shall be ex - tolled.
Hail, Christ the Lord! Your peo - ple pray, Come quick - ly, King of kings!

WORDS: Ancient Greek hymn; tr. John Brownlie, 1859-1925
MUSIC: Traditional American melody; *Kentucky Harmony*, Part Second, 1813

MORNING SONG
C.M.

LONGING FOR CHRIST'S RETURN

There is no coming of Christ to the heart, there is no coming of Christ to the Church, there is no coming of Christ to the world, that can satisfy the longing for His personal return.

A.B. Simpson (1843-1919), *Serving the King*

It should be noted that there is a vast difference between the doctrine of Christ's coming and the hope of His coming. The first we may hold without feeling a trace of the second. Indeed there are multitudes of Christians today who hold the doctrine of the second coming. What I have talked about here is that overwhelming sense of anticipation that lifts the life onto a new plane and fills the heart with rapturous optimism. This is what we today lack.

A.W. Tozer (1897-1963), *Man, the Dwelling Place of God*

JESUS IS COMING SOON

MEDLEY

Jesus Is Coming Again
Soon and Very Soon

190 Jesus Is Coming Again

Therefore keep watch, because you do not know the day or the hour. Matthew 25:13

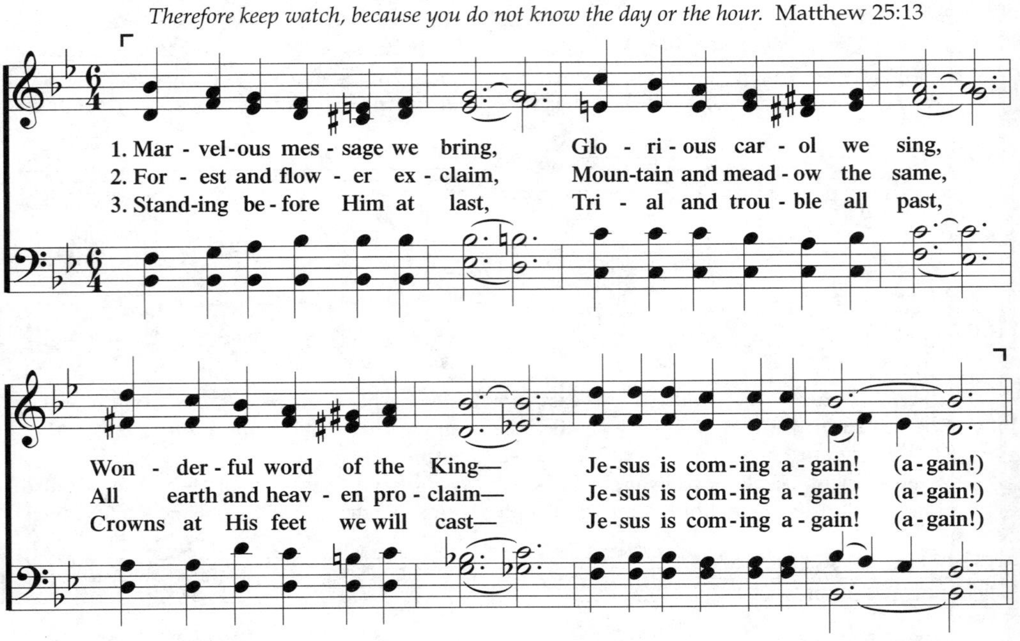
1. Mar - vel-ous mes - sage we bring, Glo - ri - ous car - ol we sing,
2. For - est and flow - er ex - claim, Moun-tain and mead - ow the same,
3. Stand-ing be - fore Him at last, Tri - al and trou - ble all past,
Won - der - ful word of the King— Je-sus is com-ing a - gain! (a - gain!)
All earth and heav - en pro - claim— Je-sus is com-ing a - gain! (a - gain!)
Crowns at His feet we will cast— Je-sus is com-ing a - gain! (a - gain!)

WORDS: John W. Peterson, b. 1921
MUSIC: John W. Peterson, b. 1921

COMING AGAIN
7.7.7.7. with Refrain

Refrain
Com - ing a - gain, com - ing a - gain;
May - be morn - ing, may - be noon, May - be eve - ning and may - be soon!
Com - ing a - gain, com - ing a - gain;
O, what a won - der - ful day it will be— Je - sus is com - ing a - gain!
Optional transition to "Soon and Very Soon"

191 Soon and Very Soon

"Yes, I am coming soon." Amen. Come, Lord Jesus. Revelation 22:20

WORDS: Andraé Crouch, b. 1947
MUSIC: Andraé Crouch, b. 1947

SOON AND VERY SOON
Irregular

Is It the Crowning Day? 192

When the Chief Shepherd appears, you will receive the crown. 1 Peter 5:4

1. Je - sus may come to - day, Glad day! Glad day! And I would see my Friend; Dan - gers and trou-bles would end If Je - sus should come to - day.
2. I may go home to - day. Glad day! Glad day! Al - most I hear their song; Hail to the ra - di - ant throng! If I should go home to - day.
3. Why should I anx - ious be? Glad day! Glad day! Lights ap - pear on the shore, Storms will a - larm nev - er - more, For He is "at hand" to - day.
4. Faith - ful I'll be to - day, Glad day! Glad day! And I will free - ly tell Why I should love Him so well, For He is my all to - day.
Refrain
Glad day! Glad day! Is it the crown - ing day? I'll live for to - day, nor anx - ious be, Je - sus, my Lord, I soon shall see. Glad day! Glad day! Is it the crown - ing day?

WORDS: George W. Whitcomb, 19th century, alt.
MUSIC: Charles H. Marsh, 1886-1956

CROWNING DAY
Irregular with Refrain

OUR KING IS COMING

MEDLEY

My Lord, What a Morning
The King Is Coming

193 My Lord, What a Morning

I watched as he opened the sixth seal . . . and the stars in the sky fell to earth.
Revelation 6:12-13

Refrain
My Lord, what a morn-ing. My Lord, what a morn-ing.
My Lord, what a morn-ing When the stars be-gin to fall.
fine
1. You'll hear the trum-pet sound to wake the na-tions un-der-ground,
2. You'll hear the sin-ner cry to wake the na-tions un-der-ground,
3. You'll hear the Chris-tian shout to wake the na-tions un-der-ground,
Look-ing to my God's right hand when the stars be-gin to fall.
D.C.
Optional transition to "The King Is Coming."
rit.

WORDS: African-American spiritual
MUSIC: African-American spiritual

BURLEIGH
Irregular

The King Is Coming 194

The Lord is coming with thousands upon thousands of his holy ones. Jude 14

O, the King is com-ing, the King is com-ing! I just
heard the trum-pets sound-ing, And now His face I see. O, the King is
com-ing, the King is com-ing! Praise God, He's com-ing for me!

WORDS: Gloria Gaither, b. 1942; William J. Gaither, b. 1936; Charles Millhuff, b. 1938
MUSIC: William J. Gaither, b. 1936

KING IS COMING
Irregular

King of Kings and Lord of Lords 195

I saw heaven standing open and there before me was a white horse, whose rider is called Faithful and True. With justice he judges and makes war.

His eyes are like blazing fire, and on his head are many crowns. He has a name written on him that no one knows but he himself.

He is dressed in a robe dipped in blood, and his name is the Word of God.

The armies of heaven were following him, riding on white horses and dressed in fine linen, white and clean.

Out of his mouth comes a sharp sword with which to strike down the nations. "He will rule them with an iron scepter."

He treads the winepress of the fury of the wrath of God Almighty. On his robe and on his thigh he has this name written: KING OF KINGS AND LORD OF LORDS.

Revelation 19:11-16

Then I saw a new heaven and a new earth, for the first heaven and the first earth had passed away, and there was no longer any sea. I saw the Holy City, the new Jerusalem, coming down out of heaven from God, prepared as a bride beautifully dressed for her husband. And I heard a loud voice from the throne saying,

"Now the dwelling of God is with men, and he will live with them. They will be his people, and God himself will be with them and be their God. He will wipe every tear from their eyes. There will be no more death or mourning or crying or pain, for the old order of things has passed away."

Revelation 21:1-4

196 At the Name of Jesus

. . . every knee should bow. Philippians 2:10

1. At the name of Je - sus Ev - ery knee shall bow,
2. Hum - bled for a sea - son To re - ceive a name
3. In your hearts en - throne Him; There let Him re - move
4. Watch, for this Lord Je - sus Shall re - turn a - gain

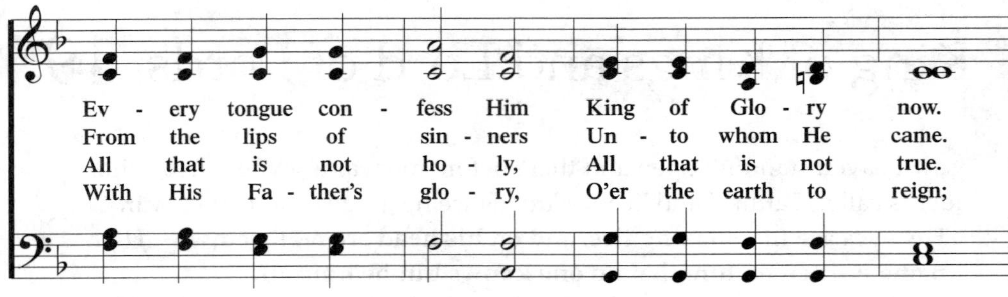
Ev - ery tongue con - fess Him King of Glo - ry now.
From the lips of sin - ners Un - to whom He came.
All that is not ho - ly, All that is not true.
With His Fa - ther's glo - ry, O'er the earth to reign;

WORDS: Caroline M. Noel, 1817-1877
MUSIC: James Mountain, 1843-1933

WYE VALLEY (abridged)
6.5.6.5.D.

'Tis the Fa - ther's plea - sure We should call Him Lord,
Faith - ful - ly He bore it, Spot - less to the last,
Crown Him as your cap - tain In temp - ta - tion's hour.
For the day is com - ing When each knee shall bow,
Who from the be - gin - ning Was the might - y Word.
Brought it back vic - to - rious When from death He passed.
Let His will en - fold you In its light and power.
All our hearts con - fess Him King of Glo - ry now.

Even So, Come, Lord Jesus 197

[Jesus said] "And behold, I am coming quickly, and My reward is with Me, to give to every one according to his work. I am the Alpha and the Omega, the Beginning and the End, the First and the Last."

Blessed are those who do His commandments, that they may have the right to the tree of life, and may enter through the gates into the city. But outside are dogs and sorcerers and sexually immoral and murderers and idolaters, and whoever loves and practices a lie.

"I, Jesus, have sent My angel to testify to you these things in the churches. I am the Root and the Offspring of David, the Bright and Morning Star."

And the Spirit and the bride say, "Come!" And let him who hears say, "Come!" And let him who thirsts come. Whoever desires, let him take the water of life freely.

For I testify to everyone who hears the words of the prophecy of this book: If anyone adds to these things, God will add to him the plagues that are written in this book;

And if anyone takes words away from the words of the book of this prophecy, God shall take away his part from the Book of Life, from the holy city, and from the things which are written in this book.

He who testifies to these things says, "Surely I am coming quickly."

Amen. Even so, come, Lord Jesus!

The grace of our Lord Jesus be with you all.

Amen.

Revelation 22:12-21, NKJV

198 Even So

The Spirit and the bride say, "Come!" And let him who hears say, "Come!" Revelation 22:17

1. There's a sweet and sa - cred prayer On the Bi - ble's fi - nal page,
2. "E - ven so." We sel - dom dream What these might - y words im - ply,
3. "E - ven so," O bless - ed Hope! Lift our souls to things on high.
4. Let us live our bless - ed Hope, And af - firm our Ad - vent prayer.
Breathed by John on Pat - mos' Isle, Left to us from age to age.
How they tell of lives con - formed To a Hope, so great, so high!
Let our hearts be cen - tered there. Hold our treas - ures in the sky.
Let us watch, and work, and live, For His com - ing to pre - pare.
Ech - o of the Mas - ter's voice: "Lo I come, I quick - ly come."
Tell of hearts trans - formed and free, Read - y at His call to go.
Let us walk as strang - ers here, And in - scribe on all be - low:
Let us send the gos - pel forth, Till the world His name shall know,
And the Bride re - peats the cry: "E - ven so, Lord Je - sus, come."
All our life one liv - ing page; "Come, Lord Je - sus, e - ven so."
"None of earth we call our own; Christ is com - ing, e - ven so."
And the Bride com - plete shall cry: "Come, Lord Je - sus, e - ven so!"

(For different harmony, see No. 503)

WORDS: Albert B. Simpson, 1843-1919
MUSIC: American melody; harm. Eldon McBride, b. 1962

BEACH SPRING
8.7.8.7.D.

We Come, O Christ, to You 199

Jesus answered, "I am the way and the truth and the life." John 14:6

1. We come, O Christ, to You, True Son of God and
2. You are the Way to God, Your blood our ran - som
3. You are the liv - ing Truth! All wis - dom dwells in
4. You on - ly are true Life, To know You is to
5. We wor - ship You, Lord Christ, Our Sav - ior and our
man, By whom all things con - sist, In whom all
paid. In You we face our Judge And Mak - er
You, The source of ev - ery skill, The one e -
live The more a - bun - dant life That earth can
King; To You our youth and strength A - dor - ing -
life be - gan: In You a - lone we
un - a - fraid. Be - fore the throne ab -
ter - nal True! O great I Am! In
nev - er give. O ris - en Lord! We
ly we bring: So fill our hearts that
live and move, And have our be - ing in Your love.
solved we stand, Your love has met Your law's de - mand.
You we rest, Sure ans - wer to our ev - ery quest.
live in You; In us each day Your life re - new!
all may view Your life in us, and turn to You!

WORDS: Margaret Clarkson, b. 1915; rev.1984
MUSIC: John Darwall, 1731-1789

DARWALL
6.6.6.6.4.4.8.

200 The Supremacy of Christ

He is the image of the invisible God, the firstborn over all creation.

For by him all things were created: things in heaven and on earth, visible and invisible, whether thrones or powers or rulers or authorities; all things were created by him and for him.

He is before all things, and in him all things hold together.

And he is the head of the body, the church; he is the beginning and the firstborn from among the dead, so that in everything he might have the supremacy.

For God was pleased to have all his fullness dwell in him,

And through him to reconcile to himself all things, whether things on earth or things in heaven, by making peace through his blood, shed on the cross.

Colossians 1:15-20

201 O, for a Thousand Tongues

FIRST TUNE

Praise be to his glorious name forever. Psalm 72:19

1. O, for a thou - sand tongues to sing My great Re - deem - er's praise, My great Re - deem - er's praise,
2. My gra - cious Mas - ter and my God, As - sist me to pro - claim, As - sist me to pro - claim,
3. Je - sus! the Name that charms our fears, That bids our sor - rows cease, That bids our sor - rows cease;
4. He breaks the power of can - celed sin, He sets the pris - oner free, He sets the pris - oner free,

WORDS: Charles Wesley, 1707-1788
MUSIC: Thomas Jarman, 1776-1861

LYNGHAM
8.6.6.8. with repeats

The glo - ries of my God and King, The
To spread through all the earth a - broad, The
'Tis mu - sic in the sin - ner's ears, 'Tis
His blood can make the foul - est clean, His
1. The tri - umphs of His
2. The hon - ors of Thy
3. 'Tis life and health and
4. His blood a - vailed for
tri - umphs of His grace, The tri - umphs of His
hon - ors of Thy Name, The hon - ors of Thy
life and health and peace, 'Tis life and health and
blood a - vailed for me, His blood a - vailed for
grace, The tri - umphs of His grace, The
Name, The hon - ors of Thy Name, The
peace, 'Tis life and health and peace, 'Tis
me, His blood a - vailed for me, His
grace, The tri - umphs of His grace.
Name, The hon - ors of Thy Name.
peace, 'Tis life and health and peace.
me, His blood a - vailed for me.
tri - umphs of His grace, The tri - umphs of His grace.
hon - ors of Thy Name, The hon - ors of Thy Name.
life and health and peace, 'Tis life and health and peace.
blood a - vailed for me, His blood a - vailed for me.

THE PRAYER OF ST. PATRICK

. . . I bind this today to me forever
By power of faith, Christ's incarnation;
His baptism in Jordan river,
His death on Cross for my salvation;
His bursting from the spiced tomb,
His riding up the heavenly way,
His coming at the day of doom
I bind unto myself today . . .

Christ be with me, Christ within me,
Christ behind me, Christ before me,
Christ beside me, Christ to win me,
Christ to comfort and restore me.
Christ beneath me, Christ above me,
Christ in quiet, Christ in danger,
Christ in hearts of all that love me,
Christ in mouth of friend and stranger.

St. Patrick (389-461), from *The Breastplate*

202 O, for a Thousand Tongues

SECOND TUNE

My tongue will speak . . . of your praises all day long. Psalm 35:28

1. O, for a thou - sand tongues to sing My great Re - deem - er's praise, The glo - ries of my God and King, The tri - umphs of His grace.
2. My gra - cious Mas - ter and my God, As - sist me to pro - claim, To spread through all the earth a - broad, The hon - ors of Thy Name.
3. *Je - sus! the Name that charms our fears, That bids our sor - rows cease; 'Tis mu - sic in the sin - ner's ears, 'Tis life and health and peace.*
4. He breaks the power of can - celed sin, He sets the pris - oner free, His blood can make the foul - est clean, His blood a - vailed for me.
5. Glo - ry to God, and praise, and love Be ev - er, ev - er given By saints be - low and saints a - bove, The Church in earth and heaven.

(For higher key, see No. 170) Optional segue to "Let There Be Honor and Glory and Praises." No transition required.

WORDS: Charles Wesley, 1707-1788
MUSIC: Carl G. Gläser, 1784-1829; adapt. Lowell Mason, 1792-1872

AZMON
C.M.

Let There Be Glory and Honor and Praises 203

To the Lamb be praise and honor and glory and power. Revelation 5:13

Let there be glo - ry and hon - or and prais - es,
Glo - ry and hon - or to Je - sus.
Glo - ry, hon - or,
Glo - ry and hon - or to Him.

WORDS: Elizabeth Greenelsh, b. 1949; James Greenelsh, b. 1940
MUSIC: Elizabeth Greenelsh, b. 1949; James Greenelsh, b. 1940

LET THERE BE GLORY
Irregular

204 Come, Christians, Join to Sing

Come, let us sing for joy to the LORD. Psalm 95:1

1. Come, Chris-tians, join to sing Al - le - lu - ia! A - men!
2. Come, lift your hearts on high. Al - le - lu - ia! A - men!
3. Praise yet our Christ a - gain. Al - le - lu - ia! A - men!
Loud praise to Christ our King. Al - le - lu - ia! A - men!
Let prais - es fill the sky. Al - le - lu - ia! A - men!
Life shall not end the strain. Al - le - lu - ia! A - men!
Let all with heart and voice, Be - fore His throne re - joice;
He is our guide and friend. To us He'll con - de - scend.
On heav - en's bliss - ful shore His good - ness we'll a - dore,
Praise is His gra - cious choice. Al - le - lu - ia! A - men!
His love shall nev - er end. Al - le - lu - ia! A - men!
Sing - ing for - ev - er - more, Al - le - lu - ia! A - men!

WORDS: Christian H. Bateman, 1813-1889
MUSIC: Spanish folk melody; arr. David Evans, 1874-1948

MADRID
6.6.6.6.D.

When Morning Gilds the Skies 205

In the morning, O LORD, you hear my voice. Psalm 5:3

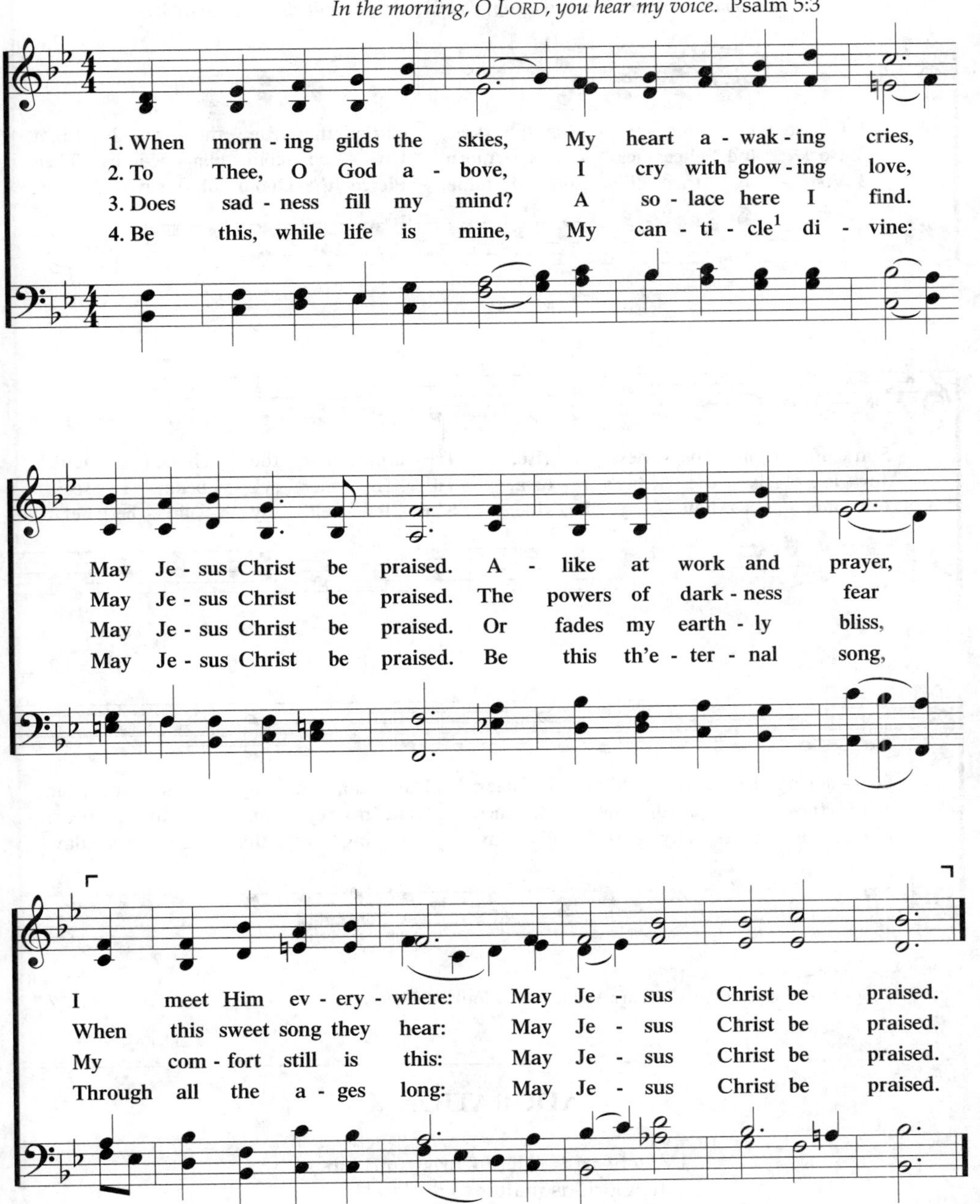
1. When morn - ing gilds the skies, My heart a - wak - ing cries, May Je - sus Christ be praised. A - like at work and prayer, I meet Him ev - ery - where: May Je - sus Christ be praised.
2. To Thee, O God a - bove, I cry with glow - ing love, May Je - sus Christ be praised. The powers of dark - ness fear When this sweet song they hear: May Je - sus Christ be praised.
3. Does sad - ness fill my mind? A so - lace here I find. May Je - sus Christ be praised. Or fades my earth - ly bliss, My com - fort still is this: May Je - sus Christ be praised.
4. Be this, while life is mine, My can - ti - cle[1] di - vine: May Je - sus Christ be praised. Be this th'e - ter - nal song, Through all the a - ges long: May Je - sus Christ be praised.

WORDS: German, 19th century; tr. Edward Caswall, 1814-1878, alt.
MUSIC: Joseph Barnby, 1838-1896

LAUDES DOMINI
6.6.6.D.

1. *canticle: song*

206 Christ, Whose Glory Fills the Skies

For you who revere my name, the sun of righteousness will rise. Malachi 4:2

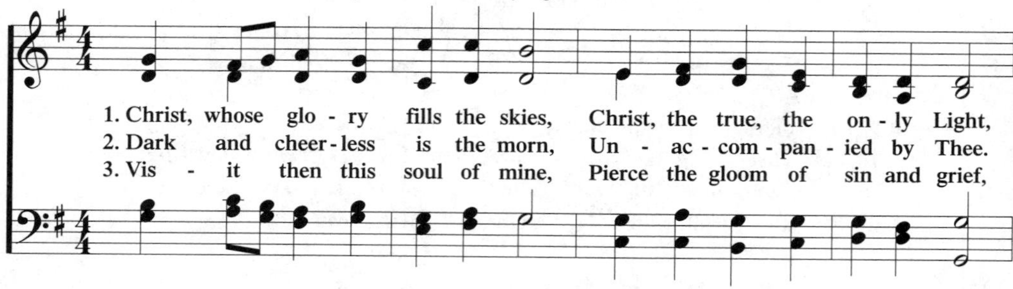
1. Christ, whose glo - ry fills the skies, Christ, the true, the on - ly Light,
2. Dark and cheer - less is the morn, Un - ac - com - pan - ied by Thee.
3. Vis - it then this soul of mine, Pierce the gloom of sin and grief,

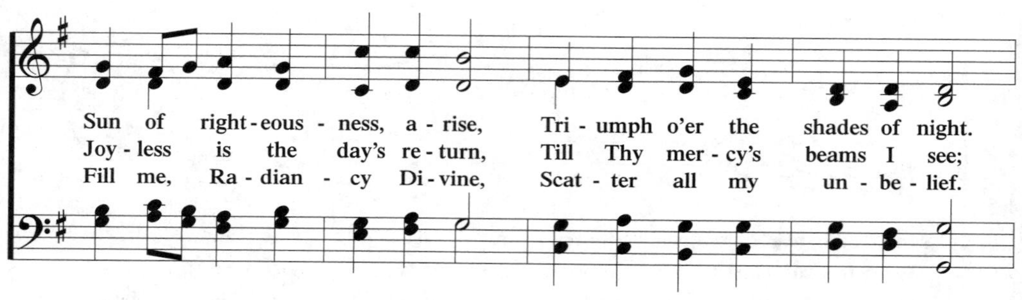
Sun of right - eous - ness, a - rise, Tri - umph o'er the shades of night.
Joy - less is the day's re - turn, Till Thy mer - cy's beams I see;
Fill me, Ra - dian - cy Di - vine, Scat - ter all my un - be - lief.

Day - spring from on high, be near; Day - star, in my heart ap - pear.
Till they in - ward light im - part, Glad my eyes, and warm my heart.
More and more Thy - self dis - play, Shin - ing to the per - fect day.

WORDS: Charles Wesley, 1707-1788
MUSIC: Conrad Kocher, 1786-1872, arr. William H. Monk, 1823-1889

DIX
7.7.7.7.7.7.

ADORATION

My heart is full of Christ, and longs
Its glorious matter to declare!
Of Him I make my loftier songs,
I cannot from His praise forbear;
My ready tongue makes haste to sing
The glories of my heavenly King.

Charles Wesley (1707-1788), *Psalms and Hymns I*, 1743

I Will Praise Him 207

Praise be to his glorious name forever. Psalm 72:19

1. When I saw the cleans-ing foun-tain O-pen wide for all my sin,
2. Though the way seemed straight and nar-row, All I claimed was swept a-way.
3. Then God's fire up-on the al-tar Of my heart was set a-flame.
4. Glo-ry, glo-ry to the Fa-ther! Glo-ry, glo-ry to the Son!
I o-beyed the Spir-it's woo-ing When He said, "Will you be clean?"
My am-bi-tions, plans, and wish-es At my feet in ash-es lay.
I shall nev-er cease to praise Him. Glo-ry, glo-ry to His name!
Glo-ry, glo-ry to the Spir-it! Glo-ry to the Three-in-One!
Refrain
I will praise Him! I will praise Him! Praise the Lamb for sin-ners slain!
Give Him glo-ry, all you peo-ple, For His blood can wash a-way each stain.

WORDS: Margaret J. Harris, 19th century, alt.
MUSIC: Margaret J. Harris, 19th century

I WILL PRAISE HIM
8.7.8.7. with Refrain

208 Praise Him! Praise Him!

. . . according to His excellent greatness! Psalm 150:2, NKJV

1. Praise Him! Praise Him! Je-sus, our bless-ed Re - deem-er! Sing, O earth; His won-der-ful love pro-claim! Hail Him! Hail Him! High-est arch-an-gels in glo - ry; Strength and hon - or give to His ho - ly name! Like a shep - herd, Je-sus will guard His chil-dren; In His arms He car-ries them all day long.
2. Praise Him! Praise Him! Je-sus, our bless-ed Re - deem-er! For our sins He suf - fered, and bled and died; He, our Rock, our Hope of e - ter-nal sal - va - tion. Hail Him! Hail Him! Je - sus, the cru - ci - fied. Sound His prais - es— Je-sus who bore our sor-rows, Love un - bound-ed, won-der-ful, deep, and strong!
3. Praise Him! Praise Him! Je-sus our bless-ed Re - deem-er! Heaven - ly por - tals loud with ho-san-nas ring. Je - sus, Sav - ior, reign-eth for-ev - er and ev - er. Crown Him! Crown Him! Proph-et, and Priest, and King! Christ is com - ing, o - ver the world vic - to - rious. Power and glo - ry un - to the Lord be - long.

WORDS: Fanny J. Crosby, 1820-1915
MUSIC: Chester G. Allen, 1838-1878

JOYFUL SONG
Irregular with Refrain

Refrain
Praise Him! Praise Him! Tell of His ex - cel - lent great - ness.
Praise Him! Praise Him, ev - er in joy - ful song!

Praise the Savior, We Who Know Him 209

. . . to the praise of his glorious grace, which he has freely given us in the One he loves.
Ephesians 1:6

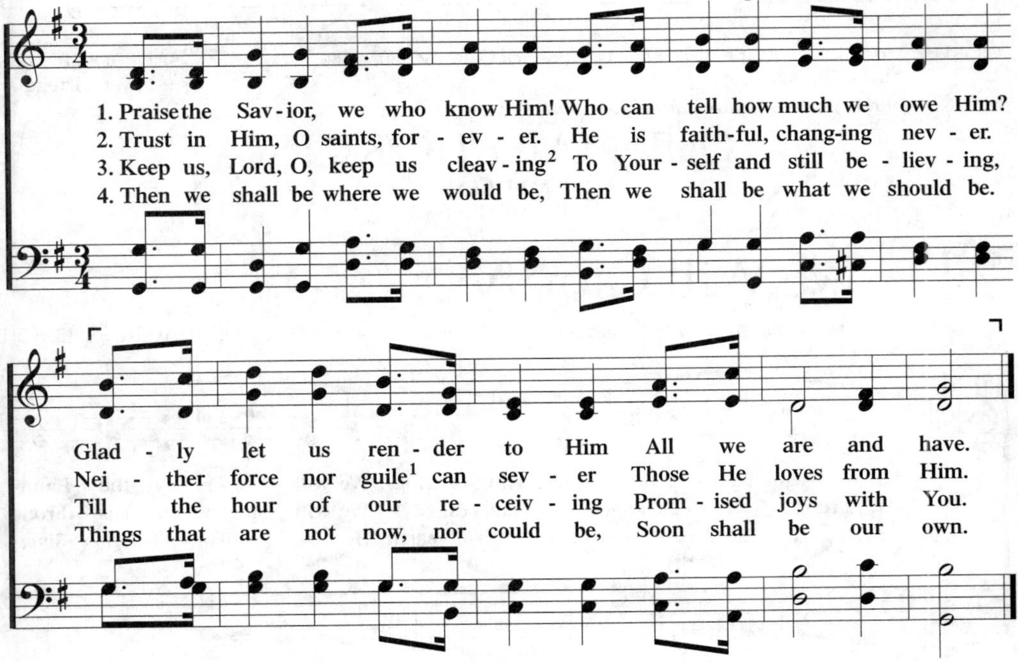

1. Praise the Sav - ior, we who know Him! Who can tell how much we owe Him?
Glad - ly let us ren - der to Him All we are and have.

2. Trust in Him, O saints, for - ev - er. He is faith-ful, chang-ing nev - er.
Nei - ther force nor guile[1] can sev - er Those He loves from Him.

3. Keep us, Lord, O, keep us cleav - ing[2] To Your - self and still be - liev - ing,
Till the hour of our re - ceiv - ing Prom - ised joys with You.

4. Then we shall be where we would be, Then we shall be what we should be.
Things that are not now, nor could be, Soon shall be our own.

WORDS: Thomas Kelly, 1769-1855, alt.
MUSIC: German melody

ACCLAIM
8.8.8.5.

1. *guile: deceit*
2. *cleaving: clinging*

210 O Come, Let Us Adore Him

We . . . have come to worship him. Matthew 2:2

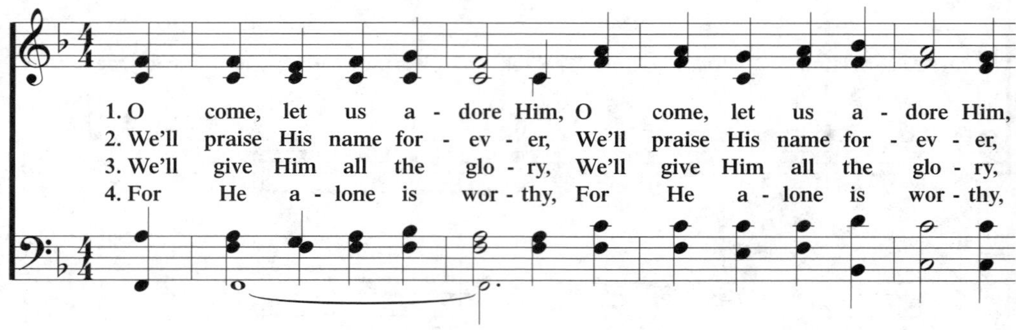
1. O come, let us a - dore Him, O come, let us a - dore Him,
2. We'll praise His name for - ev - er, We'll praise His name for - ev - er,
3. We'll give Him all the glo - ry, We'll give Him all the glo - ry,
4. For He a - lone is wor - thy, For He a - lone is wor - thy,

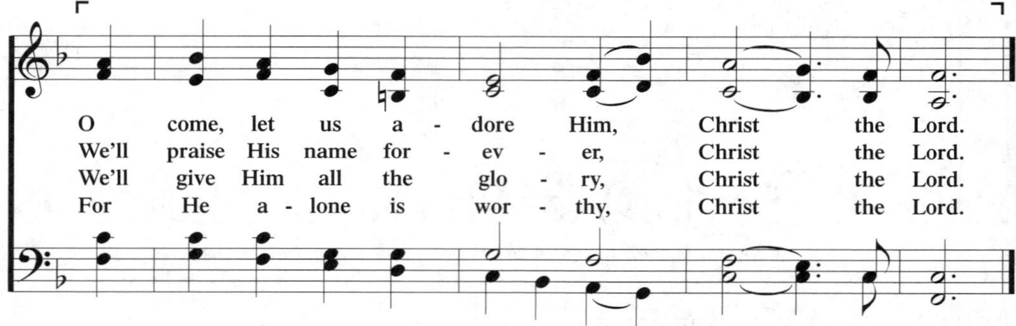
O come, let us a - dore Him, Christ the Lord.
We'll praise His name for - ev - er, Christ the Lord.
We'll give Him all the glo - ry, Christ the Lord.
For He a - lone is wor - thy, Christ the Lord.

WORDS: Attrib. John F. Wade, 1711-1786; tr. Frederick Oakeley, 1802-1880; stanzas 2-4, anonymous
MUSIC: John F. Wade's *Cantus Diversi*, 1751

ADESTE FIDELES
Irregular

OUR MAJESTIC KING

MEDLEY
We Will Glorify
Majesty

211 We Will Glorify

To him who sits on the throne and to the Lamb be praise and honor and glory. Revelation 5:13

1. We will glo - ri - fy the King of kings, We will glo - ri - fy the Lamb;
2. Lord Je - ho - vah reigns in maj - es - ty, We will bow be-fore His throne;
3. He is Lord of heav - en, Lord of earth, He is Lord of all who live;

WORDS: Twila Paris, b. 1958
MUSIC: Twila Paris, b. 1958

WE WILL GLORIFY
Irregular

1, 2.
We will glo - ri - fy the Lord of lords, For He is the great I Am.
We will wor - ship Him in right-eous-ness, We will wor - ship Him a - lone.
He is Lord a - bove the u - ni - verse, All praise to Him we
3. rit.
give.
4. Hal - le - lu - jah to the King of kings, Hal - le - lu - jah to the
Lamb; Hal - le - lu - jah to the Lord of lords, For He is the great I Am.
Song Ending
Optional transition to "Majesty"
3
3
Am.

212 Majesty

They shall lift up their voice, they shall sing; for the majesty of the LORD *they shall cry aloud.*
Isaiah 24:14, NKJV

Maj - es - ty, wor-ship His maj - es - ty. Un - to
Je - sus be all glo - ry, pow - er and praise.
Maj - es - ty, king-dom au - thor - i - ty flow from His
throne un - to His own, His an - them raise. So, ex -

WORDS: Jack Hayford, b. 1934
MUSIC: Jack Hayford, b. 1934

MAJESTY
Irregular

3
alt, lift up on high the name of Je - sus. Mag - ni -
fy, come glo - ri - fy, Christ Je - sus, the King.
Maj - es - ty, wor - ship His maj - es - ty. Je - sus, who
died, now glo - ri - fied, King of all kings.

OUR BEAUTIFUL SAVIOR

MEDLEY

Fairest Lord Jesus
You Are My All in All

213 Fairest Lord Jesus

Your eyes will see the king in his beauty. Isaiah 33:17

1. Fair - est Lord Je - sus, Rul - er of all na - ture, O Thou of God and man the Son. Thee will I cher - ish, Thee will I hon - or, Thou my soul's glo - ry, joy, and crown.
2. Fair are the mead - ows, Fair - er still the wood - lands, Robed in the bloom - ing garb of spring. Je - sus is fair - er, Je - sus is pur - er, Who makes the woe - ful heart to sing.
3. Fair is the sun - shine, Fair - er still the moon - light, And fair the twin - kling, star - ry host. Je - sus shines bright - er, Je - sus shines pur - er, Than all the an - gels heaven can boast.
4. All fair - est beau - ty Heav - en - ly and earth - ly, Won - drous - ly, Je - sus, is found in Thee. None can be near - er, Fair - er or dear - er, Than Thou, my Sav - ior, art to me.
5. Beau - ti - ful Sav - ior, Lord of all the na - tions, Son of God and Son of Man! Glo - ry and hon - or, praise, ad - o - ra - tion Now and for - ev - er - more be Thine!
Optional transition to "You Are My All in All"
rit.

WORDS: *Münster Gesangbuch*, 1677; stanzas 1-4 tr. source unknown; stanza 5 tr. Joseph A. Seiss, 1823-1904.
MUSIC: From *Schlesische Volkslieder*, 1842; arr. Richard Willis, 1819-1900

CRUSADERS' HYMN
5.6.8.5.5.8.

You Are My All in All 214

Christ is all, and is in all. Colossians 3:11

1. You are my strength when I am weak, You are the trea-sure that I seek; You are my all in all.
2. Tak-ing my sin, my cross, my shame, Ris-ing a-gain I bless Your name; You are my all in all.
Seek-ing You as a pre-cious jewel, Lord, to give up, I'd be a fool; You are my all in all.
When I fall down, You pick me up; When I am dry, You fill my cup; You are my all in all.
Refrain*
Je-sus, Lamb of God, Wor-thy is Your name!
Je-sus, Lamb of God, Wor-thy is Your name!

*The verses and the Refrain may be sung as a round.

WORDS: Dennis L. Jernigan, b. 1959
MUSIC: Dennis L. Jernigan, b. 1959

JERNIGAN
8.8.5.8.8.5. with Refrain

215 Alleluia, Alleluia! Give Thanks

Thanks be to God! He gives us the victory through our Lord Jesus Christ.
1 Corinthians 15:57

Refrain
Al - le - lu - ia, al - le - lu - ia! Give thanks to the
ris - en Lord, Al - le - lu - ia, al - le - lu - ia! Give praise to His name!
fine
1. Je - sus is Lord of all the earth.
2. Spread the good news o'er all the earth:
3. We have been cru - ci - fied with Christ.
4. Come, let us praise the liv - ing God;
D.C. al fine
He is the King of cre - a - tion.
Je - sus has died and has ris - en.
Now we shall live for - ev - er.
Joy - ful - ly sing to our Sav - ior.

WORDS: Donald Fishel, b. 1950
MUSIC: Donald Fishel, b. 1950

ALLELUIA NO. 1
Irregular

His Name Is Wonderful 216

No one can say, "Jesus is Lord," except by the Holy Spirit. 1 Corinthians 12:3

His name is Won-der-ful, His name is Won-der-ful, His name is Won-der-ful,
Je-sus, my Lord. He is the Might-y King, Mas-ter of ev-ery-thing,
His name is Won-der-ful, Je-sus, my Lord. He's the great Shep-herd, the Rock of all
ag-es, Al-might-y God is He. Bow down be-fore Him,
Love and a-dore Him. His name is Won-der-ful, Je-sus, my Lord.

WORDS: Audrey Mieir, 1916-1996
MUSIC: Audrey Mieir, 1916-1996

MIEIR
Irregular

OUR PRECIOUS SAVIOR

MEDLEY

Shout to the Lord
More Precious Than Silver

217 Shout to the Lord

Shout for joy to the LORD, all the earth. Psalm 98:4

1. My Je - sus, my Sav - ior, Lord, there is none like you.
2. My com - fort, my shel - ter, tow - er of ref - uge and strength;
All of my days, I want to praise the won - ders of Your
Let ev - ery breath, all that I am,
1.
might - y love.
2.
nev - er cease to wor - ship You.
Refrain
Shout to the Lord, all the earth; let us sing
pow - er and maj - es - ty, praise to the King.

WORDS: Darlene Zschech, b. 1965
MUSIC: Darlene Zschech, b. 1965

SHOUT TO THE LORD
Irregular

Moun-tains bow down and the seas will roar at the
sound of Your name! I sing for joy at the work
of Your hands. For-ev-er I'll love You, for-ev - er I'll stand.
Song Ending
Noth-ing com-pares to the prom - ise I have in You!
Optional transition to "More Precious Than Silver"

218 More Precious Than Silver

Earth has nothing I desire besides you. Psalm 73:25

Lord, You are more pre-cious than sil-ver,
Lord, You are more cost-ly than gold.
Lord, You are more beau-ti-ful than dia-monds, And
noth-ing I de-sire com-pares with You.

WORDS: Lynn DeShazo, b. 1956
MUSIC: Lynn DeShazo, b. 1956

MORE PRECIOUS
Irregular

Isn't He? 219

Your eyes will see the king in his beauty. Isaiah 33:17

Is-n't He beau-ti-ful? Beau-ti-ful, is-n't He?
Is-n't He won-der-ful? Won-der-ful, is-n't He?
1.
Prince of Peace, Son of God, is-n't He?
Coun-sel-or, Al-might-y God,
2.
is-n't He, is-n't He, is-n't
He, is-n't He?

Optional segue to "Holy and Anointed One." No transition required.

WORDS: John Wimber, 1934-1997
MUSIC: John Wimber, 1934-1997

ISN'T HE
Irregular

220 Holy and Anointed One

Exalt the LORD our God and worship at his footstool; he is holy. Psalm 99:5

Je - sus, Je - sus, Ho-ly and A - noint-ed One,
Je - sus, Je - sus, Ris-en and Ex - alt - ed One,
1. fine
2.
Je - sus.
Je -
sus. Your name is like hon - ey on my lips;
Your Spir-it like wa - ter to my soul. Your word is a lamp
D.C. al fine
un-to my feet. Je-sus, I love You, I love You.

WORDS: John Barnett, 20th century
MUSIC: John Barnett, 20th century

HOLY AND ANOINTED ONE
Irregular

Blessed Be the Name 221

May the name of the LORD be praised. Job 1:21

1. All praise to Him who reigns a - bove In maj - es - ty su - preme,
2. His name a - bove all names shall stand, Ex - alt - ed more and more,
3. Re - deem - er, Sav - ior, Friend of man Once ru - ined by the Fall,
4. His name shall be the Coun - sel - or, The might - y Prince of Peace;
Who gave His Son for man to die, That He might man re - deem!
At God the Fa - ther's own right hand, Where an - gel hosts a - dore.
You have de - vised sal - va - tion's plan, For You have died for all.
Of all earth's king-doms Con - quer - or, Whose reign shall nev - er cease.
Refrain
Bless-ed be the name, bless-ed be the name, Bless-ed be the name of the Lord.
Bless-ed be the name, bless-ed be the name; Bless-ed be the name of the Lord.

WORDS: William H. Clark, 19th century, alt.;
Refrain, Ralph E. Hudson, 1843-1901

MUSIC: Anonymous; arr. Ralph E. Hudson, 1843-1901 and William J. Kirkpatrick, 1838-1921

BLESSED BE THE NAME
C.M. with Refrain

222 He Is the Radiance of God's Glory

In the past God spoke to our forefathers through the prophets at many times and in various ways, but in these last days he has spoken to us by his Son, whom he appointed heir of all things, and through whom he made the universe.

The Son is the radiance of God's glory and the exact representation of his being, sustaining all things by his powerful word.

After he had provided purification for sins, he sat down at the right hand of the Majesty in heaven. So he became as much superior to the angels as the name he has inherited is superior to theirs.

For to which of the angels did God ever say, "You are my Son; today I have become your Father"? Or again, "I will be his Father, and he will be my Son"?

And again, when God brings his firstborn into the world, he says, "Let all God's angels worship him." In speaking of the angels he says, "He makes his angels winds, his servants flames of fire."

But about the Son he says, "Your throne, O God, will last for ever and ever, and righteousness will be the scepter of your kingdom. You have loved righteousness and hated wickedness; therefore God, your God, has set you above your companions by anointing you with the oil of joy."

He also says, "In the beginning, O Lord, you laid the foundations of the earth, and the heavens are the work of your hands. They will perish, but you remain; they will all wear out like a garment.

You will roll them up like a robe; like a garment they will be changed. But you remain the same, and your years will never end." *Hebrews 1:1-12*

223 How Sweet the Name of Jesus Sounds

The name he has inherited is superior to theirs. Hebrews 1:4

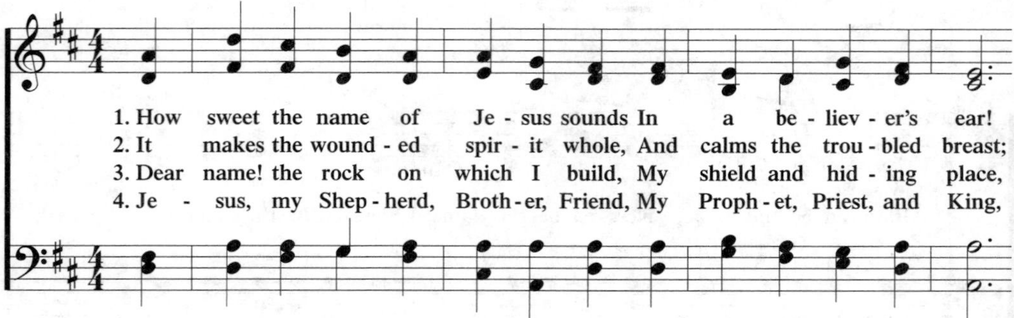
1. How sweet the name of Je - sus sounds In a be - liev - er's ear!
2. It makes the wound - ed spir - it whole, And calms the trou - bled breast;
3. Dear name! the rock on which I build, My shield and hid - ing place,
4. Je - sus, my Shep - herd, Broth - er, Friend, My Proph - et, Priest, and King,

WORDS: John Newton, 1725-1807
MUSIC: Alexander R. Reinagle, 1799-1877

ST. PETER
C.M.

It soothes his sor-rows, heals his wounds, And drives a-way his fear.
'Tis man-na to the hun-gry soul, And to the wea-ry, rest.
My nev-er-fail-ing trea-sury filled With bound-less stores of grace.
My Lord, my Life, my Way, my End, Ac-cept the praise I bring.

Jesus, Thou Joy of Loving Hearts 224

He . . . fills the hungry with good things. Psalm 107:9

1. Jesus, Thou Joy of loving hearts,
Thou Fount of life, Thou Light of men,
From the best bliss that earth imparts
We turn unfilled to Thee again.

2. Thy truth unchanged hath ever stood.
Thou savest those that on Thee call.
To them that seek Thee Thou art good,
To them that find Thee all in all.

3. *We taste Thee, O Thou living Bread,
And long to feast upon Thee still.
We drink of Thee, the Fountainhead,
And thirst our souls from Thee to fill.*

4. Our restless spirits yearn for Thee,
Where'er our changeful lot is cast,
Glad when Thy gracious smile we see,
Blest when our faith can hold Thee fast.

5. O Jesus, ever with us stay.
Make all our moments calm and bright.
Chase the dark night of sin away.
Shed o'er the world Thy holy light.

WORDS: Attrib. Bernard of Clairvaux, 1091-1153; tr. Ray Palmer, 1808-1887
MUSIC: Henry Baker, 1835-1910

QUEBEC
L.M.

OUR ROCK

MEDLEY

A Shelter in the Time of Storm
Praise the Name of Jesus
There's Something About That Name

225 A Shelter in the Time of Storm

. . . the shadow of a great rock in a weary land. Isaiah 32:2, NKJV

1. The Lord's our rock, in Him we hide, A shel-ter in the time of storm;
2. A shade by day, de - fense by night, A shel-ter in the time of storm;
3. The rag - ing storms may round us beat, A shel-ter in the time of storm;
4. O Rock di - vine, O Ref - uge dear, A shel-ter in the time of storm;
Se - cure what - ev - er ill be - tide, A shel-ter in the time of storm.
No fears a - larm, no fears af - fright, A shel-ter in the time of storm.
We'll nev - er leave our safe re - treat, A shel-ter in the time of storm.
Lord, be our help - er ev - er near, A shel-ter in the time of storm.
Refrain
O, Je-sus is a rock in a wea-ry land, A wea-ry land, a wea-ry land.
O, Je-sus is a rock in a wea-ry land, A shel-ter in the time of storm.

WORDS: Vernon J. Charlesworth, 1839-1915, alt.
MUSIC: Ira D. Sankey, 1840-1908

SHELTER
L.M. with Refrain

Praise the Name of Jesus 226

The LORD is my rock, my fortress and my deliverer. Psalm 18:2

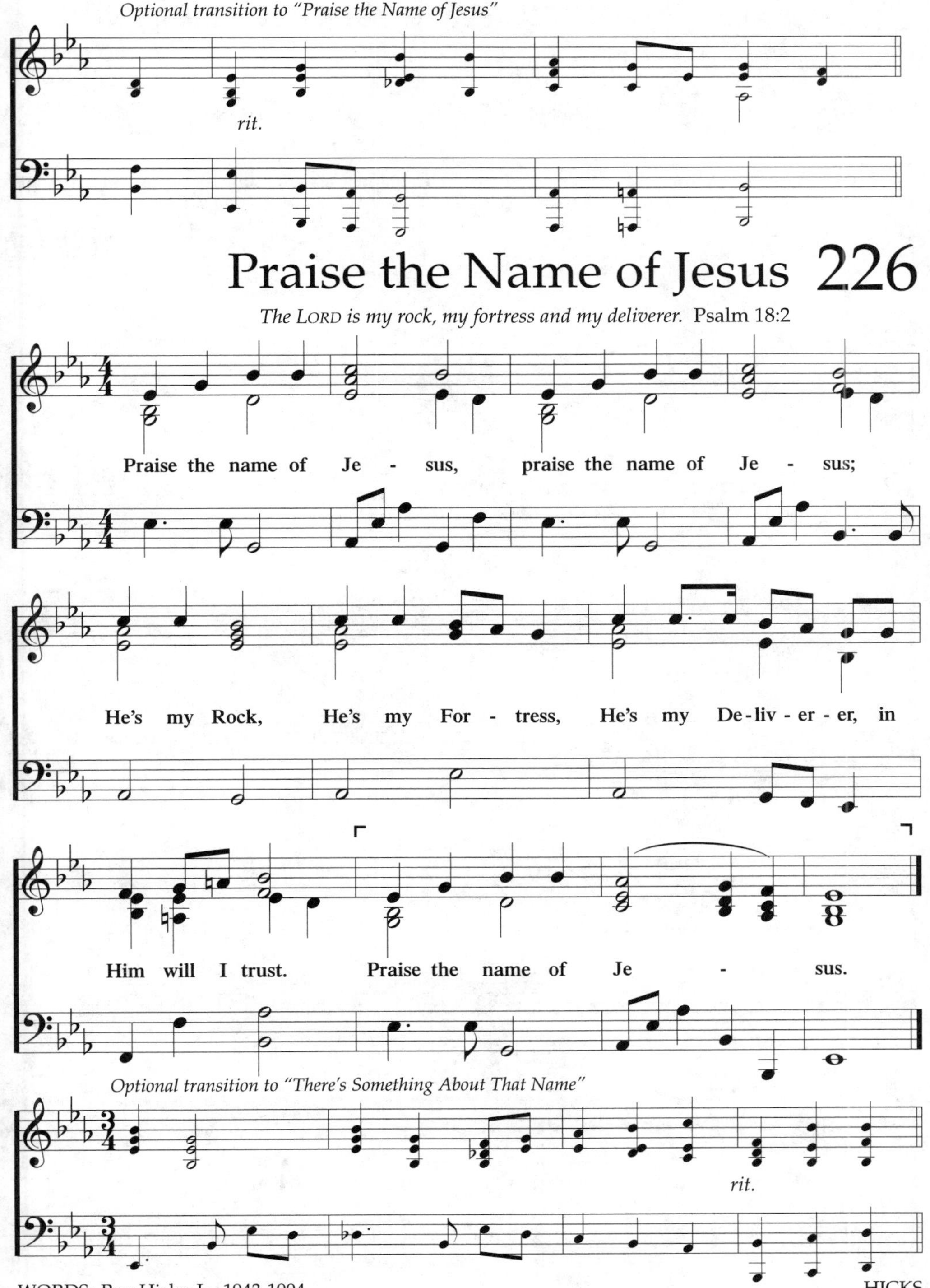
Optional transition to "Praise the Name of Jesus"
rit.
Praise the name of Je - sus, praise the name of Je - sus;
He's my Rock, He's my For - tress, He's my De-liv - er - er, in
Him will I trust. Praise the name of Je - sus.
Optional transition to "There's Something About That Name"
rit.

WORDS: Roy Hicks, Jr., 1943-1994
MUSIC: Roy Hicks, Jr., 1943-1994

HICKS
Irregular

227 There's Something About That Name

There is no other name . . . by which we must be saved. Acts 4:12

Je-sus, Je-sus, Je - sus; There's just some-thing a - bout that
name! Mas-ter, Sav-ior, Je - sus; Like the fra-grance
af - ter the rain. Je-sus, Je-sus, Je - sus, Let all
heav-en and earth pro - claim: Kings and king-doms will
all pass a - way, But there's some-thing a - bout that name!

WORDS: William J. Gaither, b. 1936; Gloria Gaither, b. 1942
MUSIC: William J. Gaither, b. 1936

THAT NAME
Irregular

Jesus, the Very Thought of Thee 228

You believe in him and are filled with an inexpressible and glorious joy. 1 Peter 1:8

1. Je - sus, the ver - y thought of Thee With sweet-ness fills my breast;
2. No voice can sing, no heart can frame, Nor can the mem - ory find
3. O hope of ev - ery con - trite heart, O joy of all the meek,
4. But what to those who find? Ah, this No tongue nor pen can show:
5. Je - sus, our on - ly joy be Thou, As Thou our prize wilt be.
But sweet - er far Thy face to see, And in Thy pres - ence rest.
A sweet - er sound than Thy blest name, O Sav - ior of man - kind!
To those who fall, how kind Thou art! How good to those who seek!
The love of Je - sus, what it is None but His loved ones know.
Je - sus, be Thou our glo - ry now, And through e - ter - ni - ty.

WORDS: Attrib. Bernard of Clairvaux, 1091-1153; tr. Edward Caswall, 1814-1878
MUSIC: John B. Dykes, 1823-1876

ST. AGNES
C.M.

PRAYER OF REMEMBRANCE FOR CHRIST'S SACRIFICE

O Jesus Christ, the mirror of all gentleness of mind,
the example of highest obedience and patience,
grant us Your servants with true devotion to consider how You,
innocent and undefiled Lamb,
were bound, taken and hauled away to death for our sins;
how well content You were to suffer such things,
not opening Your mouth in impatience, but willingly offering Yourself unto death.
O gracious God, how vilely were You mishandled for our sakes!
O Lord, let this never come out of our hearts.
Expel through it coldness and sloth;
stir up love and fervency towards You;
provoke us to earnest prayer and make us cheerful and diligent in Your will. . . . Amen.

Miles Coverdale (ca. 1488-1569)

OUR WONDERFUL LORD

MEDLEY

What a Wonderful Savior
He Is Lord

229 What a Wonderful Savior

We know that this man really is the Savior of the world. John 4:42

1. Christ has for sin a - tone - ment made, What a won - der - ful Sav - ior!
2. I praise Him for the cleans - ing blood, What a won - der - ful Sav - ior!
3. He cleansed my heart from all its sin, What a won - der - ful Sav - ior!
4. He walks be - side me all the way, What a won - der - ful Sav - ior!
5. He gives me o - ver - com - ing power, What a won - der - ful Sav - ior!
We are re - deemed! The price is paid! What a won - der - ful Sav - ior!
That rec - on - ciled my soul to God. What a won - der - ful Sav - ior!
And now He reigns and rules there - in. What a won - der - ful Sav - ior!
And keeps me faith - ful day by day. What a won - der - ful Sav - ior!
And tri - umph in each try - ing hour. What a won - der - ful Sav - ior!
Refrain
What a won - der - ful Sav - ior is Je - sus, my Je - sus!
What a won - der - ful Sav - ior is Je - sus, my Lord!
Song Ending

WORDS: Elisha A. Hoffman, 1839-1929
MUSIC: Elisha A. Hoffman, 1839-1929

BENTON HARBOR
8.7.8.7. with Refrain

Optional transition to "He Is Lord"
Lord!
rit.

He Is Lord 230

Every knee should bow . . . and every tongue confess that Jesus Christ is Lord.
Philippians 2:10-11

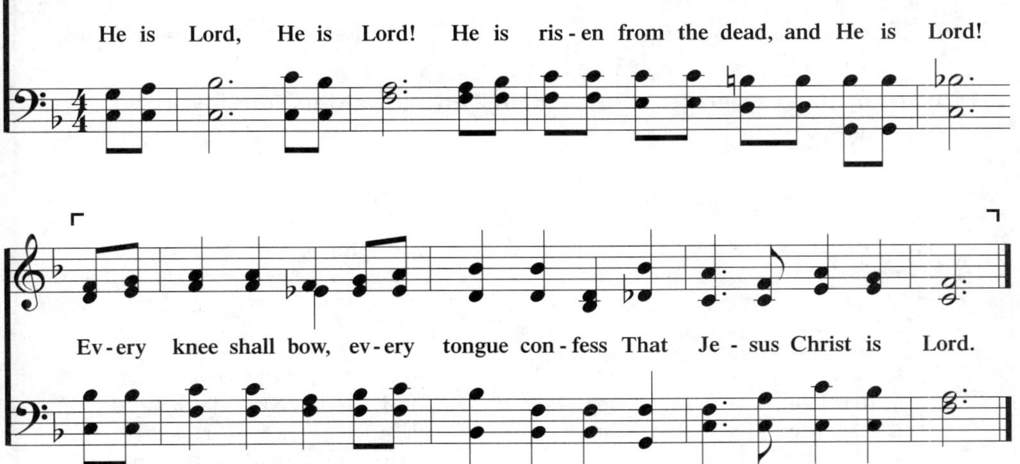
He is Lord, He is Lord! He is ris-en from the dead, and He is Lord!
Ev-ery knee shall bow, ev-ery tongue con-fess That Je-sus Christ is Lord.

WORDS: Marvin V. Frey, 1918-1992*
MUSIC: Marvin V. Frey, 1918-1992

HE IS LORD
Irregular

**formerly Anonymous*

CHRIST TRANSCENDS HARD HEARTS

There are people today who, though they disdain the church, Christianity and religion, have limitless admiration for Jesus Christ, and are ready to listen to what He said, and to what is said about Him by persons they have learned to respect.

John A. Mackay (1889-1983)

231 Worthy Is the Lamb

And they sang a new song:

"You are worthy to take the scroll and to open its seals, because you were slain, and with your blood you purchased men for God from every tribe and language and people and nation. You have made them to be a kingdom and priests to serve our God, and they will reign on the earth."

Then I looked and heard the voice of many angels, numbering thousands upon thousands, and ten thousand times ten thousand. They encircled the throne and the living creatures and the elders. In a loud voice they sang:

"Worthy is the Lamb, who was slain, to receive power and wealth and wisdom and strength and honor and glory and praise!"

Then I heard every creature in heaven and on earth and under the earth and on the sea, and all that is in them, singing:

"To him who sits on the throne and to the Lamb be praise and honor and glory and power, for ever and ever!"

The four living creatures said, "Amen," and the elders fell down and worshiped.

Revelation 5:9-14

232 Worthy Is the Lamb

Christ, our Passover lamb, has been sacrificed. 1 Corinthians 5:7

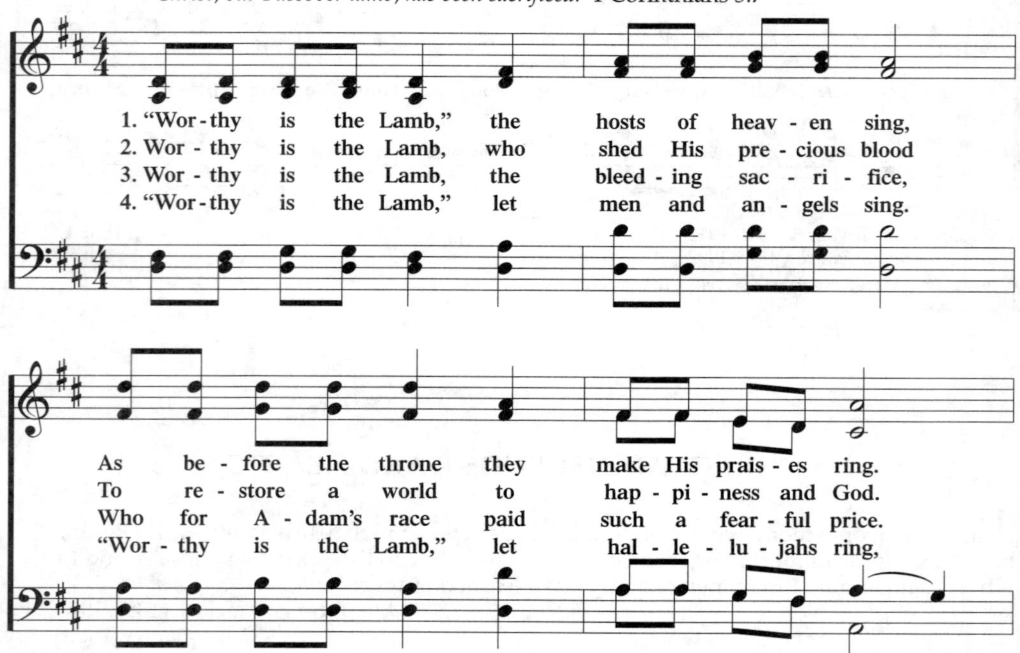
1. "Wor-thy is the Lamb," the hosts of heav - en sing,
2. Wor - thy is the Lamb, who shed His pre - cious blood
3. Wor - thy is the Lamb, the bleed - ing sac - ri - fice,
4. "Wor-thy is the Lamb," let men and an - gels sing.
As be - fore the throne they make His prais - es ring.
To re - store a world to hap - pi - ness and God.
Who for A - dam's race paid such a fear - ful price.
"Wor - thy is the Lamb," let hal - le - lu - jahs ring,

WORDS: Johnson Oatman, Jr., 1856-1926
MUSIC: George C. Hugg, 1848-1907

HUGG
11.11.11.11. with Refrain

"Wor - thy is the Lamb the book to o - pen wide.
When no eye could pit - y and no arm could save,
Wor - thy is the Lamb, the pas - chal[1] Lamb of God,
And when life is past, up - on the gold - en shore,
Wor - thy is the Lamb who once was cru - ci - fied."
Je - sus, for our ran - som, Him - self free - ly gave.
For the world re - ceived re - demp - tion through His blood.
"Wor - thy is the Lamb," we'll shout for - ev - er - more.
Refrain
O, this bleed - ing Lamb, O, this bleed - ing Lamb, O, this dy - ing Lamb, He
was found wor - thy! O, this bleed - ing Lamb, O, this bleed - ing Lamb,
O, this dy - ing Lamb, He was found wor - thy!

1. *paschal: Passover*

233 Glory to the Lamb

Look, the Lamb of God, who takes away the sin of the world! John 1:29

1. Glo - ry, glo - ry, glo - ry to the Lamb. Glo - ry, glo - ry, glo - ry to the Lamb.
2. Wor - thy, wor - thy, wor - thy is the Lamb. Wor - thy, wor - thy, wor - thy is the Lamb.
3. Ho - ly, ho - ly, ho - ly is the Lamb. Ho - ly, ho - ly, ho - ly is the Lamb.
Refrain
For He is glo - ri - ous and wor - thy to be praised, The Lamb up - on the throne; And un - to Him we lift our voice in praise, The Lamb up - on the throne.

WORDS: Larry Dempsey, 1946-1995
MUSIC: Larry Dempsey, 1946-1995

DEMPSEY
Irregular

Worthy Is the Lamb 234

. . . who was slain, to receive . . . honor and glory and praise! Revelation 5:12

Wor-thy is the Lamb that was slain, Wor-thy is the Lamb that was
slain, Wor-thy is the Lamb that was slain to re-ceive
Pow-er and rich-es and wis-dom and strength, Hon-or and glo-ry and
bless-ing! Wor-thy is the Lamb, wor-thy is the Lamb,
Wor-thy is the Lamb that was slain, Wor-thy is the Lamb!

WORDS: Don Wyrtzen, b. 1942; based on Rev. 5:12
MUSIC: Don Wyrtzen, b. 1942

WORTHY IS THE LAMB
Irregular

235 Worthy, You Are Worthy

The Lamb will overcome them because he is Lord of lords and King of kings. Revelation 17:14

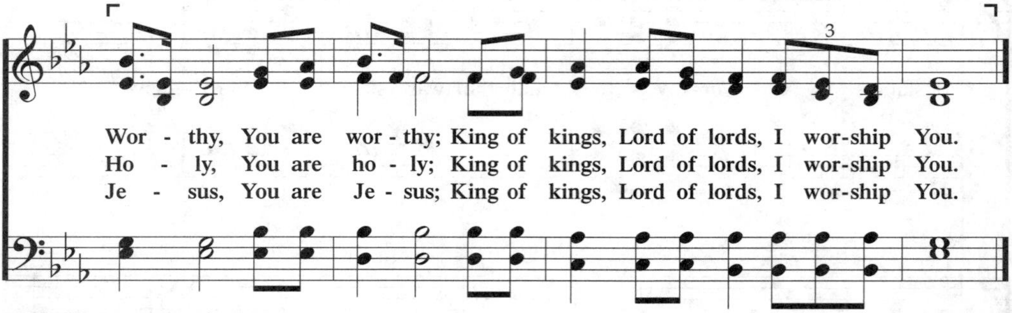

1. Wor - thy, You are wor - thy; King of kings, Lord of lords, You are wor - thy.
Wor - thy, You are wor - thy; King of kings, Lord of lords, I wor-ship You.

2. Ho - ly, You are ho - ly; King of kings, Lord of lords, You are ho - ly.
Ho - ly, You are ho - ly; King of kings, Lord of lords, I wor-ship You.

3. Je - sus, You are Je - sus; King of kings, Lord of lords, You are Je - sus.
Je - sus, You are Je - sus; King of kings, Lord of lords, I wor-ship You.

WORDS: Don Moen, b. 1950
MUSIC: Don Moen, b. 1950

WORTHY
6.6.4.6.6.4.

236 Alleluia

And they cried: "Amen, Hallelujah!" Revelation 19:4

1. Al - le - lu - ia, al - le - lu - ia, Al - le - lu - ia, al - le -
lu - ia, Al - le - lu - ia, al - le - lu - ia, Al - le - lu - ia, al - le - lu - ia.
2. He's my Savior.
3. He is worthy.
4. I will praise Him.

WORDS: Jerry Sinclair, 1943-1993
MUSIC: Jerry Sinclair, 1943-1993

ALLELUIA
L.M.

Blessed Quietness 237

The peace of God . . . will guard your hearts and your minds in Christ Jesus. Philippians 4:7

1. Joys are flow - ing like a riv - er, Since the Com - fort - er has come. He a - bides with us for - ev - er, Makes the trust - ing heart His home.
2. Bring - ing life and health and glad - ness All a - round, this heaven - ly Guest Ban - ished un - be - lief and sad - ness, Changed our wea - ri - ness to rest.
3. Like the rain that falls from heav - en, Like the sun - light from the sky, So the Ho - ly Spir - it's giv - en, Com - ing on us from on high.
4. See a fruit - ful field is grow - ing Bless - ed fruits of right - eous - ness, And the streams of life are flow - ing In the lone - ly wil - der - ness.
5. What a won - der - ful sal - va - tion Where we al - ways see His face! What a per - fect hab - i - ta - tion! What a qui - et rest - ing place!
Refrain
Bless - ed qui - et - ness, ho - ly qui - et - ness– What as - sur - ance in my soul! On the storm - y sea He speaks peace to me. How the bil - lows[1] cease to roll!

WORDS: Manie P. Ferguson, 1850-1932, alt.
MUSIC: W. S. Marshall, 19th century; arr. James M. Kirk, 1854-1945

BLESSED QUIETNESS
8.7.8.7. with Refrain

1. *billows: waves*

238 The Comforter Has Come

When the Comforter is come, whom I will send unto you from the Father . . . John 15:26, KJV

1. O, spread the tidings 'round wherever man is found,
Wherever human hearts and human woes abound.
Let every Christian tongue proclaim the joyful sound:
The Comforter has come!

2. The long, long night is past, the morning breaks at last,
And hushed the dreadful wail and fury of the blast,
As o'er the golden hills the day advances fast!
The Comforter has come!

3. Lo, the great King of kings, with healing in His wings,
To every captive soul a full deliverance brings,
And through the vacant cells the song of triumph rings:
The Comforter has come!

4. O boundless love divine! How shall this tongue of mine
To wondering mortals tell the matchless grace divine—
That I, a child of hell, should in His image shine?
The Comforter has come!

Refrain

The Comforter has come, The Comforter has come! The Holy Ghost from

WORDS: Frank Bottome, 1823-1894
MUSIC: William J. Kirkpatrick, 1838-1921

COMFORTER
12.12.12.6. with Refrain

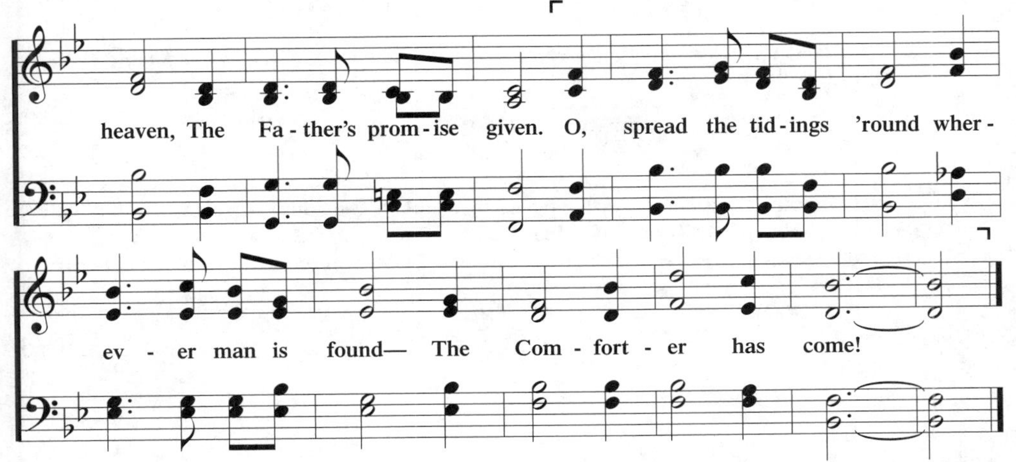
heaven, The Fa - ther's prom - ise given. O, spread the tid - ings 'round wher -
ev - er man is found— The Com - fort - er has come!

The Promised Comforter 239

"I [the LORD] will give you a new heart and put a new spirit in you; I will remove from you your heart of stone and give you a heart of flesh.

And I will put my Spirit in you and move you to follow my decrees and be careful to keep my laws." *Ezekiel 36:26-27*

"I [Jesus] will ask the Father, and he will give you another Counselor to be with you forever—

the Spirit of truth. The world cannot accept him, because it neither sees him nor knows him. But you know him, for he lives with you and will be in you.

I will not leave you as orphans; I will come to you.

Before long, the world will not see me anymore, but you will see me. Because I live, you also will live.

On that day you will realize that I am in my Father, and you are in me, and I am in you.

Whoever has my commands and obeys them, he is the one who loves me. He who loves me will be loved by my Father, and I too will love him and show myself to him."

Then Judas (not Judas Iscariot) said, "But, Lord, why do you intend to show yourself to us and not to the world?"

Jesus replied, "If anyone loves me, he will obey my teaching. My Father will love him, and we will come to him and make our home with him.

He who does not love me will not obey my teaching. These words you hear are not my own; they belong to the Father who sent me.

All this I have spoken while still with you. But the Counselor, the Holy Spirit, whom the Father will send in my name, will teach you all things and will remind you of everything I have said to you." *John 14:16-26*

240 Holy Spirit, Ever Dwelling

I will ask the Father, and he will give you another Counselor to be with you forever.
John 14:16

1. Ho-ly Spir-it, ev-er dwell-ing in the ho-liest realms of light;
2. Ho-ly Spir-it, ev-er liv-ing as the Church's ve-ry life;
3. Ho-ly Spir-it, ev-er work-ing through the Church's min-is-try;
Ho-ly Spir-it, ev-er brood-ing o'er a world of gloom and night;
Ho-ly Spir-it, ev-er striv-ing through us in a cease-less strife;
Quick-ening, strength-ening, and ab-solv-ing, set-ting cap-tive sin-ners free;
Ho-ly Spir-it, ev-er rais-ing those of earth to thrones on high;
Ho-ly Spir-it, ev-er form-ing in the Church the mind of Christ,
Ho-ly Spir-it, ev-er bind-ing age to age and soul to soul
Liv-ing, life-im-part-ing Spir-it, You we praise and mag-ni-fy.
You we praise with end-less wor-ship for Your fruits and gifts un-priced.
In com-mun-ion nev-er end-ing, You we wor-ship and ex-tol.

WORDS: Timothy Rees, 1874-1939
MUSIC: Netherlands folk melody, 18th century

IN BABILONE
8.7.8.7.D.

Thy Holy Spirit, Lord, Alone 241

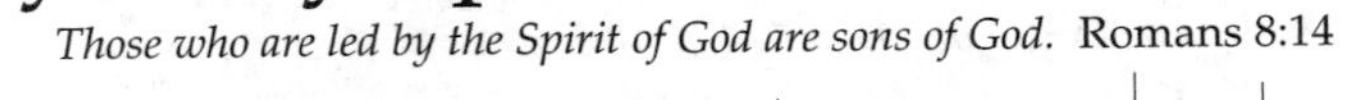

Those who are led by the Spirit of God are sons of God. Romans 8:14

1. Thy Holy Spirit, Lord, alone Can turn our hearts from sin.
His power alone can sanctify And keep us pure within.

2. Thy Holy Spirit, Lord, alone Can deeper love inspire.
His power alone within our souls Can light the sacred fire.

3. Thy Holy Spirit, Lord, can bring The gifts we seek in prayer.
His voice can words of comfort speak And still each wave of care.

4. Thy Holy Spirit, Lord, can give The grace we need this hour,
And while we wait, O Spirit, come In sanctifying power.

Refrain

1–3. O Spirit of faith and love, Come in our midst, we pray,
And purify each waiting heart; Baptize us with power today.

4. O Spirit of love, descend. Come in our midst, we pray,
And like a rushing, mighty wind Sweep over our souls today.

WORDS: Fanny J. Crosby, 1820-1915
MUSIC: William J. Kirkpatrick, 1838-1921

THY HOLY SPIRIT
C.M. with Refrain

242 Be Still, for the Spirit of the Lord

Be still, and know that I am God. Psalm 46:10

1. Be still, for the *Spir-it of the Lord, the Ho-ly One, is here.
2. Be still, for the glo-ry of the Lord is shin-ing all a-round.
3. Be still, for the pow-er of the Lord is mov-ing in this place.
Come, bow be-fore Him now, with rev-erence and with fear.
He burns with ho-ly fire, with splen-dor He is crowned.
He comes to cleanse and heal, to min-is-ter His grace.
In Him no sin is found, we stand on ho-ly ground.
How awe-some is the sight, our ra-diant King of light!
No work too hard for Him, in faith re-ceive from Him.
Be still, for the Spir-it of the Lord, the Ho-ly One, is here.
Be still, for the glo-ry of the Lord is shin-ing all a-round.
Be still, for the pow-er of the Lord is mov-ing in this place.

* *or: presence*

Optional segue to "Where the Spirit of the Lord Is." No transition required.

WORDS: David Evans, b. 1957
MUSIC: David Evans, b. 1957

BE STILL
Irregular

Where the Spirit of the Lord Is 243

The Lord is the Spirit, and where the Spirit of the Lord is, there is freedom.
2 Corinthians 3:17

Where the Spir - it of the Lord is, there is peace.
Where the Spir - it of the Lord is, there is love.
There is com - fort in life's dark - est hour, there is light and life, There is
help and pow - er in the Spir - it, in the Spir - it of the Lord.

WORDS: Stephen R. Adams, b. 1943
MUSIC: Stephen R. Adams, b. 1943

THERE IS PEACE
Irregular

244 Holy Spirit Filled (Pentecost)

When the day of Pentecost came, they were all together in one place.

Suddenly a sound like the blowing of a violent wind came from heaven and filled the whole house where they were sitting.

They saw what seemed to be tongues of fire that separated and came to rest on each of them.

All of them were filled with the Holy Spirit and began to speak in other tongues as the Spirit enabled them.

Now there were staying in Jerusalem God-fearing Jews from every nation under heaven.

When they heard this sound, a crowd came together in bewilderment, because each one heard them speaking in his own language.

Utterly amazed, they asked: "Are not all these men who are speaking Galileans?

Then how is it that each of us hears them in his own native language?

Parthians, Medes and Elamites; residents of Mesopotamia, Judea and Cappadocia, Pontus and Asia, Phrygia and Pamphylia, Egypt and the parts of Libya near Cyrene; visitors from Rome, (both Jews and converts to Judaism); Cretans and Arabs—we hear them declaring the wonders of God in our own tongues!"

Amazed and perplexed, they asked one another, "What does this mean?" Some, however, made fun of them and said, "They have had too much wine." Then Peter stood up with the Eleven, raised his voice and addressed the crowd:

"Fellow Jews and all of you who live in Jerusalem, let me explain this to you; listen carefully to what I say. These men are not drunk, as you suppose. It's only nine in the morning! No, this is what was spoken by the prophet Joel:

'In the last days, God says,
I will pour out my Spirit on all people.
Your sons and daughters will prophesy,
your young men will see visions,
your old men will dream dreams.
Even on my servants, both men and women,
I will pour out my Spirit in those days,
and they will prophesy.'"

Acts 2:1-18

On Pentecost They Gathered 245

They all joined together constantly in prayer. Acts 1:14

1. On Pen - te - cost they gath - ered quite ear - ly in the day,
2. The peo - ple all a - round them were star - tled and a - mazed
3. God pours the Ho - ly Spir - it on all who would be - lieve,
4. O Spir - it, sent from heav - en on that day long a - go,
A band of Christ's dis - ci - ples, to wor - ship, sing and pray.
To un - der - stand their lan - guage, as Christ the Lord they praised.
On wom - en, men, and chil - dren who would God's grace re - ceive.
Re - kin - dle faith a - mong us in all life's ebb and flow.
A might - y wind came blow - ing, filled all the swirl - ing air,
What u - ni - ver - sal mes - sage, what great good news was here?
That Spir - it knows no lim - it, be - stow - ing life and power.
O, give us ears to lis - ten and tongues a - flame with praise,
And tongues of fire a - glow - ing in - spired each per - son there.
That Christ, once dead, is ris - en to van - quish all our fear.
The Church, formed and re - form - ing, re - sponds in ev - ery hour.
So peo - ple of all na - tions glad songs of joy shall raise.

(For higher key, see No. 302)

WORDS: Jane Parker Huber, b. 1926
MUSIC: *Neuvermehrtes Gesangbuch*, 1693; harm. Felix Mendelssohn, 1809-1847

MUNICH
7.6.7.6.D.

246 Pentecostal Power

In the last days, God says, I will pour out my Spirit. Acts 2:17

1. Lord, as of old at Pen - te - cost You did Your power dis - play,
2. For might - y works for You, pre - pare And strength - en ev - ery heart.
3. All self con - sume, all sin de - stroy! With ear - nest zeal en - due
4. Speak, Lord; be - fore Your throne we wait. Your prom - ise we be - lieve,
With cleans - ing, pu - ri - fy - ing flame, De - scend on us to - day.
Come, take pos - ses - sion of Your own, And nev - er - more de - part.
Each wait - ing heart to work for You. O Lord, our faith re - new!
And will not let You go un - til The bless - ing we re - ceive.
Refrain
Lord, send the old - time pow - er, the Pen - te - cos - tal pow - er! Your flood - gates of
bless - ing on us throw o - pen wide! Lord, send the old - time pow - er, the
Pen - te - cos - tal pow - er, That sin - ners be con - vert - ed and Your name glo - ri - fied!

WORDS: Charles H. Gabriel, 1856-1932, alt.
MUSIC: Charles H. Gabriel, 1856-1932

PENTECOSTAL POWER
C.M. with Refrain

Old Time Power 247

He will baptize you with the Holy Spirit and with fire. Matthew 3:11

1. We are gath-ered for Your bless-ing. We will wait up - on our God.
2. We will glo - ry in Your pow - er. We will sing of won-drous grace.
3. Bring us low in prayer be - fore You, And with faith our souls in - spire,
We will trust in Him who loved us, And who bought us with His blood.
In our midst, as You have prom-ised, Come, O, come and take Your place.
Till we claim, by faith, the prom - ise Of the Ho - ly Ghost and fire.
Refrain
Spir - it, now melt and move All of our hearts with love,
Breathe on us from a - bove With old - time power.

WORDS: Paul Rader, 1879-1938, alt.
MUSIC: Paul Rader, 1879-1938

TABERNACLE
8.7.8.7. with Refrain

248 Breathe Upon Us

He breathed on them and said, "Receive the Holy Spirit." John 20:22

1. Breathe up - on us, Lord, from heav - en, Fill us with the Ho - ly Ghost.
2. While the Spir - it hov - ers near us, O - pen all our hearts, we pray.
3. Lift us, Lord, O, lift us high - er, From the car - nal mind set free.

Prom - ise of the Fa - ther giv - en, Send us now a Pen - te - cost.
To Your im - age, Lord, re - store us. Wit - ness in our souls to - day.
Fill us with re - fin - ing fire. Give us per - fect lib - er - ty.

Refrain

Breathe up - on us, breathe up - on us; With Your love our hearts in - spire.

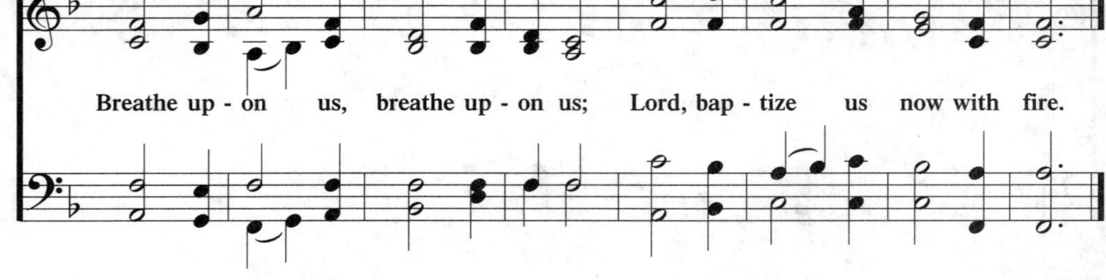
Breathe up - on us, breathe up - on us; Lord, bap - tize us now with fire.

WORDS: Russell K. Carter, 1849-1928, alt.
MUSIC: Russell K. Carter, 1849-1928; arr. J. Buchanan MacMillan, 1915-1983

BREATHE UPON US
8.7.8.7. with Refrain

Holy Spirit Power 249

In my former book, Theophilus, I wrote about all that Jesus began to do and to teach

until the day he was taken up to heaven, after giving instructions through the Holy Spirit to the apostles he had chosen.

After his suffering, he showed himself to these men and gave many convincing proofs that he was alive. He appeared to them over a period of forty days and spoke about the kingdom of God.

On one occasion, while he was eating with them, he gave them this command: "Do not leave Jerusalem, but wait for the gift my Father promised, which you have heard me speak about.

For John baptized with water, but in a few days you will be baptized with the Holy Spirit."

So when they met together, they asked him, "Lord, are you at this time going to restore the kingdom to Israel?"

He said to them: "It is not for you to know the times or dates the Father has set by his own authority.

But you will receive power when the Holy Spirit comes on you; and you will be my witnesses in Jerusalem, and in all Judea and Samaria, and to the ends of the earth."

After he said this, he was taken up before their very eyes, and a cloud hid him from their sight.

Acts 1:1-9

THE GIFT OF THE HOLY SPIRIT

[Jesus] has left us the same power which He possessed. He has bequeathed to the Church the very Holy Spirit that lived and worked in Him. Let us accept this mighty gift. Let us believe in Him and His all-sufficiency. Let us receive Him and give Him room, and let us go forth to reproduce the life and ministry of Jesus and perpetrate the divine miracles of our holy Christianity through the power of the blessed Comforter.

A.B. Simpson (1843-1919), *The Holy Spirit*

---

250 Come, Blessed Holy Spirit

". . . how much more will your Father in heaven give the Holy Spirit to those who ask him!"
Luke 11:13

1. Come, Ho - ly Spir - it, heaven - ly Dove,
2. Spir - it of life, the dead a - wake.
3. Ce - les - tial Dove of peace and rest,
Spir - it of light and life and love,
The slum - bering sin - ner's shack - les break,
Hide us be - neath Your brood - ing breast,

WORDS: Albert B. Simpson, 1843-1919; adapt. David Hahn, b. 1956
MUSIC: David Hahn, b. 1956; Gelsie Hahn, b. 1958

HEAVENLY DOVE
8.8.6.6. with Refrain

Re - vive our souls we pray,
And set the cap - tive free!
Bid all our doubts to cease,
And fill our hearts to - day.
Your great sal - va - tion see.
And keep our hearts in peace.
Refrain
Come with the
power of Pen - te - cost,
Come as the

Bless-ed Ho - ly Ghost! Come and save us
to the ut - ter - most, And fill our hearts to - day.
1, 2, 3.
3rd to D.S.
4.
hearts to - day.

Holy Spirit, with Light Divine 251

Christ . . . will also give life to your mortal bodies through his Spirit. Romans 8:11

1. Ho - ly Spir - it, with light di - vine,
2. Ho - ly Spir - it, with power di - vine,
3. Ho - ly Spir - it, with joy di - vine,
4. Ho - ly Spir - it, O, All Di - vine,

Shine up - on this heart of mine.
Cleanse this guilt - y heart of mine.
Cheer this sad - dened heart of mine.
Dwell with - in this heart of mine.

Chase the shades of night a - way,
Long has sin, with - out con - trol,
Bid my man - y woes de - part,
Cast down ev - ery i - dol throne,

Turn my dark - ness in - to day.
Held do - min - ion o'er my soul.
Heal my wound - ed, bleed - ing heart.
Reign su - preme and reign a - lone.

WORDS: Andrew Reed, 1787-1862, alt.
MUSIC: Louis M. Gottschalk, 1829-1869; arr. Edwin P. Parker, 1836-1925

LAST HOPE
8.7.7.7.

SPIRIT OF GOD, DESCEND

MEDLEY

Spirit of God, Descend upon My Heart
Spirit of the Living God

252 Spirit of God, Descend upon My Heart

Live by the Spirit, and you will not gratify the desires of the sinful nature. Galatians 5:16

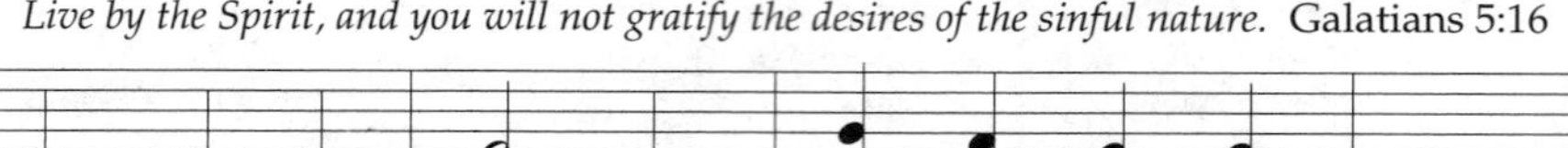

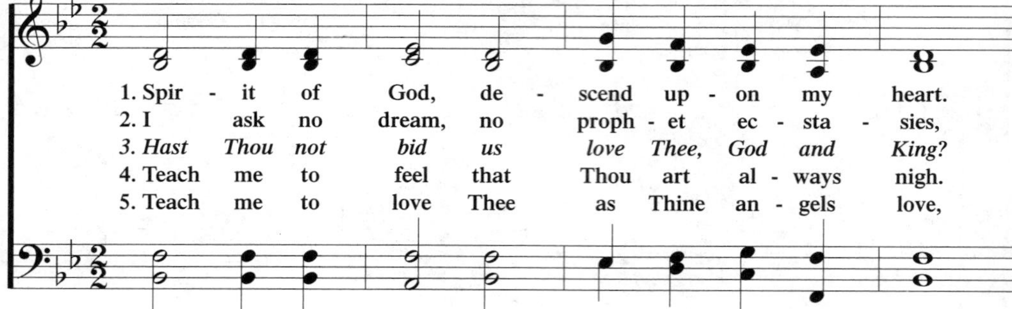
1. Spir - it of God, de - scend up - on my heart.
2. I ask no dream, no proph - et ec - sta - sies,
3. Hast Thou not bid us love Thee, God and King?
4. Teach me to feel that Thou art al - ways nigh.
5. Teach me to love Thee as Thine an - gels love,

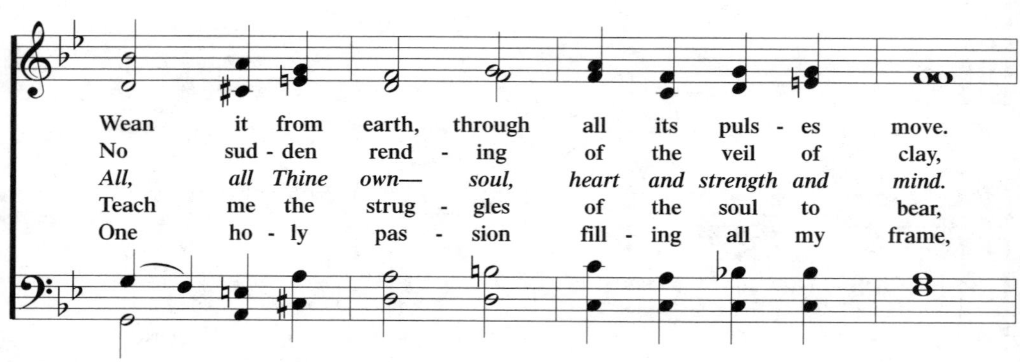
Wean it from earth, through all its puls - es move.
No sud - den rend - ing of the veil of clay,
All, all Thine own— soul, heart and strength and mind.
Teach me the strug - gles of the soul to bear,
One ho - ly pas - sion fill - ing all my frame,

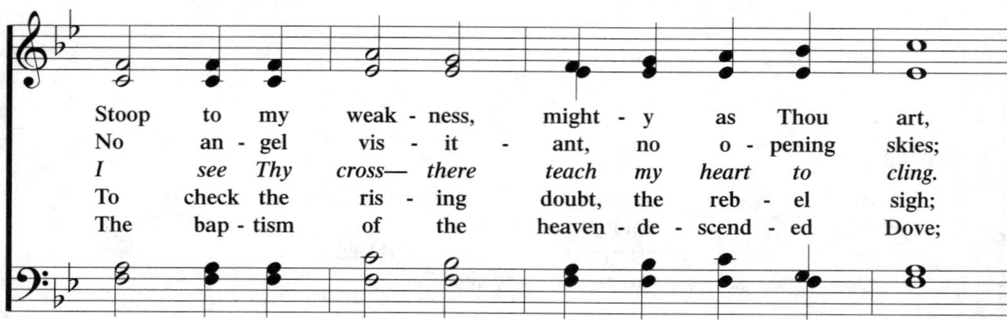
Stoop to my weak - ness, might - y as Thou art,
No an - gel vis - it - ant, no o - pening skies;
I see Thy cross— there teach my heart to cling.
To check the ris - ing doubt, the reb - el sigh;
The bap - tism of the heaven - de - scend - ed Dove;

WORDS: George Croly, 1780-1860
MUSIC: Frederick C. Atkinson, 1841-1897

MORECAMBE
10.10.10.10.

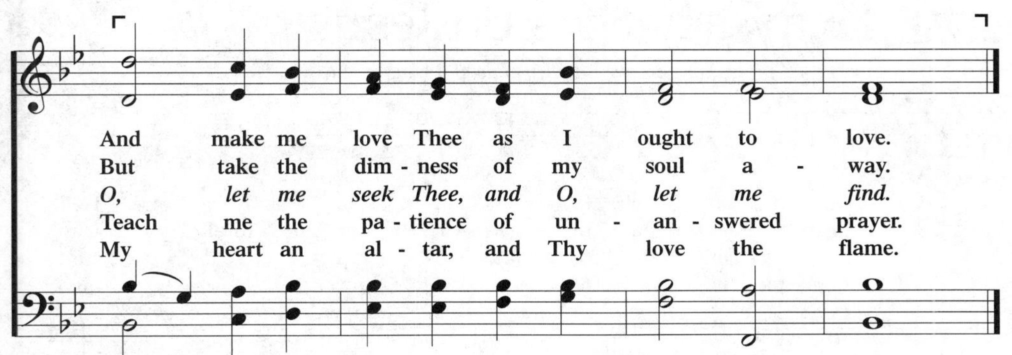
And make me love Thee as I ought to love.
But take the dim - ness of my soul a - way.
O, let me seek Thee, and O, let me find.
Teach me the pa - tience of un - an - swered prayer.
My heart an al - tar, and Thy love the flame.

Optional transition to "Spirit of the Living God."

rit.

Spirit of the Living God 253

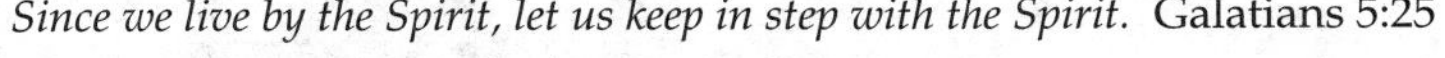

Since we live by the Spirit, let us keep in step with the Spirit. Galatians 5:25

Spir - it of the liv - ing God, Fall fresh on me. Spir - it of the liv - ing God, Fall fresh on me. Melt me, Mold me, Fill me, Use me. Spir - it of the liv - ing God, Fall fresh on me.

WORDS: Daniel Iverson, 1890-1977
MUSIC: Daniel Iverson, 1890-1977

LIVING GOD
7.4.7.4.4.4.7.4

254 I Lay My Sins on Jesus

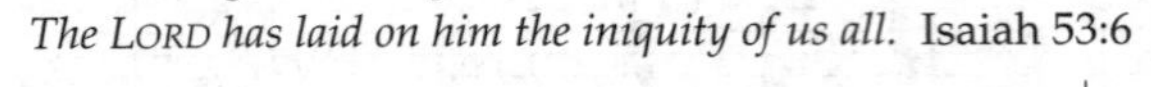

The LORD has laid on him the iniquity of us all. Isaiah 53:6

1. I lay my sins on Je - sus, The spot - less Lamb of God.
2. I lay my wants on Je - sus. All full - ness dwells in Him.
3. I rest my soul on Je - sus, This wea - ry soul of mine.
4. I long to be like Je - sus— Meek, lov - ing, low - ly, mild.

He bears them all, and frees us From the ac - curs - ed load.
He heals all my dis - eas - es. He doth my soul re - deem.
His right hand me em - brac - es, I on His breast re - cline.
I long to be, like Je - sus, The Fa - ther's ho - ly child.

I bring my guilt to Je - sus To wash my crim - son stains
I lay my griefs on Je - sus, My bur - dens, and my cares—
I love the name of Je - sus, Em - man - uel, Christ, the Lord.
I long to be with Je - sus A - mid the heaven - ly throng,

White in His blood most pre - cious, Till not a spot re - mains.
He from them all re - leas - es, He all my sor - rows shares.
Like fra - grance on the breez - es, His name a - broad is poured.
To sing with saints His prais - es, To learn the an - gels' song.

WORDS: Horatius Bonar, 1808-1889
MUSIC: Chrétien Urban, 1790-1845; arr. Edward F. Rimbault, 1816-1876

RUTHERFORD
7.6.7.6.D.

Depth of Mercy! Can There Be 255

He saved us . . . because of his mercy. Titus 3:5

1. Depth of mer - cy! Can there be Mer - cy still re - served for me?
2. I have long with - stood His grace, Long pro - voked Him to His face,
3. Lord, in - cline me to re - pent. Let me now my fall la - ment,
4. Still for me the Sav - ior stands, Shows His wounds, and spreads His hands.
Can my God His wrath for - bear? Me, the chief of sin - ners spare?
Would not hear - ken to His calls, Grieved Him by a thou - sand falls.
Deep - ly my re - volt de - plore, Weep, be - lieve and sin no more.
God is love, I know, I feel. Je - sus weeps, and loves me still.

WORDS: Charles Wesley, 1707-1788
MUSIC: Carl M. von Weber, 1786-1826

WEBER
7.7.7.7.

PRAYER OF CONFESSION

Most holy and merciful Father:
We confess in Your presence the sinfulness of our nature,
and our shortcomings and offenses against You.
You alone know how often we have sinned,
in wandering from Your ways,
in wasting Your gifts,
in forgetting Your love.
Have mercy, O Lord, upon us,
who are ashamed and sorry for all we have done to displease You;
and forgive our sins, through Jesus Christ, Your Son, our Savior. Amen.

Traditional prayer

256 Whiter Than Snow

Wash me, and I will be whiter than snow. Psalm 51:7

1. Lord Je-sus, I long to be per - fect - ly whole. I want You for - ev - er to live in my soul. Break down ev - ery i - dol, cast out ev - ery foe. Now wash me, and I shall be whit - er than snow.
2. Lord Je-sus, look down from Your throne in the skies, And help me to make a com - plete sac - ri - fice. I give up my - self, and what - ev - er I know— Now wash me, and I shall be whit - er than snow.
3. Lord Je-sus, for this I most hum - bly en - treat. I wait, bless - ed Lord, at Your cru - ci - fied feet. By faith, for my cleans - ing, I see Your blood flow— Now wash me, and I shall be whit - er than snow.
4. Lord Je-sus, You see how I pa - tient - ly wait. Come now, and with - in me a new heart cre - ate. To those who have sought You, You nev - er said "No." Now wash me, and I shall be whit - er than snow.
Refrain
Whit - er than snow, yes, whit - er than snow; Now wash me, and I shall be whit - er than snow.

Optional segue to "Change My Heart, O God." No transition required.

WORDS: James L. Nicholson, 1828-1876, alt.
MUSIC: William G. Fischer, 1835-1912

FISCHER
11.11.11.11. with Refrain

Change My Heart, O God 257

Create in me a pure heart, O God, and renew a steadfast spirit within me. Psalm 51:10

Change my heart, O God,
Make it ev - er true.
Change my heart, O God,
3rd time to Coda
May I be like
1.
You.
2.
You.
You are the Pot - ter,
I am the clay.
Mold me and make me,
This is what I pray.
D.C. al Coda
CODA
rit.
You.

WORDS: Eddie Espinosa, b. 1953
MUSIC: Eddie Espinosa, b. 1953

CHANGE MY HEART
Irregular

258 Nothing But the Blood

The blood of Jesus, his Son, purifies us from all sin. 1 John 1:7

1. What can wash a - way my sin? Noth - ing but the blood of Je - sus.
2. For my par - don this I see— Noth - ing but the blood of Je - sus.
3. Noth - ing can for sin a - tone— Noth - ing but the blood of Je - sus.
4. This is all my hope and peace— Noth - ing but the blood of Je - sus.
What can make me whole a - gain? Noth - ing but the blood of Je - sus.
For my cleans - ing, this my plea— Noth - ing but the blood of Je - sus.
Naught of good that I have done— Noth - ing but the blood of Je - sus.
This is all my right - eous - ness— Noth - ing but the blood of Je - sus.
Refrain
O, pre - cious is the flow That makes me white as snow.
No oth - er fount I know, Noth - ing but the blood of Je - sus.

Optional segue to "O, the Blood of Jesus." No transition required.

WORDS: Robert Lowry, 1826-1899
MUSIC: Robert Lowry, 1826-1899

PLAINFIELD
7.8.7.8. with Refrain

O, the Blood of Jesus 259

They have washed their robes and made them white in the blood of the Lamb. Revelation 7:14

1. O, the blood of Je - sus, O, the blood of Je - sus,
2. O, the cross of Je - sus, O, the cross of Je - sus,
3. O, the love of Je - sus, O, the love of Je - sus,
O, the blood of Je - sus, It wash - es white as snow.
O, the cross of Je - sus, His death brings life to me.
O, the love of Je - sus, He free - ly gives to
1, 2.
3.
me.
4. O, the blood of Je - sus, O, the blood of
Je - sus, O, the blood of Je - sus, It wash-es white as snow.

WORDS: Stanzas 1, 4, Traditional; stanzas 2,3, Brenda Barker, b. 1959
MUSIC: Traditional, arr. Ken Barker, b. 1955

O, THE BLOOD OF JESUS
6.6.6.6.

260 If My People

I will forgive their wickedness and will remember their sins no more. Jeremiah 31:34

1. If My peo - ple (If My peo - ple) called by My name
2. We, Your peo - ple (We, Your peo - ple) called by Your name
(called by My name) turn from e - vil (turn from e - vil) and
(called by Your name) turn from e - vil (turn from e - vil) and
seek My face. (and seek My face.) If My peo-ple (If My peo-ple)
seek Your face. (and seek Your face.) We, Your peo-ple (We, Your peo-ple)
called by My name (called by My name) turn from e - vil
called by Your name (called by Your name) turn from e - vil
(turn from e - vil) and seek My face, (and seek My face,) I will hear,
(turn from e - vil) and seek Your face. (and seek Your face.) Hear our cry,

WORDS: Eddie Smith, 20th century, based on 2 Chronicles 7:14
MUSIC: Eddie Smith, 20th century

IF MY PEOPLE
Irregular

(I will hear,) I'll for - give, (I'll for - give,)
(hear our cry) Lord, for - give, (Lord, for - give,)
I will heal, (I will heal) will heal their land, (will
come and heal, (come and heal) come heal our land, (come
heal their land.) I will hear, (I will hear) I'll for-give,
heal our land.) Hear our cry, (hear our cry) Lord, for-give,
(I'll for-give,) I will heal, I will heal their land.
(Lord, for-give,) come and heal, come and heal our land.

261 Kingdom Prayer

He has filled the hungry with good things. Luke 1:53

1. Lord, we're bro - ken, bro - ken - heart - ed, tired of go - ing our own way. We've been proud and self - suf - fi - cient, but we're bro - ken here to - day.
2. Lord, we're mourn - ing, mourn - ing chil - dren, mourn - ing o'er the sins in - side, For they're al - ways right be - fore us, much too great for us to hide.
3. Lord, we hun - ger and we thirst for right - eous - ness that's not our own. For we see our self - ish mo - tives; we need You to take Your throne.
Lord, we need Your power with - in us, for we have none of our own.
Lord, we need Your power with - in us, for we have none of our own.
Lord, we need Your power with - in us, for we have none of our own.
D.S. Lord, make us Your king - dom peo - ple, for we're noth - ing on our own.

WORDS: Dan Adler, b. 1960
MUSIC: Dan Adler, b. 1960; arr. David Hahn, b. 1956

KINGDOM PRAYER
8.7.8.7.D. with Coda

Take this bro - ken heart and mend it with Your power and
Take this mourn - ing heart and com - fort, with Your power and
Take this hun - gry heart and fill it with Your power and
Do Your will and bring Your king - dom, fill our hearts and
1, 2.
3.
D.S.
Yours a - lone.
Yours a - lone.
Yours a - lone.
4.
take Your throne.

THE BETTER WAY

This principle of death and resurrection is the real philosophy of the plan of salvation. God does not pass over our former sin, but He judges it and punishes it in the person of Christ, with whom we are recognized and so identified that His death is practically our execution. This is the ground of our justification. God does not pass by our sin, but fully deals with it and slays us for it, and the soul that enters into life is counted a newborn soul that never participated in the sins of the past.

It is as impossible for man to purify his heart as it is for him to cancel the judgment of God against his sins; and so God has to let us strive and struggle chiefly that we may find out our own inability, and give up the struggle for the better way of Christ and His divine and complete salvation.

A.B. Simpson (1843-1919), *The Christ in the Bible Commentary, Vol. 1 and 2*

262 The Blood Will Never Lose Its Power

This is my blood . . . which is poured out for many for the forgiveness of sins. Matthew 26:28

1. The blood that Je - sus shed for me,
2. It soothes my doubts and calms my fears,
Way back on Cal - va - ry, The blood that gives me strength from
And it dries all my tears. The blood that gives me strength from
day to day, It will nev - er lose its power.
day to day, It will nev - er lose its power.
Refrain
It reach - es to the high - est moun - tain. It
flows to the low - est val - ley. The blood that gives me

WORDS: Andraé Crouch, b. 1947
MUSIC: Andraé Crouch, b. 1947

THE BLOOD
Irregular

strength from day to day, It will nev - er lose its power.

The New Birth 263

Now there was a man of the Pharisees named Nicodemus, a member of the Jewish ruling council.

He came to Jesus at night and said, "Rabbi, we know you are a teacher who has come from God. For no one could perform the miraculous signs you are doing if God were not with him."

In reply Jesus declared, "I tell you the truth, no one can see the kingdom of God unless he is born again."

"How can a man be born when he is old?" Nicodemus asked. "Surely he cannot enter a second time into his mother's womb to be born!"

Jesus answered, "I tell you the truth, no one can enter the kingdom of God unless he is born of water and the Spirit.

Flesh gives birth to flesh, but the Spirit gives birth to spirit.

You should not be surprised at my saying, 'You must be born again.'

The wind blows wherever it pleases. You hear its sound, but you cannot tell where it comes from or where it is going. So it is with everyone born of the Spirit."

"How can this be?" Nicodemus asked.

"You are Israel's teacher," said Jesus, "and do you not understand these things?

I tell you the truth, we speak of what we know, and we testify to what we have seen, but still you people do not accept our testimony.

I have spoken to you of earthly things and you do not believe; how then will you believe if I speak of heavenly things?

No one has ever gone into heaven except the one who came from heaven—the Son of Man.

Just as Moses lifted up the snake in the desert, so the Son of Man must be lifted up,

that everyone who believes in him may have eternal life.

For God so loved the world that he gave his one and only Son, that whoever believes in him shall not perish but have eternal life."

John 3:1-16

OUR REDEEMER

MEDLEY
There Is a Redeemer
I Will Sing of My Redeemer

264 There Is a Redeemer

In him we have redemption through his blood. Ephesians 1:7

1. There is a Re - deem - er, Je - sus, God's own Son,
2. Je - sus, my Re - deem - er, Name a - bove all names,
3. When I stand in glo - ry I will see His face, and
Pre - cious Lamb of God, Mes - si - ah, Ho - ly One.
Pre - cious Lamb of God, Mes - si - ah, Hope for sin - ners slain.
There I'll serve my King for - ev - er, In that ho - ly place.
Refrain
Thank You, O my Fa - ther, for giv - ing us Your Son; And
leav - ing Your Spir - it 'til the work on earth is done.
Optional transition to "I Will Sing of My Redeemer."
accel.

WORDS: Melody Green-Sievright, b. 1946
MUSIC: Melody Green-Sievright, b. 1946

GREEN
Irregular

I Will Sing of My Redeemer 265

. . . Christ Jesus, . . . our righteousness, holiness and redemption. 1 Corinthians 1:30

1. I will sing of my Re - deem - er And His won - drous love to me.
2. I will tell the won - drous sto - ry, How my lost es - tate to save,
3. I will praise my dear Re - deem - er, His tri - um - phant power I'll tell,
4. I will sing of my Re - deem - er And His heaven - ly love for me.
On the cru - el cross He suf - fered, From the curse to set me free.
In His bound - less love and mer - cy, He the ran - som free - ly gave.
How the vic - to - ry He giv - eth O - ver sin, and death, and hell.
He from death to life hath brought me, Son of God with Him to be.
Refrain
Sing, O, sing of my Re - deem - er, With His blood He pur - chased me.
On the cross He sealed my par - don, Paid the debt, and made me free.

WORDS: Philip P. Bliss, 1838-1876
MUSIC: Rowland H. Prichard, 1811-1887

HYFRYDOL
8.7.8.7. with Refrain

266 And Can It Be That I Should Gain

Christ died for sins once for all . . . to bring you to God. 1 Peter 3:18

1. And can it be that I should gain An in - terest
2. 'Tis mys-tery all! Th'Im - mor - tal dies! Who can ex -
3. He left His Fa - ther's throne a - bove, So free, so
4. Long my im - pris - oned spir - it lay Fast - bound in
5. No con-dem - na - tion now I dread. Je - sus, and
in the Sav - ior's blood? Died He for me, who caused His
plore His strange de - sign? In vain the first - born ser - aph1
in - fi - nite His grace. Emp - tied Him - self of all but
sin and na - ture's night. Thine eye dif - fused3 a quick - ening4
all in Him, is mine! A - live in Him, my liv - ing
pain, For me, who Him to death pur - sued?
tries To sound2 the depths of love di - vine!
love, And bled for A - dam's help - less race.
ray. I woke, the dun - geon flamed with light.
Head, And clothed in right - eous - ness di - vine,
A - maz - ing love! How can it be That Thou, my
'Tis mer - cy all! Let earth a - dore. Let an - gel
'Tis mer - cy all, im - mense and free! For, O my
My chains fell off, my heart was free. I rose, went
Bold I ap - proach th'e - ter - nal throne, And claim the

WORDS: Charles Wesley, 1707-1788, alt.
MUSIC: Thomas Campbell, 1777-1844

SAGINA
8.8.8.8.8.8. with Refrain

1. *seraph: angelic beings* 2. *sound: measure*
3. *diffused: sent out* 4. *quickening: brightly shining*

Refrain
God, should die for me?
minds in - quire no more.
God, it found out me.
forth, and fol - lowed Thee.
crown through Christ, my own.
A - maz - ing love! How
A - maz-ing love!
can it be That Thou, my God, should die for me!
How can it be That Thou, my God, should die for me!

THE REMEDY FOR THE WORLD

Jesus Christ came in the fullness of time to be God's salvation. He was to be God's cure for all that was wrong with the human race.

He came to deliver us from our moral and spiritual disorders—but it must also be said He came to deliver us from our own remedies.

A.W. Tozer (1897-1963), *Tragedy in the Church*

267 O Redeeming One

[Hmong Title: *Au Tug Cawmseej**]

While we were still sinners, Christ died for us. Romans 5:8

1. Je - sus, You are Light in the dark - est place. In a
2. Je - sus, You are Hope in a hope - less land. You're my
3. Je - sus, You are Truth in a world turned gray. You're the
Ye - xus Koj pum - kev rua qhov tsaus ntuj nti. Huv lub
world of sor - row, You're my Song of praise. You're the
Sol - id Rock when there's sink - ing sand. You're my
Lamp that guides all a - long the way. Though I
neej kws txom - nyem, Koj yog zaaj nkauj qhuas. Koj yog
Sac - ri - fice that has saved my soul. You're the Heal - ing Balm that has
Shel - ter from ev - ery trou - bled storm. In the cold - est night Your love
fall in sin still You pick me up. When I thirst for You, You will
tug theej hab cawm kuv tug ntsuj - plig, Koj yog tug khu kuv

WORDS: Dan Adler, b. 1960
MUSIC: Dan Adler, b. 1960; arr. David Hahn, b. 1956

O REDEEMING ONE
Irregular

*originally in Hmong and English for *Heart of the City Worship Band*

Refrain
made me whole.
keeps me warm.
fill my cup.
zoo tag tag.
O Re - deem - ing One! You have
Au tug Cawm - seej Koj, tau -
set me free, For You know me well, yet You still love me. I will
tso kuv dlim Koj paub kuv ua txhum, Los Koj tseem hlub kuv. Kuv yuav
sing Your praise 'til Your face I see!
hu nkauj qhuas txug thaus kuv pum Koj.
Then I'll be with You and You'll be with
Kuv yuav nyob nrug Koj, Koj yuav nyob nrug
1, 2.
me.
kuv.
3.
rit.
me.
kuv.

268 Hallelujah for the Cross

May I never boast except in the cross of our Lord Jesus Christ. Galatians 6:14
1. The cross is stand - ing fast, Hal-le - lu-jah! Hal-le - lu-jah! De - fy - ing ev - ery blast. Hal-le - lu-jah! Hal-le - lu-jah! The winds of hell have blown, The world its hate has shown, Yet it is not o - ver - thrown. Hal-le - lu-jah for the cross!
2. It is the old cross still. Hal-le - lu-jah! Hal-le - lu-jah! Its tri-umph let us tell. Hal-le - lu-jah! Hal-le - lu-jah! The grace of God here shone Through Christ the bless-ed Son, Who did for sin a - tone. Hal-le - lu-jah for the cross!
3. 'Twas here the debt was paid. Hal-le - lu-jah! Hal-le - lu-jah! Our sins on Je - sus laid. Hal-le - lu-jah! Hal-le - lu-jah! So round the cross we sing Of Christ, our of - fer - ing, Of Christ, our liv - ing King. Hal-le - lu-jah for the cross!
Refrain
Hal - le - lu - jah, hal - le - lu - jah, hal - le - lu - jah for the cross!
Hal - le - lu - jah, hal - le - lu - jah, it shall nev - er suf - fer loss!

WORDS: Horatius Bonar, 1808-1889, alt.
MUSIC: James McGranahan, 1840-1907

KINSMAN
6.8.6.8.6.6.6.7. with Refrain

O Boundless Salvation 269

It is the power of God for the salvation of everyone who believes. Romans 1:16

1. O bound-less sal - va - tion, deep o - cean of love! O full - ness of
2. My sins, they are man - y, their stains are so deep, And bit - ter the
3. The tide now is flow - ing, I'm touch - ing the wave. I hear the loud
4. And now, hal - le - lu - jah! the rest of my days Shall glad - ly be
mer - cy Christ brought from a - bove, The whole world re - deem - ing, so
tears of re - morse that I weep; But weep - ing is use - less– thou
call of "the Might - y to save." My faith's grow - ing bold - er– de -
spent in pro - mot - ing His praise, Who o - pened His bos - om to
rich and so free, Now flow - ing for all men, Now flow - ing for
great crim - son sea, Thy wa - ters can cleanse me, Thy wa - ters can
liv - ered I'll be! I plunge 'neath the wa - ters, I plunge 'neath the
pour out this sea Of bound - less sal - va - tion, Of bound - less sal-
all men, Now flow - ing for all men– Come, roll o - ver me!
cleanse me, Thy wa - ters can cleanse me– Come, roll o - ver me!
wa - ters, I plunge 'neath the wa - ters– They roll o - ver me!
va - tion, Of bound - less sal - va - tion, For you and for me!

WORDS: William Booth, 1829-1912
MUSIC: J. Ellis, 19th century

BOOTH
11.11.11.12.11.

270 Wonderful Grace of Jesus

You know the grace of our Lord Jesus Christ. 2 Corinthians 8:9

1. Won - der - ful grace of Je - sus, Great - er than all my sin.
2. Won - der - ful grace of Je - sus, Reach - ing to all the lost.
3. Won - der - ful grace of Je - sus, Reach - ing the most de - filed.
How shall my tongue des - cribe it? Where shall its praise be - gin?
By it I have been par - doned, Saved to the ut - ter - most.
By its trans - form - ing pow - er, Mak - ing him God's dear child,
Tak - ing a - way my bur - den, Set - ting my spir - it free;
Chains have been torn a - sun - der, Giv - ing me lib - er - ty;
Pur - chas - ing peace and heav - en For all e - ter - ni - ty;
For the won - der - ful grace of Je - sus reach - es me.
Refrain
Won - der - ful the match - less grace, the match - less grace of Je - sus;
Won - der - ful the match - less grace of Je - sus;

WORDS: Haldor Lillenas, 1885-1959
MUSIC: Haldor Lillenas, 1885-1959

WONDERFUL GRACE
Irregular with Refrain

Deep - er than the might - y roll - ing sea, the roll - ing sea.
Deep - er than the might - y roll - ing sea.
Won - der - ful grace, all - suf - fi - cient for me, for e - ven me.
High - er than the moun - tain, spark - ling like a foun - tain; All - suf - fi - cient grace for e - ven me.
Broad - er than the scope of my trans - gres - sions; Great - er far than all my sin and shame.
Broad - er than the scope of my trans - gres - sions, sing it! Great - er far than all my sin and shame, my sin and shame.
O, mag - ni - fy the pre - cious name of Je - sus; Praise His name!
O, mag - ni - fy the pre - cious name of Je - sus; Praise His name!

271 Grace Greater Than Our Sin

Where sin increased, grace increased all the more. Romans 5:20

1. Mar - vel - ous grace of our lov - ing Lord, Grace that ex - ceeds our
2. Sin and de - spair, like the sea waves cold, Threat - en the soul with
3. Dark is the stain that we can - not hide. What can a - vail to
4. Mar - vel - ous, in - fi - nite, match - less grace Free - ly be - stowed on
sin and our guilt, Yon - der on Cal - va - ry's mount out - poured,
in - fi - nite loss. Grace that is great - er, yes, grace un - told,
wash it a - way? Look! There is flow - ing a crim - son tide.
all who be - lieve! You that are long - ing to see His face,
There where the blood of the Lamb was spilt.
Points to the ref - uge, the might - y cross.
Whit - er than snow you may be to - day.
Will you this mo - ment His grace re - ceive?
Refrain
Grace, grace,
Mar - vel - ous grace,
God's grace, Grace that will par - don and cleanse with - in. Grace,
in - fi - nite grace,
Mar - vel - ous
grace, God's grace, Grace that is great - er than all our sin!
grace, in - fi - nite grace,

Optional segue to "Amazing Grace." No transition required.

WORDS: Julia H. Johnston, 1849-1919
MUSIC: Daniel B. Towner, 1850-1919

MOODY
9.9.9.9. with Refrain

Amazing Grace 272

God is able to make all grace abound to you. 2 Corinthians 9:8

1. A - maz - ing grace, how sweet the sound That saved a wretch like me! I once was lost, but now am found; Was blind, but now I see.
2. 'Twas grace that taught my heart to fear, And grace my fears re - lieved. How pre - cious did that grace ap - pear The hour I first be - lieved!
3. Through man - y dan - gers, toils, and snares I have al - read - y come. 'Tis grace has brought me safe thus far, And grace will lead me home.
4. The Lord has prom - ised good to me. His Word my hope se - cures. He will my shield and por - tion be As long as life en - dures.
5. And when this flesh and heart shall fail, And mor - tal life shall cease, I shall pos - sess with - in the veil A life of joy and peace.
6. When we've been there ten thou - sand years, Bright shin - ing as the sun, We've no less days to sing God's praise Than when we first be - gun.

WORDS: John Newton, 1725-1807; stanza 6, John P. Rees, 1828-1900
MUSIC: American melody, from Carrell and Clayton's *Virginia Harmony*, 1831; arr. Edwin O. Excell, 1851-1921

AMAZING GRACE
C.M.

TRANSFORMATION

Salvation must include a judicial change of status, but what is overlooked by most teachers is that it also includes an actual change in the life of the individual. And by this we mean more than a surface change, we mean a transformation as deep as the roots of his human life.

A.W. Tozer (1897-1963), *The Divine Conquest*

---

273 I Cannot Tell

Christ loved us and gave himself up for us. Ephesians 5:2

1. I can-not tell why He, the King of Heav - en, Should leave the
2. I can-not tell why He, the Joy of Heav - en, Should give Him -
3. I can-not tell when He will rule the na - tions, How He will
peace of all e - ter - ni - ty, Why God Him - self should lay a - side His
self to suf - fer for my sin, Why Ho - ly God should love me in my
claim His loved ones as His own, And who can tell the ho - ly ju - bi -
splen - dor To leave the Fa - ther's side and come to me.
shame - ful - ness, Why He should die to draw my soul to Him.
la - tion When all His chil - dren gath - er 'round His throne.
But this I know: our si - lence filled with sing - ing, And all our
But this I know: that Christ the Lord is ris - en, And praise His
But this I know: all flesh will see His glo - ry, And skies will

WORDS: Ken Bible, b. 1950; inspired by William Y. Fullerton, 1857-1932
MUSIC: Traditional Irish melody; arr. Camp Kirkland, b. 1946

LONDONDERRY AIR
11.10.11.10.11.10.11.12.

dark - ness fled from heav - en's light When Christ the Lord, so hu - man, yet so
name, He's ris - en now in me! Be - cause He lives, I'll rise to life e -
burst as all cre - a - tion sings. The Son will rise on one e - ter - nal
ho - ly, In love was born a child for me that ho - ly night.
ter - nal! He took my guilt - y heart, and I'm for - ev - er free!
morn - ing When Christ, the Sav - ior of the world, is Lord and King!
There's a Wideness in God's Mercy
274
Let me fall into the hands of the LORD, for his mercy is very great. 1 Chronicles 21:13
1. There's a wide - ness in God's mer - cy, Like the wide - ness of the sea.
2. There is wel - come for the sin - ner, And more grac - es for the good.
3. For the love of God is broad - er Than the meas - ure of our mind,
4. If our love were but more sim - ple, We should take Him at His word,
There's a kind - ness in His jus - tice, Which is more than lib - er - ty.
There is mer - cy with the Sav - ior. There is heal - ing in His blood.
And the heart of the E - ter - nal Is most won - der - ful - ly kind.
And our lives would be all sun - shine In the sweet - ness of our Lord.

WORDS: Frederick W. Faber, 1814-1863, alt.
MUSIC: Lizzie S. Tourjée, 1858-1913

WELLESLEY
8.7.8.7.

275 Rock of Ages

I will put you in a cleft in the rock and cover you with my hand. Exodus 33:22

1. Rock of A - ges, cleft for me, Let me hide my - self in Thee.
2. Not the la - bors of my hands Can ful - fil Thy law's de - mands.
3. Noth - ing in my hand I bring, Sim - ply to Thy cross I cling;
4. While I draw this fleet - ing breath, When mine eyes shall close in death,
Let the wa - ter and the blood From Thy riv - en1 side which flowed,
Could my zeal no res - pite2 know, Could my tears for - ev - er flow,
Na - ked, come to Thee for dress, Help - less, look to Thee for grace.
When I soar to realms un - known, See Thee on Thy judg - ment throne,
Be of sin the dou - ble cure; Save me from its guilt and power.
All for sin could not a - tone. Thou must save, and Thou a - lone.
Foul, I to the foun - tain fly. Wash me, Sav - ior, or I die.
Rock of A - ges, cleft for me, Let me hide my - self in Thee.

WORDS: Augustus M. Toplady, 1740-1778
MUSIC: Thomas Hastings, 1784-1872

TOPLADY
7.7.7.7.7.7.

1. *riven: split open*
2. *respite: rest*

276 In God I Trust

To you, O LORD, I lift up my soul; in you I trust, O my God.
Do not let me be put to shame, nor let my enemies triumph over me.
No one whose hope is in you will ever be put to shame,
but they will be put to shame who are treacherous without excuse.

Show me your ways, O LORD, teach me your paths;

guide me in your truth and teach me, for you are God my Savior, and my hope is in you all day long.

Remember, O LORD, your great mercy and love, for they are from of old.

Remember not the sins of my youth and my rebellious ways; according to your love remember me, for you are good, O LORD.

Good and upright is the LORD; therefore he instructs sinners in his ways.

He guides the humble in what is right and teaches them his way.

All the ways of the LORD are loving and faithful for those who keep the demands of his covenant.

For the sake of your name, O LORD, forgive my iniquity, though it is great.

Who, then, is the man that fears the LORD? He will instruct him in the way chosen for him.

He will spend his days in prosperity, and his descendants will inherit the land.

The LORD confides in those who fear him; he makes his covenant known to them.

My eyes are ever on the LORD, for only he will release my feet from the snare.

Psalm 25:1-15

O, for a Faith That Will Not Shrink 277

Lord, I believe; help my unbelief! Mark 9:24, NKJV

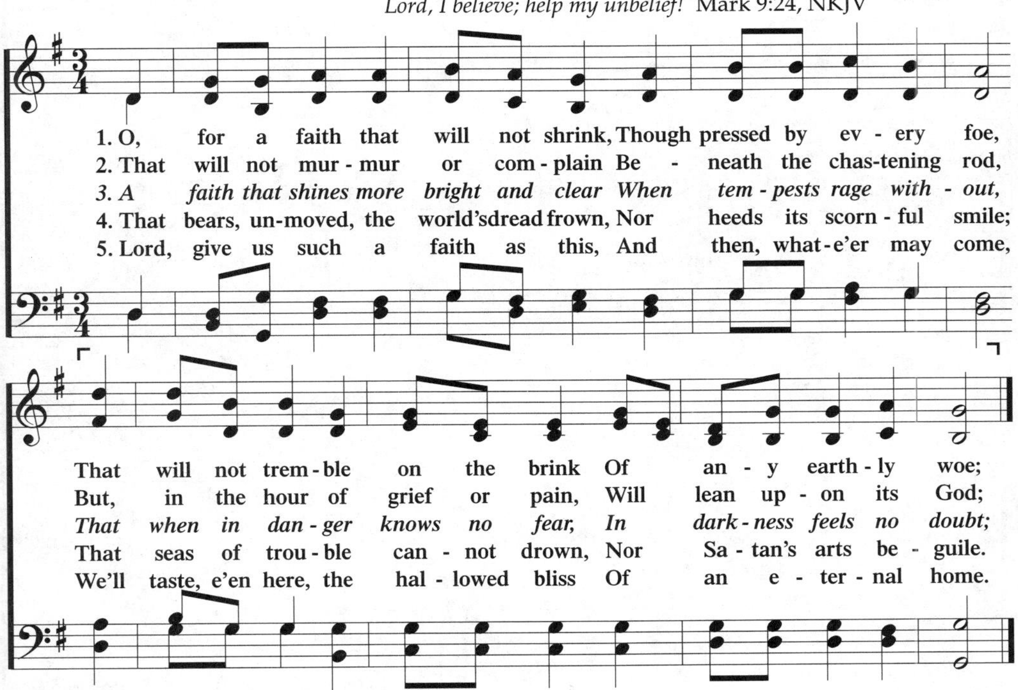
1. O, for a faith that will not shrink, Though pressed by ev - ery foe,
That will not trem - ble on the brink Of an - y earth - ly woe;
2. That will not mur - mur or com - plain Be - neath the chas-tening rod,
But, in the hour of grief or pain, Will lean up - on its God;
3. A faith that shines more bright and clear When tem - pests rage with - out,
That when in dan - ger knows no fear, In dark - ness feels no doubt;
4. That bears, un-moved, the world's dread frown, Nor heeds its scorn - ful smile;
That seas of trou - ble can - not drown, Nor Sa - tan's arts be - guile.
5. Lord, give us such a faith as this, And then, what - e'er may come,
We'll taste, e'en here, the hal - lowed bliss Of an e - ter - nal home.

WORDS: William H. Bathurst, 1796-1877, alt.
MUSIC: Carl G. Gläser, 1784-1829; adapt. Lowell Mason, 1792-1872

AZMON
C.M.

278 My Life Is in You, Lord

Love the Lord your God with all your heart . . . soul and . . . strength. Deuteronomy 6:5

My life is in You, Lord, My strength is in You, Lord, My
hope is in You Lord, in You, it's in You. My
life is in You, Lord, My strength is in You, Lord, My
Last time to Coda
hope is in You Lord, in You, it's in You. I will
praise You with all of my life, I will

WORDS: Daniel Gardner, b. 1956
MUSIC: Daniel Gardner, b. 1956

MY LIFE IS IN YOU
Irregular

praise You with all of my strength. With
all of my life, with all of my strength,
D.S. al Coda
All of my hope is in You. My
CODA
You, it's in You, in You.

A PRAYER FOR PEACE

O God, You who are the Author of love and the Lover of pure peace and affection, let all who are terrified by fears, afflicted by poverty, harassed by tribulation, worn down by illness, be set free by Your indulgent tenderness, raised up by renewal of life and cherished by Your daily compassion.

Traditional prayer (9th century)

279 My Faith Looks Up to Thee

Let us fix our eyes on Jesus, the author and perfecter of our faith. Hebrews 12:2

1. My faith looks up to Thee, Thou Lamb of
2. May Thy rich grace im - part Strength to my
3. While life's dark maze I tread And griefs a -
4. When ends life's tran - sient dream, When death's cold,
Cal - va - ry, Sav - ior di - vine. Now hear me
faint - ing heart, My zeal in - spire. As Thou hast
round me spread, Be Thou my guide. Bid dark - ness
sul - len stream Shall o'er me roll, Blest Sav - ior,
while I pray, Take all my guilt a - way.
died for me, O, may my love to Thee
turn to day, Wipe sor - row's tears a - way,
then, in love, Fear and dis - trust re - move.
O, let me from this day Be whol - ly Thine!
Pure, warm, and change - less be, A liv - ing fire!
Nor let me ev - er stray From Thee a - side.
O, bear me safe a - bove, A ran - somed soul!

WORDS: Ray Palmer, 1808-1887
MUSIC: Lowell Mason, 1792-1872

OLIVET
6.6.4.6.6.6.4.

A PRAYER FOR PEACE

O God, You who are the Author of love and the Lover of pure peace and affection, let all who are terrified by fears, afflicted by poverty, harassed by tribulation, worn down by illness, be set free by Your indulgent tenderness, raised up by renewal of life and cherished by Your daily compassion.

Traditional prayer (9th century)

279 My Faith Looks Up to Thee

Let us fix our eyes on Jesus, the author and perfecter of our faith. Hebrews 12:2

1. My faith looks up to Thee, Thou Lamb of Calvary, Savior divine. Now hear me while I pray, Take all my guilt away. O, let me from this day Be wholly Thine!
2. May Thy rich grace impart Strength to my fainting heart, My zeal inspire. As Thou hast died for me, O, may my love to Thee Pure, warm, and changeless be, A living fire!
3. While life's dark maze I tread And griefs around me spread, Be Thou my guide. Bid darkness turn to day, Wipe sorrow's tears away, Nor let me ever stray From Thee aside.
4. When ends life's transient dream, When death's cold, sullen stream Shall o'er me roll, Blest Savior, then, in love, Fear and distrust remove. O, bear me safe above, A ransomed soul!

WORDS: Ray Palmer, 1808-1887
MUSIC: Lowell Mason, 1792-1872

OLIVET
6.6.4.6.6.6.4.

Come, Thou Fount 280

A fountain will be opened . . . to cleanse them from sin and impurity. Zechariah 13:1

1. Come, Thou Fount of ev - ery bless-ing, Tune my heart to sing Thy grace.
2. Hith - er - to Thy love has blest me, Thou hast brought me to this place,
3. O, to grace how great a debt - or, Dai - ly I'm con-strained[2] to be!
Streams of mer - cy nev - er ceas - ing, Call for songs of loud - est praise.
And I know Thy hand will bring me Safe - ly home by Thy good grace.
Let Thy good - ness, as a fet - ter,[3] Bind my wan - dering heart to Thee.
Teach me some me - lo - dious son - net,[1] Sung by flam - ing tongues a - bove.
Je - sus sought me when a strang - er, Wan - dering from the fold of God.
Prone to wan - der, Lord, I feel it, Prone to leave the God I love.
Praise the mount– I'm fixed up - on it– Mount of Thy re - deem - ing love.
He, to res - cue me from dan - ger Bought me with His pre - cious blood.
Here's my heart, O take and seal[4] it– Seal it for Thy courts a - bove.

WORDS: Robert Robinson, 1735-1790
MUSIC: American melody, from John Wyeth's *Repository of Sacred Music*, 1813

NETTLETON
8.7.8.7.D.

1. sonnet: poem 2. constrained: obligated
3. fetter: chain, shackle 4. seal: secure

281 Only Believe

Everything is possible for him who believes. Mark 9:23

1. Fear not, lit-tle flock, from the cross to the throne, From death in-to life He went for His own. All pow-er in earth, all pow-er a-bove, Is giv-en to Him for the flock of His love.
2. Fear not, lit-tle flock, He go-eth a-head, Your Shep-herd se-lect-eth the path you must tread. The wa-ters of Ma-rah[1] He'll sweet-en for thee— He drank all the bit-ter in Geth-sem-a-ne.
3. Fear not, lit-tle flock, what-ev-er your lot, He en-ters all rooms, "the doors be-ing shut." He nev-er for-sakes, He nev-er is gone— So count on His pres-ence in dark-ness and dawn.
Refrain
On-ly be-lieve, on-ly be-lieve. All things are pos-si-ble, on-ly be-lieve.
On-ly be-lieve, on-ly be-lieve. All things are pos-si-ble, on-ly be-lieve.

WORDS: Paul Rader, 1879-1938
MUSIC: Paul Rader, 1879-1938

ONLY BELIEVE
Irregular with Refrain

1. *Marah: refers to the bitter water in the desert in Exodus 15:23*

Wonderful Peace 282

We have peace with God through our Lord Jesus Christ. Romans 5:1

1. Far a - way in the depths of my spir - it to - night Rings a
2. I am rest - ing to - night in this won - der - ful peace, Rest - ing
3. And I think when I rise to that cit - y of peace, Where the
4. O dear soul, are you here with - out com - fort and rest, March - ing
mel - o - dy sweet - er than psalm, And in heav - en - ly strains it un -
sweet - ly in Je - sus' con - trol, For I'm kept from all dan - ger by
Au - thor of peace I shall see, That one strain of the song which the
down the rough path - way of time? Make Je - sus your friend ere the
ceas - ing - ly falls O'er my soul like an in - fin - ite calm.
night and by day, And His glo - ry is flood - ing my soul!
ran - somed will sing In that heav - en - ly king - dom will be:
sha - dows grow dark, O, ac - cept now this peace so sub - lime!
Refrain
Peace, peace, won-der-ful peace, Com-ing down from the Fa-ther a - bove. Sweep
o - ver my spir - it for - ev - er, I pray, In fath - om - less bil - lows[1] of love.

WORDS: W.D. Cornell, 19th century, alt.
MUSIC: W.G. Cooper, 19th century

WONDERFUL PEACE
12.9.12.9. with Refrain

1. *billows: waves*

283 Thou Wilt Keep Him in Perfect Peace

. . . whose mind is stayed on thee. Isaiah 26:3, KJV

1. "Thou wilt keep him in per - fect peace, Whose mind is stayed on Thee."
2. In the shad - ow of the might - y rock I lay me down to sleep.
3. 'Tis the prom - ise of the Ho - ly One, "My peace I give to thee."
When the shad - ows come and dark - ness falls, He giv - eth in - ward peace.
He who watch - es o - ver Is - ra - el So faith - ful - ly will keep.
Though the storm of life in fu - ry rage, Thy ref - uge sure is He.
Refrain
O, He is the on - ly per - fect rest - ing place! He giv - eth per - fect peace.
"Thou wilt keep him in per - fect peace, Whose mind is stayed on Thee."

WORDS: Stanza 1, Vivian Kretz Amsler, 20th century;
stanzas 2-3, Floyd W. Hawkins, 20th century
MUSIC: Vivian Kretz Amsler, 20th century; arr. Floyd W. Hawkins, 20th century

PERFECT PEACE
8.6.9.6. with Refrain

Dear Lord and Father of Mankind 284

Commit your way to the LORD; trust in him. Psalm 37:5

1. Dear Lord and Fa - ther of man - kind, For - give our fool - ish
2. In sim - ple trust like theirs who heard, Be - side the Syr - ian
3. O Sab - bath rest by Gal - i - lee! O calm of hills a -
4. Drop Thy still dews of qui - et - ness Till all our striv - ings
5. Breathe through the heats of our de - sire Thy cool - ness and Thy

ways. Re - clothe us in our right - ful mind, In pur - er lives Thy
sea, The gra - cious call - ing of the Lord, Let us, like them, with -
bove, Where Je - sus knelt to share with Thee The si - lence of e -
cease. Take from our souls the strain and stress, And let our or - dered
balm. Let sense be dumb, let flesh re - tire; Speak through the earth - quake,

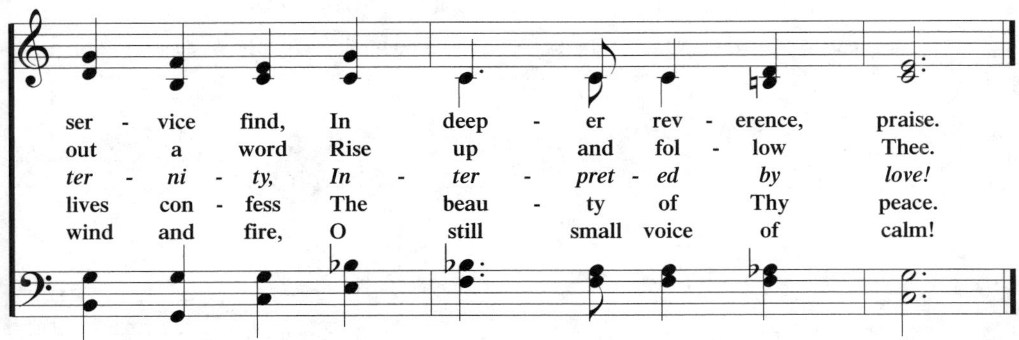
ser - vice find, In deep - er rev - erence, praise.
out a word Rise up and fol - low Thee.
ter - ni - ty, In - ter - pret - ed by love!
lives con - fess The beau - ty of Thy peace.
wind and fire, O still small voice of calm!

WORDS: John G. Whittier, 1807-1892
MUSIC: Frederick C. Maker, 1844-1927

REST (Maker)
8.6.8.8.6.

285 In My Heart There Rings a Melody

Sing and make music in your heart to the Lord. Ephesians 5:19

1. I have a song that Je - sus gave me, It was sent from heaven a - bove.
2. I love the Christ who died on Cal-vary, For He washed my sins a - way.
3. 'Twill be my end - less theme in glo - ry, With the an - gels I will sing.
There nev - er was a sweet - er mel - o - dy, 'Tis a mel - o - dy of love.
He put with - in my heart a mel - o - dy, And I know it's there to stay.
'Twill be a song with glo - rious har-mo-ny, When the courts of heav - en ring.
Refrain
In my heart there rings a mel - o - dy, There rings a mel - o - dy with heav - en's har - mo - ny.
In my heart there rings a mel - o - dy, There rings a mel - o - dy of love.

WORDS: Elton M. Roth, 1891-1951
MUSIC: Elton M. Roth, 1891-1951

HEART MELODY
Irregular with Refrain

Wonderful, Wonderful Jesus 286

You . . . surround me with songs of deliverance. Psalm 32:7

1. There is nev - er a day so drea - ry, There is nev - er a night so long, But the soul that is trust - ing Je - sus Will some - where find a song.
2. There is nev - er a cross so heav - y, There is nev - er a weight of woe, But that Je - sus will help to car - ry Be - cause He lov - eth so.
3. There is nev - er a care or bur - den, There is nev - er a grief or loss, But that Je - sus in love will light - en When car - ried to the cross.
4. There is nev - er a guilt - y sin - ner, There is nev - er a wan - dering one, But that God can in mer - cy par - don Through Je - sus Christ, His Son.
Refrain
Won - der - ful, won - der - ful Je - sus, In the heart He im - plant - eth a song; A song of de - liv - erance, of cour - age, of strength. In the heart He im - plant - eth a song.

WORDS: Anna B. Russell, 1862-1954
MUSIC: Ernest O. Sellers, 1869-1952

NEW ORLEANS
Irregular

287 The Joy of the Lord

FIRST TUNE

The joy of the LORD is your strength. Nehemiah 8:10

1. The joy of the Lord is the strength of His peo - ple,
2. The joy of the Lord is our strength for life's bur - dens,
3. The joy of the Lord is our strength for life's tri - als,
4. The joy of the Lord is the hope of our call - ing,
The sun - shine that ban - ish - es sad - ness and gloom,
And gives to each du - ty a heav - en - ly zest.
And lifts the crushed heart a - bove sor - row and care.
And, O, for His com - ing how fond - ly we pray!
The foun - tain that bursts in the des - ert of sor - row,
It sets to sweet mu - sic the task of the toil - er,
Like night - in - gales' notes, it can sing in the dark - ness,
When we shall re - turn with re - joic - ing to Zi - on,
And sheds o'er the wil - der - ness glad - ness and bloom.
And soft - ens the couch of the la - bor - er's rest.
And e - ven re - joice when the fig tree is bare.
And sor - row and sigh - ing shall van - ish a - way.

WORDS: Albert B. Simpson, 1843-1919, alt.
MUSIC: Albert B. Simpson, 1843-1919

JOY OF THE LORD
12.11.12.11 with Refrain

Refrain
O, the joy of the Lord is our strength and our song,
Our sor - row and sigh - ing are o'er. We'll re - joice in the Lord,
We'll re - joice in the Lord, We'll re - joice in the Lord ev - er - more.

COUNT IT ALL JOY

It is a great thing to learn to count it all joy. Counting is not the language of poetry or sentiment but of cold, unerring calculation. It adds up the column thus: sorrow, temptation, difficulty, opposition, depression, desertion, danger, discouragement on every side, but at the bottom of the column God's presence, God's will, God's joy, God's promise, God's recompense.

A.B. Simpson (1843-1919), *In Step with the Spirit*

288 The Joy of the Lord

SECOND SETTING

The joy of the LORD is your strength. Nehemiah 8:10

1. The joy of the Lord is the strength of His peo - ple, The
joy of the Lord is our strength for life's tri - als, And
joy of the Lord is the hope of our call - ing, And,
sun - shine that ban - ish - es sad - ness and gloom, The
lifts the crushed heart a - bove sor - row and care. Like
O, for His com - ing how fond - ly we pray! When
foun - tain that bursts in the des - ert of sor - row, And
night - in - gales' notes, it can sing in the dark - ness, And
we shall re - turn with re - joic - ing to Zi - on, And
sheds o'er the wil - der - ness glad - ness and bloom.
e - ven re - joice when the fig tree is bare.
sor - row and sigh - ing shall van - ish a - way.

WORDS: Albert B. Simpson, 1843-1919, alt.
MUSIC: R.C. Filsinger, b. 1950; arr. Tim Shuey, b. 1954

REJOICE EVERMORE
12.11.12.11 with Refrain

Refrain
O, the joy of the Lord is our strength and our song, Our
sor - row and sigh - ing are o - ver. We'll re -
joice in the Lord, We'll re - joice in the Lord, re - joice in the Lord ev - er -
more. ev - er - more.
1, 2.
3.
2. The
3. The

289 Holy Spirit Led

Therefore, there is now no condemnation for those who are in Christ Jesus,

because through Christ Jesus the law of the Spirit of life set me free from the law of sin and death.

For what the law was powerless to do in that it was weakened by the sinful nature, God did by sending his own Son in the likeness of sinful man to be a sin offering. And so he condemned sin in sinful man,

in order that the righteous requirements of the law might be fully met in us, who do not live according to the sinful nature but according to the Spirit.

Those who live according to the sinful nature have their minds set on what that nature desires; but those who live in accordance with the Spirit have their minds set on what the Spirit desires.

The mind of sinful man is death, but the mind controlled by the Spirit is life and peace;

the sinful mind is hostile to God. It does not submit to God's law, nor can it do so.

Those controlled by the sinful nature cannot please God.

You, however, are controlled not by the sinful nature but by the Spirit, if the Spirit of God lives in you. And if anyone does not have the Spirit of Christ, he does not belong to Christ.

But if Christ is in you, your body is dead because of sin, yet your spirit is alive because of righteousness.

And if the Spirit of him who raised Jesus from the dead is living in you, he who raised Christ from the dead will also give life to your mortal bodies through his Spirit, who lives in you.

Therefore, brothers, we have an obligation—but it is not to the sinful nature, to live according to it.

For if you live according to the sinful nature, you will die; but if by the Spirit you put to death the misdeeds of the body, you will live,

because those who are led by the Spirit of God are sons of God.

For you did not receive a spirit that makes you a slave again to fear, but you received the Spirit of sonship. And by him we cry, "*Abba*, Father."

The Spirit himself testifies with our spirit that we are God's children.

Now if we are children, then we are heirs—heirs of God and co-heirs with Christ, if indeed we share in his sufferings in order that we may also share in his glory.

I consider that our present sufferings are not worth comparing with the glory that will be revealed in us. *Romans 8:1-18*

Have Thine Own Way, Lord! 290

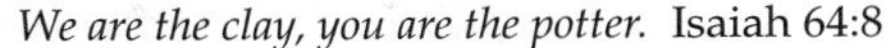

We are the clay, you are the potter. Isaiah 64:8

1. Have Thine own way, Lord! Have Thine own way!
Thou art the Pot - ter, I am the clay.
Mold me and make me After Thy will,
While I am wait - ing Yield - ed and still.

2. Have Thine own way, Lord! Have Thine own way!
Search me and try me, Mas - ter, to - day.
Whit - er than snow, Lord, Wash me just now,
As in Thy pres - ence Hum - bly I bow.

3. Have Thine own way, Lord! Have Thine own way!
Wound - ed and wea - ry, Help me I pray!
Pow - er— all pow - er— Sure - ly is Thine!
Touch me and heal me, Sav - ior di - vine!

4. Have Thine own way, Lord! Have Thine own way!
Hold o'er my be - ing Ab - so - lute sway!
Fill with Thy Spir - it Till all shall see
Christ on - ly, al - ways, Liv - ing in me!

WORDS: Adelaide A. Pollard, 1862-1934
MUSIC: George C. Stebbins, 1846-1945

ADELAIDE
5.4.5.4.D.

291 Refiner's Fire

He will be like a refiner's fire . . . and refine them like gold and silver. Malachi 3:2-3

1. Pur - i - fy my heart, let me be as gold and pre - cious sil - ver.
2. Pur - i - fy my heart, cleanse me from with - in and make me ho - ly.
Pur - i - fy my heart, let me be as gold, pure gold.
Pur - i - fy my heart, cleanse me from my sin, deep with - in.
Refrain
Re - fin - er's fire; my heart's one de - sire is to
be ho - ly, Set a - part for you,

WORDS: Brian Doerksen, b. 1965
MUSIC: Brian Doerksen, b. 1965

REFINER'S FIRE
Irregular

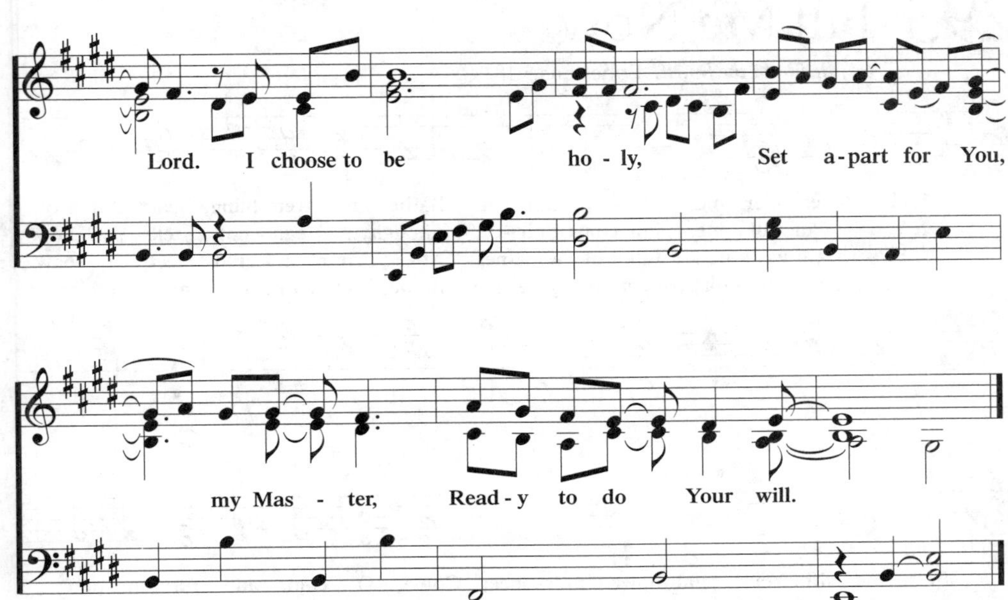
Lord. I choose to be ho - ly, Set a-part for You,
my Mas - ter, Read - y to do Your will.

Breathe on Me, Breath of God 292

He breathed on them and said, "Receive the Holy Spirit." John 20:22

1. Breathe on me, Breath of God, Fill me with life a - new,
That I may love what - e'er You love, And do what You would do.

2. Breathe on me, Breath of God, Un - til my heart is pure,
Un - til with You I will one will To do and to en - dure.

3. Breathe on me, Breath of God, So that Your will is mine,
Till all this earth - ly part of me Glows with Your fire di - vine.

4. Breathe on me, Breath of God, So shall I nev - er die,
But live with You the per - fect life Of Your e - ter - ni - ty.

WORDS: Edwin Hatch, 1835-1889, alt.
MUSIC: Robert Jackson, 1842-1914

TRENTHAM
S.M.

293 Fill Me Now

Be filled with the Spirit. Ephesians 5:18

1. Hov - er o'er me, Ho - ly Spir - it, Bathe my trem-bling heart and brow.
2. You can fill me, gra-cious Spir - it, Though I can - not tell You how.
3. I am weak-ness, full of weak-ness. At Your sa - cred feet I bow.
4. Cleanse and com - fort, bless and save me. Bathe, O bathe my heart and brow.
Fill me with Your hal - lowed pres - ence; Come, O come and fill me now.
But I need You, great - ly need You; Come, O come and fill me now.
Blest, di - vine, e - ter - nal Spir - it, Fill with power, and fill me now.
You are com - fort - ing and sav - ing. You are sweet - ly fill - ing now.
Refrain
Fill me now, fill me now, Je - sus, come and fill me now.
Fill me with Your hal - lowed pres - ence; Come, O come and fill me now.

WORDS: Elwood H. Stokes, 1815-1895, alt.
MUSIC: John R. Sweney, 1837-1899

FILL ME NOW
8.7.8.7. with Refrain

Not I, But Christ 294

FIRST TUNE

I no longer live, but Christ lives in me. Galatians 2:20

1. Not I, but Christ be hon-ored, loved, ex-alt-ed. Not I, but Christ be seen, be known, be heard. Christ, on-ly Christ in ev-ery look and ac-tion. Christ, on-ly Christ in ev-ery thought and word.
2. Not I, but Christ to gent-ly soothe in sor-row. Not I, but Christ to wipe the fall-ing tear. Christ, on-ly Christ to lift the wea-ry bur-den. Christ, on-ly Christ to calm my small-est fear.
3. Not I, but Christ my ev-ery need sup-ply-ing. Not I, but Christ my strength and health to be. Christ, on-ly Christ for bod-y, soul, and spir-it. Christ, on-ly Christ, live then Your life in me.
4. Christ, on-ly Christ some day will fill my vi-sion. Glo-ry ex-cel-ling soon, full soon I'll see. Christ, on-ly Christ my ev-ery hope ful-fill-ing. Christ, on-ly Christ my all and all to be.
Refrain
O, to be saved from my-self, dear Lord! O, to be lost in Thee!
O, that it might be no more I, but Christ that lives in me!

WORDS: Ada A. Whiddington, 19th century, alt.
MUSIC: Albert B. Simpson, 1843-1919

WHIDDINGTON
11.10.11.10. with Refrain

295 Not I, But Christ

SECOND TUNE

I no longer live, but Christ lives in me. Galatians 2:20

1. Not I, but Christ be hon - ored, loved, ex - alt - ed. Not I, but Christ be seen, be known, be heard. Christ, on - ly Christ in ev - ery look and ac - tion. Christ, on - ly
(2.) Christ to gen - tly soothe in sor - row. Not I, but Christ to wipe the fall - ing tear. Christ, on - ly Christ to lift the wea - ry bur - den. Christ, on - ly
(3.) Christ my ev - ery need sup - ply - ing. Not I, but Christ my strength and health to be. Christ, on - ly Christ for bod - y, soul, and spir - it. Christ, on - ly
(4.) Christ some day will fill my vi - sion. Glo - ry ex - cel - ling soon, full soon I'll see. Christ, on - ly Christ my ev - ery hope ful - fill - ing. Christ, on - ly

WORDS: Ada A. Whiddington, 19th century, alt.
MUSIC: Jean Sibelius, 1865-1957; arr. Eldon McBride, b. 1962

FINLANDIA
11.10.11.10. with Coda

1, 2, 3.
Christ in ev - ery thought and word.
Christ to calm my small - est fear.
Christ, live then Thy life in me.
Christ my
4.
2. Not I, but
3. Not I, but all and all to be.
4. Christ, on - ly
Christ, on - ly Christ my ev - ery hope ful - fill - ing.
Christ, on - ly Christ my all and all to be.

296 Jesus, I My Cross Have Taken

Anyone who does not take his cross and follow me is not worthy of me. Matthew 10:38

1. Je - sus, I my cross have tak - en, All to leave, and fol - low Thee.
2. Let the world de - spise and leave me. They have left my Sav - ior, too.
3. Has-ten on from grace to glo - ry, Armed by faith and winged by prayer.

Des - ti - tute, de - spised, for - sak - en, Thou from hence my all shall be.
Hu - man hearts and looks de - ceive me. Thou art not, like man, un - true.
Heaven's e - ter - nal days be - fore me, God's own hand shall guide me there.

Per - ish ev - ery fond am - bi - tion, All I've sought, and hoped, and known.
And while Thou shalt smile up - on me, God of wis - dom, love, and might,
Soon shall close my earth - ly mis - sion, Swift shall pass my pil - grim days.

Yet, how rich is my con - di - tion: God and heaven are still my own!
Foes may hate, and friends may shun me; Show Thy face and all is bright.
Hope shall change to glad fru - i - tion, Faith to sight, and prayer to praise.

WORDS: Henry F. Lyte, 1793-1847
MUSIC: Attrib.Wolfgang A. Mozart, 1756-1791;
from Joshua Leavitt's *The Christian Lyre*, 1831; arr. Hubert P. Main, 1839-1925

ELLESDIE
8.7.8.7.D.

Christ in Me 297

FIRST TUNE

Christ in you, the hope of glory. Colossians 1:27

1. This is my won-der-ful sto-ry— Christ to my heart has come.
2. Was there a sto-ry so mov-ing, Sto-ry of love and pain?
3. I am so glad I re-ceived Him, Je-sus, my heart's dear King.
4. How can I ev-er be lone-ly? How can I ev-er fall?
5. Now in His close-ness con-fid-ing, This my glad song shall be:
Je-sus, the King of all glo-ry, Finds in my heart a home.
Was there a Bride-groom so lov-ing, Seek-ing our hearts to gain?
I, who so of-ten have grieved Him, All to His feet would bring.
What can I want, if on-ly Christ is my all in all?
I am in Je-sus a-bid-ing, Je-sus a-bides in me.
Refrain
Christ in me, Christ in me, Christ in me—O, won-der-ful sto-ry!
Christ in me, Christ in me, Christ in me, the hope of glo-ry!

WORDS: Albert B. Simpson, 1843-1919, alt.
MUSIC: Albert B. Simpson, 1843-1919

CHRIST IN ME
Irregular

298 Christ in Me

SECOND TUNE

Christ in you, the hope of glory. Colossians 1:27

1. This is my won-der-ful sto - ry, Christ to my heart has
2. Was there a sto-ry so mov - ing— sto-ry of love and
3. I am so glad I re-ceived Him, Je-sus, my heart's pre-cious
4. How can I ev-er be lone - ly? How can I stum-ble and
5. Now in His close-ness con-fid - ing, this my glad song shall
come. Je - sus the King of all glo - ry
pain? Was there a Bride-groom so lov - ing,
King. I, who so of - ten have grieved Him,
fall? What can I want if on - ly
be: I am in Je - sus a - bid - ing,
finds in my heart a home.
seek - ing our hearts to gain?
all to His feet would bring.
Christ is my all in all?
Je - sus a-bides in me.
Refrain
Christ in me, Christ in me, Christ in

WORDS: Albert B. Simpson, 1843-1919, alt.
MUSIC: Dan Adler, b. 1960; arr. David Hahn, b. 1956

HOPE OF GLORY
Irregular

me, O, what a won-der-ful sto - ry! Christ in
me, Christ in me, Christ in
me, the Hope, the Hope of glo - ry!

CHRIST POSSESSES OUR BEING

And now in the light of His revealing we behold Christ, the perfect One, who walked in sinless perfection through the world of His incarnation, waiting to come and enter our hearts, and dwell in us, and walk in us as the very substance of our new life, while we simply abide in Him and walk in His very steps. It is not merely imitating an example, but it is living the very life of another. It is to have the very person of Christ possessing our being—the thoughts of Christ, the desire of Christ, the will of Christ, the faith of Christ, the purity of Christ, the love of Christ, the unselfishness of Christ, the single aim of Christ, the obedience of Christ, the humility of Christ, the submission of Christ, the meekness of Christ, the patience of Christ, the gentleness of Christ, the zeal of Christ—and the works of Christ manifest in our mortal flesh.

A.B. Simpson (1843-1919), *In Step with the Spirit*

299 More About Jesus

Grow in the grace and knowledge of our Lord and Savior Jesus Christ. 2 Peter 3:18

1. More a - bout Je - sus would I know, More of His grace to oth - ers show,
2. More a - bout Je - sus let me learn, More of His ho - ly will dis - cern.
3. More a - bout Je - sus in His Word— Hold - ing com - mun - ion with my Lord,
4. More a - bout Je - sus on His throne, Rich - es in glo - ry all His own,
More of His sav - ing full - ness see, More of His love who died for me.
Spir - it of God, my teach - er be, Show-ing the things of Christ to me.
Hear-ing His voice in ev - ery line, Mak - ing each faith - ful say - ing mine.
More of His king-dom's sure in - crease, More of His com - ing, Prince of Peace.
Refrain
More, more a - bout Je - sus, More, more a - bout Je - sus!
More of His sav - ing full - ness see, More of His love who died for me!

WORDS: Eliza E. Hewitt, 1851-1920
MUSIC: John R. Sweney, 1837-1899

SWENEY
L.M. with Refrain

Jesus Only 300

His divine power has given us everything we need for life and godliness. 2 Peter 1:3

1. Je - sus on - ly is our mes - sage. Je - sus all our theme shall be.
2. Je - sus on - ly is our Sav - ior, All our guilt He bore a - way.
3. Je - sus is our Sanc - ti - fi - er, Cleans - ing us from self and sin,
4. Je - sus on - ly is our Heal - er. All our sick - ness - es He bore,
5. Je - sus on - ly is our pow - er; His the gift of Pen - te - cost.
6. And for Je - sus we are wait - ing, List' - ning for the ad - vent call.
We will lift up Je - sus ev - er. Je - sus on - ly will we see.
All our right - eous-ness He gives us, All our strength from day to day.
And with all His Spir - it's full - ness Fill - ing all our hearts with - in.
And His ris - en life and full - ness All His mem - bers still may share.
Je - sus, breathe Thy pow - er up - on us, Fill us with the Ho - ly Ghost.
Still it will be Je - sus on - ly, Je - sus ev - er, all in all.
Refrain
Je - sus on - ly, Je - sus ev - er, Je - sus all in all we sing.
Sav - ior, Sanc - ti - fi - er, and Heal - er, Glo - ri - ous Lord and com - ing King.

WORDS: A.B. Simpson, 1843-1919, alt.
MUSIC: J.H. Burke, 19th century

JESUS ONLY
Irregular with Refrain

301 Jesus Only

SECOND SETTING

1. Je - sus on - ly is our mes - sage. Je - sus all our theme shall be. We will lift up Je - sus ev - er. Je - sus on - ly will we see.
2. Je - sus on - ly is our Sav - ior, All our guilt He bore a - way. All our right - eous - ness He gives us, All our strength from day to day.
3. Je - sus is our Sanc - ti - fi - er, Cleans - ing us from self and sin, And with all His Spir - it's full - ness Fill - ing all our hearts with - in.
4. Je - sus on - ly is our Heal - er. All our sick - ness - es He bore, And His ris - en life and full - ness All His mem - bers still may share.
5. Je - sus on - ly is our pow - er; His the gift of Pen - te - cost. Je - sus, breathe Thy pow - er up - on us, Fill us with the Ho - ly Ghost.
6. And for Je - sus we are wait - ing, List' - ning for the ad - vent call. Still it will be Je - sus on - ly, Je - sus ev - er, all in all.
3

WORDS: A.B. Simpson, 1843-1919, alt.
MUSIC: J.H. Burke, 19th century; arr. Don Marsh, b. 1943

JESUS ONLY
Irregular with Refrain

Refrain
Je - sus on - ly, Je - sus ev - er, Je - sus all in all we
sing. Sav - ior, Sanc - ti - fi - er, and Heal - er, Glo - ri - ous
Lord and com - ing King.
1 - 5.
6.
Glo - ri - ous
Lord and com - ing King.

302 My Spirit, Soul and Body

May your whole spirit, soul and body be kept blameless at the coming of our Lord Jesus Christ.
1 Thessalonians 5:23

1. My spir - it, soul and bod - y, Je - sus, I give to Thee,
2. O Je - sus, might - y Sav - ior, I trust in Thy great name.
3. O, bliss - ful self - sur - ren - der To live, my Lord, by Thee!
A con - se - crat - ed of - fering Thine ev - er - more to be.
I look for Thy sal - va - tion, Thy prom - ise now I claim.
Now, Son of God, my Sav - ior, Live out Thy life in me.
My all is on the al - tar; Lord, I am all Thine own.
My Lord, I yield my mem - bers, From sin's do - min - ion free,
I'm Thine, O bless - ed Je - sus, Washed in Thy pre - cious blood,
O, may my faith ne'er fal - ter! Lord, keep me Thine a - lone.
For war - fare and for tri - umph, As weap - ons un - to Thee.
Sealed by Thy Ho - ly Spir - it, A sac - ri - fice to God.

(For lower key, see No. 245)

WORDS: Attrib. Mary D. James, 1810-1883
MUSIC: From *Neuvermehrtes Gesangbuch*, 1693; harm. Felix Mendelssohn, 1809-1847

MUNICH
7.6.7.6.D

Himself 303

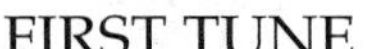

FIRST TUNE

Christ is all, and is in all. Colossians 3:11

1. Once it was the bless-ing, Now it is the Lord. Once it was the feel-ing,
2. Once 'twas pain - ful try - ing, Now it's per - fect trust. Once a half sal - va-tion,
3. Once 'twas bus - y plan-ning, Now it's trust - ful prayer. Once 'twas anx - ious car-ing,
4. Once it was my work-ing, His it hence shall be. Once I tried to use Him,
5. Once I hoped for Je - sus, Now I know He's mine. Once my lamps were dy - ing,

Now it is His Word. Once His gifts I want-ed, Now the Giv - er own.
Now the ut - ter - most![1] Once 'twas cease-less hold-ing, Now He holds me fast.
Now He has the care. Once 'twas what I want-ed, Now what Je - sus says.
Now He us - es me. Once the power I want-ed, Now the Might-y One.
Now they bright-ly shine. Once for death I wait-ed, Now His com-ing hail.

Once I sought for heal - ing, Now Him-self a - lone.
Once'twas con - stant drift - ing, Now my an - chor's cast.
Once'twas con - stant ask - ing, Now it's cease-less praise.
Once for self I la - bored, Now for Him a - lone.
And my hopes are an-chored Safe with - in the veil.[2]

Refrain

All in all for - ev - er, Je - sus will I sing. Ev-ery-thing in Je - sus, And Je-sus ev-ery - thing.

WORDS: Albert B. Simpson, 1843-1919, alt.
MUSIC: Albert B. Simpson, 1843-1919

HIMSELF
6.5.6.5.D. with Refrain

1. *Refers to Christ's work in our lives not only as Savior, but as Sanctifier, Healer and Coming King.*
2. *Hebrews 6:19. Refers to the Holy of Holies, which was covered by the Tabernacle veil.*

304 Himself

SECOND TUNE

Christ is all, and is in all. Colossians 3:11

1. Once it was the bless - ing, Now it is the Lord.
2. Once 'twas pain - ful try - ing, Now it's per - fect trust.
3. *Once 'twas bus - y plan - ning, Now it's trust - ful prayer.*
4. Once it was my work - ing, His it hence shall be.
5. Once I hoped for Je - sus, Now I know He's mine.

Once it was the feel - ing, Now it is His Word.
Once a half sal - va - tion, Now the ut - ter - most![1]
Once 'twas anx - ious car - ing, Now He has the care.
Once I tried to use Him, Now He us - es me.
Once my lamps were dy - ing, Now they bright - ly shine.

Once His gifts I want - ed, Now the Giv - er own.
Once 'twas cease - less hold - ing, Now He holds me fast.
Once 'twas what I want - ed, Now what Je - sus says.
Once the power I want - ed, Now the Might - y One.
Once for death I wait - ed, Now His com - ing hail.

Once I sought for heal - ing, Now Him - self a - lone.
Once 'twas con - stant drift - ing, Now my an - chor's cast.
Once 'twas con - stant ask - ing, Now it's cease - less praise.
Once for self I la - bored, Now for Him a - lone.
And my hopes are an - chored Safe with - in the veil.[2]

(For different harmony, see No. 340)

WORDS: Albert B. Simpson, 1843-1919, alt.
MUSIC: James Mountain, 1843-1933; arr. Eldon McBride, b. 1962

WYE VALLEY
6.5.6.5.D. with Refrain

1. *Refers to Christ's work in our lives not only as Savior, but as Sanctifier, Healer and Coming King.*
2. *Hebrews 6:19. Refers to the Holy of Holies, which was covered by the Tabernacle veil.*

Refrain
All in all for - ev - er, Je - sus will I sing.
Ev - ery - thing in Je - sus, And Je - sus ev - ery - thing.

PRAYER OF ST. FRANCIS

Lord, make me an instrument of Your peace.
Where there is hatred let me sow love;
Where there is injury, pardon;
Where there is doubt, faith;
Where there is despair, hope;
Where there is darkness, light;
Where there is sadness, joy.
O Divine Master,
Grant that I may not seek so much
To be consoled as to console;
To be understood as to understand;
To be loved as to love.
For it is in giving that we receive;
In pardoning that we are pardoned;
And in dying that we are born to eternal life.

St. Francis of Assisi (1182-1226)

305 Himself

THIRD SETTING

Christ is all, and is in all. Colossians 3:11

1. Once it was the bless - ing, Now it is the Lord.
2. Once was pain - ful try - ing, Now it's per - fect trust.
3. Once was bus - y plan - ning, Now it's trust - ful prayer.
4. Once it was my work - ing, His it hence shall be.
5. Once I hoped for Je - sus, Now I know He's mine.
Once it was the feel - ing, Now it is His Word.
Once a half sal - va - tion, Now the ut - ter - most.1
Once it was anx - ious car - ing, Now He has the care.
Once I tried to use Him, Now He us - es me.
Once my lamps were dy - ing, Now they bright - ly shine.

WORDS: Albert B. Simpson, 1843-1919, alt.
MUSIC: K. Richard Cogbill, b. 1956; arr. David Hahn, b. 1956

EVERYTHING
Irregular

1. *Refers to Christ's work in our lives not only as Savior, but as Sanctifier, Healer and Coming King.*

Once His gifts I want - ed, Now the Giv - er own.
Once was cease - less hold - ing, Now He holds me fast.
Once was what I want - ed, Now what Je - sus says.
Once the power I want - ed, Now the Might - y One.
Once for death I wait - ed, Now His com - ing hail.
Once I sought for heal - ing, Now Him - self a - lone.
Once was con - stant drift - ing, Now my an - chor's cast.
Once was con - stant ask - ing, Now it's cease - less praise.
Once for self I la - bored, Now for Him a - lone.
And my hopes are an - chored Safe with - in the veil.2
Refrain
All in all for - ev - er, Je - sus will I sing.

2. *Hebrews 6:19. Refers to the Holy of Holies, which was covered by the Tabernacle veil.*

Ev-ery-thing in Je-sus, and Je-sus ev-ery-thing.
All in all for-ev-er, Je-sus will I sing.
1, 2, 3, 4.
5.
Ev-ery-thing in Je-sus and Je-sus ev-ery-thing.
thing.

Jesus, I Am Resting, Resting 306

You will find rest for your souls. Jeremiah 6:16

1. Je - sus, I am rest - ing, rest - ing In the joy of what Thou art.
2. O, how great Thy lov - ing kind-ness, Vast - er, broad - er than the sea!
3. Sim - ply trust - ing Thee, Lord Je - sus, I be - hold Thee as Thou art,
4. Ev - er lift Thy face up - on me, As I work and wait for Thee,
Ref: Je - sus, I am rest - ing, rest - ing In the joy of what Thou art.
fine
I am find - ing out the great - ness Of Thy lov - ing heart.
O, how mar - vel - ous Thy good - ness Lav - ished all on me!
And Thy love, so pure, so change - less, Sat - is - fies my heart;
Rest - ing 'neath Thy smile, Lord Je - sus, Earth's dark shad - ows flee.
I am find - ing out the great - ness Of Thy lov - ing heart.
Thou hast bid me gaze up - on Thee, And Thy beau - ty fills my soul,
Yes, I rest in Thee, Be - lov - ed, Know what wealth of grace is Thine,
Sat - is - fies its deep - est long - ings, Meets, sup - plies its ev - ery need,
Bright - ness of my Fa - ther's glo - ry, Sun - shine of my Fa - ther's face,
D.C. for Refrain
For, by Thy trans - form - ing pow - er, Thou hast made me whole.
Know Thy cer - tain - ty of prom - ise, And have made it mine.
And sur - rounds my life with bless - ings: Thine is love in - deed!
Keep me ev - er trust - ing, rest - ing, Fill me with Thy grace.

WORDS: Jean S. Pigott, 1845-1882, alt.
MUSIC: James Mountain, 1843-1933

TRANQUILITY
8.7.8.5.D. with Refrain

OUR LIFE AND BREATH

MEDLEY

Abiding and Confiding
Breathing Out and Breathing In

307 Abiding and Confiding

Abide in Me, and I in you. John 15:4, NKJV

1. I have learned the wondrous secret Of abiding in the Lord.
I have tasted life's pure fountain, I am drinking of His Word.
I have found the strength and sweetness Of abiding 'neath the blood.
I have lost myself in Jesus, I am sinking into God.
2. I am crucified with Jesus, And He lives and dwells with me.
I have ceased from all my struggling, 'Tis no longer I, but He.
All my will is yielding to Him, And His Spirit reigns within,
And His precious blood each moment Keeps me cleansed and free from sin.
3. All my sicknesses I bring Him, And He bears them all away.
All my fears and griefs I tell Him, All my cares from day to day,
All my strength I draw from Jesus, By His breath I live and move.
E'en His very mind He gives me, And His faith, and life and love.
4. For my words I take His wisdom, For my works His Spirit's power,
For my ways His ceaseless presence Guards and guides me every hour.
Of my heart the Satisfier, Of my joy the boundless spring;
Savior, Sanctifier, Healer, Glorious Lord and coming King.

WORDS: Albert B. Simpson, 1843-1919, alt.
MUSIC: American melody, from Wyeth's *Repository of Sacred Music*, Part Second, 1813

NETTLETON
8.7.8.7.D.

Optional transition to "Breathing Out and Breathing In."

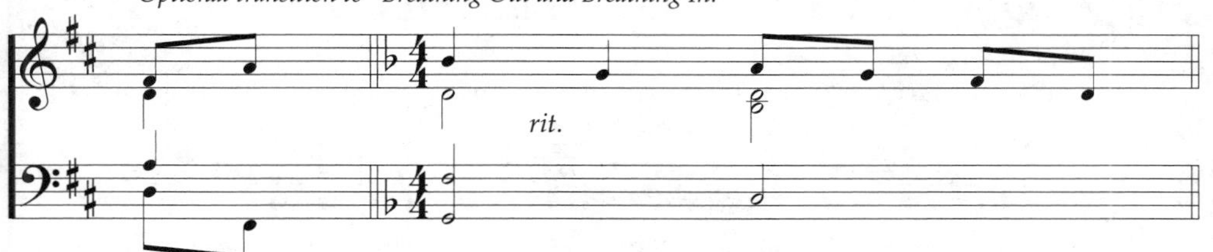

Breathing Out and Breathing In 308

Put off your old self . . . to be made new in the attitude of your minds. Ephesians 4:22-23

1. Je - sus, breathe Thy Spir - it on me, Teach me how to breathe Thee in,
2. Breath - ing out my sin - ful na - ture, Thou hast borne it all for me;
3. I am breath - ing out my long - ings, In Thy lis - tening lov - ing ear,

Help me pour from deep with - in me All my life of self and sin.
Tak - ing in Thy cleans - ing full - ness, Find - ing all my life in Thee.
And re - ceiv - ing ten - der an - swers, Still - ing ev - ery doubt and fear.

I am breath - ing out my own life, That I may be filled with Thine;
I am breath - ing out my sor - row, On Thy kind and gen - tle breast;
I am breath - ing ev - ery mo - ment, Draw - ing all my life from Thee;

Let - ting go my strength and weak - ness, Breath - ing in Thy life di - vine.
Draw - ing in Thy joy and com - fort, Draw - ing in Thy peace and rest.
Breath by breath I live up - on Thee, Bless - ed Spir - it, breathe in me.

WORDS: Albert B. Simpson, 1843-1919, alt.
MUSIC: William Moore, 19th century; arr. Eldon McBride, b. 1962

HOLY MANNA
8.7.8.7.D.

309 Breathing Out and Breathing In

ORIGINAL SETTING

Put off your old self . . . to be made new in the attitude of your minds. Ephesians 4:22-23

1. Je - sus, breathe Thy Spir - it on me, Teach me how to breathe Thee in,
2. Breath-ing out my sin - ful na - ture, Thou hast borne it all for me;
3. I am breath - ing out my long - ings, In Thy lis - tening lov - ing ear,
Help me pour from deep with - in me All my life of self and sin.
Tak - ing in Thy cleans - ing full - ness, Find - ing all my life in Thee.
And re - ceiv - ing ten - der an - swers, Still - ing ev - ery doubt and fear.
I am breath - ing out my own life, That I may be filled with Thine;
I am breath - ing out my sor - row, On Thy kind and gen - tle breast;
I am breath - ing ev - ery mo - ment, Draw - ing all my life from Thee;
Let - ting go my strength and weak - ness, Breath-ing in Thy life di - vine.
Draw - ing in Thy joy and com - fort, Draw - ing in Thy peace and rest.
Breath by breath I live up - on Thee, Bless - ed Spir - it, breathe in me.

WORDS: Albert B. Simpson, 1843-1919, alt.
MUSIC: William Moore, 19th century

HOLY MANNA
8.7.8.7.D.

Jesus, Master, Whose I Am 310

With your blood you purchased men for God. Revelation 5:9

1. Je - sus, Mas - ter, whose I am, Pur - chased Thine a - lone to be,
2. Oth - er lords have long held sway. Now Thy name a - lone to bear,
3. Je - sus, Mas - ter, I am Thine. Keep me faith - ful, keep me near.
By Thy blood, O spot - less Lamb, Shed so will - ing - ly for me.
Thy dear voice a - lone o - bey, Is my dai - ly, hour - ly prayer.
Let Thy pres - ence in me shine All my home - ward way to cheer.
Let my heart be all Thine own, Let me live to Thee a - lone.
Whom have I in heaven but Thee? Noth - ing else my joy can be.
Je - sus, at Thy feet I fall, O, be Thou my all in all.

WORDS: Frances R. Havergal, 1836-1879
MUSIC: Conrad Kocher, 1786-1872; arr. William H. Monk, 1823-1889

DIX
7.7.7.7.7.7.

GRACE FOR GRACE

[The Holy Spirit] takes the gifts and graces of Christ and brings them into our lives as we need and receive them day by day. Thus we receive of His fullness even grace for grace: His grace for our grace; His supply for our need; His strength for our strength; His body for our body; His Spirit for our spirit.

A.B. Simpson (1843-1919), *Seeing the Invisible*

---

311 Jesus, All for Jesus

We take captive every thought to make it obedient to Christ. 2 Corinthians 10:5

Je - sus, all for Je - sus, All I am and have
1.
and ev-er hope to be.
2.
and ev-er hope to
be. All of my am-bi-tions, hopes and plans,
I sur-ren - der these
1.
in-to Your hands.

WORDS: Robin Mark, 20th century, Jennifer Atkinson, 20th century
MUSIC: Robin Mark, 20th century, Jennifer Atkinson, 20th century

JESUS, ALL FOR JESUS
Irregular

2.
into Your hands. For it's
only in Your will that I am free. For it's only in
Your will that I am free. Jesus,
all for Jesus, All I am and have
and ever hope to be.
1.
For it's
2.

Optional segue to "I Surrender All." No transition required.

312 I Surrender All

We have left everything to follow you! Mark 10:28

1. All to Je - sus I sur - ren - der, All to Him I free - ly give.
2. All to Je - sus I sur - ren - der, Hum - bly at His feet I bow,
3. All to Je - sus I sur - ren - der, Make me, Sav - ior, whol - ly Thine.
4. All to Je - sus, I sur - ren - der, Lord, I give my - self to Thee.
I will ev - er love and trust Him, In His pres - ence dai - ly live.
World - ly pleas - ures all for - sak - en. Take me, Je - sus, take me now.
Let me feel the Ho - ly Spir - it, Tru - ly know that Thou art mine.
Fill me with Thy love and pow - er, Let Thy bless - ing fall on me.
Refrain
I sur - ren - der all. I sur - ren - der all.
All to Thee, my bless - ed Sav - ior, I sur - ren - der all.

WORDS: Judson W. Van De Venter, 1855-1939
MUSIC: Winfield S. Weeden, 1847-1908

SURRENDER
8.7.8.7. with Refrain

A Pleasing Sacrifice 313

Therefore, I urge you, brothers, in view of God's mercy, to offer your bodies as living sacrifices, holy and pleasing to God—this is your spiritual act of worship.

Do not conform any longer to the pattern of this world, but be transformed by the renewing of your mind. Then you will be able to test and approve what God's will is—his good, pleasing and perfect will. *Romans 12:1-2*

Since, then, you have been raised with Christ, set your hearts on things above, where Christ is seated at the right hand of God.

Set your minds on things above, not on earthly things.

For you died, and your life is now hidden with Christ in God.

When Christ, who is your life, appears, then you also will appear with him in glory. *Colossians 3:1-4*

Therefore, as God's chosen people, holy and dearly loved, clothe yourselves with compassion, kindness, humility, gentleness and patience.

Bear with each other and forgive whatever grievances you may have against one another. Forgive as the Lord forgave you.

And over all these virtues put on love, which binds them all together in perfect unity.

Let the peace of Christ rule in your hearts, since as members of one body you were called to peace. And be thankful.

Let the word of Christ dwell in you richly as you teach and admonish one another with all wisdom, and as you sing psalms, hymns and spiritual songs with gratitude in your hearts to God.

And whatever you do, whether in word or deed, do it all in the name of the Lord Jesus, giving thanks to God the Father through him.

Colossians 3:12-17

PRAYER FOR DISCERNMENT

Grant me, O Lord, to know what I ought to know,
to love what I ought to love,
to praise what delights You the most,
to value what is precious in your sight,
to hate what is offensive to You.
Do not allow me to judge according to the sight of my eyes,
nor pass sentence according to the hearing of the ears of ignorant persons,
but to discern with true judgment between things visible and spiritual,
and above all, always to inquire what is the good pleasure of Your will. Amen.

Thomas á Kempis (15th century)

OUR EXAMPLE

MEDLEY

O, to Be Like Thee, Blessed Redeemer
Let the Beauty of Jesus

314 O, to Be Like Thee, Blessed Redeemer

Be imitators of God . . . and live a life of love, just as Christ loved us. Ephesians 5:1

1. O, to be like Thee! bless-ed Re-deem-er, This is my con-stant long-ing and prayer. Glad-ly I'll for-feit all of earth's treas-ures, Je-sus, Thy per-fect like-ness to wear.
2. O, to be like Thee! full of com-pas-sion, Lov-ing, for-giv-ing, ten-der, and kind, Help-ing the help-less, cheer-ing the faint-ing, Seek-ing the wan-dering sin-ner to find.
3. O, to be like Thee! low-ly in spir-it, Ho-ly and harm-less, pa-tient and brave, Meek-ly en-dur-ing cru-el re-proach-es, Will-ing to suf-fer oth-ers to save.
4. O, to be like Thee! while I am plead-ing, Pour out Thy Spir-it, fill with Thy love. Make me a tem-ple fit for Thy dwell-ing, Fit me for life and heav-en a-bove.
Refrain
O, to be like Thee! O, to be like Thee, Bless-ed Re-deem-er, pure as Thou art! Come in Thy

WORDS: Thomas O. Chisholm, 1866-1960
MUSIC: William J. Kirkpatrick, 1838-1921

RONDINELLA
10.9.10.9. with Refrain

Song Ending
sweet-ness, come in Thy full-ness. Stamp Thine own im-age deep on my heart.
Optional transition to "Let the Beauty of Jesus."
heart.
rit.

Let the Beauty of Jesus 315

We . . . are being transformed into his likeness. 2 Corinthians 3:18

Let the beau-ty of Je-sus be seen in me,
All His won-der-ful pas-sion and pu - ri - ty.
O Thou Spir-it di-vine, All my na-ture re-fine
Till the beau-ty of Je-sus be seen in me.

WORDS: Albert Osborn, 1886-1967
MUSIC: Arr. Richard Hainsworth, 1885-1959

BEAUTY OF JESUS
Irregular

316 Search Me, O God

. . . and know my heart. Psalm 139:23

1. Search me, O God, search me and know my heart.
2. Christ is the same, yes - ter - day and to - day.
3. Change my de - sire, cause me to on - ly love
4. Lord, let my work stand through the test - ing day
Try me and prove me in the hid - den part.
O, make His life in me the same al - ways.
That which for - ev - er shall a - bid - ing prove.
Which will con - sume the stub - ble and the hay.
Cleanse me and make me ho - ly as Thou art, And
Take from my heart the things that pass a - way, And
Help me to lay my treas - ures up a - bove, And
Help me to build up - on the rock, I pray, And
lead me in the way ev - er - last - ing, And
lead me in the way ev - er - last - ing, And
lead me in the way ev - er - last - ing, And
lead me in the way ev - er - last - ing, And

WORDS: Albert B. Simpson, 1843-1919; adapt. Gene Rivard, b. 1949
MUSIC: Albert B. Simpson, 1843-1919; adapt. Gene Rivard, b. 1949; harm. Eldon McBride, b. 1962

SEARCH ME
Irregular with Refrain

lead me in the way ev - er - last - ing.
lead me in the way ev - er - last - ing.
lead me in the way ev - er - last - ing.
lead me in the way ev - er - last - ing.
Optional Refrain
Lead me, lead me, lead me in the way ev - er - last - ing;
Keep me from the things that with-er and de-cay; Give to me the things that
can-not pass a-way— And lead me in the way ev - er - last - ing.

OUR SURRENDER

MEDLEY

Take My Life, and Let It Be Consecrated
Sanctuary

317 Take My Life, and Let It Be Consecrated

Consecrate yourselves and be holy, because I am holy. Leviticus 11:44

1. Take my life, and let it be Con - se - crat - ed, Lord, to Thee. Take my mo - ments and my days, Let them flow in cease - less praise, Let them flow in cease - less praise.
2. Take my hands, and let them move At the im - pulse of Thy love. Take my feet, and let them be Swift and beau - ti - ful for Thee, Swift and beau - ti - ful for Thee.
3. Take my voice, and let me sing Al - ways, on - ly for my King. Take my lips, and let them be Filled with mes - sag - es from Thee, Filled with mes - sag - es from Thee.
4. Take my sil - ver and my gold, Not a mite[1] would I with - hold. Take my in - tel - lect, and use Ev - ery power as Thou shalt choose, Ev - ery power as Thou shalt choose.
5. Take my will, and make it Thine. It shall be no long - er mine. Take my heart; it is Thine own. It shall be Thy roy - al throne, It shall be Thy roy - al throne.
6. Take my love; my Lord, I pour At Thy feet its treas - ure store. Take my - self, and I will be Ev - er, on - ly, all for Thee, Ev - er, on - ly, all for Thee.
Song ending

WORDS: Frances R. Havergal, 1836-1879
MUSIC: Henri A.C. Malan, 1787-1864

HENDON
7.7.7.7. with repeat

1. *mite: the smallest coin*

Optional transition to "Sanctuary."
all for Thee.
rit.
Sanctuary 318
We are the temple of the living God. 2 Corinthians 6:16
Lord, pre - pare me to be a sanc - tu - ar - y, pure and
ho - ly, tried and true; With thanks - giv - ing, I'll be a
liv - ing sanc - tu - ar - y for you.

WORDS: John Thompson, b. 1950; Randy Scruggs, 20th century
MUSIC: John Thompson, b. 1950; Randy Scruggs, 20th century

SANCTUARY
Irregular

319 Ho, Everyone That Is Thirsty

I will pour water on him who is thirsty. Isaiah 44:3, NKJV

1. Ho, ev-ery - one that is thirst - y in spir - it! Ho, ev-ery - one that is wea-ry and sad! Come to the foun-tain; there's full-ness in Je - sus— All that you're long-ing for, come and be glad.
2. Child of the world, are you tired of your bond-age? Wea - ry of earth-joys, so false, so un - true? Thirst-ing for God, and His full-ness of bless - ing? Hear the great prom-ise— a mes-sage for you.
3. Child of the king-dom, be filled with the Spir - it. Noth-ing but full - ness your long-ing can meet. 'Tis the en - dow-ment for life and for ser - vice— Yours is the prom-ise, so cer-tain, so sweet.
Refrain
"I will pour wa - ter on him who is thirst - y, I will pour

WORDS: Lucy J. Rider, 1849-1922, alt.
MUSIC: Lucy J. Rider, 1849-1922

RIDER
11.10.11.10. with Refrain

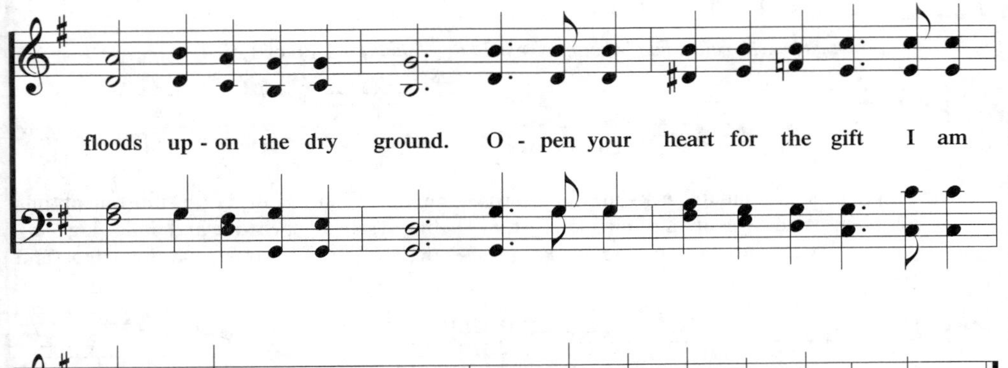
floods up - on the dry ground. O - pen your heart for the gift I am

bring - ing, While you are seek - ing me, I will be found."

Holy Spirit Fruit 320

So I say, live by the Spirit, and you will not gratify the desires of the sinful nature.

For the sinful nature desires what is contrary to the Spirit, and the Spirit what is contrary to the sinful nature. They are in conflict with each other, so that you do not do what you want.

But if you are led by the Spirit, you are not under law.

The acts of the sinful nature are obvious: sexual immorality, impurity and debauchery;

idolatry and witchcraft; hatred, discord, jealousy, fits of rage, selfish ambition, dissensions, factions and envy;

drunkenness, orgies, and the like. I warn you, as I did before, that those who live like this will not inherit the kingdom of God.

But the fruit of the Spirit is love, joy, peace, patience, kindness, goodness, faithfulness, gentleness and self-control.

Against such things there is no law.

Those who belong to Christ Jesus have crucified the sinful nature with its passions and desires.

Since we live by the Spirit, let us keep in step with the Spirit. Let us not become conceited, provoking and envying each other.

Galatians 5:16-26

321 I Want to Be Holy

Just as he who called you is holy, so be holy in all you do. 1 Peter 1:15

1. O souls that are seek-ing for pleas - ure, Who emp-ty a-muse-ments pur-
2. I am wea-ry of sin-ning and stum - bling, Re - pent-ing and fall - ing a -
3. I want to be pa-tient and gen - tle, True - heart-ed, and lov - ing, and
sue, Who strive for the priz - es of for - tune, Such
gain. I am tired of re - solv - ing and striv - ing, And
kind, As quick to ac - know - ledge my fail - ings As
tri - fles may an - swer for you. But mine is a no - bler am -
find - ing the strug - gle so vain. I long for an arm to up -
I to an - oth - er's am blind. I want to be qui - et and
bi - tion, I seek for a rich - er re - ward. I
hold me, A will that is strong - er than mine. A
peace - ful, Though tem - pests a - round me may roll; The

WORDS: Albert B. Simpson, 1843-1919; adapt. Gene Rivard, b. 1949
MUSIC: Gene Rivard, b. 1949; arr. Eldon McBride, b. 1962

REGINA
Irregular

want to be Christ-like and ho - ly, I want to be just like my
Sav - ior to cleanse me and fill me, And keep me by pow - er di -
still - ness of Je - sus with - in me, Pos - sess - ing and fill - ing my
Refrain
Lord.
vine. I long, O, I long to be ho - ly, Con -
soul.
formed to His will and His Word. O, I want to be gen - tle and
Christ - like, I want to be just like my Lord.

322 Bring Your Vessels, Not a Few

Ask all your neighbors for empty jars. Don't ask for just a few. 2 Kings 4:3

1. Are you long-ing for the full-ness of the bless - ing of the Lord
2. Bring your emp - ty earth - en ves - sels, clean through Je - sus' pre - cious blood.
3. Like the jar of oil un - fail - ing is His grace for - ev - er - more,
In your heart and life to - day? Claim the prom - ise of your Fa - ther, come ac -
Come, ye need - y, one and all, And in hum - ble con - se - cra - tion wait be -
And His love un - chang - ing still, And ac - cord - ing to His prom - ise with the
cord - ing to His Word In the bless - ed old - time way.
fore the throne of God Till the Ho - ly Ghost shall fall.
Ho - ly Ghost and power, He will ev - ery ves - sel fill.
Refrain
He will fill your heart to - day to ov - er - flow - ing,
He will fill your heart to ov - er - flow - ing,

WORDS: Lelia N. Morris, 1862-1929, alt.
MUSIC: Lelia N. Morris, 1862-1929

VESSELS
Irregular

As the Lord com-mand - eth you, "Bring your ves - sels, not a few,"
He will fill your heart to-day to ov - er - flow - ing
He will fill your heart to ov - er-flow - ing,
With the Ho - ly Ghost and power.

PRAYER OF LONGING FOR GOD

God, I have tasted Your goodness,
and it has both satisfied me and made me thirsty for more.
I am painfully conscious of my need for further grace.
I am ashamed of my lack of desire.
O God, the triune God, I want to want You; I long to be filled with longing;
I thirst to be made more thirsty still.
Show me Your glory, I pray, so that I may know You indeed.
Begin in mercy a new work of love within me.
Say to my soul, "Rise up, my love, my fair one, and come away."
Then give me grace to rise and follow You
up from this misty lowland where I have wandered so long.
In Jesus' name, Amen.

A.W. Tozer (1897-1963), *The Pursuit of God* (adapt.)

323 As the Deer

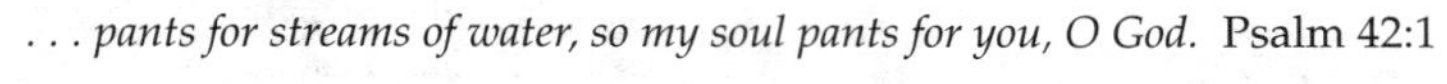
. . . pants for streams of water, so my soul pants for you, O God. Psalm 42:1

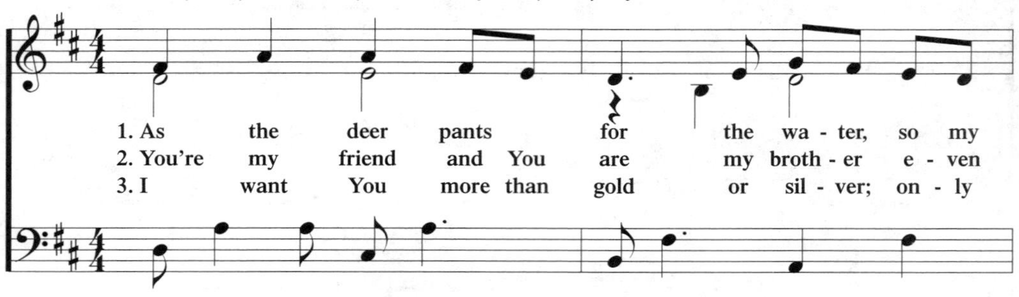
1. As the deer pants for the wa - ter, so my
2. You're my friend and You are my broth - er e - ven
3. I want You more than gold or sil - ver; on - ly

soul longs af - ter You. You a - lone are my
though You are a King. I love you more than
You can sat - is - fy. You a - lone are the

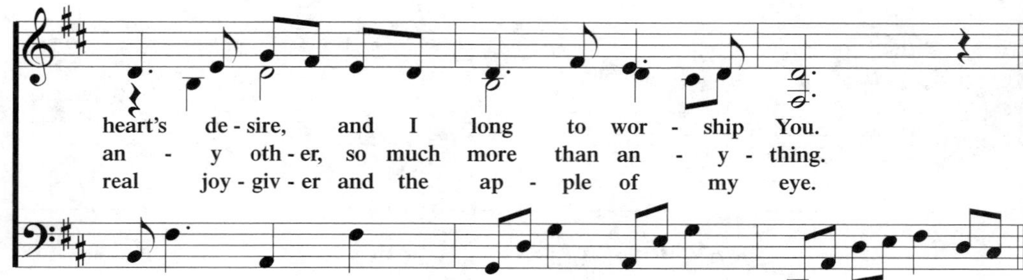
heart's de - sire, and I long to wor - ship You.
an - y oth - er, so much more than an - y - thing.
real joy - giv - er and the ap - ple of my eye.

Refrain
You a - lone are my strength, my shield. To You a - lone may my

WORDS: Martin Nystrom, b. 1956
MUSIC: Martin Nystrom, b. 1956

AS THE DEER
Irregular

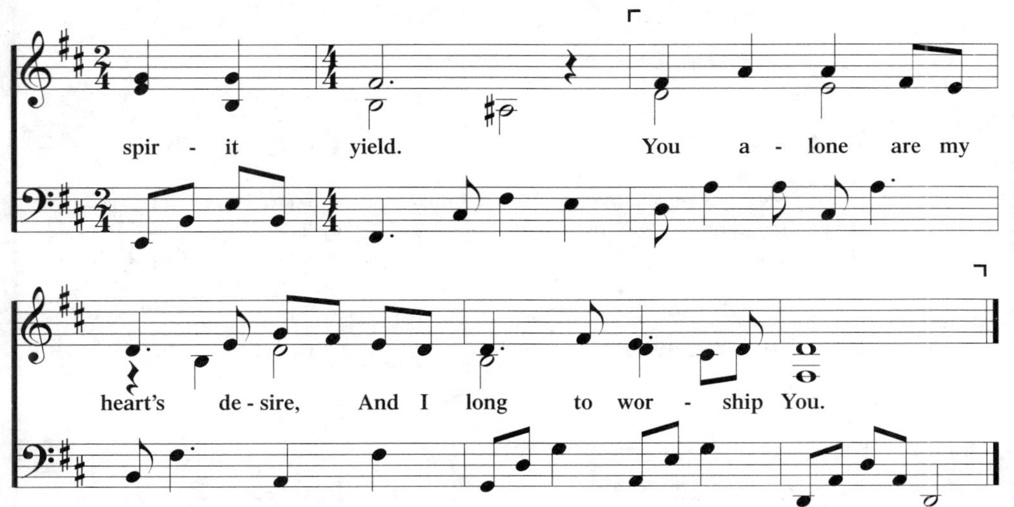
spir - it yield. You a - lone are my
heart's de - sire, And I long to wor - ship You.

Jesus Calls Us 324

"Come follow me," Jesus said. Matthew 4:19

1. Je - sus calls us o'er the tu - mult Of our life's wild, rest - less sea.
Day by day His voice is sound - ing, Say - ing, "Chris - tian, fol - low Me."

2. Je - sus calls us from the wor - ship Of the vain world's gold - en store,
From each i - dol that would keep us, Say - ing, "Chris - tian, love Me more."

3. In our joys and in our sor - rows, Days of toil and hours of ease,
Still He calls, in cares and plea - sures, "Chris - tian, love Me more than these."

4. Je - sus calls us. By Your mer - cies, Sav - ior, may we hear Your call;
Give our hearts to Your o - be - dience, Serve and love You best of all.

WORDS: Cecil F.H. Alexander, 1818-1895, alt.
MUSIC: William H. Jude, 1852-1922

GALILEE
8.7.8.7.

325 Open My Eyes That I May See

. . . wonderful things in your law. Psalm 119:18

1. O - pen my eyes that I may see Glimp - ses of truth Thou hast for me;
2. O - pen my mind that I may read More of Thy love in word and deed.
3. O - pen my way that I may bring Tro - phies of grace to Christ, my King;
Place in my hands the won - der - ful key That shall un-clasp and set me free.
What shall I fear while yet Thou dost lead? On - ly for light from Thee I plead.
Ech - oed in love Thy Word shall out-ring, Sweet as the note that an - gels sing.
Refrain
Si - lent - ly now I wait for Thee, Read - y, my God, Thy will to see;
Si - lent - ly now I wait for Thee, Read - y, my God, Thy will to see;
Si - lent - ly now I wait for Thee, Read - y, my God, Thy will to see;
O - pen my eyes, il - lu - mine me, Spir - it di - vine!
O - pen my mind, il - lu - mine me, Spir - it di - vine!
O - pen my way, il - lu - mine me, Spir - it di - vine!

WORDS: Clara H. Scott, 1841-1897, alt.
MUSIC: Clara H. Scott, 1841-1897

SCOTT
Irregular

How Blest Are They 326

For the LORD knows the way of the righteous . . . Psalm 1:6, NKJV

1. How blest are they who turn from sin, In whom God's word dwells deep within. Rejecting wrong, they love the right, And hear His voice both day and night.
2. They shall be like tall lovely trees, Who spread their green, undying leaves, And drinking deep from flowing streams, They bear sweet fruit, and God is pleased.
3. But those who choose unrighteousness Walk aimless paths, alone, unblessed. For God attends His children's way, Watching in love, how blest are they.
1, 2.
3.

(For different harmony and higher key, see No. 451)

WORDS: Gene Rivard, b. 1949; para. Psalm 1
MUSIC: Traditional English melody; arr. Gene Rivard, b. 1949

O WALY WALY
L.M.

327 My Goal Is God Himself

. . . so that God may be all in all. 1 Corinthians 15:28

1. My goal is God Him - self— not joy, nor peace,
2. So faith bounds for - ward to its goal in God,
3. No mat - ter if the way be some - times dark,
4. One thing I know, I can - not turn a - way.
Nor e - ven bless - ing, but Him - self, my God.
And love can trust her Lord to lead her there.
No mat - ter though the cost be of - ten great,
One thing I do, I press to - wards my Lord.
'Tis His to lead me there, not mine, but His;
Up - held by Him, my soul is fol - lowing hard,
Well does He know the path to reach the mark;
My God my glo - ry here from day to day,
"At an - y cost, dear Lord, by an - y road!"
Till God has full ful - filled my deep - est prayer.
The way that leads me to Him must be straight.
And in the glo - ry there, my great re - ward.

WORDS: F. Brook, 19th century, alt.
MUSIC: William H. Monk, 1823-1889

EVENTIDE
10.10.10.10.

Be Thou My Vision 328

Blessed are those . . . who walk in the light of your presence, O Lord. Psalm 89:15

1. Be Thou my Vi - sion, O Lord of my heart,
2. Be Thou my Wis - dom and Thou my true Word,
3. Rich - es I heed not, nor man's emp - ty praise,
4. High King of heav - en, my vic - to - ry won,
Nought be all else to me, save that Thou art;
I ev - er with Thee and Thou with me, Lord;
Thou mine In - her - it - ance now and al - ways;
May I reach heav - en's joys, O bright heaven's Sun!
Thou my best thought by day or by night,
Thou my great Fa - ther, I Thy true son,
Thou and Thou on - ly, first in my heart,
Heart of my own heart, what - ev - er be - fall,
Wak - ing or sleep - ing, Thy pres - ence my light.
Thou in me dwell - ing, and I with Thee one.
High King of heav - en, my Treas - ure Thou art.
Still be my Vi - sion, O Rul - er of all.

WORDS: Irish hymn, 8th century; tr. Mary E. Byrne, 1880-1931; adapt. Eleanor H. Hull, 1860-1935
MUSIC: Irish melody; arr. Norman Johnson, b. 1928

SLANE
10.10.9.10.

329 Draw Me Nearer

Come near to God and he will come near to you. James 4:8

1. I am Thine, O Lord, I have heard Thy voice, And it
2. Con - se - crate me now to Thy ser - vice, Lord, By the
3. O, the pure de - light of a sin - gle hour That be -
4. There are depths of love that I can - not know Till I
told Thy love to me. But I long to rise in the
power of grace di - vine. Let my soul look up with a
fore Thy Throne I spend, When I kneel in prayer, and with
cross the nar - row sea.1 There are heights of joy that I
arms of faith And be clos - er drawn to Thee
stead - fast hope, And my will be lost in Thine.
Thee my God, I com - mune as friend with friend!
may not reach Till I rest in peace with Thee.
Refrain
Draw me near - er,
near - er, bless - ed Lord, To the cross where Thou hast died. Draw me
near - er, near - er, near - er bless - ed Lord, To Thy pre - cious, bleed - ing side.

WORDS: Fanny J. Crosby, 1820-1915
MUSIC: William H. Doane, 1832-1915

I AM THINE
10.7.10.7. with Refrain

1. *pass from this life to the next*

Higher Ground 330

I press on toward the goal to win the prize. Philippians 3:14

1. I'm press - ing on the up - ward way, New heights I'm gain - ing every day. Still pray - ing as I on - ward bound, "Lord, plant my feet on high - er ground."
2. I want to live a - bove the world, Though Sa - tan's darts at me are hurled. For faith has caught the joy - ful sound, The song of saints on high - er ground.
3. I want to scale the ut - most height And catch a gleam of glo - ry bright. But still I'll pray till heaven I've found, "Lord, lead me on to high - er ground."
Refrain
Lord, lift me up, and let me stand By faith on heav - en's ta - ble - land; A high - er plane than I have found— Lord, plant my feet on high - er ground.

WORDS: Johnson Oatman, Jr., 1856-1926
MUSIC: Charles H. Gabriel, 1856-1932

HIGHER GROUND
L.M. with Refrain

331 Deeper and Deeper

Blessed are those who hunger and thirst for righteousness, for they will be filled. Matthew 5:6

1. In - to the heart of Je - sus, deep - er and deep - er I go,
2. In - to the will of Je - sus, deep - er and deep - er I go,
3. In - to the cross of Je - sus, deep - er and deep - er I go,
4. In - to the joy of Je - sus, deep - er and deep - er I go,
5. In - to the love of Je - sus, deep - er and deep - er I go,
Seek - ing to know the rea - son why He should love me so,
Pray - ing for grace to fol - low, seek - ing His way to know,
Fol - low - ing through the gar - den, fac - ing the dread - ed foe,
Ris - ing with soul en - rap - tured far from the world be - low,
Prais - ing the One who brought me out of my sin and woe,
Why He should stoop to lift me up from the mir - y clay,
Bow - ing in full sur - ren - der low at His bless - ed feet,
Drink - ing the cup of sor - row, sob - bing with bro - ken heart,
Joy in the place of sor - row, peace in the midst of pain,
And through e - ter - nal a - ges grate - ful - ly I shall sing,
Sav - ing my soul, mak - ing me whole, Though I had wan - dered a - way.
Bid - ding Him take, break me and make, Till I am mold - ed and meet.
"O Sav - ior, help! Dear Sav - ior, help! Grace for my weak - ness im - part."
Je - sus will give, Je - sus will give, He will up - hold and sus - tain.
"O, how He loved! O, how He loved! Je - sus, my Lord and my King!"

WORDS: Oswald J. Smith, 1889-1986
MUSIC: Oswald J. Smith, 1889-1986

DEEPER
7.7.7.6.7.6.4.4.6.

Fully Surrendered 332

Offer your bodies as living sacrifices, holy and pleasing to God. Romans 12:1

1. Ful - ly sur - ren - dered, Lord, I would be,
2. Ful - ly sur - ren - dered— life, time and all,
3. Ful - ly sur - ren - dered— sil - ver and gold,
4. Ful - ly sur - ren - dered, Lord, I am Thine;
Ful - ly sur - ren - dered, dear Lord, to Thee.
All Thou hast given me held at Thy call.
His, who hath given me rich - es un - told.
Ful - ly sur - ren - dered, Sav - ior di - vine!
All on the al - tar laid, Sur - ren - der ful - ly made,
Speak but the word to me, Glad - ly I'll fol - low Thee,
All, all be - long to Thee, For Thou didst pur - chase me,
Live Thou Thy life in me; All full - ness dwells in Thee;
Thou hast my ran - som paid; I yield to Thee.
Now and e - ter - nal - ly O - bey my Lord.
Thine ev - er - more to be, Je - sus, my Lord.
Not I, but Christ in me, Christ all in all.

WORDS: Alfred C. Snead, 1884-1961
MUSIC: George C. Stebbins, 1846-1945

FULLY SURRENDERED
Irregular

333 May the Mind of Christ, My Savior

Your attitude should be the same as that of Christ Jesus. Philippians 2:5

1. May the mind of Christ, my Sav - ior, Live in me from day to day,
2. May the Word of God dwell rich - ly In my heart from hour to hour,
3. May the peace of God, my Fa - ther, Rule my life in ev - ery - thing,
4. May the love of Je - sus fill me, As the wa - ters fill the sea;
5. May I run the race be - fore me, Strong and brave to face the foe,
6. May His beau - ty rest up - on me As I seek the lost to win,
By His love and power con - trol - ling All I do and say.
So that all may see I tri - umph On - ly through His power.
That I may be calm to com - fort Sick and sor - row - ing.
Him ex - alt - ing, self a - bas - ing— This is vic - to - ry.
Look - ing on - ly un - to Je - sus As I on - ward go.
And may they for - get the chan - nel, See - ing on - ly Him.

WORDS: Kate B. Wilkinson, 1859-1928
MUSIC: Arthur C. Barham-Gould, 1891-1953

ST. LEONARDS
8.7.8.5.

THE PRACTICE OF THE PRESENCE OF GOD

There is not in the world a kind of life more sweet and more delightful than that of continual walk with God; those only can comprehend it who practice and experience it. Yet I do not advise you to do it from that motive, it is not pleasure that we ought to seek in this exercise; but let us do it from the motive of love, and because God would have us so walk.

Were I a preacher, I should preach above all other things, the practice of the Presence of God: Were I a teacher, I should advise all the world to it; so necessary do I think it, and so easy.

Nicholas Herman [Brother Lawrence] (1611-1691)

I Need Thee Every Hour 334

Hear, O LORD, and answer me, for I am poor and needy. Psalm 86:1

1. I need Thee ev - ery hour, Most gra - cious Lord.
2. I need Thee ev - ery hour; Stay Thou near by.
3. I need Thee ev - ery hour, In joy or pain.
4. I need Thee ev - ery hour, Most Ho - ly One.
No ten - der voice like Thine Can peace af - ford.
Temp - ta - tions lose their power When Thou art nigh.
Come quick - ly and a - bide, Or life is vain.
O, make me Thine in - deed, Thou bless - ed Son!
Refrain
I need Thee, oh, I need Thee! Ev - ery hour I need Thee!
Oh, bless me now, my Sav - ior, I come to Thee!

WORDS: Annie S. Hawks, 1835-1918; Refrain, Robert Lowry, 1826-1899
MUSIC: Robert Lowry, 1826-1899

NEED
6.4.6.4. with Refrain

335 Knowing You

I consider everything a loss compared to the surpassing greatness of knowing Christ Jesus my Lord. Philippians 3:8

1. All I once held dear, built my life up - on, All this
(2.) heart's de - sire is to know You more, To be
(3.) know the power of Your ris - en life, And to
world re - veres, and wars to own, All I once thought gain I have
found in You and known as Yours, To pos - sess by faith what I
know You in Your suf - fer - ings. To be - come like You in Your
count - ed loss, Spent and worth - less now, com - pared to
could not earn, All - sur - pass - ing gift of right - eous -
death, my Lord, So with You to live and nev - er
this.
ness.
die.
Refrain
Know - ing You, Je - sus, know - ing You; There

WORDS: Graham Kendrick, b. 1950
MUSIC: Graham Kendrick, b. 1950

KNOWING YOU
Irregular

is no great - er thing. You're my all, You're the best, You're my
1, 2.
joy, my right-eous-ness, And I love You, Lord.
2. Now my
3. O, to
3.
love You, Lord, love You, Lord.

HOW CAN WE LIVE LIVES ACCEPTABLE TO GOD?

Vacate the throne room of your heart and enthrone Jesus there. Set Him in the focus of your heart's attention and stop wanting to be a hero. Make Him your all in all and try yourself to become less and less. Dedicate your entire life to His honor alone and shift the motives of your life from self to God. Let the reason back of your daily conduct be Christ and His glory, not yourself, not your family nor your country nor your church. In all things let Him have the preeminence.

A.W. Tozer (1897-1963), *Born After Midnight*

336 I Am Crucified with Christ

I no longer live, but Christ lives in me. Galatians 2:20

1. When Je - sus died on Cal - va - ry, I too was
rose with life di - vine, I too was
comes some day for me, I shall be
there, I too was there. There in my
there, I too was there. His res - ur -
there, I shall be there. With Him and
place He hung for me, And now ac - cept - ed just as
rec - tion power is mine, And as the branch - es on the
like Him I shall be, And all His glo - rious maj - es -
He, His name I bear.
vine, His life I share. I am
ty, I too shall share.
Refrain

WORDS: Albert B. Simpson, 1843-1919; adapt. Gene Rivard, b. 1949
MUSIC: Gene Rivard, b. 1949; arr. Eldon McBride, b. 1962

SANCTIFIER
Irregular with Refrain

cru - ci - fied with Christ, but Christ now lives in me. I
live by faith in the Son of God who gave His life for me, Who
gave His life for me.
1, 2.
me.
2. When Je - sus
3. When Je - sus
3.
me.

PRAYER FOR A GODLY LIFE

Steadfast hearts, which no unworthy thought can drag downwards;
Unconquered hearts, which no tribulations can wear out;
Upright hearts, which no unworthy purpose may tempt aside;
Bestow upon us also, O Lord God,
Understanding to know You,
Diligence to seek You,
Wisdom to find You,
And a faithfulness that may finally embrace You,
Through Jesus Christ our Lord, Amen.

Thomas á Kempis (15th century)

337 Revive Us Again

Revive us, and we will call on your name. Psalm 80:18

1. We praise Thee, O God, for the Son of Thy love,
2. We praise Thee, O God, for Thy Spir - it of light,
3. All glo - ry and praise to the Lamb that was slain,
4. Re - vive us a - gain, fill each heart with Thy love.
For Je - sus who died and is now gone a - bove.
Who has shown us our Sav - ior and scat - tered our night.
Who has borne all our sins and has cleansed ev - ery stain.
May each soul be re - kin - dled with fire from a - bove.
Refrain
Hal - le - lu - jah! Thine the glo - ry, Hal - le - lu - jah! A - men.
Hal - le - lu - jah! Thine the glo - ry; Re - vive us a - gain.

WORDS: William P. Mackay, 1839-1885
MUSIC: John J. Husband, 1760-1825

REVIVE US AGAIN
11.11. with Refrain

Send Refreshing 338

Christ loved the church . . . cleansing her by the washing with water through the word.
Ephesians 5:25-26

1. Heaven-ly Fa-ther, we Your child-ren, Gath-ered round our ris-en Lord,
2. Gra-cious gales of heaven-ly bless-ing In Your love to us af-ford.
3. Weak and wea-ry in the con-flict, Wres-tling "not with flesh and blood,"
4. With Your strength, O Mas-ter, gird us; Be our guide and be our guard;
Lift our hearts in ear-nest plead-ing— O, re-vive us by Your Word!
Let us feel Your Spir-it's pres-ence— O, re-vive us by Your Word!
Help us, Lord, as faint we fal-ter— O, re-vive us by Your Word!
Fill us with Your Ho-ly Spir-it— O, re-vive us by Your Word!
Refrain
Send re-fresh-ing, send re-fresh-ing From Your pres-ence, gra-cious Lord!
Send re-fresh-ing, send re-fresh-ing And re-vive us by Your Word!

WORDS: Daniel W. Whittle, 1840-1901, alt.
MUSIC: Arthur B. Hunt, 1890-1971

SEND REFRESHING
8.7.8.7. with Refrain

339 The Solid Rock

No one can lay any foundation other than . . . Jesus Christ. 1 Corinthians 3:11

1. My hope is built on noth-ing less Than Je - sus' blood and right - eous - ness.
2. When dark-ness veils His love - ly face, I rest on His un - chang - ing grace.
3. His oath, His cov - e - nant, His blood Sup - port me in the whelm-ing flood.
4. When He shall come with trum-pet sound, O, may I then in Him be found.
I dare not trust the sweet - est frame[1] But whol - ly lean on Je - sus' name.
In ev - ery high and storm - y gale My an - chor holds with - in the veil.[2]
When all a - round my soul gives way He then is all my hope and stay.
Dressed in His right-eous - ness a - lone, Fault - less to stand be - fore the throne!
Refrain
On Christ, the sol - id rock I stand; All oth - er ground is sink - ing sand, All oth - er ground is sink - ing sand.

WORDS: Edward Mote, 1797-1874
MUSIC: William B. Bradbury, 1816-1868

SOLID ROCK
L.M. with Refrain

1. *sweetest frame: best made structure*
2. *anchor holds within the veil: refers to the Holy of Holies, which was covered by the Tabernacle veil (Hebrews 6:19).*

Like a River Glorious 340

I will extend peace to her like a river. Isaiah 66:12

1. Like a riv-er glo-rious Is God's per-fect peace, O - ver all vic-to-rious In its bright in-crease. Per-fect, yet it flow-eth Ful-ler ev-ery day. Per-fect, yet it grow-eth Deep-er all the way.
2. Hid-den in the hol-low Of His bless-ed hand, Nev - er foe can fol-low, Nev-er trai-tor stand. Not a surge of wor-ry, Not a shade of care, Not a blast of hur-ry Touch the spir-it there.
3. Ev-ery joy or tri-al Fall-eth from a-bove, Traced up-on our di-al By the Sun of love. We may trust Him ful-ly, All for us to do. They who trust Him whol-ly Find Him whol-ly true.
Refrain
Stayed up-on Je-ho-vah Hearts are ful-ly blest, Find-ing as He prom-ised, Per-fect peace and rest.

(For alternate harmony, see No. 304)

WORDS: Frances R. Havergal, 1836-1879
MUSIC: James Mountain, 1843-1933

WYE VALLEY
6.5.6.5.D. with Refrain

341 'Tis So Sweet to Trust in Jesus

Do not let your hearts be troubled. Trust in God; trust also in me. John 14:1

1. 'Tis so sweet to trust in Je - sus, Just to take Him at His word,
2. O, how sweet to trust in Je - sus, Just to trust His cleans - ing blood,
3. Yes, 'tis sweet to trust in Je - sus, Just from sin and self to cease,
4. I'm so glad I learned to trust Thee, Pre - cious Je - sus, Sav - ior, Friend;
Just to rest up - on His prom - ise, Just to know, "Thus saith the Lord."
Just in sim - ple faith to plunge me 'Neath the heal - ing, cleans - ing flood.
Just from Je - sus sim - ply tak - ing Life and rest, and joy and peace.
And I know that Thou art with me, Will be with me to the end.
Refrain
Je - sus, Je - sus, how I trust Him, How I've proved Him o'er and o'er;
Je - sus, Je - sus, pre - cious Je - sus! O, for grace to trust Him more.

Optional segue to "He Is Able." No transition required

WORDS: Louisa M.R. Stead, 1850-1917
MUSIC: William J. Kirkpatrick, 1838-1921

TRUST IN JESUS
8.7.8.7. with Refrain

He Is Able 342

Now to him who is able to do immeasurably more than all we ask or imagine. Ephesians 3:20

He is a-ble, more than a-ble To ac-com-plish what con-cerns me to-day.
He is a-ble, more than a-ble To han-dle an-y-thing that comes my way.
He is a-ble, more than a-ble To do much more than I could ev - er dream.
He is a-ble, more than a-ble To make me what He wants me to be.

WORDS: Rory Noland, 20th century; Greg Ferguson, 20th century
MUSIC: Rory Noland, 20th century; Greg Ferguson, 20th century

HE IS ABLE
Irregular

343 Trusting Jesus

Trust in the L*ORD with all your heart.* Proverbs 3:5

1. Sim - ply trust - ing ev - ery day, Trust-ing through a storm - y way,
2. Bright - ly does His Spir - it shine In - to this poor heart of mine.
3. Sing - ing if my way is clear, Pray - ing if the path be drear,
4. Trust - ing Him while life shall last, Trust-ing Him till earth be past,
E - ven when my faith is small, Trust - ing Je - sus, that is all.
While He leads I can - not fall, Trust - ing Je - sus, that is all.
If in dan - ger, for Him call, Trust - ing Je - sus, that is all.
Till with - in the jas - per wall,1 Trust - ing Je - sus, that is all.
Refrain
Trust - ing as the mo - ments fly, Trust - ing as the days go by,
Trust - ing Him what - e'er be - fall, Trust - ing Je - sus, that is all.

WORDS: Edgar P. Stites, 1836-1921, alt.
MUSIC: Ira D. Sankey, 1840-1908

TRUSTING JESUS
7.7.7.7. with Refrain

1. *jasper wall: refers to Revelation 21:18, the jeweled walls of the new Jerusalem*

Blessed Assurance 344

Let us draw near to God with a sincere heart in full assurance of faith. Hebrews 10:22

1. Bless - ed as - sur - ance, Je - sus is mine! O, what a fore - taste of glo - ry di - vine! Heir of sal - va - tion, pur - chase of God, Born of His Spir - it, washed in His blood.
2. Per - fect sub - mis - sion, per - fect de - light, Vi - sions of rap - ture now burst on my sight. An - gels de - scend - ing, bring from a - bove Ech - oes of mer - cy, whis - pers of love.
3. Per - fect sub - mis - sion, all is at rest. I in my Sav - ior am hap - py and blest, Watch - ing and wait - ing, look - ing a - bove, Filled with His good - ness, lost in His love.
Refrain
This is my sto - ry, this is my song: Prais - ing my Sav - ior all the day long.
This is my sto - ry, this is my song: Prais - ing my Sav - ior all the day long.

WORDS: Fanny J. Crosby, 1820-1915
MUSIC: Phoebe P. Knapp, 1839-1908

ASSURANCE
9.10.9.9. with Refrain

345 Day by Day

My grace is sufficient for you, for my power is made perfect in weakness. 2 Corinthians 12:9

1. Day by day and with each pass - ing mo - ment Strength I find to meet my tri - als here; Trust - ing in my Fa - ther's wise be - stow - ment, I've no cause for wor - ry or for fear. He whose heart is kind be - yond all mea - sure Gives un -
2. Ev - ery day the Lord Him - self is near me, With a spe - cial mer - cy for each hour; All my cares He wants to bear, to cheer me, He whose name is Coun - sel - or and Power. The pro - tec - tion of His child and trea - sure Is a
3. Help me then in ev - ery tri - bu - la - tion So to trust Your prom - is - es, O Lord, That I lose not faith's sweet con - so - la - tion Of - fered me with - in Your ho - ly Word. Help me, Lord, when toil and trou - ble meet - ing, E'er to

WORDS: Carolina V.S. Berg, 1832-1903; tr. Andrew L. Skoog, 1856-1934, alt.
MUSIC: Oscar Ahnfelt, 1813-1882

BLOTT EN DAG
Irregular

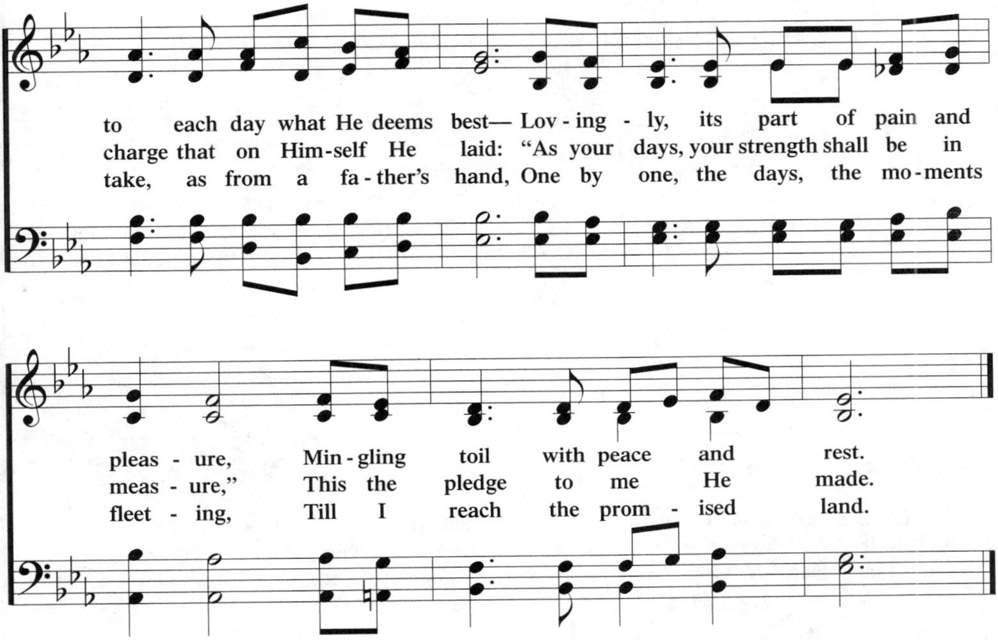

to each day what He deems best— Lov - ing - ly, its part of pain and
charge that on Him-self He laid: "As your days, your strength shall be in
take, as from a fa - ther's hand, One by one, the days, the mo-ments

pleas - ure, Min - gling toil with peace and rest.
meas - ure," This the pledge to me He made.
fleet - ing, Till I reach the prom - ised land.

My Times Are in Thy Hand 346

Deliver me from the hand of my enemies. Psalm 31:15, NKJV

1. My times are in Thy hand. My God, I wish them there. My life, my friends, my soul I leave En - tire - ly to Thy care.
2. My times are in Thy hand, What - ev - er they may be, Pleas - ing or pain - ful, dark or bright, As best may seem to Thee.
3. My times are in Thy hand, Je - sus, the cru - ci - fied! Those hands my cru - el sins had pierced Are now my guard and guide.
4. My times are in Thy hand, I'll al - ways trust in Thee, And af - ter death at Thy right hand I shall for - ev - er be.

WORDS: William F. Lloyd, 1791-1853
MUSIC: Lowell Mason, 1792-1872

BOYLSTON
S.M.

347 Trust and Obey

If you obey me fully . . . you will be my treasured possession. Exodus 19:5

1. When we walk with the Lord In the light of His Word, What a glo - ry He sheds on our way! While we do His good will, He a - bides with us still And with all who will trust and o - bey.
2. Not a shad - ow can rise, Not a cloud in the skies, But His smile quick - ly drives it a - way. Not a doubt nor a fear, Not a sigh nor a tear Can a - bide while we trust and o - bey.
3. But we nev - er can prove The de - lights of His love Un - til all on the al - tar we lay; For the fa - vor He shows And the joy He be - stows Are for them who will trust and o - bey.
4. Then in fel - low-ship sweet We will sit at His feet, Or we'll walk by His side in the way. What He says we will do, Where He sends we will go— Nev - er fear, on - ly trust and o - bey.
Refrain
Trust and o - bey, for there's no oth - er way To be hap - py in Je - sus, But to trust and o - bey.

Optional segue to "Yes, Lord, Yes." No transition required.

WORDS: John H. Sammis, 1846-1919
MUSIC: Daniel B. Towner, 1850-1919

TRUST AND OBEY
6.6.9.D. with Refrain

Yes, Lord, Yes 348

Speak, LORD, for your servant is listening. 1 Samuel 3:9

I'll say yes, Lord, yes to Your will and to Your way.
I'll say yes, Lord, yes; I will trust You and o-bey.
When Your Spir-it speaks to me, With my whole heart I'll a-gree,
And my an-swer will be yes, Lord, yes. (Lord, yes)

WORDS: Lynn Keesecker, b. 1953
MUSIC: Lynn Keesecker, b. 1953

YES, LORD, YES
Irregular

349 Jesus Never Fails

Heaven and earth will pass away, but my words will never pass away. Matthew 24:35

1. Earth - ly friends may prove un - true, Doubts and fears as - sail.[1]
2. Though the sky be dark and drear, Fierce and strong the gale,
3. In life's dark and bit - ter hour Love will still pre - vail.
One still loves and care for you, One who will not fail.
Just re - mem - ber He is near And He will not fail.
Trust His ev - er - last - ing power. Je - sus will not fail.
Refrain
Je - sus nev - er fails. Je - sus nev - er fails.
Heaven and earth may pass a - way, But Je - sus nev - er fails.

WORDS: Arthur A. Luther, 1891-1960
MUSIC: Arthur A. Luther, 1891-1960

JESUS NEVER FAILS
7.5.7.5. with Refrain

1. *assail: attack*

Turn Your Eyes upon Jesus 350

Let us fix our eyes on Jesus, the author and perfecter of our faith. Hebrews 12:2

1. O soul, are you wea - ry and trou - bled? No light in the dark-ness you see? There's light for a look at the Sav - ior, And life more a - bun - dant and free!
2. Through death in - to life ev - er - last - ing He passed, and we fol - low Him there. O - ver us sin no more has do - min - ion— For more than con - querors we are!
3. His Word shall not fail you— He prom - ised. Be - lieve Him and all will be well. Then go to a world that is dy - ing, His per - fect sal - va - tion to tell!
Refrain
Turn your eyes up - on Je - sus, Look full in His won - der - ful face, And the things of earth will grow strange - ly dim In the light of His glo - ry and grace.

WORDS: Helen H. Lemmel, 1864-1961
MUSIC: Helen H. Lemmel, 1864-1961

LEMMEL
9.8.9.8. with Refrain

351 Hiding in Thee

Lead me to the rock that is higher than I. For you have been my refuge. Psalm 61:2, 3
1. O, safe to the Rock that is high - er than I,
2. In the calm of the noon - tide, in sor - row's lone hour,
3. How oft in the con - flict, when pressed by the foe,
My soul in its con - flicts and sor - rows would fly. So
In times when temp - ta - tion casts o'er me its power, In the
I have fled to my Re - fuge and breathed out my woe. How
sin - ful, so wea - ry, Thine, Thine would I be! Thou
tem - pests of life, on its wide, heav - ing sea, Thou
of - ten, when tri - als like sea bil - lows[1] roll, Have I
blest Rock of A - ges, I'm hid - ing in Thee.
blest Rock of A - ges, I'm hid - ing in Thee.
hid - den in Thee, O Thou Rock of my soul.
Refrain
Hid - ing in Thee,
Hid - ing in Thee, Thou blest Rock of A - ges, I'm hid - ing in Thee.

WORDS: William O. Cushing, 1823-1902
MUSIC: Ira D. Sankey, 1840-1908
1. billows: waves

HIDING IN THEE
11.11.11.11. with Refrain

It Is Well with My Soul 352

Let the peace of Christ rule in your hearts. Colossians 3:15

1. When peace like a river attendeth my way, When sorrows like sea billows[1] roll, Whatever my lot, Thou hast taught me to say, "It is well, it is well with my soul."
2. Though Satan should buffet,[2] though trials should come, Let this blest assurance control, That Christ hath regarded my helpless estate, And hath shed His own blood for my soul.
3. My sin— O, the bliss of this glorious thought— My sin, not in part but the whole, Is nailed to His cross and I bear it no more! Praise the Lord, praise the Lord, O my soul!
4. And, Lord, haste the day when the faith shall be sight, The clouds be rolled back as a scroll, The trump shall resound, and the Lord shall descend! Even so— it is well with my soul!
Refrain
It is well (It is well) with my soul (with my soul); It is well, it is well with my soul.

WORDS: Horatio G. Spafford, 1828-1888
MUSIC: Philip P. Bliss, 1838-1876

VILLE DU HAVRE
11.8.11.9. with Refrain

1. *billows: waves*
2. *buffet: hit with force*

353 Moment by Moment

There is a friend who sticks closer than a brother. Proverbs 18:24

1. Dy-ing with Je-sus, by death reck-oned mine, Liv-ing with Je-sus, a new life di-vine, Look-ing to Je-sus till glo-ry shall shine, Mo-ment by mo-ment, O Lord, I am Thine.
2. Nev-er a tri-al that He is not there, Nev-er a bur-den that He does not bear, Nev-er a sor-row that He does not share, Mo-ment by mo-ment I'm un-der His care.
3. Nev-er a heart-ache and nev-er a groan, Nev-er a tear-drop and nev-er a moan, Nev-er a dan-ger but there on the throne, Mo-ment by mo-ment, He thinks of His own.
4. Nev-er a weak-ness that He does not feel, Nev-er a sick-ness that He can-not heal. Mo-ment by mo-ment, in woe or in weal,[1] Je-sus, my Sav-ior, a-bides with me still.
Refrain
Mo-ment by mo-ment I'm kept in His love. Mo-ment by mo-ment I've life from a-bove. Look-ing to Je-sus till glo-ry shall shine, Mo-ment by mo-ment, O Lord, I am Thine.

WORDS: Daniel W. Whittle, 1840-1901, alt.
MUSIC: May W. Moody, 1870-1963

WHITTLE
10.10.10.10. with Refrain

1. weal: well-being

Keep His Commandments 354

Love the LORD your God and keep his requirements, his decrees, his laws and his commands always. *Deuteronomy 11:1*

Now what I [The LORD] am commanding you today is not too difficult for you or beyond your reach. It is not up in heaven, so that you have to ask, "Who will ascend into heaven to get it and proclaim it to us so we may obey it?"

Nor is it beyond the sea, so that you have to ask, "Who will cross the sea to get it and proclaim it to us so we may obey it?"

No, the word is very near you; it is in your mouth and in your heart so you may obey it. *Deuteronomy 30:11-14*

Do not let this Book of the Law depart from your mouth; meditate on it day and night, so that you may be careful to do everything written in it. Then you will be prosperous and successful. *Joshua 1:8*

Does the LORD delight in burnt offerings and sacrifices as much as in obeying the voice of the LORD?

To obey is better than sacrifice, and to heed is better than the fat of rams. *1 Samuel 15:22*

[Jesus said] "Whoever has my commands and obeys them, he is the one who loves me. He who loves me will be loved by my Father, and I too will love him and show myself to him."

"If anyone loves me, he will obey my teaching. My Father will love him, and we will come to him and make our home with him." *John 14:21, 23*

We know that we have come to know him if we obey his commands. *1 John 2:3*

355 Under His Wings

Under his wings you will find refuge. Psalm 91:4

1. Un-der His wings I am safe-ly a-bid-ing, Though the night deep-ens and tem-pests are wild, Still I can trust Him, I know He will keep me. He has re-deemed me, and I am His child.
2. Un-der His wings— what a ref-uge in sor-row! How the heart yearn-ing-ly turns to His rest! Of-ten when earth has no balm for my heal-ing, There I find com-fort, and there I am blest.
3. Un-der His wings— O, what pre-cious en-joy-ment! There will I hide till life's tri-als are o'er. Shel-tered, pro-tect-ed, no e-vil can harm me, Rest-ing in Je-sus I'm safe ev-er-more.
Refrain
Un-der His wings, un-der His wings, Who from His love can sev-er?
Un-der His wings my soul shall a-bide, Safe-ly a-bide for-ev-er.

WORDS: William O. Cushing, 1823-1902
MUSIC: Ira D. Sankey, 1840-1908

HINGHAM
11.10.11.10. with Refrain

Nearer, Still Nearer 356

Come near to God and he will come near to you. James 4:8

1. Near - er, still near - er, close to Thy heart, Draw me, my Sav - ior, so pre - cious Thou art. Fold me, O fold me close to Thy breast, Shel - ter me safe in that ha - ven of rest, Shel - ter me safe in that ha - ven of rest.
2. Near - er, still near - er— noth - ing I bring, Naught[1] as an of - fering to Je - sus, my King— On - ly my sin - ful, now con - trite heart. Grant me the cleans - ing Thy blood doth im - part, Grant me the cleans - ing Thy blood doth im - part.
3. Near - er, still near - er, Lord, to be Thine. Sin, with its fol - lies, I glad - ly re - sign, All of its plea - sures, pomp and its pride. Give me but Je - sus, my Lord cru - ci - fied, Give me but Je - sus, my Lord cru - ci - fied.
4. Near - er, still near - er, while life shall last, Till safe in glo - ry my an - chor is cast. Through end - less a - ges ev - er to be Near - er, my Sav - ior, still near - er to Thee, Near - er, my Sav - ior, still near - er to Thee.

WORDS: Lelia N. Morris, 1862-1929
MUSIC: Lelia N. Morris, 1862-1929

MORRIS
9.10.9.10. with repeat

1. naught: nothing

357 Leaning on the Everlasting Arms

The eternal God is your refuge, and underneath are the everlasting arms. Deuteronomy 33:27

1. What a fel - low - ship, what a joy di - vine, Lean - ing on the ev - er - last - ing arms. What a bless - ed - ness, what a peace is mine, Lean - ing on the ev - er - last - ing arms.
2. O, how sweet to walk in this pil - grim way, Lean - ing on the ev - er - last - ing arms. O, how bright the path grows from day to day, Lean - ing on the ev - er - last - ing arms.
3. What have I to dread, what have I to fear, Lean - ing on the ev - er - last - ing arms? I have bless - ed peace with my Lord so near, Lean - ing on the ev - er - last - ing arms.
Refrain
Lean - ing, Lean - ing on Je - sus, lean - ing, lean - ing on Je - sus, Safe and se - cure from all a - larms; Lean - ing, Lean - ing on Je - sus, lean - ing, lean - ing on Je - sus, Lean - ing on the ev - er - last - ing arms.

WORDS: Elisha A. Hoffman, 1839-1929
MUSIC: Anthony J. Showalter, 1858-1924

SHOWALTER
10.9.10.9. with Refrain

Learning to Lean 358

Come to me, all you who are weary and burdened, and I will give you rest. Matthew 11:28
Refrain
Learn-ing to lean, learn-ing to lean, I'm learn-ing to lean on Je - sus;
Find-ing more pow-er than I'd ev-er dreamed, I'm learn-ing to lean on Je - sus.
fine
1. A joy I can't ex - plain is fill - ing my soul Since the day I met Je - sus, my King. His bless - ed Ho - ly Spir - it is lead - ing my way— He is teach - ing, and I'm learn - ing to lean.
2. There's glo - ri - ous vic - tory each day now for me As I dwell in His peace so se - rene. He helps me with each task if on - ly I ask— Ev - ery day now I am learn - ing to lean.
D.C.

WORDS: John Stallings, b. 1938
MUSIC: John Stallings, b. 1938

LEARNING TO LEAN
Irregular

359 Standing on the Promises

He has given us his very great and precious promises. 2 Peter 1:4

1. Stand-ing on the prom-is-es of Christ, my King, Through e-ter-nal a-ges let His prais-es ring. Glo-ry in the high-est, I will shout and sing, Stand-ing on the prom-is-es of God.
2. Stand-ing on the prom-is-es that can-not fail, When the howl-ing storms of doubt and fear as-sail, By the liv-ing Word of God I shall pre-vail, Stand-ing on the prom-is-es of God.
3. Stand-ing on the prom-is-es of Christ the Lord, Bound to Him e-ter-nal-ly by love's strong cord, O-ver-com-ing dai-ly with the Spir-it's sword, Stand-ing on the prom-is-es of God.
4. Stand-ing on the prom-is-es I can-not fall, Lis-tening ev-ery mo-ment to the Spir-it's call, Rest-ing in my Sav-ior as my all in all, Stand-ing on the prom-is-es of God.
Refrain
Stand-ing, stand-ing, Standing on the
Stand-ing on the prom-is-es, stand-ing on the prom-is-es,

WORDS: Russell K. Carter, 1849-1928
MUSIC: Russell K. Carter, 1849-1928

PROMISES
11.11.11.9. with Refrain

prom - is - es of God, my Sav - ior; Stand - ing,
Stand - ing on the prom - is - es,
stand - ing, I'm stand - ing on the prom - is - es of God.
stand - ing on the prom - is - es,

I Am Trusting Thee, Lord Jesus 360

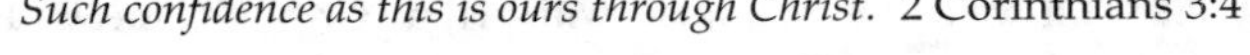
Such confidence as this is ours through Christ. 2 Corinthians 3:4

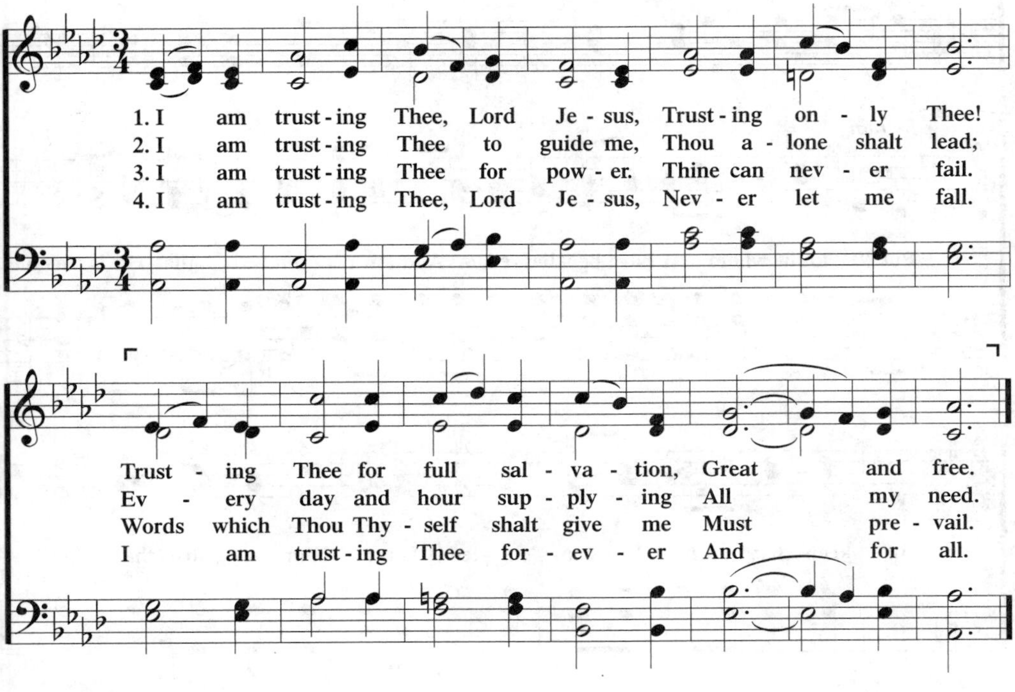

1. I am trust - ing Thee, Lord Je - sus, Trust - ing on - ly Thee!
Trust - ing Thee for full sal - va - tion, Great and free.

2. I am trust - ing Thee to guide me, Thou a - lone shalt lead;
Ev - ery day and hour sup - ply - ing All my need.

3. I am trust - ing Thee for pow - er. Thine can nev - er fail.
Words which Thou Thy - self shalt give me Must pre - vail.

4. I am trust - ing Thee, Lord Je - sus, Nev - er let me fall.
I am trust - ing Thee for - ev - er And for all.

WORDS: Frances R. Havergal, 1836-1879
MUSIC: Ethelbert W. Bullinger, 1837-1913

BULLINGER
8.5.8.3.

361 I Know Whom I Have Believed

. . . and am persuaded that He is able. 2 Timothy 1:12, NKJV

1. I know not why God's won-drous grace To me He hath made known,
2. I know not how this sav-ing faith To me He did im-part,
3. I know not how the Spir-it moves, Con-vinc-ing men of sin,
4. I know not what of good or ill May be re-served for me,
5. I know not when my Lord may come, At night or noon-day fair,
Nor why— un-wor-thy— Christ in love Re-deemed me for His own.
Nor how be-liev-ing in His Word Wrought peace with-in my heart.
Re-veal-ing Je-sus through the Word, Cre-at-ing faith in Him.
Of wea-ry ways or gold-en days, Be-fore His face I see.
Nor if I'll walk the vale[1] with Him Or meet Him in the air.
Refrain
But "I know whom I have be-liev-ed, And am per-suad-ed that He is a-ble
To keep that which I've com-mit-ted Un-to Him a-gainst that day."

WORDS: Daniel W. Whittle, 1840-1901
MUSIC: James McGranahan, 1840-1907

EL NATHAN
C.M. with Refrain

1. walk the vale: experience death

O Thou, in Whose Presence 362

You will fill me with joy in your presence. Psalm 16:11

1. O Thou, in whose pres - ence my soul takes de - light, On
2. Where dost Thou, dear Shep - herd, re - sort with Thy sheep, To
3. O, why should I wan - der, an a - lien from Thee, Or
4. He looks! And the thou - sands of an - gels re - joice, And
5. Dear Shep - herd, I hear and will fol - low Thy call. I
whom in af - flic - tion I call, My com - fort by day and my
feed them in pas - tures of love? Say, why in the val - ley of
cry in the des - ert for bread? Thy foes will re - joice when my
myr - i - ads wait for His word. He speaks! And e - ter - ni - ty,
know the sweet sound of Thy voice. Re - store and de - fend me, for
song in the night, My hope, my sal - va - tion, my all!
death should I weep, Or a - lone in this wil - der - ness rove?
sor - rows they see, And smile at the tears I have shed.
filled with His voice, Re - ech - oes the praise of the Lord.
Thou art my all, And in Thee I will ev - er re - joice.

WORDS: Joseph Swain, 1761-1796
MUSIC: Freeman Lewis, 1780-1859

MEDITATION
11.8.11.8.

363 Be Still, My Soul

Be still, and know that I am God. Psalm 46:10

1. Be still, my soul, the Lord is on thy side. Bear pa - tient - ly the
2. Be still, my soul, thy God doth un - der - take To guide the fu - ture
3. Be still, my soul, the hour is has-tening on When we shall be for -
cross of grief or pain. Leave to thy God to or - der or pro - vide.
as He has the past. Thy hope, thy con - fi - dence let noth-ing shake.
ev - er with the Lord, When dis - ap - point-ment, grief and fear are gone,
In ev - ery change He faith - ful will re - main. Be still, my soul, thy
All now mys - te - rious shall be bright at last. Be still, my soul, the
Sor - row for - got, love's pur - est joys re - stored. Be still my soul, when
best, thy heaven - ly Friend Through thorn - y ways leads to a joy - ful end.
waves and winds still know His voice who ruled them while He dwelt be - low.
change and tears are past, All safe and bless - ed we shall meet at last.

WORDS: Katharina A.D. von Schlegel, 18th century; tr. Jane L. Borthwick, 1813-1897
MUSIC: Jean Sibelius, 1865-1957; arr. *Hymnal* 1933

FINLANDIA
10.10.10.10.10.10.

Jesus, Lover of My Soul 364

As the Father has loved me, so have I loved you. John 15:9

1. Je - sus, Lov - er of my soul, Let me to Thy bos - om fly
2. Oth - er ref - uge have I none; Hangs my help-less soul on Thee.
3. Thou, O Christ, art all I want. More than all in Thee I find.
4. Plen - teous grace with Thee is found, Grace to cov - er all my sin.
While the near - er wa - ters roll, While the tem-pest still is high.
Leave, ah, leave me not a - lone; Still sup - port and com - fort me.
Raise the fall - en, cheer the faint, Heal the sick, and lead the blind.
Let the heal - ing streams a - bound. Make and keep me pure with - in.
Hide me, O my Sav - ior, hide Till the storm of life is past.
All my trust on Thee is stayed, All my help from Thee I bring.
Just and ho - ly is Thy name; I am all un - right-eous - ness.
Thou of life the Foun-tain art, Free - ly let me take of Thee.
Safe in - to the ha - ven guide; O, re - ceive my soul at last!
Cov - er my de - fense-less head With the shad - ow of Thy wing.
False and full of sin I am. Thou art full of truth and grace.
Spring Thou up with - in my heart, Rise to all e - ter - ni - ty.

WORDS: Charles Wesley, 1707-1788
MUSIC: Joseph Parry, 1841-1903

ABERYSTWYTH
7.7.7.7.D.

365 Would You Live for Jesus?

To me, to live is Christ and to die is gain. Philippians 1:21

1. Would you live for Je - sus and be al - ways pure and good?
2. Would you have Him make you free and fol - low at His call?
3. Would you in His king - dom find a place of con - stant rest?
Would you walk with Him with - in the nar - row road?
Would you know the peace that comes by giv - ing all?
Would you prove Him true in prov - i - den - tial test?
Would you have Him bear your bur - den, car - ry all your load?
Would you have Him save you so that you need nev - er fall?
Would you in His ser - vice la - bor al - ways at your best?
Let Him have His way with thee.
Let Him have His way with thee.
Let Him have His way with thee.
Refrain
His power can make you what you ought to be. His

WORDS: Cyrus S. Nusbaum, 1861-1937
MUSIC: Cyrus S. Nusbaum, 1861-1937

NUSBAUM
13.11.13.7. with Refrain

blood can cleanse your heart and make you free. His love can fill our soul and
you will see 'Twas best for Him to have His way with thee.

The Christian Walk 366

As a prisoner for the Lord, then, I urge you to live a life worthy of the calling you have received.

Be completely humble and gentle; be patient, bearing with one another in love.

Make every effort to keep the unity of the Spirit through the bond of peace.

There is one body and one Spirit—just as you were called to one hope when you were called—

one Lord, one faith, one baptism;

one God and Father of all, who is over all and through all and in all.

But to each one of us grace has been given as Christ apportioned it.

This is why it says: "When he ascended on high, he led captives in his train and gave gifts to men."

What does "he ascended" mean except that he also descended to the lower, earthly regions?

He who descended is the very one who ascended higher than all the heavens, in order to fill the whole universe.

It was he who gave some to be apostles, some to be prophets, some to be evangelists, and some to be pastors and teachers,

to prepare God's people for works of service, so that the body of Christ may be built up

until we all reach unity in the faith and in the knowledge of the Son of God and become mature, attaining to the whole measure of the fullness of Christ.

Then we will no longer be infants, tossed back and forth by the waves, and blown here and there by every wind of teaching and by the cunning and craftiness of men in their deceitful scheming.

Instead, speaking the truth in love, we will in all things grow up into him who is the Head, that is, Christ.

Ephesians 4:1-15

OUR GUIDE

MEDLEY

Teach Me Thy Way, O Lord
Step By Step

367 Teach Me Thy Way, O Lord

I will walk in your truth. Psalm 86:11

1. Teach me Thy way, O Lord, Teach me Thy way!
2. When I am sad at heart, Teach me Thy way!
3. When doubts and fears a - rise, Teach me Thy way!
4. Long as my life shall last, Teach me Thy way!
Thy guid - ing grace af - ford— Teach me Thy way!
When earth - ly joys de - part, Teach me Thy way!
When storms o'er - spread the skies, Teach me Thy way!
Wher - e'er my lot be cast, Teach me Thy way!
Help me to walk a - right, More by faith, less by sight.
In hours of lone - li - ness, In times of dire dis - tress,
Shine through the cloud and rain, Through sor - row, toil and pain,
Un - til the race is run, Un - til the jour - ney's done,
Song ending
Lead me with heaven - ly light, Teach me Thy way!
In fail - ure or suc - cess, Teach me Thy way!
Make Thou my path - way plain, Teach me Thy way!
Un - til the crown is won, Teach me Thy way!

WORDS: Benjamin M. Ramsey, 1849-1923
MUSIC: Benjamin M. Ramsey, 1849-1923

CAMACHA
6.4.6.4.6.6.6.4.

Optional transition to "Step By Step."
way!

Step by Step 368

This God is our God for ever and ever. Psalm 48:14

O God, You are my God, and I will ev-er praise You. O

God, You are my God, and I will ev-er praise You. I will

seek You in the morn-ing, And I will learn to walk in Your ways, And

step by step You'll lead me, And I will fol-low You all of my days.

WORDS: Beaker, 20th century
MUSIC: Beaker, 20th century

BEAKER
Irregular

369 It Is Glory Just to Walk with Him

God . . . will be our guide even to the end. Psalm 48:14

1. It is glo-ry just to walk with Him whose blood has ran-somed me. It is
2. It is glo-ry when the shad-ows fall to know that He is near. O, what
3. 'Twill be glo-ry when I walk with Him on heav-en's gold - en shore, Nev - er
rap - ture for my soul each day. It is joy di-vine to feel Him near where-
joy to sim-ply trust and pray! It is glo-ry to a - bide in Him when
from His side a - gain to stray. 'Twill be glo-ry, won-drous glo - ry with the
e'er my path may be. Bless the Lord, it's glo - ry all the way!
skies a - bove are clear; Yes, with Him, it's glo - ry all the way!
Sav - ior ev - er - more, Ev - er - last - ing glo - ry all the way!
Refrain
It is glo - ry just to walk with Him, It is
walk with Him,
glo - ry just to walk with Him. He will
walk with Him.

WORDS: Avis M.B. Christiansen, 1895-1966
MUSIC: Haldor Lillenas, 1885-1959

WALK WITH HIM
15.9.15.9. with Refrain

guide my steps a - right, Through the vale and o'er the height; It is
glo - ry just to walk with Him.
walk with Him.

Just a Closer Walk with Thee 370

I can do everything through him who gives me strength. Philippians 4:13

1. I am weak but Thou art strong. Je - sus, keep me from all wrong.
2. Through this world of toil and snares, If I fal - ter, Lord, who cares?
3. When my fee - ble life is o'er, Time for me will be no more.

Refrain: Just a clos - er walk with Thee, Grant it, Je - sus, is my plea.

I'll be sat - is - fied as long As I walk, let me walk close to Thee.
Who with me my bur - den shares? None but Thee, dear Lord, none but Thee.
Guide me gen - tly, safe - ly o'er To Thy king - dom shore, to Thy shore.
Dai - ly walk - ing close to Thee, Let it be, dear Lord, let it be.

D.C. for Refrain

WORDS: Anonymous
MUSIC: Anonymous

CLOSER WALK
Irregular

371 Step by Step

We walk by faith, not by sight. 2 Corinthians 5:7, NKJV

1. O, how
sweet to walk with Je - sus, Step by step and day by day, Step - ping
step I'll walk with Je - sus, Just a mo - ment at a time. Heights I
keep me clos - er to You, Step by step and day by day, Step - ping
in His ver - y foot - prints, Walk - ing with Him all the
have no wings to soar to Step by step my feet can
in Your ver - y foot - prints, Walk - ing with You all the
way.
climb.
way.
Refrain
Step by step, step by step, I would walk with

WORDS: Albert B. Simpson, 1843-1919
MUSIC: David Hahn, b. 1956

STEP BY STEP
8.7.8.7. with Refrain

Je - sus. All the day, all the way, Keep - ing step with
1, 2.
3.
Je - sus. 2. Step by Je - sus.
3. Je - sus,

Must Jesus Bear the Cross Alone? 372

He must deny himself and take up his cross and follow me. Matthew 16:24

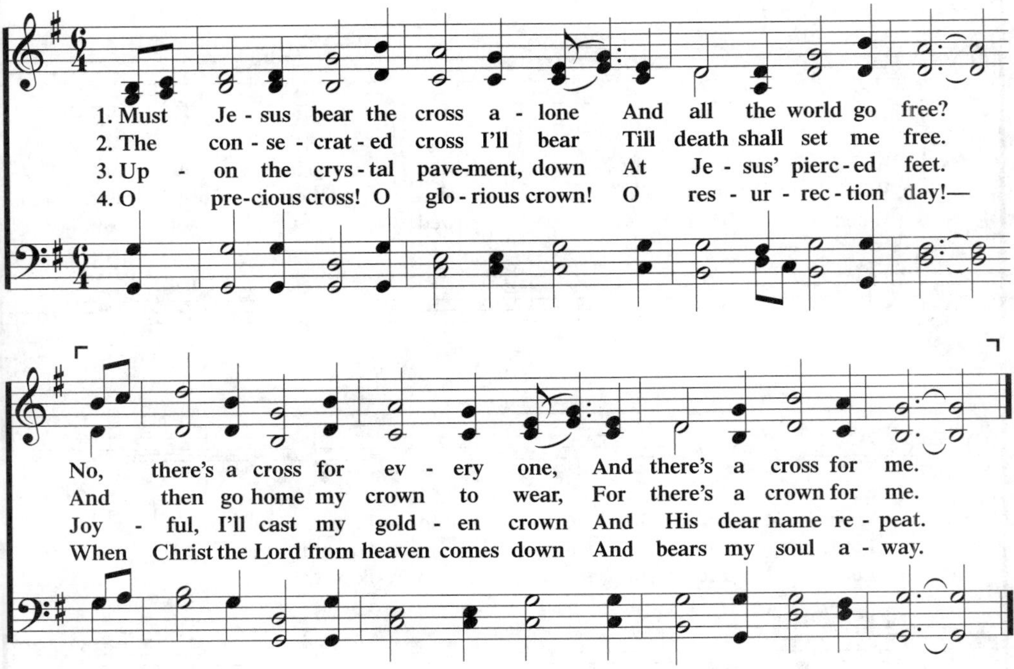

1. Must Jesus bear the cross alone
And all the world go free?
No, there's a cross for every one,
And there's a cross for me.

2. The consecrated cross I'll bear
Till death shall set me free.
And then go home my crown to wear,
For there's a crown for me.

3. Upon the crystal pavement, down
At Jesus' pierced feet.
Joyful, I'll cast my golden crown
And His dear name repeat.

4. O precious cross! O glorious crown!
O resurrection day!—
When Christ the Lord from heaven comes down
And bears my soul away.

WORDS: Thomas Shepherd, 1665-1739 (and others)
MUSIC: George N. Allen, 1812-1877

MAITLAND
C.M.

373 I Want Jesus to Walk with Me

Jesus himself came up and walked along with them. Luke 24:15

1. I want Je - sus to walk with me.
2. In my tri - als, Lord, walk with me.
3. When I'm trou - bled, Lord, walk with me.
I want Je - sus to walk with me.
In my tri - als, Lord, walk with me.
When I'm trou - bled, Lord, walk with me.
All a - long my pil - grim jour - ney,
When my heart is al - most break - ing,
When my head is bowed in sor - row,
Lord, I want Je - sus to walk with me.
Lord, I want Je - sus to walk with me.
Lord, I want Je - sus to walk with me.

WORDS: African-American spiritual
MUSIC: African-American spiritual; arr. Mark Blankenship, b. 1943

SOJOURNER
Irregular

Where He Leads Me 374

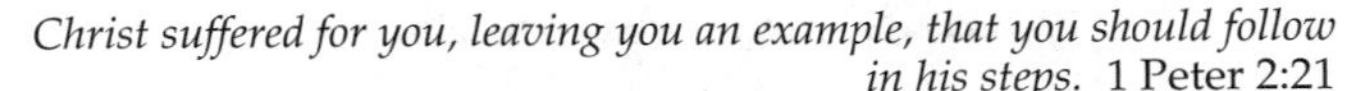

Christ suffered for you, leaving you an example, that you should follow in his steps. 1 Peter 2:21

1. I can hear the Sav - ior call - ing, I can
2. I'll go with Him through the gar - den, I'll go
3. I'll go with Him through the judg - ment, I'll go
4. He will give me grace and glo - ry, He will

Refrain: Where He leads me I will fol - low, Where He

hear the Sav - ior call - ing, I can hear the Sav - ior
with Him through the gar - den, I'll go with Him through the
with Him through the judg - ment, I'll go with Him through the
give me grace and glo - ry, He will give me grace and

leads me I will fol - low, Where He leads me I will

D.C. for Refrain
call - ing, "Take thy cross and fol - low, fol - low Me."
gar - den, I'll go with Him, with Him all the way.
judg - ment, I'll go with Him, with Him all the way.
glo - ry, And go with me, with me all the way.
fol - low, I'll go with Him, with Him all the way.

WORDS: E.W. Blandy, 19th century
MUSIC: John S. Norris, 1844-1907

NORRIS
8.8.8.9. with Refrain

375 We're Marching to Zion

Let the people of Zion be glad in their King. Psalm 149:2

1. Come, we that love the Lord, And let our joys be known. Join
2. Let those re - fuse to sing Who nev - er knew our God, But
3. The hill of Zi - on yields A thou-sand sa - cred sweets, Be -
4. Then let our songs a - bound And ev - ery tear be dry. We're
in a song with sweet ac - cord, Join in a song with sweet ac -
chil - dren of the heaven - ly King, But chil - dren of the heaven - ly
fore we reach the heaven - ly fields, Be - fore we reach the heaven - ly
march - ing through Em - man - uel's ground, We're march - ing through Em - man - uel's
cord, And thus sur - round the throne, And thus sur - round the throne.
King, May speak their joys a - broad, May speak their joys a - broad.
fields, Or walk the gold - en streets, Or walk the gold - en streets.
ground, To fair - er worlds on high, To fair - er worlds on high.
Refrain
We're march - ing to Zi - on,1 Beau - ti - ful, beau - ti - ful Zi - on. We're
We're march - ing on to Zi - on, Beau - ti - ful, beau - ti - ful Zi - on. We're

WORDS: Isaac Watts, 1674-1748; Refrain, Robert Lowry, 1826-1899
MUSIC: Robert Lowry, 1826-1899

1. *Zion: refers to the heavenly Jerusalem, Hebrews 12:22*

MARCHING TO ZION
6.6.8.8.6.6.with Refrain

march-ing up-ward to Zi - on, The beau-ti-ful cit-y of God.
march-ing up-ward to Zi-on, Zi-on, The beau-ti-ful cit-y of God.

The Lord's My Shepherd 376

I shall not be in want. Psalm 23:1

1. The Lord's my Shep-herd, I'll not want. He makes me down to lie
In pas-tures green; He lead-eth me The qui-et wa-ters by.

2. My soul He doth re-store a-gain, And me to walk doth make
With-in the paths of right-eous-ness, Even for His own name's sake.

3. Yea, though I walk through death's dark vale, Yet will I fear no ill,
For Thou art with me, and Thy rod And staff me com-fort still.

4. My ta-ble Thou hast fur-nish-ed In pres-ence of my foes.
My head Thou dost with oil a-noint, And my cup o-ver-flows.

5. Good-ness and mer-cy all my life Shall sure-ly fol-low me,
And in God's house for-ev-er-more My dwell-ing place shall be.

(For lower key, see. No. 468)

WORDS: From *The Scottish Psalter*, 1650
MUSIC: Jessie S. Irvine, 1836-1887; arr. David Grant, 1833-1893

CRIMOND
C.M.

377 The Lord My Shepherd Guards Me Well

He restores my soul. Psalm 23:3

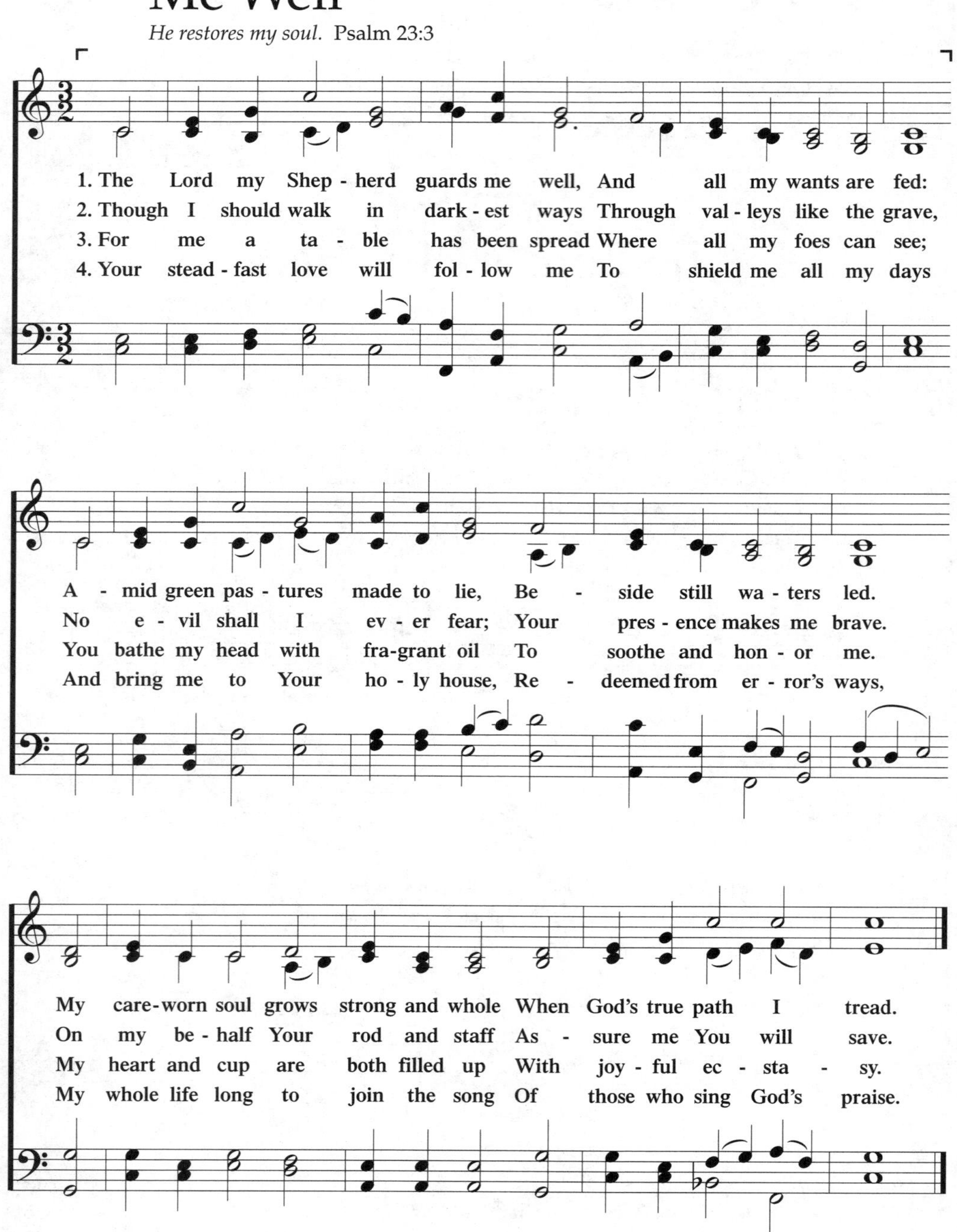
1. The Lord my Shep - herd guards me well, And all my wants are fed:
2. Though I should walk in dark - est ways Through val - leys like the grave,
3. For me a ta - ble has been spread Where all my foes can see;
4. Your stead - fast love will fol - low me To shield me all my days
A - mid green pas - tures made to lie, Be - side still wa - ters led.
No e - vil shall I ev - er fear; Your pres - ence makes me brave.
You bathe my head with fra-grant oil To soothe and hon - or me.
And bring me to Your ho - ly house, Re - deemed from er - ror's ways,
My care-worn soul grows strong and whole When God's true path I tread.
On my be - half Your rod and staff As - sure me You will save.
My heart and cup are both filled up With joy - ful ec - sta - sy.
My whole life long to join the song Of those who sing God's praise.

WORDS: Carl P. Daw, Jr., b. 1944; para. Psalm 23
MUSIC: James L. Bain, 1840-1925; arr. Gordon Jacob, 1895-1984

BROTHER JAMES' AIR
8.6.8.6.8.6.

Savior, Like a Shepherd, Lead Us 378

I am the good shepherd; I know my sheep. John 10:14

1. Sav - ior, like a shep-herd, lead us, Much we need Thy ten - der care.
2. We are Thine; do Thou be - friend us, Be the guard-ian of our way.
3. Thou hast prom-ised to re - ceive us, Poor and sin - ful though we be.
4. Ear - ly let us seek Thy fa - vor, Ear - ly let us do Thy will.
In Thy pleas - ant pas - tures feed us, For our use Thy folds pre -
Keep Thy flock, from sin de - fend us, Seek us if we go a -
Thou hast mer - cy to re - lieve us, Grace to cleanse and power to
Bless - ed Lord and on - ly Sav - ior, With Thy love our bos - oms
pare. Bless-ed Je - sus, bless-ed Je - sus, Thou hast bought us, Thine we
stray. Bless-ed Je - sus, bless-ed Je - sus, Hear, O, hear us when we
free. Bless-ed Je - sus, bless-ed Je - sus, Ear - ly let us turn to
fill. Bless-ed Je - sus, bless-ed Je - sus, Thou hast loved us, love us
are. Bless-ed Je - sus, bless-ed Je - sus, Thou hast bought us, Thine we are.
pray. Bless-ed Je - sus, bless-ed Je - sus, Hear, O, hear us when we pray.
Thee. Bless-ed Je - sus, bless-ed Je - sus, Ear - ly let us turn to Thee.
still. Bless-ed Je - sus, bless-ed Je - sus, Thou hast loved us, love us still.

Optional segue to "Lead Me, Lord." No transition required.

WORDS: From *Hymns for the Young*, 1836, attrib. Dorothy A. Thrupp, 1779-1847, alt.
MUSIC: William B. Bradbury, 1816-1868

BRADBURY
8.7.8.7.D.

379 Lead Me, Lord (I Will Follow)

My sheep listen to my voice; I know them, and they follow me. John 10:27

Lead me, Lord, I will fol - low. Lead me, Lord,
I will go. You have called me— I will
an - swer. Lead me, Lord, I will go.

WORDS: Wayne Goodine, b. 1954; Elizabeth Goodine, b.1962
MUSIC: Wayne Goodine, b. 1954; Elizabeth Goodine, b.1962

GOODINE
Irregular

380 Lead Me, Lord

Make straight your way before me. Psalm 5:8

Lead me, Lord, lead me in Your right - eous - ness.

WORDS: Samuel S. Wesley, 1810-1876, alt.; based on Psalm 5:8
MUSIC: Samuel S. Wesley, 1810-1876

LEAD ME, LORD
Irregular

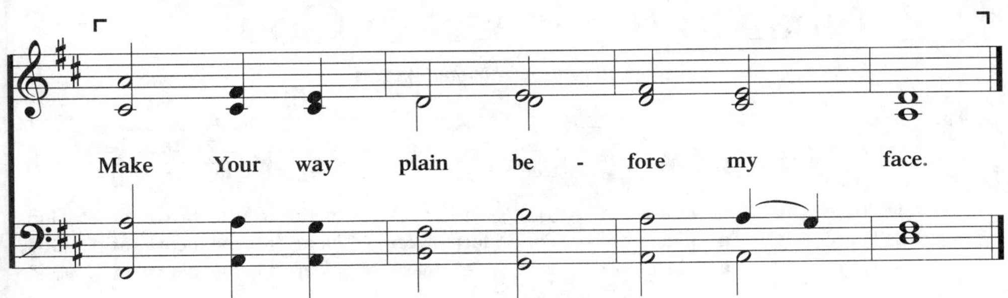
Make Your way plain be - fore my face.

Show Me Your Ways, O Lord 381

. . . teach me your paths. Psalm 25:4

Show me Your ways, O Lord, and teach me Your paths.

Guide me in ev - er - last - ing truth, O Lord, and teach me.

For You are God, You are my Sav - ior.

My faith, my trust, my hope is in You all day long.

WORDS: Gene Rivard, b. 1949; from Psalm 25:4-5
MUSIC: Gene Rivard, b. 1949

PSALM 25
Irregular

382 Near to the Heart of God

Come near to God and he will come near to you. James 4:8

1. There is a place of qui - et rest Near to the heart of God,
2. There is a place of com - fort sweet Near to the heart of God,
3. There is a place of full re - lease Near to the heart of God,
A place where sin can - not mo - lest, Near to the heart of God.
A place where we our Sav - ior meet, Near to the heart of God.
A place where all is joy and peace, Near to the heart of God.
Refrain
O Je - sus, blest Re - deem - er, Sent from the heart of God,
Hold us, who wait be - fore Thee, Near to the heart of God.

Optional segue to "Seek Ye First." No transition required.

WORDS: Cleland B. McAfee, 1866-1944
MUSIC: Cleland B. McAfee, 1866-1944

MCAFEE
C.M. with Refrain

Seek Ye First 383

Seek first his kingdom and his righteousness. Matthew 6:33

Descant
Al - le - lu - ia, al - le - lu - ia, al - le - lu - ia, al - le - lu - ia.
1. Seek ye first the king - dom of God and His right - eous - ness, And all these things shall be add - ed un - to you. Al - le - lu, al - le - lu - ia.
2. Ask, and it shall be giv - en un - to you. Seek and ye shall find. Knock, and the door shall be o - pened un - to you. Al - le - lu, al - le - lu - ia.
3. Man shall not live by bread a - lone, but by ev - ery word That pro - ceeds from the mouth of God. Al - le - lu, al - le - lu - ia.

WORDS: Karen Lafferty, b. 1948; from Matthew 6:33, 7:7 and Deuteronomy 8:3
MUSIC: Karen Lafferty, b. 1948

LAFFERTY
Irregular

384 Guide Me, O Thou Great Jehovah

He will be our guide even to the end. Psalm 48:14

1. Guide me, O Thou great Je - ho - vah, Pil - grim through this bar - ren land. I am weak, but Thou art might - y. Hold me with Thy power - ful hand. Bread of heav - en, Bread of heav - en, Feed me till I want no more, Feed me till I want no more.
2. O - pen now the crys - tal foun - tain, Whence the heal - ing stream doth flow. Let the fire and cloud - y pil - lar Lead me all my jour - ney through. Strong De - liv - erer, strong De - liv - erer, Be Thou still my strength and shield, Be Thou still my strength and shield.
3. When I tread the verge of Jor - dan, Bid my anx - ious fears sub - side. Death of death, and hell's de - struc - tion, Land me safe on Ca - naan's side. Songs of prais - es, songs of prais - es I will ev - er give to Thee, I will ev - er give to Thee.

(For lower key, see No. 385.)

WORDS: From the Welsh of William Williams, 1717-1791; stanza 1 tr. Peter Williams, 1722-1796; stanzas 2-3 tr. William Williams, 1717-1791
MUSIC: John Hughes, 1873-1932

CWM RHONDDA
8.7.8.7.8.7.7.

God of Grace and God of Glory 385

Be strong and courageous . . . for the LORD *your God will be with you.* Joshua 1:9

1. God of grace and God of glo - ry, On Your peo - ple pour Your power.
2. Lo! the hosts of e - vil round us Scorn Your Christ, as - sail[1] His ways!
3. Heal Your chil - dren's war - ring mad - ness, Bend our pride to Your con - trol.
4. Save us from weak res - ig - na - tion To the e - vils we de - plore.
Crown Your an - cient Church - 's sto - ry, Bring its bud to glo - rious flower.
Fears and doubts too long have bound us— Free our hearts to work and praise.
Shame our wan - ton,[2] self - ish glad - ness, Rich in things and poor in soul.
Let the gift of Your sal - va - tion Be our glo - ry ev - er - more.
Grant us wis - dom, grant us cour - age For the fac - ing of this
Grant us wis - dom, grant us cour - age For the liv - ing of these
Grant us wis - dom, grant us cour - age Lest we miss Your king - dom's
Grant us wis - dom, grant us cour - age Serv - ing You whom we a -
hour, (of this hour,) For the fac - ing of this hour.
days, (of these days,) For the liv - ing of these days.
goal, (king - dom's goal,) Lest we miss Your king - dom's goal.
dore, (we a - dore,) Serv - ing You whom we a - dore.

(For a higher key, see No. 384.)

WORDS: Harry E. Fosdick, 1878-1969, alt.
MUSIC: John Hughes, 1873-1932

CWM RHONDDA
8.7.8.7.8.7.7.

1. *assail: attack*
2. *wanton: unruly*

386 I Would Be Like Jesus

Those God foreknew he also predestined to be conformed to the likeness of his Son. Romans 8:29

1. Earth - ly plea - sures vain - ly call me, I would be like Je - sus;
2. He has bro - ken ev - ery fet - ter,[2] I would be like Je - sus;
3. All the way from earth to glo - ry, I would be like Je - sus;
4. That in heav - en He may meet me, I would be like Je - sus;
Noth - ing world - ly shall en - thrall[1] me, I would be like Je - sus.
That my soul may serve Him bet - ter, I would be like Je - sus.
Tell - ing o'er and o'er the sto - ry, I would be like Je - sus.
That His words, "Well done," may greet me, I would be like Je - sus.
Refrain
Be like Je - sus, this my song, In the home and in the throng;
Be like Je - sus all day long! I would be like Je - sus.

WORDS: James Rowe, 1865-1933
MUSIC: Bentley D. Ackley, 1872-1958

SPRING HILL
C.M. with Refrain

1. *enthrall: charm*
2. *fetter: chain, shackle*

Lord Jesus, Think on Me 387

According to your love remember me. Psalm 25:7

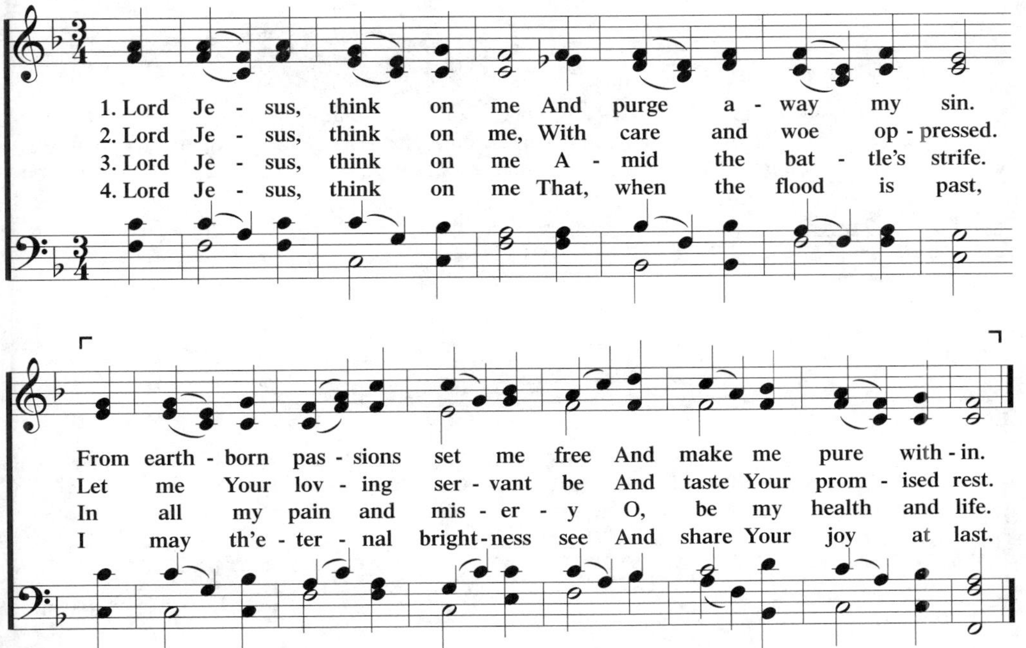
1. Lord Je - sus, think on me And purge a - way my sin.
2. Lord Je - sus, think on me, With care and woe op - pressed.
3. Lord Je - sus, think on me A - mid the bat - tle's strife.
4. Lord Je - sus, think on me That, when the flood is past,
From earth - born pas - sions set me free And make me pure with - in.
Let me Your lov - ing ser - vant be And taste Your prom - ised rest.
In all my pain and mis - er - y O, be my health and life.
I may th'e - ter - nal bright - ness see And share Your joy at last.

WORDS: Synesius of Cyrene, 375-430; tr. Allen W. Chatfield, 1808-1896, alt.
MUSIC: Johann H.G. Nageli, 1768-1836; arr. Lowell Mason, 1792-1872

DENNIS
S.M.

GOD, OUR PROTECTOR AND DELIVERER

God has put a Savior against sin, a heaven against a hell, light against darkness, good against evil, and the breadth and length and depth and height of the grace that is in Himself against all the power and the strength and cleverness of every enemy of my soul.

I have noticed that rich people's young children go nowhere without their nurses close beside them. If they go outside, their nurses go with them; if they go to eat their meals, their nurses go with them; if they go to bed, their nurses go with them; even if they fall asleep, their nurses stand nearby them. Oh, my brothers and sisters, those little ones who worship the Lord are the children of the richest Parent; therefore, they go nowhere by themselves. If they go to their spiritual meal, if they go to their sickbeds or to their graves, the salvation of their God is close to them, ready to deliver them from any danger.

John Bunyan (1628-1688)

388 Close to Thee

Whoever claims to live in him must walk as Jesus did. 1 John 2:6

1. Thou, my ev - er - last - ing por - tion,[1] More than friend or life to me,
2. Not for ease or world - ly pleas - ure, Nor for fame my prayer shall be.
3. Lead me through the vale of shad - ows, Bear me o'er life's fit - ful sea.
All a - long my pil - grim jour - ney, Sav - ior, let me walk with Thee.
Glad - ly will I toil and suf - fer, On - ly let me walk with Thee.
Then the gate of life e - ter - nal May I en - ter, Lord, with Thee.
Close to Thee, close to Thee, Close to Thee, close to Thee;
Close to Thee, close to Thee, Close to Thee, close to Thee;
Close to Thee, close to Thee, Close to Thee, close to Thee;
All a - long my pil - grim jour - ney, Sav - ior, let me walk with Thee.
Glad - ly will I toil and suf - fer, On - ly let me walk with Thee.
Then the gate of life e - ter - nal May I en - ter, Lord, with Thee.

WORDS: Fanny J. Crosby, 1820-1915
MUSIC: Silas J. Vail, 1818-1884

CLOSE TO THEE
8.7.8.7.6.6.8.7.

1. *portion: allotment*

Take the Name of Jesus with You 389

Whatever you do . . . do it all in the name of the Lord Jesus. Colossians 3:17

1. Take the name of Je - sus with you, Child of sor - row and of woe—
2. Take the name of Je - sus ev - er As a shield from ev - ery snare.
3. O, the pre - cious name of Je - sus, How it thrills our souls with joy,
4. At the name of Je - sus bow - ing, Fall - ing pros - trate at His feet,
It will joy and com - fort give you, Take it then wher - e'er you go.
If temp - ta - tions 'round you gath - er, Breathe that ho - ly name in prayer.
When His lov - ing arms re - ceive us And His songs our tongues em - ploy!
King of kings in heaven we'll crown Him When our jour - ney is com - plete.
Refrain
Pre-cious name, O, how sweet! Hope of earth and joy of heaven.
Pre-cious name, O, how sweet!
Pre-cious name, O, how sweet— Hope of earth and joy of heaven.
Pre - cious name, O, how sweet, how sweet

WORDS: Lydia Baxter, 1809-1874
MUSIC: William H. Doane, 1832-1915

PRECIOUS NAME
8.7.8.7. with Refrain

390 Jesus, I Would Faithful Be

Show me the way I should go. Psalm 143:8

1. Je - sus, I would faith - ful be— Give me the power, Give me the power.
2. Je - sus, I would talk with Thee While in the way, While in the way;
3. Give me, Lord, Thy burn - ing heart To dwell with - in, To dwell with - in.
4. Thus my dai - ly walk shall be In Thy sweet will, In Thy sweet will.
Je - sus, I would walk with Thee Each pass - ing hour, Each pass - ing hour.
Joy - ful, while Thy smile I see Each hap - py day, Each hap - py day.
Thine own na - ture, Lord, im - part To free from sin, To free from sin.
Je - sus on - ly, on - ly Thee, My heart can fill, My heart can fill.
Refrain
In Thy foot - steps place my feet, As Thou dost will, As Thou dost will;
And if thorns my path - way meet, Bid me be still, be still.

WORDS: J.O. Hillyer, 19th century
MUSIC: J.O. Hillyer, 19th century

HILLYER
Irregular with Refrain

Find Us Faithful 391

Those who have been given a trust must prove faithful. 1 Corinthians 4:2

O, may all who come be-hind us find us faith - ful;
May the fire of our de-vo - tion light their way.
May the foot-prints that we leave lead them to be - lieve
And the lives we live in - spire them to o - bey.
O, may all who come be-hind us find us faith - ful.

WORDS: Jon Mohr, b. 1955
MUSIC: Jon Mohr, b. 1955

FIND US FAITHFUL
Irregular

392 Faith Is the Victory

This is the victory that has overcome the world, even our faith. 1 John 5:4

1. En - camped a - long the hills of light, You Chris - tian sol - diers, rise!
2. His ban - ner o - ver us is love, Our sword the Word of God.
3. On ev - ery hand the foe we find Drawn up in dread ar - ray.
4. To we that o - ver - come the foe White rai - ment shall be given.
And press the bat - tle ere the night Shall veil the glow - ing skies.
We tread the road the saints a - bove With shouts of tri - umph trod.
Let tents of ease be left be - hind, And on - ward to the fray.
Be - fore the an - gels we shall know Our names con - fessed in heaven.
A - gainst the foe in vales be - low, Let all our strength be hurled.
By faith they, like a whirl-wind's breath, Swept on o'er ev - ery field.
Sal - va - tion's hel - met on each head, With truth all girt a - bout.
Then on - ward from the hills of light Our hearts with love a - flame.
Faith is the vic - to - ry, we know, That o - ver - comes the world.
The faith by which they con - quered death Is still our shin - ing shield.
The earth shall trem - ble 'neath our tread And ech - o with our shout.
We'll van - quish all the hosts of night In Je - sus' con - quering name.

WORDS: John H. Yates, 1837-1900, alt.
MUSIC: Ira D. Sankey, 1840-1908

SANKEY
C.M.D. with Refrain

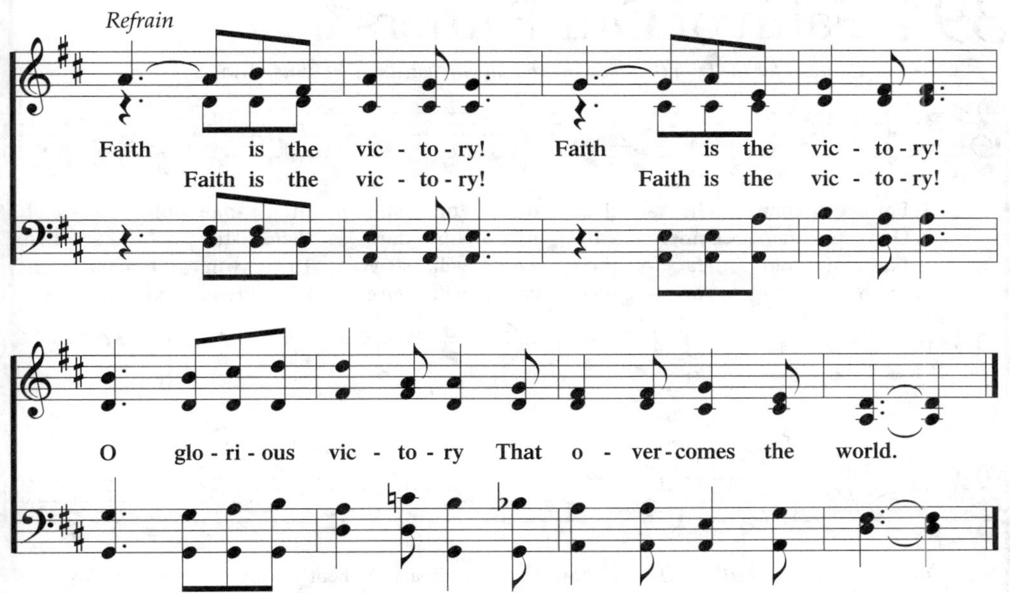
Refrain
Faith is the vic - to - ry! Faith is the vic - to - ry!
Faith is the vic - to - ry! Faith is the vic - to - ry!
O glo - ri - ous vic - to - ry That o - ver - comes the world.

More Than Conquerors 393

Give ear to my words, O LORD, consider my sighing. Listen to my cry for help, my King and my God, for to you I pray.

In the morning, O LORD, you hear my voice; in the morning I lay my requests before you and wait in expectation. *Psalm 5:1-3*

As the deer pants for streams of water, so my soul pants for you, O God. My soul thirsts for God, for the living God. When can I go and meet with God?

My tears have been my food day and night, while men say to me all day long, "Where is your God?" *Psalm 42:1-3*

He gives strength to the weary and increases the power of the weak. Even youths grow weary, and young men stumble and fall; but those who hope in the LORD will renew their strength.

They will soar on wings of eagles; they will run and not grow weary, they will walk and not faint. *Isaiah 40:29-31*

What, then, shall we say in response to this? If God is for us, who can be against us? He who did not spare his own Son, but gave him up for us all—how will he not also, along with him, graciously give us all things?

No, in all these things we are more than conquerors through him who loved us. *Romans 8:31-32, 37*

394 Faith of Our Fathers

Contend for the faith that was once for all entrusted to the saints. Jude 3

1. Faith of our fa - thers, liv - ing still In spite of dun - geon, fire, and sword! O, how our hearts beat high with joy When - e'er we hear that glo - rious word.
2. Our fa - thers, chained in pris - on dark, Were still in heart and con - science free. Lord, grant their chil - dren strength and love, Like them, to live and die for Thee.
3. Faith of our fa - thers, we will strive To win all na - tions un - to Thee, And through the truth that comes from God Man - kind shall then in - deed be free.
4. Faith of our fa - thers! We will love Both friend and foe in all our strife, And preach thee, too, as love knows how By kind - ly words and vir - tuous life.
Refrain
Faith of our fa - thers, ho - ly faith! We will be true to thee till death.

WORDS: Frederick W. Faber, 1814-1863, alt.
MUSIC: Henri F. Hemy, 1818-1888; arr. James G. Walton, 1821-1905

ST. CATHERINE
L.M. with Refrain

Sound the Battle Cry! 395

Be strong in the Lord and in his mighty power. Ephesians 6:10

1. Sound the bat - tle cry! See, the foe is nigh. Raise the stand-ard high
2. Strong to meet the foe, March-ing on we go, While our cause we know
3. O Thou God of all, Hear us when we call. Help us one and all
For the Lord! Gird your ar - mor on, Stand firm ev - ery one,
Must pre - vail. Shield and ban - ner bright, Gleam - ing in the light,
By Thy grace. When the bat - tle's done And the vic - tory won,
Rest your cause up - on His ho - ly Word!
Bat - tling for the right we ne'er can fail!
May we wear the crown be - fore Thy face!
Refrain
Rouse then, sol - diers,
ral - ly round the ban-ner! Read-y, stead-y, pass the word a-long. On-ward! For-ward!
Shout a loud Ho-san - na! Christ is Cap-tain of the might-y throng!

WORDS: William F. Sherwin, 1826-1888
MUSIC: William F. Sherwin, 1826-1888

SOUND THE BATTLE CRY
Irregular

396 Dare to Be a Daniel

Be on your guard; stand firm in the faith. 1 Corinthians 16:13

1. Stand-ing by a pur-pose true, Heed-ing God's com-mand,
2. Man-y might-y men are lost, Dar-ing not to stand,
3. Man-y gi-ants, great and tall, Stalk-ing through the land,
4. Hold the gos-pel ban-ner high On to vic-tory grand!
Hon-or them, the faith-ful few! All hail to Dan-iel's band!
Who for God had been a host By join-ing Dan-iel's band!
Head-long to the earth would fall If met by Dan-iel's band!
Sa-tan and his host de-fy And shout for Dan-iel's band!
Refrain
Dare to be a Dan-iel, Dare to stand a-lone,
Dare to have a pur-pose firm, Dare to make it known!

WORDS: Philip P. Bliss, 1838-1876
MUSIC: Philip P. Bliss, 1838-1876

DANIEL
7.5.7.6. with Refrain

OUR BATTLE

MEDLEY

Onward, Christian Soldiers
The Battle Belongs to the Lord

Onward, Christian Soldiers 397

Endure hardship with us like a good soldier of Christ Jesus. 2 Timothy 2:3

1. On - ward, Chris - tian sol - diers, March - ing as to war,
2. Like a might - y ar - my Moves the Church of God.
3. Crowns and thrones may per - ish, King - doms rise and wane,[1]
4. On - ward, then, you peo - ple, Join our hap - py throng,
With the cross of Je - sus Go - ing on be - fore.
Chris - tians, we are tread - ing Where the saints have trod.
But the Church of Je - sus Con - stant will re - main.
Blend with ours your voic - es In the tri - umph song.
Christ, the roy - al Mas - ter, Leads a - gainst the foe.
We are not di - vid - ed, All one bod - y we,
Gates of hell can nev - er 'Gainst that Church pre - vail.
Glo - ry, laud,[2] and hon - or Un - to Christ the King;
For - ward in - to bat - tle, See His ban - ners go.
One in hope and doc - trine, One in char - i - ty.
We have Christ's own prom - ise, And that can - not fail.
This through count - less a - ges Men and an - gels sing.

WORDS: Sabine Baring-Gould, 1834-1924, alt.
MUSIC: Arthur S. Sullivan, 1842-1900

ST. GERTRUDE
6.5.6.5.D. with Refrain

1. *wane: decrease*
2. *laud: praise*

Refrain

On-ward, Chris-tian sol - diers, March-ing as to war,

With the cross of Je - sus Go - ing on be - fore.

Song ending

Optional transition to "The Battle Belongs to the Lord."

fore.

398 The Battle Belongs to the Lord

The battle is not yours, but God's. 2 Chronicles 20:15

1. In heav-en-ly ar - mor we'll en - ter the land, The
2. When the pow-er of dark - ness comes in like a flood, The
3. When your en - e - my press - es in hard, do not fear, The

WORDS: Jamie Owens-Collins, b. 1955
MUSIC: Jamie Owens-Collins, b. 1955

THE BATTLE
Irregular

bat-tle be-longs to the Lord. No weap-on that's fash-ioned a-gainst us will stand, The bat-tle be-longs to the Lord.
bat-tle be-longs to the Lord. He's raised up a stand-ard, the power of His blood, The bat-tle be-longs to the Lord.
bat-tle be-longs to the Lord. Take cour-age, my friend, your re-demp-tion is near, The bat-tle be-longs to the Lord.
Refrain
And we sing glo-ry, hon-or, pow-er and strength to the Lord. We sing glo-ry, hon-or, pow-er and strength to the Lord.

399 We Choose to Bow

At the name of Jesus every knee should bow. Philippians 2:10

1. Though a
(2. Though the)
(3. Though the)
mil - lion voic - es choose to de - ny You, We choose to
powers of dark - ness rage all a - round us, We choose to
cost is great to the call set be - fore us, We choose to
bow. Though a thou - sand thoughts seek to rise a - bove You,
bow. Though tri - als come and temp - ta - tions sur - round us,
bow. Though the world may hate us, our God is for us,
We cast them down. Though they de - ny that we
We choose to bow. Though we may stum - ble or
We choose to bow. Though we may strug - gle or

WORDS: Dan Adler, b. 1960
MUSIC: Dan Adler, b. 1960; arr. David Hahn, b. 1956

WE CHOOSE TO BOW
Irregular

are all sin - ful, Though they pro - claim God is in us all.
we may fal - ter, Though we have wan - dered and gone a - stray.
we may pros - per, Though we have lit - tle or man - y things,
Though we are told we don't need a Sav - ior, Hum - bly now at Your
Mer - cy is giv - en to all who call You, Mer - cy is giv - en to
You are our God and there is no oth - er Worth - y now of the
feet we fall.
all who say:
song we sing!
Refrain
We choose to bow, we choose to sing, We choose to
crown You the King of kings. "We are not God," we say out loud. On - ly to

1, 2.
You do we choose to bow, Do we choose to bow.
3.
2. Though the
3. Though the
bow. No oth - er god, no oth - er king, On - ly to
You do we choose to sing. O ho - ly God, we praise You now! On - ly to
You do we choose to bow! Do we choose to bow!

Stand Up, Stand Up for Jesus 400

Stand firm in the faith. 1 Corinthians 16:13

1. Stand up, stand up for Je - sus, You sol - diers of the cross.
2. Stand up, stand up for Je - sus, The trum - pet call o - bey.
3. Stand up, stand up for Je - sus, Stand in His strength a - lone.
4. Stand up, stand up for Je - sus— The strife will not be long.
Lift high His roy - al ban - ner, It must not suf - fer loss.
Forth to the might - y con - flict, In this His glo - rious day!
The arm of flesh will fail you, You dare not trust your own.
This day the noise of bat - tle, The next the vic - tor's song.
From vic - tory un - to vic - tory His ar - my shall He lead,
You that are His, now serve Him A - gainst un - num - bered foes.
Put on the gos - pel ar - mor, Each piece put on with prayer.
To him that o - ver - com - eth A crown of life shall be.
Till ev - ery foe is van - quished And Christ is Lord in - deed.
Let cour - age rise with dan - ger And strength to strength op - pose.
Where du - ty calls, or dan - ger, Be nev - er want - ing there.
He, with the King of glo - ry Shall reign e - ter - nal - ly.

WORDS: George Duffield, 1818-1888, alt.
MUSIC: George J. Webb, 1803-1887

WEBB
7.6.7.6.D.

401 Who Is on the Lord's Side?

Put on the full armor of God, so that . . . you may be able to stand your ground. Ephesians 6:13

1. Who is on the Lord's side? Who will serve the King?
2. Not for weight of glo - ry, Not for crown or palm,
3. Je - sus, Thou hast bought us, Not with gold or gem,
4. Fierce may be the con - flict, Strong may be the foe,
Who will be His help - ers, Oth - er lives to bring? Who will leave the
En - ter we the ar - my, Raise the war - rior psalm, But for love that
But with Thine own life - blood, For Thy di - a - dem.1 With Thy bless - ing
But the King's own ar - my None can o - ver - throw. Round His stand - ard
world's side? Who will face the foe? Who is on the
claim - eth Lives for whom He died; He whom Je - sus
fill - ing Each who comes to Thee, Thou hast made us
rang - ing Vic - tory is se - cure; For His truth un -
Lord's side? Who for Him will go? By Thy call of mer - cy,
nam - eth Must be on His side. By Thy love con - strain - ing,
will - ing, Thou hast made us free. By Thy grand re - demp - tion,
chang - ing Makes the tri - umph sure. Joy - ful - ly en - list - ing

WORDS: Frances R. Havergal, 1836-1879
MUSIC: C. Luise Reichardt, 1780-1826; arr. John Goss, 1800-1880

ARMAGEDDON
6.5.6.5.D. with Refrain

1. *diadem: crown*

By Thy grace di - vine, We are on the Lord's side; Sav-ior, we are Thine.
By Thy grace di - vine, We are on the Lord's side; Sav-ior, we are Thine.
By Thy grace di - vine, We are on the Lord's side; Sav-ior, we are Thine.
By Thy grace di - vine, We are on the Lord's side; Sav-ior, we are Thine.

Am I a Soldier of the Cross? 402

Be men of courage; be strong. 1 Corinthians 16:13

1. Am I a sol - dier of the cross, A fol - lower of the Lamb? And shall I fear to own His cause, Or blush to speak His name?
2. Must I be car - ried to the skies On flower - y beds of ease, While oth - ers fight to win the prize And sail through blood - y seas?
3. Are there no foes for me to face? Must I not stem the flood? Is this vile world a friend to grace To help me on to God?
4. Since I must fight if I would reign, In - crease my cour - age, Lord. I'll bear the toil, en - dure the pain, Sup - port - ed by Your Word.

(For higher key, see No. 477)

Optional segue to "Soldiers of Christ, Arise." No transition required.

WORDS: Isaac Watts, 1674-1748, alt.
MUSIC: Thomas A. Arne, 1710-1778

ARLINGTON
C.M.

403 Soldiers of Christ, Arise

Put on the full armor of God. Ephesians 6:13

1. Sol - diers of Christ, a - rise And put your ar - mor on,
2. Stand, then in His great might, With all His strength en - dued,
3. Leave no un - guard - ed place, No weak - ness of the soul.
Strong in the strength which God sup - plies, Through His e - ter - nal Son.
And take, to arm you for the fight, The pan - o - ply[1] of God.
Take ev - ery vir - tue, ev - ery grace And for - ti - fy the whole.
Strong in the Lord of Hosts, And in His might - y power,
That, hav - ing all things done And all your con - flicts past,
From strength to strength go on, Wres - tle and fight and pray.
Who in the strength of Je - sus trusts Is more than con - quer - or.
You may o'er - come through Christ a - lone And stand com - plete at last.
Tread all the powers of dark - ness down And win the well-fought day.

WORDS: Charles Wesley, 1707-1788, alt.
MUSIC: George J. Elvey, 1816-1893

DIADEMATA
S.M.D.

1. panoply: a complete suit of armor

Lead On, O King Eternal 404

I am the LORD *your God . . . who directs you in the way you should go.* Isaiah 48:17

1. Lead on, O King E - ter - nal, The day of march has come.
2. Lead on, O King E - ter - nal, To lands of deep - est night.
3. Lead on, O King E - ter - nal, We fol - low not with fears,
Hence - forth in fields of con - quest Your tents shall be our home.
We fol - low where You lead us As her - alds of the light.
For glad - ness breaks like morn - ing Wher - e'er Your face ap - pears.
Through days of prep - a - ra - tion Your grace has made us strong,
May we to souls im - mor - tal Your Word of life con - vey
Your cross is lift - ed o'er us, We jour - ney in its light.
And now, O King E - ter - nal, We lift our bat - tle song.
And o - pen heav - en's por - tal Through Christ, the Truth, the Way.
The crown a - waits the con - quest. Lead on, O God of might.

WORDS: Ernest W. Shurtleff, 1862-1917, alt.
MUSIC: Henry T. Smart, 1813-1879

LANCASHIRE
7.6.7.6.D.

405 My Anchor Holds

We have this hope as an anchor for the soul, firm and secure. Hebrews 6:19

1. Though the an - gry sur - ges roll On my tem - pest - driv - en soul,
2. Might - y tides a - bout me sweep, Per - ils lurk with - in the deep,
3. I can feel the an - chor fast As I meet each sud - den blast,
4. Trou - bles al - most 'whelm the soul, Griefs like bil - lows1 o'er me roll,
I am peace - ful, for I know, Wild - ly though the winds may blow,
An - gry clouds o'er - shade the sky, And the tem - pest ris - es high.
And the ca - ble, though un - seen, Bears the heav - y strain be - tween.
Tempt - ers seek to lure a - stray, Storms ob - scure the light of day—
I've an an - chor safe and sure That can ev - er - more en - dure.
Still I stand the tem - pest's shock, For my an - chor grips the rock.
Through the storm I safe - ly ride Till the turn - ing of the tide.
But in Christ I can be bold. I've an an - chor that shall hold.
Refrain
And it holds, my an - chor holds. Blow your wild - est, then, O
And it holds, my an - chor holds. Blow your wild - est,

WORDS: W.C. Martin, 19th century
MUSIC: Daniel B. Towner, 1850-1919

MY ANCHOR HOLDS
7.7.7.7.7.7. with Refrain

1. *billows: waves*

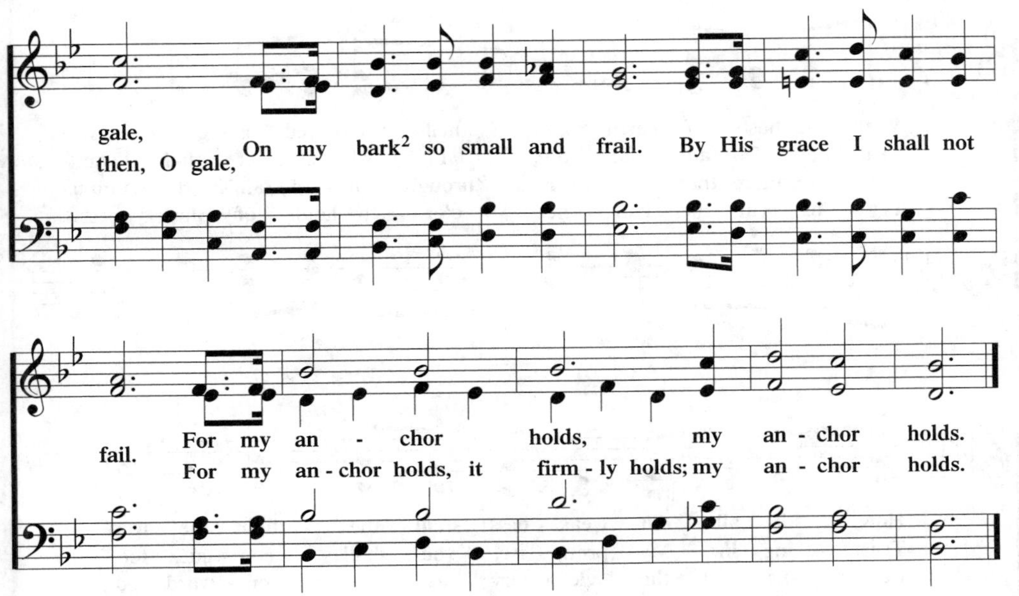
gale,
then, O gale,
On my bark² so small and frail. By His grace I shall not
fail.
For my an - chor holds, my an - chor holds.
For my an - chor holds, it firm - ly holds; my an - chor holds.

2. bark: small sailing vessel

Jesus Giveth Us the Victory 406

He gives us the victory through our Lord Jesus Christ. 1 Corinthians 15:57

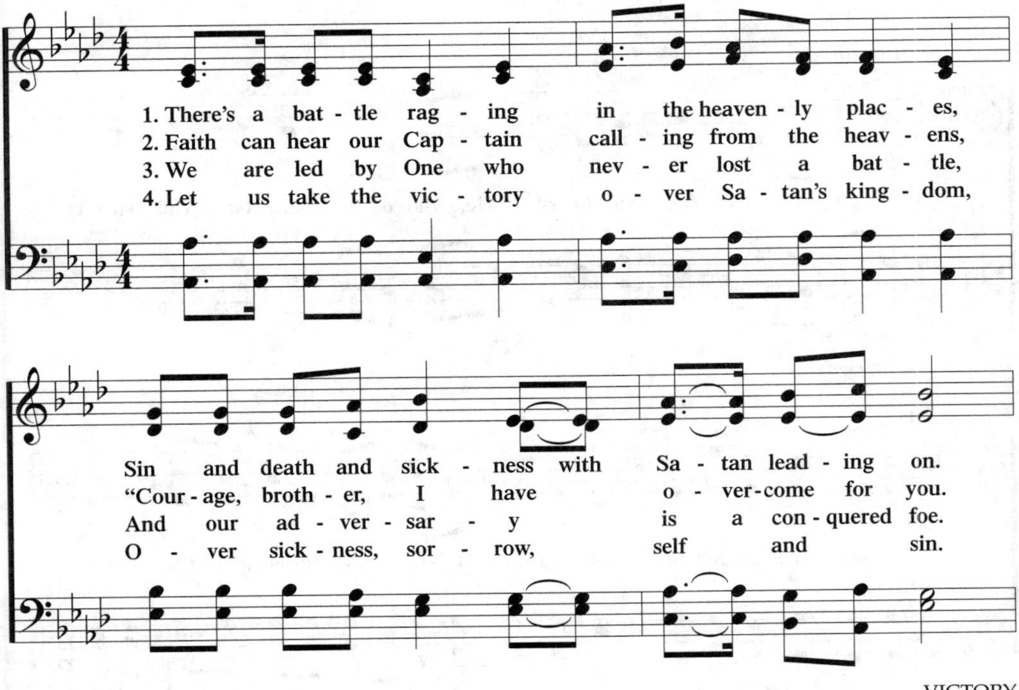

1. There's a bat - tle rag - ing in the heaven - ly plac - es,
Sin and death and sick - ness with Sa - tan lead - ing on.

2. Faith can hear our Cap - tain call - ing from the heav - ens,
"Cour - age, broth - er, I have o - ver-come for you.

3. We are led by One who nev - er lost a bat - tle,
And our ad - ver - sar - y is a con - quered foe.

4. Let us take the vic - tory o - ver Sa - tan's king - dom,
O - ver sick - ness, sor - row, self and sin.

WORDS: Albert B. Simpson, 1843-1919
MUSIC: Albert B. Simpson, 1843-1919

VICTORY
6.6.6.5.D. with Refrain

With the hosts of earth and hell ar-rayed a-gainst us,
Fear not, I am with you, I will nev-er fail you.
We are more than con-querors through our Cap-tain's tri-umph.
Let us bear the ban-ner o'er the lands of dark-ness,
How in all our weak-ness shall the fight be won?
Trust-ing in My prom-ise, you shall con-quer, too."
Let us shout the vic-tory as we on-ward go.
Till the foes' last strong-hold we for Christ shall win.
Refrain
Je-sus giv-eth us the vic-to-ry. He, who o-ver-came on Cal-va-ry,
O-ver-comes a-gain in you and me. Hal-le-lu-jah! Je-sus gives the vic-to-ry!

Healing 407

When [Jesus] came down from the mountainside, large crowds followed him.

A man with leprosy came and knelt before him and said, "Lord, if you are willing, you can make me clean."

Jesus reached out his hand and touched the man. "I am willing," he said. "Be clean!" Immediately he was cured of his leprosy.

Then Jesus said to him, "See that you don't tell anyone. But go, show yourself to the priest and offer the gift Moses commanded, as a testimony to them."

When Jesus had entered Capernaum, a centurion came to him, asking for help.

"Lord," he said, "my servant lies at home paralyzed and in terrible suffering."

Jesus said to him, "I will go and heal him."

The centurion replied, "Lord, I do not deserve to have you come under my roof. But just say the word, and my servant will be healed.

For I myself am a man under authority, with soldiers under me. I tell this one, 'Go,' and he goes; and that one, 'Come,' and he comes. I say to my servant, 'Do this,' and he does it."

When Jesus heard this, he was astonished and said to those following him, "I tell you the truth, I have not found anyone in Israel with such great faith.

I say to you that many will come from the east and the west, and will take their places at the feast with Abraham, Isaac and Jacob in the kingdom of heaven.

But the subjects of the kingdom will be thrown outside, into the darkness, where there will be weeping and gnashing of teeth."

Then Jesus said to the centurion, "Go! It will be done just as you believed it would." And his servant was healed at that very hour. . . .

When evening came, many who were demon-possessed were brought to him, and he drove out the spirits with a word and healed all the sick.

This was to fulfill what was spoken through the prophet Isaiah:

"He took up our infirmities and carried our diseases."

Matthew 8:1-13, 16-17

Is any one of you sick? He should call the elders of the church to pray over him and anoint him with oil in the name of the Lord. And the prayer offered in faith will make the sick person well; the Lord will raise him up.

James 5:14-15

408 Blessed Be the Glorious Tidings

By his wounds we are healed. Isaiah 53:5

1. Bless - ed be the glo - rious tid - ings To a suf - fering world re - vealed. Christ has made a full a - tone - ment. By His wounds we may be healed.
2. Je - sus ev - er wel - comed suf - ferers To His mer - cy who ap - pealed. Still He bids us bring our sick - ness. By His wounds we may be healed.
3. Sa - cred is His blest a - noint - ing Through the Ho - ly Spir - it sealed. Je - sus, lay Your hand up - on us. By Your wounds we may be healed.
4. Sav - ior, from the fi - ery ar - rows Be our ref - uge and our shield. Safe - ly shall we walk through dan - ger. By Your wounds we may be healed.
5. Je - sus, to Your glo - ry ev - er All our - selves we glad - ly yield. Nev - er ceas - ing to re - mem - ber— By Your wounds we may be healed.
Refrain
Bless - ed be the great a - tone - ment To a suf - fering world re -

(For alternate harmony, see No. 265)

WORDS: Albert B. Simpson, 1843-1919; adapt. Gene Rivard, b. 1949
MUSIC: Rowland Prichard, 1811-1887; arr. Eldon McBride, b. 1962

HYFRYDOL
8.7.8.7. with Refrain

vealed. Bless - ed be the Great Phy - si - cian,
By whose wounds we may be healed.

Heal Me, Hands of Jesus 409

Lord, if you are willing, you can make me clean. Matthew 8:2

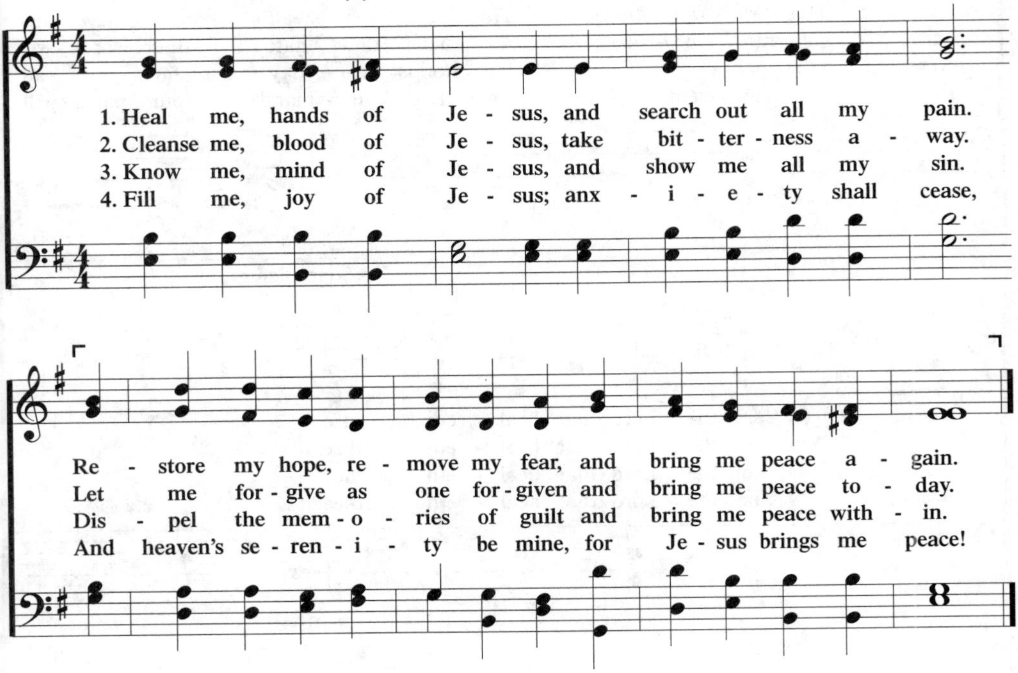

1. Heal me, hands of Je - sus, and search out all my pain.
Re - store my hope, re - move my fear, and bring me peace a - gain.

2. Cleanse me, blood of Je - sus, take bit - ter - ness a - way.
Let me for - give as one for - given and bring me peace to - day.

3. Know me, mind of Je - sus, and show me all my sin.
Dis - pel the mem - o - ries of guilt and bring me peace with - in.

4. Fill me, joy of Je - sus; anx - i - e - ty shall cease,
And heaven's se - ren - i - ty be mine, for Je - sus brings me peace!

WORDS: Michael Perry, 1942-1996
MUSIC: Herbert S. Irons, 1834-1905

SOUTHWELL
S.M.

OUR HEALER

MEDLEY

The Branch of Healing
I Am the God That Healeth Thee

410 The Branch of Healing

. . . for I am the LORD that healeth Thee. Exodus 15:26, KJV

1. There is a heal - ing branch that grows Where ev - ery bit - ter Ma - rah[1] flows; This is our health - re - new - ing tree. "I am the Lord that heal - eth thee."
2. There is an old ap - point - ed way For those who hark - en and o - bey; A - bove the gate these words we see: "I am the Lord that heal - eth thee."
3. There is an ord' - nance that has stood Since Is - rael crossed the part - ed flood; It stands to - day for you and me— "I am the Lord that heal - eth thee."
4. There is a great Phy - si - cian still Whose hand has all its an - cient skill; At His com - mand our pains will flee— "I am the Lord that heal - eth thee."
Song ending

(For alternate tune, see No. 444.)

WORDS: Albert B. Simpson, 1843-1919
MUSIC: Twila Paris, b. 1958

LAMB OF GOD (abbrev.)
L.M.

1. *Marah: refers to the bitter water in Exodus 15:23*

Optional transition to "I Am the God That Healeth Thee."
thee."

I Am the God That Healeth Thee 411

. . . who forgives all your sins and heals all your diseases. Psalm 103:3

1. I am the God that heal - eth thee,
I am the Lord, your heal - er.
I sent my Word and healed your dis - ease,
I am the Lord, your heal - er.

2. You are the God that heal - eth me,
You are the Lord, my heal - er.
You sent Your Word and healed my dis - ease,
You are the Lord, my heal - er.
You are the Lord, my heal - er.

WORDS: Don Moen, b. 1950
MUSIC: Don Moen, b. 1950

HEALETH THEE
Irregular

412 Healing in His Wings

To you who fear My name, the Sun of Righteousness shall arise with healing in His wings.
Malachi 4:2, NKJV

1. To those who fear God's ho - ly name, How sweet the words the proph - et brings: "The Sun of Right - eous - ness shall rise With heal - ing in His wings, With heal - ing in His wings."
2. It is to those who fear His name His heal - ing power the Sav - ior brings. O let us hide with con - trite hearts Be - neath His heal - ing wings, Be - neath His heal - ing wings.
3. Christ is the Son of Right - eous - ness, But if to sin our spir - it clings, We can - not know His heal - ing touch, Or rest be - neath His wings, Or rest be - neath His wings.
4. For yes, He loves to heal our pains, And soothe the ser - pent's poi - soned stings. Close to His bo - som we must press To feel His heal - ing wings, To feel His heal - ing wings.
Refrain
There is heal - ing, heal - ing in His

WORDS: Albert B. Simpson, 1843-1919; adapt. Gene Rivard, b. 1949
MUSIC: Gene Rivard, b. 1949; harm. Eldon McBride, b. 1962

HEALING WINGS
8.8.8.6.6. with Refrain

wings; Cov-ered and sur-round-ed by the peace that Je-sus
brings. I am rest - ing, while my spir-it
sings, There is heal-ing, heal-ing in His wings.

HEALING GLORIFIES GOD

The true doctrine of healing through the Lord Jesus Christ is most humbling, holy and practical. It exalts no man, it spares no sin, it offers no promises to the disobedient, it gives no strength for selfish indulgence or worldly ends. Rather it exalts the name of Jesus, glorifies God, inspires the soul with faith and power, summons to a life of self-denial and holy service. It awakens a slumbering church and an unbelieving world with the solemn signals of a living God and risen Christ.

A.B. Simpson (1843-1919), *The Gospel of Healing*

413 I Will Change Your Name

You will be called by a new name that the mouth of the LORD will bestow. Isaiah 62:2

I will change your name.
I will change your name.
You shall no long - er be called
Your new name shall be
wound - ed, out - cast,
con - fi - dence, joy - ful - ness,
lone - ly or a - fraid.
o - ver - com - ing one,

WORDS: D.J. Butler, 20th century
MUSIC: D.J. Butler, 20th century

BUTLER
Irregular

faith - ful - ness, friend of God,
one who seeks My face.

His Strength Is Perfect 414

My grace is sufficient for you, for my power is made perfect in weakness.
2 Corinthians 12:9

His strength is per - fect when our strength is gone.

He'll car - ry us when we can't car - ry on.

WORDS: Steven Curtis Chapman, b. 1962; Jerry Shalley, 20th century
MUSIC: Steven Curtis Chapman, b. 1962; Jerry Shalley, 20th century

HIS STRENGTH IS PERFECT
Irregular

Raised in His pow - er, the weak be-come strong.
His strength is per - fect, His strength is per - fect.

415 Healer of My Soul

Evening, morning and noon I cry out in distress, and he hears my voice. Psalm 55:17

1, 3. Heal - er of my soul,
2. Keep - er of my soul, on

keep me at eve-ning. Keep me at morn - ing,
rough course far - ing. Help and safe - guard my

WORDS: John Michael Talbot, b. 1954
MUSIC: John Michael Talbot, b. 1954

HEALER OF MY SOUL
Irregular

1, 3.
Fine
keep me at noon, Heal - er of my soul.
means this night, Keep - er of my
2.
soul. I am tired, a - stray and stum - bling.
to verse 3
Shield my soul from the snare of sin.

STRENGTH FROM DAY TO DAY

There is nothing that has so chastening, humbling, heart-searching and sanctifying an influence over our spiritual life as to live a life of dependence upon Christ for our bodily strength from day to day. . . . God's highest method of working still is to put into human bodies a kind of physical energy for which there is no way of accounting apart from the Holy Spirit.

A.B. Simpson (1843-1919), *The Lord for the Body*

416 Healing in Jesus

He . . . healed those who needed healing. Luke 9:11

1. There is
cleans - ing in Je - sus for guilt and for sin. There's a
heal - ing in Je - sus, the same as of old. There is
glad - ness in Je - sus that nev - er grows old. There's a
foun - tain that wash - es us whit - er than snow. There's a
heal - ing for all who be - lieve and o - bey, For the
sun - shine that nev - er shall van - ish a - way. O, the
Spir - it that's will - ing to fill us with - in Till the
love and com - pas - sion that nev - er grow cold Are as
rest and the sweet - ness can nev - er be told Of the

WORDS: Albert B. Simpson, 1843-1919
MUSIC: Dan Adler, b. 1960; arr. David Hahn, b. 1956

HEALING IN JESUS
12.12.12.12. with Refrain

depths of our be - ing His cleans - ing shall know.
a - ble and will - ing to help us to - day.
hearts that have learned to be - lieve and o - bey.
Refrain
There is heal - ing in Je - sus, heal - ing for thee,
Heal - ing for all who be - lieve and o - bey. There is
heal - ing in Je - sus, heal - ing for me— Je - sus, I take Thee for
1, 2.
heal - ing to - day.
2. There is
3. There is

3.
heal - ing to - day.
417 O Christ, the Healer
By his wounds you have been healed. 1 Peter 2:24
1. O Christ, the heal - er, we have come to pray for health, to plead for friends. How can we fail to be re - stored when reached by love that nev - er ends?
2. From ev - ery ail - ment flesh en - dures our bod - ies clam - or to be freed. Yet in our hearts we would con - fess that whole - ness is our deep - est need.
3. How strong, O Lord, are our de - sires, how weak our knowl - edge of our - selves! Re - lease in us those heal - ing truths un - con - scious pride re - sists or shelves.
4. In con - flicts that de - stroy our health we re - cog - nize the world's dis - ease; Our com - mon life de - clares our ills. Is there no cure, O Christ, for these?
5. Grant that we all, made one in faith, in Your com - mun - i - ty may find The whole - ness that, en - rich - ing us, shall reach the whole of hu - man - kind.

WORDS: Fred Pratt Green, 1903-2000
MUSIC: Robert A. Schumann, 1810-1856

CANONBURY
L.M.

OUR HOPE

MEDLEY

Come, Ye Disconsolate
God Will Make a Way

Come, Ye Disconsolate 418

Let us then approach the throne of grace with confidence . . . and find grace to help us in our time of need. Hebrews 4:16

1. Come, ye dis - con - so - late, wher - e'er ye lan - guish,[1]
2. Joy of the des - o - late, light of the stray - ing,
3. Here see the Bread of Life, see wa - ters flow - ing
Come to the mer - cy seat, fer - vent - ly kneel.
Hope of the pen - i - tent, fade - less and pure!
Forth from the throne of God, pure from a - bove.
Here bring your wound - ed hearts, here tell your an - guish.
Here speaks the Com - fort - er, ten - der - ly say - ing,
Come to the feast of love, come, ev - er know - ing
Song ending
Earth has no sor - rows that heaven can - not heal.
"Earth has no sor - rows that heaven can - not cure."
Earth has no sor - rows but heaven can re - move.

WORDS: Thomas Moore, 1779-1882; alt. Thomas Hastings, 1784-1872
MUSIC: Samuel Webbe, Sr., 1740-1816

CONSOLATION
11.10.11.10.

1. *languish: fade or weaken*

Optional transition to "God Will Make a Way."
move.

419 God Will Make a Way

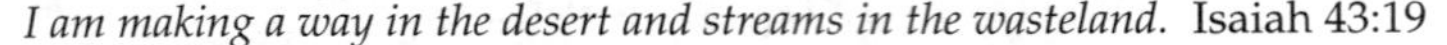
I am making a way in the desert and streams in the wasteland. Isaiah 43:19

God will make a way where there seems to be no way. He works in ways we
can-not see, He will make a way for me. He will be my guide, hold me
close-ly to His side. With love and strength for each new day,
He will make a way, He will make a way.

WORDS: Don Moen, b. 1950
MUSIC: Don Moen, b. 1950

HE WILL MAKE A WAY
Irregular

The Resurrection 420

If Christ has not been raised, your faith is futile; you are still in your sins.

Then those also who have fallen asleep in Christ are lost.

If only for this life we have hope in Christ, we are to be pitied more than all men.

But Christ has indeed been raised from the dead, the firstfruits of those who have fallen asleep.

For since death came through a man, the resurrection of the dead comes also through a man.

For as in Adam all die, so in Christ all will be made alive.

But each in his own turn: Christ, the firstfruits; then, when he comes, those who belong to him.

Then the end will come, when he hands over the kingdom to God the Father after he has destroyed all dominion, authority and power.

For he must reign until he has put all his enemies under his feet.

The last enemy to be destroyed is death. *1 Corinthians 15:17-26*

Listen, I tell you a mystery: We will not all sleep, but we will all be changed—

in a flash, in the twinkling of an eye, at the last trumpet. For the trumpet will sound, the dead will be raised imperishable, and we will be changed.

For the perishable must clothe itself with the imperishable, and the mortal with immortality.

When the perishable has been clothed with the imperishable, and the mortal with immortality, then the saying that is written will come true: "Death has been swallowed up in victory."

"Where, O death, is your victory? Where, O death, is your sting?"

The sting of death is sin, and the power of sin is the law.

But thanks be to God! He gives us the victory through our Lord Jesus Christ.

Therefore, my dear brothers, stand firm. Let nothing move you. Always give yourselves fully to the work of the Lord, because you know that your labor in the Lord is not in vain. *1 Corinthians 15:51-58*

421 When the Roll Is Called Up Yonder

We will be with the Lord forever. 1 Thessalonians 4:17

1. When the trum - pet of the Lord shall sound and time shall be no more,
2. On that bright and cloud - less morn - ing when the dead in Christ shall rise,
3. Let us la - bor for the Mas - ter from the dawn to set - ting sun,
And the morn - ing breaks e - ter - nal bright and fair;
And the glo - ry of His re - sur - rec - tion share;
Let us talk of all His won - drous love and care.
When the saved of earth shall gath - er o - ver on the oth - er shore,
When His cho - sen ones shall gath - er to their home be - yond the skies,
Then when all of life is o - ver, and our work on earth is done,
And the roll is called up yon - der, I'll be there.
And the roll is called up yon - der, I'll be there.
And the roll is called up yon - der, we'll be there.
Refrain
When the roll
When the roll

WORDS: James M. Black, 1856-1938
MUSIC: James M. Black, 1856-1938

ROLL CALL
15.11.15.11. with Refrain

is called up yon - der, When the roll is called up
is called up yon - der, I'll be there When the roll is called up
yon - der, When the roll is called up yon - der, When the
yon - der, I'll be there When the roll is called up
roll is called up yon - der, I'll be there.

Optional segue to "I'll Fly Away." No transition required.

MORTALITY AND IMMORTALITY

It is God Almighty who puts eternity in a man's breast and tomorrow in a man's heart and gives His people immortality, so what you see down here really is not much. But when the bird of immortality takes to the wing, she sails on and on, over the horizon and out into the everlasting tomorrows and never comes down and never dies.

A.W. Tozer (1897-1963), *Who Put Jesus on the Cross?*

422 I'll Fly Away

We . . . would prefer to be away from the body and at home with the Lord. 2 Corinthians 5:8

1. Some glad morn - ing when this life is o'er,
2. When the shad - ows of this life have gone,
3. Just a few more wea - ry days and then,
I'll fly a - way;
fly a-way, fly a-way;
To a home on God's ce - les - tial shore,
Like a bird from pris - on bars have flown,
To a land where joys shall nev - er end.
I'll fly a - way.
fly a-way, fly a-way.
Refrain
I'll fly a - way, O, glo-ry,
fly a-way,
I'll fly a - way;
fly a-way,
in the morn - ing;
When I die, hal - le - lu - jah, by and by,
I'll fly a - way.
fly a-way, fly a-way.

WORDS: Albert E. Brumley, 1905-1977
MUSIC: Albert E. Brumley, 1905-1977

I'LL FLY AWAY
9.4.9.4. with Refrain

When We All Get to Heaven 423

In My Father's house are many mansions. John 14:2, NKJV

1. Sing the won-drous love of Je-sus, Sing His mer-cy
2. While we walk the pil-grim path-way, Clouds will o-ver-
3. Let us then be true and faith-ful, Trust-ing, serv-ing
4. On-ward to the prize be-fore us! Soon His beau-ty
and His grace. In the man-sions bright and bless-ed,
spread the sky. But when trav-eling days are o-ver,
ev-ery day. Just one glimpse of Him in glo-ry
we'll be-hold. Soon the pearl-y gates will o-pen;
He'll pre-pare for us a place.
Not a shad-ow, not a sigh.
Will the toils of life re-pay.
We shall tread the streets of gold.
1. for us a place.
Refrain
When we all get to
When we all
heav-en, What a day of re-joic-ing that will be! When we
What a day of re-joic-ing that will be!
all see Je-sus, We'll sing and shout the vic-to-ry.
When we all and shout the vic-to-ry.

WORDS: Eliza E. Hewett, 1851-1920
MUSIC: Emily D. Wilson, 1865-1942

HEAVEN
8.7.8.7.with Refrain

424 My Savior First of All

Blessed are those who have not seen and yet have believed. John 20:29

1. When my life work is end - ed and I cross the swell - ing tide,
2. O, the soul - thrill - ing rap - ture when I view His bless - ed face
3. O, the dear ones in glo - ry, how they beck - on me to come,
4. Through the gates to the cit - y in a robe of spot - less white,
When the bright and glo - rious morn - ing I shall see, I shall
And the lus - ter of His kind - ly beam - ing eye. How my
And our part - ing at the riv - er I re - call. To the
He will lead me where no tears shall ev - er fall. In the
know my Re - deem - er when I reach the oth - er side, And His
full heart will praise Him for the mer - cy, love, and grace That pre -
sweet vales of E - den they will sing my wel - come home, But I
glad song of a - ges I shall min - gle with de - light, But I
smile will be the first to wel - come me.
pares for me a man - sion in the sky.
long to meet my Sav - ior first of all.
long to meet my Sav - ior first of all.
Refrain
I shall know Him, I shall
I shall know Him,

WORDS: Fanny J. Crosby, 1820-1915
MUSIC: John R. Sweney, 1837-1899

I SHALL KNOW HIM
14.11.14.11. with Refrain

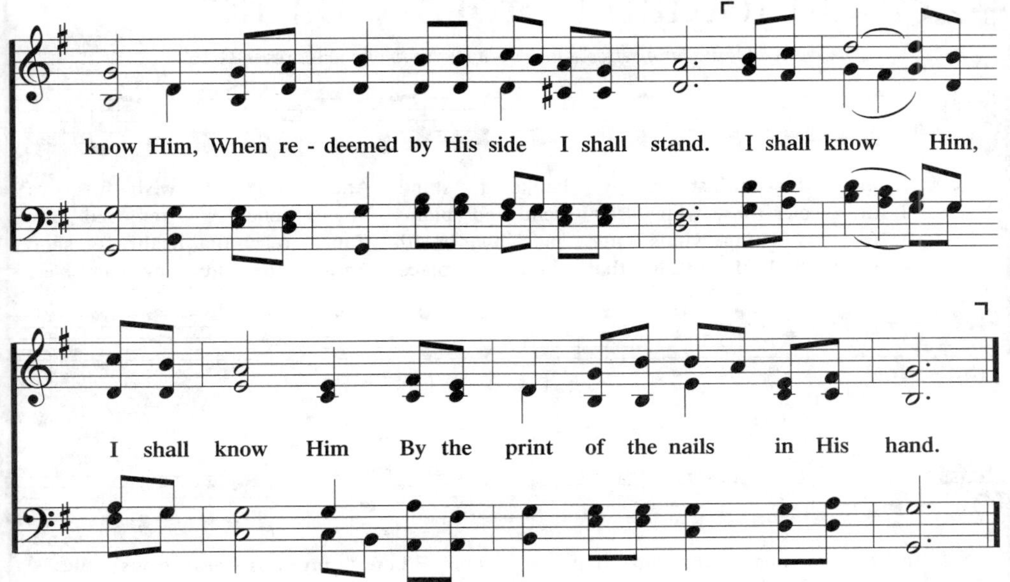
know Him, When re - deemed by His side I shall stand. I shall know Him,
I shall know Him By the print of the nails in His hand.

Life Everlasting 425

Just as Moses lifted up the snake in the desert, so the Son of Man must be lifted up, that everyone who believes in him may have eternal life.

For God so loved the world that he gave his one and only Son, that whoever believes in him shall not perish but have eternal life. *John 3:14-16*

I tell you the truth, whoever hears my word and believes him who sent me has eternal life and will not be condemned; he has crossed over from death to life. *John 5:24*

Whoever believes in the Son has eternal life, but whoever rejects the Son will not see life, for God's wrath remains on him. *John 3:36*

My sheep listen to my voice; I know them, and they follow me. I give them eternal life, and they shall never perish; no one can snatch them out of my hand. My Father, who has given them to me, is greater than all; no one can snatch them out of my Father's hand. *John 10:27-29*

And this is the testimony: God has given us eternal life, and this life is in his Son. He who has the Son has life; he who does not have the Son of God does not have life.

I write these things to you who believe in the name of the Son of God so that you may know that you have eternal life. *1 John 5:11-13*

426 On Jordan's Stormy Banks

They were longing for a better country—a heavenly one. Hebrews 11:16

1. On Jor - dan's storm - y banks I stand And cast a wish - ful eye
2. All o'er those wide - ex - tend - ed plains Shines one e - ter - nal day.
3. No chill - ing winds nor pois' - nous breath Can reach that health - ful shore.
4. When shall I reach that hap - py place And be for - ev - er blest?

To Ca - naan's fair and hap - py land Where my pos - ses - sions lie.
There God the Son for - ev - er reigns And scat - ters night a - way.
Sick - ness and sor - row, pain and death Are felt and feared no more.
When shall I see my Fa - ther's face And in His bos - om rest?

Refrain

I am bound for the Prom - ised Land. I am bound for the Prom - ised Land.

O, who will come and go with me? I am bound for the Prom - ised Land.

WORDS: Samuel Stennett, 1727-1795
MUSIC: American folk hymn; arr. Rigdon M. McIntosh, 1836-1899

PROMISED LAND
C.M. with Refrain

O, That Will Be Glory 427

We shall see him as he is. 1 John 3:2

1. When all my la - bors and tri - als are o'er And I am safe on that beau - ti - ful shore, Just to be near the dear Lord I a - dore Will through the a - ges be glo - ry for me.
2. When, by the gift of His in - fin - ite grace, I am ac - cord - ed in heav - en a place, Just to be there and to look on His face Will through the a - ges be glo - ry for me.
3. Friends will be there I have loved long a - go, Joy like a riv - er a - round me will flow. Yet, just a smile from my Sav - ior, I know, Will through the a - ges be glo - ry for me.
Refrain
O, that will be glo - ry for me, Glo - ry for me, glo - ry for me!
O, that will be glo - ry for me, Glo - ry for me, glo - ry for me!
When by His grace I shall look on His face, That will be glo - ry, be glo - ry for me!
rit.

WORDS: Charles H. Gabriel, 1856-1932
MUSIC: Charles H. Gabriel, 1856-1932

GLORY SONG
10.10.10.10. with Refrain

428 Safe in the Arms of Jesus

Whoever trusts in the LORD *is kept safe.* Proverbs 29:25

1. Safe in the arms of Je - sus, Safe on His gen - tle breast,
2. Safe in the arms of Je - sus, Safe from cor - rod - ing care,
3. Je - sus, my heart's dear ref - uge, Je - sus has died for me.
There, by His love o'er - shad - ed, Sweet - ly my soul shall rest.
Safe from the world's temp - ta - tions— Sin can - not harm me there.
Firm on the Rock of A - ges Ev - er my trust shall be.
Hark! 'Tis the voice of an - gels Borne in a song to me O - ver the
Free from the blight of sor - row, Free from my doubts and fears. On - ly a
Here let me wait with pa-tience, Wait till the night is o'er, Wait till I
fields of glo - ry, O - ver the crys - tal sea.
few more tri - als, On - ly a few more tears!
see the morn-ing Break on the gold - en shore.
Refrain
Safe in the arms of Je - sus,
Safe on His gen-tle breast, There, by His love o'er-shad - ed, Sweet - ly my soul shall rest.

WORDS: Fanny J. Crosby, 1820-1915, alt.
MUSIC: William H. Doane, 1832-1915

ARMS OF JESUS
7.6.7.6.D. with Refrain

Face to Face 429

Now I know in part; then I shall know fully. 1 Corinthians 13:12

1. Face to face with Christ, my Sav - ior, Face to face—what will it be—
2. On - ly faint - ly now I see Him With the dark - ling veil be - tween,
3. What re - joic - ing in His pres - ence When are ban - ished grief and pain,
4. Face to face! O bliss - ful mo - ment! Face to face— to see and know!
When with rap - ture I be - hold Him, Je - sus Christ, who died for me?
But a bless - ed day is com - ing When His glo - ry shall be seen.
When the crook - ed ways are straight-ened, And the dark things shall be plain!
Face to face with my Re - deem - er, Je - sus Christ, who loves me so!
Refrain
Face to face shall I be - hold Him, Far be - yond the star - ry sky.
Face to face in all His glo - ry, I shall see Him by and by!

WORDS: Carrie E. Breck, 1855-1934
MUSIC: Grant Colfax Tullar, 1869-1950

FACE TO FACE
8.7.8.7. with Refrain

430 He the Pearly Gates Will Open

Blessed are those who wash their robes, that they . . . may go through the gates into the city.
Revelation 22:14

1. Love di-vine, so great and won-drous, Deep and might-y, pure, sub-lime;
Com-ing from the heart of Je-sus—Just the same through tests of time.
2. Like a dove when hunt-ed, fright-ened, As a wound-ed fawn was I;
Bro-ken-heart-ed, yet He healed me—He will heed the sin-ner's cry.
3. Love di-vine, so great and won-drous— All my sins He then for-gave.
I will sing His praise for-ev-er For His blood, His power to save.
4. In life's e-ven-tide, at twi-light, At His door I'll knock and wait.
By the pre-cious love of Je-sus, I shall en-ter heav-en's gate.
Refrain
He the pearl-y gates will o-pen So that I may en-ter in;
For He pur-chased my re-demp-tion And for-gave me all my sin.

WORDS: Frederick A. Blom, 1867-1927; tr. Nathaniel Carlson, 1879-1957
MUSIC: Elsie Ahlwen, 1905-1986

PEARLY GATES
8.7.8.7. with Refrain

Sun of My Soul, Our Savior Dear 431

The night will shine like the day, for darkness is as light to you. Psalm 139:12

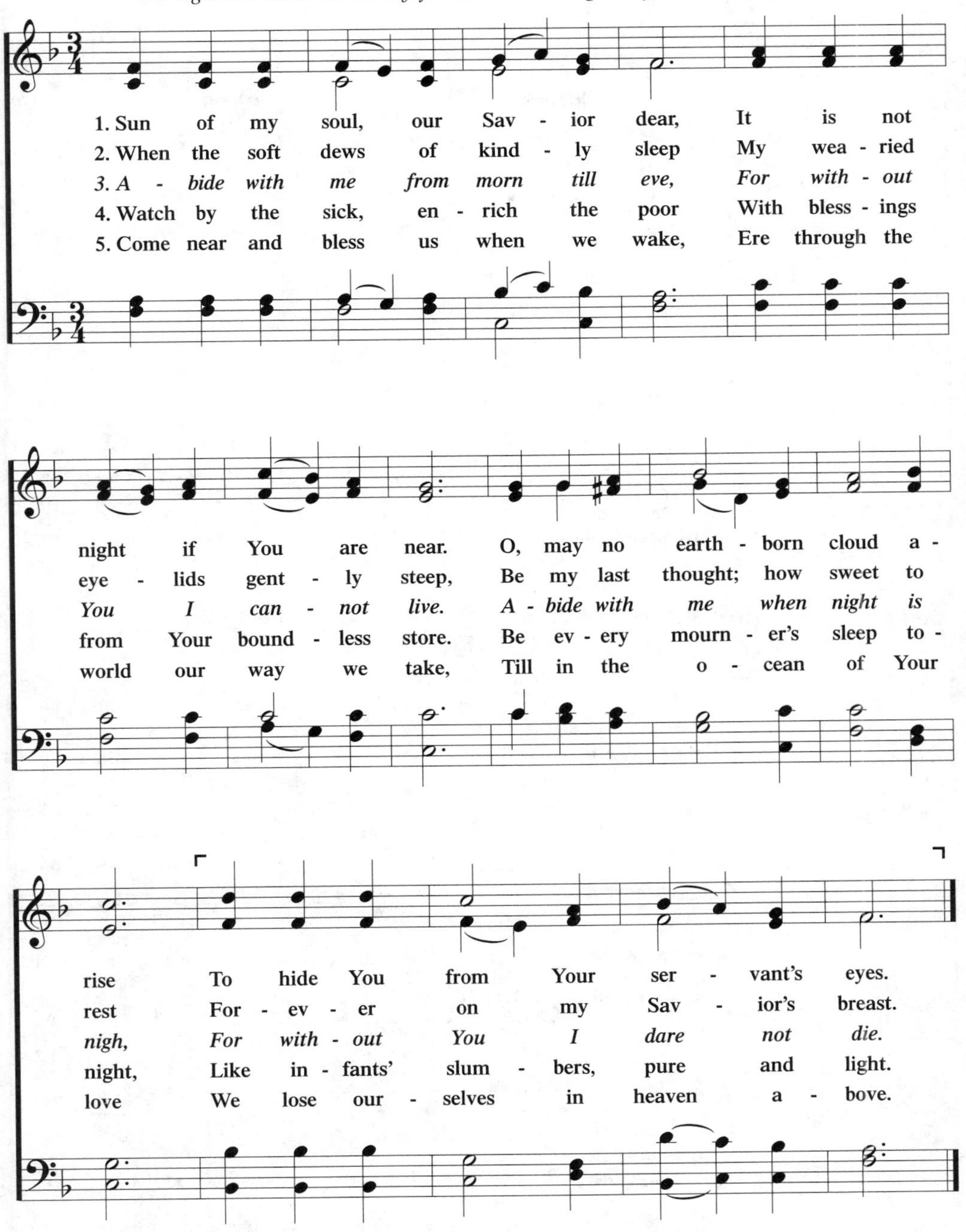
1. Sun of my soul, our Sav - ior dear, It is not night if You are near. O, may no earth - born cloud a - rise To hide You from Your ser - vant's eyes.
2. When the soft dews of kind - ly sleep My wea - ried eye - lids gent - ly steep, Be my last thought; how sweet to rest For - ev - er on my Sav - ior's breast.
3. A - bide with me from morn till eve, For with - out You I can - not live. A - bide with me when night is nigh, For with - out You I dare not die.
4. Watch by the sick, en - rich the poor With bless - ings from Your bound - less store. Be ev - ery mourn - er's sleep to - night, Like in - fants' slum - bers, pure and light.
5. Come near and bless us when we wake, Ere through the world our way we take, Till in the o - cean of Your love We lose our - selves in heaven a - bove.

WORDS: John Keble, 1792-1866, alt.
MUSIC: *Katholisches Gesangbuch*, Vienna, 1774; adapted from *Metrical Psalter*, 1855

HURSLEY
L.M.

432 Saved By Grace

For it is by grace you have been saved, through faith. Ephesians 2:8

1. Some day the sil - ver cord will break, And I no more as now shall sing, But, O, the joy when I shall wake With - in the pal - ace of the King!
2. Some day my earth - ly house will fall— I can - not tell how soon 'twill be. But this I know— my All in All Has now a place in heaven for me.
3. Some day, when fades the gold - en sun Be - neath the ros - y - tint - ed west, My bless - ed Lord will say, "Well done!" And I shall en - ter in - to rest.
4. Some day— till then I'll watch and wait, My lamp all trimmed and burn - ing bright, That when my Sav - ior opes the gate, My soul to Him may take its flight.
Refrain
And I shall see Him face to face And tell the sto - ry— saved by grace.
And I shall see Him face to face And tell the sto - ry— saved by grace.

WORDS: Fanny J. Crosby, 1820-1915
MUSIC: George C. Stebbins, 1846-1945

SAVED BY GRACE
L.M. with Refrain

Swing Low 433

We are looking for the city that is to come. Hebrews 13:14

Refrain
Swing low, sweet char - i - ot, Com-ing for to car-ry me home.
Swing low, sweet char - i - ot, Com-ing for to car-ry me home.
1. I looked o - ver Jor - dan and what did I see,
2. If you get there be - fore I do,
3. I'm some - times up, I'm some - times down,
Com-ing for to car - ry me home? A band of an - gels
Com-ing for to car - ry me home, Tell all my friends I'm
Com-ing for to car - ry me home; But still my soul feels
to Refrain
com - ing af - ter me, Com-ing for to car - ry me home.
com - ing, too, Com-ing for to car - ry me home.
heav - en - ly bound, Com-ing for to car - ry me home.

WORDS: African-American spiritual
MUSIC: African-American spiritual

SWING LOW
Irregular with Refrain

434 Nearer, My God, to Thee

It is good to be near God. I have made the Sovereign LORD my refuge. Psalm 73:28

1. Near - er, my God, to Thee, Near - er to Thee!
2. There let the way ap - pear Steps un - to heaven;
3. Then, with my wak - ing thoughts Bright with Thy praise,
E'en though it be a cross That rais - eth me;
All that Thou send - est me In mer - cy given;
Out of my ston - y griefs, Beth - el I'll raise;
Still all my song shall be, Near - er, my God, to Thee,
An - gels to beck - on me Near - er, my God, to Thee,
So by my woes to be Near - er, my God, to Thee,
Near - er, my God, to Thee, Near - er to Thee.
Near - er, my God, to Thee, Near - er to Thee.
Near - er, my God, to Thee, Near - er to Thee.

WORDS: Sarah F. Adams, 1805-1848; based on Genesis 28:10-22
MUSIC: Lowell Mason, 1792-1872

BETHANY
6.4.6.4.6.6.6.4.

Abide with Me 435

They urged him strongly, "Stay with us." Luke 24:29

1. A - bide with me— fast falls the e - ven - tide.
2. Swift to its close ebbs out life's lit - tle day.
3. I need Thy pres - ence ev - ery pass - ing hour.
4. I fear no foe with Thee at hand to bless.
5. Hold Thou Thy cross be - fore my clos - ing eyes.
The dark - ness deep - ens— Lord, with me a - bide!
Earth's joys grow dim, its glo - ries pass a - way.
What but Thy grace can foil the tempt - er's power?
Ills have no weight, and tears no bit - ter - ness.
Shine through the gloom, and point me to the skies.
When oth - er help - ers fail and com - forts flee,
Change and de - cay in all a - round I see.
Who, like Thy - self, my guide and stay can be?
Where is death's sting? Where, grave, thy vic - to - ry?
Heaven's morn - ing breaks and earth's vain shad - ows flee!
Help of the help - less, O, a - bide with me!
O Thou, who chang - est not, a - bide with me!
Through cloud and sun - shine, O, a - bide with me!
I tri - umph still if Thou a - bide with me!
In life, in death, O Lord, a - bide with me!

WORDS: Henry F. Lyte, 1793-1847
MUSIC: William H. Monk, 1823-1889

EVENTIDE
10.10.10.10.

436 Sweet Hour of Prayer

Peter and John were going up to the temple at the time of prayer. Acts 3:1

1. Sweet hour of prayer, sweet hour of prayer That calls me from a world of care,
And bids me at my Father's throne, Make all my wants and wishes known.
In seasons of distress and grief, My soul has often found relief,
And oft escaped the tempter's snare, By thy return, sweet hour of prayer!

2. Sweet hour of prayer, sweet hour of prayer, Thy wings shall my petition bear
To Him whose truth and faithfulness Engage the waiting soul to bless.
And since He bids me seek His face, Believe His Word, and trust His grace,
I'll cast on Him my every care And wait for thee, sweet hour of prayer!

3. Sweet hour of prayer, sweet hour of prayer, May I thy consolation share
Till, from Mount Pisgah's[1] lofty height, I view my home and take my flight.
This robe of flesh[2] I'll drop, and rise To seize the everlasting prize,
And shout, while passing through the air, "Farewell, farewell, sweet hour of prayer!"

WORDS: William W. Walford, 1772-1850
MUSIC: William B. Bradbury, 1816-1868

HOUR OF PRAYER
L.M.D.

1. *Mount Pisgah: the place where Moses looked at the Promised Land. (Deuteronomy 34:1)*
2. *robe of flesh: physical body*

A New Day Dawns 437

In the morning you will see the glory of the L*ORD*. Exodus 16:7

1. A new day dawns at Your command,
A precious gift from Your own hand.
O, give us eyes that we might see
What You have willed for us to be.

2. Too often, Lord, we start the day
Without a thought of what You'd say
Through us if we would fully give
Our lives to You each day we live.

3. Resolved to start each day with prayer,
We'll take Your gift, use it with care.
Within the grasp of Your strong hand
We'll do the work that You have planned.

4. May Your light shine throughout this day,
In all we think and do and say;
And with full hearts we now will raise
Our song, our lives to You in praise.

(For alternate arrangement, see No. 451)

WORDS: Ron Sprunger, b. 1939
MUSIC: Traditional English melody

O WALY WALY
L.M.

438 Take Time to Be Holy

Make every effort . . . to be holy. Hebrews 12:14

1. Take time to be ho - ly— Speak oft with thy Lord.
2. Take time to be ho - ly— The world rush - es on.
3. Take time to be ho - ly— Let Him be thy guide,
4. Take time to be ho - ly— Be calm in thy soul,
A - bide in Him al - ways, And feed on His Word.
Spend much time in se - cret With Je - sus a - lone.
And run not be - fore Him What - ev - er be - tide.
Each thought and each mo - tive Be - neath His con - trol.
Make friends of God's chil - dren, Help those who are weak,
By look - ing to Je - sus, Like Him thou shalt be;
In joy or in sor - row, Still fol - low thy Lord,
Thus, led by His Spir - it To foun - tains of love,
For - get - ting in noth - ing His bless - ing to seek.
Thy friends in thy con - duct His like - ness shall see.
And, look - ing to Je - sus, Still trust in His Word.
Thou soon shalt be fit - ted For ser - vice a - bove.

WORDS: William D. Longstaff, 1822-1894
MUSIC: George C. Stebbins, 1846-1945

HOLINESS
6.5.6.5.D.

OUR FRIEND

MEDLEY

What a Friend We Have in Jesus
I Must Tell Jesus

What a Friend We Have in Jesus 439

By prayer and petition, with thanksgiving, present your requests to God. Philippians 4:6

1. What a friend we have in Je - sus, All our sins and griefs to bear!
2. Have we tri - als and temp - ta - tions? Is there trou - ble an - y - where?
3. Are we weak and heav - y - la - den, Cum-bered with a load of care?
What a priv - i - lege to car - ry Ev - ery - thing to God in prayer!
We should nev - er be dis - cour - aged— Take it to the Lord in prayer.
Pre - cious Sav - ior, still our ref - uge— Take it to the Lord in prayer.
O, what peace we of - ten for - feit, O, what need - less pain we bear,
Can we find a friend so faith - ful Who will all our sor - rows share?
Do thy friends de - spise, for - sake thee? Take it to the Lord in prayer.
Song ending
All be - cause we do not car - ry Ev - ery - thing to God in prayer.
Je - sus knows our ev - ery weak - ness— Take it to the Lord in prayer.
In His arms He'll take and shield thee; Thou wilt find a sol - ace there.

WORDS: Joseph M. Scriven, 1819-1886
MUSIC: Charles C. Converse, 1832-1918

CONVERSE
8.7.8.7.D.

Optional transition to "I Must Tell Jesus."
there.

440 I Must Tell Jesus

He is able to help those who are being tempted. Hebrews 2:18

1. I must tell Jesus all of my trials; I cannot bear these burdens alone. In my distress He kindly will help me; He ever loves and cares for His own.
2. I must tell Jesus all of my troubles; He is a kind, compassionate friend. If I but ask Him, He will deliver, Make of my troubles quickly an end.
3. Tempted and tried, I need a great Savior, One who can help my burdens to bear. I must tell Jesus, I must tell Jesus; He all my cares and sorrows will share.
4. O, how the world to evil allures me! O, how my heart is tempted to sin! I must tell Jesus, and He will help me Over the world the victory to win.

Refrain

I must tell Jesus! I must tell

WORDS: Elisha A. Hoffman, 1839-1929
MUSIC: Elisha A. Hoffman, 1839-1929

ORWIGSBURG
10.9.10.9. with Refrain

Je - sus! I can-not bear my bur-dens a - lone. I must tell
Je - sus! I must tell Je - sus! Je-sus can help me, Je-sus a - lone.

Prayer 441

Ask and it will be given to you; seek and you will find; knock and the door will be opened to you.

For everyone who asks receives; he who seeks finds; and to him who knocks, the door will be opened.

Which of you, if his son asks for bread, will give him a stone?

Or, if he asks for a fish, will give him a snake?

If you, then, though you are evil, know how to give good gifts to your children, how much more will your Father in heaven give good gifts to those who ask him!

Matthew 7:7-11

But when you pray, go into your room, close the door and pray to your Father, who is unseen. Then your Father, who sees what is done in secret, will reward you.

Matthew 6:6

442 Prayer Is the Soul's Sincere Desire

Pray in the Spirit on all occasions. Ephesians 6:18

1. Prayer is the soul's sin - cere de - sire, Un - ut - tered or ex - pressed, The mo - tion of a hid - den fire That trem - bles in the breast.
2. Prayer is the bur - den of a sigh, The fall - ing of a tear, The up - ward glanc - ing of an eye When none but God is near.
3. Prayer is the Chris - tian's vi - tal breath, The Chris - tian's na - tive air, Our watch - word at the gates of death— We en - ter heaven with prayer.
4. O Christ, by whom we come to God, The Life, the Truth, the Way, The path of prayer You too have trod— Lord, teach us how to pray.

WORDS: James Montgomery, 1771-1854, alt.
MUSIC: William H. Havergal, 1793-1870

EVAN
C.M.

443 Hear My Prayer, O LORD

Hear, O LORD, and answer me,
for I am poor and needy.
Bring joy to your servant,
for to you, O Lord, I lift up my soul.
You are forgiving and good, O Lord,
abounding in love to all who call to you.
Hear my prayer, O LORD;
listen to my cry for mercy.
In the day of my trouble I will call to you,
for you will answer me.

Among the gods there is none like you, O Lord;
no deeds can compare with yours.
All the nations you have made
will come and worship before you, O LORD;
they will bring glory to your name.
For you are great and do marvelous deeds;
you alone are God.
Give me a sign of your goodness,
that my enemies may see it and be put to shame,
for you, O LORD, have helped me and comforted me.

Psalm 86:1, 4-10, 17

The LORD has heard my cry for mercy;
the LORD accepts my prayer.

Psalm 6:9

From Every Stormy Wind That Blows 444

I will speak with you from above the mercy seat. Exodus 25:22, NKJV

1. From every stormy wind that blows, From every swelling tide of woes, There is a calm, a sure retreat, 'Tis found beneath the mercy seat.
2. There is a place where Jesus sheds The oil of gladness on our heads, A place than all besides more sweet, It is the blood-bought mercy seat.
3. There is a scene where spirits blend, Where friend holds fellowship with friend; Though sundered far, by faith they meet Around the common mercy seat.
4. There, there, on eagle's wings we soar, And sin and sense seem all no more, And heaven comes down our souls to greet, And glory crowns the mercy seat.

WORDS: Hugh Stowell, 1799-1865
MUSIC: Thomas Hastings, 1784-1872

RETREAT
L.M.

445 The Lord's Prayer

This, then, is how you should pray. Matthew 6:9

R.H.
Our Father, which art in heaven, Hallowed be Thy name.
R.H.
Thy kingdom come, Thy will be done on earth as it is in heaven.
Give us this day our daily bread, And forgive us our debts as
3

WORDS: Matthew 6:9-13, KJV
MUSIC: Albert Hay Malotte, 1895-1964; arr. Donald P. Hustad, b. 1918

MALOTTE
Irregular

we for-give our debt-ors.
And lead us not in-to temp-
ta-tion but de-liv-er us from e-vil. For Thine is the
king - dom, and the pow - er, and the
glo - ry, for-ev - er.
A - men, A - men.

446 Our Father

Pray to your Father, who is unseen. Matthew 6:6

Our Fa - ther, who art in heav - en, hal - lowed be Thy
name. Thy king-dom come, Thy will be done on
earth as it is in heaven. Give us this
day our dai - ly bread, and for -

WORDS: Based on Matthew 6:9-13
MUSIC: Gene Rivard, b. 1949

OUR FATHER
Irregular

give us our debts as we for-give our debt-ors.
And lead us not in-to temp-ta-tion but de-
liv-er us from e-vil. For Thine is the
king-dom, the pow-er, and the glo-ry, for
ev-er and ev-er. A-men.

447 Open Our Eyes, Lord

Blessed are the pure in heart, for they will see God. Matthew 5:8

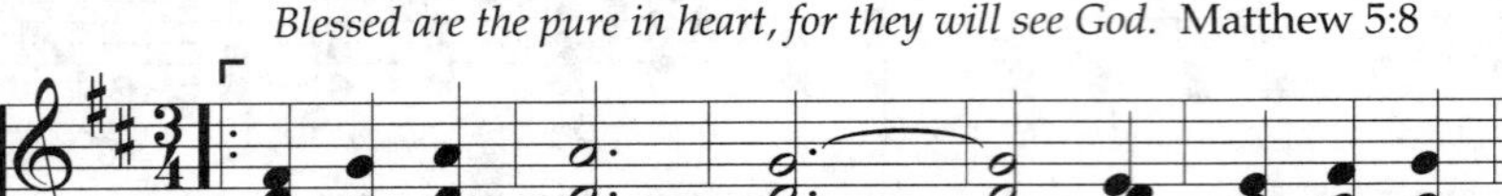
O - pen our eyes, Lord, we want to see Je - sus,
O - pen our ears, Lord, and help us to lis - ten.

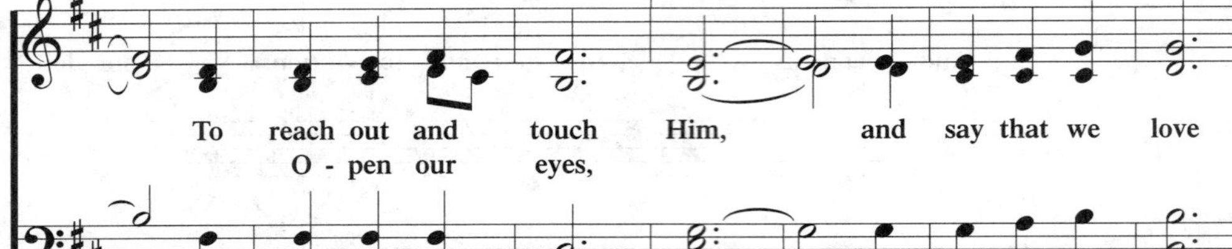
1.
To reach out and touch Him, and say that we love
O - pen our eyes,

2.
Him. Lord, we want to see Je - sus.

WORDS: Bob Cull, b. 1949
MUSIC: Bob Cull, b. 1949; arr. David Allen, b. 1941

OPEN OUR EYES
Irregular

THE LORD'S PRAYER

Our Father, Who art in heaven
Hallowed be Thy name.
Thy kingdom come, Thy will be done
On earth as it is in heaven.
Give us this day our daily bread,
And forgive us our trespasses
As we forgive those who trespass against us.
And lead us not into temptation,
But deliver us from evil.
For Thine is the kingdom, and the power, and the glory
Forever. Amen.

Based on Matthew 6:9-13

Love Divine, All Loves Excelling 448

Over all these virtues put on love. Colossians 3:14

1. Love di - vine, all loves ex - cel - ling, Joy of heaven, to earth come down.
2. Breathe, O, breathe Thy lov - ing Spir - it In - to ev - ery trou - bled breast.
3. Come, Al - might - y, to de - liv - er, Let us all Thy life re - ceive.
4. Fin - ish, then, Thy new cre - a - tion, Pure and spot - less let us be.
Fix in us Thy hum - ble dwell - ing, All Thy faith - ful mer - cies crown.
Let us all in Thee in - her - it, Let us find the prom - ised rest.
Sud - den - ly re - turn, and nev - er, Nev - er - more Thy tem - ples leave.
Let us see Thy great sal - va - tion Per - fect - ly re - stored in Thee.
Je - sus, Thou art all com - pas - sion, Pure, un - bound - ed love Thou art—
Take a - way the love of sin - ning. Al - pha and O - me - ga[1] be;
Thee we would be al - ways bless - ing, Serve Thee as Thy hosts a - bove,
Changed from glo - ry in - to glo - ry Till in heaven we take our place,
Vis - it us with Thy sal - va - tion, En - ter ev - ery trem - bling heart.
End of faith, as its be - gin - ning, Set our hearts at lib - er - ty.
Pray and praise Thee with - out ceas - ing, Glo - ry in Thy per - fect love.
Till we cast our crowns be - fore Thee, Lost in won - der, love and praise.

WORDS: Charles Wesley, 1707-1788
MUSIC: John Zundel, 1815-1882

BEECHER
8.7.8.7.D.

1. Alpha and Omega: first and last letters in the Greek alphabet; a name of God

449 O Love That Will Not Let Me Go

I have loved you with an everlasting love. Jeremiah 31:3

1. O Love that will not let me go, I rest my wea - ry soul in Thee. I give Thee back the life I owe, That in Thine o - cean depths its flow May rich - er, full - er be.
2. O Light that fol - lowest all my way, I yield my flick - ering torch to Thee. My heart re - stores its bor - rowed ray, That in Thy sun - shine's blaze its day May bright - er, fair - er be.
3. O Joy that seek - est me through pain, I can - not close my heart to Thee. I trace the rain - bow through the rain, And feel the prom - ise is not vain That morn shall tear - less be.
4. O Cross that lift - est up my head, I dare not ask to fly from Thee. I lay in dust life's glo - ry dead, And from the ground there blos - soms red Life that shall end - less be.

WORDS: George Matheson, 1842-1906
MUSIC: Albert L. Peace, 1844-1912

ST. MARGARET
8.8.8.8.6.

The King of Love My Shepherd Is 450

The Lord is my shepherd, I shall not be in want. Psalm 23:1

1. The King of love my Shep - herd is, Whose
2. Where streams of liv - ing wa - ter flow My
3. Per - verse and fool - ish oft I strayed, But
4. In death's dark vale I fear no ill With
5. Thou spreadst a ta - ble in my sight. Thy
6. And so through all the length of days Thy
good - ness fail - eth nev - er. I noth - ing lack if
ran - somed soul He lead - eth, And where the ver - dant
yet in love He sought me, And on His shoul - der
Thee, dear Lord, be - side me. Thy rod and staff my
unc - tion grace be - stow - eth. And O, what trans - port
good - ness fail - eth nev - er. Good Shep - herd, may I
I am His And He is mine for - ev - er.
pas - tures grow, With food cel - es - tial feed - eth.
gent - ly laid, And home, re - joic - ing, brought me.
com - fort still, Thy cross be - fore to guide me.
of de - light From Thy pure chal - ice flow - eth.
sing Thy praise With - in Thy house for - ev - er.

WORDS: Henry W. Baker, 1821-1877
MUSIC: John B. Dykes, 1823-1876

DOMINUS REGIT ME
8.7.8.7.

451 The Gift of Love

But the greatest of these is love. 1 Corinthians 13:13

1. Though I may speak with brav - est fire, And have the gift to all in - spire, And have not
2. Though I may give all I pos - sess, And striv - ing so my love pro - fess, But not be
3. Come, Spir - it, come, our hearts con - trol, Our spir - its long to be made whole. Let in - ward
mf
f

WORDS: Hal H. Hopson, b. 1933; para. 1 Corinthians 13
MUSIC: Traditional English melody; adapt. Hal H. Hopson, b. 1933

GIFT OF LOVE
L.M.

love, my words are vain,
given by love with - in,
love guide ev - ery deed;
1, 2.
As sound - ing brass, and hope - less gain.
The prof - it soon turns strange - ly thin.
By this we wor - ship, and are
1, 2.
3.
freed.
3.
rit.
pp

452 What Wondrous Love Is This

Praise be to the LORD, for he showed his wonderful love to me. Psalm 31:21

Unison
1. What wondrous love is this, O my soul, O my soul, What wondrous love is this, O my soul! What wondrous love is this that caused the Lord of bliss To bear the dread-ful curse for my soul, for my soul, To bear the dread-ful curse for my soul.
2. What wondrous love is this, O my soul, O my soul, What wondrous love is this, O my soul! What wondrous love is this, that caused the Lord of life To lay a-side his crown for my soul, for my soul, To lay a-side his crown for my soul.
3. To God and to the Lamb I will sing, I will sing, To God and to the Lamb, I will sing. To God and to the Lamb who is the great I AM, While mil-lions join the theme I will sing, I will sing, While mil-lions join the theme I will sing.
4. And when from death I'm free, I'll sing on, I'll sing on, And when from death I'm free, I'll sing on. And when from death I'm free, I'll sing and joy-ful be, And through e-ter-ni-ty I'll sing on, I'll sing on, And through e-ter-ni-ty I'll sing on.

WORDS: American folk hymn
MUSIC: William Walker's *Southern Harmony*, 1835

WONDROUS LOVE
12.9.12.12.9.

OUR MODEL OF LOVE

MEDLEY

Here Is Love
In Moments Like These

Here Is Love 453

Greater love has no one than this, that he lay down his life for his friends. John 15:13

1. Here is love, vast as the o - cean, Lov - ing - kind - ness as the flood,
2. On the mount of cru - ci - fix - ion, Foun-tains o - pened deep and wide;
3. Let me all Your love ac - cept - ing Love You ev - er all my days.
When the Prince of Life, our Ran - som, Shed for us His pre - cious blood.
Through the flood - gates of God's mer - cy Flowed a vast and gra - cious tide.
Let me seek Your king - dom on - ly, All my life be to Your praise.
Who His love will not re - mem - ber? Who can cease to sing His praise?
Grace and love, like might - y riv - ers, Poured in - ces - sant from a - bove,
You a - lone shall be my glo - ry, Noth - ing in the world I see.
Song ending
He can nev - er be for - got - ten, Through-out heaven's e - ter - nal days.
And heaven's peace and per - fect jus - tice Kissed a guilt - y world in love.
You have cleansed and sanc - ti - fied me, You a - lone have set me free.

WORDS: William Rees, 1802-1883; tr. William Edwards, 1848-1929, from Welsh
MUSIC: Robert Lowry, 1826-1899

CYMRAEG
8.7.8.7.D.

Optional transition to "In Moments Like These."
free.

454 In Moments Like These

I love you, O LORD, my strength. Psalm 18:1

In mo - ments like these, I sing out a song, I

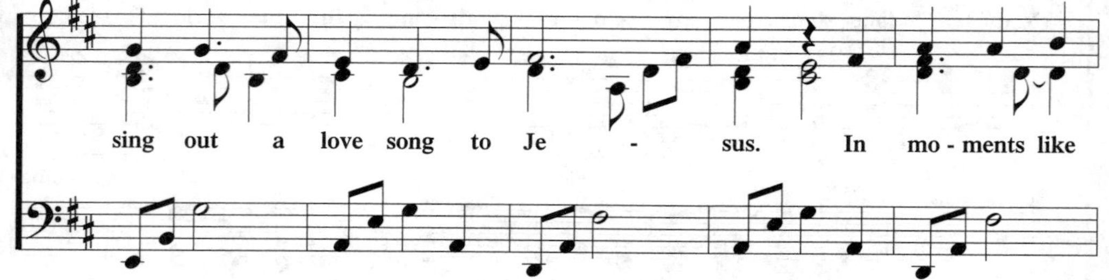
sing out a love song to Je - sus. In mo - ments like

WORDS: David Graham, b. 1948
MUSIC: David Graham, b. 1948

GRAHAM
Irregular

these, I lift up my hands, I lift up my hands to the
Lord. Sing - ing, "I love You, Lord."
Sing - ing, "I love You, Lord."
Sing - ing, "I love You, Lord.
I love You."

455 How Great Is Your Love

How wide and long and high and deep is the love of Christ. Ephesians 3:18

1. No eye has seen and no ear has heard, And
2. Ob - jects of mer - cy, who should have known wrath, We're
no mind has ev - er con - ceived The
filled with un - speak - a - ble joy,
glo - ri - ous things that You have pre - pared For
Rich - es of wis - dom, un - search - a - ble wealth, And the
ev - ery - one who has be - lieved.
won - der of know - ing Your voice.
You brought us
You are our

WORDS: Mark Altrogge, b. 1950
MUSIC: Mark Altrogge, b. 1950

HOW GREAT IS YOUR LOVE
Irregular

near and You called us Your own And made us joint
trea - sure and our great re - ward, Our hope and our
heirs with Your Son.
glo - ri - ous King.
Refrain
How high and how wide, how
deep and how long, How sweet and how strong is Your love.
How lav - ish Your grace, how faith - ful Your ways, How
great is Your love, O Lord!

456 The Love of God

I have loved you with an everlasting love. Jeremiah 31:3

1. The love of God is great - er far Than tongue or pen can ev - er tell.
2. When years of time shall pass a - way And earth - ly thrones and king-doms fall,
3. Could we with ink the o - cean fill And were the skies of parch-ment made,
It goes be - yond the high - est star, And reach - es to the low - est hell.
When men who here re - fuse to pray, On rocks and hills and moun - tains call,
Were ev - ery stalk on earth a quill And ev - ery man a scribe by trade,
The guilt - y pair, bowed down with care, God gave His Son to win.
God's love so sure shall still en - dure, All mea - sure - less and strong;
To write the love of God a - bove Would drain the o - cean dry;
His err - ing child He re - con - ciled, And par - doned from his sin.
Re - deem-ing grace to Ad - am's race— The saints' and an - gels' song.
Nor could the scroll con - tain the whole, Though stretched from sky to sky.

WORDS: Frederick M. Lehman, 1868-1953; stanza 3, Meir Ben Isaac Nehorai, 11th century
MUSIC: Frederick M. Lehman, 1868-1953

LOVE OF GOD
Irregular

Refrain
O love of God, how rich and pure! How mea - sure - less and
strong! It shall for - ev - er - more en - dure— The saints' and an - gels' song!

Love 457

If I speak in the tongues of men and of angels, but have not love, I am only a resounding gong or a clanging cymbal.

If I have the gift of prophecy and can fathom all mysteries and all knowledge, and if I have a faith that can move mountains, but have not love, I am nothing.

If I give all I possess to the poor and surrender my body to the flames, but have not love, I gain nothing.

Love is patient, love is kind. It does not envy, it does not boast, it is not proud.

It is not rude, it is not self-seeking, it is not easily angered, it keeps no record of wrongs.

Love does not delight in evil but rejoices with the truth. It always protects, always trusts, always hopes, always perseveres. Love never fails.

But where there are prophecies, they will cease; where there are tongues, they will be stilled; where there is knowledge, it will pass away.

For we know in part and we prophesy in part, but when perfection comes, the imperfect disappears.

When I was a child, I talked like a child, I thought like a child, I reasoned like a child. When I became a man, I put childish ways behind me.

Now we see but a poor reflection as in a mirror; then we shall see face to face.

Now I know in part; then I shall know fully, even as I am fully known.

And now these three remain: faith, hope and love. But the greatest of these is love.

1 Corinthians 13

458 O, the Deep, Deep Love of Jesus

He now showed them the full extent of his love. John 13:1

1. O, the deep, deep love of Je - sus, Vast, un - mea - sured, bound - less, free, Roll - ing as a might - y o - cean In its full - ness o - ver me. Un - der - neath me, all a - round me, Is the cur - rent of Thy love, Lead - ing on - ward,
2. O, the deep, deep love of Je - sus, Spread His praise from shore to shore. How He loves us, ev - er loves us, Chang - es nev - er, nev - er - more. How He watch - es o'er His loved ones, Died to call them all His own, How for them He's
3. O, the deep, deep love of Je - sus, Love of ev - ery love the best. 'Tis an o - cean vast of bless - ing, 'Tis a ha - ven sweet of rest. O, the deep, deep love of Je - sus, 'Tis a heaven of heavens to me, And it lifts me
3
3
3

WORDS: Samuel T. Francis, 1834-1925, alt.
MUSIC: Thomas J. Williams, 1869-1944

EBENEZER
8.7.8.7.D.

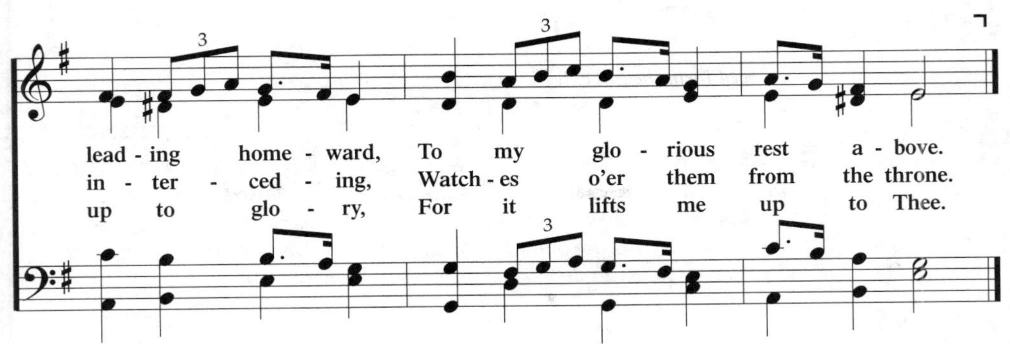
3
3
lead - ing home - ward, To my glo - rious rest a - bove.
in - ter - ced - ing, Watch - es o'er them from the throne.
up to glo - ry, For it lifts me up to Thee.
3

Jesus Loves Me 459

Let the little children come to me, and do not hinder them. Mark 10:14

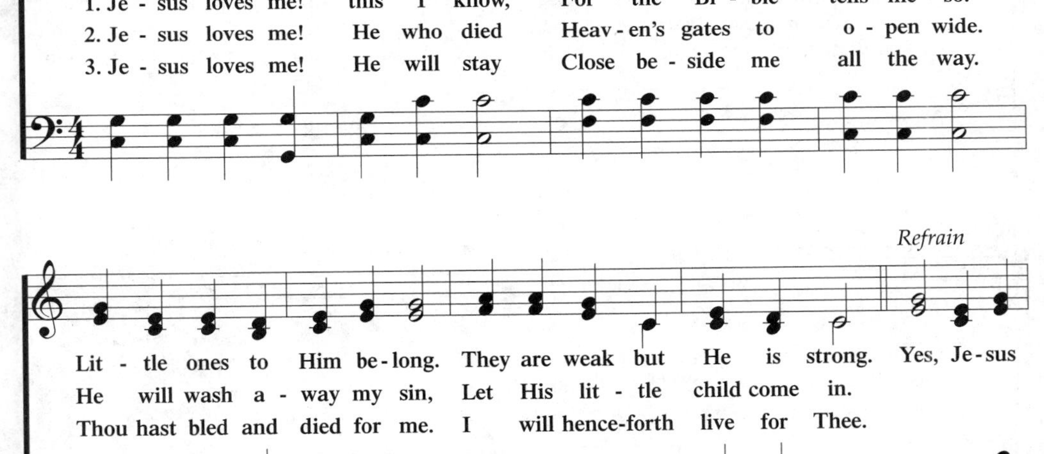
1. Je - sus loves me! this I know, For the Bi - ble tells me so.
2. Je - sus loves me! He who died Heav - en's gates to o - pen wide.
3. Je - sus loves me! He will stay Close be - side me all the way.
Refrain
Lit - tle ones to Him be - long. They are weak but He is strong. Yes, Je - sus
He will wash a - way my sin, Let His lit - tle child come in.
Thou hast bled and died for me. I will hence-forth live for Thee.

loves me. Yes, Je - sus loves me. Yes, Je - sus loves me. The Bi - ble tells me so.

WORDS: Anna B. Warner, 1820-1915
MUSIC: William B. Bradbury, 1816-1868

JESUS LOVES ME
7.7.7.7. with Refrain

460 O Love Divine

Love never fails. 1 Corinthians 13:8

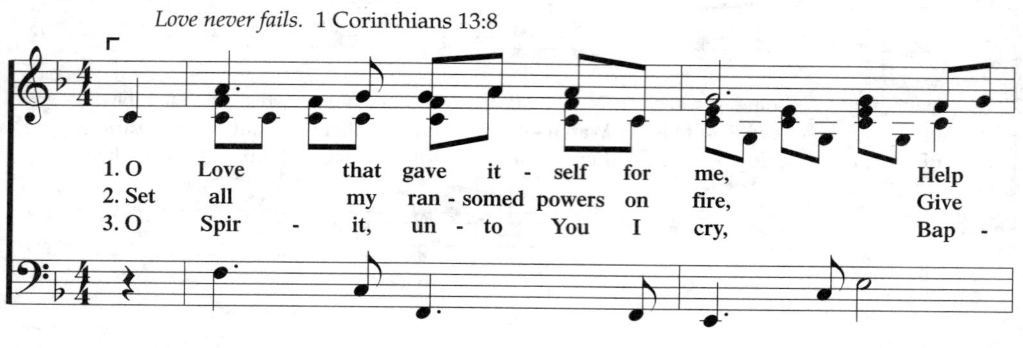
1. O Love that gave it - self for me, Help
2. Set all my ran - somed powers on fire, Give
3. O Spir - it, un - to You I cry, Bap -

me to love and live like Thee, And kin - dle in this heart of
me the love that will not tire, And kin - dle in this heart of
tize with pow - er from on high, And kin - dle in this heart of

mine The pas - sion fire of love di - vine.
mine The liv - ing fire of zeal di - vine.
mine The liv - ing fire of power di - vine.

Refrain
O Love di - vine, O Love di - vine, Re - vive this long - ing heart of mine, And

WORDS: Albert B. Simpson, 1843-1919, alt.
MUSIC: David Hahn, b. 1956

O LOVE DIVINE
L.M. with Refrain

kin - dle in me from a - bove The liv - ing fire of heav - en's love.

His Love Endures Forever 461

Give thanks to the LORD, for he is good.
His love endures forever.
Give thanks to the God of gods.
His love endures forever.
Give thanks to the Lord of lords.
His love endures forever.

Psalm 136:1-3

And now, O Israel, what does the LORD your God ask of you but to fear the LORD your God, to walk in all his ways,
to love him, to serve the LORD your God with all your heart and with all your soul.

Deuteronomy 10:12

I love you, O LORD, my strength. The LORD is my rock, my fortress and my deliverer; my God is my rock, in whom I take refuge.
Be exalted, O LORD, in your strength; we will sing and praise your might.

Psalm 18:1-2; 21:13

Though you have not seen him, you love him; and even though you do not see him now, you believe in him and are filled with inexpressible and glorious joy,
for you are receiving the goal of your faith, the salvation of your souls.

1 Peter 1:8-9

He sent his one and only Son into the world that we might live through him. This is love: not that we loved God,
but that he loved us and sent his Son as an atoning sacrifice for our sins.
Thanks be to God for his indescribable gift!

1 John 4:9-10; 2 Corinthians 9:15

462 He Giveth More Grace

Grace has been given as Christ apportioned it. Ephesians 4:7

1. He giv - eth more grace when the bur - dens grow great - er. He send - eth more
2. When we have ex - haust - ed our store of en - dur - ance, When our strength has
strength when the la - bors in - crease. To add - ed af - flic - tion He
failed ere the day is half done, When we reach the end of our
add - eth His mer - cy, To mul - ti - plied tri - als, His mul - ti - plied peace.
hoard - ed re - sourc - es, Our Fa - ther's full giv - ing is on - ly be - gun.
Refrain
His love has no lim - it, His grace has no mea - sure. His power has no

WORDS: Annie J. Flint, 1862-1932
MUSIC: Hubert Mitchell, 20th century

HE GIVETH MORE GRACE
12.11.12.11. with Refrain

bound - a - ry known un - to men. For out of His in - fi - nite
rich - es in Je - sus, He giv - eth, and giv - eth, and giv - eth a - gain!

WHERE LOVE BEGINS

We are not responsible to feel but we are responsible to love, and true spiritual love begins in the will. We should set our hearts to love God supremely, however cold or hard they may seem to be, and go on to confirm our love by careful and happy obedience to His Word. Enjoyable emotions are sure to follow. Bird song and blossoms do not make the spring, but when the spring comes they come with it.

A.W. Tozer (1897-1963), adapted from *God Tells the Man Who Cares*

463 Such Love

. . . that the love you have for me may be in them. John 17:26

3
1. Such love, pure as the whit - est snow;
2. Such love, still - ing my rest - less - ness;
3. Such love springs from e - ter - ni - ty;
3
Such love weeps for the shame I know;
Such love, fill - ing my emp - ti - ness;
Such love, stream - ing through his - to - ry;
3
Such love, pay - ing the debt I owe;
Such love, show - ing me ho - li - ness;
Such love, foun - tain of life to me;
O Je - sus, such love.
O Je - sus, such love.
O Je - sus, such love.

WORDS: Graham Kendrick, b. 1950
MUSIC: Graham Kendrick, b. 1950

SUCH LOVE
Irregular

How Can I Help but Love Him? 464

For God so loved the world that he gave his one and only Son. John 3:16

1. Down from His splen - dor in glo - ry He came In - to a world of woe,
2. I am un - wor - thy to take of His grace, Won - der - ful grace so free.
3. He is the fair - est of thou - sands to me, His love is sweet and true.
Took on Him - self all my guilt and my shame— Why should He love me so?
Yet Je - sus suf - fered and died in my place, E'en for a soul like me.
Won - der - ful beau - ty in Him I now see, More than I ev - er knew.
Refrain
How can I help but love Him When He loved me so?
How can I help but love Him When He loved me so?

WORDS: Elton M. Roth, 1891-1951
MUSIC: Elton M. Roth, 1891-1951

ROTH
10.6.10.6 with Refrain

465 Jesus Loves Even Me

Christ Jesus came into the world to save sinners—of whom I am the worst. 1 Timothy 1:15

1. I am so glad that our Fa-ther in heaven Tells of His love in the Book He has given. Won-der-ful things in the Bi-ble I see; This is the dear-est, that Je-sus loves me.
2. Though I for-get Him and wan-der a-way, Still He doth love me wher-ev-er I stray. Back to His dear, lov-ing arms would I flee When I re-mem-ber that Je-sus loves me.
3. O, if there's on-ly one song I can sing When in His beau-ty I see the great King. This shall my song in e-ter-ni-ty be; "O, what a won-der that Je-sus loves me!"
Refrain
I am so glad that Je-sus loves me, Je-sus loves me, Je-sus loves me!
I am so glad that Je-sus loves me, Je-sus loves ev-en me!
WORDS: Philip P. Bliss, 1838-1876
MUSIC: Philip P. Bliss, 1838-1876
GLADNESS
10.10.10.10. with Refrain

More Love to Thee 466

This is my prayer: that your love may abound more and more. Philippians 1:9

1. More love to Thee, O Christ, More love to Thee!
2. Once earth - ly joy I craved, Sought peace and rest.
3. Let sor - row do its work, Send grief and pain.
4. Then shall my lat - est breath Whis - per Thy praise.
Hear Thou the prayer I make On bend - ed knee.
Now Thee a - lone I seek, Give what is best.
Sweet are Thy mes - sen - gers, Sweet their re - frain,
This be the part - ing cry My heart shall raise.
This is my ear - nest plea, More love, O Christ, to Thee,
This all my prayer shall be, More love, O Christ, to Thee,
When they can sing with me, More love, O Christ, to Thee,
This still its prayer shall be, More love, O Christ, to Thee,
More love to Thee, More love to Thee.
More love to Thee, More love to Thee.
More love to Thee, More love to Thee.
More love to Thee, More love to Thee.

Optional segue to "O, How I Love Jesus." No transition required.

WORDS: Elizabeth P. Prentiss, 1818-1878
MUSIC: William H. Doane, 1832-1915

MORE LOVE TO THEE
6.4.6.4.6.6.4.4.

467 O, How I Love Jesus

Though you have not seen him, you love him. 1 Peter 1:8

1. There is a name I love to hear, I love to sing its worth.
2. It tells me of a Sav-ior's love, Who died to set me free.
3. It tells me what my Fa-ther has In store for ev-ery day.
4. It tells of One whose lov-ing heart Can feel my deep-est woe,
It sounds like mu-sic in my ear, The sweet-est name on earth.
It tells me of His pre-cious blood, The sin-ner's per-fect plea.
And though I tread a dark-some path, Yields sun-shine all the way.
Who in each sor-row bears a part, That none can bear be-low.
Refrain
O, how I love Je-sus, O, how I love Je-sus,
O, how I love Je-sus, Be-cause He first loved me.

WORDS: Frederick Whitfield, 1829-1904
MUSIC: Anonymous

O HOW I LOVE JESUS
C.M. with Refrain

O Jesus, Jesus 468

I love you, O LORD. Psalm 18:1

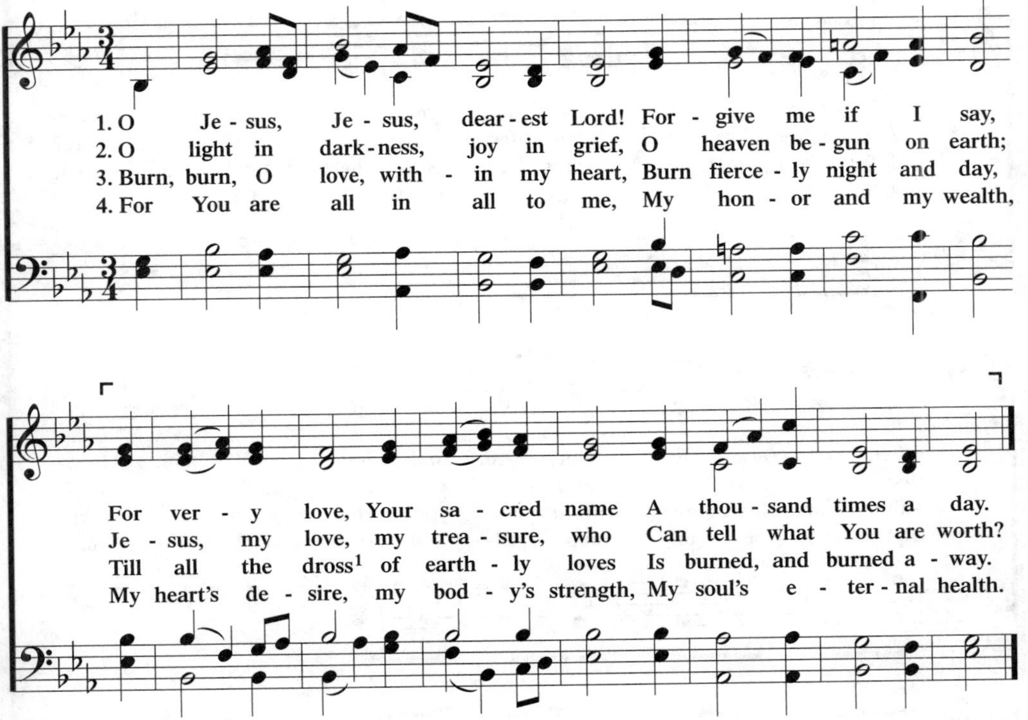
1. O Je - sus, Je - sus, dear - est Lord! For - give me if I say,
2. O light in dark - ness, joy in grief, O heaven be - gun on earth;
3. Burn, burn, O love, with - in my heart, Burn fierce - ly night and day,
4. For You are all in all to me, My hon - or and my wealth,
For ver - y love, Your sa - cred name A thou - sand times a day.
Je - sus, my love, my trea - sure, who Can tell what You are worth?
Till all the dross[1] of earth - ly loves Is burned, and burned a - way.
My heart's de - sire, my bod - y's strength, My soul's e - ter - nal health.

(*For higher key, see No. 376*)

WORDS: Frederick W. Faber, 1814-1863, alt.
MUSIC: Jessie S. Irvine, 1836-1887; arr. David Grant, 1833-1893

CRIMOND
C.M.

1. dross: impurity

PRAYER OF GRATITUDE FOR GOD'S TENDER MERCIES

Honor and praise be unto You, O Lord our God, for all Your tender mercies again bestowed upon us throughout another week.
Continual thanks be unto You for creating us in Your own likeness;
for redeeming us by the precious blood of Your dear Son when we were lost;
and for sanctifying us with the Holy Spirit.

John Knox (1505-1572)

469 Count Your Blessings

Many, O LORD my God, are the wonders you have done. Psalm 40:5

1. When up - on life's bil - lows[1] you are tem - pest - tossed,
2. Are you ev - er bur - dened with a load of care?
3. When you look at oth - ers with their lands and gold,
4. So, a - mid the con - flict, wheth - er great or small,

When you are dis - cour - aged, think - ing all is lost,
Does the cross seem heav - y you are called to bear?
Think that Christ has prom - ised you His wealth un - told.
Do not be dis - cour - aged— God is o - ver all.

Count your man - y bless - ings, name them one by one,
Count your man - y bless - ings, ev - ery doubt will fly,
Count your man - y bless - ings, wealth can nev - er buy
Count your man - y bless - ings, an - gels will at - tend,

And it will sur - prise you what the Lord has done.
And you will keep sing - ing as the days go by.
Your re - ward in heav - en, nor your home on high.
Help and com - fort give you to your jour - ney's end.

WORDS: Johnson Oatman, Jr., 1856-1926
MUSIC: Edwin O. Excell, 1851-1921

BLESSINGS
11.11.11.11. with Refrain

1. billows: waves

Refrain
Count your bless-ings; name them one by one.
Count your man-y bless-ings; name them one by one.
Count your bless-ings; see what God has done!
Count your man-y bless-ings; see what God has done!
Count your bless-ings; name them one by one.
Count your man-y bless-ings; name them one by one.
Count your man-y bless-ings; see what God has done.

470 I Love Thee, I Love Thee

Lord, you know all things; you know that I love you. John 21:17

1. I love Thee, I love Thee, I love Thee, my Lord.
I love Thee, my Savior, I love Thee, my God.
I love Thee, I love Thee, and that Thou dost know,
But how much I love Thee my actions will show.

2. I'm happy, I'm happy. O, wondrous account!
My joys are immortal, I stand on the mount.
I gaze on my treasure and long to be there,
With Jesus and angels and kindred so dear.

3. O Jesus, my Savior, with Thee I am blest,
My life and salvation, my joy and my rest.
Thy name be my theme, and Thy love be my song.
Thy grace shall inspire both my heart and my tongue.

4. O, who's like my Savior? He's Salem's bright King.[1]
He smiles and He loves me and helps me to sing.
I'll praise Him, I'll praise Him with notes loud and clear,
While rivers of pleasure my spirit shall cheer.

WORDS: Anonymous
MUSIC: From Jeremiah Ingall's *Christian Harmony*, 1805

I LOVE THEE
11.11.11.11.

1. *Salem's bright King: reference to Melchizedek, priest/king of Genesis 14:18 (Hebrews 7)*

I Love You, Lord 471

Love the Lord your God with all your heart. Matthew 22:37

I love You, Lord, and I lift my voice to
wor - ship You, O my soul re - joice. Take
joy, my King, in what You hear. May it be a
sweet, sweet sound in Your ear.

Optional segue to "My Jesus, I Love Thee." No transition required.

WORDS: Laurie Klein, b. 1950
MUSIC: Laurie Klein, b. 1950

I LOVE YOU, LORD
Irregular

472 My Jesus, I Love Thee

We love Him because He first loved us. 1 John 4:19, NKJV

1. My Je - sus, I love Thee, I know Thou art mine,
2. I love Thee be - cause Thou hast first lov - ed me,
3. I'll love Thee in life, I will love Thee in death,
4. In man - sions of glo - ry and end - less de - light,
For Thee all the fol - lies of sin I re - sign.
And pur - chased my par - don on Cal - va - ry's tree.
And praise Thee as long as Thou lend - est me breath,
I'll ev - er a - dore Thee in heav - en so bright.
My gra - cious Re - deem - er, my Sav - ior art Thou.
I love Thee for wear - ing the thorns on Thy brow.
And say, when the death - dew lies cold on my brow,
I'll sing with a glit - ter - ing crown on my brow,
If ev - er I loved Thee, my Je - sus, 'tis now.
If ev - er I loved Thee, my Je - sus, 'tis now.
If ev - er I loved Thee, my Je - sus, 'tis now.
If ev - er I loved Thee, my Je - sus, 'tis now.

WORDS: William R. Featherstone, 1846-1873
MUSIC: Adoniram J. Gordon, 1836-1895

GORDON
11.11.11.11.

The Church's One Foundation 473

No one can lay any foundation other than . . . Jesus Christ. 1 Corinthians 3:11

1. The Church - 's one Foun - da - tion is Je - sus Christ her Lord.
2. E - lect from ev - ery na - tion, yet one o'er all the earth,
3. Though with a scorn - ful won - der men see her sore op - pressed
4. 'Mid toil and trib - u - la - tion and tu - mult of her war,
5. Yet she on earth hath un - ion with God the Three - in - One,
She is His new cre - a - tion by wa - ter and the Word.
Her char - ter of sal - va - tion, one Lord, one faith, one birth,
By schis - ms rent a - sun - der, by her - e - sies dis - tressed.
She waits the con - sum - ma - tion of peace for - ev - er - more,
And mys - tic sweet com - mun - ion with those whose rest is won.
From heaven He came and sought her to be His ho - ly bride,
One ho - ly name she bless - es, par - takes one ho - ly food,
Yet saints their watch are keep - ing, their cry goes up— "How long?"
Till with the vi - sion glo - rious her long - ing eyes are blest,
O, hap - py ones and ho - ly! Lord, give us grace that we,
With His own blood He bought her, and for her life He died.
And to one hope she press - es, with ev - ery grace en - dued.
But soon the night of weep - ing shall be the morn of song.
And the great Church vic - to - rious shall be the Church at rest.
Like them, the meek and low - ly, on high may dwell with Thee.

WORDS: Samuel J. Stone, 1839-1900
MUSIC: Samuel S. Wesley, 1810-1876

AURELIA
7.6.7.6.D.

474 Christ Is Made the Sure Foundation

See, I lay a . . . precious cornerstone for a sure foundation. Isaiah 28:16

1. Christ is made the sure foun - da - tion, Christ, the
2. To this tem - ple, where we call You, Come, O
3. Grant, we pray, to all Your ser - vants What they
4. Praise and hon - or to the Fa - ther, Praise and
head and cor - ner - stone, Cho - sen of the Lord and pre - cious,
Lord of hosts, to - day. Come, with all Your lov - ing kind - ness
ask of You to gain; What they gain from You for - ev - er
hon - or to the Son, Praise and hon - or to the Spir - it—
Bind - ing all the Church in one; Ho - ly Zi - on's[1]
Hear Your peo - ple as they pray, And Your full - est
With the bless - ed to re - tain; And here - af - ter
Ev - er Three and ev - er One, One in might and
help for - ev - er, And her con - fi - dence a - lone.
ben - e - dic - tion Shed with - in these walls al - way.
in Your glo - ry Ev - er - more with You to reign.
One in glo - ry, While un - end - ing a - ges run!

WORDS: Latin, 7th century; tr. John M. Neale, 1818-1866, alt.
MUSIC: John Goss, 1800-1880

LAUDA ANIMA
8.7.8.7.8.7.

1. Zion: the church

Glorious Things of Thee Are Spoken 475

Glorious things are said of you, O city of God. Psalm 87:3

1. Glo-rious things of thee are spo - ken, Zi - on, cit - y of our God;
2. See, the streams of liv - ing wa - ters, Spring - ing from e - ter - nal love,
3. Blest in - hab - i - tants of Zi - on, Washed in our Re - deem-er's blood;
4. Sav - ior, if of Zi - on's cit - y I, through grace, a mem - ber am,

He whose word can - not be bro - ken Formed you for His own a - bode.
Well sup - ply your sons and daugh-ters, And all fear of want re - move.
Je - sus, whom our souls re - ly on, Makes us kings and priests to God.
Let the world de - ride or pi - ty— I will glo - ry in Your name.

On the Rock of A - ges found - ed, What can shake your sure re - pose?
Who can faint, when such a riv - er Ev - er will their thirst as - suage;[1]
By sur - pass - ing love He lifts us O - ver self to reign as kings;
Fad - ing are the world's best plea - sures, All its boast - ed pomp and show.

With sal - va - tion's walls sur-round-ed, You may smile at all your foes.
Grace, which like the Lord, the giv - er, Nev - er fails from age to age.
And as priests, His sol - emn prais - es, We for thank - ful of - fering bring.
Sol - id joys and last - ing trea - sure None but Zi - on's chil - dren know.

(For different harmony, see No. 661)

WORDS: John Newton, 1725-1807, alt.
MUSIC: Franz Joseph Haydn, 1732-1809

AUSTRIA
8.7.8.7.D.

1. assuage: quench

476 O Church of God, United

That they may be one as we are one. John 17:22

1. O Church of God, u - nit - ed to serve one com - mon Lord, Pro - claim to all one mes - sage, with hearts in glad ac - cord. Christ ev - er goes be - fore us; we fol - low day by day With
2. From ev - ery land and na - tion the or - dered ranks ap - pear; To serve one val - iant Lead - er they come from far and near. They chant their one con - fes - sion, they praise one liv - ing Lord, And
3. Though creeds and tongues may dif - fer, they speak, O Christ, of Thee; And in Thy lov - ing Spir - it we shall one peo - ple be. Lord, may our faith - ful ser - vice and sin - gle - ness of aim Pro -
4. May Thy great prayer be an - swered that we may all be one, Close bound, by love u - nit - ed in Thee, God's bless - ed Son; To bring a sin - gle wit - ness, to make the path - way bright, That

(For higher key, see No. 33.)

WORDS: Frederick B. Morley, 20th century
MUSIC: From *Gesangbuch der Herzogl*, Württemberg, 1784, alt.

ELLACOMBE
C.M.D.

strong and ea - ger foot - steps a - long the up - ward way.
place their sure de - pen - dence up - on His sav - ing Word.
claim to all the pow - er of Thy re - deem - ing name.
souls which grope in dark - ness may find the one true Light.

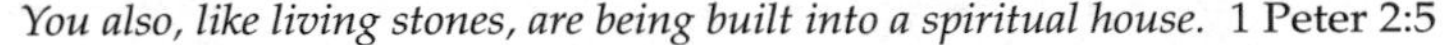

Living Stones 477

You also, like living stones, are being built into a spiritual house. 1 Peter 2:5

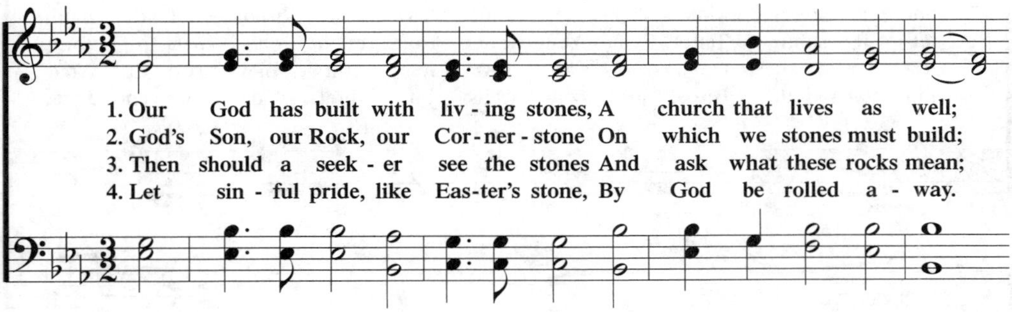

1. Our God has built with liv - ing stones, A church that lives as well;
2. God's Son, our Rock, our Cor - ner - stone On which we stones must build;
3. Then should a seek - er see the stones And ask what these rocks mean;
4. Let sin - ful pride, like Eas - ter's stone, By God be rolled a - way.

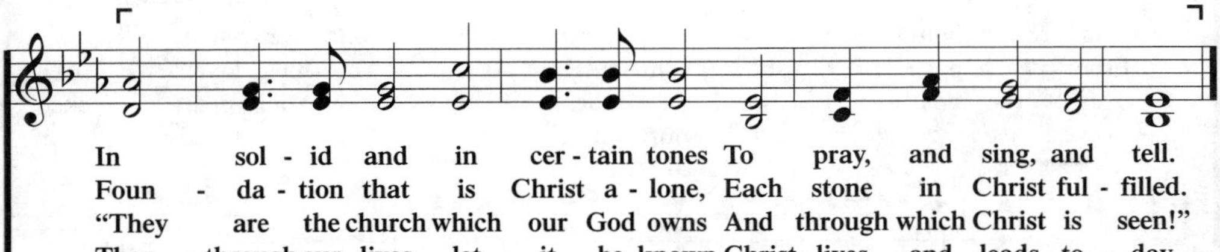

In sol - id and in cer - tain tones To pray, and sing, and tell.
Foun - da - tion that is Christ a - lone, Each stone in Christ ful - filled.
"They are the church which our God owns And through which Christ is seen!"
Then through our lives let it be known Christ lives and leads to - day.

(For lower key, see No. 402.)

WORDS: Terry W. York, b. 1949
MUSIC: Thomas A. Arne, 1710-1778

ARLINGTON
C.M.

478 Renew Your Church

Repent and do the things you did at first. Revelation 2:5

1. Re - new Your Church, her min - is - tries re - store, Both to serve
2. Teach us Your Word, re - veal its truth di - vine, On our path
3. Teach us to pray, for You are ev - er near, Your still voice
4. Teach us to love, with strength of heart and mind, Each and all,
and a - dore. Make her a - gain as salt through - out the land,
let it shine. Tell of Your works, Your might - y acts of grace,
let us hear. Our souls are rest - less till they rest in You,
hu - man - kind. Break down old walls of prej - u - dice and hate,
And as light from a stand. 'Mid som - ber shad - ows
From each page show Your face. As You have loved us,
This the goal we pur - sue. Be - fore Your pres - ence
Leave us not to our fate. As You have loved and
of the night, Where greed and ha - treds spread their blight, O,
sent Your Son, And our sal - va - tion now is won, O,
keep us still That we may find for us Your will, And
given Your life To end hos - til - i - ty and strife, O,

WORDS: Kenneth L. Cober, 20th century, alt.
MUSIC: From *The Sacred Harp*, 1844

ALL IS WELL
10.6.10.6.8.8.8.6.

send us forth with power en - dued, Help us, Lord, be re - newed.
let our hearts with love be stirred, Help us, Lord, know Your Word.
seek Your guid - ance ev - ery day, Teach us Lord, how to pray.
share Your grace from heaven a - bove, Teach us, Lord, how to love.

Revival 479

When the people heard [Peter's sermon] they were cut to the heart and said to Peter and the other apostles,

"Brothers, what shall we do?"

Peter replied, "Repent and be baptized, every one of you, in the name of Jesus Christ for the forgiveness of your sins. And you will receive the gift of the Holy Spirit.

The promise is for you and your children and for all who are far off—for all whom the Lord our God will call."

With many other words he warned them; and he pleaded with them, "Save yourselves from this corrupt generation."

Those who accepted his message were baptized, and about three thousand were added to their number that day.

They devoted themselves to the apostles' teaching and to the fellowship, to the breaking of bread and to prayer.

Everyone was filled with awe, and many wonders and miraculous signs were done by the apostles.

All the believers were together and had everything in common.

Selling their possessions and goods, they gave to anyone as he had need.

Every day they continued to meet together in the temple courts. They broke bread in their homes and ate together with glad and sincere hearts,

praising God and enjoying the favor of all the people. And the Lord added to their number daily those who were being saved. *Acts 2:38-47*

480 O Breath of Life

I stand in awe of your deeds, O LORD. Renew them in our day. Habakkuk 3:2

1. O Breath of Life, come sweep - ing through us,
2. O Wind of God, come bend us, break us,
3. O Breath of Love, come breathe with - in us,
4. Re - vive us, Lord! Is zeal a - bat - ing
Re - vive Thy church with life and power.
Till hum - bly we con - fess our need.
Re - new - ing thought and will and heart.
While har - vest fields are vast and white?
O Breath of Life, come, cleanse, re - new us,
Then in Thy ten - der - ness re - make us,
Come, Love of Christ, a - fresh to win us,
Re - vive us Lord, the world is wait - ing,
And fit Thy Church to meet this hour.
Re - vive, re - store, for this we plead.
Re - vive Thy Church in ev - ery part.
E - quip Thy Church to spread the light.

WORDS: Bessie P. Head, 1850-1936
MUSIC: Mary J. Hammond, 1878-1964

SPIRITUS VITAE
9.8.9.8.

A Revival Hymn 481

Will you not revive us again, that your people may rejoice in you? Psalm 85:6

1. Re - vive Thy work, O Lord! And man - i - fest Thy power.
2. Re - vive Thy work, O Lord! And ev - ery soul in - spire.
3. Re - vive Thy work, O Lord! And give a - bound - ing joy.
4. Re - vive Thy work, O Lord! And make Thy ser - vants bold.
5. Re - vive Thy work, O Lord! Ful - fill Thy prom - ise true.
Thy work, O Lord!
O, come up - on Thy church and give A pen - i - ten - tial shower!
O, kin - dle in each heart, we pray, The Pen - te - cos - tal fire!
O, fill our hearts with per - fect love And burn out all al - loy!
Con - vict of sin and work once more As in the days of old.
Let Je - sus Christ be glo - ri - fied And great things for us do.
Refrain
Re - vive Thy work, O Lord, Come now and an - swer prayer;
an - swer prayer;
O, come in Ho - ly Spir - it power And save men ev - ery - where.

WORDS: Oswald J. Smith, 1889-1986
MUSIC: Bentley D. Ackley, 1872-1958

REVIVAL HYMN
S.M. with Refrain

THE BODY OF CHRIST—THE CHURCH

482 I Love Your Kingdom, Lord

I love the place . . . where your glory dwells. Psalm 26:8

1. I love Your king - dom, Lord, The house of Your a - bode,
2. I love the Church, O God! Her walls be - fore You stand,
3. *For her my tears shall fall, For her my prayers as - cend,*
4. Be - yond my high - est joy I prize her heaven - ly ways,
5. Sure as Your truth shall last, To Zi - on shall be given,

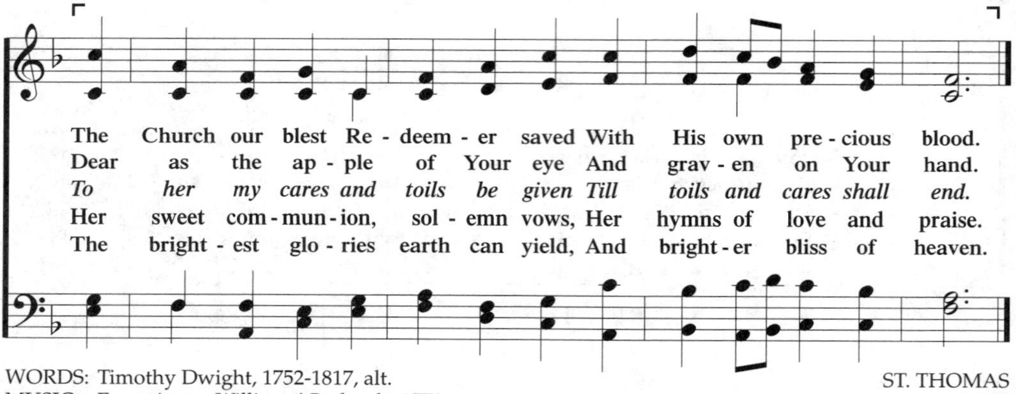

The Church our blest Re - deem - er saved With His own pre - cious blood.
Dear as the ap - ple of Your eye And grav - en on Your hand.
To her my cares and toils be given Till toils and cares shall end.
Her sweet com - mun - ion, sol - emn vows, Her hymns of love and praise.
The bright - est glo - ries earth can yield, And bright - er bliss of heaven.

WORDS: Timothy Dwight, 1752-1817, alt.
MUSIC: From Aaron Williams' *Psalmody*, 1770

ST. THOMAS
S.M.

THE BODY OF CHRIST—FELLOWSHIP OF BELIEVERS

483 Blest Be the Tie That Binds

You are all one in Christ Jesus. Galatians 3:28

1. Blest be the tie that binds Our hearts in Chris - tian love. The
2. Be - fore our Fa - ther's throne We pour our ar - dent prayers. Our
3. We share our mu - tual woes, Our mu - tual bur - dens bear, And
4. When we a - sun - der part It gives us in - ward pain, But

WORDS: John Fawcett, 1740-1817
MUSIC: Johann G. Nägeli, 1773-1836; arr. Lowell Mason, 1792-1872

DENNIS
S.M.

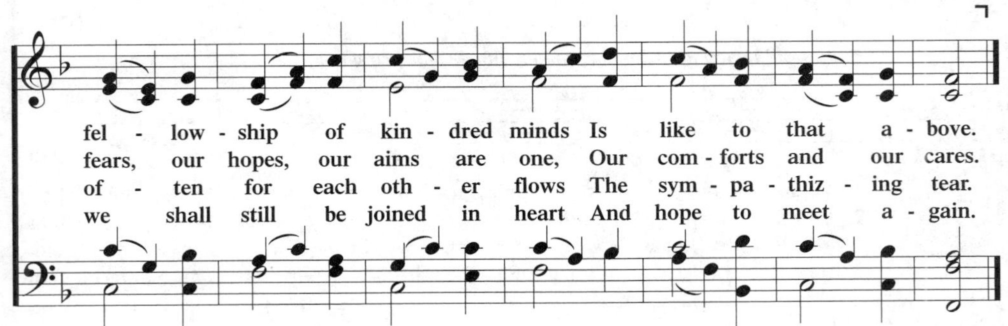
fel - low - ship of kin - dred minds Is like to that a - bove.
fears, our hopes, our aims are one, Our com - forts and our cares.
of - ten for each oth - er flows The sym - pa - thiz - ing tear.
we shall still be joined in heart And hope to meet a - gain.

Fellowship of Believers 484

A new command I give you: Love one another. As I have loved you, so you must love one another.

By this all men will know that you are my disciples, if you love one another.

John 13:34-35

If you have any encouragement from being united with Christ, if any comfort from his love, if any fellowship with the Spirit, if any tenderness and compassion,

then make my joy complete by being like-minded, having the same love, being one in spirit and purpose.

Do nothing out of selfish ambition or vain conceit, but in humility consider others better than yourselves.

Each of you should look not only to your own interests, but also to the interest of others.

Philippians 2:1-4

Carry each other's burdens and in this way you will fulfill the law of Christ.

Galatians 6:2

And let us consider how we may spur one another on toward love and good deeds.

Let us not give up meeting together, as some are in the habit of doing,

but let us encourage one another—and all the more as you see the Day approaching.

Hebrews 10:24-25

485 They'll Know We Are Christians

By this all men will know that you are my disciples, if you love one another. John 13:35

1. We are one in the Spir - it, we are one in the Lord,
2. We will walk with each oth - er, we will walk hand in hand,
3. We will work with each oth - er, we will work side by side,
4. All praise to the Fa - ther, from whom all things come,
We are one in the Spir - it, we are one in the Lord,
We will walk with each oth - er, we will walk hand in hand,
We will work with each oth - er, we will work side by side,
And all praise to Christ Je - sus, His on - ly Son,
And we pray that all u - ni - ty may one day be re - stored.
And to - geth - er we'll spread the news that God is in our land.
And we'll guard each one's dig - ni - ty and save each one's pride.
And all praise to the Spir - it, who makes us one.
Refrain
And they'll know we are Chris - tians by our love, by our love,
Yes, they'll know we are Chris - tians by our love.

WORDS: Peter Scholtes, b. 1938
MUSIC: Peter Scholtes, b. 1938

ST. BRENDAN'S
Irregular with Refrain

For All the Saints 486

They will rest from their labor. Revelation 14:13

1. For all the saints who from their la - bors rest,
2. Thou wast their rock, their for - tress, and their might;
3. O blest com - mu - nion, fel - low - ship di - vine!
4. And when the strife is fierce, the war - fare long,
5. But lo! there breaks a yet more glo - rious day.
6. From earth's wide bounds, from o - cean's far - thest coast,
Who Thee by faith be - fore the world con - fessed, Thy
Thou, Lord, their cap - tain in the well - fought fight;
We fee - bly strug - gle, they in glo - ry shine. Yet
Steals on the ear the dis - tant tri - umph song, And
The saints tri - um - phant rise in bright ar - ray. The
Through gates of pearl stream in the count - less host,
name, O Je - sus, be for - ev - er blest.
Thou, in the dark - ness drear, their one true light.
all are one in Thee, for all are Thine.
hearts are brave a - gain and arms are strong.
King of glo - ry pass - es on His way.
Sing - ing to Fa - ther, Son and Ho - ly Ghost.
Al - le - lu - ia! Al - le - lu - ia!

WORDS: William W. How, 1823-1897
MUSIC: Ralph Vaughan Williams, 1872-1958

SINE NOMINE
10.10.10.4.4.

487 The Family of God

We are God's children . . . heirs of God and co-heirs with Christ. Romans 8:16-17

I'm so glad I'm a part of the fam-ily of God— I've been washed in the
foun-tain, cleansed by His blood! Joint heirs with Je-sus as we trav-el this
sod; For I'm part of the fam-ily, the fam-ily of God.

WORDS: William J. Gaither, b. 1936; Gloria Gaither, b. 1942
MUSIC: William J. Gaither, b. 1936

FAMILY OF GOD
Irregular

THE CHURCH AS THE GLORY OF THE WORLD

The doctrine of the gospel is like the dew, like the mist that moistens the tender grass, making it flourish, keeping it green. Christians are like all the different flowers in a garden, each of them having the dew of heaven. When the flowers are shaken by the wind, they let their dew fall on each other's roots—and as a result they are all nourished, for they are nourishers of one another.

Church fellowship, when it is healthy and productive, is the glory of the world. No place, no community, no fellowship is decorated and spangled with such beauties as the church is when it is rightly knit together with their Head, each lovingly serving the other.

John Bunyan (1628-1688)

The Word of God 488

The law of the LORD is perfect, reviving the soul.
The statutes of the LORD are trustworthy, making wise the simple.
The precepts of the LORD are right, giving joy to the heart.
The commands of the LORD are radiant, giving light to the eyes.
The fear of the LORD is pure, enduring forever.
The ordinances of the LORD are sure and altogether righteous.
They are more precious than gold, than much pure gold;
they are sweeter than honey, than honey from the comb.
By them is your servant warned;
in keeping them there is great reward.

Psalm 19:7-11

How can a young man keep his way pure?
By living according to your word.
I seek you with all my heart;
do not let me stray from your commands.
I have hidden your word in my heart
that I might not sin against you.

Psalm 119:9-11

But as for you, continue in what you have learned and have become convinced of, because you know those from whom you learned it,
and how from infancy you have known the holy Scriptures, which are able to make you wise for salvation through faith in Christ Jesus.
All Scripture is God-breathed and is useful for teaching, rebuking, correcting and training in righteousness,
so that the man of God may be thoroughly equipped for every good work.

2 Timothy 3:14-17

THE LIVING BOOK

Read it much, read it often, brood over it, think over it, meditate over it—meditate on the Word of God day and night. When you are awake at night, think of a helpful verse. When you get up in the morning, no matter how you feel, think of a verse and make the Word of God the important element in your day. The Holy Ghost wrote the Word, and if you make much of the Word, He will make much of you. It is through the Word that He reveals Himself. Between those covers is a living Book. God wrote it and it is still vital and effective and alive. God is in this Book, the Holy Ghost is in this Book, and if you want to find Him, go into this Book.

A.W. Tozer (1897-1963), *The Tozer Pulpit*

---

489 How Firm a Foundation

The word of the Lord stands forever. 1 Peter 1:25

1. How firm a foun - da - tion, you saints of the Lord,
2. "Fear not, I am with you. O, be not dis - mayed,
3. "When through the deep wa - ters I call you to go,
4. "When through fi - ery tri - als your path - way shall lie,
5. "The soul that on Je - sus has leaned for re - pose,
Is laid for your faith in His ex - cel - lent Word!
For I am your God, I will still give you aid.
The riv - ers of sor - row shall not o - ver - flow,
My grace all - suf - fi - cient shall be your sup - ply.
I will not, I will not de - sert to his foes.
What more can He say than to you He has said,
I'll strength - en you, help you, and cause you to stand,
For I will be with you, your tri - als to bless,
The flame shall not hurt you, I on - ly de - sign
That soul, though all hell should en - deav - or to shake,
To you who for ref - uge to Je - sus have fled?
Up - held by My gra - cious, om - nip - o - tent hand.
And sanc - ti - fy to you your deep - est dis - tress.
Your dross1 to con - sume and your gold to re - fine.
I'll nev - er, no nev - er, no nev - er for - sake!"

WORDS: From John Rippon's *Selection of Hymns*, 1787, alt.
MUSIC: American melody, from Mercer's *Cluster of Spiritual Songs*, 1817

FOUNDATION
11.11.11.11.

1. dross: impurity

OUR BREAD OF LIFE

MEDLEY
Break Thou the Bread of Life
Thy Word

Break Thou the Bread of Life 490

Then he opened their minds so they could understand the Scriptures. Luke 24:45

1. Break Thou the bread of life, Dear Lord to me,
2. Bless now the truth, dear Lord, To me, to me,
3. Thou art the bread of life, O Lord, to me;
4. O, send Thy Spir - it, Lord, Now un - to me,
As Thou once broke the loaves Be - side the sea.
As Thou once blessed the bread By Gal - i - lee.
Thy ho - ly Word, the truth That still saves me.
That He may touch my eyes And make me see.
Be - yond the sa - cred page I seek Thee, Lord.
Then shall all bond - age cease, All fet - ters1 fall,
Give me to eat and live With Thee a - bove.
Show me the truth con - cealed With - in Thy Word,
Song ending
My spir - it pants for Thee, O liv - ing Word.
And I shall find my peace, My all in all.
Teach me to love Thy truth For Thou art love.
And in Thy Book re - vealed, I see Thee, Lord.

(For higher key, see No. 634)

WORDS: Stanzas 1-2, Mary A. Lathbury, 1841-1913, alt.; stanzas 3-4, Alexander Groves, 1843-1909, alt.

MUSIC: William F. Sherwin, 1826-1888

BREAD OF LIFE
6.4.6.4.D.

1. fetters: chains, shackles

Optional transition to "Thy Word."
Lord.
491 Thy Word
Your word is a lamp to my feet and a light for my path. Psalm 119:105
Refrain
Thy Word is a lamp un-to my feet and a light un - to my path.
Thy Word is a lamp un-to my feet and a light un - to my path.
last time fine

WORDS: Amy Grant, b. 1960; para. Psalm 119:105
MUSIC: Michael W. Smith, b. 1957

THY WORD
Irregular

1. When I feel a - fraid, and I think I've lost my way,
2. I will not for - get Your love for me, and yet my
Still You're there right be - side me. Noth - ing will I fear as
heart for - ev - er is wan - der - ing. Je - sus, be my guide and
long as You are near. Please be near me
hold me to Your side, I will love You
to the end.
to the end.
D.C. twice

492 O Word of God Incarnate

The unfolding of your words gives light. Psalm 119:130

1. O Word of God in - car - nate, O Wis - dom from on high,
2. The Church from her dear Mas - ter Re - ceived the gift di - vine,
3. O, make Your Church, dear Sav - ior, A lamp of pur - est gold,
O Truth un - changed, un - chang - ing, O Light of our dark sky;
And still that light is lift - ed O'er all the earth to shine.
To bear be - fore the na - tions Your true light, as of old.
We praise You for the ra - diance That from the hal - lowed page,
It is the gold - en cas - ket Where gems of truth are stored.
O, teach Your wan - dering pil - grims By this their path to trace,
A lan - tern to our foot - steps, Shines on from age to age.
It is the heaven - drawn pic - ture Of Christ, the liv - ing Word.
Till, clouds and dark - ness end - ed, They see You face to face.

(For alternate tune, see No. 302)

WORDS: William W. How, 1823-1897, alt.
MUSIC: Samuel S. Wesley, 1810-1876

AURELIA
7.6.7.6.D.

Trust in the Word 493

May your unfailing love come to me, O LORD, your salvation according to your promise;

then I will answer the one who taunts me, for I trust in your word.

Do not snatch the word of truth from my mouth, for I have put my hope in your laws.

I will always obey your law, for ever and ever.

I will walk about in freedom, for I have sought out your precepts.

I will speak of your statutes before kings and will not be put to shame,

for I delight in your commands because I love them.

I lift up my hands to your commands, which I love, and I meditate on your decrees.

In the night I remember your name, O LORD, and I will keep your law.

Psalm 119:41-48, 55

How Precious Is the Book Divine 494

Your word is a lamp to my feet. Psalm 119:105

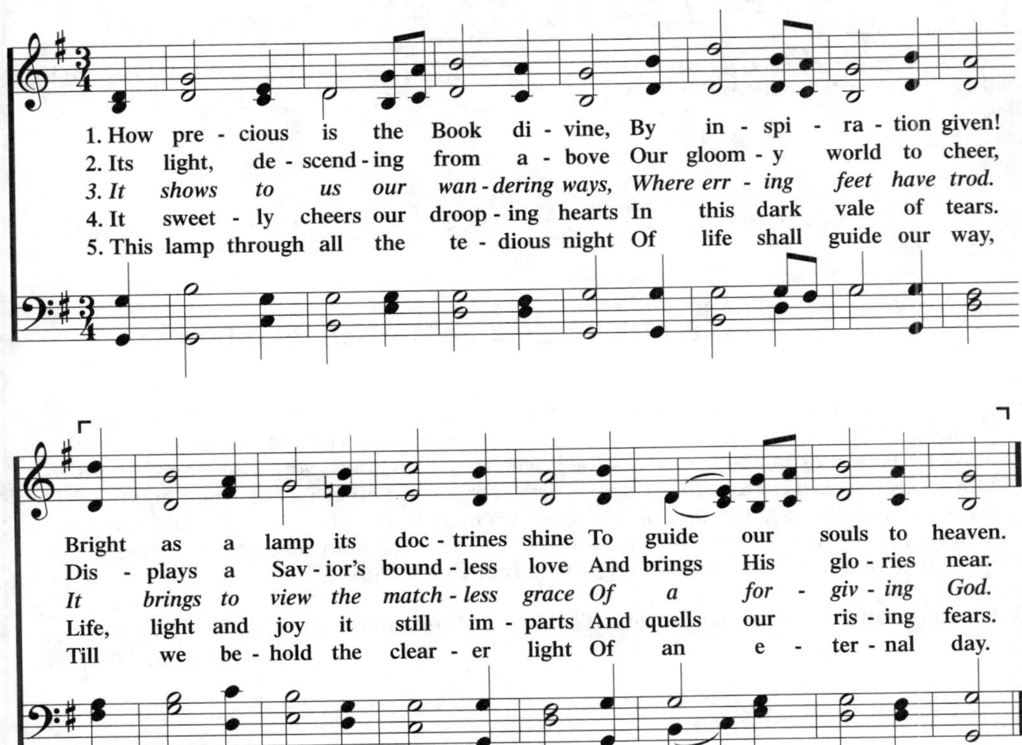

1. How pre - cious is the Book di - vine, By in - spi - ra - tion given!
2. Its light, de - scend - ing from a - bove Our gloom - y world to cheer,
3. It shows to us our wan - dering ways, Where err - ing feet have trod.
4. It sweet - ly cheers our droop - ing hearts In this dark vale of tears.
5. This lamp through all the te - dious night Of life shall guide our way,
Bright as a lamp its doc - trines shine To guide our souls to heaven.
Dis - plays a Sav - ior's bound - less love And brings His glo - ries near.
It brings to view the match - less grace Of a for - giv - ing God.
Life, light and joy it still im - parts And quells our ris - ing fears.
Till we be - hold the clear - er light Of an e - ter - nal day.

WORDS: John Fawcett, 1740-1817, alt.
MUSIC: Hugh Wilson, 1764-1824

MARTYRDOM
C.M.

495 Holy Bible, Book Divine

Oh, how I love your law! I meditate on it all day long. Psalm 119:97

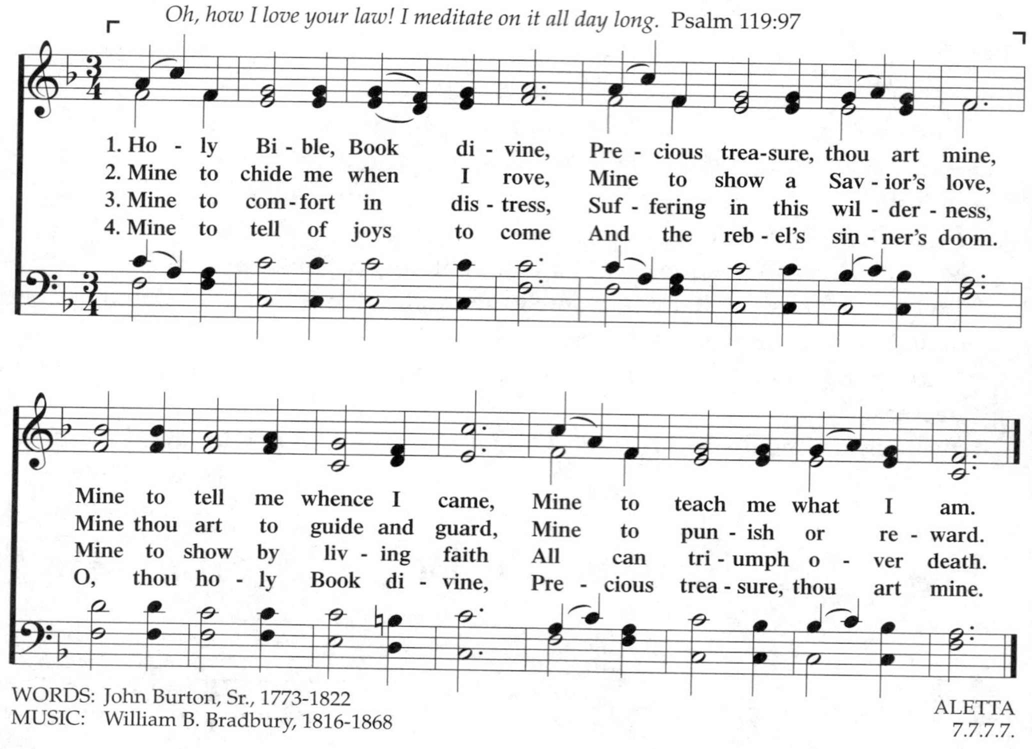
1. Ho - ly Bi - ble, Book di - vine, Pre - cious trea-sure, thou art mine,
2. Mine to chide me when I rove, Mine to show a Sav - ior's love,
3. Mine to com - fort in dis - tress, Suf - fering in this wil - der - ness,
4. Mine to tell of joys to come And the reb - el's sin - ner's doom.
Mine to tell me whence I came, Mine to teach me what I am.
Mine thou art to guide and guard, Mine to pun - ish or re - ward.
Mine to show by liv - ing faith All can tri - umph o - ver death.
O, thou ho - ly Book di - vine, Pre - cious trea - sure, thou art mine.

WORDS: John Burton, Sr., 1773-1822
MUSIC: William B. Bradbury, 1816-1868

ALETTA
7.7.7.7.

GOD'S WORD TRANSCENDS THE WORLD

The Holy Scriptures surpass in effectiveness all the arts and all the sciences of the philosophers and lawyers. These, though good and necessary to life here below, are vain and of no effect as to what concerns the life eternal. The Bible should be regarded with wholly different eyes from those with which we view all other works. They that wholly renounce themselves, and do not rely solely on mere human reason, will make good progress in the Scriptures. The world, however, does not comprehend them, due to ignorance of that selflessness which is the gift of God's Word.

Can they who do not understand God's Word understand God's works?

Martin Luther (1483-1546), *Table Talk*

Wonderful Words of Life 496

The words I have spoken to you are spirit and they are life. John 6:63

1. Sing them o - ver a - gain to me, Won - der - ful words of life!
2. Christ, the bless - ed One, gives to all Won - der - ful words of life!
3. Sweet - ly ech - o the gos - pel call, Won - der - ful words of life!
Let me more of their beau - ty see, Won - der - ful words of life!
Sin - ner, list to the lov - ing call, Won - der - ful words of life!
Of - fer par - don and peace to all, Won - der - ful words of life!
Words of life and beau - ty, Teach me faith and du - ty!
All so free - ly giv - en, Woo - ing us to heav - en!
Je - sus, on - ly Sav - ior, Sanc - ti - fy for - ev - er!
Refrain
Beau - ti - ful words! Won - der - ful words! Won - der - ful words of life!
Beau - ti - ful words! Won - der - ful words! Won - der - ful words of life!

WORDS: Philip P. Bliss, 1838-1876
MUSIC: Philip P. Bliss, 1838-1876

WORDS OF LIFE
8.6.8.6.6.6. with Refrain

497 Stewardship

Honor the LORD with your wealth,
with the firstfruits of all your crops;
then your barns will be filled to overflowing,
and your vats will brim with new wine. *Proverbs 3:9-10*

"Bring in the whole tithe into the storehouse, that there may be food in my house. Test me in this," says the LORD Almighty,
"and see if I will not throw open the floodgates of heaven and pour out so much blessing that you will not have room enough for it." *Malachi 3:10*

Remember this: Whoever sows sparingly will also reap sparingly, and whoever sows generously will also reap generously.
Each man should give what he has decided in his heart to give, not reluctantly or under compulsion, for God loves a cheerful giver.
And God is able to make all grace abound to you, so that in all things at all times, having all that you need, you will abound in every good work.
2 Corinthians 9:6-8

Above all, love each other deeply, because love covers over a multitude of sins.
Offer hospitality to one another without grumbling.
Each one should use whatever gift he has received to serve others, faithfully administering God's grace in its various forms. *1 Peter 4:8-10*

498 We Give Thee but Thine Own

We have given you only what comes from your hand. 1 Chronicles 29:14

1. We give Thee but Thine own, What - e'er the gift may be.
2. May we Thy boun - ties thus As stew - ards true re - ceive,
All that we have is Thine a - lone, A trust, O Lord, from Thee.
And glad - ly, as Thou bless - est us, To Thee our first fruits give.

WORDS: William W. How, 1823-1897
MUSIC: From *Harmonischer Liederschatz*, 1738; adapt. William H. Havergal, 1793-1870

FRANCONIA
S.M.

God, Whose Giving Knows No Ending 499

Ask God, who gives generously to all. James 1:5

1. God, whose giv - ing knows no end - ing, From Your rich and end - less store—
2. Skills and time are ours for press - ing Toward the goals of Christ, Your Son:
3. Trea - sure, too, You have en - trust - ed, Gain through powers Your grace con - ferred;
Na - ture's won - der, Je - sus' wis - dom, Cost - ly cross, grave's shat - tered door—
All at peace in health and free - dom, Rac - es joined, the Church made one.
Ours to use for home and kin - dred, And to spread the gos - pel word.
Gift - ed by You, we turn to You, Of - fering up our - selves in praise.
Now di - rect our dai - ly la - bor, Lest we strive for self a - lone.
O - pen wide our hands in shar - ing, As we heed Christ's age - less call,
Thank - ful song shall rise for - ev - er, Gra - cious Do - nor of our days.
Born with ta - lents, make us ser - vants Fit to an - swer at Your throne.
Heal - ing, teach - ing, and re - claim - ing, Serv - ing You by serv - ing all.

WORDS: Robert L. Edwards, b. 1915
MUSIC: Rowland Prichard, 1811-1887; arr. Ralph Vaughan Williams, 1872-1958

HYFRYDOL
8.7.8.7.D.

500 Lord, You Love the Cheerful Giver

God loves a cheerful giver. 2 Corinthians 9:7

1. Lord, You love the cheer-ful giv - er, Who with o - pen heart and hand
2. We are Yours, Your mer - cy sought us, Found us in death's dread - ful way,
3. Blest by You with gifts and grac - es, May we heed Your church - 's call.
4. Sav - ior, You have free - ly giv - en All the bless - ings we en - joy,
Bless - es free - ly, as a riv - er That re - fresh - es all the land.
To the fold in safe - ty brought us, Nev - er - more from You to stray.
Glad - ly in all times and plac - es Give to You who gave us all.
Earth - ly store and bread of heav - en, Love and peace with - out al - loy.
Grant us then the grace of giv - ing With a spir - it large and free,
Your own life You free - ly gave us As an of - fering on the cross.
You have bought us, and no long - er Can we claim to be our own.
Hum - bly now we bow be - fore You, And our all to You re - sign,
That our life and all our liv - ing We may con - se - crate to Thee.
We have sinned and You have saved us From e - ter - nal shame and loss.
Ev - er free and ev - er strong - er, We shall serve You, Lord a - lone.
For the king - dom, power, and glo - ry Are, O Lord, for - ev - er Thine!

WORDS: Robert Murray, 1832-1910, alt.
MUSIC: John Zundel, 1815-1882

BEECHER
8.7.8.7.D.

A Life of Service 501

Therefore, my dear brothers, stand firm. Let nothing move you. Always give yourselves fully to the work of the Lord, because you know that your labor in the Lord is not in vain. *1 Corinthians 15:58*

So we make it our goal to please him, whether we are at home in the body or away from it. *2 Corinthians 5:9*

We continually remember before our God and Father your work produced by faith, your labor prompted by love, and your endurance inspired by hope in our Lord Jesus Christ. *1 Thessalonians 1:3*

For Christ's love compels us, because we are convinced that one died for all, and therefore all died.

And he died for all, that those who live should no longer live for themselves but for him who died for them and was raised again. . .

We are therefore Christ's ambassadors, as though God were making his appeal through us. We implore you on Christ's behalf: Be reconciled to God. *2 Corinthians 5:14-15, 20*

The man who plants and the man who waters have one purpose, and each will be rewarded according to his own labor.

For we are God's fellow workers; you are God's field, God's building.

By the grace God has given me, I laid a foundation as an expert builder, and someone else is building on it. But each one should be careful how he builds.

For no one can lay any foundation other than the one already laid, which is Jesus Christ.

If any man builds on this foundation using gold, silver, costly stones, wood, hay or straw,

his work will be shown for what it is, because the Day will bring it to light. It will be revealed with fire, and the fire will test the quality of each man's work.

If what he has built survives, he will receive his reward.

If it is burned up, he will suffer loss; he himself will be saved, but only as one escaping through the flames. *1 Corinthians 3:8-15*

502 Let It Be Said of Us

I have fought the good fight, I have finished the race, I have kept the faith. 2 Timothy 4:7

1. Let it be said of us that the Lord was our pas - sion, That with
2. Let it be said of us: We were marked by for - give - ness, We were
glad - ness we bore ev - ery cross we were giv - en, That we
known by our love, and de - light - ed in meek - ness. We were
fought the good fight, that we fin - ished the course Know - ing with -
ruled by His peace, heed - ing u - ni - ty's call; Joined as one
in us the power of the ris - en Lord.
bo - dy that Christ would be seen by all.
Refrain
Let the cross be our glo - ry and the

WORDS: Steve Fry, b. 1954
MUSIC: Steve Fry, b. 1954

LET IT BE SAID
Irregular with Refrain

Lord be our song, By mer - cy made ho - ly, by the Spir - it made
strong. Let the cross be our glo - ry and the Lord be our song 'Til the
like - ness of Je - sus be through us made known. Let the
cross be our glo - ry and the Lord be our song.

503 Come, All Christians, Be Committed

I urge you . . . to offer your bodies as living sacrifices. Romans 12:1

1. Come, all Chris-tians, be com - mit - ted To the ser - vice of the Lord.
2. Of your time and tal - ents give Him, They are gifts from God a - bove,
3. God's com - mand to love each oth - er Is re - quired of ev - ery - one.
4. Come in praise and ad - o - ra - tion, All who on Christ's name be - lieve.
Make your lives for Him more fit - ted, Tune your hearts with one ac - cord.
To be used by Chris-tians free - ly To pro - claim His won - drous love.
Show - ing mer - cy to each oth - er Mir - rors His re - deem - ing Son.
Wor - ship Him with con - se - cra - tion, Grace and love will you re - ceive.
Come in - to His courts with glad - ness, Each His sa - cred vows re - new.
Come a - gain to serve the Sav - ior, Tithes and of - ferings with you bring.
In com - pas - sion He has giv - en Of His love that is di - vine,
For His grace give Him the glo - ry, For the Spir - it and the Word,
Turn a - way from sin and sad - ness, Be trans - formed with life a - new.
In your work, with Him find fa - vor, And with joy His prais - es sing.
On the cross were sins for - giv - en, Joy and peace are ful - ly thine.
And re - peat the gos - pel sto - ry Till the world His name has heard.

(For different harmony, see No. 198)

WORDS: Eva B. Lloyd, b. 1912, alt.
MUSIC: American melody from *The Sacred Harp*, 1844; arr. James H. Wood, b. 1921

BEACH SPRING
8.7.8.7.D.

Rise Up, O Church of God 504

Serve him with all your heart and with all your soul. Deuteronomy 11:13

1. Rise up, O Church of God! Have done with less - er things.
2. Rise up, O Church of God! His king - dom tar - ries long.
3. Rise up, O saints of God! The Church for you doth wait,
4. Lift high the cross of Christ, Tread where His feet have trod.
Give heart and soul and mind and strength To serve the King of kings.
Bring in the day of broth - er - hood And end the night of wrong.
Her strength un - e - qual to her task; Rise up and make her great!
As fol - lowers of the Son of Man, Rise up, O Church of God!

WORDS: William P. Merrill, 1867-1954, alt.
MUSIC: William H. Walter, 1825-1893

FESTAL SONG
S.M.

THE TRUE SOURCE OF SERVICE

God does not want anything that has to be pressed from an unwilling giver. The prayer that is offered God from a sense of duty, the work that is done just because we have to do it, the word that is spoken because we are expected to be ministers and to be consistent with our profession, are dead, cold and comparatively worthless. True service springs from a full and joyful heart, and runs over like the broad and boundless river.

This is the true secret of power for service—the heart filled and satisfied with Jesus and so baptized with the Holy Spirit that it is impelled by the fullness of its joy and love to impart to others what it has so abundantly received.

A. B. Simpson (1843-1919), *The Holy Spirit; Days of Heaven and Earth*

505 I'll Go Where You Want Me to Go

Here am I. Send me! Isaiah 6:8

1. It may not be on the moun-tain's height Or o - ver the storm-y sea.
2. Per - haps to-day there are lov - ing words Which Je - sus would have me speak.
3. There's sure-ly some-where a low - ly place In earth's har-vest fields so wide,
It may not be at the bat-tle's front My Lord will have need of me.
There may be now in the paths of sin Some wan-derer whom I should seek.
Where I may la-bor through life's short day For Je - sus, the Cru - ci - fied.
But if by a still, small voice He calls To paths I do not know,
O Sav-ior, if Thou will be my Guide, Though dark and rug-ged the way,
So trust-ing my all un - to Thy care, I know Thou lov - est me!
I'll an-swer, dear Lord, with my hand in Thine, I'll go where You want me to go.
My voice shall ech - o the mes - sage sweet—I'll say what You want me to say.
I'll do Thy will with a heart sin - cere, I'll be what You want me to be.

WORDS: Stanza 1, Mary A. Brown, 19th century; stanzas 2-3, Charles E. Prior, 1856-1927
MUSIC: Carrie E. Rounsefell, 1861-1930

MANCHESTER
Irregular with Refrain

Refrain
I'll go where You want me to go, dear Lord, O'er moun-tain, or plain, or sea.
I'll say what You want me to say, dear Lord, I'll be what You want me to be.

Lord, Be Glorified 506

Christ will be exalted in my body, whether by life or by death. Philippians 1:20

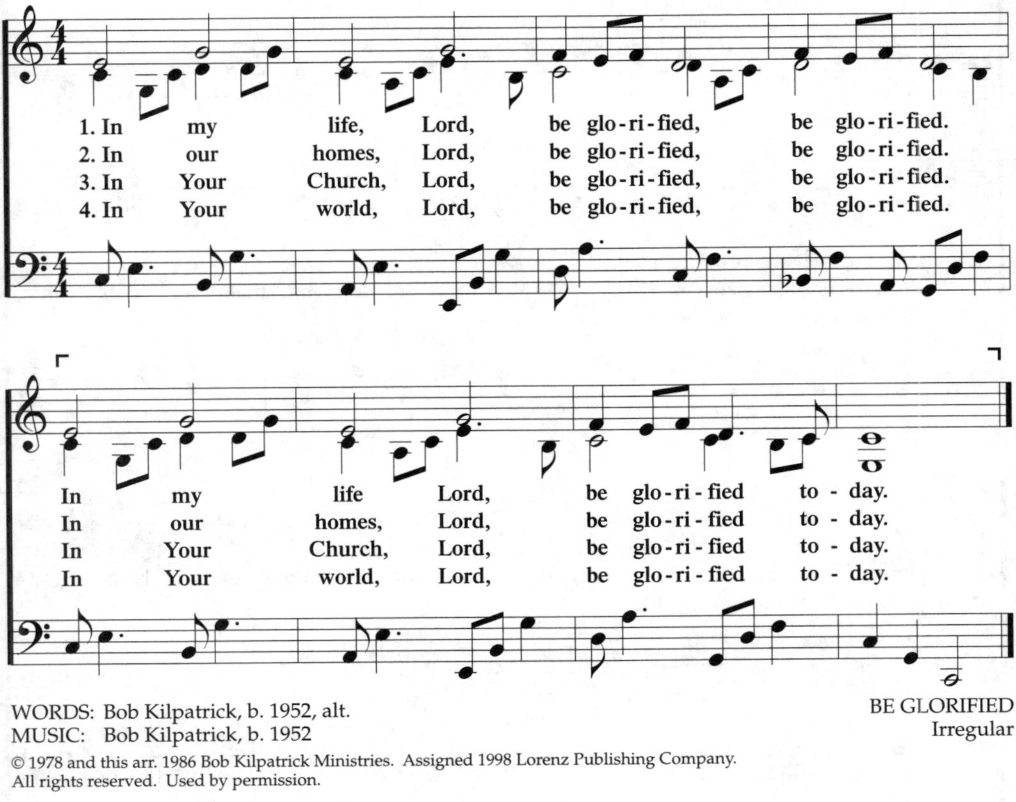

1. In my life, Lord, be glo-ri-fied, be glo-ri-fied.
   In my life Lord, be glo-ri-fied to-day.
2. In our homes, Lord, be glo-ri-fied, be glo-ri-fied.
   In our homes, Lord, be glo-ri-fied to-day.
3. In Your Church, Lord, be glo-ri-fied, be glo-ri-fied.
   In Your Church, Lord, be glo-ri-fied to-day.
4. In Your world, Lord, be glo-ri-fied, be glo-ri-fied.
   In Your world, Lord, be glo-ri-fied to-day.

WORDS: Bob Kilpatrick, b. 1952, alt.
MUSIC: Bob Kilpatrick, b. 1952

BE GLORIFIED
Irregular

507 Make Me a Blessing

Strengthen the feeble hands, steady the knees that give way. Isaiah 35:3

1. Out in the high-ways and by-ways of life, Man-y are wea-ry and sad. Car-ry the sun-shine where dark-ness is rife, Mak-ing the sor-row-ing glad.
2. Tell the sweet sto-ry of Christ and His love, Tell of His power to for-give. Oth-ers will trust Him if on-ly you prove True, ev-ery mo-ment you live.
3. Give as 'twas giv-en to you in your need, Love as the Mas-ter loved you. Be to the help-less a help-er in-deed, Un-to your mis-sion be true.
are wea-ry and sad.
His power to for-give.
the Mas-ter loved you.
Refrain
Make me a bless-ing, make me a bless-ing, Out of my life, may Je-sus shine. Make me a bless-ing, O
out of my life

WORDS: Ira B. Wilson, 1880-1950
MUSIC: George S. Schuler, 1882-1973

SCHULER
10.7.10.7. with Refrain

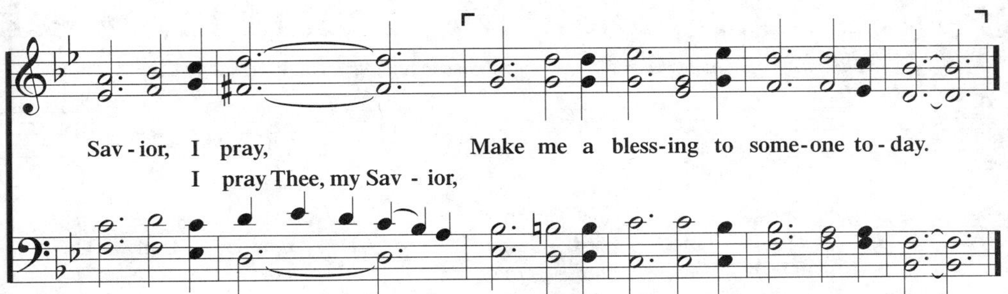
Sav - ior, I pray, Make me a bless-ing to some-one to - day.
I pray Thee, my Sav - ior,

The Servant Song 508

Serve one another in love. Galatians 5:13

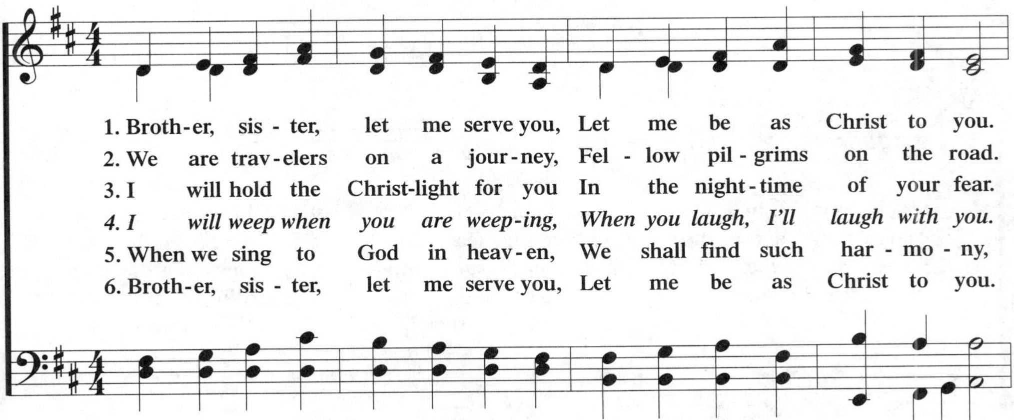

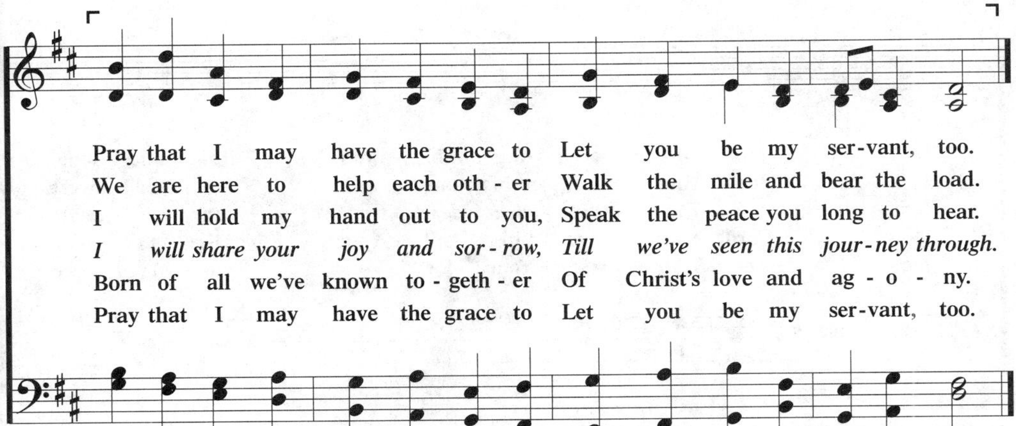

1. Broth-er, sis - ter, let me serve you, Let me be as Christ to you. Pray that I may have the grace to Let you be my ser-vant, too.
2. We are trav-elers on a jour-ney, Fel - low pil - grims on the road. We are here to help each oth - er Walk the mile and bear the load.
3. I will hold the Christ-light for you In the night-time of your fear. I will hold my hand out to you, Speak the peace you long to hear.
4. *I will weep when you are weep-ing, When you laugh, I'll laugh with you. I will share your joy and sor - row, Till we've seen this jour-ney through.*
5. When we sing to God in heav-en, We shall find such har - mo - ny, Born of all we've known to - geth - er Of Christ's love and ag - o - ny.
6. Broth-er, sis - ter, let me serve you, Let me be as Christ to you. Pray that I may have the grace to Let you be my ser-vant, too.

(For alternate setting, see No. 503; combine two verses of "The Servant Song" into one verse of No. 503.)

WORDS: Richard Gillard, b.1953
MUSIC: Richard Gillard, b.1953

THE SERVANT SONG
8.7.8.7.

509 Lord, Speak to Me, That I May Speak

The things you have heard me say . . . entrust to reliable men. 2 Timothy 2:2

1. Lord, speak to me, that I may speak In
2. O, lead me, Lord, that I may lead The
3. O, teach me, Lord, that I may teach The
4. O, fill me with Your full - ness, Lord, Un -
5. O, use me, Lord, use e - ven me Just
liv - ing ech - oes of Your tone. As You have sought, so
wan - dering and the wa - vering feet. O, feed me, Lord, that
pre - cious things that You im - part, And wing my words, that
til my ve - ry heart o'er - flow In kin - dling thought and
as You will, and when and where; Un - til Your bless - ed
let me seek Your err - ing chil - dren, lost and lone.
I may feed Your hun - gering ones with man - na sweet.
they may reach The hid - den depth of many a heart.
glow - ing word, Your love to tell, Your praise to show.
face I see, Your rest, Your joy, Your glo - ry share.

WORDS: Frances R. Havergal, 1836-1879, alt.
MUSIC: Robert A. Schumann, 1810-1856

CANONBURY
L.M.

Channels Only 510

He will be an instrument . . . useful to the Master. 2 Timothy 2:21

1. How I praise Thee, pre - cious Sav - ior, That Thy love laid hold of me.
2. Emp-tied that Thou should - est fill me, A clean ves - sel in Thy hand;
3. Wit - ness - ing Thy power to save me, Set - ting free from self and sin,
4. Je - sus, fill now with Thy Spir - it Hearts that full sur - ren - der know,
Thou hast saved and cleansed and filled me That I might Thy chan - nel be.
With no power but as Thou giv - est Gra - cious - ly with each com - mand.
Thou who bought - est to pos - sess me, In Thy full - ness, Lord, come in.
That the streams of liv - ing wa - ter From our in - ner man may flow.
Refrain
Chan - nels on - ly, bless - ed Mas - ter, But with all Thy won - drous power
Flow - ing through us, Thou canst use us Ev - ery day and ev - ery hour.

(For lower key, see No. 533)

WORDS: Mary E. Maxwell, 1827-1915
MUSIC: Ada R. Gibbs, 1865-1905

CHANNELS
8.7.8.7. with Refrain

511 Freely, Freely

Freely you have received, freely give. Matthew 10:8

1. God for - gave my sin in Je - sus' name, I've been born a - gain in
2. All power is given in Je - sus' name, In earth and heaven in
Je - sus' name, And in Je - sus' name I come to you, To share His
Je - sus' name, And in Je - sus' name I come to you, To share His
love as He told me to.
power as He told me to.
Refrain
He said, "Free - ly, free - ly you have re - ceived; free - ly, free - ly give. Go in My name, and be - cause you be - lieve, oth - ers will know that I live."

WORDS: Carol Owens, b. 1931
MUSIC: Carol Owens, b. 1931

FREELY, FREELY
9.9.9.9 with Refrain

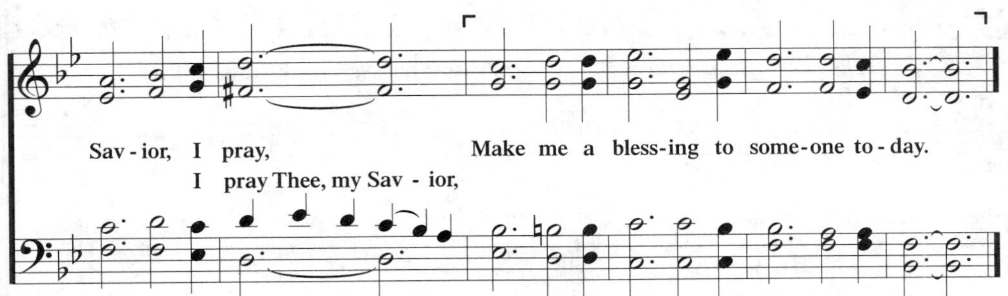

The Servant Song 508

Serve one another in love. Galatians 5:13

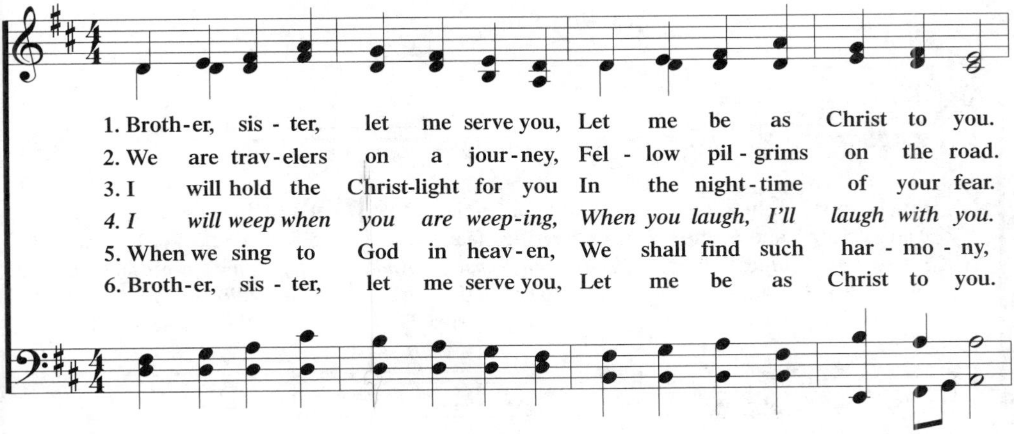

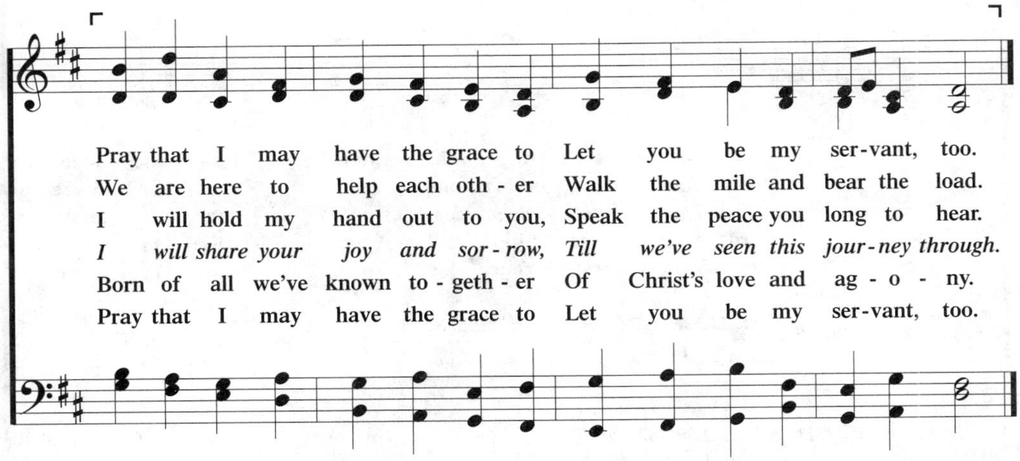

1. Broth-er, sis - ter, let me serve you, Let me be as Christ to you.
Pray that I may have the grace to Let you be my ser-vant, too.

2. We are trav-elers on a jour-ney, Fel - low pil - grims on the road.
We are here to help each oth - er Walk the mile and bear the load.

3. I will hold the Christ-light for you In the night-time of your fear.
I will hold my hand out to you, Speak the peace you long to hear.

4. I will weep when you are weep-ing, When you laugh, I'll laugh with you.
I will share your joy and sor - row, Till we've seen this jour-ney through.

5. When we sing to God in heav-en, We shall find such har - mo - ny,
Born of all we've known to - geth - er Of Christ's love and ag - o - ny.

6. Broth-er, sis - ter, let me serve you, Let me be as Christ to you.
Pray that I may have the grace to Let you be my ser-vant, too.

(For alternate setting, see No. 503; combine two verses of "The Servant Song" into one verse of No. 503.)

WORDS: Richard Gillard, b.1953
MUSIC: Richard Gillard, b.1953

THE SERVANT SONG
8.7.8.7.

509 Lord, Speak to Me, That I May Speak

The things you have heard me say . . . entrust to reliable men. 2 Timothy 2:2

WORDS: Frances R. Havergal, 1836-1879, alt.
MUSIC: Robert A. Schumann, 1810-1856

CANONBURY
L.M.

O Jesus, I Have Promised 512

Whoever serves me must follow me. John 12:26

1. O Je - sus, I have prom - ised To serve Thee to the end.
2. O, let me feel Thee near me, The world is ev - er near.
3. O, let me hear Thee speak - ing In ac - cents clear and still,
4. O Je - sus, Thou hast prom - ised To all who fol - low Thee,
Be Thou for - ev - er near me, My Mas - ter and my Friend.
I see the sights that daz - zle, The tempt - ing sounds I hear.
A - bove the storms of pas - sion, The mur - murs of self - will.
That where Thou art in glo - ry, There shall Thy ser - vant be.
I shall not fear the bat - tle If Thou art by my side,
My foes are ev - er near me, A - round me and with - in,
O, speak to re - as - sure me, To has - ten or con - trol.
And, Je - sus, I have prom - ised To serve Thee to the end.
Nor wan - der from the path - way If Thou wilt be my guide.
But, Je - sus, draw Thou near - er, And shield my soul from sin.
O, speak, and make me lis - ten, Thou guard - ian of my soul.
O, give me grace to fol - low, My Mas - ter and my Friend.

(For alternate tune, see No. 404)

WORDS: John E. Bode, 1816-1874
MUSIC: Arthur H. Mann, 1850-1929

ANGEL'S STORY
7.6.7.6.D.

513 Use Me Today

Serve him with wholehearted devotion. 1 Chronicles 28:9

1. Use me to - day, O Sav - ior di - vine! Cleanse and re -
2. Use me to - day, Lord, use e - ven me— Use me to
3. Use me to - day to scat - ter the seed, Bring - ing the

new this ser - vant of Thine. Lord, with Thy Spir - it fill me, I
lead some lost one to Thee. Lead where Thou wilt, Lord, o - pen the
bless - ing some - one may need. Wheth - er I toil or qui - et - ly

pray. Then, in Thy ser - vice, use me to - day.
way, And to Thy glo - ry, use me to - day.
pray, Bless - ed Lord Je - sus, use me to - day.

WORDS: Gertrude R. Dugan, 1873-1948
MUSIC: George C. Stebbins, 1846-1945

USE ME TODAY
9.9.9.9.

514 Make Them a Blessing

The grace of the Lord Jesus Christ be with you. 1 Corinthians 16:23

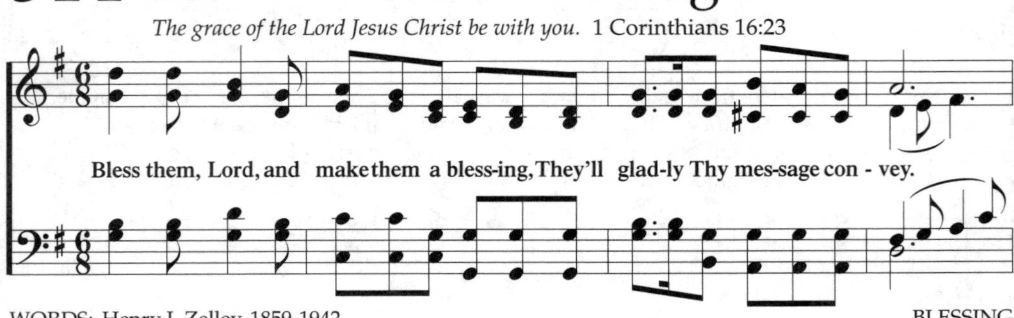
Bless them, Lord, and make them a bless-ing, They'll glad-ly Thy mes-sage con - vey.

WORDS: Henry J. Zelley, 1859-1942
MUSIC: Henry L. Gilmour, 1837-1920

BLESSING
Irregular

Use them to help a great man-y souls, And make them a bless-ing each day.

O Master, Let Me Walk with Thee 515

Come . . . let us walk in the light of the LORD. Isaiah 2:5

1. O Mas - ter, let me walk with Thee In low - ly
2. Help me the slow of heart to move By some clear,
3. Teach me Thy pa - tience! Still with Thee In clos - er,
4. In hope that sends a shin - ing ray Far down the

paths of ser - vice free. Tell me Thy se - cret;
win - ning word of love. Teach me the way - ward
dear - er com - pa - ny, In work that keeps faith
fu - ture's broad - ening way, In peace that on - ly

help me bear The strain of toil, the fret of care.
feet to stay, And guide them in the home - ward way.
sweet and strong, In trust that tri - umphs o - ver wrong,
Thou canst give, With Thee, O Mas - ter, let me live.

WORDS: Washington Gladden, 1836-1918
MUSIC: Henry P. Smith, 1825-1898

MARYTON
L.M.

OUR MESSAGE

MEDLEY
Lift High the Cross
All Heaven Declares

516 Lift High the Cross

I, when I am lifted up from the earth, will draw all men to myself. John 12:32

Refrain
Lift high the cross, the love of Christ proclaim, Till all the world adore His sacred name.
Song ending fine
1. Come, Christians, follow where our Savior trod, Our King victorious, Christ, the Son of God.
2. Led on their way by this triumphant sign, The hosts of God in conquering ranks combine.
3. O Lord, once lifted on this glorious tree, As Thou hast promised, draw men unto Thee.
4. Set up Thy throne, that earth's despair may cease Beneath the shadow of its healing peace.
5. For Thy blest cross which doth for all atone, Creation's praises rise before Thy throne.
D.C.

WORDS: George W. Kitchin, 1827-1912; rev. Michael R. Newbolt, 1874-1956
MUSIC: Sydney H. Nicholson, 1875-1947

CRUCIFER
10.10.10.10.

All Heaven Declares 517

The heavens declare the glory of God. Psalm 19:1

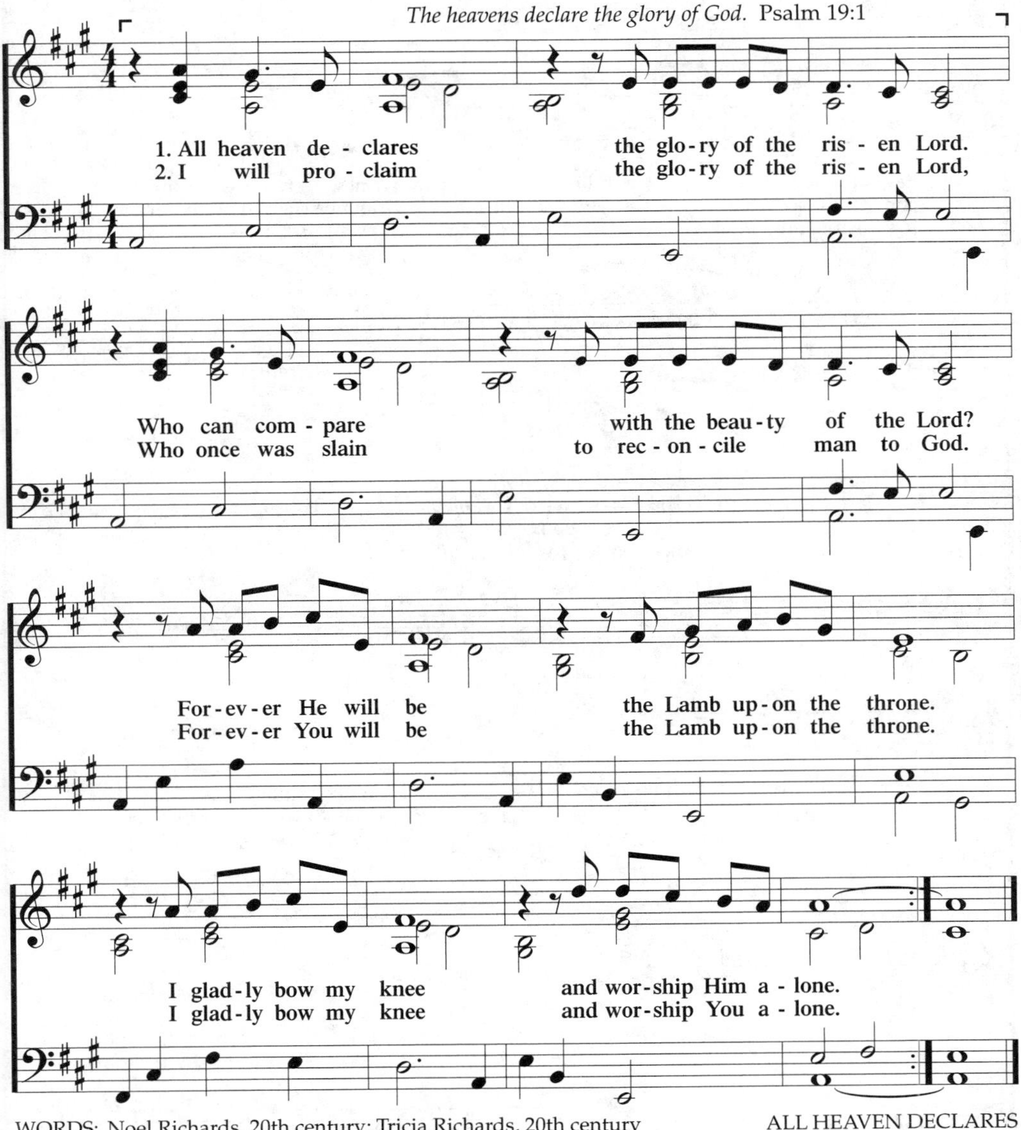

1. All heaven de - clares the glo - ry of the ris - en Lord.
Who can com - pare with the beau - ty of the Lord?
For - ev - er He will be the Lamb up - on the throne.
I glad - ly bow my knee and wor - ship Him a - lone.

2. I will pro - claim the glo - ry of the ris - en Lord,
Who once was slain to rec - on - cile man to God.
For - ev - er You will be the Lamb up - on the throne.
I glad - ly bow my knee and wor - ship You a - lone.

WORDS: Noel Richards, 20th century; Tricia Richards, 20th century
MUSIC: Noel Richards, 20th century; Tricia Richards, 20th century

ALL HEAVEN DECLARES
Irregular

518 The Regions Beyond

Therefore go and make disciples of all nations. Matthew 28:19

1. To the re - gions be - yond I must go, I must go, Where the sto - ry has
2. To the hard - est of plac - es He calls me to go, Not think - ing of
3. O you that are spend - ing your lei - sure and powers In plea - sures so
4. There are oth - er lost sheep that the Mas - ter must bring, And to them must the
nev - er been told. To the mil - lions that nev - er have heard of His love,
com - fort or ease. The world may pro - nounce me a dream - er, a fool—
fool - ish and fond, A - wake from your self - ish - ness, fol - ly and sin,
mes - sage be told. He sends me to gath - er them out of all lands,
I must tell the sweet sto - ry of old.
E - nough if the Mas - ter I please.
And go to the re - gions be - yond.
And wel - come them back to His fold.
Refrain
To the re - gions be - yond, I must go, I must go Till the world, all the world, His sal - va - tion shall know.
I must go, I must go, To the re - gions be - yond I must go, Till the world, all the world, His sal - va - tion shall know.

WORDS: Albert B. Simpson, 1843-1919
MUSIC: Margaret M. Simpson, 1876-1958

REGIONS BEYOND
Irregular

Hark, the Voice of Jesus Calling 519

The harvest is plentiful but the workers are few. Matthew 9:37

1. Hark, the voice of Je - sus call - ing— "Who will go and work to - day?
2. If you can - not cross the o - cean And the dis - tant lands ex - plore,
3. If you can - not speak like an - gels, If you can - not preach like Paul,
4. Let none hear you i - dly say - ing, "There is noth - ing I can do,"
Fields are white and har - vests wait - ing, Who will bear the sheaves a - way?"
You can find the lost ones near - er, You can help them at your door.
You can tell the love of Je - sus, You can say He died for all.
While the lost of earth are dy - ing And the Mas - ter calls for you.
Loud and long the Mas - ter calls you, Rich re - ward He of - fers free.
If you can - not give your thou - sands, You can give the wid - ow's mite,
If you can - not rouse the wick - ed With the judg - ment's dread a - larms,
Take the task He gives you glad - ly; Let His work your plea - sure be.
Who will an - swer, glad - ly say - ing, "Here am I, send me, send me"?
And the least you give for Je - sus Will be pre - cious in His sight.
You can lead the lit - tle chil - dren To the Sav - ior's wait - ing arms.
An - swer quick - ly when He calls you, "Here am I, send me, send me."

WORDS: Daniel March, 1816-1909, alt.
MUSIC: Rowland Prichard, 1811-1887

HYFRYDOL
8.7.8.7.D.

520 All Nations Will Worship God

In my vision at night I looked, and there before me was one like a son of man, coming with the clouds of heaven. He approached the Ancient of Days and was led into his presence. He was given authority, glory and sovereign power;

all peoples, nations and men of every language worshipped him.

Daniel 7:13-14

And they sang a new song:

"You are worthy to take the scroll and to open its seals, because you were slain, and with your blood you purchased men for God from every tribe and language and people and nation." *Revelation 5:9*

After this I looked and there before me was a great multitude that no one could count,

from every nation, tribe, people and language,

standing before the throne and in front of the Lamb. They were wearing white robes and were holding palm branches in their hands. And they cried out in a loud voice:

"Salvation belongs to our God, who sits on the throne, and to the Lamb."

All the angels were standing around the throne and around the elders and the four living creatures. They fell down on their faces before the throne and worshipped God, saying:

"Amen! Praise and glory and wisdom and thanks and honor and power and strength be to our God for ever and ever. Amen!" *Revelation 7:9-12*

OUR MISSION

MEDLEY

We've a Story to Tell to the Nations
Song for the Nations

521 We've a Story to Tell to the Nations

This gospel of the kingdom will be preached in the whole world. Matthew 24:14

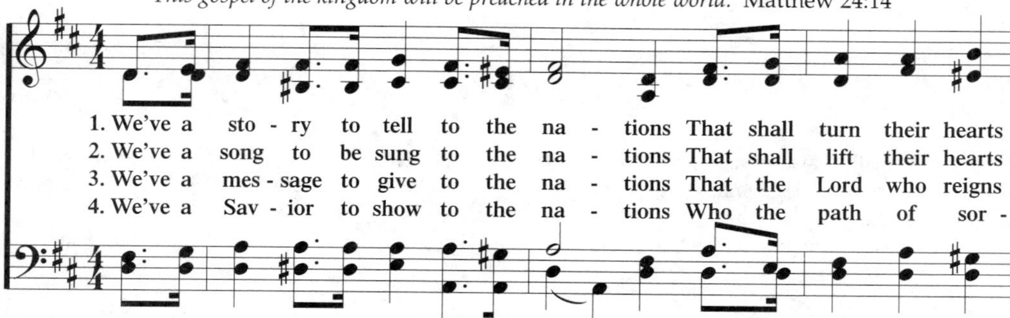
1. We've a sto - ry to tell to the na - tions That shall turn their hearts
2. We've a song to be sung to the na - tions That shall lift their hearts
3. We've a mes - sage to give to the na - tions That the Lord who reigns
4. We've a Sav - ior to show to the na - tions Who the path of sor -

WORDS: Henry E. Nichol, 1862-1928, alt.
MUSIC: Henry E. Nichol, 1862-1928

MESSAGE
10.8.8.7.7. with Refrain

to the right, A sto - ry of truth and mer - cy, A sto - ry of
to the Lord, A song that shall con - quer e - vil And shat - ter the
high a - bove Has sent us His Son to save us And show us that
row has trod, That all of the world's great peo - ples Might come to the
Refrain
peace and light, A sto - ry of peace and light.
spear and sword, And shat - ter the spear and sword.
God is love, And show us that God is love.
truth of God, Might come to the truth of God.
For the
dark - ness shall turn to dawn - ing, And the dawn - ing to noon - day bright, And
Christ's great king - dom shall come to earth, The king - dom of love and
Song ending
light.
Optional transition to "Song for the Nations."
light.
rit.

522 Song for the Nations

Repentance and forgiveness of sins will be preached in his name to all nations. Luke 24:47

1. May we be a shin - ing light to the na - tions, A
2. May we bring a word of hope to the na - tions, A
3. May we be a heal - ing balm to the na - tions, A
4. May we sing a song of joy to the na - tions, A
5. May Your king - dom come to the na - tions, Your
shin - ing light to the peo - ples of the earth; Till the
word of life to the peo - ples of the earth; Till the
heal - ing balm to the peo - ples of the earth; Till the
song of praise to the peo - ples of the earth; Till the
will be done in the peo - ples of the earth; Till the
whole world sees the glo - ry of Your name.
whole world knows there's sal - va - tion through Your name.
whole world knows the pow - er of Your name.
whole world rings with the prais - es of Your name.
whole world knows that Je - sus Christ is Lord.
May Your pure light shine through us!
May Your mer - cy flow through us!
May Your heal - ing flow through us!
May Your song be sung through us!
May Your king - dom come on earth!

WORDS: Chris Christensen, b. 1957
MUSIC: Chris Christensen, b. 1957; arr. Tom Fettke, b. 1941

SONG FOR THE NATIONS
Irregular

Christ for the World! We Sing 523

Go into all the world and preach the good news to all creation. Mark 16:15

1. Christ for the world! we sing; The world to Christ we bring With loving zeal— The poor and them that mourn, The faint and overborne,[1] Sin-sick and sorrow-worn, For Christ to heal.
2. Christ for the world! we sing; The world to Christ we bring With fervent prayer— The wayward and the lost, By restless passions tossed, Redeemed at countless cost From dark despair.
3. Christ for the world! we sing; The world to Christ we bring With one accord— With us the work to share, With us reproach to dare, With us the cross to bear, For Christ our Lord.
4. Christ for the world! we sing; The world to Christ we bring With joyful song— The newborn souls whose days, Reclaimed from error's ways, Inspired with hope and praise, To Christ belong.

WORDS: Samuel Wolcott, 1813-1886
MUSIC: Felice de Giardini, 1716-1796

ITALIAN HYMN
6.6.4.6.6.6.4.

1. overborne: oppressed

MISSIONARIES ARE THE "SCAFFOLDING"

I look upon foreign missionaries as the scaffolding around a rising building. The sooner it can be dispensed with, the better; or rather, the sooner it can be transferred to other places, to serve the same temporary use, the better.

Hudson Taylor (1832-1905)

524 Let All the World in Every Corner Sing

Sing to the LORD, all the earth. Psalm 96:1

1. Let all the world in ev - ery cor - ner sing: My God and King!
2. Let all the world in ev - ery cor - ner sing: My God and King!
The heavens are not too high, His praise may thith - er fly; The
The church with psalms must shout, No door can keep them out; But
earth is not too low, His prais - es there may grow. Let
more than all, the heart Must bear the long - est part. Let
all the world in ev - ery cor - ner sing: My God and King!
all the world in ev - ery cor - ner sing: My God and King!

WORDS: George Herbert, 1593-1633
MUSIC: Robert G. McCutchan, 1877-1958

ALL THE WORLD
Irregular

O Zion, Haste 525

O Zion, You who bring good tidings . . . lift up your voice. Isaiah 40:9, NKJV

1. O Zi - on, haste, your mis-sion high ful - fill - ing, To tell to all the
2. Pro - claim to ev - ery peo - ple, tongue and na - tion That God, in whom they
3. Send sons and daugh-ters with the mes - sage glo-rious, Give of your wealth to
world that God is light, That He who made all na - tions is not will - ing
live and move, is love. Tell how He stooped to save His lost cre - a - tion,
speed them on their way. Pour out your soul for them in prayer vic - to - rious,
Refrain
One soul should per - ish, lost in shades of night.
And died on earth that man might live a - bove.
And all your spend - ing Je - sus will re - pay.
Pub - lish glad tid - ings,
Tid - ings of peace, Tid - ings of Je - sus, re - demp-tion and re - lease.

WORDS: Mary A. Thomson, 1834-1923, alt.
MUSIC: James Walch, 1837-1901

TIDINGS
11.10.11.10. with Refrain

526 This Is the Gospel of Christ

I am not ashamed of the gospel of Christ, for it is the power of God to salvation for everyone who believes. Romans 1:16, NKJV

To de - stroy the works of the e-vil one And the king-dom of dark-ness with
light, And to res - cue men from the law and sin, This
is the gos - pel of Christ. To pro - claim good news un -
to the poor, And the bro - ken - heart - ed new life, And, for
those who mourn heav - en's Child is born, This is the gos - pel of

WORDS: Scott Wesley Brown, 20th century
MUSIC: Scott Wesley Brown, 20th century

GOSPEL OF CHRIST
Irregular

Christ. And to God be the glo - ry, and to God be the glo-
ry; And to God be the glo - ry, this is the gos - pel of
1.
2.
Christ. And to Christ. To re - deem a peo - ple He
calls His own From ev-ery na-tion, tongue, and tribe, Pur-chased
by the blood He shed with love, This is the gos - pel of

Christ. And to rise a-gain and to con-quer death, He'll re-
turn like a thief in the night, And He will reign on high, for-ev-er
with His Bride, This is the gos - pel of Christ. And to God be the glory, and to God be the glo - ry; And to God be the glo-
ry, this is the gos - pel of Christ. And to Christ.
1.
2.
3

Macedonia 527

Look at the fields! They are ripe for harvest. John 4:35

1. The vi - sion of a dy - ing world Is vast be - fore our eyes.
2. The sav - age hugs his god of stone And fears de - scent of night.
3. To - day, as un - der - stand - ing's bounds Are stretched on ev - ery hand,
4. The warn - ing bell of judg - ment tolls, A - bove us looms the cross,
We feel the heart - beat of its need, We hear its fee - ble cries.
The cit - y dwell - er cring - es lone A - mid the gar - ish light.
O, clothe Thy Word in bright, new sounds, And speed it o'er the land.
A - round are ev - er - dy - ing souls— How great, how great the loss!
Lord Je - sus Christ, re - vive Thy Church In this, her cru - cial hour!
Lord Je - sus Christ, a - rouse Thy Church To see their mute dis - tress!
Lord Je - sus Christ, em - pow - er us To preach by ev - ery means!
O Lord, con - strain and move Thy Church The glad news to im - part!
Lord Je - sus Christ, a - wake Thy Church With Spir - it - giv - en power.
Lord Je - sus Christ, e - quip Thy Church With love and ten - der - ness.
Lord Je - sus Christ, em - bold - en us In near and dis - tant scenes.
And Lord, as Thou dost stir Thy Church, Be - gin with - in my heart.

WORDS: Anne Ortlund, b. 1923
MUSIC: Henry S. Cutler, 1824-1902

ALL SAINTS, NEW
C.M.D.

528 Jesus Saves

All the ends of the earth will see the salvation of our God. Isaiah 52:10

1. We have heard the joy - ful sound: Je - sus saves! Je - sus saves!
2. Waft it on the roll - ing tide; Je - sus saves! Je - sus saves!
3. Sing a - bove the bat - tle's strife, Je - sus saves! Je - sus saves!
4. Give the winds a might - y voice, Je - sus saves! Je - sus saves!
Spread the tid - ings all a - round: Je - sus saves! Je - sus saves!
Tell to sin - ners far and wide: Je - sus saves! Je - sus saves!
By His death and end - less life. Je - sus saves! Je - sus saves!
Let the na - tions now re - joice, Je - sus saves! Je - sus saves!
Bear the news to ev - ery land, Climb the steeps and cross the waves;
Sing, you is - lands of the sea, Ech - o back, you o - cean caves;
Sing it soft - ly through the gloom, When the heart for mer - cy craves;
Shout sal - va - tion full and free, High - est hills and deep - est caves—
On - ward— 'tis our Lord's com - mand. Je - sus saves! Je - sus saves!
Earth shall keep her ju - bi - lee— Je - sus saves! Je - sus saves!
Sing in tri - umph o'er the tomb, Je - sus saves! Je - sus saves!
This our song of vic - to - ry: Je - sus saves! Je - sus saves!

WORDS: Priscilla J. Owens, 1829-1907, alt.
MUSIC: William J. Kirkpatrick, 1838-1921

JESUS SAVES
7.6.7.6.7.7.7.6.

One Race, One Gospel, One Task 529

He has committed to us the message of reconciliation. We are therefore Christ's ambassadors.
2 Corinthians 5:19-20

1. One is the race of man - kind un - der sin's con - dem -
2. One is the Word that can speak to our fall - en con -
3. One is the task that our Lord to His Church has com -
4. One is the hope of e - ter - nal re - joic - ing be -
na - tion. One is the gos - pel that frees us from
di - tion: Je - sus a - lone can re - deem us and
mit - ted. His is the Spir - it by whom for His
fore us. One is the song we shall share in God's
death's dom - i - na - tion. One is our task— sin, death and
give sin's re - mis - sion. His sav - ing name we must for -
work we are fit - ted. No more our own, we serve one
heav - en - ly chor - us. Till that glad day let us Christ's
hell to un - mask, Show - ing God's way of sal - va - tion.
ev - er pro - claim, On - ly in Christ is sal - va - tion.
Mas - ter a - lone— Je - sus, who won our sal - va - tion!
man - date o - bey— Tell the whole world of sal - va - tion!

WORDS: Margaret Clarkson, b. 1915
MUSIC: *Stralsund Gesangbuch*, 1665

LOBE DEN HERREN
14.14.4.7.8.

530 Go Forth and Tell!

You will be my witnesses . . . to the ends of the earth. Acts 1:8
1. Go forth and tell! O Church of God, a - wake!
God's sav - ing news to all the na - tions take.
Pro - claim Christ Je - sus, Sav - ior, Lord and King,
That all the world His wor - thy praise may sing.
2. Go forth and tell! God's love em - brac - es all.
He will in grace re - spond to all who call.
How shall they call if they have nev - er heard
The gra - cious in - vi - ta - tion of His Word?
3. Go forth and tell! Men still in dark - ness lie;
In wealth or want, in sin they live and die.
Give us, O Lord, con - cern of heart and mind—
A love like Yours which cares for all man - kind.
4. Go forth and tell! The doors are o - pen wide.
Share God's good gifts; let no one be de - nied.
Live out your life as Christ your Lord shall choose;
Your ran - somed powers for His sole glo - ry use.
5. Go forth and tell! O Church of God, a - rise!
Go in the strength which Christ your Lord sup - plies.
Go till all na - tions His great name a - dore,
And serve Him— Lord and King for - ev - er - more.
Optional segue to "Lift Up Our Eyes." No transition required.

WORDS: James E. Seddon, 1915-1983
MUSIC: George W. Warren, 1828-1902

NATIONAL HYMN
10.10.10.10.

Lift Up Our Eyes 531

Lift up your eyes and look at the fields, for they are already white for harvest!
John 4:35, NKJV

1. Lift up our eyes, Lord, un - to the fields,
2. Lift up our eyes, Lord, un - to the world,
White un - to har - vest, read - y to yield.
And to the mil - lions who've nev - er heard.
Lift up our hearts, Lord, be - yond our cares.
Lift up our hands, Lord Je - sus, de - clare.
Lift up our eyes, Lord, and lead us there.
Lift up our eyes, Lord, and lead us there.

WORDS: Scott Wesley Brown, 20th century
MUSIC: Scott Wesley Brown, 20th century

LIFT UP OUR EYES
9.9.9.9.

532 You Servants of God, Your Master Proclaim

Ascribe to the LORD the glory due his name. Psalm 96:8

1. You ser - vants of God, your Mas - ter pro - claim,
2. God rules from on high, al - might - y to save,
3. "Sal - va - tion to God, who sits on the throne,"
4. Then let us a - dore, and give Him His right,
And pub - lish a - broad His won - der - ful name.
And still He is nigh— His pres - ence we have.
Let all cry a - loud and hon - or the Son.
All glo - ry and power, all wis - dom and might;
The name all vic - to - rious of Je - sus ex - tol.
The great con - gre - ga - tion His tri - umph shall sing,
The prais - es of Je - sus the an - gels pro - claim,
All hon - or and bless - ing, with an - gels a - bove,
His King - dom is glo - rious, He rules o - ver all.
As - crib - ing sal - va - tion to Je - sus our King.
Fall down on their fac - es, and wor - ship the Lamb.
And thanks nev - er ceas - ing, and in - fi - nite love.

WORDS: Charles Wesley, 1707-1788, alt.
MUSIC: William Croft, 1678-1727

HANOVER
10.10.11.11.

Go and Tell Them 533

Go and proclaim the kingdom of God. Luke 9:60

1. Send the gos - pel of sal - va - tion To a world of dy - ing men.
2. 'Tis the Church - 's great com - mis - sion, 'Tis the Mas - ter's last com - mand.
3. Christ is gath - ering out a peo - ple To His name from ev - ery race.
4. Give the gos - pel as a wit - ness To a world of sin - ful men,
Tell it out to ev - ery na - tion Till the Lord shall come a - gain.
Christ has died for ev - ery crea - ture, Tell it out in ev - ery land.
Haste to give the in - vi - ta - tion Ere shall end the day of grace.
Till the Bride shall be com - plet - ed And the Lord shall come a - gain.
Refrain
Go and tell them, go and tell them Je - sus died for sin - ful men;
Go and tell them, go and tell them He is com - ing back a - gain.

(For higher key, see No. 510.)
WORDS: Albert B. Simpson, 1843-1919
MUSIC: Ada R. Gibbs, 1865-1905

CHANNELS
8.7.8.7. with Refrain

534 Our God Reigns

How beautiful . . . are the feet of those who bring good news. . . . "Your God reigns!"
Isaiah 52:7

1. How love - ly on the moun - tains are the feet of him
2. He had no state - ly form, He had no maj - es - ty
3. Out of the tomb He came with grace and maj - es - ty;
Who brings good news, good news, An - nounc - ing
That we should be drawn to Him. He was de -
He is a - live, He is a - live. God loves us
peace, pro - claim - ing news of hap - pi - ness, Our God
spised and we took no ac - count of Him, Yet now He
so, see here His hands, His feet, His side. Yes, we
reigns, our God reigns!
reigns with the Most High. Our God reigns!
know He is a - live.
Refrain

WORDS: Leonard E. Smith, Jr., b. 1942
MUSIC: Leonard E. Smith, Jr., b. 1942

OUR GOD REIGNS
Irregular with Refrain

Our God reigns! Our God reigns! Our God reigns!

Optional Stanzas: *May be sung after stanza 2 as stanzas 3 and 4.*

It was our sin and guilt that bruised and wounded Him.
It was our sin that brought Him down.
When we like sheep had gone astray our Shepherd came
And on His shoulders bore our shame.
Refrain

Meek as a lamb that's led out to the slaughterhouse,
Dumb as a sheep before its shearer,
His life ran down upon the ground like pouring rain
That we might be born again.
Refrain

I've Come to Tell 535

Te Vengo a Decir

Love the Lord your God with all your heart. Matthew 22:37

I've come to tell, I've come to tell, O Sav-ior di - vine,
Te ven - go a de - cir, te ven - go a de - cir, oh mi Sal - va - dor,
How much I love You, how much I love You, with all of my heart.
Que yo te a - mo a ti, que yo te a - mo a ti, con el co - ra - zón.

WORDS: Juan M. Isáis, 1926-2002; tr. Frank Sawyer, b. 1946
MUSIC: Juan M. Isáis, 1926-2002; harm. Dale Grotenhuis, b. 1931

TE VENGO
Irregular

I've come to tell, I've come to tell, to tell You the truth:
Te ven-go a de-cir, te ven-go a de-cir to-da la ver-dad;
fine
I love You, O Lord, I wor-ship You, Lord, with all of my heart.
Te quie-ro, Se-ñor, te a-mo, Se-ñor, con el co-ra-zón.
I want to sing, I want to sing from hap-pi-ness;
Yo quie-ro can-tar, yo quie-ro can-tar de go-zo y de paz;
D.S. al fine
I want to cry, I want to cry from joy and peace.
Yo quie-ro llo-rar, yo quie-ro llo-rar de fe-li-ci-dad.

We Are Singing, for the Lord Is Our Light 536

(Siyahamba)

The LORD is my light and my salvation. Psalm 27:1

We are sing - ing* for the Lord is our light.
Si - ya - hamb' e - ku - kha - ny - en' kwen - khos'.
We are sing - ing for the Lord is our light.
Si - ya - hamb' e - ku - kha - ny - en' kwen - khos'.
We are sing - ing, O, we are
Si - ya - ham - ba, Oo si - ya -
We are sing - ing, sing - ing, we are sing - ing, sing - ing, We are
Si - ya - ham - ba, ham - ba, si - ya - ham - ba, ham - ba, Si - ya -
we are
si - ya -
sing - ing for the Lord is our light. We are
hamb' e - ku-kha - ny - en' kwen-khos. Si - ya
1.
2.
our light.
kwen-khos.
sing - ing for the Lord is, for the Lord is our light. We are our light.
hamb' e - ku-kha - ny - en' kwen, kha - ny - en' kwen-khos. Si - ya kwen-khos.
sing - ing for the Lord is our light. We are our light.
hamb' e - ku-kha - ny - en' kwen-khos. Si - ya kwen-khos.

*marching/praying

WORDS: "Siyahamba" tr. Hal H. Hopson, b. 1933
MUSIC: Hal H. Hopson, b. 1933; based on Zulu traditional song

SIYAHAMBA
Irregular

537 O, Sing to the Lord

Cantad al Señor

They sang a new song: "You are worthy." Revelation 5:9

1. Cantad al Señor un cántico nuevo.
Cantad al Señor un cántico nuevo.
Cantad al Señor un cántico nuevo.
¡Cantad al Señor, cantad al Señor!

2. Pues nuestro Señor ha hecho prodigios.
Pues nuestro Señor ha hecho prodigios.
Pues nuestro Señor ha hecho prodigios.
¡Cantad al Señor, cantad al Señor!

3. Es él que nos da el Espiritu Santo.
Es él que nos da el Espiritu Santo.
Es él que nos da el Espiritu Santo.
¡Cantad al Señor, cantad al Señor!

4. ¡Jesús es Señor, ¡Amén, Alleluya!
¡Jesús es Señor, ¡Amén, Alleluya!
¡Jesús es Señor, ¡Amén, Alleluya!
¡Cantad al Señor, cantad al Señor!

WORDS: Brazilian folk song, "Cantai ao Senhor";
Spanish and English tr. Gerhard Cartford, b. 1923, alt.
MUSIC: Brazilian folk melody; arr. Jack Schrader, b. 1942

CANTAD AL SEÑOR
Irregular

The Call for Reapers 538

Ask the Lord of the harvest . . . to send out workers into his harvest field. Luke 10:2

1. Far and near the fields are teem - ing With the waves of ri - pened grain.
2. Send them forth with morn's first beam - ing, Send them in the noon - tide's glare.
3. O thou, whom thy Lord is send - ing, Gath - er now the sheaves of gold.
Far and near their gold is gleam - ing O'er the sun - ny slope and plain.
When the sun's last rays are gleam - ing, Bid them gath - er ev - ery - where.
Heaven-ward then at eve-ning wend - ing, Thou shalt come with joy un - told.
Refrain
Lord of har - vest, send forth reap - ers! Hear us, Lord, to Thee we cry.
Send them now the sheaves to gath - er, Ere the har - vest time pass by.

WORDS: John O. Thompson, 1782-1818
MUSIC: J.B.O. Clemm, 19th century

HARVESTTIME
8.7.8.7. with Refrain

539 King of the Nations

All nations will come and worship before you. Revelation 15:4

1. Come, let us wor - ship Je - sus, King of na - tions,
2. Lav - ish our heart's af - fec - tion, Deep - est love and
3. Bring trib - utes from the na - tions, Come in joy - ful
4. Come, Lord, and fill Your tem - ple, Glo - ri - fy Your
5. Fear God and give Him glo - ry For His hour of
Lord of all; Mag - ni - fi - cent and glo - rious,
high - est praise; Voice, race and lan - guage blend - ing,
cav - al - cades; One thun - derous ac - cla - ma - tion,
dwell - ing place Till na - tions see Your splen - dor
judg - ment comes; Cre - a - tor, Lord Al - might - y,
Just and mer - ci - ful.
All the world a - mazed.
One ban - ner raised.
And seek Your face.
Wor - ship Him a - lone.
Refrain
Je - sus,
King of the na - tions, Je - sus, Lord of all.

WORDS: Graham Kendrick, b. 1950
MUSIC: Graham Kendrick, b. 1950

KING OF THE NATIONS
Irregular

1, 2, 3, 4.
Je - sus, King of the na - tions, Lord of
5.
all. wor - ship Him a - lone.

Go and Make Disciples 540

Then the eleven disciples went to Galilee, to the mountain where Jesus had told them to go.

When they saw him, they worshiped him; but some doubted.

Then Jesus came to them and said, "All authority in heaven and on earth has been given to me. Therefore go and make disciples of all nations, baptizing them in the name of the Father and of the Son and of the Holy Spirit,

and teaching them to obey everything I have commanded you. And surely I am with you always, to the very end of the age." *Matthew 28:16-20*

Then he said to his disciples, "The harvest is plentiful but the workers are few.

Ask the Lord of the harvest, therefore, to send out workers into his harvest field." *Matthew 9:37-38*

But what does it say? "The word is near you; it is in your mouth and in your heart," that is, the word of faith we are proclaiming: That if you confess with your mouth, "Jesus is Lord," and believe in your heart that God raised him from the dead, you will be saved.

For it is with your heart that you believe and are justified, and it is with your mouth that you confess and are saved.

As the Scripture says, "Anyone who trusts in him will never be put to shame." For there is no difference between Jew and Gentile—the same Lord is Lord of all and richly blesses all who call on him,

. . . for, "Everyone who calls on the name of the Lord will be saved."

How, then, can they call on the one they have not believed in? And how can they believe in the one of whom they have not heard? And how can they hear without someone preaching to them?

And how can they preach unless they are sent? As it is written, "How beautiful are the feet of those who bring good news!" *Romans 10:8-15*

541 Let Your Heart Be Broken

When he saw the crowds, he had compassion on them. Matthew 9:36

1. Let your heart be bro - ken For a world in need— Feed the mouths that hun - ger, Soothe the wounds that bleed, Give the cup of wa - ter And the loaf of bread— Be the hands of Je - sus, Serv - ing in His stead.
2. Here on earth ap - ply - ing Prin - ci - ples of love— Vis - i - ble ex - pres - sion God still rules a - bove, Liv - ing il - lus - tra - tion Of the Liv - ing Word To the minds of all who've Nev - er seen and heard.
3. Add to your be - liev - ing Deeds that prove it true— Know - ing Christ as Sav - ior, Make Him Mas - ter too: Fol - low in His foot - steps, Go where He has trod, In the world's great trou - ble Risk your - self for God.
4. Let your heart be ten - der And your vi - sion clear— See man - kind as God sees, Serve Him far and near. Let your heart be bro - ken By an - oth - er's pain, Share your rich re - sourc - es— Give and give a - gain.

WORDS: Bryan Jeffery Leech, b. 1931
MUSIC: James Mountain, 1844-1933

WYE VALLEY (abridged)
6.5.6.5.D.

Send the Light 542

Send forth your light and your truth. Psalm 43:3

1. There's a call comes ring-ing o'er the rest-less wave, "Send the light!
2. We have heard the Mac-e-do-nian call to-day, "Send the light!
3. Let us not grow wea-ry in the work of love. Send the light!
Send the light!
Send the light!" There are souls to res-cue, there are souls to save.
Send the light!" And a gold-en of-fering at the cross we lay.
Send the light! Let us gath-er jew-els for a crown a-bove.
Refrain
Send the light! Send the light!
Send the light! Send the light! Send the light, the bless-ed
Send the light! Send the light!
Send the light!
gos-pel light, Let it shine from shore to shore. Send the light,
the bless-ed gos-pel light, Let it shine for-ev-er-more.

WORDS: Charles H. Gabriel, 1856-1932
MUSIC: Charles H. Gabriel, 1856-1932

MCCABE
11.6.11.6. with Refrain

543 Let Us Go

The important thing is that in every way . . . Christ is preached. Philippians 1:18

1. Let us go and preach the gos - pel as a wit - ness
2. Let us pray as well as la - bor, God the sav - ing
3. Let us give to send the gos - pel as a wit - ness
to the world.
work can do.
ev - ery - where.
And for ev - ery tongue and peo - ple
Pray that He will send forth reap - ers,
We can help to send the work - ers,
let Christ's ban - ner be un - furled.
for the lab - or - ers are few.
and their toils and tri - umphs share.
He is wait - ing
O, for such a
Sac - ri - fice is
(D.S.) Let us go now,
till earth's mil - lions shall His full sal - va - tion know.
great bap - tis - m as will bring the Ad - vent day!
high - est ser - vice; on - ly while we love we live.
pray now, give now; ser - vants of the Com - ing King.

(For different harmony and higher key, see No. 50.)

WORDS: Albert B. Simpson, 1843-1919; adapt. Gene Rivard, b. 1949
MUSIC: Ludwig van Beethoven, 1770-1827; arr. Eldon McBride, b. 1962

HYMN TO JOY
8.7.8.7.D. with Coda

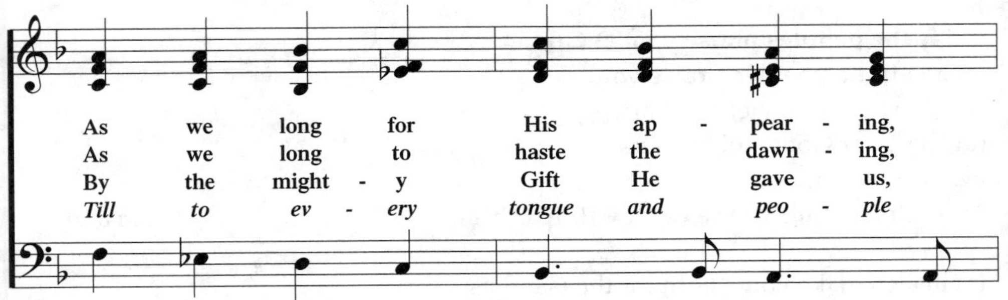
As we long for His ap - pear - ing,
As we long to haste the dawn - ing,
By the might - y Gift He gave us,
Till to ev - ery tongue and peo - ple

let us go, O, let us go.
let us pray, O, let us pray.
let us give, O, let us give. D.S.
God's great mes - sage we shall bring.

I Will Be Exalted among the Nations 544

The LORD had said to Abram, "Leave your country, your people and your father's household and go to the land I will show you. I will make you into a great nation and I will bless you; I will make your name great, and you will be a blessing. I will bless those who bless you, and whoever curses you I will curse;

and all peoples on earth will be blessed through you." *Genesis 12:1-3*

"Be still, and know that I am God;
I will be exalted among the nations,
I will be exalted in the earth." *Psalm 46:10*

May God be gracious to us and bless us
and make his face shine upon us,
that your ways may be known on earth,
your salvation among all nations.
May the peoples praise you, O God;
may all the peoples praise you.
May the nations be glad and sing for joy,
for you rule the peoples justly and guide the nations of the earth.

May the peoples praise you, O God;
may all the peoples praise you.
Then the land will yield its harvest,
and God, our God, will bless us.
God will bless us,
and all the ends of the earth will fear him. *Psalm 67:1-7*

"I will also make you a light for the Gentiles,
that you may bring my salvation to the ends of the earth." *Isaiah 49:6*

545 God Calls Us

How can they believe in the one of whom they have not heard? Romans 10:14

1. Be - cause so man - y need to know, It's up to you and me to go. Be - cause so man - y need to know, God calls us, God calls us.
2. Be - cause so man - y need to see That God a - lone can make them free; Be - cause so man - y need to see, God calls us, God calls us.
3. Be - cause so man - y need to hear, I want to be a vol - un - teer. Be - cause so man - y need to hear, God calls us, God calls us.

WORDS: Linda Rebuck, 20th century
MUSIC: Tom Fettke, b. 1941

GOD CALLS US
Irregular

Lord of the Living Harvest 546

Ask the Lord of the harvest . . . to send out workers into his harvest field. Matthew 9:38

1. Lord of the liv - ing har - vest That whit - ens o'er the plain,
2. As la - borers in Thy vine - yard, Send them out, Christ, to be
3. Be with them, God the Fa - ther; Be with them, God the Son;

Where an - gels soon shall gath - er Their sheaves of gold - en grain,
Con - tent to bear the bur - den Of wea - ry days for Thee,
Be with them, God the Spir - it, E - ter - nal Three - in - One!

Ac - cept fresh hands to la - bor, Fresh hearts to trust and love,
Con - tent to ask no wag - es When Thou shalt call them home,
Make them a roy - al priest - hood, Thee right - ly to a - dore,

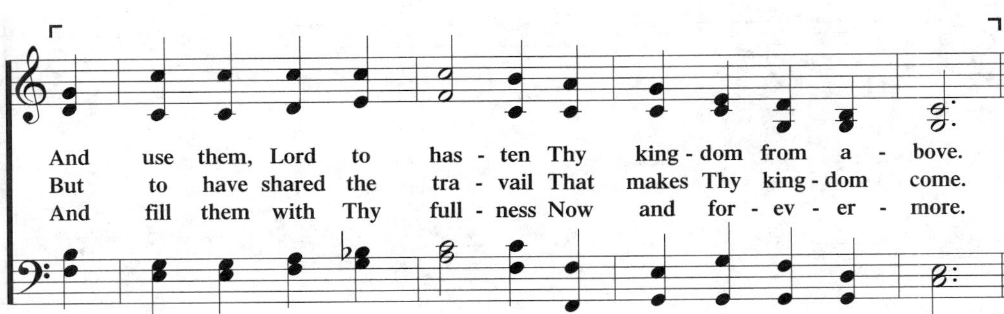
And use them, Lord to has - ten Thy king - dom from a - bove.
But to have shared the tra - vail That makes Thy king - dom come.
And fill them with Thy full - ness Now and for - ev - er - more.

WORDS: John S.B. Monsell, 1811-1875, alt.
MUSIC: Henry T. Smart, 1813-1879

LANCASHIRE
7.6.7.6.D.

547 Shine, Jesus, Shine

I am the light of the world. John 8:12

1. Lord, the light of Your love is shin - ing, In the midst of the dark - ness shin - ing. Je - sus, Light of the world, shine up - on us, Set us free by the truth You now bring us, Shine on me, shine on me.
2. Lord, I come to Your awe - some pres - ence, From the shad - ows in - to Your ra - di - ance. By the blood I may en - ter Your bright - ness. Search me, try me, con - sume all my dark - ness, Shine on me, shine on me.
3. As we gaze on Your king - ly bright - ness, So our fac - es dis - play Your like - ness. Ev - er chang - ing from glo - ry to glo - ry, Mir - rored here, may our lives tell Your sto - ry, Shine on me, shine on me.

WORDS: Graham Kendrick, b. 1950
MUSIC: Graham Kendrick, b. 1950

SHINE
Irregular

Refrain
Shine, Je - sus, shine, fill this land with the Fa - ther's glo - ry.
Blaze, Spir - it, blaze, set our hearts on fire.
Flow, riv - er, flow, flood the na - tions with grace and mer - cy.
Send forth Your Word, Lord, and let there be light.
1, 2.
3.

Optional segue to "Heart for the Nations." No transition required.

548 Heart for the Nations

Wherever you send us we will go. Joshua 1:16

Give us Your heart for the na - tions, Let us be light
to the world. Use us to de - clare Your sal - va - tion To the peo -
ple of the earth. May we be moved by com - pas -
sion, Let us know Your love for the lost. Lord, use us to

WORDS: Martin J. Nystrom, b.1956, and Gary Sadler, b. 1954
MUSIC: Martin J. Nystrom, b.1956, and Gary Sadler, b. 1954

HEART FOR THE NATIONS
Irregular

lead them to the cross.
Fa-ther, here we are,
stand-ing in Your pres - ence,
Send us forth to
lead them to the cross.
Spir-it, here we are,
fill us with Your pow - er,
Send us forth
to lead them to the cross.

549 Speak, My Lord

FIRST TUNE

Speak, LORD, for your servant is listening. 1 Samuel 3:9

1. Hear the Lord of har - vest sweet - ly call - ing, "Who will go and work for Me to - day? Who will bring to me the lost and dy - ing? Who will point them to the nar - row way?"
2. When the coal of fire touched the proph - et, Mak - ing him as pure, as pure can be, When the voice of God said, "Who'll go for us?" Then he an - swered, "Here I am, send me."
3. Mil - lions now in sin and shame are dy - ing, Lis - ten to their sad and bit - ter cry. Has - ten, Chris - tian, has - ten to the res - cue, Quick - ly an - swer, "Mas - ter, here am I."
4. Soon the time for reap - ing will be o - ver. Soon we'll gath - er for the har - vest home. May the Lord of har - vest smile up - on us, May we hear His bless - ed, "Child, well done."
Refrain
Speak, my Lord, speak, my Lord, Speak, and I'll be quick to an - swer Thee.
Speak, my Lord, speak, my Lord,
to an - swer Thee.
Speak, my Lord, speak, my Lord, Speak, and I will an - swer, "Lord, send me."
"Lord, send me."

WORDS: George Bennard, 1873-1958, alt.
MUSIC: George Bennard, 1873-1958

BENNARD
10.9.10.9. with Refrain

Speak, My Lord 550

SECOND TUNE

I said, "Here am I. Send me!" Isaiah 6:8

1. Hear the Lord of har - vest sweet - ly call - ing,
2. When the coal of fi - re touched the proph - et,
3. Mil - lions now in sin and shame are dy - ing,
4. Soon the time for reap - ing will be o - ver.
"Who will go and work for Me to - day?
Mak - ing him as pure, as pure can be,
Lis - ten to their sad and bit - ter cry.
Soon we'll gath - er for the har - vest home.
Who will bring to me the lost and dy - ing?
When the voice of God said, "Who'll go for us?"
Has - ten, Chris - tian, has - ten to the res - cue,
May the Lord of har - vest smile up - on us,

WORDS: George Bennard, 1873-1958, alt.
MUSIC: Michael B. Davis, Sr., b. 1958; arr. David Hahn, b. 1956

DAVIS
10.9.10.9. with Refrain

Who will point them to the nar - row way?"
Then he an - swered, "Here am I, send me."
Quick - ly an - swer, "Mas - ter, here am I."
May we hear His bless - ed, "Child, well done."
Refrain
Speak, my Lord, speak, my Lord,
Speak, and I'll be quick to an - swer Thee. Speak, my
Lord, speak, my Lord,

1, 2, 3.
Speak, and I will an - swer, "Lord, send me."
4
Speak, and I will an - swer, "Lord, send me."
rit.
Speak, and I will an - swer, "Lord, send me."
rit.

A PRAYER FOR MISSIONARIES

O God our Savior,
who wills that all should be saved and come to the knowledge of the truth,
prosper Your servants who labor in distant lands.
Protect them in all perils by land and sea and air;
support them in loneliness and in the hour of trial;
give them grace to bear faithful witness to You,
and endue them with burning zeal and love,
that they may turn many to righteousness and finally obtain a crown of glory;
through Jesus Christ, our Lord. Amen.

Scottish Book of Common Prayer, 1912, alt.

551 The Breaking of the Bread

He gave thanks and broke the loaves. Then he gave them to the disciples. Matthew 14:19

1. A - long the shores of Gal - i - lee When Christ five thou - sand
2. Long years have passed and few have heard That Je - sus Christ has
3. Great God, Who gave Thine on - ly Son, Help us, now Spir - it
fed Not one was o - mit - ted In the break - ing of the
bled, That they might feed on Him Who died To be that Liv - ing
led, To tell the sto - ry of Thy love To those who ask for
bread. To - day they die in hea - then lands, They die in want and
Bread. To gods of stone and wood they cry, Yet they are nev - er
bread. Then glad - ly will we go or send, Till this blest news has
dread, For they have been o - mit - ted in the
fed, For they have been o - mit - ted in the
spread, And they have been in - clud - ed in the

WORDS: Beatrice B. Bixler, b. 1916
MUSIC: Beatrice B. Bixler, b. 1916

BREAKING BREAD
Irregular

Refrain
break - ing of the Bread.
break - ing of the Bread.
break - ing of the Bread.
Lord, I would give them the
Bread of Life, The Liv - ing Wa - ter too.
My heart cries out, "O,
here am I, Read - y Thy will to do."

PROCLAIM THE GOSPEL TO EVERY NATION, TRIBE AND TONGUE

Jesus' Great Commission has never yet been fully realized. It contemplates a worldwide evangelization so glorious and complete that no nation, tribe or tongue will be overlooked! It calls us to focus especially on the nations rather than on the isolated individual; unevangelized peoples should be the first objects of our care. Nor are we to rest until this glorious gospel shall have been proclaimed in every tongue spoken by man. God wants representatives from every nation to herald the return of the Son of man!

A.B. Simpson (1843-1919), *Missionary Messages*

552 Here I Am, Lord

"Whom shall I send?" . . . I said, "Here am I. Send me!" Isaiah 6:8

1. I, the Lord of sea and sky, I have heard My people cry. All who dwell in dark and sin My hand will save.
2. I, the Lord of snow and rain, I have borne My people's pain. I have wept for love of them. They turn away.
3. I, the Lord of wind and flame, I will tend the poor and lame, I will set a feast for them. My hand will save.
I, who made the stars of night, I will make their dark - ness bright. Who will bear My
I will break their hearts of stone, give them hearts for love a - lone. I will speak My
Fin - est bread I will pro - vide till their hearts be sat - is - fied. I will give My

WORDS: Daniel L. Schutte, b. 1947; based on Isaiah 6:8
MUSIC: Daniel L. Schutte, b. 1947

HERE I AM, LORD
7.7.7.4.D. with Refrain

PROCLAIM THE GOSPEL TO EVERY NATION, TRIBE AND TONGUE

Jesus' Great Commission has never yet been fully realized. It contemplates a worldwide evangelization so glorious and complete that no nation, tribe or tongue will be overlooked! It calls us to focus especially on the nations rather than on the isolated individual; unevangelized peoples should be the first objects of our care. Nor are we to rest until this glorious gospel shall have been proclaimed in every tongue spoken by man. God wants representatives from every nation to herald the return of the Son of man!

A.B. Simpson (1843-1919), *Missionary Messages*

552 Here I Am, Lord

"Whom shall I send?" . . . I said, "Here am I. Send me!" Isaiah 6:8

1. I, the Lord of sea and sky, I have heard My people cry. All who dwell in dark and sin My hand will save. I, who made the stars of night, I will make their dark - ness bright. Who will bear My
2. I, the Lord of snow and rain, I have borne My peo - ple's pain. I have wept for love of them. They turn a - way. I will break their hearts of stone, give them hearts for love a - lone. I will speak My
3. I, the Lord of wind and flame, I will tend the poor and lame, I will set a feast for them. My hand will save. Fin - est bread I will pro - vide till their hearts be sat - is - fied. I will give My

WORDS: Daniel L. Schutte, b. 1947; based on Isaiah 6:8
MUSIC: Daniel L. Schutte, b. 1947

HERE I AM, LORD
7.7.7.4.D. with Refrain

rit.
light to them? Whom shall I send?
word to them. Whom shall I send?
life to them. Whom shall I send?
Refrain
a tempo
Here I am, Lord. Is it I, Lord? I have
heard You call - ing in the night. I will
go, Lord, if You lead me. I will
hold Your peo - ple in my heart.

553 Our Heart

All the nations you have made will come and worship before you, O LORD. Psalm 86:9

Refrain
Our heart, our de-sire, is to see the na-tions
wor - ship. Our cry, our prayer, is to
sing Your praise to the ends of the earth, That with one might - y
voice ev-ery tribe and tongue re - joic - es. Our heart,
our de-sire, is to see the na - tions wor-ship You.
fine

WORDS: John Chisum, 20th century, and George Searcy, 20th century
MUSIC: John Chisum, 20th century, and George Searcy, 20th century

OUR HEART
Irregular

Heav - en - ly Fa - ther, Your mer - cy show - ers
down up-on Your peo-ple, ev-ery race up-on this earth. May Your
Spir - it pierce the dark - ness, may it break the chains of death up -
on us. Let us rise in hon-est wor - ship, to de -
D.S. al fine
clare Your match - less worth. Our heart,

554 My Trust

Those who have been given a trust must prove faithful. 1 Corinthians 4:2

1. Lord, You have giv - en me a trust, A high and ho - ly dis - pen -
2. We all are debt - ors to our race. God holds us bound to one an -
sa - tion; To tell the world, and tell I must The
oth - er. The gifts and bless - ings of His grace Were
sto - ry of Your great sal - va - tion. You might have sent from heaven a -
giv - en us to give our broth - er. We owe to ev - ery - one in
bove An - gel - ic hosts to tell the sto - ry, But
sin One chance, at least, for hope of heav - en. O,

WORDS: Albert B. Simpson, 1843-1919; adapt. Gene Rivard, b. 1949
MUSIC: Gene Rivard, b. 1949; arr. Eldon McBride, b. 1962

MY TRUST
Irregular

in Your wis-dom and Your love On us You have con-ferred the
by the love that brought us in, Let help and hope to them be
Refrain
glo - ry. Let me be faith-ful to my trust, Tell - ing the world the
giv - en.
sto - ry. Press on my heart the woe.
Give me the will to go. Let me be faith - ful
to my trust, And use me for Your glo - ry.

OUR LORD SHALL REIGN

MEDLEY

Jesus Shall Reign
To the Ends of the Earth

555 Jesus Shall Reign

He will reign for ever and ever. Revelation 11:15

1. Je - sus shall reign wher - e'er the sun Doth his suc -
2. To Him shall end - less prayer be made, And prais - es
3. Peo - ple and realms of ev - ery tongue Dwell on His
4. Let ev - ery crea - ture rise and sing Hon - or and
ces - sive jour - neys run. His king-dom stretch from shore to
throng to crown His head. His name like sweet per - fume shall
love with sweet - est song, And in - fant voic - es shall pro -
glo - ry to our King. An - gels de - scend with songs a -
shore, Till moons shall wax and wane no more.
rise With ev - ery morn - ing sac - ri - fice.
claim Their ear - ly bless - ings on His name.
gain, And earth re - peat the long A - men.
Song ending
Optional transition to "To the Ends of the Earth."
men.

WORDS: Isaac Watts, 1674-1748, alt.
MUSIC: John Hatton, 1710-1793

DUKE STREET
L.M.

To the Ends of the Earth 556

I have made you a light for the Gentiles, that you may bring salvation to the ends of the earth. Acts 13:47

To the ends of the earth You are Lord. From the
heav - ens, all glo - ry is Yours. We ex -
alt You, O Christ, as we car - ry Your
light To the ends of the earth, O Lord.

WORDS: Scott Wesley Brown, 20th century; David Hampton, 20th century
MUSIC: Scott Wesley Brown, 20th century; David Hampton, 20th century

ENDS OF THE EARTH
Irregular

557 All Around Your Throne

With your blood you purchased men for God from every tribe and language and people and nation. Revelation 5:9

Refrain
All a-round Your throne, we come from ev - ery language and na-tion; Mak-ing Your glo - ries known,
lift-ing a-loud our song of sal - va-tion All a-round Your throne,
1.
all a - round Your throne.

WORDS: Lynn DeShazo, b. 1956, and Ed Kerr, 20th century
MUSIC: Lynn DeShazo, b. 1956, and Ed Kerr, 20th century

AROUND YOUR THRONE
Irregular

2, 3.
all a - round Your throne.
1. From the North and the South we come, all a - round Your throne;
2. From the dark to the light we come, all a - round Your throne;
From the East and the West we come,
We re - joice in the Ho - ly One,
all a - round Your throne.
all a - round Your throne.
4.
all a - round Your throne.

558 So Send I You

As the Father has sent me, I am sending you. John 20:21

1. So send I you— by grace made strong to triumph O'er hosts of hell, o'er dark-ness, death and sin, My name to bear, and in that name to con-quer— So send I you, My vic-to-ry to win.
2. So send I you— to take to souls in bond-age The Word of truth that sets the cap-tive free, To break the bonds of sin, to loose death's fet-ters— So send I you, to bring the lost to Me.
3. So send I you— My strength to know in weak-ness, My joy in grief, My per-fect peace in pain, To prove My power, My grace, My prom-ised pres-ence— So send I you, e-ter-nal fruit to gain.
4. So send I you— to bear My cross with pa-tience, And then one day with joy to lay it down, To hear My voice, "Well done, My faith-ful ser-vant— Come, share My throne, My king-dom and My crown!" "As the Fa-ther has sent Me, so send I you."
1, 2, 3.
4.

WORDS: E. Margaret Clarkson, b. 1915
MUSIC: John W. Peterson, b. 1921

TORONTO
11.10.11.10. with Coda

Thy Kingdom Come 559

Your will be done on earth as it is in heaven. Matthew 6:10

1. O Christ, my Lord and King, This is the prayer I bring, This is the song I sing: "Thy king - dom come, Thy king - dom come!"
2. Help me to work and pray, Help me to live each day That all I do may say, "Thy king - dom come, Thy king - dom come!"
3. Up - on my heart's high throne, Rule Thou, and Thou a - lone. Let me be all Thine own! "Thy king - dom come, Thy king - dom come!"
4. Through all the earth a - broad, Where hu - man - kind has trod, Send forth Thy word, O God— "Thy king - dom come, Thy king - dom come!"
5. Soon may our King ap - pear! Haste bright mil - len - nial year! We live to bring it near. "Thy king - dom come, Thy king - dom come!"

WORDS: Albert B. Simpson, 1843-1919, alt.
MUSIC: Albert B. Simpson, 1843-1919

PAROUSIA
6.6.6.4.4.

560 Our Great Savior

. . . a friend of tax collectors and "sinners." Luke 7:34

1. Je - sus, what a friend for sin - ners! Je - sus, Lov - er of my soul.
2. Je - sus, what a strength in weak - ness! Let me hide my - self in Him.
3. Je - sus, what a help in sor - row! While the bil - lows o'er me roll,
4. Je - sus, what a guide and keep - er! While the tem - pest still is high,
5. Je - sus! I do now re - ceive Him, More than all in Him I find.
Friends may fail me, foes as - sail me, He, my Sav - ior, makes me whole.
Tempt - ed, tried, and some-times fail - ing, He, my strength, my vic - tory wins.
E - ven when my heart is break - ing, He, my com - fort, helps my soul.
Storms a - bout me, night o'er - takes me, He, my pi - lot, hears my cry.
He hath grant - ed me for - give - ness. I am His, and He is mine.
Refrain
Hal - le - lu - jah! What a Sav - ior! Hal - le - lu - jah! What a friend!
Sav - ing, help - ing, keep - ing, lov - ing, He is with me to the end.

WORDS: J. Wilbur Chapman, 1859-1918
MUSIC: Rowland H. Prichard, 1811-1887, arr. Robert Harkness, 1880-1961

HYFRYDOL
8.7.8.7. with Refrain

Calvary Covers It All 561

He forgave us all our sins. Colossians 2:13

1. Far dear - er than all that the world can im - part Was the mes-sage that came to my heart, How that Je - sus a - lone for my sin did a - tone, And Cal - va - ry cov - ers it all.
2. The stripes that He bore and the thorns that He wore Told His mer - cy and love ev - er - more, And my heart bowed in shame as I called on His name,
3. How match-less the grace, when I looked on the face Of this Je - sus, my cru - ci-fied Lord. My re - demp - tion com - plete I then found at His feet,
4. How bless - ed the thought, that my soul, by Him bought, Shall be His in the glo - ry on high, Where with glad - ness and song I'll be one of the throng,
Refrain
Cal - va - ry cov - ers it all, My past with its sin and shame. My guilt and de - spair Je - sus took on Him there, And Cal - va - ry cov - ers it all.

WORDS: Mrs. Walter G. Taylor, 20th century
MUSIC: Mrs. Walter G. Taylor, 20th century

CALVARY COVERS IT ALL
Irregular

562 Since I Have Been Redeemed

I will exalt you and praise your name. Isaiah 25:1

1. I have a song I love to sing, Since I have been re - deemed,
2. I have a Christ that sat - is - fies, Since I have been re - deemed,
3. I have a wit - ness bright and clear, Since I have been re - deemed,
4. I have a joy I can't ex - press, Since I have been re - deemed,
5. I have a home pre - pared for me, Since I have been re - deemed,
Of my Re - deem - er, Sav - ior, King— Since I have been re - deemed.
To do His will my high - est prize— Since I have been re - deemed.
Dis - pel - ling ev - ery doubt and fear— Since I have been re - deemed.
All through His blood and right - eous - ness— Since I have been re - deemed.
Where I shall dwell e - ter - nal - ly— Since I have been re - deemed.
Refrain
Since I have been re - deemed, Since I have been redeemed,
Since I have been re-deemed, since I have been re-deemed,
I will glo - ry in His name. Since I have been re -
Since I have been re - deemed, since

WORDS: Edwin O. Excell, 1851-1921
MUSIC: Edwin O. Excell, 1851-1921

OTHELLO
C.M. with Refrain

Calvary Covers It All 561

He forgave us all our sins. Colossians 2:13

WORDS: Mrs. Walter G. Taylor, 20th century
MUSIC: Mrs. Walter G. Taylor, 20th century

CALVARY COVERS IT ALL
Irregular

562 Since I Have Been Redeemed

I will exalt you and praise your name. Isaiah 25:1

WORDS: Edwin O. Excell, 1851-1921
MUSIC: Edwin O. Excell, 1851-1921

OTHELLO
C.M. with Refrain

deemed, I will glo - ry in the Sav - ior's name.
I have been re - deemed,
The Cleansing Wave 563
A fountain will be opened . . . to cleanse them from sin and impurity. Zechariah 13:1
1. O, now I see the cleans - ing wave! The foun - tain deep and wide.
2. I rise to walk in heaven's own light A - bove the world of sin,
3. A - maz - ing grace! 'Tis heaven be - low To feel the blood ap - plied,
Je - sus, my Lord, might - y to save, Points to His wound - ed side.
With heart made pure and gar - ments white, With Christ en - throned with - in.
And Je - sus, on - ly Je - sus know—My Je - sus cru - ci - fied.
Refrain
The cleans - ing stream, I see, I see. I plunge, and O, it cleans - es me!
O, praise the Lord, it cleans - es me! It cleans - es me— yes, cleans - es me.
WORDS: Phoebe Worrall Palmer, 1807-1874, alt.
MUSIC: Phoebe Palmer Knapp, 1839-1908
KNAPP
Irregular

OUR STORY

MEDLEY

My Faith Has Found a Resting Place
God Is So Good

564 My Faith Has Found a Resting Place

While we were still sinners, Christ died for us. Romans 5:8

1. My faith has found a rest - ing place, Not in de - vice nor creed.
2. E - nough for me that Je - sus saves— This ends my fear and doubt.
3. My heart is lean - ing on the Word, The writ - ten Word of God,
4. My great Phy - si - cian heals the sick, The lost He came to save.
I trust the ev - er - liv - ing One, His wounds for me shall plead.
A sin - ful soul, I come to Him, He'll nev - er cast me out.
Sal - va - tion by my Sav - ior's name, Sal - va - tion through His blood.
For me His pre - cious blood He shed, For me His life He gave.
Refrain
I need no oth - er ar - gu - ment, I need no oth - er plea.
It is e - nough that Je - sus died, And that He died for me.
Song ending

WORDS: Lidie H. Edmunds, 1851-1920
MUSIC: Norwegian folk melody; arr. William J. Kirkpatrick, 1838-1921

LANDAS
C.M. with Refrain

Optional transition to "God Is So Good."
me.

God Is So Good 565

Give thanks to the LORD, for he is good. Psalm 107:1

1. God is so good, God is so good, God is so good, He's so good to me! me!
2. He answers prayer, He answers prayer, He answers prayer, He's so good to

3. He cares for me, He cares for me, He cares for me, He's so good to me!
4. I love Him so, I love Him so, I love Him so, He's so good to me!

WORDS: Traditional
MUSIC: Traditional

GOD IS SO GOOD
Irregular

566 My Tribute

How can I repay the LORD for all his goodness to me? Psalm 116:12

How can I say thanks for the things You have done for me— Things so un-de-
served, yet You give to prove Your love for me? The voic-es of a mil-lion
an-gels could not ex-press my grat-i-tude— All that I am and ev-er hope to
be, I owe it all to Thee.
Refrain
To God be the glo-ry, To

WORDS: Andraé Crouch, b. 1947
MUSIC: Andraé Crouch, b. 1947

MY TRIBUTE
Irregular

God be the glo - ry, To God be the glo-ry For the things He has
done! With His blood He has saved me, With His power He has
fine
raised me— To God be the glo - ry For the things He has done!
* On introduction, hold 4 beats
Just let me live my life— Let it be pleas-ing, Lord, to
D.S. al fine
Thee, And should I gain an-y praise, Let it go to Cal - va - ry. With His

567 Redeemed

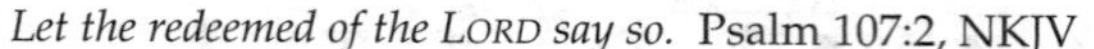
Let the redeemed of the LORD say so. Psalm 107:2, NKJV

1. Re-deemed–how I love to pro-claim it! Re-deemed by the blood of the Lamb.
Re-deemed through His in-fi-nite mer-cy, His child, and for-ev-er, I am.

2. Re-deemed and so hap-py in Je-sus, No lan-guage my rap-ture can tell.
I know that the light of His pres-ence With me doth con-tin-ual-ly dwell.

3. I think of my bless-ed Re-deem-er, I think of Him all the day long.
I sing, for I can-not be si-lent. His love is the theme of my song.

4. I know I shall see in His beau-ty The King in whose law I de-light,
Who lov-ing-ly guards all my foot-steps And gives me a song in the night.

Refrain

Re-deemed, re-deemed, re-deemed, re-deemed, Re-deemed by the blood of the Lamb.
Re-deemed, re-deemed, re-deemed, re-deemed, His child, and for-ev-er, I am.

WORDS: Fanny J. Crosby, 1820-1915
MUSIC: William J. Kirkpatrick, 1838-1921

REDEEMED
9.8.9.8. with Refrain

Jesus Paid It All 568

Though your sins are like scarlet, they shall be as white as snow. Isaiah 1:18

1. I hear the Savior say, "Your strength indeed is small.
Child of weakness, watch and pray. Find in Me your all in all."

2. Lord, now indeed I find Your power, and Yours alone,
Can change the leper's spots And melt the heart of stone.

3. For nothing good have I Whereby Your grace to claim—
I'll wash my garments white In the blood of Calv'ry's Lamb.

4. And when, before the throne, I stand in Him complete,
"Jesus died my soul to save," My lips shall still repeat.

Refrain

Jesus paid it all, All to Him I owe.
Sin had left a crimson stain; He washed it white as snow.

Optional segue to "My Redeemer." No transition required.

WORDS: Elvina M. Hall, 1820-1889
MUSIC: John T. Grape, 1835-1915

ALL TO CHRIST
6.6.7.7. with Refrain

569 My Redeemer

Jesus Christ, who gave himself for us to redeem us. Titus 2:13, 14

1. I will sing of my Re - deem-er And His won - drous love to me.
2. I will tell the won - drous sto - ry, How my lost es - tate to save,
3. I will sing of my Re - deem-er And His heaven - ly love for me.
On the cru - el cross He suf - fered, From the curse to set me free.
In His bound-less love and mer - cy, He the ran - som free - ly gave.
He from death to life hath brought me, Son of God with Him to be.
Refrain
Sing, O, sing of my Re - deem - er,
of my Re-deem - er, Sing, O, sing of my Re-deem - er,
With His blood He pur - chased me,
He pur-chased me, With His blood He pur-chased me,
On the cross He sealed my par - don,
He sealed my par - don, On the cross He sealed my par - don,

WORDS: Philip P. Bliss, 1838-1876
MUSIC: James McGranahan, 1840-1907

MY REDEEMER
8.7.8.7. with Refrain

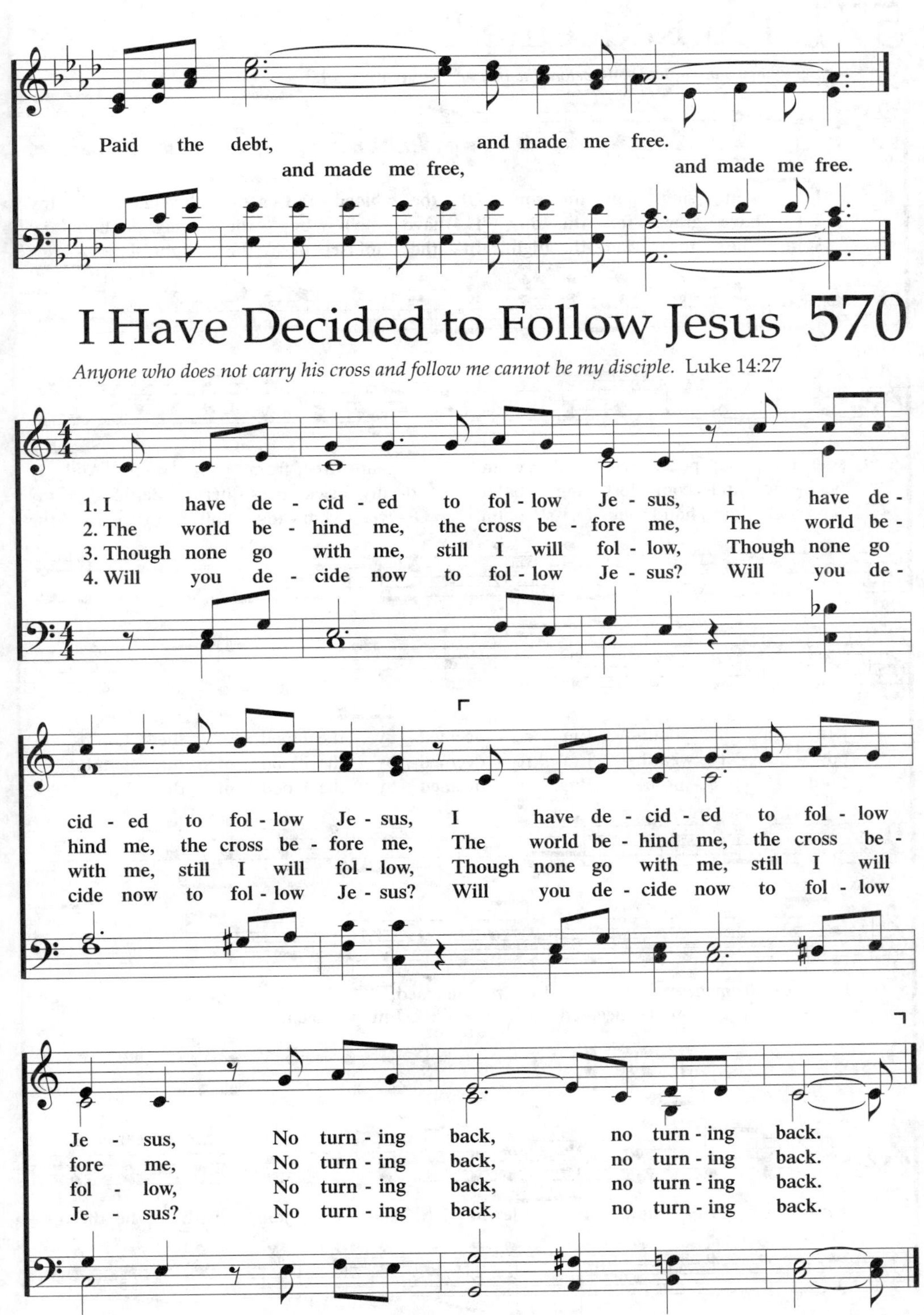
Paid the debt, and made me free.
and made me free, and made me free.
I Have Decided to Follow Jesus 570
Anyone who does not carry his cross and follow me cannot be my disciple. Luke 14:27
1. I have de - cid - ed to fol - low Je - sus, I have de - cid - ed to fol - low Je - sus, I have de - cid - ed to fol - low Je - sus, No turn - ing back, no turn - ing back.
2. The world be - hind me, the cross be - fore me, The world be - hind me, the cross be - fore me, The world be - hind me, the cross be - fore me, No turn - ing back, no turn - ing back.
3. Though none go with me, still I will fol - low, Though none go with me, still I will fol - low, Though none go with me, still I will fol - low, No turn - ing back, no turn - ing back.
4. Will you de - cide now to fol - low Je - sus? Will you de - cide now to fol - low Je - sus? Will you de - cide now to fol - low Je - sus? No turn - ing back, no turn - ing back.
WORDS: Anonymous
MUSIC: Indian folk tune
ASSAM
10.10.10.8.

571 I'm Redeemed

They sang a new song before the throne. Revelation 14:3

1. I can sing now the song Of the blood-ran-somed throng. In my
2. I have grace for the day, I have help by the way. There is
3. In the storm and the night, In the midst of the fight, Je-sus
soul there is peace, rest and calm. I am free from all doubt And I
heal-ing and com-fort-ing balm. For my sick-ness there's health, For my
puts in my hand vic-tory's palm. O-ver-com-ing all foes, In the
join in the shout— I'm re-deemed by the blood of the Lamb.
pov-er-ty wealth— I'm re-deemed by the blood of the Lamb.
Lord I re-pose— I'm re-deemed by the blood of the Lamb.
Refrain
I'm re-deemed, I'm re-deemed, Jesus saves me and
I'm re-deemed, I'm re-deemed,
keeps me just now, Hal-le-lu-jah, And I join with the throng

WORDS: Russell K. Carter, 1849-1928
MUSIC: Russell K. Carter, 1849-1928

I'M REDEEMED
6.6.9.D. with Refrain

round the throne in the song— I'm re - deemed by the blood of the Lamb.
Satisfied 572
He satisfies the thirsty and fills the hungry with good things. Psalm 107:9
1. All my life long I had pant - ed For a drink from some cool spring
2. Feed - ing on the husks a - round me Till my strength was al - most gone.
3. Poor I was, and sought for rich - es, Some-thing that would sat - is - fy,
4. Well of wa - ter, ev - er spring-ing, Bread of life, so rich and free,
That I hoped would quench the burn - ing Of the thirst I felt with - in.
Longed my soul for some - thing bet - ter, On - ly still to hun - ger on.
But the dust I gath - ered round me On - ly mocked my soul's sad cry.
Un - told wealth that nev - er fail - eth, My Re - deem - er is to me.
Refrain
Hal - le - lu - jah! I have found Him Whom my soul so long has craved!
Je - sus sat - is - fies my long - ings. Through His blood I now am saved.
WORDS: Clara T. Williams, 1858-1937
MUSIC: Ralph E. Hudson, 1843-1901
SATISFIED
8.7.8.7. with Refrain

573 The Old Rugged Cross

Jesus . . . endured the cross, scorning its shame. Hebrews 12:2

1. On a hill far a - way stood an old rug-ged cross, The em - blem of
2. O, that old rug-ged cross, so de - spised by the world, Has a won - drous at -
3. In the old rug-ged cross, stained with blood so di - vine, A won - drous
4. To the old rug-ged cross I will ev - er be true, Its shame and re -
suf - fering and shame. And I love that old cross where the dear - est and best
trac - tion for me, For the dear Lamb of God left His glo - ry a - bove
beau - ty I see, For 'twas on that old cross Je - sus suf-fered and died
proach glad - ly bear. Then He'll call me some day to my home far a - way,
For a world of lost sin - ners was slain.
To bear it to dark Cal - va - ry.
To par - don and sanc - ti - fy me.
Where His glo - ry for - ev - er I'll share.
Refrain
So I'll cher - ish the old rug - ged cross, the
cross, Till my tro - phies at last I lay down. I will cling to the
old rug - ged cross,

WORDS: George Bennard, 1873-1958
MUSIC: George Bennard, 1873-1958

OLD RUGGED CROSS
Irregular with Refrain

old rug - ged cross, And ex - change it some day for a crown.
cross, the old rug - ged cross,

I Am Not Skilled to Understand 574

The Lord will give you insight into all this. 2 Timothy 2:7

1. I am not skilled to understand
What God has willed, what God has planned.
I only know at His right hand
Is One who is my Savior!

2. I take Him at His Word indeed
"Christ died for sinners"—this I read.
For in my heart I find a need
Of Him to be my Savior!

3. That He should leave His place on high
And come for sinful man to die.
You count it strange? So once did I
Before I knew my Savior!

4. And O, that He fulfilled may see
The travail of His soul in me,
And with His work contented be,
As I with my dear Savior!

5. Yes, living, dying, let me bring
My strength, my solace from this spring
That He who lives to be my King
Once died to be my Savior!

WORDS: Dora Greenwell, 1821-1882, alt.
MUSIC: William J. Kirkpatrick, 1838-1921

GREENWELL
8.8.8.7.

575 He Hideth My Soul

I have . . . covered you with the shadow of my hand. Isaiah 51:16

1. A won - der - ful Sav - ior is Je - sus, my Lord, A
2. A won - der - ful Sav - ior is Je - sus, my Lord, He
3. With num - ber - less bless - ings each mo - ment He crowns, And,
4. When clothed in his bright - ness, trans - port - ed I rise To
won - der - ful Sav - ior to me. He hid - eth my soul in the
tak - eth my bur - den a - way. He hold - eth me up, and I
filled with His full - ness di - vine, I sing in my rap - ture, O,
meet Him in clouds of the sky. His per - fect sal - va - tion, His
cleft of the rock Where riv - ers of plea - sure I see.
shall not be moved. He giv - eth me strength as my day.
glo - ry to God For such a Re - deem - er as mine!
won - der - ful love I'll shout with the mil - lions on high.
Refrain
He hid - eth my soul in the cleft of the rock That shad - ows a

WORDS: Fanny J. Crosby, 1820-1915
MUSIC: William J. Kirkpatrick, 1838-1921

KIRKPATRICK
11.8.11.8. with Refrain

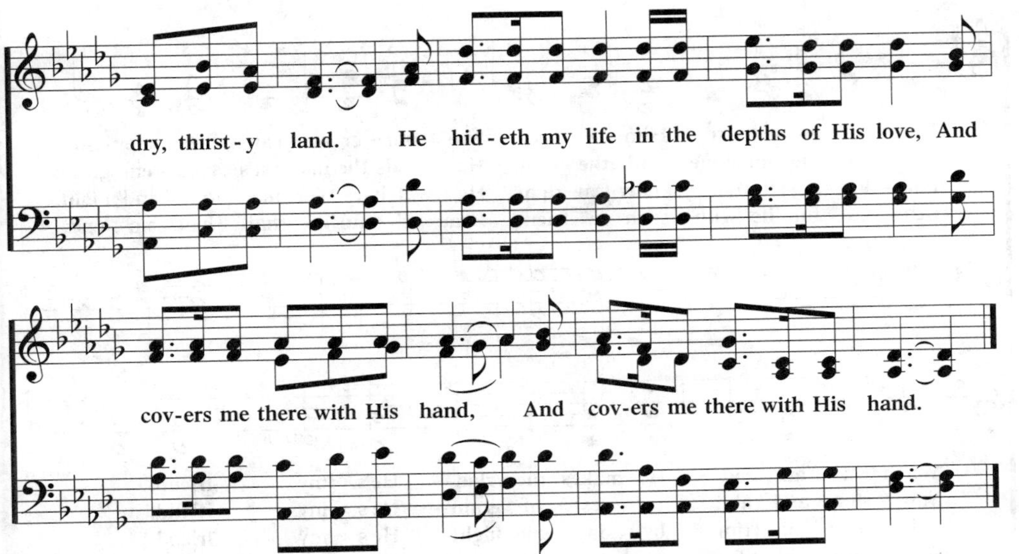
dry, thirst-y land. He hid-eth my life in the depths of His love, And
cov-ers me there with His hand, And cov-ers me there with His hand.

Jesus Is All the World to Me 576

There is a friend who sticks closer than a brother. Proverbs 18:24

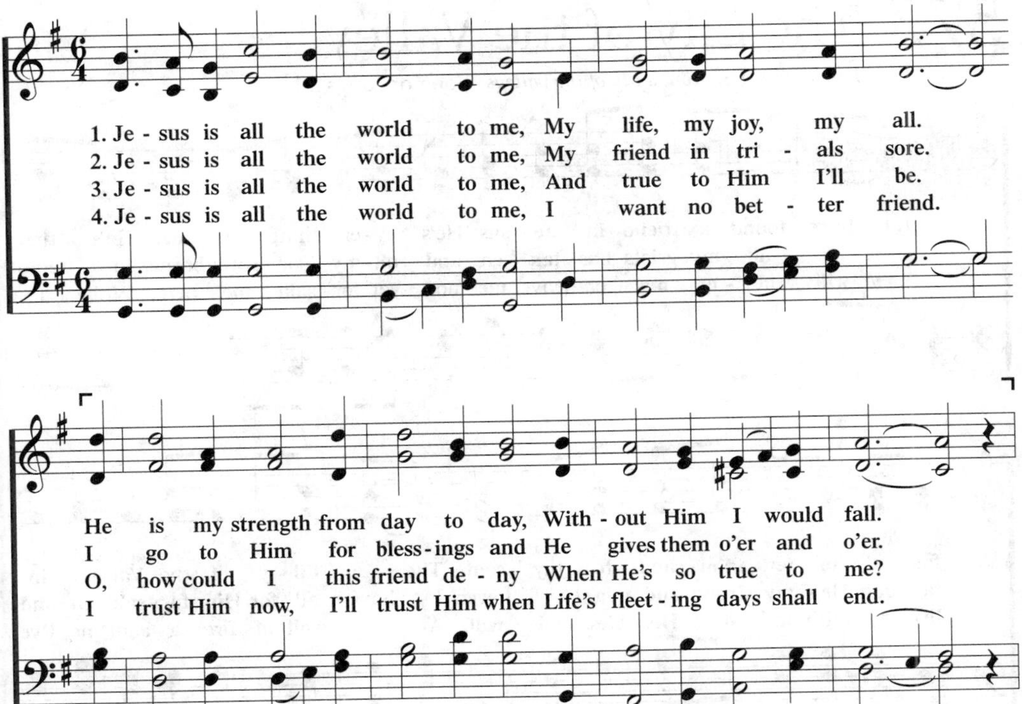

1. Jesus is all the world to me, My life, my joy, my all. He is my strength from day to day, Without Him I would fall.
2. Jesus is all the world to me, My friend in trials sore. I go to Him for blessings and He gives them o'er and o'er.
3. Jesus is all the world to me, And true to Him I'll be. O, how could I this friend deny When He's so true to me?
4. Jesus is all the world to me, I want no better friend. I trust Him now, I'll trust Him when Life's fleeting days shall end.

WORDS: Will L. Thompson, 1847-1909
MUSIC: Will L. Thompson, 1847-1909

ELIZABETH
Irregular

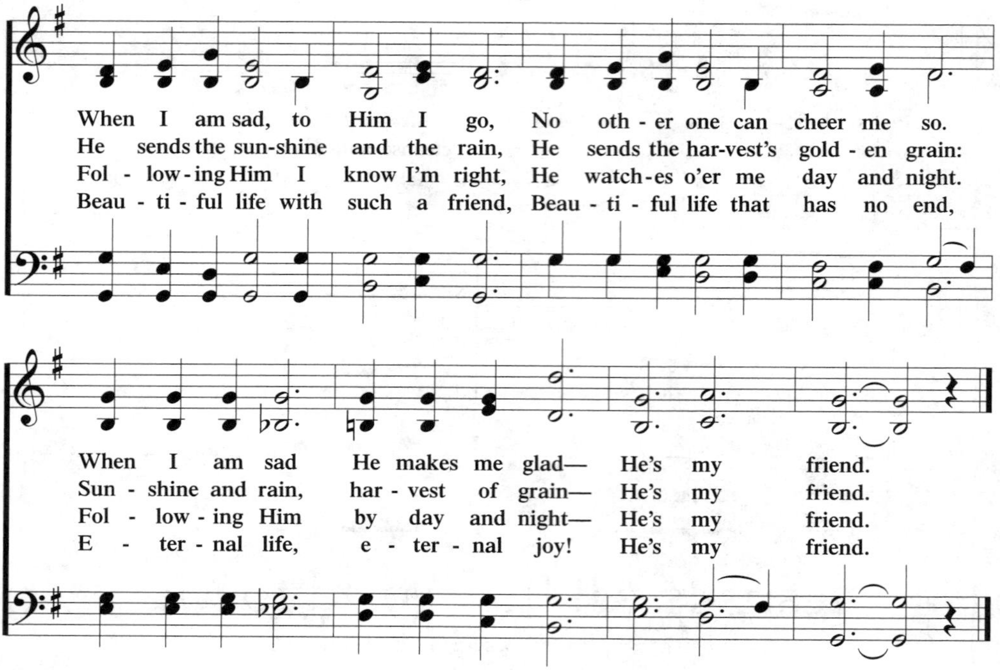

When I am sad, to Him I go, No oth - er one can cheer me so.
He sends the sun-shine and the rain, He sends the har-vest's gold - en grain:
Fol - low - ing Him I know I'm right, He watch - es o'er me day and night.
Beau - ti - ful life with such a friend, Beau - ti - ful life that has no end,

When I am sad He makes me glad— He's my friend.
Sun - shine and rain, har - vest of grain— He's my friend.
Fol - low - ing Him by day and night— He's my friend.
E - ter - nal life, e - ter - nal joy! He's my friend.

577 The Lily of the Valley

I am a rose of Sharon, a lily of the valleys. Song of Songs 2:1

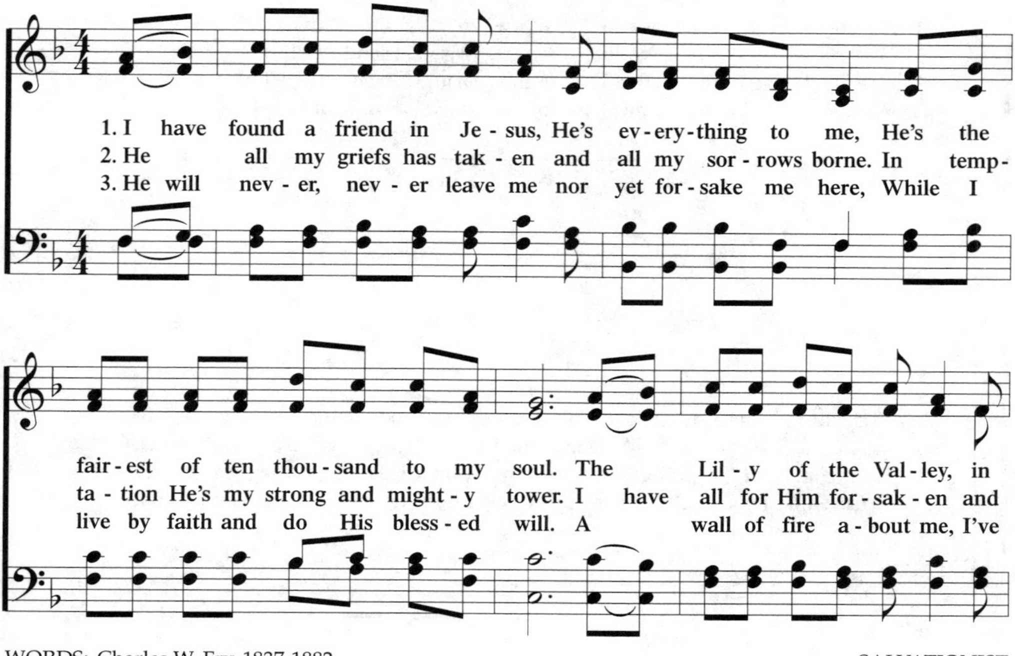

1. I have found a friend in Je - sus, He's ev - ery - thing to me, He's the fair - est of ten thou - sand to my soul. The Lil - y of the Val - ley, in
2. He all my griefs has tak - en and all my sor - rows borne. In temp - ta - tion He's my strong and might - y tower. I have all for Him for - sak - en and
3. He will nev - er, nev - er leave me nor yet for - sake me here, While I live by faith and do His bless - ed will. A wall of fire a - bout me, I've

WORDS: Charles W. Fry, 1837-1882
MUSIC: William S. Hays, 1837-1907

SALVATIONIST
Irregular with Refrain

Him a - lone I see All I need to cleanse and make me ful - ly whole.
all my i - dols torn From my heart, and now He keeps me by His power.
noth - ing now to fear. With His man - na He my hun - gry soul shall fill.
In sor - row He's my com - fort, in trou - ble He's my stay. He
Though all the world for - sake me and Sa - tan tempt me sore, Through
Then sweep - ing up to glo - ry to see His bless - ed face, Where
tells me ev - ery care on Him to roll.
Je - sus I shall safe - ly reach the goal.
riv - ers of de - light shall ev - er roll.
Refrain
He's the Lil - y of the Val - ley,
the bright and Morn - ing Star, He's the fair - est of ten thou - sand to my soul.

578 I'd Rather Have Jesus

I consider everything a loss compared to the surpassing greatness of knowing Christ.
Philippians 3:8

1. I'd rath - er have Je - sus than sil - ver or gold, I'd rath - er be
2. I'd rath - er have Je - sus than men's ap - plause, I'd rath - er be
3. He's fair - er than lil - ies of rar - est bloom, He's sweet - er than
His than have rich - es un - told, I'd rath - er have Je - sus than hous - es or
faith - ful to His dear cause, I'd rath - er have Je - sus than world - wide
hon - ey from out of the comb, He's all that my hun - ger - ing spir - it
land, I'd rath - er be led by His nail - pierced hand:
fame, I'd rath - er be true to His ho - ly name:
needs— I'd rath - er have Je - sus and let Him lead:
Refrain
Than to be the
king of a vast do - main Or be held in sin's dread sway! I'd
rath - er have Je - sus than an - y - thing This world af - fords to - day.

WORDS: Rhea F. Miller, 1894-1966
MUSIC: George Beverly Shea, b. 1909

I'D RATHER HAVE JESUS
Irregular with Refrain

Glory to His Name 579

Not to us, O LORD . . . but to your name be the glory. Psalm 115:1

1. Down at the cross where my Sav - ior died, Down where for cleans - ing from sin I cried— There to my heart was the blood ap - plied, Glo - ry to His name!
2. I am so won - drous - ly saved from sin. Je - sus so sweet - ly a - bides with - in. There at the cross where He took me in, Glo - ry to His name!
3. O, pre - cious foun - tain that saves from sin! I am so glad I have en - tered in. There Je - sus saves me and keeps me clean, Glo - ry to His name!
4. Come to this foun - tain so rich and sweet. Cast your poor soul at the Sav - ior's feet. Plunge in to - day and be made com - plete, Glo - ry to His name!
Refrain
Glo - ry to His name, Glo - ry to His name.
There to my heart was the blood ap - plied, Glo - ry to His name!
Optional segue to "Victory in Jesus." No transition required.

WORDS: Elisha A. Hoffman, 1839-1929, alt.
MUSIC: John H. Stockton, 1813-1877

GLORY TO HIS NAME
9.9.9.5. with Refrain

580 Victory in Jesus

He gives us the victory through our Lord Jesus Christ. 1 Corinthians 15:57

1. I heard an old, old sto - ry, how a Sav - ior came from glo - ry,
2. I heard a - bout His heal - ing, of His cleans - ing power re - veal - ing,
3. I heard a - bout a man - sion He has built for me in glo - ry,
How He gave His life on Cal - va - ry to save a wretch like me.
How He made the lame to walk a - gain and caused the blind to see.
And I heard a - bout the streets of gold be - yond the crys - tal sea.
I heard a - bout His groan - ing, of His pre - cious blood's a - ton - ing,
And then I cried, "Dear Je - sus, come and heal my bro - ken spir - it,"
A - bout the an - gels sing - ing, and the old re - demp - tion sto - ry,
Then I re - pent - ed of my sins and won the vic - to - ry.
And some - how Je - sus came and brought to me the vic - to - ry.
And some sweet day I'll sing up there the song of vic - to - ry.

WORDS: Eugene M. Bartlett, 1885-1941
MUSIC: Eugene M. Bartlett, 1885-1941

HARTFORD
15.15.15.14. with Refrain

Refrain
O, vic - to-ry in Je - sus, my Sav - ior, for - ev - er!
He sought me and bought me with His re - deem - ing blood.
He loved me ere I knew Him, and all my love is due Him.
He plunged me to vic - to-ry be - neath the cleans - ing flood.

LIVING LIKENESSES OF CHRIST

As we become occupied with Christ and abide in His fellowship, His glorious likeness is reproduced in us, and we stand before the world, not only living epistles but living likenesses of our blessed Lord.

A.B. Simpson (1843-1919), *The Holy Spirit*

581 Love Lifted Me

There is no fear in love. 1 John 4:18
1. I was sink - ing deep in sin, Far from the peace - ful shore, Ver - y
2. All my heart to Him I give. Ev - er to Him I'll cling, In His
3. Souls in dan - ger, look a - bove; Je - sus com - plete - ly saves. He will
deep - ly stained with - in, Sink - ing to rise no more. But the Mas - ter
bless - ed pres - ence live, Ev - er His prais - es sing. Love so might - y
lift you by His love Out of the an - gry waves. He's the Mas - ter
of the sea Heard my de - spair - ing cry, From the wa - ters lift - ed me—
and so true Mer - its my soul's best songs. Faith - ful, lov - ing ser - vice, too,
of the sea, Bil - lows His will o - bey. He your Sav - ior wants to be—
Now safe am I.
To Him be - longs.
Be saved to - day.
Refrain
Love lift - ed me! Love lift - ed me!
Love lift - ed e - ven me! Love lift - ed e - ven me!

WORDS: James Rowe, 1865-1933
MUSIC: Howard E. Smith, 1863-1918

SAFETY
7.6.7.6.7.6.7.4. with Refrain

1.
2.
When noth - ing else could help, Love lift - ed me.
Love lift - ed me.

Because He Lives 582

Because I live, you also will live. John 14:19

1. God sent His Son, they called Him Je - sus. He came to love, heal, and for - give. He lived and died to buy my par - don. An emp - ty grave is there to prove my Sav - ior lives.
2. How sweet to hold a new - born ba - by, And feel the pride and joy he gives. But great - er still the calm as - sur - ance, This child can face un - cer - tain days be - cause He lives.
3. And then one day I'll cross the riv - er. I'll fight life's fi - nal war with pain. And then as death gives way to vic - tory, I'll see the lights of glo - ry and I'll know He reigns.

WORDS: William J. Gaither, b. 1936; Gloria Gaither, b. 1942
MUSIC: William J. Gaither, b. 1936

RESURRECTION
9.8.9.12. with Refrain

Refrain
Be-cause He lives, I can face to-mor-row. Be-cause He lives, all fear is gone. Be-cause I know He holds the fu-ture, And life is worth the liv-ing just be-cause He lives.
583 He Lives
He has risen! He is not here. Mark 16:6
1. I serve a ris-en Sav-ior, He's in the world to-day. I know that He is liv-ing, what-ev-er men may say. I see His
2. In all the world a-round me I see His lov-ing care, And though my heart grows wea-ry, I nev-er will de-spair. I know that
3. Re-joice, re-joice, O Chris-tian, lift up your voice and sing E-ter-nal hal-le-lu-jahs to Je-sus Christ the King! The hope of

WORDS: Alfred H. Ackley, 1887-1960
MUSIC: Alfred H. Ackley, 1887-1960

ACKLEY
13.13.13.11. with Refrain

hand of mer - cy, I hear His voice of cheer. And just the time I
He is lead - ing through all the storm - y blast. The day of His ap-
all who seek Him, the help of all who find. None oth - er is so
Refrain
need Him He's al - ways near. He lives, He lives, Christ
pear - ing will come at last.
lov - ing, so good and kind. He lives, He lives,
Je - sus lives to - day! He walks with me and talks with me A - long life's
nar - row way. He lives, He lives, sal - va - tion to im - part!
He lives, He lives,
rit.
You ask me how I know He lives! He lives with - in my heart.

584 Love Found a Way

For God so loved the world that he gave his one and only Son. John 3:16

1. Won - der - ful love that res - cued me, Sunk deep in sin,
2. Love brought my Sav - ior here to die, On Cal - va - ry
3. Love o - pened wide the gates of light To heaven's do - main,
Guilt - y and vile as I could be— No hope with - in.
For such a sin - ful wretch as I— How can it be?
Where in e - ter - nal power and might Je - sus shall reign.
When ev - ery ray of light had fled— O, glo - rious day!
Love bridged the gulf twixt me and heaven, Taught me to pray.
Love lift - ed me from depth of woe To end - less day.
Rais - ing my soul from out the dead, Love found a way.
I am re - deemed, set free, for - given— Love found a way.
There was no help in earth be - low— Love found a way.
Refrain
Love found a way to re - deem my soul, Love found a
a way to re - deem my soul,

WORDS: Avis M.B. Christiansen, 1895-1966
MUSIC: Harry D. Loes, 1892-1965

LOVE FOUND A WAY
Irregular

way that could make me whole. Love sent my Lord to the
a way could make me whole. my Lord
cross of shame, Love found a way— O, praise His ho-ly name!
to the cross of shame,

THE HEART STRANGELY WARMED

In the evening I went very unwillingly to a society in Aldersgate Street, where one was reading Luther's preface to the Epistles to the Romans. About a quarter before nine, while he was describing the change which God works in the heart through faith in Christ, I felt my heart strangely warmed. I felt I did trust in Christ, Christ alone for salvation; and an assurance was given me that He had taken away my sins, even mine, and saved me from the law of sin and death.

I began to pray with all my might for those who had in a more especial manner despitefully used and persecuted me. I then testified openly to all there what I now first felt in my heart. But it was not long before the enemy suggested, "This cannot be faith; for where is your joy?" Then was I taught that peace and victory over sin are essential to faith in the Captain of our salvation; but that, as to the transports of joy that usually attend the beginnings of it, especially in those who have mourned deeply, God sometimes gives, sometimes withholds them, according to the counsels of His own will.

After my return home, I was much buffeted with temptations; but cried out, and they fled away. They returned again and again. I as often lifted up my eyes, and He "sent me help from his holy place." And herein I found the difference between this and my former state chiefly consisted. I was striving, yea, fighting with all my might under the law, as well as under grace. But then I was sometimes, if not often, conquered; now, I was always conqueror.—May 24, 1738

John Wesley (1703-1791)

585 Give Me Jesus

I consider everything a loss compared to . . . knowing Christ Jesus my Lord. Philippians 3:8

1. In the morn-ing when I rise,
when I am a-lone,
when I come to die,
In the morn-ing when I rise,
O, and when I am a-lone,
O, and when I come to die,
In the morn-ing when I rise,
And when I am a-lone,
And when I come to die,
Give me Je - sus.
Give me Je - sus.
Give me Je - sus.
Refrain
Give me Je - sus, give me Je - sus;
You can have all this world, but give me Je - sus.
1, 2.
2. And
3. And
3.
sus.

WORDS: African-American spiritual
MUSIC: African-American spiritual; arr. Scott A. Simpson, b. 1966

GIVE ME JESUS
Irregular

He Keeps Me Singing 586

Sing and make music in your heart to the Lord. Ephesians 5:19

1. There's with - in my heart a mel - o - dy Je - sus whis - pers sweet and low, "Fear not, I am with thee, peace be still," In all of life's ebb and flow.
2. All my life was wrecked by sin and strife. Dis - cord filled my heart with pain. Je - sus swept a - cross the bro - ken strings, Stirred the slum - bering chords a - gain.
3. Feast - ing on the rich - es of His grace, Rest - ing 'neath His shel - tering wing, Al - ways look - ing on His smil - ing face— That is why I shout and sing.
4. Though some - times He leads through wa - ters deep, Tri - als fall a - cross the way, Though some - times the path seems rough and steep, See His foot - prints all the way.
5. Soon He's com - ing back to wel - come me Far be - yond the star - ry sky. I shall wing my flight to worlds un - known, I shall reign with Him on high.
Refrain
Je - sus, Je - sus, Je - sus, Sweet - est name I know, Fills my ev - ery long - ing, Keeps me sing - ing as I go.

WORDS: Luther B. Bridgers, 1884-1948
MUSIC: Luther B. Bridgers, 1884-1948

SWEETEST NAME
9.7.9.7. with Refrain

587 Since Jesus Came Into My Heart

The old has gone, the new has come. 2 Corinthians 5:17

1. What a won-der-ful change in my life has been wrought, Since Je-sus came in-to my heart! I have light in my soul for which long I have sought, Since Je-sus came in-to my heart!
2. I have ceased from my wan-dering and go-ing a-stray, Since Je-sus came in-to my heart! And my sins, which were man-y, are all washed a-way, Since Je-sus came in-to my heart!
3. I shall go there to dwell in that Cit-y, I know, Since Je-sus came in-to my heart! And I'm hap-py, so hap-py, as on-ward I go, Since Je-sus came in-to my heart!
Refrain
Since Je-sus came in-to my heart, Since Je-sus came in-to my heart, Floods of joy o'er my soul like the sea bil-lows roll, Since Je-sus came in-to my heart.

WORDS: Rufus H. McDaniel, 1850-1940
MUSIC: Charles H. Gabriel, 1856-1932

MCDANIEL
12.8.12.8. with Refrain

He Touched Me 588

Filled with compassion, Jesus reached out his hand and touched the man. Mark 1:41

1. Shack - led by a heav - y bur - den, 'Neath a load of guilt and shame, Then the hand of Je - sus touched me, And now I am no long - er the same.
2. Since I met this bless - ed Sav - ior, Since He cleansed and made me whole, I will nev - er cease to praise Him. I'll shout it while e - ter - ni - ty rolls.
Refrain
He touched me, O, He touched me, And O, the joy that floods my soul. Some - thing hap - pened, and now I know, He touched me and made me whole.

WORDS: William J. Gaither, b. 1936
MUSIC: William J. Gaither, b. 1936

HE TOUCHED ME
Irregular

589 Fill My Cup, Lord

. . . the fullness of him who fills everything in every way. Ephesians 1:23

1. Like the wom - an at the well I was seek - ing For things that could not sat - is - fy. And then I heard my Sav - ior speak-ing, "Draw from My well that nev - er shall run dry."
2. There are mil - lions in this world who are crav - ing The plea - sure earth - ly things af - ford. But none can match the won-drous trea - sure That I find in Je - sus Christ my Lord.
3. So, my broth - er, if the things this world gave you Leave hun - gers that won't pass a - way, My bless - ed Lord will come and save you, If you kneel to Him and hum - bly pray.
Refrain
Fill my cup, Lord, I lift it up, Lord! Come and quench this thirst - ing of my soul. Bread of heav - en, feed me till I want no more. Fill my cup, fill it up and make me whole!

WORDS: Richard Blanchard, b. 1925
MUSIC: Richard Blanchard, b. 1925

FILL MY CUP
11.8.9.9. with Refrain

In the Garden 590

Jesus said to her, "Mary." She turned toward him and cried out in Aramaic, "Rabboni!" John 20:16

1. I come to the gar - den a - lone, While the dew is
2. He speaks, and the sound of His voice Is so sweet the
3. I'd stay in the gar - den with Him Though the night a -
still on the ros - es, And the voice I hear, fall - ing on my ear,
birds hush their sing - ing, And the mel - o - dy that He gave to me
round me be fall - ing, But He bids me go, through the voice of woe;
Refrain
The Son of God dis - clos - es.
With - in my heart is ring - ing. And He walks with me, and He
His voice to me is call - ing.
talks with me, And He tells me I am His own, And the joy we
share as we tar - ry there None oth - er has ev - er known.

WORDS: C. Austin Miles, 1868-1946
MUSIC: C. Austin Miles, 1868-1946

GARDEN
Irregular

591 O Happy Day!

Rejoice in the Lord always. Philippians 4:4

1. O hap - py day that fixed my choice On Thee, my Sav - ior and my God!
2. O hap - py bond that seals my vows To Him who mer - its all my love!
3. 'Tis done, the great trans - ac - tion's done! I am the Lord's and He is mine.
4. High heaven, that heard the sol - emn vow, That vow re - newed shall dai - ly hear
Well may this glow - ing heart re - joice And tell its rap - tures all a - broad.
Let cheer - ful an - thems fill His house, While to that sa - cred shrine I move.
He drew me, and I fol - lowed on, Charmed to con - fess the voice di - vine.
Till in life's lat - est hour I bow, And bless in death a bond so dear.
Refrain
Hap - py day, hap - py day, When Je - sus washed my sins a - way!
He taught me how to watch and pray And live re - joic - ing ev - ery day.
Hap - py day, hap - py day, When Je - sus washed my sins a - way!

WORDS: Philip Doddridge, 1702-1751
MUSIC: Attrib. Edward F. Rimbault, 1816-1876

HAPPY DAY
L.M. with Refrain

I Am His, and He Is Mine 592

Neither death nor life . . . will be able to separate us from the love of God.
Romans 8:38, 39

1. Loved with ev - er - last - ing love, Led by grace that love to know.
2. Heaven a - bove is soft - er blue, Earth a - round is sweet - er green.
3. Things that once were wild a - larms Can - not now dis - turb my rest,
4. His for - ev - er, on - ly His. Who, the Lord and me shall part?

Spir - it, breath - ing from a - bove, You have taught me it is so!
Some - thing lives in ev - ery hue Christ - less eyes have nev - er seen.
Closed in ev - er - last - ing arms, Pil - lowed on the lov - ing breast.
Ah, with what a rest of bliss Christ can fill the lov - ing heart!

O, this full and per - fect peace! O, this trans - port all di - vine!
Birds with glad - der songs o'er - flow, Flowers with deep - er beau - ties shine,
O, to lie for - ev - er here, Doubt and care and self re - sign,
Heaven and earth may fade and flee, First - born light in gloom de - cline,

In a love which can - not cease, I am His, and He is mine.
Since I know, as now I know, I am His, and He is mine.
While He whis - pers in my ear— I am His, and He is mine.
But while God and I shall be, I am His, and He is mine.

WORDS: George W. Robinson, 1838-1877, alt.
MUSIC: James Mountain, 1843-1933

EVERLASTING LOVE
7.7.7.7.D.

593 I Will Sing the Wondrous Story

Sing to him . . . tell of all his wonderful acts. 1 Chronicles 16:9

1. I will sing the won-drous sto - ry Of the Christ who died for me,
2. I was lost, but Je - sus found me, Found the sheep that went a - stray,
3. I was bruised, but Je - sus healed me. Faint was I from many a fall.
4. Days of dark - ness still come o'er me, Sor - row's paths I of - ten tread,
5. He will keep me till the riv - er Rolls its wa - ters at my feet.
How He left His home in glo - ry For the cross of Cal - va - ry.
Threw His lov - ing arms a - round me, Drew me back in - to His way.
Sight was gone, and fears pos - sessed me, But He freed me from them all.
But the Sav - ior still is with me, By His hand I'm safe - ly led.
Then He'll bear me safe - ly o - ver Where the loved ones I shall meet.
Refrain
Yes, I'll sing the won - drous sto - ry Of the Christ who died for me—
Sing it with the saints in glo - ry, Gath - ered by the crys - tal sea.

WORDS: Francis H. Rowley, 1854-1952
MUSIC: Peter P. Bilhorn, 1861-1936

WONDROUS STORY
8.7.8.7. with Refrain

At Calvary 594

When they had come to the place called Calvary, there they crucified Him.
Luke 23:33, NKJV

1. Years I spent in vanity and pride, Caring not my Lord was crucified, Knowing not it was for me He died On Calvary.
2. By God's Word at last my sin I learned. Then I trembled at the law I'd spurned, Till my guilty soul imploring turned To Calvary.
3. Now I've given to Jesus everything. Now I gladly own Him as my King. Now my raptured soul can only sing Of Calvary.
4. O, the love that drew salvation's plan! O, the grace that brought it down to man! O, the mighty gulf that God did span At Calvary!
Refrain
Mercy there was great, and grace was free. Pardon there was multiplied to me. There my burdened soul found liberty At Calvary.

WORDS: William R. Newell, 1868-1956
MUSIC: Daniel B. Towner, 1850-1919

CALVARY
9.9.9.4. with Refrain

595 There Is Power in the Blood

We have redemption through His blood. Colossians 1:14, NKJV

1. Would you be free from the bur - den of sin? There's power in the blood,
2. Would you be free from your pas - sion and pride? There's power in the blood,
3. Would you be whit - er, much whit - er than snow? There's power in the blood,
4. Would you do ser - vice for Je - sus, your King? There's power in the blood,
power in the blood. Would you o'er e - vil a vic - to - ry win? There's
power in the blood. Come for a cleans - ing to Cal - va - ry's tide. There's
power in the blood. Sin stains are lost in its life - giv - ing flow. There's
power in the blood. Would you live dai - ly His prais - es to sing? There's
won - der - ful power in the blood.
won - der - ful power in the blood.
won - der - ful power in the blood.
won - der - ful power in the blood.
Refrain
There is power, power, Won - der - work - ing
there is power,
power In the blood of the Lamb.
In the blood of the Lamb.
There is power, power,
there is power,
Won - der - work - ing power In the pre - cious blood of the Lamb.

WORDS: Lewis E. Jones, 1865-1936
MUSIC: Lewis E. Jones, 1865-1936

POWER IN THE BLOOD
10.9.10.8. with Refrain

There Shall Be Showers of Blessing 596

I will send down showers in season; there will be showers of blessing. Ezekiel 34:26

1. There shall be show-ers of bless-ing— This is the prom-ise of love.
2. There shall be show-ers of bless-ing— Send them up-on us, O Lord!
3. There shall be show-ers of bless-ing— O, that to-day they might fall,
4. There shall be show-ers of bless-ing, If we but trust and o-bey.
There shall be sea-sons re-fresh-ing Sent from the Sav-ior a-bove.
Grant to us now a re-fresh-ing. Come, and now hon-or Thy Word.
Now as to God we're con-fess-ing, Now as on Je-sus we call!
There shall be sea-sons re-fresh-ing, If we let God have His way.
Refrain
Show - ers of bless-ing, Show-ers of bless-ing we need.
Show - ers, show-ers of bless-ing,
Mer-cy drops round us are fall-ing, But for the show-ers we plead.

WORDS: Daniel W. Whittle, 1840-1901
MUSIC: James McGranahan, 1840-1907

SHOWERS OF BLESSING
8.7.8.7. with Refrain

597 Rescue the Perishing

The Son of Man came to seek and to save what was lost. Luke 19:10

1. Res - cue the per - ish - ing, Care for the dy - ing, Snatch them in pit - y from
2. Though they are slight-ing Him, Still He is wait-ing, Wait - ing the pen - i - tent
3. Down in the hu - man heart, Crushed by the tempt - er, Feel - ings lie bur-ied that
4. Res - cue the per - ish - ing, Du - ty de-mands it. Strength for thy la - bor the
sin and the grave. Weep o'er the err - ing one, Lift up the fall - en,
child to re - ceive. Plead with them ear-nest - ly, Plead with them gent - ly,
grace can re - store. Touched by a lov - ing heart, Wak - ened by kind - ness,
Lord will pro - vide. Back to the nar-row way Pa - tient - ly win them.
Refrain
Tell them of Je - sus the might - y to save.
He will for - give if they on - ly be - lieve.
Chords that were bro - ken will vi - brate once more.
Tell the poor wan-derer a Sav - ior has died.
Res-cue the per-ish-ing,
Care for the dy - ing. Je - sus is mer - ci - ful, Je - sus will save.

WORDS: Fanny J. Crosby, 1820-1915
MUSIC: William H. Doane, 1832-1915

RESCUE
11.10.11.10. with Refrain

Whosoever Will May Come 598

Whoever wishes, let him take the free gift of the water of life. Revelation 22:17

1. "Who-so-ev-er hear-eth," shout, shout the sound! Spread the bless-ed tid - ings
2. Who - so-ev-er com - eth need not de - lay, Now the door is o - pen,
3. "Who-so-ev-er will," the prom-ise is se - cure. "Who - so - ev - er will," for -
all the world a - round. Tell the joy - ful news wher - ev - er man is found,
en - ter while you may. Je - sus is the true, the on - ly liv - ing Way,
ev - er must en - dure. "Who - so - ev - er will," 'tis life for - ev - er - more.
"Who - so - ev - er will may come."
Refrain
"Who - so - ev - er will, who - so - ev - er will!"
Send the proc - la - ma - tion o - ver vale and hill. 'Tis a lov - ing
Fa - ther calls the wan - derer home, "Who - so - ev - er will may come."

WORDS: Philip P. Bliss, 1838-1876
MUSIC: Philip P. Bliss, 1838-1876

WHOSOEVER
Irregular with Refrain

599 I Love to Tell the Story

Let me tell you what he has done for me. Psalm 66:16

1. I love to tell the story Of unseen things above,
Of Jesus and His glory, Of Jesus and His love.
I love to tell the story Because I know 'tis true.
It satisfies my longings As nothing else can do.
2. I love to tell the story, More wonderful it seems
Than all the golden fancies Of all our golden dreams.
I love to tell the story, It did so much for me,
And that is just the reason I tell it now to thee.
3. I love to tell the story, 'Tis pleasant to repeat
What seems, each time I tell it, More wonderfully sweet.
I love to tell the story, For some have never heard
The message of salvation From God's own holy Word.
4. I love to tell the story, For those who know it best
Seem hungering and thirsting To hear it like the rest.
And when, in scenes of glory, I sing the new, new song,
'Twill be the old, old story That I have loved so long.

WORDS: Arabella C. Hankey, 1834-1911
MUSIC: William G. Fischer, 1835-1912

HANKEY
7.6.7.6.D. with Refrain

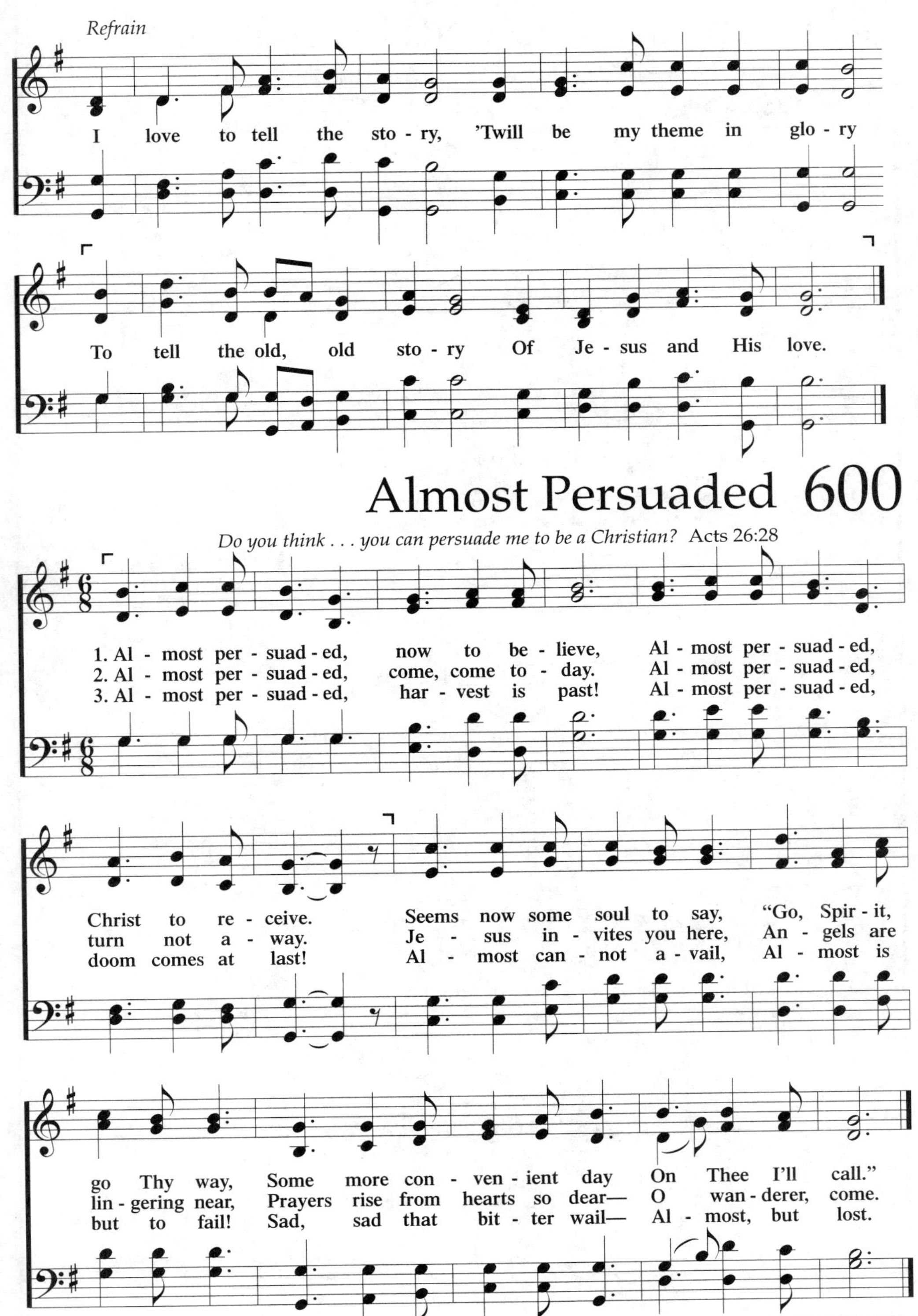
Refrain
I love to tell the sto - ry, 'Twill be my theme in glo - ry
To tell the old, old sto - ry Of Je - sus and His love.
Almost Persuaded 600
Do you think . . . you can persuade me to be a Christian? Acts 26:28
1. Al - most per - suad - ed, now to be - lieve, Al - most per - suad - ed, Christ to re - ceive. Seems now some soul to say, "Go, Spir - it, go Thy way, Some more con - ven - ient day On Thee I'll call."
2. Al - most per - suad - ed, come, come to - day. Al - most per - suad - ed, turn not a - way. Je - sus in - vites you here, An - gels are lin - gering near, Prayers rise from hearts so dear— O wan - derer, come.
3. Al - most per - suad - ed, har - vest is past! Al - most per - suad - ed, doom comes at last! Al - most can - not a - vail, Al - most is but to fail! Sad, sad that bit - ter wail— Al - most, but lost.
WORDS: Philip P. Bliss, 1838-1876
MUSIC: Philip P. Bliss, 1838-1876
ALMOST PERSUADED
9.9.6.6.6.4.

601 Christ Receiveth Sinful Men

This man welcomes sinners and eats with them. Luke 15:2

1. Sin - ners Je - sus will re - ceive. Sound this word of grace to all
2. Come, and He will give you rest. Trust Him, for His Word is plain.
3. Now my heart con-demns me not. Pure be - fore the law I stand.
4. Christ re - ceiv - eth sin - ful men, E - ven me with all my sin.
Who the heaven - ly path - way leave, All who lin - ger, all who fall.
He will take the sin - ful - est. Christ re - ceiv - eth sin - ful men.
He who cleansed me from all spot Sat - is - fied its last de - mand.
Purged from ev - ery spot and stain, Heaven with Him I en - ter in.
Refrain
Sing it o'er and o'er a - gain, Christ re -
Sing it o'er a - gain, sing it o'er a - gain, Christ re -
ceiv - eth sin - ful men. Make the mes - sage
ceiv-eth sin-ful men, Christ re - ceiv-eth sin-ful men. Make the mes-sage plain,
clear and plain: Christ re - ceiv - eth sin - ful men.
make the mes - sage plain:

WORDS: Erdmann Neumeister, 1671-1756; tr. Emma F. Bevan, 1827-1909
MUSIC: James McGranahan, 1840-1907

NEUMEISTER
7.7.7.7. with Refrain

Come Unto Me, Ye Weary 602

I will give you rest. Matthew 11:28

1. "Come un - to Me, ye wea - ry, And I will give you rest."
2. "Come un - to Me, ye wan - derers, And I will give you light."
3. "Come un - to Me, ye faint - ing, And I will give you life."
4. "And who - so - ev - er com - eth I will not cast him out."
O bless - ed voice of Je - sus, Which comes to hearts op - pressed!
O lov - ing voice of Je - sus, Which comes to cheer the night!
O cheer - ing voice of Je - sus, Which comes to aid our strife!
O wel - come voice of Je - sus, Which drives a - way our doubt,
It tells of ben - e - dic - tion, Of par - don, grace and peace,
Our hearts were filled with sad - ness, And we had lost our way,
The foe is stern and ea - ger, The fight is fierce and long,
Which calls us, ver - y sin - ners, Un - wor - thy though we be
Of joy that hath no end - ing, Of love which can - not cease.
But morn - ing brings us glad - ness, And songs the break of day.
But Thou hast made us might - y, And strong - er than the strong.
Of love so free and bound - less, To come, dear Lord, to Thee!

WORDS: William C. Dix, 1837-1898
MUSIC: Samuel S. Wesley, 1810-1876

AURELIA
7.6.7.6.D.

603 The Great Physician

. . . who forgives all your sins and heals all your diseases. Psalm 103:3

1. The great Phy - si - cian now is near, The sym - pa - thiz - ing Je - sus.
2. Your man - y sins are all for - given— O, hear the voice of Je - sus.
3. All glo - ry to the dy - ing Lamb, I now be - lieve in Je - sus.
4. His name dis - pels my guilt and fear, No oth - er name but Je - sus.
He speaks the droop - ing heart to cheer— O, hear the voice of Je - sus.
Go on your way in peace to heaven And wear a crown with Je - sus.
I love the bless - ed Sav - ior's name, I love the name of Je - sus.
O, how my soul de - lights to hear The charm - ing name of Je - sus.
Refrain
Sweet - est note in ser - aph[1] song, Sweet - est name on mor - tal tongue,
Sweet - est car - ol ev - er sung— Je - sus, bless - ed Je sus.

WORDS: William Hunter, 1811-1877
MUSIC: John H. Stockton, 1813-1877

GREAT PHYSICIAN
8.7.8.7. with Refrain

1. *seraph: angelic being*

The Way of the Cross Leads Home 604

Narrow [is] the road that leads to life. Matthew 7:14

1. I must needs go home by the way of the cross, There's no oth - er
2. I must needs go on in the blood - sprin - kled way, The path that the
3. Then I bid fare - well to the way of the world To walk in it
way but this. I shall ne'er get sight of the gates of light,
Sav - ior trod, If I ev - er climb to the heights sub - lime,
nev - er - more, For my Lord says, "Come," and I seek my home
If the way of the cross I miss.
Where the soul is at home with God.
Where He waits at the o - pen door.
Refrain
The way of the cross leads
home, The way of the cross leads home.
leads home, leads home.
It is
sweet to know, as I on - ward go, The way of the cross leads home.

WORDS: Jessie B. Pounds, 1861-1921
MUSIC: Charles H. Gabriel, 1856-1932

THE WAY OF THE CROSS
11.7.10.8. with Refrain

605 Are You Washed in the Blood?

The blood of Jesus, his Son, purifies us from all sin. 1 John 1:7

1. Have you been to Je - sus for the cleans - ing power? Are you washed
2. Are you walk - ing dai - ly by the Sav - ior's side? Are you washed
3. When the Bride-groom com - eth, will your robes be white, Pure and white
4. Lay a - side the gar - ments that are stained with sin And be washed
in the blood of the Lamb? Are you ful - ly trust - ing in His grace this hour?
in the blood of the Lamb? Do you rest each mo - ment in the Cru - ci - fied?
in the blood of the Lamb? Will your souls be read - y for the man - sions bright
in the blood of the Lamb. There's a foun - tain flow - ing for the soul un - clean.
Are you washed in the blood of the Lamb?
Are you washed in the blood of the Lamb?
And be washed in the blood of the Lamb?
O, be washed in the blood of the Lamb.
Refrain
Are you washed in the blood,
Are you washed in theblood,
In the soul-cleans-ing blood of the Lamb?
of the Lamb?
Are your gar-ments spot-less? Are they white as snow? Are you washed in the blood of the Lamb?

WORDS: Elisha A. Hoffman, 1839-1929
MUSIC: Elisha A. Hoffman, 1839-1929

WASHED IN THE BLOOD
11.9.11.9. with Refrain

Once for All 606

We have been made holy through the sacrifice of the body of Jesus Christ once for all.
Hebrews 10:10

1. Free from the law— O, hap - py con - di - tion! Je - sus has bled, and there is re - mis - sion. Cursed by the law and bruised by the fall, Grace has re - deemed us once for all.
2. There on the cross your bur - den up - bear - ing, Thorns on His brow your Sav - ior is wear - ing. Nev - er a - gain your sin need ap - pall, You have been par - doned once for all.
3. Now are we free— there's no con - dem - na - tion. Je - sus pro - vides a per - fect sal - va - tion. "Come un - to me," O, hear His sweet call, Come, and He saves us once for all.
4. Chil - dren of God— O, glo - ri - ous call - ing, Sure - ly His grace will keep us from fall - ing. Pass - ing from death to life at His call, Bless - ed sal - va - tion once for all.
Refrain
Once for all— O sin - ner, re - ceive it. Once for all— O doubt - er, be - lieve it. Cling to the cross, the bur - den will fall, Christ has re - deemed us once for all.

WORDS: Philip P. Bliss, 1838-1876, alt.
MUSIC: Philip P. Bliss, 1838-1876

ONCE FOR ALL
10.10.9.8. with Refrain

607 Only Trust Him

Blessed is the man who makes the LORD his trust. Psalm 40:4

1. Come, ev - ery soul by sin op - pressed, There's mer - cy with the Lord,
2. For Je - sus shed His pre - cious blood, Rich bless - ings to be - stow.
3. Yes, Je - sus is the truth, the way That lead you in - to rest.
4. Come, then, and join this ho - ly band And on to glo - ry go,
And He will sure - ly give you rest By trust - ing in His Word.
Plunge now in - to the crim - son flood That wash - es white as snow.
Be - lieve in Him with - out de - lay And you are ful - ly blest.
To dwell in that ce - les - tial land Where joys im - mor - tal flow.
Refrain
On - ly trust Him, on - ly trust Him, On - ly trust Him now.
He will save you, He will save you, He will save you now.

WORDS: John H. Stockton, 1813-1877
MUSIC: John H. Stockton, 1813-1877

MINERVA
C.M. with Refrain

Pass Me Not 608

Let your ears be attentive to my cry for mercy. Psalm 130:2

1. Pass me not, O gen - tle Sav - ior, Hear my hum - ble cry.
2. Let me at the throne of mer - cy Find a sweet re - lief.
3. Trust - ing on - ly in Thy mer - it, Would I seek Thy face.
4. Thou, the Spring of all my com - fort, More than life to me,
While on oth - ers Thou art call - ing, Do not pass me by.
Kneel - ing there in deep con - tri - tion, Help my un - be - lief.
Heal my wound - ed, bro - ken spir - it, Save me by Thy grace.
Whom have I on earth be - side Thee? Whom in heaven but Thee?
Refrain
Sav - ior, Sav - ior, Hear my hum - ble cry.
While on oth - ers Thou art call - ing, Do not pass me by.

WORDS: Fanny J. Crosby, 1820-1915
MUSIC: William H. Doane, 1832-1915

PASS ME NOT
8.5.8.5. with Refrain

609 Softly and Tenderly

Come to me, all you who are weary and burdened, and I will give you rest. Matthew 11:28

1. Soft - ly and ten - der - ly Je - sus is call - ing,
2. Why should we tar - ry when Je - sus is plead - ing,
3. Time is now fleet - ing, the mo - ments are pass - ing,
4. O, for the won - der - ful love He has prom - ised,

Call - ing for you and for me. See on the por - tals He's
Plead - ing for you and for me? Why should we lin - ger and
Pass - ing from you and from me. Shad - ows are gath - er - ing,
Prom - ised for you and for me! Though we have sinned, He has

wait - ing and watch - ing, Watch - ing for you and for me.
heed not His mer - cies, Mer - cies for you and for me?
death's night is com - ing, Com - ing for you and for me.
mer - cy and par - don, Par - don for you and for me.

Refrain

Come home, come home, Ye who are wea-ry, come home.
Come home, come home.

WORDS: Will L. Thompson, 1847-1909
MUSIC: Will L. Thompson, 1847-1909

THOMPSON
11.7.11.7. with Refrain

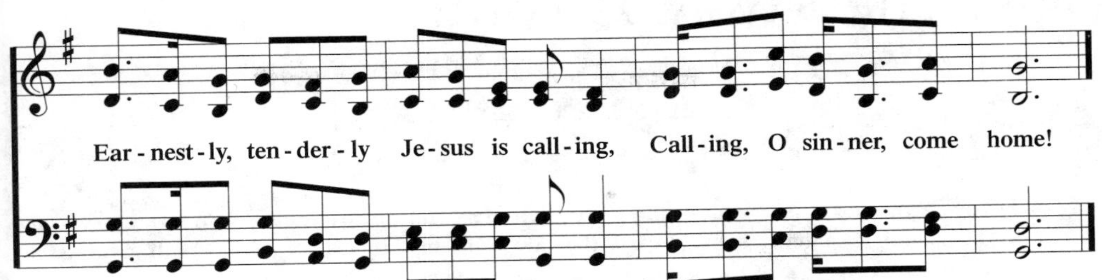
Ear - nest - ly, ten - der - ly Je - sus is call - ing, Call - ing, O sin - ner, come home!

People Need the Lord 610

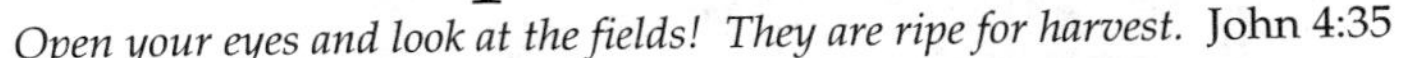
Open your eyes and look at the fields! They are ripe for harvest. John 4:35

1. Peo - ple need the Lord, Peo - ple need the Lord. At the end of bro - ken dreams, He's the o - pen door.
2. Peo - ple need the Lord, Peo - ple need the Lord. When will we re - al - ize, Peo - ple need the Lord.

WORDS: Greg Nelson, b. 1948; Phil McHugh, b. 1951
MUSIC: Greg Nelson, b. 1948; Phil McHugh, b. 1951; arr. David Allen, b. 1941

PEOPLE NEED THE LORD
Irregular

611 The Savior Is Waiting

The LORD longs to be gracious to you. Isaiah 30:18

1. The Sav - ior is wait - ing to en - ter your heart— Why don't you
2. If you'll take one step toward the Sav - ior, my friend, You'll find His
let Him come in? There's noth - ing in this world to keep you a -
arms o - pen wide. Re - ceive Him, and all of your dark - ness will
part— What is your an - swer to Him?
end, With - in your heart He'll a - bide.
Refrain
Time af - ter time He has
wait - ed be - fore, And now He is wait - ing a - gain To see if you're
will - ing to o - pen the door. O, how He wants to come in.

Optional segue to "Come Just as You Are." No transition required.

WORDS: Ralph R. Carmichael, b. 1927
MUSIC: Ralph R. Carmichael, b. 1927

CARMICHAEL
11.7.11.7. with Refrain

Come Just as You Are 612

Come! . . . Whoever wishes, let him take the free gift of the water of life. Revelation 22:17

1, 3. Come just as you are, Hear the Spir - it call.
2, 4. Come just as you are, Hear the Spir - it call.
Come just as you are, Come and see, come, re-ceive,
Come just as you are, Come, re-ceive Christ, the King,
1, 3.
2, 4.
last time fine
Come and live for - ev - er.
Come and live for - ev - er - more.
Life ev-er - last-ing, and strength for to - day;
D.C. al fine
(to stanza 3)
Taste the Liv-ing Wa-ter, and nev - er thirst a - gain.

WORDS: Joseph Sabolick, b. 1958
MUSIC: Joseph Sabolick, b. 1958

SABOLICK
Irregular

613 Jesus, I Come

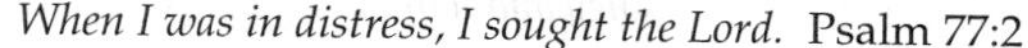

When I was in distress, I sought the Lord. Psalm 77:2

1. Out of my bondage, sorrow and night, Jesus, I come, Jesus, I come.
Into Thy freedom, gladness and light, Jesus, I come to Thee.
Out of my sickness into Thy health, Out of my want and into Thy wealth,
Out of my sin and into Thyself, Jesus, I come to Thee.

2. Out of my shameful failure and loss, Jesus, I come, Jesus, I come.
Into the glorious gain of Thy cross, Jesus, I come to Thee.
Out of earth's sorrows into Thy balm, Out of life's storms and into Thy calm,
Out of distress to jubilant psalm, Jesus, I come to Thee.

3. Out of unrest and arrogant pride, Jesus, I come, Jesus, I come.
Into Thy blessed will to abide, Jesus, I come to Thee.
Out of myself to dwell in Thy love, Out of despair into raptures above,
Upward for aye on wings like a dove, Jesus I come to Thee.

4. Out of the fear and dread of the tomb, Jesus, I come, Jesus, I come.
Into the joy and light of my home, Jesus, I come to Thee.
Out of the depths of ruin untold, Into the peace of Thy sheltering fold,
Ever Thy glorious face to behold, Jesus, I come to Thee.

WORDS: William T. Sleeper, 1819-1904
MUSIC: George C. Stebbins, 1846-1945

JESUS, I COME
Irregular

Just As I Am 614

Come . . . without money and without cost. Isaiah 55:1

1. Just as I am, with - out one plea, But that Thy blood was shed for me, And that Thou bidd'st me come to Thee, O Lamb of God, I come, I come!
2. Just as I am and wait - ing not To rid my soul of one dark blot, To Thee, whose blood can cleanse each spot, O Lamb of God, I come, I come!
3. Just as I am, though tossed a - bout With many a con - flict, many a doubt, Fight - ings and fears with - in, with - out, O Lamb of God, I come, I come!
4. Just as I am, Thou wilt re - ceive, Wilt wel - come, par - don, cleanse, re - lieve, Be - cause Thy prom - ise I be - lieve, O Lamb of God, I come, I come!
5. Just as I am, Thy love un - known Hath bro - ken ev - ery bar - rier down. Now, to be Thine, yea, Thine a - lone, O Lamb of God, I come, I come!

WORDS: Charlotte Elliott, 1789-1871
MUSIC: William B. Bradbury, 1816-1868

WOODWORTH
L.M.

615 Lord, I Want to Be a Christian

If you confess . . . and believe . . . you will be saved. Romans 10:9

WORDS: African-American spiritual;
adapt. John W. Work, Jr., 1872-1925 and Frederick J. Work, 1879-1942
MUSIC: African-American spiritual; adapt. Frederick J. Work, 1879-1942

I WANT TO BE A CHRISTIAN
Irregular

OUR CALL TO WORSHIP

MEDLEY

We Bring the Sacrifice of Praise
He Has Made Me Glad (I Will Enter His Gates)
This Is the Day

We Bring the Sacrifice of Praise 616

Let us continually offer to God a sacrifice of praise. Hebrews 13:15

We bring the sac-ri-fice of praise in-to the house of the
Lord. We bring the sac-ri-fice of praise in-to the house of the
Lord. And we of - fer up to You the sac-ri-fic - es of
thanks-giv-ing, And we of - fer up to You the sac-ri-fic - es of joy.

WORDS: Kirk Dearman, b. 1952
MUSIC: Kirk Dearman, b. 1952

WE BRING THE SACRIFICE
Irregular

Optional transition to "He Has Made Me Glad."

617 He Has Made Me Glad

(I Will Enter His Gates)

Enter his gates with thanksgiving and his courts with praise. Psalm 100:4

I will enter His gates with thanks-giving in my heart, I will enter His courts with praise. I will say, "This is the day that the Lord has made!" I will rejoice for He has made me glad.

WORDS: Leona Von Brethorst, b. 1923
MUSIC: Leona Von Brethorst, b. 1923

HE HAS MADE ME GLAD
Irregular

He has made me glad, He has made me glad, I
will re - joice for He has made me glad.
He has made me glad, He has made me glad, I
will re - joice for He has made me glad.
Song Ending
Optional transition to "This Is the Day."
glad.

618 This Is the Day

This is the day the L*ORD has made; let us rejoice and be glad in it.* Psalm 118:24

This is the day, this is the day that the Lord has made, that the
Lord has made. We will re-joice, we will re-joice and be
glad in it, and be glad in it. This is the day that the Lord has
made. We will re-joice and be glad in it. This is the day,
this is the day that the Lord has made.

WORDS: Les Garrett, b.1944; from Psalm 118:24
MUSIC: Les Garrett, b.1944

THE LORD'S DAY
Irregular

God Himself Is With Us 619

And surely I am with you always. Matthew 28:20

1. God Him-self is with us; Let us now a - dore Him, And with awe ap - pear be - fore Him. God is in His tem - ple, All with - in keep si - lence, And be - fore Him bow with rev - erence. Him a - lone do we own As our God and Sav - ior; Praise His name for - ev - er.
2. God Him-self is with us; Hear the harps re - sound-ing! See the crowds the throne sur - round - ing! "Ho - ly, ho - ly, ho - ly," Hear the hymn as - cend - ing, An - gels, saints, their voic - es blend - ing! Bow Your ear to us here. Hear, O Christ, the prais - es That Your Church now rais - es.
3. Fount of ev - ery bless-ing, Pu - ri - fy my spir - it, Trust-ing on - ly in Your mer - it. Like the ho - ly an - gels Who be - hold Your glo - ry, May I cease - less - ly a - dore You, And in all, great and small, Seek to do most near - ly What You love so dear - ly.

WORDS: Gerhardt Tersteegen, 1697-1769; tr. composite, alt.
MUSIC: Joachim Neander, 1650-1680

ARNSBERG
6.6.8.6.6.8.6.6.6.

620 Come, Now Is the Time to Worship

Today, if you hear his voice, do not harden your hearts. Hebrews 4:7

Come, now is the time to wor - ship.
Come, now is the time to give your heart.
Come, just as you are to wor - ship.
Last time to Coda
Come, just as you are be-fore your God.
Come.
One day, ev - ery tongue will con - fess

WORDS: Brian Doerksen, b. 1965
MUSIC: Brian Doerksen, b. 1965

NOW IS THE TIME
Irregular

God Himself Is With Us 619

And surely I am with you always. Matthew 28:20

1. God Him-self is with us; Let us now a - dore Him, And with awe ap-
2. God Him-self is with us; Hear the harps re - sound-ing! See the crowds the
3. Fount of ev-ery bless-ing, Pu - ri - fy my spir - it, Trust-ing on - ly
pear be - fore Him. God is in His tem-ple, All with - in keep
throne sur - round - ing! "Ho - ly, ho - ly, ho - ly," Hear the hymn as -
in Your mer - it. Like the ho - ly an - gels Who be - hold Your
si - lence, And be - fore Him bow with rev - erence. Him a - lone
cend - ing, An - gels, saints, their voic - es blend - ing! Bow Your ear
glo - ry, May I cease - less - ly a - dore You, And in all,
do we own As our God and Sav - ior; Praise His name for - ev - er.
to us here. Hear, O Christ, the prais - es That Your Church now rais - es.
great and small, Seek to do most near - ly What You love so dear - ly.

WORDS: Gerhardt Tersteegen, 1697-1769; tr. composite, alt.
MUSIC: Joachim Neander, 1650-1680

ARNSBERG
6.6.8.6.6.8.6.6.6.

620 Come, Now Is the Time to Worship

Today, if you hear his voice, do not harden your hearts. Hebrews 4:7

WORDS: Brian Doerksen, b. 1965
MUSIC: Brian Doerksen, b. 1965

NOW IS THE TIME
Irregular

You are God.
One day, ev - ery knee will bow.
Still, the great - est treas - ure re - mains
for those who glad - ly choose You now.
CODA
Come.
Come.

EARTH'S CRAMMED WITH HEAVEN

Earth's crammed with heaven,
And every common bush afire with God;
But only he who sees, takes off his shoes—
The rest sit round it and pluck blackberries.

Elizabeth Barrett Browning (1806-1861)

621 As We Gather

Let us not give up meeting together. Hebrews 10:25

As we gath-er may Your Spir-it work with-in us, As we gath-er may we
glo-ri-fy Your name. Know-ing well that as our hearts be-gin to wor-ship,
We'll be blessed be-cause we came, We'll be blessed be-cause we came.

WORDS: Mike Fay, 20th century, and Tom Coomes, b. 1946
MUSIC: Mike Fay, 20th century, and Tom Coomes, b. 1946

AS WE GATHER
Irregular

622 Jesus, Stand Among Us

Jesus himself stood among them. Luke 24:36

1. Je - sus, stand a - mong us in Your ris - en power.
2. Breathe the Ho - ly Spir - it in - to ev - ery heart.

WORDS: William Pennefather, 1816-1873
MUSIC: Friedrich Filitz, 1804-1876

BEMERTON
6.5.6.5

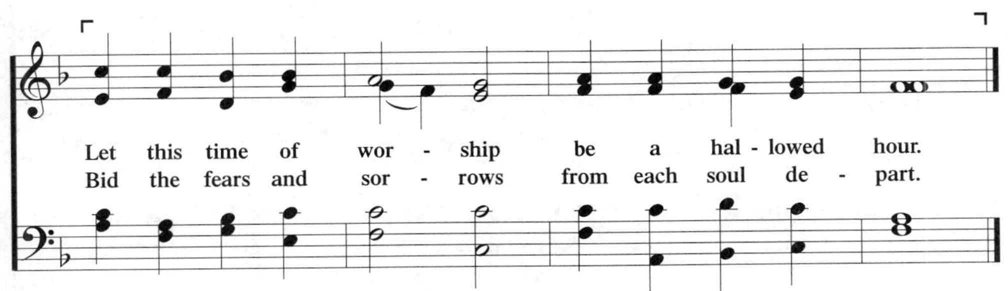
Let this time of wor - ship be a hal - lowed hour.
Bid the fears and sor - rows from each soul de - part.

The Day of Thy Power 623

Power and might are in your hand. 2 Chronicles 20:6

May I stand, O Lord, in this ho - ly place. May I wor - ship
Thee and be - hold Thy face. May I be trans - formed by Thy
Word and Thy Spir - it And be - hold the day of Thy power.

WORDS: Jack W. Hayford, b. 1934, based on Psalm 110:3
MUSIC: Jack W. Hayford, b. 1934

THY POWER
Irregular

624 Sent Forth by God's Blessing

As the Father has sent me, I am sending you. John 20:21

1. Sent forth by God's bless-ing our true faith con - fess-ing, The
2. With praise and thanks - giv-ing to God ev - er liv-ing, The
peo - ple of God from this dwell-ing take leave. The
tasks of our ev - ery - day life we will face. Our
ser - vice is end - ed, O, now be ex - tend - ed The
faith ev - er shar - ing, in love ev - er car - ing, Em -
fruits of our wor - ship in all who be - lieve. The
brac - ing God's chil - dren of each tribe and race. With

(For a different harmony, see No. 659.)

WORDS: Omer Westendorf, 1916-1998
MUSIC: Welsh folk tune; arr. Leland Sateren, b. 1913

ASH GROVE
12.11.12.11.D.

seed of the teach - ing, re - cep - tive souls reach - ing, Shall
Your grace You feed us, with Your light now lead us; U -
blos - som in ac - tion for God and for all. God's
nite us as one in this life that we share. Then
grace did in - vite us, and love shall u - nite us To
may all the liv - ing with praise and thanks - giv - ing Give
work for God's king - dom and an - swer the call.
hon - or to Christ and that name which we bear.

625 Now May the God of Hope

May the God of hope fill you with all joy and peace. Romans 15:13

Now may the God of hope Fill you with joy and peace in be -
liev-ing. May you a - bound in all joy. May you a - bound
in all hope by the power of the Spir - it, The Spir - it of
God in you.
you.
1.
2.

WORDS: Ron Sprunger, b. 1939; para. Romans 15:13
MUSIC: Ron Sprunger (1999), b. 1939

HOLMES
Irregular

The Lord Bless You and Keep You 626

The LORD blesses his people with peace. Psalm 29:11

The Lord bless you and keep you. The Lord lift His coun - te-nance up -
on you,
and give you peace,
and give you peace,
and give you
The Lord make His face to shine up -
and give you peace. The Lord make His face to shine up -
peace.
on you, and be gra - cious un - to you, be gra - cious.
on you, and be gra-cious, and be gra - cious.
The Lord be gra-cious, gra-cious un - to you. A - men.

WORDS: From Numbers 6:24-26
MUSIC: Peter C. Lutkin, 1858-1931

BENEDICTION
Irregular

627 God Be with You till We Meet Again

May the LORD *keep watch between you and me when we are away from each other.*
Genesis 31:49

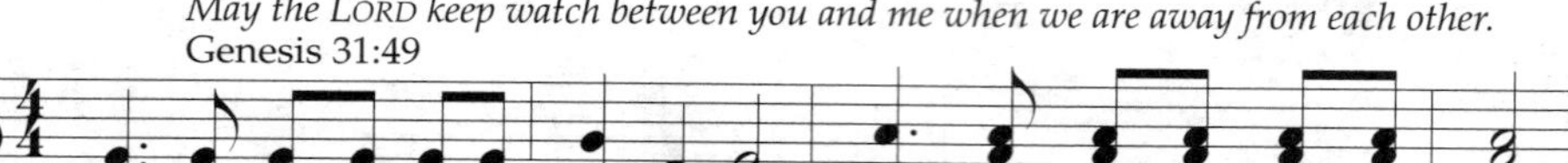
1. God be with you till we meet a-gain, By His coun-sels guide, up - hold you,
2. God be with you till we meet a-gain, 'Neath His wings pro - tect - ing hide you,
3. God be with you till we meet a-gain, When life's per - ils thick con - found you,

With His sheep se - cure - ly fold you, God be with you till we meet a-gain.
Dai - ly man - na still pro - vide you, God be with you till we meet a-gain.
Put His arms un - fail - ing round you, God be with you till we meet a-gain.

WORDS: Jeremiah E. Rankin, 1828-1904
MUSIC: William G. Tomer, 1833-1896

GOD BE WITH YOU
Irregular

628 The Lord's Supper

For I received from the Lord what I also passed on to you: The Lord Jesus, on the night he was betrayed, took bread, and when he had given thanks, he broke it and said,

"This is my body, which is for you; do this in remembrance of me."

In the same way, after supper he took the cup, saying,

"This cup is the new covenant in my blood; do this, whenever you drink it, in remembrance of me."

For whenever you eat this bread and drink this cup, you proclaim the Lord's death until he comes. Therefore, whoever eats the bread or drinks the cup of the Lord in an unworthy manner will be guilty of sinning against the body and blood of the Lord.

A man ought to examine himself before he eats of the bread and drinks of the cup. For anyone who eats and drinks without recognizing the body of the Lord eats and drinks judgment on himself. *1 Corinthians 11:23-29*

Jesus, at Your Holy Table 629

A man ought to examine himself before he eats. 1 Corinthians 11:28

1. Je - sus, at Your ho - ly ta - ble, May our hearts u - nit - ed be.
2. Christ, re - mind us of Your pas - sion, Of Your pre - cious life out - poured,
3. Lift your hearts and raise your voic - es, Cel - e - brate this won-drous love.
Bind us with Your grace and pres - ence That re - deem and set us free.
Of the love which none can fath - om, And our vic - tory ev - er - more.
Join the cho - rus with all Chris - tians, And with saints who live a - bove.
Cru - ci - fy our pride and ha - tred, Light the path on which we walk.
Bread of heav - en, wine of prom - ise, Feed us with Your ho - ly Word.
Si - lent lips now sing with glad - ness, Blind - ed eyes are filled with sight.
Teach us how to love each oth - er, In the way that You have taught.
Nour - ish us with Your strong pres - ence, Ris - en Sav - ior, on - ly Lord.
Je - sus' love has pierced our dark - ness, Brought us home to peace and light.

(For a different harmony, see No. 198.)

WORDS: Tom Allen, b. 1958
MUSIC: *The Sacred Harp*, 1844; harm. James H. Wood, b. 1921

BEACH SPRING
8.7.8.7.D.

630 Come to the Table

Unless you eat the flesh of the Son of Man and drink his blood, you have no life in you.
John 6:53

Come to the ta - ble of mer - cy, pre - pared with the wine and the bread.

All who are hun - gry and thirst - y, come and your souls will be fed.

Come at the Lord's in - vi - ta - tion, re -

WORDS: Claire Cloninger, b. 1942; Martin J. Nystrom, b. 1956
MUSIC: Claire Cloninger, b. 1942; Martin J. Nystrom, b. 1956

COME TO THE TABLE
8.8.8.7.D.

ceive from His nail - scarred hand. Eat of the bread of sal - va -
tion, drink of the blood of the Lamb.

I Will Remember Thee 631

This is my body given for you; do this in remembrance of me. Luke 22:19

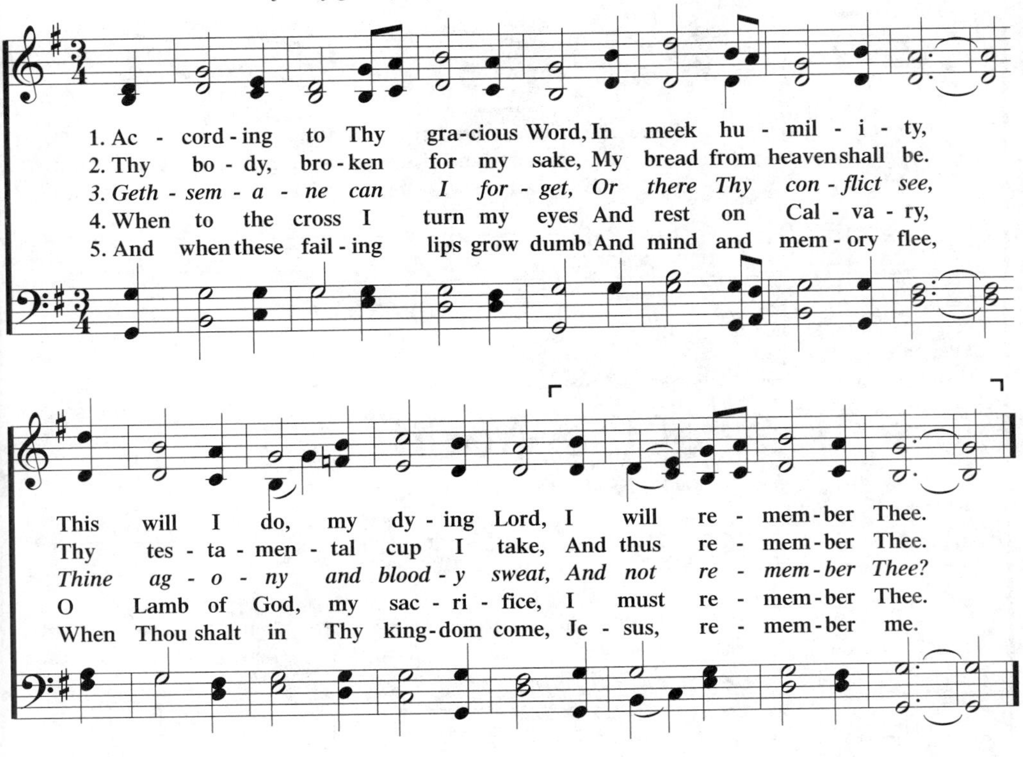

1. Ac - cord - ing to Thy gra - cious Word, In meek hu - mil - i - ty,
This will I do, my dy - ing Lord, I will re - mem - ber Thee.

2. Thy bo - dy, bro - ken for my sake, My bread from heaven shall be.
Thy tes - ta - men - tal cup I take, And thus re - mem - ber Thee.

3. *Geth - sem - a - ne can I for - get, Or there Thy con - flict see,*
Thine ag - o - ny and blood - y sweat, And not re - mem - ber Thee?

4. When to the cross I turn my eyes And rest on Cal - va - ry,
O Lamb of God, my sac - ri - fice, I must re - mem - ber Thee.

5. And when these fail - ing lips grow dumb And mind and mem - ory flee,
When Thou shalt in Thy king - dom come, Je - sus, re - mem - ber me.

WORDS: James Montgomery, 1771-1854
MUSIC: Hugh Wilson, 1764-1824

MARTYRDOM
C.M.

632 Come, Share the Lord

Is not the bread that we break a participation in the body of Christ? 1 Corinthians 10:16

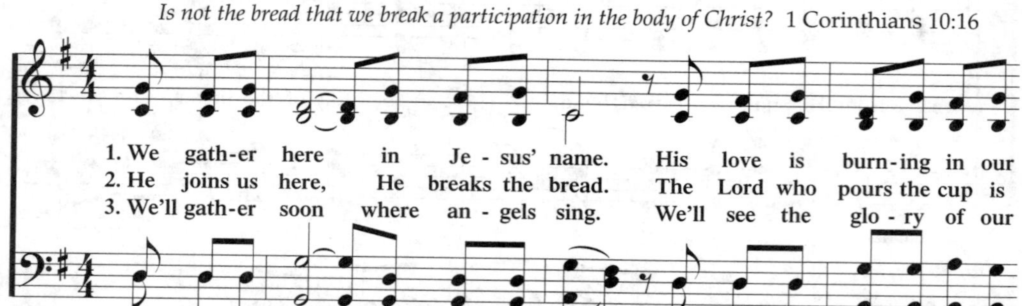

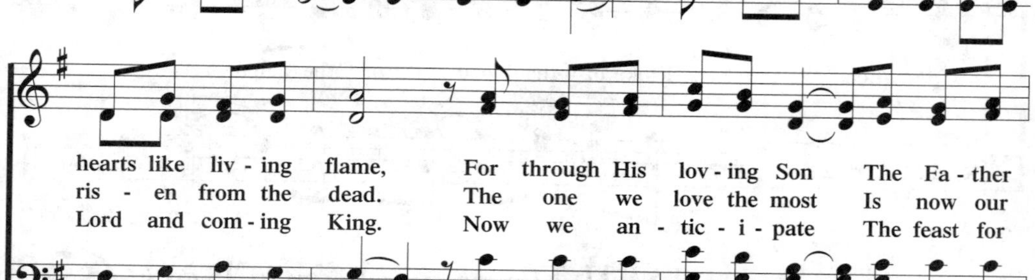

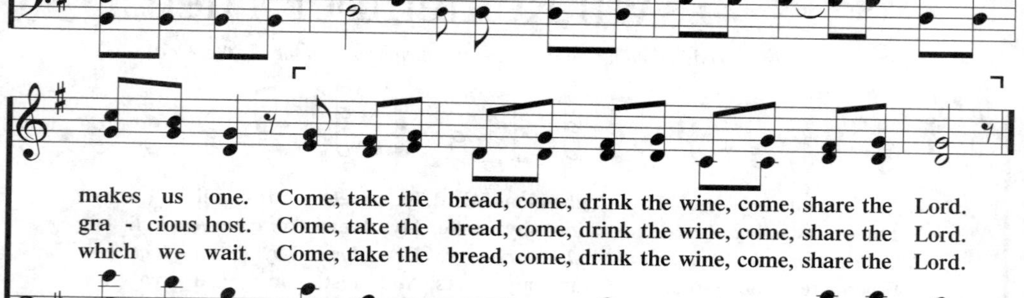

1. We gath-er here in Je - sus' name. His love is burn-ing in our hearts like liv - ing flame, For through His lov - ing Son The Fa - ther makes us one. Come, take the bread, come, drink the wine, come, share the Lord.
2. He joins us here, He breaks the bread. The Lord who pours the cup is ris - en from the dead. The one we love the most Is now our gra - cious host. Come, take the bread, come, drink the wine, come, share the Lord.
3. We'll gath-er soon where an - gels sing. We'll see the glo - ry of our Lord and com - ing King. Now we an - tic - i - pate The feast for which we wait. Come, take the bread, come, drink the wine, come, share the Lord.

WORDS: Bryan Jeffery Leech, b. 1931
MUSIC: Bryan Jeffery Leech, b. 1931

DIVERNON (abridged)
Irregular

633 Bread of the World

Jesus declared, "I am the bread of life." John 6:35

1. Bread of the world in mer - cy bro - ken, Wine of the
2. Look on the heart by sor - row bro - ken, Look on the

WORDS: Reginald Heber, 1783-1826
MUSIC: John S.B. Hodges, 1830-1915

EUCHARISTIC HYMN
9.8.9.8.

soul in mer - cy shed, By whom the words of life were
tears by sin - ners shed, And be Your feast to us the
spo - ken, And in whose death our sins are dead:
to - ken That by Your grace our souls are fed.

Here, at Your Table, Lord 634

Take this and divide it among you. Luke 22:17

1. Here, at Your ta - ble, Lord, This sa - cred hour, O, let us
feel You near, In lov - ing power, Call - ing our thoughts a - way
From self and sin, As to Your ban - quet hall We en - ter in.

2. Come then, O ho - ly Christ, Feed us, we pray. Touch with Your
pierc - ed hand Each com - mon day, Mak - ing this earth - ly life
Full of Your grace, Till, in the home of heaven, We find our place.

(For lower key, see No. 490.)

Optional segue to "Let Us Break Bread Together." No transition required.

WORDS: May P. Hoyt, 19th century
MUSIC: William F. Sherwin, 1826-1888

BREAD OF LIFE
6.4.6.4.D.

635 Let Us Break Bread Together

They devoted themselves . . . to the breaking of bread and to prayer. Acts 2:42

1. Let us break bread to - geth - er on our knees. (on our knees.)
2. Let us drink the cup to - geth - er on our knees. (on our knees.)
3. Let us praise God to - geth - er on our knees. (on our knees.)
Let us break bread to - geth - er on our knees. (on our knees.)
Let us drink the cup to - geth - er on our knees. (on our knees.)
Let us praise God to - geth - er on our knees. (on our knees.)
Refrain
When I fall on my knees with my face to the ris - ing sun,
O Lord, have mer - cy on me. (on me.)

WORDS: African-American spiritual
MUSIC: African-American spiritual; arr. Keith Phillips, b. 1941

LET US BREAK BREAD
Irregular

As We Gather Around the Table 636

Do this in remembrance of me. Luke 22:19

1. As we gath - er a - round the ta - ble of our Lord,
2. As we gath - er a - round the ta - ble of our Lord,
3. As we gath - er a - round the ta - ble of our Lord,
We re - call His hum - ble birth in Beth - le - hem.
We re - call His ag - o - ny up - on the cross.
We re - call the emp - ty tomb where He was laid.
As the an - gels sang, as the shep - herds came,
Here our Sav - ior died, a - lone was cru - ci - fied.
He is liv - ing still, our long - ing hearts to fill.
Let us a - dore and wor - ship the Lord, Let us re - mem - ber Him.
Let us a - dore and wor - ship the Lord, Let us re - mem - ber Him.
Let us a - dore and wor - ship the Lord, Let us re - mem - ber Him.

WORDS: Mark Blankenship, b. 1943
MUSIC: Mark Blankenship, b. 1943

NORTH PHOENIX
Irregular

637 For the Bread which You Have Broken

He took bread, gave thanks and broke it. Luke 22:19

1. For the bread which You have bro-ken, For the wine which You have poured, For the words which You have spo-ken, Now we give You thanks, O Lord, Now we give You thanks, O Lord.
2. By these pledg-es that You love us, By Your gift of peace re-stored, By Your call to heaven a-bove us, Con-se-crate our lives, O Lord, Con-se-crate our lives, O Lord.
3. In Your ser-vice, Lord, de-fend us, Help us now o-bey Your Word. In the world to which You send us Let Your king-dom come, O Lord, Let Your king-dom come, O Lord.

WORDS: Louis F. Benson, 1855-1930
MUSIC: Gene Rivard, b. 1949; arr. Bill Fasig, 1929-2002

COMMUNION
8.7.8.7.7.

PRAYER AFTER COMMUNION

Master almighty, You created all things for Your name's sake; You gave food and drink to all for enjoyment, that they might give thanks to You; but to us You freely gave spiritual food and drink and life eternal through Your Servant. Before all things we thank You that You are mighty; to You be the glory for ever.

Remember, Lord, Your Church, to deliver it from all evil and to make it perfect in Your love, and gather it from the four winds, sanctified for Your kingdom which You have prepared for it; for Yours is the power and the glory for ever. Let grace come, and let this world pass away. Hosanna to the Son of David! If any one is holy, let him come; if any one is not so, let him repent. Maranatha. Amen.

from *The Didache (Teaching of the Twelve Apostles)*, ca. 1st Century

In Remembrance of Thee 638

Do this in remembrance of me. 1 Corinthians 11:24

1. In re - mem - brance of Thee do we gath - er to - day, 'Round Thy ta - ble of mer - cy so free. For as oft as we eat, and as oft as we drink, Do we come in re - mem - brance of Thee.
2. Here a ta - ble is spread of for - give - ness and grace, Here our needs and our wants He doth meet. He took bread and gave thanks, and He broke it for them, He said: "Take of my bod - y and eat."
3. There He drank of the cup of our sin and our death, Let us come and for - give - ness re - ceive Through His blood which was shed for re - mis - sion of sin, Let us come, eat and drink and be - lieve.
4. When He comes for His Church what a joy it will be To par - take of the cup from His hand. We will sit at His feet as we wor - ship our Lord, From all tongues and all tribes and all lands.
Final Ending
In re - mem-brance of Thee, We do show the Lord's death till He come.

WORDS: Doris R. Horn, b. 1918
MUSIC: Doris R. Horn, b. 1918

MILLER
12.9.12.9. with Coda

639 Hallelujah! We Sing Your Praises

Haleluya! Pelo Tso Rona [South Africa]

This cup is the new covenant in my blood. Luke 22:20

Refrain
Hal - le - lu - jah! We sing Your prais - es, All our hearts are filled with glad - ness. Hal - le - lu - jah! We sing Your prais - es, All our hearts are filled with glad - ness.
fine
1. Christ the Lord to us said: "I am wine, I am bread, I am wine, I am bread." Give to all who thirst and hun - ger.
2. Now He sends us all out, Strong in faith, free of doubt, Strong in faith, free of doubt. Tell to all the joy - ful gos - pel.
D.C. al fine

WORDS: South African
MUSIC: South African

HALELUYA! PELO TSO RONA
Irregular

Baptized into His Death 640

Don't you know that all of us . . . were baptized into his death? Romans 6:3

1. A - round Your grave, Lord Je - sus, The emp - ty grave, we stand,
2. O Lord, You now are ris - en, Your a - gon - y is o'er.
3. In - to Your death we're bap - tized, With You to sin we died,
With hearts all full of prais - es, To keep Your blest com - mand.
For sin You once have suf - fered, And live to die no more.
With You we now are ris - en— And shall be glo - ri - fied.
By faith our souls, re - joic - ing, Re - trace Your path of love
Sin, death and hell are van - quished By You, the Church - 's Head;
From sin, the world, and Sa - tan, Now ran - somed by Your blood,
Through death's dark, an - gry wa - ters Up to the throne a - bove.
And Lord, we share Your tri - umph, O First - born from the dead!
We walk on earth as stran - gers A - live with You, to God.

WORDS: James G. Deck, 1802-1884, alt.
MUSIC: *Neuvermehrtes Gesangbuch*, 1693; harm. Felix Mendelssohn, 1809-1847

MUNICH
7.6.7.6.D.

641 We Bless the Name of Christ the Lord

Then Jesus came from Galilee to the Jordan to be baptized by John. Matthew 3:13

1. We bless the name of Christ the Lord, We bless Him
2. We fol - low Him with pure de - light To sanc - ti -
3. Bap - tized in God the Fa - ther, Son And Ho - ly
4. By grace we "Ab - ba, Fa - ther" cry; By grace the
for His ho - ly Word, Who loved to do His
fy His sa - cred rite, And thus our faith with
Spir - it, Three - in - One. With con - science free, we
Com - fort - er comes nigh, And for Thy grace our
Fa - ther's will And all His right - eous - ness ful - fill.
wa - ter seal, To prove o - be - dience that we feel.
rest in God, In love and peace through Je - sus' blood.
love shall be For - ev - er, on - ly, Lord, for Thee.

WORDS: Samuel F. Coffman, 1872-1954
MUSIC: Thomas Hastings, 1784-1872

RETREAT
L.M.

642 Baptism

Be completely humble and gentle; be patient, bearing with one another in love. Make every effort to keep the unity of the Spirit through the bond of peace.

There is one body and one Spirit—just as you were called to one hope when you were called—one Lord, one faith, one baptism; one God and Father of all, who is over all and through all and in all. *Ephesians 4:2-6*

What shall we say, then? Shall we go on sinning so that grace may increase?

By no means! We died to sin; how can we live in it any longer? Or don't

Baptized into His Death 640

Don't you know that all of us . . . were baptized into his death? Romans 6:3

WORDS: James G. Deck, 1802-1884, alt.
MUSIC: *Neuvermehrtes Gesangbuch*, 1693; harm. Felix Mendelssohn, 1809-1847

MUNICH
7.6.7.6.D.

641 We Bless the Name of Christ the Lord

Then Jesus came from Galilee to the Jordan to be baptized by John. Matthew 3:13

1. We bless the name of Christ the Lord, We bless Him for His holy Word, Who loved to do His Father's will And all His righteousness fulfill.
2. We follow Him with pure delight To sanctify His sacred rite, And thus our faith with water seal, To prove obedience that we feel.
3. Baptized in God the Father, Son And Holy Spirit, Three-in-One. With conscience free, we rest in God, In love and peace through Jesus' blood.
4. By grace we "Abba, Father" cry; By grace the Comforter comes nigh, And for Thy grace our love shall be Forever, only, Lord, for Thee.

WORDS: Samuel F. Coffman, 1872-1954
MUSIC: Thomas Hastings, 1784-1872

RETREAT
L.M.

642 Baptism

Be completely humble and gentle; be patient, bearing with one another in love. Make every effort to keep the unity of the Spirit through the bond of peace.

There is one body and one Spirit—just as you were called to one hope when you were called—one Lord, one faith, one baptism; one God and Father of all, who is over all and through all and in all. *Ephesians 4:2-6*

What shall we say, then? Shall we go on sinning so that grace may increase?

By no means! We died to sin; how can we live in it any longer? Or don't

you know that all of us who were baptized into Christ Jesus were baptized into his death?

We were therefore buried with him through baptism into death in order that, just as Christ was raised from the dead through the glory of the Father, we too may live a new life.

If we have been united with him like this in his death, we will certainly also be united with him in his resurrection.

For we know that our old self was crucified with him so that the body of sin might be done away with, that we should no longer be slaves to sin—because anyone who has died has been freed from sin.

Now if we died with Christ, we believe that we will also live with him.

Romans 6:1-8

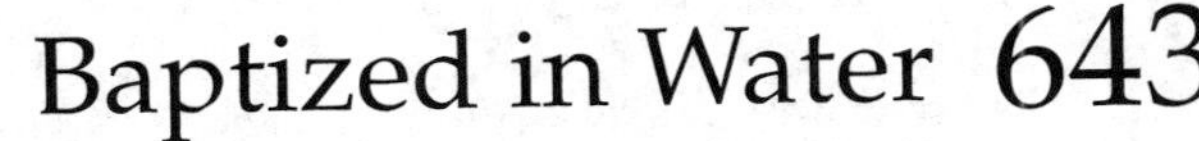

Baptized in Water 643

Those who accepted his message were baptized. Acts 2:41

1. Bap-tized in wa - ter, sealed by the Spir - it, Cleansed by the blood of Christ, our King; Heirs of sal - va - tion, trust - ing His prom - ise, Faith - ful - ly now God's praise we sing.
2. Bap-tized in wa - ter, sealed by the Spir - it, Dead in the tomb with Christ, our King; One with His ris - ing, freed and for - giv - en, Thank - ful - ly now God's praise we sing.
3. Bap-tized in wa - ter, sealed by the Spir - it, Marked with the sign of Christ, our King; Born of one Fa - ther, we are His chil - dren, Joy - ful - ly now God's praise we sing.

WORDS: Michael Saward, b. 1932
MUSIC: Traditional Gaelic melody; harm. David Evans, 1874-1948

BUNESSAN
5.5.5.4.D.

644 Come, Holy Spirit, Dove Divine

He saw the Spirit of God descending like a dove and lighting on him. Matthew 3:16

1. Come, Ho - ly Spir - it, Dove di - vine, On these bap - tis - mal wa - ters shine, And teach our hearts, in high - est strain, To praise the Lamb for sin - ners slain.
2. We love Your name, we love Your laws, And joy - ful - ly em - brace Your cause. We love Your cross, the shame, the pain, O Lamb of God for sin - ners slain.
3. We sink be - neath the wa - ter's face, And thank You for Your sav - ing grace. We die to sin and seek a grave With You, be - neath the yield - ing wave.
4. And as we rise with You to live, O, let the Ho - ly Spir - it give The seal - ing unc - tion from a - bove, The joy of life, the fire of love!

WORDS: Adoniram Judson, 1788-1850, alt.
MUSIC: Henry P. Smith, 1825-1898

MARYTON
L.M.

A BAPTISM PRAYER

Father in heaven,
at the baptism of Jesus in the River Jordan,
You proclaimed Him Your Beloved Son
and anointed Him with the Holy Spirit.
Grant that all who are baptized into His name
may keep the covenant they have made,
and boldly confess Him as Lord and Savior,
who with You and the Holy Spirit lives and reigns,
One God, in glory everlasting. Amen.

From *The Book of Common Prayer*, alt.

When He Cometh 645

They will be mine . . . in the day when I make up my treasured possession. Malachi 3:17

1. When He com - eth, when He com - eth To make up His jew - els,
2. He will gath - er, He will gath - er The gems for His king - dom.
3. Lit - tle chil - dren, lit - tle chil - dren, Who love their Re - deem - er,
All His jew - els, pre - cious jew - els, His loved and His own:
All the pure ones, all the bright ones, His loved and His own.
Are the jew - els, pre - cious jew - els, His loved and His own.
Refrain
Like the stars of the morn - ing, His bright crown a - dorn - ing,
They shall shine in their beau - ty— Bright gems for His crown.

WORDS: William O. Cushing, 1823-1902
MUSIC: George F. Root, 1820-1895

JEWELS
8.6.8.5. with Refrain

646 Christ and the Children

At that time the disciples came to Jesus and asked, "Who is the greatest in the kingdom of heaven?"

He called a little child and had him stand among them.

And he said: "I tell you the truth, unless you change and become like little children, you will never enter the kingdom of heaven.

Therefore, whoever humbles himself like this child is the greatest in the kingdom of heaven.

And whoever welcomes a little child like this in my name welcomes me.

But if anyone causes one of these little ones who believe in me to sin, it would be better for him to have a large millstone hung around his neck and to be drowned in the depths of the sea."

Matthew 18:1-6

People were bringing little children to Jesus to have him touch them, but the disciples rebuked them.

When Jesus saw this, he was indignant. He said to them, "Let the little children come to me, and do not hinder them, for the kingdom of God belongs to such as these.

I tell you the truth, anyone who will not receive the kingdom of God like a little child will never enter it."

And he took the children in his arms, put his hands on them and blessed them.

Mark 10:13-16

647 Good Shepherd, Take This Little Child

People were also bringing babies to Jesus to have him touch them. Luke 18:15

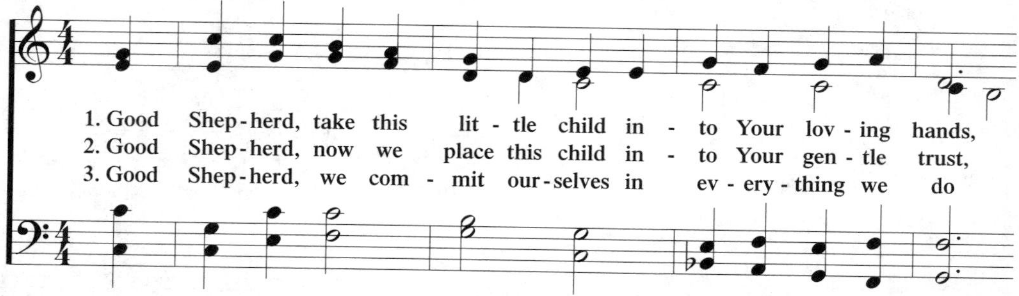
1. Good Shep-herd, take this lit - tle child in - to Your lov - ing hands,
2. Good Shep-herd, now we place this child in - to Your gen - tle trust,
3. Good Shep-herd, we com - mit our-selves in ev - ery - thing we do

WORDS: Claire Cloninger, b. 1942
MUSIC: Ken Barker, b. 1955

AMY
C.M.

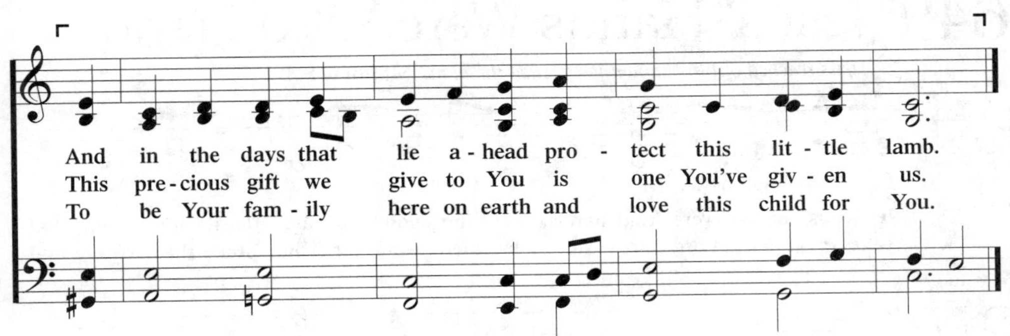
And in the days that lie a-head pro-tect this lit-tle lamb.
This pre-cious gift we give to You is one You've giv-en us.
To be Your fam-ily here on earth and love this child for You.

This Child We Dedicate to Thee 648

I prayed for this child. . . . So now I give him to the LORD. 1 Samuel 1:27, 28

1. This child we ded-i-cate to Thee,
O God of grace and pu-ri-ty!
In Thy great love its life pro-long,
Shield it, we pray, from sin and wrong.

2. O may Thy Spir-it gent-ly draw
Its will-ing soul to keep Thy law.
May vir-tue, pi-e-ty and truth
Dawn e-ven with its dawn-ing youth.

WORDS: Anonymous, German; tr. Samuel Gilman, 1791-1858, alt.
MUSIC: Henry K. Oliver, 1800-1885

FEDERAL STREET
L.M.

649 Jesus' Hands Were Kind Hands

Jesus reached out his hand and touched the man. Matthew 8:3

1. Je - sus' hands were kind hands, do - ing good to all, Heal - ing pain and
2. Take my hands, Lord Je - sus, let them work for You; Make them strong and
sick - ness, bless - ing chil - dren small, Wash - ing tired feet, and
gen - tle, kind in all I do. Let me watch You, Je - sus,
sav - ing those who fall; Je - sus' hands were kind hands, do - ing good to all.
till I'm gen - tle, too, Till my hands are kind hands, quick to work for You.

WORDS: Margaret Cropper, 1886-1980
MUSIC: French melody

AU CLAIR DE LA LUNE
11.11.11.11.

A CHARGE TO PARENTS

I charge you in the presence of God and this congregation to love your child as much as your own life. Never allow him/her to ever have any doubts of the depths of your love. Teach him/her to love and obey God. Let him/her see in your life evidences of the working of your personal Savior. Make spiritual things the topic of conversation, the focus of family life and the basis for personal development.

From "Dedication of a Baby or Child," *The Pastor's Handbook*

Friend of the Home 650

Little children were brought to Jesus for him to place his hands on them. Matthew 19:13

1. Friend of the home, as when, in Gal - i - lee,
2. Lord, may Thy Church, as with a moth - er's care,
3. Draw, through the child, the par - ents near - er Thee,
The moth - ers brought their lit - tle ones to Thee,
For Thee the lambs with - in her bos - om bear,
En - due their home with grow - ing sanc - ti - ty,
So we, dear Lord, would now the chil - dren bring,
And grant, as morn - ing grows to noon, that they
And gath - er all, by earth - ly homes made one,
And seek for them the shel - ter of Thy wing.
Still in her love and ho - ly ser - vice stay.
In heaven, O Christ, when earth - ly days are done.

WORDS: Howell E. Lewis, 1860-1953
MUSIC: William H. Monk, 1823-1889

EVENTIDE
10.10.10.10.

651 God's Blessing on the Family

These are all the commands, decrees and laws that the LORD your God directed me to teach you to observe in the land that you are crossing the Jordan to possess, so that you, your children and their children after them may fear the LORD your God as long as you live by keeping all his decrees and commands that I give you, and so that you may enjoy long life.

Hear, O Israel: The LORD our God, the LORD is one. Love the LORD your God with all your heart and with all our soul and with all your strength.

These commandments that I give you today are to be upon your hearts.

Impress them on your children. Talk about them when you sit at home and when you walk along the road, when you lie down and when you get up.

Tie them as symbols on your hands and bind them on your foreheads. Write them on the doorframes of your houses and on your gates.

Deuteronomy 6:1-9

See, I set before you today life and prosperity, death and destruction.

For I command you today to love the LORD your God, to walk in his ways, and to keep his commands, decrees and laws;

Then you will live and increase, and the LORD your God will bless you in the land you are entering to possess.

But if your heart turns away and you are not obedient, and if you are drawn away to bow down to other gods and worship them, I declare to you this day that you will certainly be destroyed. *Deuteronomy 30:15-18*

As for me and my household, we will serve the LORD. *Joshua 24:15*

652 Happy the Home When God Is There

Today salvation has come to this house. Luke 19:9

1. Hap - py the home when God is there And love fills ev - ery breast,
2. Hap - py the home where Je - sus' name Is sweet to ev - ery ear,
3. Hap - py the home where prayer is heard And prais - es of - ten rise,
4. Lord, let us in our homes pur - sue This bless - ed peace to gain.

WORDS: Henry Ware, Jr., 1794-1843, alt.
MUSIC: John B. Dykes, 1823-1876

ST. AGNES
C.M.

When one their wish and one their prayer And one their heaven - ly rest.
Where chil-dren ear - ly lisp His fame And par-ents hold Him dear.
Where par-ents love the sa-cred Word And all its wis - dom prize.
U - nite our hearts in love to You, And love to all will reign.

Faith of Our Mothers 653

I have been reminded of your sincere faith, which first lived in your grandmother Lois and in your mother Eunice. 2 Timothy 1:5

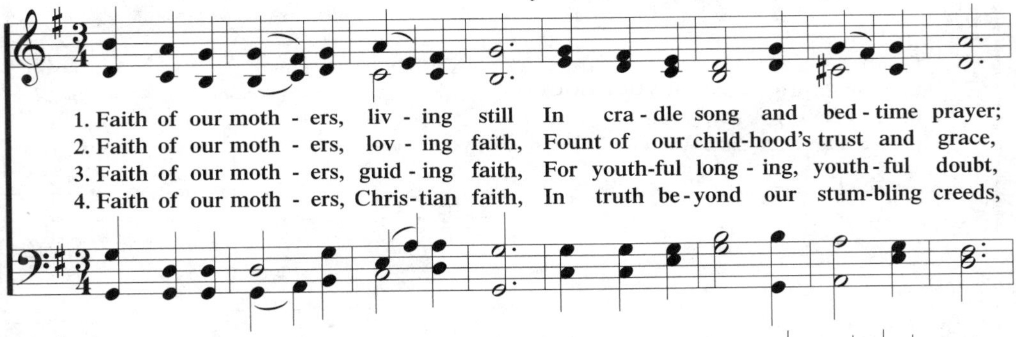

1. Faith of our moth - ers, liv - ing still In cra - dle song and bed - time prayer;
2. Faith of our moth - ers, lov - ing faith, Fount of our child-hood's trust and grace,
3. Faith of our moth - ers, guid - ing faith, For youth-ful long - ing, youth - ful doubt,
4. Faith of our moth - ers, Chris-tian faith, In truth be - yond our stum-bling creeds,

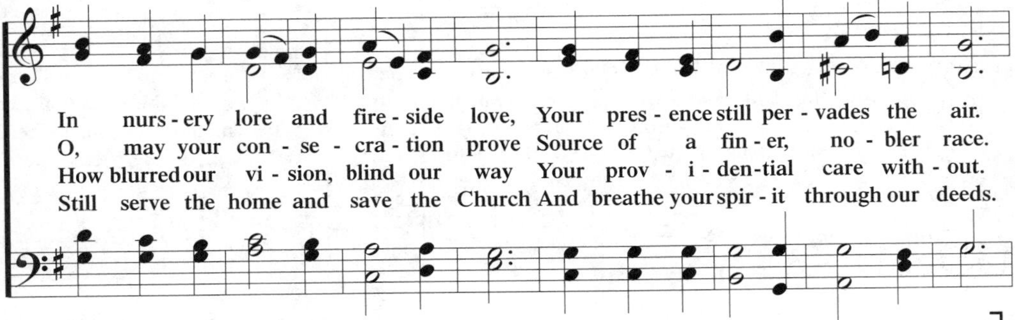

In nurs - ery lore and fire - side love, Your pres - ence still per - vades the air.
O, may your con - se - cra - tion prove Source of a fin - er, no - bler race.
How blurred our vi - sion, blind our way Your prov - i - den-tial care with - out.
Still serve the home and save the Church And breathe your spir - it through our deeds.

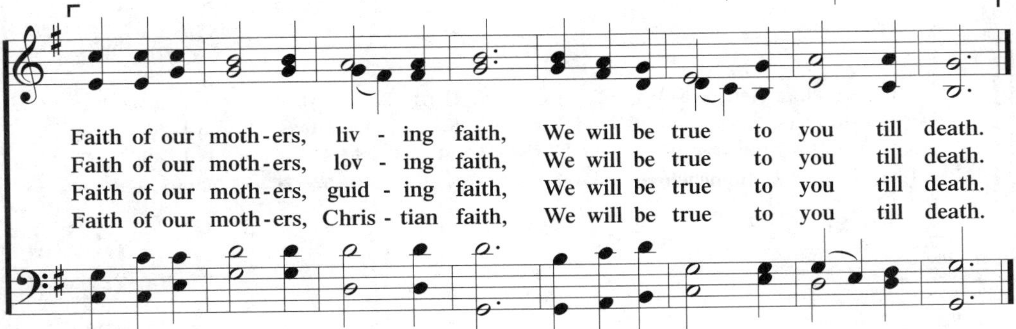

Faith of our moth-ers, liv - ing faith, We will be true to you till death.
Faith of our moth-ers, lov - ing faith, We will be true to you till death.
Faith of our moth-ers, guid - ing faith, We will be true to you till death.
Faith of our moth-ers, Chris - tian faith, We will be true to you till death.

WORDS: A.B. Patten, 1871-1938
MUSIC: Henri F. Hemy, 1818-1888; arr. James G. Walton, 1821-1905

ST. CATHERINE
8.8.8.D

654 A Christian Home

From infancy you have known the holy Scriptures. 2 Timothy 3:15

1. O, give us homes built firm up - on the Sav - ior, Where Christ is Head and
2. O, give us homes with god - ly fa - thers, moth - ers, Who al - ways place their
3. O, give us homes where Christ is Lord and Mas - ter, The Bi - ble read, the
4. O Lord, our God, our homes are Thine for - ev - er! We trust to Thee their
Coun - sel - or and Guide, Where ev - ery child is taught His love and fa - vor
hope and trust in Him, Whose ten - der pa - tience tur - moil nev - er both - ers,
pre - cious hymns still sung, Where prayer comes first in peace or in di - sas - ter,
prob - lems, toil and care. Their bonds of love no en - e - my can sev - er
And gives his heart to Christ, the Cru - ci - fied: How sweet to know that,
Whose calm and cour - age trou - ble can - not dim, A home where each finds
And praise is nat - ural speech to ev - ery tongue, Where moun - tains move be -
If Thou art al - ways Lord and Mas - ter there. Be Thou the cen - ter
though his foot - steps wa - ver, His faith - ful Lord is walk - ing by his side!
joy in serv - ing oth - ers, And love still shines, though days be dark and grim.
fore a faith that's vast - er, And Christ suf - fi - cient is for old and young.
of our least en - deav - or— Be Thou our guest, our hearts and homes to share.

WORDS: Barbara B. Hart, b. 1916
MUSIC: Jean Sibelius, 1865-1957

FINLANDIA
11.10.11.10.11.10.

Would You Bless Our Homes and Families 655

Love one another deeply, from the heart. 1 Peter 1:22

1. Would You bless our homes and fam - ilies, Source of life who calls us here.
2. When our way is un - de - mand - ing, Let us use the time that's ours
3. From the homes in which we're nur - tured, With the love that shapes us there,
4. Let us reach be - yond the bound-aries Of our dai - ly thought and care
In our world of stress and ten - sion Teach us love that con - quers fear.
To de - light in sim - ple plea - sures, Shar - ing joys in gen - tle hours.
Teach us, God, to claim as fam - ily Ev - ery one whose life we share.
'Til the fam - ily You have cho - sen Spills its love out ev - ery - where.
Help us learn to love each oth - er With a love that con - stant stays.
When our way is anx - ious walk - ing And a heav - y path we plod,
And through all that life may of - fer, May we in Your love re - main.
Help us learn to love each oth - er With a love that con - stant stays.
Teach us when we face our trou - bles, Love's ex - pressed in man - y ways.
Teach us trust in one an - oth - er And in You, our gra - cious God.
May the love we share in fam - ilies Be a - live to praise Your name.
Teach us when we face our trou - bles, Love's ex - pressed in man - y ways.

WORDS: Walter Farquharson, b. 1936
MUSIC: Wyeth's *Repository of Sacred Music, Part Second*, 1813

NETTLETON
8.7.8.7.D.

656 O Perfect Love

Love must be sincere. Romans 12:9

1. O per - fect Love, all hu - man thought tran - scend - ing,
2. O per - fect Life, be now their full as - sur - ance
3. Grant them the joy which bright - ens earth - ly sor - row.
Low - ly we kneel in prayer be - fore Your throne,
Of ten - der char - i - ty and stead - fast faith,
Grant them the peace which calms all earth - ly strife,
That theirs may be the love that has no end - ing,
Of pa - tient hope, and qui - et, brave en - dur - ance,
And to life's day the glo - rious, un - known mor - row
Whom You for - ev - er - more u - nite in one.
With child - like trust that fears no pain or death.
That dawns up - on e - ter - nal love and life.

WORDS: Dorothy F.B. Gurney, 1858-1932, alt.
MUSIC: Joseph Barnby, 1838-1896

O PERFECT LOVE
11.10.11.10.

Rejoice, You Pure in Heart 657

Be joyful always; give thanks in all circumstances. 1 Thessalonians 5:16, 18

1. Re - joice, you pure in heart, Re - joice, give thanks, and sing.
2. Bright youth and snow-crowned age, Strong souls and spir - its meek,
3. With all the an - gel choirs, With all the saints on earth,
4. Yes, on through life's long path, Still chant - ing as you go,
Your fes - tal ban - ner wave on high, The cross of Christ your King.
Raise high your free, ex - ult - ing song, God's won-drous prais - es speak.
Pour out the strains of joy and bliss, True rap - ture, no - blest mirth!
From youth to age, by night and day, In glad - ness and in woe.
Refrain
Re - joice, re - joice, Re - joice, give thanks, and sing!
Re - joice, re - joice,

WORDS: Edward H. Plumptre, 1821-1891, alt.
MUSIC: Arthur H. Messiter, 1834-1916

MARION
S.M. with Refrain

Thanksgiving 658

Observe the commands of the LORD your God, walking in his ways and revering him.

For the LORD your God is bringing you into a good land—a land with streams and pools of water, with springs flowing in the valleys and hills;

A land with wheat and barley, vines and fig trees, pomegranates, olive oil and honey;

A land where bread will not be scarce and you will lack nothing; a land where the rocks are iron and you can dig copper out of the hills.

When you have eaten and are satisfied, praise the LORD your God, for the good land he has given you.

Be careful that you do not forget the LORD your God, failing to observe his commands, his laws and his decrees that I am giving you this day.

Otherwise, when you eat and are satisfied, when you build fine houses and settle down,

And when your herds and flocks grow large and your silver and gold increase and all you have is multiplied,

Then your heart will become proud and you will forget the LORD your God, who brought you out of Egypt, out of the land of slavery.

He led you through the vast and dreadful desert, that thirsty and waterless land, with its venomous snakes and scorpions. He brought you water out of the hard rock.

He gave you manna to eat in the desert, something your fathers had never known, to humble and to test you so that in the end it might go well with you.

You may say to yourself, "My power and the strength of my hands have produced this wealth for me."

But remember the LORD your God, for it is he who gives you the ability to produce wealth,

and so confirms his covenant, which he swore to your forefathers, as it is today.

Deuteronomy 8:6-18

659 Let All Things Now Living

Let everything that has breath praise the LORD. Psalm 150:6

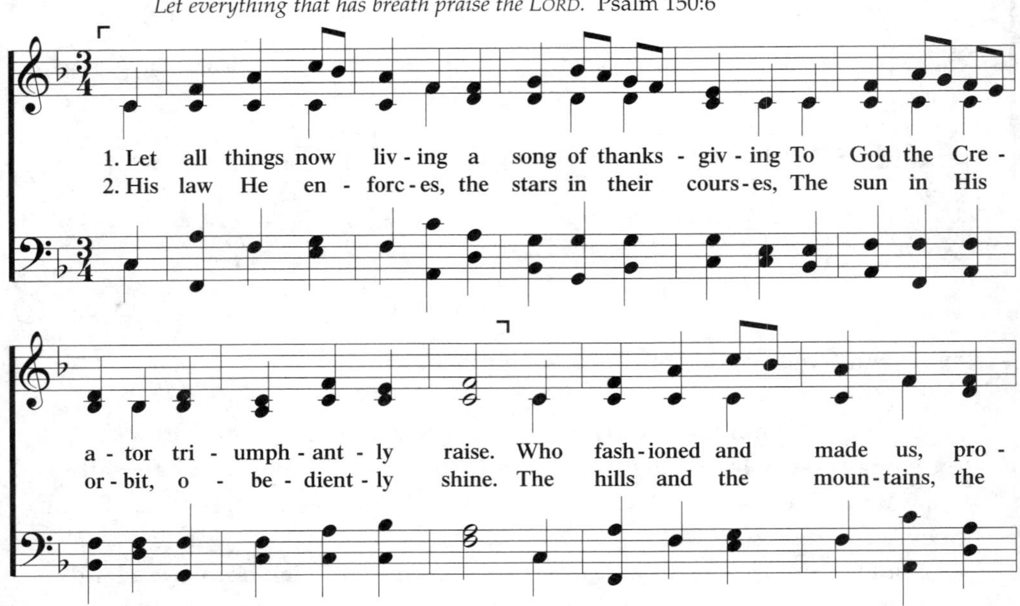
1. Let all things now liv - ing a song of thanks - giv - ing To God the Cre -
2. His law He en - forc - es, the stars in their cours - es, The sun in His
a - tor tri - umph - ant - ly raise. Who fash - ioned and made us, pro -
or - bit, o - be - dient - ly shine. The hills and the moun - tains, the

(For a different harmony, see No. 624.)

WORDS: Katherine K. Davis, 1892-1980
MUSIC: Welsh melody

ASH GROVE
12.11.12.11.D.

tect - ed and stayed us, Who guid - eth us on to the end of our days.
riv - ers and foun - tains, The deeps of the o - cean pro - claim Him Di - vine.
His ban - ners are o'er us, His light goes be - fore us, A pil - lar of
We too, should be voic-ing our love and re - joic-ing, With glad ad - or -
fire shin - ing forth in the night, Till shad - ows have van - ished and
a - tion a song let us raise, Till all things now liv - ing u -
dark-ness is ban - ished, As for - ward we trav - el from light in - to light.
nite in thanks - giv - ing To God in the high-est, ho - san - na and praise!

Optional segue to "Give Thanks." No transition required.

660 Give Thanks

The LORD has done great things for us, and we are filled with joy. Psalm 126:3

Give thanks with a grate-ful heart. Give thanks to the Ho-ly One. Give
thanks be-cause He's giv-en Je-sus Christ, His Son. Give
1.
2.
Son. And now let the weak say, "I am strong," Let the poor say, "I am
rich," Be-cause of what the Lord Has done for us. And
1.
2.
us. Give thanks!

WORDS: Henry Smith, b. 1952
MUSIC: Henry Smith, b. 1952

GIVE THANKS
Irregular

In Thanksgiving, Let Us Praise Him 661

With praise and thanksgiving they sang to the LORD. Ezra 3:11

1. From the first bright light of morn - ing To the last warm glow of dusk,
2. In the sea - son of our plen - ty, In the sea - son of our need,
3. Safe with - in His hand that guides us, Hid-den in His heal - ing wings,
Ev - ery breath we take is sa - cred, For it is God's gift to us.
We will find His grace suf - fi - cient, We will find His love com - plete.
Day by day His love pro - vides us Ev - ery good and per - fect thing.
Refrain
In thanks - giv - ing, let us praise Him. In thanks - giv - ing, let us sing
Songs of praise and ad - o - ra - tion To our gra - cious Lord and King.

(For a different harmony, see No. 475.)

WORDS: Claire Cloninger, b. 1942
MUSIC: Franz Joseph Haydn, 1732-1809

AUSTRIA
8.7.8.7.D.

662 Now Thank We All Our God

Now, our God, we give you thanks, and praise your glorious name. 1 Chronicles 29:13

1. Now thank we all our God With heart and hands and voic - es,
2. O, may this boun - teous God Through all our life be near us,
3. All praise and thanks to God The Fa - ther now be giv - en,
Who won-drous things hath done, In whom His world re - joic - es,
With ev - er joy - ful hearts And bless - ed peace to cheer us,
The Son, and Him who reigns With them in high - est heav - en,
Who from our moth - ers' arms Hath blessed us on our way
And keep us in His grace, And guide us when per - plexed,
The one e - ter - nal God, Whom earth and heaven a - dore,
With count - less gifts of love, And still is ours to - day.
And free us from all ills In this world and the next.
For thus it was, is now, And shall be ev - er - more.

WORDS: Martin Rinkart, 1586-1649; tr. Catherine Winkworth, 1827-1878
MUSIC: Johann Crüger, 1598-1662; harm. Felix Mendelssohn, 1809-1847

NUN DANKET
6.7.6.7.6.6.6.6.

Come, Ye Thankful People, Come 663

Let us come before him with thanksgiving. Psalm 95:2

1. Come, ye thank - ful peo - ple, come, Raise the song of har - vest home.
2. All the world is God's own field, Fruit un - to His praise to yield.
3. For the Lord our God shall come And shall take His har - vest home.
4. E - ven so, Lord, quick - ly come To Your fi - nal har - vest home.
All is safe - ly gath - ered in, Ere the win - ter storms be - gin.
Wheat and tares to - geth - er sown, Un - to joy or sor - row grown.
From His field shall in that day All of - fens - es purge a - way.
Gath - er all Your peo - ple in, Free from sor - row, free from sin.
God, our Mak - er, doth pro - vide For our wants to be sup - plied.
First the blade, and then the ear, Then the full corn shall ap - pear.
Give His an - gels charge at last In the fire the tares to cast,
There, for - ev - er pu - ri - fied, In Your pres - ence to a - bide:
Come to God's own tem - ple, come, Raise the song of har - vest home.
Lord of har - vest, grant that we Whole - some grain and pure may be.
But the fruit - ful ears to store In His gar - ner ev - er - more.
Come, with all Your an - gels come, Raise the glo - rious har - vest home.

WORDS: Henry Alford, 1810-1871, alt.
MUSIC: George J. Elvey, 1816-1893

ST. GEORGE'S, WINDSOR
7.7.7.7.D.

664 We Gather Together

The LORD remembers us and will bless us. Psalm 115:12

1. We gath - er to - geth - er to ask the Lord's bless - ing.
2. Be - side us to guide us, our God with us join - ing,
3. We all do ex - tol Thee, Thou Lead - er tri - um - phant,
He chas - tens and has - tens His will to make known.
Or - dain - ing, main - tain - ing His king - dom di - vine.
And pray that Thou still our de - fend - er wilt be.
The wick - ed op - press - ing now cease from dis - tress - ing.
So from the be - gin - ning the fight we were win - ning.
Let Thy con - gre - ga - tion es - cape trib - u - la - tion.
Sing prais - es to His name; He for - gets not His own.
Thou, Lord, wast at our side, all glo - ry be Thine.
Thy name be ev - er praised! O Lord, make us free!

WORDS: Netherlands folk hymn; tr. Theodore Baker, 1851-1934
MUSIC: Netherlands folk song; arr. Edward Kremser, 1838-1914

KREMSER
12.11.12.11.

God of Our Fathers 665

The LORD strong and mighty, the LORD mighty in battle. Psalm 24:8
1. God of our fa - thers, whose al - might - y
2. Thy love di - vine hath led us in the
3. From war's a - larms, from dead - ly pes - ti -
4. Re - fresh Thy peo - ple on their toil - some
hand Leads forth in beau - ty all the star - ry
past. In this free land by Thee our lot is
lence, Be Thy strong arm our ev - er sure de -
way. Lead us from night to nev - er - end - ing
band Of shin - ing worlds in splen - dor through the
cast. Be Thou our rul - er, guard - ian, guide and
fense. Thy true re - li - gion in our hearts in -
day. Fill all our lives with love and grace di -
skies, Our grate - ful songs be - fore Thy throne a - rise.
stay, Thy Word our law, Thy paths our cho - sen way.
crease, Thy boun - teous good - ness nour - ish us in peace.
vine, And glo - ry, laud and praise be ev - er Thine.

WORDS: Daniel C. Roberts, 1841-1907
MUSIC: George W. Warren, 1828-1902

NATIONAL HYMN
10.10.10.10.

666 O God, Beneath Thy Guiding Hand

May the nations be glad and sing for joy, for you rule the peoples justly. Psalm 67:4

1. O God, beneath Thy guiding hand
Our exiled fathers crossed the sea,
And when they trod the wintry strand,[1]
With prayer and psalm they worshiped Thee.

2. Thou heard, well pleased, the song, the prayer:
Thy blessing came, and still its power
Shall onward through all ages bear
The memory of that holy hour.

3. Laws, freedom, truth, and faith in God
Came with those exiles o'er the waves,
And where their pilgrim feet have trod,
The God they trusted guards their graves.

4. And here Thy name, O God of love,
Their children's children shall adore
Till these eternal hills remove
And spring adorns the earth no more.

WORDS: Leonard Bacon, 1802-1881
MUSIC: John Hatton, 1710-1793

DUKE STREET
L.M.

1. *strand: shore*

Eternal Father, Strong to Save 667

When you pass through the waters, I will be with you. Isaiah 43:2

1. E - ter - nal Fa - ther, strong to save, Whose arm hath bound the
2. O Christ, the Lord of hill and plain O'er which our traf - fic
3. O Spir - it, whom the Fa - ther sent To spread a - broad the
4. O Trin - i - ty of love and power, Thy chil - dren shield in
rest - less wave, Who bidd'st the might - y o - cean deep Its
runs a - main By moun - tain pass or val - ley low; Wher -
firm - a - ment; O Wind of heav - en, by Thy might Save
dan - ger's hour; From rock and tem - pest, fire and foe, Pro -
own ap - point - ed lim - its keep: O, hear us when we
ev - er, Lord, Thy chil - dren go, Pro - tect them by Thy
all who dare the ea - gle's flight, And keep them by Thy
tect them where - so - e'er they go; Thus ev - er - more shall
cry to Thee For those in per - il on the sea.
guard - ing hand From ev - ery per - il on the land.
watch - ful care From ev - ery per - il in the air.
rise to Thee Glad hymns of praise from land and sea.

WORDS: Stanzas 1, 4 William Whiting, 1825-1878, alt.;
stanzas 2, 3 Robert Nelson Spencer, 1877-1961
MUSIC: John B. Dykes, 1823-1876

MELITA
8.8.8.8.8.8.

668 Battle Hymn of the Republic

The truth of the Lord endures forever. Psalm 117:2, NKJV

1. Mine eyes have seen the glo - ry of the com - ing of the Lord.
He is tram - pling out the vin - tage where the grapes of wrath are stored.
He hath loosed the fate - ful light - ning of His ter - ri - ble swift sword,
His truth is march - ing on.
2. I have seen Him in the watch-fires of a hun-dred cir - cling camps.
They have build - ed Him an al - tar in the eve - ning dews and damps.
I can read His right - eous sen - tence by the dim and flar - ing lamps.
His day is march - ing on.
3. He has sound - ed forth the trum - pet that shall nev - er call re - treat.
He is sift - ing out the hearts of men be - fore His judg - ment seat.
O, be swift, my soul, to an - swer Him! Be ju - bi - lant, my feet!
Our God is march - ing on.
4. In the beau - ty of the lil - ies, Christ was born a - cross the sea,
With a glo - ry in His bos - om that trans - fig - ures you and me.
As He died to make men ho - ly, let us live to make men free
While God is march - ing on.

WORDS: Julia W. Howe, 1819-1910, alt.
MUSIC: American melody

BATTLE HYMN
15.15.15.6. with Refrain

Refrain
Glo - ry! Glo - ry! Hal - le - lu - jah! Glo - ry! Glo - ry! Hal - le - lu - jah!
Glo - ry! Glo - ry! Hal - le - lu - jah! His truth is march - ing on.

GOD ESTABLISHES ALL AUTHORITY

Everyone must submit himself to the governing authorities, for there is no authority except that which God has established. The authorities that exist have been established by God. Consequently, he who rebels against the authority is rebelling against what God has instituted, and those who do so will bring judgment on themselves. For rulers hold no terror for those who do right, but for those who do wrong.

Do you want to be free from fear of the one in authority? Then do what is right and he will commend you. For he is God's servant to do you good. But if you do wrong, be afraid, for he does not bear the sword for nothing. He is God's servant, an agent of wrath to bring punishment on the wrongdoer. Therefore, it is necessary to submit to the authorities, not only because of possible punishment but also because of conscience.

This is also why you pay taxes, for the authorities are God's servants, who give their full time to governing. Give everyone what you owe him: If you owe taxes, pay taxes; if revenue, then revenue; if respect, then respect; if honor, then honor.

Romans 13:1-7

669 The Star-Spangled Banner

With God we will gain the victory, and he will trample down our enemies. Psalm 60:12

1. O say, can you see by the dawn's ear - ly light,
2. O, thus be it ev - er when free men shall stand
What so proud - ly we hailed at the twi - light's last gleam - ing?
Be - tween their loved homes and the war's des - o - la - tion!
Whose broad stripes and bright stars through the per - il - ous fight,
Blest with vic - tory and peace, may the heaven - res - cued land
O'er the ram - parts we watched were so gal - lant - ly stream - ing?
Praise the Power that hath made and pre - served us a na - tion!

WORDS: Francis Scott Key, 1779-1843
MUSIC: Attrib. John Stafford Smith, 1750-1836

NATIONAL ANTHEM
Irregular

And the rock - ets' red glare, the bombs burst - ing in air
Then con - quer we must, when our cause it is just,
Gave proof through the night that our flag was still there.
And this be our mot - to: "In God is our trust!"
O say, does that star - span - gled ban - ner yet wave
And the star - span - gled ban - ner in tri - umph shall wave
O'er the land of the free and the home of the brave?
O'er the land of the free and the home of the brave!

670 America, the Beautiful

Blessed is the nation whose God is the LORD. Psalm 33:12

1. O beau - ti - ful for spa - cious skies, For am - ber waves of grain,
2. O beau - ti - ful for pil - grim feet, Whose stern, im - pas - sioned stress
3. O beau - ti - ful for he - roes proved In lib - er - a - ting strife,
4. O beau - ti - ful for pa - triot dream That sees be - yond the years
For pur - ple moun - tain maj - es - ties A - bove the fruit - ed plain!
A thor - ough - fare for free - dom beat A - cross the wil - der - ness!
Who more than self their coun - try loved, And mer - cy more than life!
Thine al - a - bas - ter cit - ies gleam, Un - dimmed by hu - man tears!
A - mer - i - ca! A - mer - i - ca! God shed His grace on thee,
A - mer - i - ca! A - mer - i - ca! God mend thine ev - ery flaw,
A - mer - i - ca! A - mer - i - ca! May God thy gold re - fine
A - mer - i - ca! A - mer - i - ca! God shed His grace on thee
And crown thy good with broth - er - hood From sea to shin - ing sea!
Con - firm thy soul in self - con - trol, Thy lib - er - ty in law!
Till all suc - cess be no - ble - ness And ev - ery gain di - vine!
And crown thy good with broth - er - hood From sea to shin - ing sea!

WORDS: Katherine L. Bates, 1859-1929
MUSIC: Samuel A. Ward, 1847-1903

MATERNA
C.M.D.

America 671

Righteousness exalts a nation, but sin is a disgrace to any people. Proverbs 14:34

1. My coun - try, 'tis of thee, Sweet land of lib - er - ty,
2. My na - tive coun - try, thee, Land of the no - ble, free,
3. Let mu - sic swell the breeze And ring from all the trees
4. Our fa - thers' God, to Thee, Au - thor of lib - er - ty,
Of thee I sing. Land where my fa - thers died, Land of the
Thy name I love. I love thy rocks and rills, Thy woods and
Sweet free - dom's song. Let mor - tal tongues a - wake, Let all that
To Thee we sing. Long may our land be bright With free - dom's
pil - grim's pride, From ev - ery moun - tain - side Let free - dom ring.
tem - pled hills, My heart with rap - ture thrills Like that a - bove.
breathe par - take, Let rocks their si - lence break, The sound pro - long.
ho - ly light. Pro - tect us by Thy might, Great God, our King.

(For a different harmony, see No. 673.)

WORDS: Samuel F. Smith, 1808-1895
MUSIC: *Thesaurus Musicus*, circa 1740

AMERICA
6.6.4.6.6.6.4.

672 O Canada!

It is better to take refuge in the LORD than to trust in princes. Psalm 118:9

1. O Can - a - da! Our home and na - tive land! True pa - triot love in all thy sons com - mand. With glow - ing hearts we see thee rise, The True North, strong and free. From far and wide, O Can - a - da, We stand on guard for thee.
2. Rul - er Su - preme, who hear - est hum - ble prayer, Hold our Do - min - ion in Thy lov - ing care. Help us to find, O God, in Thee A last - ing, rich re - ward, As, wait - ing for the bet - ter day, We ev - er stand on guard.
Refrain
God keep our land glo - rious and free! O Can - a - da, we stand on guard for

WORDS: R. Stanley Weir, 1856-1926
MUSIC: Calixa Lavallée, 1842-1891

O CANADA
10.10.8.6.8.6. with Refrain

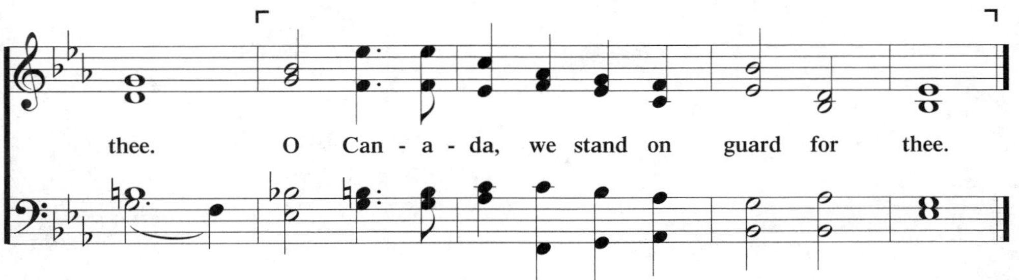
thee. O Can - a - da, we stand on guard for thee.

God Save the Queen 673

The authorities that exist have been established by God. Romans 13:1

God save our gra - cious Queen! Long live our no - ble Queen!

God save the Queen! Send her vic - to - ri - ous, Hap - py and

glo - ri - ous, Long to reign o - ver us, God save the Queen!

(For a different harmony, see No. 671)

WORDS: Anonymous, 18th century
MUSIC: *Thesaurus Musicus,* circa 1740

GOD SAVE THE QUEEN
6.6.4.6.6.6.4.

Table of Contents: Psalms
[Psalm–Number]

Psalms of Longing

13 674
42 675
142:1-5 676
143:1-11 677

Psalms of Trust

16 678
23 679
27 680
31:1-5, 15-16, 19-24 681
37:1-8, 23-31, 37 682
46 683
63 684
71:1-6, 17-24 685
86 686
91 687
121 688
127 689
130 690
139:1-12, 17-18, 23-24 691

Psalms of Penitence

38 692
51:1-17 693
85 694

Psalms of Thanksgiving for Deliverance

30 695
34 696
40:1-13, 16-17 697
57 698
66:1-9, 16-20 699
107:1-22 700
116:1-9, 12-19 701

Psalms of Thanksgiving for Forgiveness

32 702
65 703
103 704

Psalms of Praise and Calls to Worship

24 705
95 706
96 707
98 708
100 709
145 710
146 711
147:1-7 712
150 713

Psalms of Praise for Creation

8 714
19:1-6 715
104:1-10, 24-34 716

Psalms of Praise for the Word

19:7-14 717
33 718
119:1-16 719
119:89-108 720

Psalms of Zion

48 721
84 722
122 723

Psalms of God's Kingship

97 724
115 725

Psalms of the Messiah-King

2 726
22 727
72:1-7, 17-19 728
110 729

Psalms of Blessing for the People

1 730
67 731
128 732
133 733
134 734

Psalms of Longing

674
Psalm 13

1 How long, O LORD? Will you forget me forever?
How long will you hide your face from me?
2 How long must I wrestle with my thoughts
and every day have sorrow in my heart?
How long will my enemy triumph over me?
3 Look on me and answer, O LORD my God.
Give light to my eyes, or I will sleep in death;
4 my enemy will say, "I have overcome him,"
and my foes will rejoice when I fall.
5 But I trust in your unfailing love;
my heart rejoices in your salvation.
6 I will sing to the LORD,
for he has been good to me.

675
Psalm 42

1 As the deer pants for streams of water,
so my soul pants for you, O God.
2 My soul thirsts for God, for the living God.
When can I go and meet with God?
3 My tears have been my food
day and night,
while men say to me all day long,
"Where is your God?"
4 These things I remember
as I pour out my soul:
how I used to go with the multitude,
leading the procession to the house of God,
with shouts of joy and thanksgiving
among the festive throng.
5 Why are you downcast, O my soul?
Why so disturbed within me?
Put your hope in God,
for I will yet praise him,
my Savior and 6 my God.
My soul is downcast within me;
therefore I will remember you
from the land of the Jordan,
the heights of Hermon—
from Mount Mizar.
7 Deep calls to deep
in the roar of your waterfalls;
all your waves and breakers
have swept over me.
8 By day the LORD directs his love,
at night his song is with me—
a prayer to the God of my life.
9 I say to God my Rock,
"Why have you forgotten me?
Why must I go about mourning,
oppressed by the enemy?"
10 My bones suffer mortal agony
as my foes taunt me,
saying to me all day long,
"Where is your God?"
11 Why are you downcast, O my soul?
Why so disturbed within me?
Put your hope in God,
for I will yet praise him,
my Savior and my God.

676
Psalm 142 (portion)

1 I cry aloud to the LORD;
I lift up my voice to the LORD for mercy.
2 I pour out my complaint before him;
before him I tell my trouble.
3 When my spirit grows faint within me,
it is you who know my way.
In the path where I walk
men have hidden a snare for me.
4 Look to my right and see;
no one is concerned for me.
I have no refuge;
no one cares for my life.

5 I cry to you, O LORD;
I say, "You are my refuge,
my portion in the land of the living."

677
Psalm 143 (portion)

1 O LORD, hear my prayer,
listen to my cry for mercy;
in your faithfulness and righteousness
come to my relief.
2 Do not bring your servant into judgment,
for no one living is righteous before you.
3 The enemy pursues me,
he crushes me to the ground;
he makes me dwell in darkness
like those long dead.
4 So my spirit grows faint within me;
my heart within me is dismayed.
5 I remember the days of long ago;
I meditate on all your works
and consider what your hands have done.
6 I spread out my hands to you;
my soul thirsts for you like a parched land. *Selah*
7 Answer me quickly, O LORD;
my spirit faints with longing.
Do not hide your face from me
or I will be like those who go down to the pit.
8 Let the morning bring me word of your unfailing love,
for I have put my trust in you.
Show me the way I should go,
for to you I lift up my soul.
9 Rescue me from my enemies, O LORD,
for I hide myself in you.
10 Teach me to do your will,
for you are my God;
may your good Spirit
lead me on level ground.
11 For your name's sake, O LORD,
preserve my life;
in your righteousness, bring me out of trouble.

Psalms of Trust

678
Psalm 16

1 Keep me safe, O God,
for in you I take refuge.
2 I said to the LORD, "You are my Lord;
apart from you I have no good thing."
3 As for the saints who are in the land,
they are the glorious ones in whom is all my delight.
4 The sorrows of those will increase
who run after other gods.
I will not pour out their libations of blood
or take up their names on my lips.
5 LORD, you have assigned me my portion and my cup;
you have made my lot secure.
6 The boundary lines have fallen for me in pleasant places;
surely I have a delightful inheritance.
7 I will praise the LORD, who counsels me;
even at night my heart instructs me.
8 I have set the LORD always before me.
Because he is at my right hand,
I will not be shaken.
9 Therefore my heart is glad and my tongue rejoices;
my body also will rest secure,
10 because you will not abandon me to the grave,
nor will you let your Holy One see decay.
11 You have made known to me the path of life;
you will fill me with joy in your presence,
with eternal pleasures at your right hand.

679
Psalm 23

1 The LORD is my shepherd, I shall not be in want.
2 He makes me lie down in green pastures,
he leads me beside quiet waters,
3 **he restores my soul.**
He guides me in paths of righteousness
for his name's sake.
4 Even though I walk
through the valley of the shadow of death,
I will fear no evil,
for you are with me;
your rod and your staff,
they comfort me.
5 You prepare a table before me
in the presence of my enemies.
You anoint my head with oil;
my cup overflows.
6 Surely goodness and love will follow me
all the days of my life,
and I will dwell in the house of the LORD
forever.

680
Psalm 27

1 The LORD is my light and my salvation—
whom shall I fear?
The LORD is the stronghold of my life—
of whom shall I be afraid?
2 When evil men advance against me
to devour my flesh,
when my enemies and my foes attack me,
they will stumble and fall.
3 Though an army besiege me,
my heart will not fear;
though war break out against me,
even then will I be confident.
4 One thing I ask of the LORD,
this is what I seek:
that I may dwell in the house of the LORD
all the days of my life,
to gaze upon the beauty of the LORD
and to seek him in his temple.
5 For in the day of trouble
he will keep me safe in his dwelling;
he will hide me in the shelter of his tabernacle
and set me high upon a rock.
6 Then my head will be exalted
above the enemies who surround me;
at his tabernacle will I sacrifice with shouts of joy;
I will sing and make music to the LORD.
7 Hear my voice when I call, O LORD;
be merciful to me and answer me.
8 My heart says of you, "Seek his face!"
Your face, LORD, I will seek.
9 Do not hide your face from me,
do not turn your servant away in anger;
you have been my helper.
Do not reject me or forsake me,
O God my Savior.
10 Though my father and mother forsake me,
the LORD will receive me.
11 Teach me your way, O LORD;
lead me in a straight path
because of my oppressors.
12 Do not turn me over to the desire of my foes,
for false witnesses rise up against me,
breathing out violence.
13 I am still confident of this:
I will see the goodness of the LORD
in the land of the living.
14 Wait for the LORD;
be strong and take heart
and wait for the LORD.

681
Psalm 31 (portions)

1 In you, O LORD, I have taken refuge;
let me never be put to shame;
deliver me in your righteousness.
2 Turn your ear to me,
come quickly to my rescue;
be my rock of refuge,
a strong fortress to save me.
3 Since you are my rock and my fortress,
for the sake of your name lead and guide me.
4 Free me from the trap that is set for me,
for you are my refuge.
5 Into your hands I commit my spirit;
redeem me, O LORD, the God of truth. . . .
15 My times are in your hands;
deliver me from my enemies
and from those who pursue me.
16 Let your face shine on your servant;
save me in your unfailing love. . . .
19 How great is your goodness,
which you have stored up for those who fear you,
which you bestow in the sight of men
on those who take refuge in you.
20 In the shelter of your presence you hide them
from the intrigues of men;
in your dwelling you keep them safe
from accusing tongues.
21 Praise be to the LORD,
for he showed his wonderful love to me
when I was in a besieged city.
22 In my alarm I said,
"I am cut off from your sight!"
Yet you heard my cry for mercy
when I called to you for help.
23 Love the LORD, all his saints!
The LORD preserves the faithful,
but the proud he pays back in full.
24 Be strong and take heart,
all you who hope in the LORD.

682
Psalm 37 (portions)

1 Do not fret because of evil men
or be envious of those who do wrong;
2 for like the grass they will soon wither,
like green plants they will soon die away.
3 Trust in the LORD and do good;
dwell in the land and enjoy safe pasture.
4 Delight yourself in the LORD
and he will give you the desires of your heart.
5 Commit your way to the LORD;
trust in him and he will do this:
6 He will make your righteousness shine like the dawn,
the justice of your cause like the noonday sun.
7 Be still before the LORD and wait patiently for him;
do not fret when men succeed in their ways,
when they carry out their wicked schemes.
8 Refrain from anger and turn from wrath;
do not fret—it leads only to evil. . . .
23 If the LORD delights in a man's way,
he makes his steps firm;
24 though he stumble, he will not fall,
for the LORD upholds him with his hand.
25 I was young and now I am old,
yet I have never seen the righteous forsaken
or their children begging bread.
26 They are always generous and lend freely;
their children will be blessed.
27 Turn from evil and do good;
then you will dwell in the land forever.
28 For the LORD loves the just
and will not forsake his faithful ones.

They will be protected forever,
but the offspring of the wicked
will be cut off;
29 the righteous will inherit the land
and dwell in it forever.
30 The mouth of the righteous man
utters wisdom,
and his tongue speaks what is just.
31 The law of his God is in his heart;
his feet do not slip. . . .
37 Consider the blameless, observe the
upright;
there is a future for the man of
peace.

683
Psalm 46

1 God is our refuge and strength,
an ever-present help in trouble.
2 Therefore we will not fear, though
the earth give way
and the mountains fall into the
heart of the sea,
3 though its waters roar and foam
and the mountains quake with
their surging. *Selah*
4 There is a river whose streams make
glad the city of God,
the holy place where the Most
High dwells.
5 God is within her, she will not fall;
God will help her at break of day.
6 Nations are in uproar, kingdoms
fall;
he lifts his voice, the earth melts.
7 The LORD Almighty is with us;
the God of Jacob is our fortress.
Selah
8 Come and see the works of the LORD,
the desolations he has brought on
the earth.
9 He makes wars cease to the ends of
the earth;
he breaks the bow and shatters the
spear,
he burns the shields with fire.
10 "Be still, and know that I am God;
I will be exalted among the nations,
I will be exalted in the earth."
11 The LORD Almighty is with us;
the God of Jacob is our fortress.
Selah

684
Psalm 63

1 O God, you are my God,
earnestly I seek you;
my soul thirsts for you,
my body longs for you,
in a dry and weary land
where there is no water.
2 I have seen you in the sanctuary
and beheld your power and your
glory.
3 Because your love is better than life,
my lips will glorify you.
4 I will praise you as long as I live,
and in your name I will lift up my
hands.
5 My soul will be satisfied as with the
richest of foods;
with singing lips my mouth will
praise you.
6 On my bed I remember you;
I think of you through the watches
of the night.
7 Because you are my help,
I sing in the shadow of your wings.
8 My soul clings to you;
your right hand upholds me.
9 They who seek my life will be
destroyed;
they will go down to the depths of
the earth.
10 They will be given over to the sword
and become food for jackals.
11 But the king will rejoice in God;
all who swear by God's name will
praise him,
while the mouths of liars will be
silenced.

685
Psalm 71 (portions)

1 In you, O LORD, I have taken refuge;
let me never be put to shame.
2 Rescue me and deliver me in your righteousness;
turn your ear to me and save me.
3 Be my rock of refuge,
to which I can always go;
give the command to save me,
for you are my rock and my fortress.
4 Deliver me, O my God, from the hand of the wicked,
from the grasp of evil and cruel men.
5 For you have been my hope,
O Sovereign LORD,
my confidence since my youth.
6 From birth I have relied on you;
you brought me forth from my mother's womb.
I will ever praise you. . . .
17 Since my youth, O God, you have taught me,
and to this day I declare your marvelous deeds.
18 Even when I am old and gray,
do not forsake me, O God,
till I declare your power to the next generation,
your might to all who are to come.
19 Your righteousness reaches to the skies, O God,
you who have done great things.
Who, O God, is like you?
20 Though you have made me see troubles, many and bitter,
you will restore my life again;
from the depths of the earth
you will again bring me up.
21 You will increase my honor
and comfort me once again.
22 I will praise you with the harp
for your faithfulness, O my God;
I will sing praise to you with the lyre,
O Holy One of Israel.
23 My lips will shout for joy
when I sing praise to you—
I, whom you have redeemed.
24 My tongue will tell of your righteous acts
all day long,
for those who wanted to harm me
have been put to shame and confusion.

686
Psalm 86

1 Hear, O LORD, and answer me,
for I am poor and needy.
2 Guard my life, for I am devoted to you.
You are my God; save your servant who trusts in you.
3 Have mercy on me, O Lord,
for I call to you all day long.
4 Bring joy to your servant,
for to you, O Lord,
I lift up my soul.
5 You are forgiving and good, O Lord,
abounding in love to all who call to you.
6 Hear my prayer, O LORD;
listen to my cry for mercy.
7 In the day of my trouble I will call to you,
for you will answer me.
8 Among the gods there is none like you, O Lord;
no deeds can compare with yours.
9 All the nations you have made
will come and worship before you, O Lord;
they will bring glory to your name.
10 For you are great and do marvelous deeds;
you alone are God.
11 Teach me your way, O LORD,
and I will walk in your truth;
give me an undivided heart,
that I may fear your name.

12 I will praise you, O Lord my God,
with all my heart;
I will glorify your name forever.
**13 For great is your love toward me;
you have delivered me from the
depths of the grave.**
14 The arrogant are attacking me, O
God;
a band of ruthless men seeks my
life—
men without regard for you.
**15 But you, O Lord, are a compassionate
and gracious God,
slow to anger, abounding in love
and faithfulness.**
16 Turn to me and have mercy on me;
grant your strength to your servant
and save the son of your
maidservant.
**17 Give me a sign of your goodness,
that my enemies may see it and be
put to shame,
for you, O LORD, have helped me
and comforted me.**

687
Psalm 91

1 He who dwells in the shelter of the
Most High
will rest in the shadow of the
Almighty.
**2 I will say of the LORD, "He is my
refuge and my fortress,
my God, in whom I trust."**
3 Surely he will save you from the
fowler's snare
and from the deadly pestilence.
**4 He will cover you with his feathers,
and under his wings you will find
refuge;
his faithfulness will be your shield
and rampart.**
5 You will not fear the terror of night,
nor the arrow that flies by day,
**6 nor the pestilence that stalks in the
darkness,
nor the plague that destroys at
midday.**
7 A thousand may fall at your side,
ten thousand at your right hand,
but it will not come near you.
**8 You will only observe with your eyes
and see the punishment of the
wicked.**
9 If you make the Most High your
dwelling—
even the LORD, who is my refuge—
**10 then no harm will befall you,
no disaster will come near your
tent.**
11 For he will command his angels
concerning you
to guard you in all your ways;
**12 they will lift you up in their hands,
so that you will not strike your
foot against a stone.**
13 You will tread upon the lion and the
cobra;
you will trample the great lion and
the serpent.
**14 "Because he loves me," says the
LORD, "I will rescue him;
I will protect him, for he
acknowledges my name.**
15 He will call upon me, and I will
answer him;
I will be with him in trouble,
I will deliver him and honor him.
**16 With long life will I satisfy him
and show him my salvation."**

688
Psalm 121

1 I lift up my eyes to the hills—
where does my help come from?
**2 My help comes from the LORD,
the Maker of heaven and earth.**
3 He will not let your foot slip—
he who watches over you will not
slumber;
**4 indeed, he who watches over Israel
will neither slumber nor sleep.**

5 The LORD watches over you—
the LORD is your shade at your right hand;
6 the sun will not harm you by day,
nor the moon by night.
7 The LORD will keep you from all harm—
he will watch over your life;
8 the LORD will watch over your coming and going
both now and forevermore.

689

Psalm 127

1 Unless the LORD builds the house,
its builders labor in vain.
Unless the LORD watches over the city,
the watchmen stand guard in vain.
2 In vain you rise early
and stay up late,
toiling for food to eat—
for he grants sleep to those he loves.
3 Sons are a heritage from the LORD,
children a reward from him.
4 Like arrows in the hands of a warrior
are sons born in one's youth.
5 Blessed is the man
whose quiver is full of them.
They will not be put to shame
when they contend with their enemies in the gate.

690

Psalm 130

1 Out of the depths I cry to you, O LORD;
2 O Lord, hear my voice.
Let your ears be attentive
to my cry for mercy.
3 If you, O LORD, kept a record of sins,
O Lord, who could stand?
4 But with you there is forgiveness;
therefore you are feared.
5 I wait for the LORD, my soul waits,
and in his word I put my hope.
6 My soul waits for the Lord
more than watchmen wait for the morning,
more than watchmen wait for the morning.
7 O Israel, put your hope in the LORD,
for with the LORD is unfailing love
and with him is full redemption.
8 He himself will redeem Israel
from all their sins.

691

Psalm 139 (portions)

1 O LORD, you have searched me
and you know me.
2 You know when I sit and when I rise;
you perceive my thoughts from afar.
3 You discern my going out and my lying down;
you are familiar with all my ways.
4 Before a word is on my tongue
you know it completely, O LORD.
5 You hem me in—behind and before;
you have laid your hand upon me.
6 Such knowledge is too wonderful for me,
too lofty for me to attain.
7 Where can I go from your Spirit?
Where can I flee from your presence?
8 If I go up to the heavens, you are there;
if I make my bed in the depths, you are there.
9 If I rise on the wings of the dawn,
if I settle on the far side of the sea,
10 even there your hand will guide me,
your right hand will hold me fast.
11 If I say, "Surely the darkness will hide me
and the light become night around me,"
12 even the darkness will not be dark to you;

the night will shine like the day,
for darkness is as light to you. . . .

17 How precious to me are your thoughts, O God!
How vast is the sum of them!

18 Were I to count them,
they would outnumber the grains of sand.
When I awake,
I am still with you. . . .

23 Search me, O God, and know my heart;
test me and know my anxious thoughts.

24 See if there is any offensive way in me,
and lead me in the way everlasting.

Psalms of Penitence

(See also No. 276, Psalm 25)

692
Psalm 38

1 O LORD, do not rebuke me in your anger
or discipline me in your wrath.

2 For your arrows have pierced me,
and your hand has come down upon me.

3 Because of your wrath there is no health in my body;
my bones have no soundness because of my sin.

4 My guilt has overwhelmed me
like a burden too heavy to bear.

5 My wounds fester and are loathsome
because of my sinful folly.

6 I am bowed down and brought very low;
all day long I go about mourning.

7 My back is filled with searing pain;
there is no health in my body.

8 I am feeble and utterly crushed;
I groan in anguish of heart.

9 All my longings lie open before you, O Lord;
my sighing is not hidden from you.

10 My heart pounds, my strength fails me;
even the light has gone from my eyes.

11 My friends and companions avoid me because of my wounds;
my neighbors stay far away.

12 Those who seek my life set their traps,
those who would harm me talk of my ruin;
all day long they plot deception.

13 I am like a deaf man, who cannot hear,
like a mute, who cannot open his mouth;

14 I have become like a man who does not hear,
whose mouth can offer no reply.

15 I wait for you, O LORD;
you will answer, O Lord my God.

16 For I said, "Do not let them gloat
or exalt themselves over me when my foot slips."

17 For I am about to fall,
and my pain is ever with me.

18 I confess my iniquity;
I am troubled by my sin.

19 Many are those who are my vigorous enemies;
those who hate me without reason are numerous.

20 Those who repay my good with evil
slander me when I pursue what is good.

21 O LORD, do not forsake me;
be not far from me, O my God.

22 Come quickly to help me,
O Lord my Savior.

693
Psalm 51 (portion)

1 Have mercy on me, O God,
according to your unfailing love;

according to your great compassion
blot out my transgressions.
2 Wash away all my iniquity
and cleanse me from my sin.
3 For I know my transgressions,
and my sin is always before me.
4 Against you, you only, have I sinned
and done what is evil in your sight,
so that you are proved right when you speak
and justified when you judge.
5 Surely I was sinful at birth,
sinful from the time my mother conceived me.
6 Surely you desire truth in the inner parts;
you teach me wisdom in the inmost place.
7 Cleanse me with hyssop, and I will be clean;
wash me, and I will be whiter than snow.
8 Let me hear joy and gladness;
let the bones you have crushed rejoice.
9 Hide your face from my sins
and blot out all my iniquity.
10 Create in me a pure heart, O God,
and renew a steadfast spirit within me.
11 Do not cast me from your presence
or take your Holy Spirit from me.
12 Restore to me the joy of your salvation
and grant me a willing spirit, to sustain me.
13 Then I will teach transgressors your ways,
and sinners will turn back to you.
14 Save me from bloodguilt, O God,
the God who saves me,
and my tongue will sing of your righteousness.
15 O Lord, open my lips,
and my mouth will declare your praise.
16 You do not delight in sacrifice, or I would bring it;
you do not take pleasure in burnt offerings.
17 The sacrifices of God are a broken spirit;
a broken and contrite heart,
O God, you will not despise.

694
Psalm 85

1 You showed favor to your land, O LORD;
you restored the fortunes of Jacob.
2 You forgave the iniquity of your people
and covered all their sins. *Selah*
3 You set aside all your wrath
and turned from your fierce anger.
4 Restore us again, O God our Savior,
and put away your displeasure toward us.
5 Will you be angry with us forever?
Will you prolong your anger through all generations?
6 Will you not revive us again,
that your people may rejoice in you?
7 Show us your unfailing love, O LORD,
and grant us your salvation.
8 I will listen to what God the LORD will say;
he promises peace to his people, his saints—
but let them not return to folly.
9 Surely his salvation is near those who fear him,
that his glory may dwell in our land.
10 Love and faithfulness meet together;
righteousness and peace kiss each other.
11 Faithfulness springs forth from the earth,
and righteousness looks down from heaven.

12 The LORD will indeed give what is good,
and our land will yield its harvest.
13 Righteousness goes before him
and prepares the way for his steps.

Psalms of Thanksgiving for Deliverance

695
Psalm 30

1 I will exalt you, O LORD,
for you lifted me out of the depths
and did not let my enemies gloat over me.
2 O LORD my God, I called to you for help
and you healed me.
3 O LORD, you brought me up from the grave;
you spared me from going down into the pit.
4 Sing to the LORD, you saints of his;
praise his holy name.
5 For his anger lasts only a moment,
but his favor lasts a lifetime;
weeping may remain for a night,
but rejoicing comes in the morning.
6 When I felt secure, I said,
"I will never be shaken."
7 O LORD, when you favored me,
you made my mountain stand firm;
but when you hid your face,
I was dismayed.
8 To you, O LORD, I called;
to the Lord I cried for mercy:
9 "What gain is there in my destruction,
in my going down into the pit?
Will the dust praise you?
Will it proclaim your faithfulness?
10 Hear, O LORD, and be merciful to me;
O LORD, be my help."
11 You turned my wailing into dancing;
you removed my sackcloth and clothed me with joy,
12 that my heart may sing to you and not be silent.
O LORD my God, I will give you thanks forever.

696
Psalm 34

1 I will extol the LORD at all times;
his praise will always be on my lips.
2 My soul will boast in the LORD;
let the afflicted hear and rejoice.
3 Glorify the LORD with me;
let us exalt his name together.
4 I sought the LORD, and he answered me;
he delivered me from all my fears.
5 Those who look to him are radiant;
their faces are never covered with shame.
6 This poor man called, and the LORD heard him;
he saved him out of all his troubles.
7 The angel of the LORD encamps around those who fear him,
and he delivers them.
8 Taste and see that the LORD is good;
blessed is the man who takes refuge in him.
9 Fear the LORD, you his saints,
for those who fear him lack nothing.
10 The lions may grow weak and hungry,
but those who seek the LORD lack no good thing.
11 Come, my children, listen to me;
I will teach you the fear of the LORD.
12 Whoever of you loves life
and desires to see many good days,
13 keep your tongue from evil
and your lips from speaking lies.
14 Turn from evil and do good;
seek peace and pursue it.
15 The eyes of the LORD are on the righteous

and his ears are attentive to their cry;
16 the face of the LORD is against those who do evil,
to cut off the memory of them from the earth.
17 The righteous cry out, and the LORD hears them;
he delivers them from all their troubles.
18 The LORD is close to the brokenhearted
and saves those who are crushed in spirit.
19 A righteous man may have many troubles,
but the LORD delivers him from them all;
20 he protects all his bones,
not one of them will be broken.
21 Evil will slay the wicked;
the foes of the righteous will be condemned.
22 The LORD redeems his servants;
no one will be condemned who takes refuge in him.

697

Psalm 40 (portions)

1 I waited patiently for the LORD;
he turned to me and heard my cry.
2 He lifted me out of the slimy pit,
out of the mud and mire;
he set my feet on a rock
and gave me a firm place to stand.
3 He put a new song in my mouth,
a hymn of praise to our God.
Many will see and fear
and put their trust in the LORD.
4 Blessed is the man
who makes the LORD his trust,
who does not look to the proud,
to those who turn aside to false gods.
5 Many, O LORD my God,
are the wonders you have done.
The things you planned for us
no one can recount to you;
were I to speak and tell of them,
they would be too many to declare.
6 Sacrifice and offering you did not desire,
but my ears you have pierced;
burnt offerings and sin offerings
you did not require.
7 Then I said, "Here I am, I have come—
it is written about me in the scroll.
8 I desire to do your will, O my God;
your law is within my heart."
9 I proclaim righteousness in the great assembly;
I do not seal my lips,
as you know, O LORD.
10 I do not hide your righteousness in my heart;
I speak of your faithfulness and salvation.
I do not conceal your love and your truth
from the great assembly.
11 Do not withhold your mercy from me, O LORD;
may your love and your truth always protect me.
12 For troubles without number surround me;
my sins have overtaken me, and I cannot see.
They are more than the hairs of my head,
and my heart fails within me.
13 Be pleased, O LORD, to save me;
O LORD, come quickly to help me. . . .
16 May all who seek you
rejoice and be glad in you;
may those who love your salvation always say,
"The LORD be exalted!"
17 Yet I am poor and needy;
may the Lord think of me.
You are my help and my deliverer;
O my God, do not delay.

698
Psalm 57

1 Have mercy on me, O God, have mercy on me,
for in you my soul takes refuge.
I will take refuge in the shadow of your wings
until the disaster has passed.
2 I cry out to God Most High,
to God, who fulfills his purpose for me.
3 He sends from heaven and saves me,
rebuking those who hotly pursue me; *Selah*
God sends his love and his faithfulness.
4 I am in the midst of lions;
I lie among ravenous beasts—
men whose teeth are spears and arrows,
whose tongues are sharp swords.
5 Be exalted, O God, above the heavens;
let your glory be over all the earth.
6 They spread a net for my feet—
I was bowed down in distress.
They dug a pit in my path—
but they have fallen into it themselves. *Selah*
7 My heart is steadfast, O God,
my heart is steadfast;
I will sing and make music.
8 Awake, my soul!
Awake, harp and lyre!
I will awaken the dawn.
9 I will praise you, O Lord, among the nations;
I will sing of you among the peoples.
10 For great is your love, reaching to the heavens;
your faithfulness reaches to the skies.
11 Be exalted, O God, above the heavens;
let your glory be over all the earth.

699
Psalm 66 (portions)

1 Shout with joy to God, all the earth!
2 Sing the glory of his name;
make his praise glorious!
3 Say to God, "How awesome are your deeds!
So great is your power
that your enemies cringe before you.
4 All the earth bows down to you;
they sing praise to you,
they sing praise to your name." *Selah*
5 Come and see what God has done,
how awesome his works in man's behalf!
6 He turned the sea into dry land,
they passed through the waters on foot—
come, let us rejoice in him.
7 He rules forever by his power,
his eyes watch the nations—
let not the rebellious rise up against him. *Selah*
8 Praise our God, O peoples,
let the sound of his praise be heard;
9 he has preserved our lives
and kept our feet from slipping. . . .
16 Come and listen, all you who fear God;
let me tell you what he has done for me.
17 I cried out to him with my mouth;
his praise was on my tongue.
18 If I had cherished sin in my heart,
the Lord would not have listened;
19 but God has surely listened
and heard my voice in prayer.
20 Praise be to God,
who has not rejected my prayer
or withheld his love from me!

700

Psalm 107 (portion)

1 Give thanks to the LORD, for he is good;
his love endures forever.
2 Let the redeemed of the LORD say this—
those he redeemed from the hand of the foe,
3 those he gathered from the lands,
from east and west, from north and south.
4 Some wandered in desert wastelands,
finding no way to a city where they could settle.
5 They were hungry and thirsty,
and their lives ebbed away.
6 Then they cried out to the LORD in their trouble,
and he delivered them from their distress.
7 He led them by a straight way
to a city where they could settle.
8 Let them give thanks to the LORD for his unfailing love
and his wonderful deeds for men,
9 for he satisfies the thirsty
and fills the hungry with good things.
10 Some sat in darkness and the deepest gloom,
prisoners suffering in iron chains,
11 for they had rebelled against the words of God
and despised the counsel of the Most High.
12 So he subjected them to bitter labor;
they stumbled, and there was no one to help.
13 Then they cried to the LORD in their trouble,
and he saved them from their distress.
14 He brought them out of darkness and the deepest gloom
and broke away their chains.
15 Let them give thanks to the LORD for his unfailing love
and his wonderful deeds for men,
16 for he breaks down gates of bronze
and cuts through bars of iron.
17 Some became fools through their rebellious ways
and suffered affliction because of their iniquities.
18 They loathed all food
and drew near the gates of death.
19 Then they cried to the LORD in their trouble,
and he saved them from their distress.
20 He sent forth his word and healed them;
he rescued them from the grave.
21 Let them give thanks to the LORD for his unfailing love
and his wonderful deeds for men.
22 Let them sacrifice thank offerings
and tell of his works with songs of joy.

701

Psalm 116 (portions)

1 I love the LORD, for he heard my voice;
he heard my cry for mercy.
2 Because he turned his ear to me,
I will call on him as long as I live.
3 The cords of death entangled me,
the anguish of the grave came upon me;
I was overcome by trouble and sorrow.
4 Then I called on the name of the Lord:
"O LORD, save me!"
5 The LORD is gracious and righteous;
our God is full of compassion.
6 The LORD protects the simplehearted;
when I was in great need, he saved me.
7 Be at rest once more, O my soul,
for the LORD has been good to you.
8 For you, O LORD, have delivered my soul from death,

my eyes from tears,
my feet from stumbling,
9 that I may walk before the LORD
in the land of the living. . . .
12 How can I repay the LORD
for all his goodness to me?
13 I will lift up the cup of salvation
and call on the name of the LORD.
14 I will fulfill my vows to the LORD
in the presence of all his people.
15 Precious in the sight of the LORD
is the death of his saints.
16 O LORD, truly I am your servant;
I am your servant, the son of your maidservant;
you have freed me from my chains.
17 I will sacrifice a thank offering to you
and call on the name of the LORD.
18 I will fulfill my vows to the LORD
in the presence of all his people,
19 in the courts of the house of the LORD—
in your midst, O Jerusalem.
Praise the LORD.

Psalms of Thanksgiving for Forgiveness

702
Psalm 32

1 Blessed is he
whose transgressions are forgiven,
whose sins are covered.
2 Blessed is the man
whose sin the LORD does not count against him
and in whose spirit is no deceit.
3 When I kept silent,
my bones wasted away
through my groaning all day long.
4 For day and night
your hand was heavy upon me;
my strength was sapped
as in the heat of summer. *Selah*
5 Then I acknowledged my sin to you
and did not cover up my iniquity.
I said, "I will confess
my transgressions to the Lord"—
and you forgave
the guilt of my sin. *Selah*
6 Therefore let everyone who is godly pray to you
while you may be found;
surely when the mighty waters rise,
they will not reach him.
7 You are my hiding place;
you will protect me from trouble
and surround me with songs of deliverance. *Selah*
8 I will instruct you and teach you in the way you should go;
I will counsel you and watch over you.
9 Do not be like the horse or the mule,
which have no understanding
but must be controlled by bit and bridle
or they will not come to you.
10 Many are the woes of the wicked,
but the LORD's unfailing love
surrounds the man who trusts in him.
11 Rejoice in the Lord and be glad, you righteous;
sing, all you who are upright in heart!

703
Psalm 65

1 Praise awaits you, O God, in Zion;
to you our vows will be fulfilled.
2 O you who hear prayer,
to you all men will come.
3 When we were overwhelmed by sins,
you forgave our transgressions.
4 Blessed are those you choose
and bring near to live in your courts!
We are filled with the good things of your house,
of your holy temple.
5 You answer us with awesome deeds of righteousness,

O God our Savior,
the hope of all the ends of the earth
and of the farthest seas,
6 who formed the mountains by your power,
having armed yourself with strength,
7 who stilled the roaring of the seas,
the roaring of their waves,
and the turmoil of the nations.
8 Those living far away fear your wonders;
where morning dawns and evening fades
you call forth songs of joy.
9 You care for the land and water it;
you enrich it abundantly.
The streams of God are filled with water
to provide the people with grain,
for so you have ordained it.
10 You drench its furrows
and level its ridges;
you soften it with showers
and bless its crops.
11 You crown the year with your bounty,
and your carts overflow with abundance.
12 The grasslands of the desert overflow;
the hills are clothed with gladness.
13 The meadows are covered with flocks
and the valleys are mantled with grain;
they shout for joy and sing.

704
Psalm 103

1 Praise the LORD, O my soul;
all my inmost being, praise his holy name.
2 Praise the LORD, O my soul,
and forget not all his benefits—
3 who forgives all your sins
and heals all your diseases,
4 who redeems your life from the pit
and crowns you with love and compassion,
5 who satisfies your desires with good things
so that your youth is renewed like the eagle's.
6 The LORD works righteousness
and justice for all the oppressed.
7 He made known his ways to Moses,
his deeds to the people of Israel:
8 The LORD is compassionate and gracious,
slow to anger, abounding in love.
9 He will not always accuse,
nor will he harbor his anger forever;
10 he does not treat us as our sins deserve
or repay us according to our iniquities.
11 For as high as the heavens are above the earth,
so great is his love for those who fear him;
12 as far as the east is from the west,
so far has he removed our transgressions from us.
13 As a father has compassion on his children,
so the LORD has compassion on those who fear him;
14 for he knows how we are formed,
he remembers that we are dust.
15 As for man, his days are like grass,
he flourishes like a flower of the field;
16 the wind blows over it and it is gone,
and its place remembers it no more.
17 But from everlasting to everlasting
the LORD's love is with those who fear him,
and his righteousness with their children's children—
18 with those who keep his covenant
and remember to obey his precepts.
19 The LORD has established his throne in heaven,
and his kingdom rules over all.

20 Praise the LORD, you his angels,
you mighty ones who do his bidding,
who obey his word.
21 Praise the LORD, all his heavenly hosts,
you his servants who do his will.
22 Praise the LORD, all his works
everywhere in his dominion.
Praise the LORD, O my soul.

Psalms of Praise and Calls to Worship

705
Psalm 24

1 The earth is the LORD's, and everything in it,
the world, and all who live in it;
2 for he founded it upon the seas
and established it upon the waters.
3 Who may ascend the hill of the LORD?
Who may stand in his holy place?
4 He who has clean hands and a pure heart,
who does not lift up his soul to an idol
or swear by what is false.
5 He will receive blessing from the LORD
and vindication from God his Savior.
6 Such is the generation of those who seek him,
who seek your face, O God of Jacob. *Selah*
7 Lift up your heads, O you gates;
be lifted up, you ancient doors,
that the King of glory may come in.
8 Who is this King of glory?
The LORD strong and mighty,
the LORD mighty in battle.
9 Lift up your heads, O you gates;
lift them up, you ancient doors,
that the King of glory may come in.
10 Who is he, this King of glory?
The LORD Almighty—
he is the King of glory. *Selah*

706
Psalm 95

1 Come, let us sing for joy to the LORD;
let us shout aloud to the Rock of our salvation.
2 Let us come before him with thanksgiving
and extol him with music and song.
3 For the LORD is the great God,
the great King above all gods.
4 In his hand are the depths of the earth,
and the mountain peaks belong to him.
5 The sea is his, for he made it,
and his hands formed the dry land.
6 Come, let us bow down in worship,
let us kneel before the LORD our Maker;
7 for he is our God
and we are the people of his pasture,
the flock under his care.
Today, if you hear his voice,
8 do not harden your hearts as you did at Meribah,
as you did that day at Massah in the desert,
9 where your fathers tested and tried me,
though they had seen what I did.
10 For forty years I was angry with that generation;
I said, "They are a people whose hearts go astray,
and they have not known my ways."
11 So I declared on oath in my anger,
"They shall never enter my rest."

707
Psalm 96

1 Sing to the LORD a new song;
sing to the LORD, all the earth.
2 Sing to the LORD, praise his name;
proclaim his salvation day after day.
3 Declare his glory among the nations,
his marvelous deeds among all peoples.
4 For great is the LORD and most worthy of praise;
he is to be feared above all gods.
5 For all the gods of the nations are idols,
but the LORD made the heavens.
6 Splendor and majesty are before him;
strength and glory are in his sanctuary.
7 Ascribe to the LORD, O families of nations,
ascribe to the LORD glory and strength.
8 Ascribe to the LORD the glory due his name;
bring an offering and come into his courts.
9 Worship the LORD in the splendor of his holiness;
tremble before him, all the earth.
10 Say among the nations, "The LORD reigns."
The world is firmly established, it cannot be moved;
he will judge the peoples with equity.
11 Let the heavens rejoice, let the earth be glad;
let the sea resound, and all that is in it;
12 let the fields be jubilant, and everything in them.
Then all the trees of the forest will sing for joy;
13 they will sing before the LORD, for he comes,
he comes to judge the earth.
He will judge the world in righteousness
and the peoples in his truth.

708
Psalm 98

1 Sing to the LORD a new song,
for he has done marvelous things;
his right hand and his holy arm
have worked salvation for him.
2 The LORD has made his salvation known
and revealed his righteousness to the nations.
3 He has remembered his love
and his faithfulness to the house of Israel;
all the ends of the earth have seen the salvation of our God.
4 Shout for joy to the LORD, all the earth,
burst into jubilant song with music;
5 make music to the LORD with the harp,
with the harp and the sound of singing,
6 with trumpets and the blast of the ram's horn—
shout for joy before the LORD, the King.
7 Let the sea resound, and everything in it,
the world, and all who live in it.
8 Let the rivers clap their hands,
let the mountains sing together for joy;
9 let them sing before the LORD,
for he comes to judge the earth.
He will judge the world in righteousness
and the peoples with equity.

709
Psalm 100

1 Shout for joy to the LORD, all the earth.
2 Worship the LORD with gladness;
come before him with joyful songs.

3 Know that the LORD is God.
It is he who made us, and we are his;
we are his people, the sheep of his pasture.
4 Enter his gates with thanksgiving
and his courts with praise;
give thanks to him and praise his name.
5 For the LORD is good and his love endures forever;
his faithfulness continues through all generations.

710
Psalm 145

1 I will exalt you, my God the King;
I will praise your name for ever and ever.
2 Every day I will praise you
and extol your name for ever and ever.
3 Great is the LORD and most worthy of praise;
his greatness no one can fathom.
4 One generation will commend your works to another;
they will tell of your mighty acts.
5 They will speak of the glorious splendor of your majesty,
and I will meditate on your wonderful works.
6 They will tell of the power of your awesome works,
and I will proclaim your great deeds.
7 They will celebrate your abundant goodness
and joyfully sing of your righteousness.
8 The LORD is gracious and compassionate,
slow to anger and rich in love.
9 The LORD is good to all;
he has compassion on all he has made.
10 All you have made will praise you, O LORD;
your saints will extol you.
11 They will tell of the glory of your kingdom
and speak of your might,
12 so that all men may know of your mighty acts
and the glorious splendor of your kingdom.
13 Your kingdom is an everlasting kingdom,
and your dominion endures through all generations.
The LORD is faithful to all his promises
and loving toward all he has made.
14 The LORD upholds all those who fall
and lifts up all who are bowed down.
15 The eyes of all look to you,
and you give them their food at the proper time.
16 You open your hand
and satisfy the desires of every living thing.
17 The LORD is righteous in all his ways
and loving toward all he has made.
18 The LORD is near to all who call on him,
to all who call on him in truth.
19 He fulfills the desires of those who fear him;
he hears their cry and saves them.
20 The LORD watches over all who love him,
but all the wicked he will destroy.
21 My mouth will speak in praise of the LORD.
Let every creature praise his holy name
for ever and ever.

711
Psalm 146

1 Praise the LORD.
Praise the LORD, O my soul.

2 I will praise the LORD all my life;
I will sing praise to my God as long as I live.
3 Do not put your trust in princes,
in mortal men, who cannot save.
4 When their spirit departs, they return to the ground;
on that very day their plans come to nothing.
5 Blessed is he whose help is the God of Jacob,
whose hope is in the LORD his God,
6 the Maker of heaven and earth,
the sea, and everything in them—
the LORD, who remains faithful forever.
7 He upholds the cause of the oppressed
and gives food to the hungry.
The LORD sets prisoners free,
8 the LORD gives sight to the blind,
the LORD lifts up those who are bowed down,
the LORD loves the righteous.
9 The LORD watches over the alien
and sustains the fatherless and the widow,
but he frustrates the ways of the wicked.
10 The LORD reigns forever,
your God, O Zion, for all generations.
Praise the LORD.

712

Psalm 147 (portion)

1 Praise the LORD.
How good it is to sing praises to our God,
how pleasant and fitting to praise him!
2 The LORD builds up Jerusalem;
he gathers the exiles of Israel.
3 He heals the brokenhearted
and binds up their wounds.
4 He determines the number of the stars
and calls them each by name.
5 Great is our Lord and mighty in power;
his understanding has no limit.
6 The LORD sustains the humble
but casts the wicked to the ground.
7 Sing to the LORD with thanksgiving;
make music to our God on the harp.

713

Psalm 150

1 Praise the LORD.
Praise God in his sanctuary;
praise him in his mighty heavens.
2 Praise him for his acts of power;
praise him for his surpassing greatness.
3 Praise him with the sounding of the trumpet,
praise him with the harp and lyre,
4 praise him with tambourine and dancing,
praise him with the strings and flute,
5 praise him with the clash of cymbals,
praise him with resounding cymbals.
6 Let everything that has breath praise the LORD.
Praise the LORD.

Psalms of Praise for Creation

714

Psalm 8

1 O LORD, our Lord,
how majestic is your name in all the earth!
You have set your glory
above the heavens.
2 From the lips of children and infants
you have ordained praise
because of your enemies,
to silence the foe and the avenger.

3 When I consider your heavens,
the work of your fingers,
the moon and the stars,
which you have set in place,
4 what is man that you are mindful of him,
the son of man that you care for him?
5 You made him a little lower than the heavenly beings
and crowned him with glory and honor.
6 You made him ruler over the works of your hands;
you put everything under his feet:
7 all flocks and herds,
and the beasts of the field,
8 the birds of the air,
and the fish of the sea,
all that swim the paths of the seas.
9 O LORD, our Lord,
how majestic is your name in all the earth!

715

Psalm 19 (portion)

1 The heavens declare the glory of God;
the skies proclaim the work of his hands.
2 Day after day they pour forth speech;
night after night they display knowledge.
3 There is no speech or language
where their voice is not heard.
4 Their voice goes out into all the earth,
their words to the ends of the world.
In the heavens he has pitched a tent for the sun,
5 which is like a bridegroom coming forth from his pavilion,
like a champion rejoicing to run his course.
6 It rises at one end of the heavens
and makes its circuit to the other;
nothing is hidden from its heat.

716

Psalm 104 (portions)

1 Praise the LORD, O my soul.
O LORD my God, you are very great;
you are clothed with splendor and majesty.
2 He wraps himself in light as with a garment;
he stretches out the heavens like a tent
3 and lays the beams of his upper chambers on their waters.
He makes the clouds his chariot
and rides on the wings of the wind.
4 He makes winds his messengers,
flames of fire his servants.
5 He set the earth on its foundations;
it can never be moved.
6 You covered it with the deep as with a garment;
the waters stood above the mountains.
7 But at your rebuke the waters fled,
at the sound of your thunder they took to flight;
8 they flowed over the mountains,
they went down into the valleys,
to the place you assigned for them.
9 You set a boundary they cannot cross;
never again will they cover the earth.
10 He makes springs pour water into the ravines;
it flows between the mountains. . . .
24 How many are your works, O LORD!
In wisdom you made them all;
the earth is full of your creatures.
25 There is the sea, vast and spacious,
teeming with creatures beyond number—
living things both large and small.
26 There the ships go to and fro,
and the leviathan, which you formed to frolic there.
27 These all look to you
to give them their food at the proper time.

28 When you give it to them,
they gather it up;
when you open your hand,
they are satisfied with good things.
29 When you hide your face,
they are terrified;
when you take away their breath,
they die and return to the dust.
30 When you send your Spirit,
they are created,
and you renew the face of the earth.
31 May the glory of the LORD endure
forever;
may the LORD rejoice in his works—
32 he who looks at the earth, and it
trembles,
who touches the mountains, and
they smoke.
33 I will sing to the LORD all my life;
I will sing praise to my God as long
as I live.
34 May my meditation be pleasing to him,
as I rejoice in the LORD.

Psalms of Praise for the Word

717
Psalm 19 (portion)

7 The law of the LORD is perfect,
reviving the soul.
The statutes of the LORD are
trustworthy,
making wise the simple.
8 The precepts of the LORD are right,
giving joy to the heart.
The commands of the LORD are
radiant,
giving light to the eyes.
9 The fear of the LORD is pure,
enduring forever.
The ordinances of the LORD are sure
and altogether righteous.
10 They are more precious than gold,
than much pure gold;
they are sweeter than honey,
than honey from the comb.
11 By them is your servant warned;
in keeping them there is great
reward.
12 Who can discern his errors?
Forgive my hidden faults.
13 Keep your servant also from willful
sins;
may they not rule over me.
Then will I be blameless,
innocent of great transgression.
14 May the words of my mouth and the
meditation of my heart
be pleasing in your sight,
O LORD, my Rock and my
Redeemer.

718
Psalm 33

1 Sing joyfully to the LORD, you
righteous;
it is fitting for the upright to praise
him.
2 Praise the LORD with the harp;
make music to him on the
ten-stringed lyre.
3 Sing to him a new song;
play skillfully, and shout for joy.
4 For the word of the LORD is right and
true;
he is faithful in all he does.
5 The LORD loves righteousness and
justice;
the earth is full of his unfailing love.
6 By the word of the LORD were the
heavens made,
their starry host by the breath of
his mouth.
7 He gathers the waters of the sea into
jars;
he puts the deep into storehouses.
8 Let all the earth fear the LORD;
let all the people of the world
revere him.
9 For he spoke, and it came to be;
he commanded, and it stood firm.

10 The LORD foils the plans of the nations;
he thwarts the purposes of the peoples.
11 But the plans of the LORD stand firm forever,
the purposes of his heart through all generations.
12 Blessed is the nation whose God is the LORD,
the people he chose for his inheritance.
13 From heaven the LORD looks down
and sees all mankind;
14 from his dwelling place he watches
all who live on earth—
15 he who forms the hearts of all,
who considers everything they do.
16 No king is saved by the size of his army;
no warrior escapes by his great strength.
17 A horse is a vain hope for deliverance;
despite all its great strength it cannot save.
18 But the eyes of the LORD are on those who fear him,
on those whose hope is in his unfailing love,
19 to deliver them from death
and keep them alive in famine.
20 We wait in hope for the LORD;
he is our help and our shield.
21 In him our hearts rejoice,
for we trust in his holy name.
22 May your unfailing love rest upon us, O LORD,
even as we put our hope in you.

719

Psalm 119 (portion)

1 Blessed are they whose ways are blameless,
who walk according to the law of the LORD.
2 Blessed are they who keep his statutes
and seek him with all their heart.
3 They do nothing wrong;
they walk in his ways.
4 You have laid down precepts
that are to be fully obeyed.
5 Oh, that my ways were steadfast
in obeying your decrees!
6 Then I would not be put to shame
when I consider all your commands.
7 I will praise you with an upright heart
as I learn your righteous laws.
8 I will obey your decrees;
do not utterly forsake me.
9 How can a young man keep his way pure?
By living according to your word.
10 I seek you with all my heart;
do not let me stray from your commands.
11 I have hidden your word in my heart
that I might not sin against you.
12 Praise be to you, O LORD;
teach me your decrees.
13 With my lips I recount
all the laws that come from your mouth.
14 I rejoice in following your statutes
as one rejoices in great riches.
15 I meditate on your precepts
and consider your ways.
16 I delight in your decrees;
I will not neglect your word.

720

Psalm 119 (portion)

89 Your word, O LORD, is eternal;
it stands firm in the heavens.
90 Your faithfulness continues through all generations;
you established the earth, and it endures.
91 Your laws endure to this day,
for all things serve you.
92 If your law had not been my delight,
I would have perished in my affliction.
93 I will never forget your precepts,
for by them you have preserved my life.

94 Save me, for I am yours;
I have sought out your precepts.
95 The wicked are waiting to destroy me,
but I will ponder your statutes.
96 To all perfection I see a limit;
but your commands are boundless.
97 Oh, how I love your law!
I meditate on it all day long.
98 Your commands make me wiser than my enemies,
for they are ever with me.
99 I have more insight than all my teachers,
for I meditate on your statutes.
100 I have more understanding than the elders,
for I obey your precepts.
101 I have kept my feet from every evil path
so that I might obey your word.
102 I have not departed from your laws,
for you yourself have taught me.
103 How sweet are your words to my taste,
sweeter than honey to my mouth!
104 I gain understanding from your precepts;
therefore I hate every wrong path.
105 Your word is a lamp to my feet
and a light for my path.
106 I have taken an oath and confirmed it,
that I will follow your righteous laws.
107 I have suffered much;
preserve my life, O LORD,
according to your word.
108 Accept, O LORD, the willing praise of my mouth,
and teach me your laws.

Psalms of Zion

721

Psalm 48

1 Great is the LORD, and most worthy of praise,
in the city of our God, his holy mountain.
2 It is beautiful in its loftiness,
the joy of the whole earth.
Like the utmost heights of Zaphon is Mount Zion,
the city of the Great King.
3 God is in her citadels;
he has shown himself to be her fortress.
4 When the kings joined forces,
when they advanced together,
5 they saw her and were astounded;
they fled in terror.
6 Trembling seized them there,
pain like that of a woman in labor.
7 You destroyed them like ships of Tarshish
shattered by an east wind.
8 As we have heard,
so have we seen
in the city of the LORD Almighty,
in the city of our God:
God makes her secure forever.
Selah
9 Within your temple, O God,
we meditate on your unfailing love.
10 Like your name, O God,
your praise reaches to the ends of the earth;
your right hand is filled with righteousness.
11 Mount Zion rejoices,
the villages of Judah are glad
because of your judgments.
12 Walk about Zion, go around her,
count her towers,
13 consider well her ramparts,
view her citadels,
that you may tell of them to the next generation.
14 For this God is our God for ever and ever;
he will be our guide even to the end.

722

Psalm 84

1 How lovely is your dwelling place,
O LORD Almighty!

2 **My soul yearns, even faints,**
for the courts of the LORD;
my heart and my flesh cry out
for the living God.
3 Even the sparrow has found a home,
and the swallow a nest for herself,
where she may have her young—
a place near your altar,
O LORD Almighty, my King and my God.
4 Blessed are those who dwell in your house;
they are ever praising you. *Selah*
5 Blessed are those whose strength is in you,
who have set their hearts on pilgrimage.
6 **As they pass through the Valley of Baca,**
they make it a place of springs;
the autumn rains also cover it with pools.
7 They go from strength to strength,
till each appears before God in Zion.
8 **Hear my prayer, O LORD God Almighty;**
listen to me, O God of Jacob. *Selah*
9 Look upon our shield, O God;
look with favor on your anointed one.
10 Better is one day in your courts
than a thousand elsewhere;
I would rather be a doorkeeper in the house of my God
than dwell in the tents of the wicked.
11 For the LORD God is a sun and shield;
the LORD bestows favor and honor;
no good thing does he withhold
from those whose walk is blameless.
12 O LORD Almighty,
blessed is the man who trusts in you.

723
Psalm 122

1 I rejoiced with those who said to me,
"Let us go to the house of the LORD."
2 **Our feet are standing**
in your gates, O Jerusalem.
3 Jerusalem is built like a city
that is closely compacted together.
4 **That is where the tribes go up,**
the tribes of the LORD,
to praise the name of the LORD
according to the statute given to Israel.
5 There the thrones for judgment stand,
the thrones of the house of David.
6 Pray for the peace of Jerusalem:
"May those who love you be secure.
7 **May there be peace within your walls**
and security within your citadels."
8 For the sake of my brothers and friends,
I will say, "Peace be within you."
9 **For the sake of the house of the LORD our God,**
I will seek your prosperity.

Psalms of God's Kingship

(See also No. 67, Psalm 93)

724
Psalm 97

1 The LORD reigns, let the earth be glad;
let the distant shores rejoice.
2 **Clouds and thick darkness surround him;**
righteousness and justice are the foundation of his throne.
3 Fire goes before him
and consumes his foes on every side.
4 **His lightning lights up the world;**
the earth sees and trembles.

5 The mountains melt like wax before the LORD,
before the Lord of all the earth.
6 The heavens proclaim his righteousness,
and all the peoples see his glory.
7 All who worship images are put to shame,
those who boast in idols—
worship him, all you gods!
8 Zion hears and rejoices
and the villages of Judah are glad
because of your judgments, O LORD.
9 For you, O LORD, are the Most High over all the earth;
you are exalted far above all gods.
10 Let those who love the LORD hate evil,
for he guards the lives of his faithful ones
and delivers them from the hand of the wicked.
11 Light is shed upon the righteous
and joy on the upright in heart.
12 Rejoice in the LORD, you who are righteous,
and praise his holy name.

725
Psalm 115

1 Not to us, O LORD, not to us
but to your name be the glory,
because of your love and faithfulness.
2 Why do the nations say,
"Where is their God?"
3 Our God is in heaven;
he does whatever pleases him.
4 But their idols are silver and gold,
made by the hands of men.
5 They have mouths, but cannot speak,
eyes, but they cannot see;
6 they have ears, but cannot hear,
noses, but they cannot smell;
7 they have hands, but cannot feel,
feet, but they cannot walk;
nor can they utter a sound with their throats.
8 Those who make them will be like them,
and so will all who trust in them.
9 O house of Israel, trust in the LORD—
he is their help and shield.
10 O house of Aaron, trust in the LORD—
he is their help and shield.
11 You who fear him, trust in the LORD—
he is their help and shield.
12 The LORD remembers us and will bless us:
He will bless the house of Israel,
he will bless the house of Aaron,
13 he will bless those who fear the LORD—
small and great alike.
14 May the LORD make you increase,
both you and your children.
15 May you be blessed by the LORD,
the Maker of heaven and earth.
16 The highest heavens belong to the LORD,
but the earth he has given to man.
17 It is not the dead who praise the LORD,
those who go down to silence;
18 it is we who extol the LORD,
both now and forevermore.
Praise the LORD.

Psalms of the Messiah-King

726
Psalm 2

1 Why do the nations conspire
and the peoples plot in vain?
2 The kings of the earth take their stand
and the rulers gather together
against the LORD
and against his Anointed One.
3 "Let us break their chains," they say,
"and throw off their fetters."

4 The One enthroned in heaven laughs;
the Lord scoffs at them.
5 Then he rebukes them in his anger
and terrifies them in his wrath,
saying,
6 "I have installed my King
on Zion, my holy hill."
7 I will proclaim the decree of the
LORD:
He said to me, "You are my Son;
today I have become your Father.
8 Ask of me,
and I will make the nations your
inheritance,
the ends of the earth your
possession.
9 You will rule them with an iron
scepter;
you will dash them to pieces like
pottery."
10 Therefore, you kings, be wise;
be warned, you rulers of the earth.
11 Serve the LORD with fear
and rejoice with trembling.
12 Kiss the Son, lest he be angry
and you be destroyed in your way,
for his wrath can flare up in a
moment.
Blessed are all who take refuge in
him.

727
Psalm 22

1 My God, my God, why have you
forsaken me?
Why are you so far from saving me,
so far from the words of my
groaning?
2 O my God, I cry out by day, but you
do not answer,
by night, and am not silent.
3 Yet you are enthroned as the Holy
One;
you are the praise of Israel.
4 In you our fathers put their trust;
they trusted and you delivered
them.
5 They cried to you and were saved;
in you they trusted and were not
disappointed.
6 But I am a worm and not a man,
scorned by men and despised by
the people.
7 All who see me mock me;
they hurl insults, shaking their
heads:
8 "He trusts in the LORD;
let the LORD rescue him.
Let him deliver him,
since he delights in him."
9 Yet you brought me out of the womb;
you made me trust in you
even at my mother's breast.
10 From birth I was cast upon you;
from my mother's womb you have
been my God.
11 Do not be far from me,
for trouble is near
and there is no one to help.
12 Many bulls surround me;
strong bulls of Bashan encircle me.
13 Roaring lions tearing their prey
open their mouths wide against me.
14 I am poured out like water,
and all my bones are out of joint.
My heart has turned to wax;
it has melted away within me.
15 My strength is dried up like a
potsherd,
and my tongue sticks to the roof of
my mouth;
you lay me in the dust of death.
16 Dogs have surrounded me;
a band of evil men has encircled
me,
they have pierced my hands and
my feet.
17 I can count all my bones;
people stare and gloat over me.
18 They divide my garments among
them
and cast lots for my clothing.
19 But you, O LORD, be not far off;
O my Strength, come quickly to
help me.

20 **Deliver my life from the sword,**
my precious life from the power of the dogs.
21 Rescue me from the mouth of the lions;
save me from the horns of the wild oxen.
22 **I will declare your name to my brothers;**
in the congregation I will praise you.
23 You who fear the LORD, praise him!
All you descendants of Jacob, honor him!
Revere him, all you descendants of Israel!
24 For he has not despised or disdained
the suffering of the afflicted one;
he has not hidden his face from him
but has listened to his cry for help.
25 From you comes the theme of my praise in the great assembly;
before those who fear you will I fulfill my vows.
26 **The poor will eat and be satisfied;**
they who seek the LORD will praise him—
may your hearts live forever!
27 All the ends of the earth
will remember and turn to the LORD,
and all the families of the nations
will bow down before him,
28 for dominion belongs to the LORD
and he rules over the nations.
29 **All the rich of the earth will feast and worship;**
all who go down to the dust will kneel before him—
those who cannot keep themselves alive.
30 Posterity will serve him;
future generations will be told about the Lord.
31 **They will proclaim his righteousness**
to a people yet unborn—
for he has done it.

728
Psalm 72 (portions)

1 Endow the king with your justice, O God,
the royal son with your righteousness.
2 **He will judge your people in righteousness,**
your afflicted ones with justice.
3 The mountains will bring prosperity to the people,
the hills the fruit of righteousness.
4 **He will defend the afflicted among the people**
and save the children of the needy;
he will crush the oppressor.
5 He will endure as long as the sun,
as long as the moon, through all generations.
6 **He will be like rain falling on a mown field,**
like showers watering the earth.
7 In his days the righteous will flourish;
prosperity will abound till the moon is no more. . . .
17 **May his name endure forever;**
may it continue as long as the sun.
All nations will be blessed through him,
and they will call him blessed.
18 **Praise be to the LORD God, the God of Israel,**
who alone does marvelous deeds.
19 Praise be to his glorious name forever;
may the whole earth be filled with his glory.
Amen and Amen.

729
Psalm 110

1 The LORD says to my Lord:
"Sit at my right hand
until I make your enemies
a footstool for your feet."

2 The LORD will extend your mighty scepter from Zion;
you will rule in the midst of your enemies.
3 Your troops will be willing
on your day of battle.
Arrayed in holy majesty,
from the womb of the dawn
you will receive the dew of your youth.
4 The LORD has sworn
and will not change his mind:
"You are a priest forever,
in the order of Melchizedek."
5 The Lord is at your right hand;
he will crush kings on the day of his wrath.
6 He will judge the nations, heaping up the dead
and crushing the rulers of the whole earth.
7 He will drink from a brook beside the way;
therefore he will lift up his head.

Psalms of Blessing for the People

730
Psalm 1

1 Blessed is the man
who does not walk in the counsel of the wicked
or stand in the way of sinners
or sit in the seat of mockers.
2 But his delight is in the law of the LORD,
and on his law he meditates day and night.
3 He is like a tree planted by streams of water,
which yields its fruit in season
and whose leaf does not wither.
Whatever he does prospers.
4 Not so the wicked!
They are like chaff
that the wind blows away.
5 Therefore the wicked will not stand in the judgment,
nor sinners in the assembly of the righteous.
6 For the LORD watches over the way of the righteous,
but the way of the wicked will perish.

731
Psalm 67

1 May God be gracious to us and bless us
and make his face shine upon us,
Selah
2 that your ways may be known on earth,
your salvation among all nations.
3 May the peoples praise you, O God;
may all the peoples praise you.
4 May the nations be glad and sing for joy,
for you rule the peoples justly
and guide the nations of the earth.
Selah
5 May the peoples praise you, O God;
may all the peoples praise you.
6 Then the land will yield its harvest,
and God, our God, will bless us.
7 God will bless us,
and all the ends of the earth will fear him.

732
Psalm 128

1 Blessed are all who fear the LORD,
who walk in his ways.
2 You will eat the fruit of your labor;
blessings and prosperity will be yours.
3 Your wife will be like a fruitful vine
within your house;

your sons will be like olive shoots
around your table.
4 Thus is the man blessed
who fears the LORD.
5 May the LORD bless you from Zion
all the days of your life;
may you see the prosperity of Jerusalem,
6 and may you live to see your children's children.
Peace be upon Israel.

733
Psalm 133

1 How good and pleasant it is
when brothers live together in unity!
2 It is like precious oil poured on the head,
running down on the beard,
running down on Aaron's beard,
down upon the collar of his robes.
3 It is as if the dew of Hermon
were falling on Mount Zion.
For there the LORD bestows his blessing,
even life forevermore.

734
Psalm 134

1 Praise the LORD, all you servants of the LORD
who minister by night in the house of the LORD.
2 Lift up your hands in the sanctuary
and praise the LORD.
3 May the LORD, the Maker of heaven and earth,
bless you from Zion.

Worship Helps

Calls to Worship

"Be still, and know that I am God; I will be exalted among the nations, I will be exalted in the earth." *Psalm 46:10*

Exalt the LORD our God and worship at his holy mountain, for the LORD our God is holy. *Psalm 99:9*

Give thanks to the LORD, for he is good; his love endures forever. Let the redeemed of the LORD say this. *Psalm 107:1-2*

Praise the LORD, all you nations; extol him, all you peoples. For great is his love toward us, and the faithfulness of the LORD endures forever. Praise the LORD. *Psalm 117*

This is the day the LORD has made; let us rejoice and be glad in it. *Psalm 118:24*

I rejoiced with those who said to me, "Let us go to the house of the LORD." *Psalm 122:1*

Praise the LORD. Praise God in his sanctuary; praise him in his mighty heavens. . . . Let everything that has breath praise the LORD. *Psalm 150:1, 6*

The LORD is in his holy temple; let all the earth be silent before him. *Habakkuk 2:20*

A time is coming and has now come when the true worshipers will worship the Father in spirit and truth, for they are the kind of worshipers the Father seeks. *John 4:23*

God is spirit, and his worshipers must worship in spirit and in truth. *John 4:24*

Since . . . you have been raised with Christ, set your hearts on things above, where Christ is seated at the right hand of God. Set your minds on things above. *Colossians 3:1-2*

Invocations

Show me your ways, O LORD, teach me your paths; guide me in your truth and teach me, for you are God my Savior, and my hope is in you all day long. *Psalm 25:4-5*

O God, you are my God, earnestly I seek you; my soul thirsts for you, my body longs for you, in a dry and weary land where there is no water. I have seen you in the sanctuary and beheld your power and your glory. Because your love is better than life, my lips will glorify you. *Psalm 63:1-3*

Hear my prayer, O LORD; listen to my cry for mercy. In the day of my trouble I will call to you, for you will answer me. *Psalm 86:6-7*

Open my eyes that I may see wonderful things in your law. *Psalm 119:18*

Offertory Sentences

Sacrifice thank offerings to God, fulfill your vows to the Most High. *Psalm 50:14*

Ascribe to the LORD, O families of nations, ascribe to the LORD glory and strength. Ascribe to the LORD the glory due his name; bring an offering and come into his courts. *Psalm 96:7-8*

Honor the LORD with your wealth, with the firstfruits of all your crops. *Proverbs 3:9*

Bring the whole tithe into the storehouse, that there may be food in my house. "Test me in this," says the LORD Almighty, "and see if I will not throw open the floodgates of heaven and pour out so much blessing that you will not have room enough for it." *Malachi 3:10*

On the first day of every week, each one of you should set aside a sum of money in keeping with his income. *1 Corinthians 16:2*

Benedictions

The LORD bless you and keep you; the LORD make his face shine upon you and be gracious to you; the LORD turn his face toward you and give you peace. *Numbers 6:24-26*

Grace and peace to you from God our Father and from the Lord Jesus Christ. *Romans 1:7*

May the God of hope fill you with all joy and peace as you trust in him, so that you may overflow with hope by the power of the Holy Spirit. *Romans 15:13*

May the grace of the Lord Jesus Christ, and the love of God, and the fellowship of the Holy Spirit be with you all. *2 Corinthians 13:14*

Grace and peace to you from God our Father and the Lord Jesus Christ, who gave himself for our sins to rescue us from the present evil age, according to the will of our God and Father, to whom be glory for ever and ever. Amen. *Galatians 1:3-5*

Now to him who is able to do immeasurably more than all we ask or imagine, according to his power that is at work within us, to him be glory in the church and in Christ Jesus throughout all generations, for ever and ever! Amen. *Ephesians 3:20-21*

Now may the Lord of peace himself give you peace at all times and in every way. The Lord be with all of you. *2 Thessalonians 3:16*

May the God of peace, who through the blood of the eternal covenant brought back from the dead our Lord Jesus, that great Shepherd of the sheep, equip you with everything good for doing his will, and may he work in us what is pleasing to him, through Jesus Christ, to whom be glory for ever and ever. Amen.
Hebrews 13:20-21

Grace and peace be yours in abundance through the knowledge of God and of Jesus our Lord. *2 Peter 1:2*

Words of Pardon

The LORD is compassionate and gracious, slow to anger, abounding in love. He will not always accuse, nor will he harbor his anger forever; he does not treat us as our sins deserve or repay us according to our iniquities. For as high as the heavens are above the earth, so great is his love for those who fear him; as far as the east is from the west, so far has he removed our transgressions from us. *Psalm 103:8-12*

Let the wicked forsake his way and the evil man his thoughts. Let him turn to the LORD, and he will have mercy on him, and to our God, for he will freely pardon.
Isaiah 55:7

There will be more rejoicing in heaven over one sinner who repents than over ninety-nine righteous persons who do not need to repent. *Luke 15:7*

If we confess our sins, he is faithful and just and will forgive us our sins and purify us from all unrighteousness. *1 John 1:9*

The Apostles' Creed

I believe in God, the Father Almighty, Creator of heaven and earth.

I believe in Jesus Christ, His only son, our Lord, who was conceived by the Holy Spirit and born of the Virgin Mary. He suffered under Pontius Pilate, was crucified, died, and was buried; He descended to hell. The third day He rose again from the dead. He ascended to heaven and is seated at the right hand of God the Father Almighty. From there He will come to judge the living and the dead.

I believe in the Holy Spirit, the holy catholic* Church, the communion of saints, the forgiveness of sins, the resurrection of the body, and the life everlasting. Amen.

**that is, the true Christian Church of all times and all places*

The Nicene Creed

We believe in one God, the Father, the Almighty, Maker of heaven and earth, and of all that is, seen and unseen.

We believe in one Lord, Jesus Christ, the only Son of God, eternally begotten of the Father, God from God, Light from Light, true God from true God, begotten, not made, of one Being with the Father; through Him all things were made. For us and for our salvation He came down from heaven, was incarnate of the Holy Spirit and the Virgin Mary and became truly human. For our sake He was crucified under Pontius Pilate; He suffered death and was buried. On the third day He rose again in accordance with the Scriptures; He ascended into heaven and is seated at the right hand of the Father. He will come again in glory to judge the living and the dead, and His kingdom will have no end.

We believe in the Holy Spirit, the Lord, the Giver of life, who proceeds from the Father and the Son, who with the Father and the Son is worshiped and glorified, who has spoken through the prophets. We believe in the one holy catholic* and apostolic Church. We acknowledge one baptism for the forgiveness of sins. We look for the resurrection of the dead and the life of the world to come. Amen.

**that is, the true Christian Church of all times and all places*

The Ten Commandments

1. I am the LORD your God, who brought you out of Egypt, out of the land of slavery. You shall have no other gods before me.
2. You shall not make for yourself an idol in the form of anything in heaven above or on the earth beneath or in the waters below.
3. You shall not misuse the name of the LORD your God.
4. Remember the Sabbath day by keeping it holy.
5. Honor your father and your mother.
6. You shall not murder.
7. You shall not commit adultery.
8. You shall not steal.
9. You shall not give false testimony against your neighbor.
10. You shall not covet your neighbor's house. You shall not covet your neighbor's wife, or his manservant or maidservant, his ox or donkey, or anything that belongs to your neighbor.

[from *Exodus 20:2-17*]

Copyright Owners and Administrators

The use of the valid copyrights of the following publishers and individuals is gratefully acknowledged. No further use of these copyrights may be made without obtaining permission directly from the appropriate owner. Every effort has been made to determine and locate the owners of all the materials that appear in this book. The publisher regrets any errors or omissions and upon written notice will make necessary corrections in subsequent printings.

Abingdon Press, c/o The Copyright Company, 1025 16th Ave. S., Suite 204, Nashville, TN 37212: Selection 524

Albert E. Brumley & Sons, c/o Integrated Copyright Group, Inc., P.O. Box 24149, Nashville, TN, 37202: Selection 422

Bartlett, E.M., c/o Integrated Copyright Group, Inc., P.O. Box 24149, Nashville, TN 37202: Selection 580

Birdwing Music, c/o EMI Christian Music Publishing, P.O. Box 5085, Brentwood, TN 37024-5085: Selections 183, 253, 264, 391, 415

BMG Songs, Inc., c/o EMI Christian Music Publishing, P.O. Box 5085, Brentwood, TN 37024-5085: Selections 183, 264, 415

BMG Songs, Inc., c/o BMG Music Publishing, 1400-18th Ave. S., Nashville, TN 37212: Selections 62, 368, 531

Board of Publication, Lutheran Church of America, c/o Augsburg Fortress, P.O. Box 1209, Minneapolis, MN 55440-1209: Selection 40

Bob Kilpatrick Ministries, c/o Lorenz Publishing Company, 501 E. 3rd St., P.O. Box 802, Dayton, OH 45401-0802: Selection 506

Breitkopf & Haertel, Postfach 1707, D-65007 Wiesbaden, Germany: Selections 295, 363, 654

Bridge Building Music, Inc., c/o Brentwood-Benson Music Publishing, Inc., 741 Cool Springs Blvd., Franklin, TN 37067: Selection 358

Broadman Press, c/o Genevox Music Group, 127 Ninth Ave. N., Nashville, TN 37234: Selections 503, 629, 636

Bud John Songs, Inc., c/o EMI Christian Music Publishing, P.O. Box 5085, Brentwood, TN 37024-5085: Selections 14, 16, 191, 511, 566

C.A. Music (a div. of C.A. Records, Inc.), c/o Music Services, Inc., 209 Chapelwood Dr., Franklin, TN 37069: Selections 80, 454

Careers-BMG Music/Multisongs, c/o BMG Music Publishing, 1400-18th Ave. S., Nashville, TN 37212: Selection 414

Cartford, Gerhard, 2279 Commonwealth Ave., St. Paul, MN 55108: Selection 537

Celebration, P.O. Box 309, Aliquippa, PA 15001: Selection 24

Centergetic Music, c/o Integrated Copyright Group, Inc., P.O. Box 24149, Nashville, TN 37202: Selection 399

Centerville (Ohio) Community Church, 10688 Lebanon Pike, Centerville, OH 45458-4602: Selection 98

Christian Publications, Inc., 3825 Hartzdale Dr., Camp Hill, PA 17011: Selections 41, 122, 297, 298, 301, 585

Church Pension Fund, c/o Church Publishing Inc., 445 Fifth Ave., New York, NY 10016: Selection 667

Cogbill, K. R., Box 1153, Summerland, BC, V0H 1Z0, Canada: Selection 305

Contemporary Worship 4: Hymns for Baptism and Holy Communion, c/o Augsburg Fortress, P.O. Box 1209, Minneapolis, MN 55440-1209: Selection 624

Coomesietunes, c/o The Copyright Company, 1025 16th Ave. S., Suite 204, Nashville, TN 37212: Selection 621

Crouch Music, c/o EMI Christian Music Publishing, P.O. Box 5085, Brentwood, TN 37024-5085: Selection 191

David Hahn Music, 1373 Buckingham Circle, Franklin, TN 37064: Selections 250, 371, 460

Davis, Michael B., Sr., Rua Barao de Triunfo, 520 CJ72 (Brooklin), 04.602-002 Sao Paulo, SP, Brasil: Selection 550

Dayspring Music, Inc., c/o Warner/Chappell Music, Inc., 20 Music Square East, Nashville, TN 37203: Selection 176

E.C. Schirmer Music Company (a div. of ECS Publishing), 138 Ipswich Street, Boston, MA 02215: Selection 659

Ears to Hear Music, c/o EMI Christian Music Publishing, P.O. Box 5085, Brentwood, TN 37024-5085: Selection 264

F.E.L. Publications, Ltd., c/o Lorenz Publishing Company, 501 E. 3rd St., P.O. Box 802, Dayton, OH 45401-0802: Selection 485

Fairhill Music, Inc., P.O. Box 4467, Oceanside, CA 92052: Selection 398

Farquharson, Rev. Walter, P.O. Box 126, Saltcoats, SK S0A 3R0, Canada: Selection 655

Fred Bock Music Company, Inc., P.O. Box 570567, Tarzana, CA 91357: Selections 70, 632

Frey, Marvin V., c/o Mrs. Helen M. Frey, 63 Freedom Pond Land, North Chili, NY 14514: Selection 230

Full Armor Music, c/o The Kruger Organisation, Inc., 15 Rolling Way, New City, NY, 10956-6912: Selection 318

G. Schirmer, Inc., 257 Park Ave. S., New York, NY 10010: Selections 51, 445

Gaither Music Company, c/o Gaither Copyright Management, P.O. Box 737, Alexandria, IN 46001: Selection 64

Greg Nelson Music, c/o EMI Christian Music Publishing, P.O. Box 5085, Brentwood, TN 37024-5085: Selection 414

Harcourt, Inc., 6277 Sea Harbor Dr., 6th Floor, Orlando, FL 32887-6777: Selection 98

Hark! Productions, 2200 Tart Lake Road, Lino Lakes, MN 55038: Selection 13

Harold Ober Associates Incorporated, 425 Madison Ave., New York, NY 10017: Selection 32

Heart of the City Music, 810 S. 7th St., Minneapolis, MN 55415: Selections 261, 267, 298, 416

Hillsong Publishing, c/o Integrity Music, Inc., 1000 Copy Road, Mobile, AL 36695: Selection 217

Hine, S.K., c/o Manna Music, Inc., P.O. Box 218, Pacific City, OR 97135: Selection 66

His Grace Music, c/o Russell C. Filsinger, 13 Bunn St., Califon, NJ 07830: Selection 288

Hope Publishing Company, 380 S. Main Place, Carol Stream, IL 60188: Selections 25, 39, 135, 158, 159, 199, 285, 332, 377, 417, 451, 513, 516, 529, 536, 537

House of Mercy Music, c/o The Copyright Company, 1025 16th Ave. S., Suite 204, Nashville, TN 37212: Selection 471

Huber, Jane Parker, c/o Westminster John Knox Press, 100 Witherspoon St., Louisville, KY 40202-1396: Selection 245

Integrity's Hosanna! Music, c/o Integrity Music, Inc., 1000 Cody Road, Mobile, AL 36695: Selections 56, 57, 60, 65, 145, 156, 203, 218, 235, 278, 411, 419, 522, 526, 548, 553, 556, 557, 630, 660

Integrity's Praise! Music, c/o Integrity Music, Inc., 1000 Cody Road, Mobile, AL 36695: Selections 60, 455, 553

Isáis, Juan M., c/o Mrs. Juan M. Isáis, Apartado 21-200, 04100 Mexico, D.F., Mexico: Selection 535

Jabusch, Willard F., c/o New Dawn Music/OCP Publications, 5536 NE Hassalo, Portland, OR 97213: Selection 129

John T. Benson Publishing Company, c/o Brentwood-Benson Music Publishing, Inc., 741 Cool Springs Blvd., Franklin, TN 37067: Selections 148, 616

John W. Peterson Music Company, 6501 E. Greenway Parkway, Suite 102, #435, Scottsdale, AZ 85254-2065: Selection 190

Jonathan Mark Music, c/o Gaither Copyright Management, P.O. Box 737, Alexandria, IN 46001: Selection 391

Jubilate Hymns, Ltd., c/o Hope Publishing Company, 380 S. Main Place, Carol Stream, IL 60188: Selections 117, 409, 530, 643

Kids Brothers of St. Frank Publishing, c/o BMG Music Publishing, 1400-18th Ave. S., Nashville, TN 37212: Selection 368

Kingsway's Thankyou Music, c/o EMI Christian Music Publishing, P.O. Box 5085, Brentwood, TN 37024-5085: Selections 124, 144, 242, 517

Latter Rain Music, c/o EMI Christian Music Publishing, P.O. Box 5085, Brentwood, TN 37024-5085: Selection 226

Lillenas Publishing Company, c/o The Copyright Company, 1025 16th Ave. S., Suite 204, Nashville, TN 37212: Selections 283, 437, 462, 545

Make Way Music, c/o Music Services in the Western Hemisphere, 209 Chapelwood Dr., Franklin, TN, 37069: Selections 335, 463, 539, 547

Manna Music, Inc., P.O. Box 218, Pacific City, OR 97135: Selections 216, 236, 262, 348

Maranatha Praise, Inc., c/o The Copyright Company, 1025 16th Ave. S., Suite 204, Nashville, TN 37212: Selections 3, 164, 342, 612, 617

Maranatha! Music, c/o The Copyright Company, 1025 16th Ave. S., Suite 204, Nashville, TN 37212: Selections 18, 260, 311, 323, 383, 447, 471, 502, 621

McBride, Eldon, 35 Kearney Dr., Etobicoke, ON M9W 5J5, Canada: Selections 198, 295, 304, 308, 316, 408, 543

McKinney Music, Inc., c/o Genevox Music Group, 127 Ninth Ave. N., Nashville, TN 37234: Selections 83, 93, 373

Meadowgreen Music Company, c/o EMI Christian Music Publishing, P.O. Box 5085, Brentwood, TN 37024- 5085: Selections 46, 53, 491

Mercy/Vineyard Publishing, c/o Music Services, Inc., 209 Chapelwood Dr., Franklin, TN, 37069: Selections 22, 27, 128, 219, 220, 257, 291, 413

Miller, Doris R., 8552 Loyd Drive, St. Louis, MO 63114: Selection 638

Mountain Spring Music, c/o EMI Christian Music Publishing, P.O. Box 5085, Brentwood, TN 37024-5085: Selections 54, 150, 410

New Dawn Music, c/o OCP Publications, 5536 NE Hassalo, Portland, OR 97213: Selection 552

New Spring Publishing, Inc., c/o Brentwood-Benson Music Publishing, Inc., 741 Cool Springs Blvd., Franklin, TN 37067: Selection 379

OCP Publications, 5536 NE Hassalo, Portland, OR 97213: Selection 552

Ortlund, Anne, c/o Renew Ministries, 4500 Campus Dr., Suite 662, Newport Beach, CA 92660: Selection 527

Oxford University Press, 198 Madison Ave., New York, NY 10016-4314: Selections 204, 377, 643

Paragon Music, c/o Brentwood-Benson Music Publishing, Inc., 741 Cool Springs Blvd., Franklin, TN 37067: Selection 89

PDI Praise, c/o Integrity Music, Inc., 1000 Cody Road, Mobile, AL 36695: Selection 455

Pearce, Almeda J., c/o Jeanne P. Hopkins, 503 Shortridge Dr., Wynnewood, PA 19096: Selection 185

Pilot Point Music, c/o The Copyright Company, 1025 16th Ave. S., Suite 204, Nashville, TN 37212: Selections 79, 111, 243, 273, 545

Presbyterian Board of Christian Education, c/o Westminster John Knox Press, 100 Witherspoon St., Louisville, KY 40202-1396: Selection 363, 654

Prince, Nolene, Resource Christian Music Pty. Ltd., c/o The Copyright Company, 1025 16th Ave. S., Suite 204, Nashville, TN 37212: Selection 12

Redeemer Music, c/o Redeemer Presbyterian Church, 271 Madison Ave., 16th Floor, New York, NY 10016: Selection 63

Rivard, Gene, 3825 Hartzdale Dr., Camp Hill, PA 17011: Selections 182, 321, 326, 336, 381, 412, 446, 554, 637

River Oaks Music, c/o EMI Christian Music Publishing, P.O. Box 5085, Brentwood, TN 37024-5085: Selections 64, 610

Rocksmith Music, c/o Brentwood-Benson Music Publishing, Inc., 741 Cool Springs Blvd., Franklin, TN 37067: Selections 212, 623

Sanchez, Pete Jr., c/o Gabriel Music, P.O. Box 840999, Houston, TX 77282-0999: Selection 55

Sandi's Songs Music, c/o Gaither Copyright Management, P.O. Box 737, Alexandria, IN 46001: Selection 64

Scripture In Song, c/o Integrity Music, Inc., 1000 Cody Road, Mobile, AL 36695: Selections 71, 76, 508, 618

Shepherd's Fold Music, c/o EMI Christian Music Publishing, P.O. Box 5085, Brentwood, TN 37024-5085: Selection 610

Shepherd's Heart Music, Inc., c/o Dayspring Music, Inc., and Warner/Chappell Music, Inc., 20 Music Square East, Nashville, TN 37203: Selection 214

Simpson, Scott A., Perrysburg Alliance Church, 10401 Avenue Road, Perrysburg, OH 43551: Selection 17

Singspiration Music, c/o Brentwood-Benson Music Publishing, Inc., 741 Cool Springs Blvd., Franklin, TN 37067: Selections 49, 211, 234, 328, 331, 349, 551, 558, 654

Sloan, T. Lynn (Tebbutt), c/o Fairview Alliance Church, P.O. Box 325, Fairview, MT 59221-0325: Selection 9

Smith, Alfred B., address not available: Selection 11

Smith, L.E. Jr., c/o New Jerusalem Music, P.O. Box 225, Clarksboro, NJ 08020: Selection 534

Sparrow Song, c/o EMI Christian Music Publishing, P.O. Box 5085, Brentwood, TN 37024-5085: Selection 414

SpiritQuest Music, c/o Gaither Copyright Management, P.O. Box 737, Alexandria, IN 46001: Selection 611

Sprunger, Ronald L., 408 Keen Ave., Ashland, OH 44805-3844: Selection 625

Stainer & Bell Ltd., c/o Hope Publishing Company, 380 S. Main Place, Carol Stream, IL 60188: Selection 649

Straightway Music, c/o EMI Christian Music Publishing, P.O. Box 5085, Brentwood, TN 37024-5085: Selections 54, 150, 410

The Continuum International Publishing Group, 15 East 26th Street, New York, NY 10010: Selection 240

The Evangelical Covenant Church, 5101 N. Francisco Ave., Chicago, IL 60625: Selection 541

The Hymn Society, c/o Hope Publishing Company, 380 S. Main Place, Carol Stream, IL 60188: Selections 476, 499

The Pilgrim Press, 700 Prospect Ave., Cleveland, OH 44115: Selection 129

Universal-MCA Music Publishing, c/o Warner Bros. Publications U.S. Inc., 15800 NW 48th Ave., Miami, FL 33014: Selections 34, 68

Universal-Polygram International Publishing, Inc., c/o Warner Bros. Publications U.S. Inc., 15800 NW 48th Ave., Miami, FL 33014: Selection 169

Utryck, Walton Music Corp., c/o Licensing Associates, 935 Broad Street #31, Bloomfield, NJ, 07003: Selection 639

Utterbach Music, Inc., c/o Warner Bros. Publications U.S. Inc., 15800 NW 48th Ave., Miami, FL 33014: Selection 169

Van Ness Press, Inc., c/o Genevox Music Group, 127 Ninth Ave. N., Nashville, TN 37234: Selections 32, 105, 477

Vineyard Songs (UK/Eire), Mercy/Vineyard Publishing in North America, c/o Music Services, Inc., 209 Chapelwood Dr., Franklin, TN, 37069: Selection 620

Whole Armor Music, c/o The Kruger Organisation, Inc., 15 Rolling Way, New City, NY, 10956-6912: Selection 318

William J. Gaither, Inc., c/o Gaither Copyright Management, P.O. Box 737, Alexandria, IN 46001: Selections 194, 227, 487, 582, 588

Word Music, Inc., c/o Warner/Chappell Music, Inc., 20 Music Square East, Nashville, TN 37203: Selections 145, 153, 180, 259, 481, 491, 502, 507, 561, 578, 583, 589, 630, 635, 647, 661

Word of God Music, c/o The Copyright Company, 1025 16th Ave. S., Suite 204, Nashville, TN 37212: Selection 215

Word's Spirit of Praise Music, c/o The Copyright Company, 1025 16th Ave. S., Suite 204, Nashville, TN 37212: Selection 311

World Library Publications, 3825 N. Willow Road, Schiller Park, IL 60176-9936: Selection 624

Yellow House Music, c/o Brentwood-Benson Music Publishing, Inc., 741 Cool Springs Blvd., Franklin, TN 37067: Selection 89

ZionSong Music, P.O. Box 574044, Orlando, FL 32857: Selection 233

Zschech, Darlene, c/o Integrity Music, Inc., 1000 Copy Road, Mobile, AL 36695: Selection 217

Responsive Scripture Readings: Titles

A Life of Service 501
A Pleasing Sacrifice 313
All Nations Will Worship God 520
Baptism 642
Christ and the Children 646
Even So, Come, Lord Jesus 197
Father, Son and Holy Spirit 7
Fellowship of Believers 484
Go and Make Disciples 540
God's Blessing on the Family 651
God's Goodness 26
Great Is the Lord 52
He Has Blessed Us 37
He Is the Radiance of God's Glory 222
Healing 407
Hear My Prayer, O Lord 443
His Love Endures Forever 461
Holy Spirit Filled (Pentecost) 244
Holy Spirit Fruit 320
Holy Spirit Led 289
Holy Spirit Power 249
I Will Be Exalted Among the Nations 544
In God I Trust 276
Keep His Commandments 354
King of Kings and Lord of Lords 195
Life Everlasting 425
Love 457
Man of Sorrows 146
More Than Conquerors 393
Name Above All Names 179
Praise the Almighty King 45
Prayer 441
Prince of Peace 72
Revival 479
Stewardship 497
Thanksgiving 658
The Ascension 167
The Beatitudes 119
The Christian Walk 366
The Crucifixion 131
The Exaltation of Christ 168
The Heavens Declare His Glory 29
The Lord Is Robed in Majesty 67
The Lord's Return 181
The Lord's Supper 628
The Nature of the Lord 20
The New Birth 263
The Promised Comforter 239
The Resurrection 420
The Risen Savior 157
The Savior's Birth 84
The Suffering Lamb 149
The Supremacy of Christ 200
The Triumphal Entry 125
The Word Became Flesh 116
The Word of God 488
Trust in the Word 493
We Have Come to Worship 110
Worthy Is the Lamb 231

Responsive Scripture Readings: Scripture Index

Genesis
12:1-3 544

Deuteronomy
6:1-9 651
8:6-18 658
10:12 461
11:1 354
30:11-14 354
30:15-18 651

Joshua
1:8 354
24:15 651

1 Samuel
15:22 354

1 Chronicles
29:11-13 45

Psalms
1 730
2 726
5:1-3 393
6:9 443
8 714
13 674
16 678
18:1-2 461
19:1-4 29
19:1-6 715
19:7-11 488
19:7-14 717
21:13 461
22 727
23 679
24 705
25:1-15 276
27 680
30 695
31:1-5, 15-16, 19-24 681
32 702
33 718
34 696
37:1-8, 23-31, 37 682
38 692
40:1-13, 16-17 697
42 675
42:1-3 393
46 683
46:10 544
48 721
51:1-17 693
57 698
63 684
65 703
66:1-9, 16-20 699
67 731
67:1-7 544
71:1-6, 17-24 685
72:1-7, 17-19 728
84 722
85 694
86 686
86:1, 4-10, 17 443
91 687
93 67
95 706
96 707
97 724
98 708
100 709
103 704
104:1-10, 24-34 716
107: excerpts 26
107:1-22 700
110 729
115 725
116:1-9, 12-19 701
119:1-16 719
119:9-11 488
119:41-48, 55 493
119:89-108 720
121 688
122 723
127 689
128 732
130 690
133 733
134 734
136:1-3 461
139:1-18, 23-24 691
142:1-5 676
143:1-11 677
145 710
145:1-7 52
145:8-21 20
146 711
147:1-7 712
150 713

Proverbs
3:9-10 497

Isaiah
9:6-7 72
40:29-31 393
49:6 544
53:1-6 146
53:7-12 149

Ezekiel
36:26-27 239

Daniel
7:13-14 520

Malachi
3:10 497

Matthew
2:1-11 110
3:13-17 7
5:1-12 119
6:6 441
7:7-11 441
8:1-13, 16-17 407
9:37-38 540
18:1-6 646
24:44 181
28:1-10 157
28:16-20 ....7, 540

Mark
10:13-16 646
11:1-11 125

Luke
2:1-20 84
24:36-53 167

John
1:1-14 116
3:1-16 263
3:14-16 425
3:36 425
5:24 425
10:27-29 425
13:34-35 484
14:16-26 239
14:21, 23 354
14:25-26 7
19:16-30 131
20:19-20, 26-29 157

Acts
1:1-9 249
1:10-11 181
2:1-18 244
2:38-47 479

Romans
6:1-8 642
8:1-18 289
8:31-32, 37 393
10:8-15 540
11:36 37
12:1-2 313

1 Corinthians
3:8-15 501
11:23-29 628
13 457
15:17-26 420
15:51-58 420
15:58 501

2 Corinthians
5:9 501
5:14-15, 20 501
9:6-8 497
9:15 461

Galatians
5:16-26 320
6:2 484

Ephesians
1:3-14 37
4:1-15 366
4:2-6 642

Philippians
2:1-4 484
2:5-11 179
3:20 181

Colossians
1:15-20 200
3:1-4 313

3:12-17..................313

1 Thessalonians
1:3..........................501
4:15-18..................181

2 Timothy
3:14-17..................488

Hebrews
1:1-12.....................222
10:24-25................484

James
5:14-15..................407

1 Peter
1:8-9.......................461
4:8-10....................497

2 Peter
3:11-14..................181

1 John
2:3..........................354
4:9-10....................461
5:11-13..................425

Revelation
1:18........................157
5:9..........................520
5:9-14....................231
5:11-13..................168
7:9-12....................520
19:11-16................195
21:1-4....................195
22:12-21................197

Inspirational Readings and Prayers

Title	*Author/Source*	*Number*
Trinity as Family	A.B. Simpson	4a
We Live and Move in God	Augustine	8a
The Trinity	A.W. Tozer	13a
O Trinity of Blessed Light	Ambrose of Milan	15a
The Universal Presence	A.W. Tozer	23a
God's Creation, Praise Him!	Anonymous	39a
Apprehending God	A.W. Tozer	48a
Prayer of Praise to God	*Te Deum Laudamus*	49a
The Gaze of the Soul	A.W. Tozer	68a
Praise	A.B. Simpson	69a
To Be Like Jesus	Christina Rossetti	119a
Christ Reveals the Father	A.B. Simpson	130a
Christ, the Dividing Line	A.B. Simpson	141a
We Glory in Your Cross, O Lord	Ancient Prayer	144a
Jesus Is Love Itself	A.B. Simpson	153a
Christ Is Our Example	Martin Luther	158a
Longing for Christ's Return	A.B. Simpson	189a
Longing for Christ's Return	A.W. Tozer	189a
The Prayer of St. Patrick	St. Patrick	201a
Adoration	Charles Wesley	206a
Prayer of Remembrance for Christ's Sacrifice	Miles Coverdale	228a
Christ Transcends Hard Hearts	John A. Mackay	230a
The Gift of the Holy Spirit	A.B. Simpson	249a
Prayer of Confession	Traditional prayer	255a
The Better Way	A.B. Simpson	261a
The Remedy for the World	A.W. Tozer	266a
Transformation	A.W. Tozer	272a
A Prayer for Peace	Traditional Prayer	278a
Count It All Joy	A.B. Simpson	287a
Christ Possesses Our Being	A.B. Simpson	298a
Prayer of St. Francis	St. Francis of Assisi	304a
Grace for Grace	A.B. Simpson	310a
Prayer for Discernment	Thomas á Kempis	313a
Prayer of Longing for God	A.W. Tozer	322a
The Practice of the Presence of God	Nicholas Herman (Brother Lawrence)	333a
How Can We Live Lives Acceptable to God?	A.W. Tozer	335a
Prayer for a Godly Life	Thomas á Kempis	336a
God, Our Protector and Deliverer	John Bunyan	387a
Healing Glorifies God	A.B. Simpson	412a
Strength from Day to Day	A.B. Simpson	415a
Mortality and Immortality	A.W. Tozer	421a
The Lord's Prayer	Based on Matthew 6:9-13	447a
Where Love Begins	A.W. Tozer	462a
Prayer of Gratitude for God's Tender Mercies	John Knox	468a
The Church as the Glory of the World	John Bunyan	487a
The Living Book	A.W. Tozer	488a
God's Word Transcends the World	Martin Luther	495a
The True Source of Service	A.B. Simpson	504a
Missionaries Are the "Scaffolding"	Hudson Taylor	523a

A Prayer for Missionaries	*Scottish Book of Common Prayer*	550a
Proclaim the Gospel to Every Nation, Tribe and Tongue	A.B. Simpson	551a
Living Likenesses of Christ	A.B. Simpson	580a
The Heart Strangely Warmed	John Wesley	584a
Earth's Crammed with Heaven	Elizabeth Barrett Browning	620a
Prayer after Communion	The Didache	637a
A Baptism Prayer	*The Book of Common Prayer*	644a
A Charge to Parents	*The Pastor's Handbook*	649a
God Establishes All Authority	Romans 13:1-7	668a

Medleys

OUR GOD IS HOLY
Theme: God, The Holy Trinity
2 ....Holy, Holy, Holy, Lord God Almighty
3..Hide Me in Your Holiness

OUR GOD IS MIGHTY
Theme: God, The Father—His Creation, Providence and Redemption
33 ....I Sing the Mighty Power of God
34 ....Great and Mighty

OUR GOD IS EXALTED
Theme: God, The Father—His Praise
53 ....Great Is the Lord
54...He Is Exalted

OUR GOD IS WORTHY OF PRAISE
Theme: God, The Father—His Praise
56.................................Blessed Be the Name of the Lord
57..I Sing Praises

OUR GOD IS MIGHTY
Theme: God, The Father—His Praise
65 ....Mighty Is Our God
66 ....How Great Thou Art

OUR GOD IS WITH US
Theme: God, The Son—His Advent
79...God Is with Us! Alleluia!
80..Emmanuel

CHRIST IS BORN
Theme: God, The Son—His Nativity
104 ....Silent Night! Holy Night!
105 ....Child in the Manger

CHRIST IS RISEN
Theme: God, The Son—His Resurrection and Exaltation
155.......................................Christ the Lord Is Risen Today
156 ....Celebrate Jesus

LIFT UP HIS NAME
Theme: God, The Son—His Resurrection and Exaltation
163.................................All Hail the Power of Jesus' Name
164.......................................Lord, I Lift Your Name on High

CROWN HIM KING
Theme: God, The Son—His Resurrection and Exaltation
175 ....Crown Him with Many Crowns
176 ....All Hail, King Jesus

CHRIST IS RETURNING
Theme: God, The Son—His Coming in Glory
182..Christ Is Coming Back Again
183 ....Lift Up Your Heads

JESUS IS COMING SOON
Theme: God, The Son—His Coming in Glory
190 ....Jesus Is Coming Again
191...Soon and Very Soon

OUR KING IS COMING
Theme: God, The Son—His Coming in Glory
193 ....My Lord, What a Morning
194..The King Is Coming

OUR MAJESTIC KING
Theme: God, The Son—His Praise
211...We Will Glorify
212 ....Majesty

OUR BEAUTIFUL SAVIOR
Theme: God, The Son—His Praise
213...Fairest Lord Jesus
214 ....You Are My All in All

OUR PRECIOUS SAVIOR
Theme: God, The Son—His Praise
217 ....Shout to the Lord
218 ....More Precious Than Silver

OUR ROCK
Theme: God, The Son—His Praise
225 ....A Shelter in the Time of Storm
226 ....Praise the Name of Jesus
227.........................There's Something About That Name

OUR WONDERFUL LORD
Theme: God, The Son—His Praise
229...What a Wonderful Savior
230 ....He Is Lord

SPIRIT OF GOD, DESCEND
Theme: God, The Holy Spirit
252 ....Spirit of God, Descend upon My Heart
253 ....Spirit of the Living God

OUR REDEEMER
Theme: The Life in Christ—Redemption and Salvation
264...There Is a Redeemer
265 ....I Will Sing of My Redeemer

OUR LIFE AND BREATH
Theme: The Life in Christ—Sanctification, Consecration and the Deeper Life
307 ....Abiding and Confiding
308 ....Breathing Out and Breathing In

OUR EXAMPLE
Theme: The Life in Christ—Sanctification, Consecration and the Deeper Life
314...........................O, to Be Like Thee, Blessed Redeemer
315...Let the Beauty of Jesus

OUR SURRENDER
Theme: The Life in Christ—Sanctification, Consecration and the Deeper Life
317 .... Take My Life, and Let It Be Consecrated
318 .... Sanctuary

OUR GUIDE
Theme: The Life in Christ—Pilgrimage, Protection and Guidance
367 .... Teach Me Thy Way, O Lord
368 .... Step By Step

OUR BATTLE
Theme: The Life in Christ—Spiritual Conflict and Victory
397 .... Onward, Christian Soldiers
398 .... The Battle Belongs to the Lord

OUR HEALER
Theme: The Life in Christ—Divine Healing
410 .... The Branch of Healing
411 .... I Am the God That Healeth Thee

OUR HOPE
Theme: The Life in Christ—Divine Healing
418 .... Come, Ye Disconsolate
419 .... God Will Make a Way

OUR FRIEND
Theme: The Life in Christ—Prayer
439 .... What a Friend We Have in Jesus
440 .... I Must Tell Jesus

OUR MODEL OF LOVE
Theme: The Life in Christ—Love and Gratitude
453 .... Here Is Love
454 .... In Moments Like These

OUR BREAD OF LIFE
Theme: The Body of Christ—The Word of God
490 .... Break Thou the Bread of Life
491 .... Thy Word

OUR MESSAGE
Theme: The Body of Christ—Missions
516 .... Lift High the Cross
517 .... All Heaven Declares

OUR MISSION
Theme: The Body of Christ—Missions
521 .... We've a Story to Tell to the Nations
522 .... Song for the Nations

OUR LORD SHALL REIGN
Theme: The Body of Christ—Missions
555 .... Jesus Shall Reign
556 .... To the Ends of the Earth

OUR STORY
Theme: The Body of Christ—Testimony
564 .... My Faith Has Found a Resting Place
565 .... God Is So Good

OUR CALL TO WORSHIP
Theme: The Body of Christ—Gathering and Dismissal
616 .... We Bring the Sacrifice of Praise
617 .... He Has Made Me Glad (I Will Enter His Gates)
618 .... This Is the Day

Segues

From Number		To Number	
12	Holy, Holy, Holy Is the Lord of Hosts (C)	13	Glory Be to God, Creator (C)
24	The Steadfast Love of the Lord (E♭)	25	Great Is Thy Faithfulness (E♭)
47	Praise to the Lord, the Almighty (G)	48	O Worship the King (G)
75	Come, Thou Long-Expected Jesus (F)	76	Jesus, Name Above All Names (F)
88	Good Christian Friends, Rejoice (F)	89	Worship the King (B♭)
95	Angels We Have Heard on High (F)	96	Angels, from the Realms of Glory (B♭)
128	Hosanna (G)	129	The King of Glory Comes (e min.)
137	Were You There? (E♭)	138	At the Cross (E♭)
152	My Savior's Love (A♭)	153	O, How He Loves You and Me! (A♭)
202	O, for a Thousand Tongues (G)	203	Let There Be Honor and Glory and Praises (G)
219	Isn't He? (G)	220	Holy and Anointed One (G)
242	Be Still, for the Spirit of the Lord (D)	243	Where the Spirit of the Lord Is (D)
256	Whiter Than Snow (G)	257	Change My Heart, O God (C)
258	Nothing But the Blood (F)	259	O, the Blood of Jesus (F/G)
271	Grace Greater Than Our Sin (G)	272	Amazing Grace (G)
311	Jesus, All for Jesus (D)	312	I Surrender All (D)
341	'Tis So Sweet to Trust in Jesus (G)	342	He Is Able (C)
347	Trust and Obey (F)	348	Yes, Lord, Yes (F)
378	Savior, Like a Shepherd, Lead Us (C)	379	Lead Me, Lord (I Will Follow) (C)
382	Near to the Heart of God (D)	383	Seek Ye First (D)
402	Am I a Soldier of the Cross? (D)	403	Soldiers of Christ, Arise (D)
421	When the Roll Is Called Up Yonder (G)	422	I'll Fly Away (G)
466	More Love to Thee (G)	467	O, How I Love Jesus (G)
471	I Love You, Lord (F)	472	My Jesus, I Love Thee (F)
530	Go Forth and Tell! (E♭)	531	Lift Up Our Eyes (E♭)
547	Shine, Jesus, Shine (A)	548	Heart for the Nations (A)

568 Jesus Paid It All (E♭)
579 Glory to His Name (G)
611 The Savior Is Waiting (F)
634 Here, at Your Table, Lord (E♭)
659 Let All Things Now Living (F)
569 My Redeemer (A♭)
580 Victory in Jesus (G)
612 Come Just as You Are (F)
635 Let Us Break Bread Together (E♭)
660 Give Thanks (F)

Alphabetical Index of Tunes

A

ABERYSTWYTH 364
ACCLAIM 209
ACKLEY 583
ADELAIDE 290
ADESTE FIDELES 100, 210
ALETTA 495
ALL HEAVEN DECLARES 517
ALL IS WELL 478
ALL SAINTS, NEW 527
ALL THE WORLD 524
ALL TO CHRIST 568
ALLELUIA 236
ALLELUIA NO. 1 215
ALMOST PERSUADED 600
AMAZING GRACE 272
AMERICA 671
AMY 647
ANCIENT OF DAYS 60
ANDREWS 51
ANGEL'S STORY 512
ANTIOCH 81
ARLINGTON 402, 477
ARMAGEDDON 401
ARMS OF JESUS 428
ARNSBERG 619
AROUND YOUR THRONE 557
AS THE DEER 323
AS WE GATHER 621
ASH GROVE 624, 659
ASSAM 570
ASSURANCE 344
AU CLAIR DE LA LUNE 649
AURELIA 473, 492, 602
AUSTRIA 475, 661
AWAY IN A MANGER 85
AWESOME GOD 62
AZMON 61, 170, 202, 277

B

BATTLE HYMN 668
BE EXALTED 71
BE GLORIFIED 506
BE STILL 242
BE THOU EXALTED 11
BEACH SPRING 198, 503, 629
BEAKER 368
BEAUTY OF JESUS 315
BEECHER 448, 500
BEHOLD THE LAMB 148
BEMERTON 622
BENEDICTION 626
BENNARD 549
BENTON HARBOR 229
BERRY 180
BETHANY 434
BLESSED 56
BLESSED BE THE NAME 221
BLESSED QUIETNESS 237
BLESSING 514
BLESSINGS 469
BLOTT EN DAG 345
BOOTH 269
BOSTDORFF 17
BOYLSTON 346
BRADBURY 378
BREAD OF LIFE 490, 634
BREAKING BREAD 551
BREATHE UPON US 248
BROTHER JAMES' AIR 377
BULLINGER 360
BUNESSAN 32, 105, 643
BURLEIGH 193
BUTLER 413

C

CALVARY 594
CALVARY COVERS IT ALL 561
CAMACHA 367
CAMP 184
CANONBURY 417, 509
CANTAD AL SEÑOR 537
CARMICHAEL 611
CAROL 102
CELEBRATE JESUS 156
CHANGE MY HEART 257
CHANNELS 510, 533
CHAPMAN 115
CHRIST AROSE 160
CHRIST IN ME 297
CHRIST RETURNETH 186
CHRISTMAS 92
CHRISTMAS SONG 101
CLEANSING FOUNTAIN 151
CLOSE TO THEE 388
CLOSER WALK 370
COME TO THE TABLE 630
COMFORTER 238
COMING AGAIN 190
COMMUNION 637
CONSOLATION 418
CONVERSE 439
CORONATION 163
CRADLE SONG 86
CRANHAM 103
CRIMOND 376, 468
CROWNING DAY 192
CRUCIFER 516
CRUSADERS' HYMN 213
CWM RHONDDA 384, 385
CYMRAEG 453

D

DANIEL 396
DARWALL 172, 199
DAVIS 550
DEEPER 331
DEMPSEY 233
DENNIS 387, 483
DIADEM 165
DIADEMATA 175, 403
DIVERNON (abridged) 632
DIVINUM MYSTERIUM 77
DIX 30, 112, 206, 310
DOMINUS REGIT ME 450
DUKE STREET 555, 666
DUNCANNON 133
DUNDEE 23

E

EASTER HYMN 155
EBENEZER 458
EIN' FESTE BURG 35
EL NATHAN 361
ELIZABETH 576
ELLACOMBE 33, 476
ELLESDIE 296
EMMANUEL 80
ENDS OF THE EARTH 556
ES IST EIN ROS' 78
EUCHARISTIC HYMN 633
EVAN 442
EVENTIDE 327, 435, 650
EVERLASTING LOVE 592
EVERYTHING 305
EXCELL 154

F

FACE TO FACE 429
FAIRHILL 16
FAITHFUL ONE 22
FAITHFULNESS 25
FAMILY OF GOD 487
FATHER'S LOVE 144
FEDERAL STREET 648
FESTAL SONG 504
FILL ME NOW 293
FILL MY CUP 589
FIND US FAITHFUL 391
FINLANDIA 295, 363, 654
FISCHER 256
FLEMMING 8
FOUNDATION 489
FRANCONIA 498
FREELY, FREELY 511
FRENCH CAROL 93
FULLY SURRENDERED 332

G

GALILEE....324
GARDEN....590
GIFT OF LOVE....451
GIVE ME JESUS....585
GIVE THANKS....660
GLADNESS....465
GLORIA....95
GLORIA PATRI....10
GLORIFY THY NAME....18
GLORY SONG....427
GLORY TO GOD....9
GLORY TO HIS NAME....579
GO, TELL IT....82
GOD BE WITH YOU....627
GOD CALLS US....545
GOD CARES....42
GOD IS SO GOOD....565
GOD SAVE THE QUEEN....673
GOOD TO ME....27
GOODINE....379
GORDON....472
GOSPEL OF CHRIST....526
GRAHAM....454
GREAT AND MIGHTY....34
GREAT IS THE LORD....53
GREAT PHYSICIAN....603
GREEN....264
GREENSLEEVES....106
GREENWELL....574
GROSSER GOTT, WIR LOBEN DICH....5

H

HALELUYA! PELO TSO RONA....639
HAMBURG....145
HANKEY....599
HANOVER....532
HAPPY DAY....591
HARTFORD....580
HARVESTTIME....538
HE GIVETH MORE GRACE....462
HE HAS MADE ME GLAD....617
HE IS ABLE....342
HE IS EXALTED....54
HE IS LORD....230
HE LEADETH ME....43
HE TOUCHED ME....588
HE WILL MAKE A WAY....419
HEALER OF MY SOUL....415
HEALETH THEE....411
HEALING IN JESUS....416
HEALING WINGS....412
HEARN....76
HEART FOR THE NATIONS....548
HEART MELODY....285
HEAVEN....423
HEAVENLY DOVE....250
HENDON....317
HERE I AM, LORD....552
HERZLIEBSTER JESU....136
HICKS....226
HIDE ME....3
HIDING IN THEE....351
HIGHER GROUND....330
HILLYER....390
HIMSELF....303
HINGHAM....355
HIS STRENGTH IS PERFECT....414
HOLINESS....438
HOLMES....625
HOLY AND ANOINTED ONE....220
HOLY IS THE LORD....19
HOLY MANNA....308, 309
HOLY, HOLY....14
HOPE OF GLORY....298
HOSANNA....128
HOUR OF PRAYER....436
HOW GREAT IS YOUR LOVE....455
HOW MAJESTIC....46
HUDSON....138
HUGG....232
HURSLEY....431
HYFRYDOL....75, 162, 265, 408, 499, 519, 560
HYMN TO JOY....50, 159, 543

I

I AM THINE....329
I EXALT THEE....55
I LOVE THEE....470
I LOVE YOU, LORD....471
I SHALL KNOW HIM....424
I SING PRAISES....57
I WANT TO BE A CHRISTIAN....615
I WILL PRAISE HIM....207
I'D RATHER HAVE JESUS....578
IF MY PEOPLE....260
IL EST NÉ....83
I'LL FLY AWAY....422
I'M REDEEMED....571
IN BABILONE....240
IN DULCI JUBILO....88
IN THE NAME OF THE LORD....64
IRBY....107
ISN'T HE....219
ITALIAN HYMN....4, 523

J

JANICE....111
JENNINGS....63
JERNIGAN....214
JESUS, ALL FOR JESUS....311
JESUS, I COME....613
JESUS LOVES ME....459
JESUS NEVER FAILS....349
JESUS ONLY....300, 301
JESUS SAVES....528
JEWELS....645
JOY OF THE LORD....287
JOYFUL SONG....208
JUDAS MACCABEUS....173
JÜNGST....91

K

KING IS COMING....194
KING JESUS....176
KING OF THE NATIONS....539
KINGDOM PRAYER....261
KINGS OF ORIENT....109
KINGSFOLD....113
KINSMAN....268
KIRKPATRICK....575
KNAPP....563
KNOWING YOU....335
KREMSER....58, 664

L

LAFFERTY....383
LAMB OF GOD....150, 410
LANCASHIRE....127, 161, 404, 546
LANDAS....564
LASST UNS ERFREUEN....28, 79
LAST HOPE....251
LAUDA ANIMA....474
LAUDES DOMINI....205
LEAD ME, LORD....380
LEARNING TO LEAN....358
LEMMEL....350
LENOX....177
LEONI....59
LET IT BE SAID....502
LET THERE BE GLORY....203
LET US BREAK BREAD....635
LIFT UP OUR EYES....531
LIFT UP YOUR HEADS....183
LIU....98
LIVING GOD....253
LO, JESUS COMES....187
LOBE DEN HERREN....47, 529
LONDONDERRY AIR....273
LORD, I LIFT YOUR NAME....164
LOVE FOUND A WAY....584
LOVE OF GOD....456
LOWLINESS....114
LYNGHAM....201
LYONS....48

M

MADRID....204
MAITLAND....372
MAJESTY....212
MALOTTE....445
MAN OF SORROWS....134
MANCHESTER....505
MARCHING TO ZION....375
MARGARET....108
MARION....657
MARTYRDOM....38, 143, 494, 631
MARYTON....515, 644
MATERNA....670
MCAFEE....382
MCCABE....542
MCDANIEL....587
MEDITATION....362
MEEKNESS AND MAJESTY....124
MELITA....667
MENDELSSOHN....94
MESSAGE....521
MESSIAH....171
MIEIR....216
MIGHTY IS OUR GOD....65
MILES LANE....166

MILLER 638
MINERVA 607
MONTREAT 123
MOODY 271
MORE LOVE TO THEE....................466
MORE PRECIOUS 218
MORECAMBE 252
MORNING SONG 189
MORRIS 356
MUNICH 245, 302, 640
MY ANCHOR HOLDS 405
MY LIFE IS IN YOU 278
MY REDEEMER 569
MY SAVIOR'S LOVE 152
MY TRIBUTE 566
MY TRUST 554

N

NATIONAL ANTHEM 669
NATIONAL HYMN 530, 665
NEAR THE CROSS 139
NEED 334
NETTLETON 280, 307, 655
NEUMEISTER 601
NEW ORLEANS 286
NICAEA 2
NORRIS 374
NORTH PHOENIX 636
NOW IS THE TIME 620
NUN DANKET 662
NUSBAUM 365
NYACK 121, 122

O

O CANADA 672
O HOW I LOVE JESUS....................467
O LOVE DIVINE 460
O PERFECT LOVE 656
O REDEEMING ONE 267
O STORE GUD 66
O, THE BLOOD OF JESUS 259
O WALY WALY 326, 437
OLD HUNDREDTH....................6, 69
OLD RUGGED CROSS 573
OLIVE'S BROW 141
OLIVET 279
ONCE FOR ALL 606
ONLY BELIEVE 281
OPEN OUR EYES 447
ORTONVILLE 174
ORWIGSBURG 440
O'SHIELDS 68
OTHELLO 562
OUR FATHER 446
OUR GOD REIGNS....................534
OUR HEART 553

P

PAROUSIA 559
PASS ME NOT 608
PASSION CHORALE 132
PATRICIA 153
PEARCE 185
PEARLY GATES 430
PENTECOSTAL POWER 246
PEOPLE NEED THE LORD....................610
PERFECT PEACE 283
PICARDY 74
PLAINFIELD 258
POWER IN THE BLOOD 595
PRECIOUS NAME 389
PRINCE 12
PROMISED LAND 426
PROMISED ONE 129
PROMISES 359
PSALM 25 381
PUER NOBIS 15

Q

QUEBEC 224

R

RATHBUN 147
REDEEMED 567
REFINER'S FIRE 291
REGENT SQUARE....................1, 96
REGINA 321
REGIONS BEYOND 518
REJOICE EVERMORE 288
RENEWED 13
RESCUE 597
REST (Maker) 284
RESURRECTION 582
RETREAT 444, 641
REVIVAL HYMN....................481
REVIVE US AGAIN 337
RIDER 319
ROLL CALL 421
RONDINELLA 314
ROTH 464
RUTHERFORD 254

S

SABOLICK 612
SAFETY 581
SAGINA 266
SALVATIONIST 577
SANCTIFIER 336
SANCTUARY 318
SANKEY 392
SATISFIED 572
SAVED BY GRACE 432
SCHULER 507
SCOTT 325
SEARCH ME 316
SECOND COMING 188
SEND REFRESHING....................338
SERENITY 135
SHELTER 225
SHINE 547
SHOUT TO THE LORD 217
SHOWALTER 357
SHOWERS OF BLESSING 596
SINE NOMINE 486
SIYAHAMBA 536
SLANE 328
SOJOURNER 373
SOLID ROCK 339
SONG FOR THE NATIONS 522
SOON AND VERY SOON 191
SOUND THE BATTLE CRY....................395
SOUTHWELL 409
SPIRITUS VITAE 480
SPRING HILL 386
ST. AGNES 228, 652
ST. ANNE 36
ST. BRENDAN'S 485
ST. CATHERINE 394, 653
ST. CHRISTOPHER 140
ST. DENIO 21
ST. GEORGE'S, WINDSOR....................117, 663
ST. GERTRUDE 397
ST. LEONARDS 333
ST. LOUIS 97
ST. MARGARET 449
ST. PETER 223
ST. THEODULPH 126
ST. THOMAS 482
STAR OF HOPE 182
STEADFAST LOVE 24
STEP BY STEP 371
STILLE NACHT 104
STORY OF JESUS 120
SUCH LOVE 463
SURRENDER 312
SWEETEST NAME....................586
SWENEY 299
SWING LOW 433

T

TABERNACLE 247
TE VENGO 535
TERRA BEATA 31
THAT BEAUTIFUL NAME....................118
THAT NAME 227
THE BATTLE 398
THE BLOOD 262
THE FIRST NOEL 90
THE LORD'S DAY 618
THE SERVANT SONG....................508
THE WAY OF THE CROSS....................604
THERE IS PEACE 243
THOMPSON 609
THOU ART WORTHY....................70
THY HOLY SPIRIT 241
THY POWER 623
THY WORD 491
TIDINGS 525
TO GOD BE THE GLORY....................44
TOPLADY 275
TORONTO 558
TRANQUILITY 306
TRENTHAM 292
TRURO 130, 158
TRUST AND OBEY 347
TRUST IN JESUS 341
TRUSTING JESUS 343
TRYGGARE KAN INGEN VARA....................40

U

USE ME TODAY 513
UTTERBACH 169

V

VENI EMMANUEL 73
VESSELS 322
VICTORY 406
VILLE DU HAVRE 352

W

W ZLOBIE LEZY 87
WALK WITH HIM 369
WALTHAM 99, 178
WASHED IN THE BLOOD 605
WE BOW DOWN 49
WE BRING THE SACRIFICE 616
WE CHOOSE TO BOW 399
WE WILL GLORIFY 211
WEBB 400
WEBER 255
WELLESLEY 274
WERE YOU THERE 137
WHIDDINGTON 294
WHITTLE 353
WHOLE WORLD 41
WHOSOEVER 598
WONDERFUL GRACE 270
WONDERFUL PEACE 282
WONDROUS LOVE 452
WONDROUS STORY 593
WOODWORTH 614
WORDS OF LIFE 496
WORSHIP THE KING 89
WORTHY 235
WORTHY IS THE LAMB 234
WYE VALLEY 304, 340
WYE VALLEY (abridged) 196, 541

Y

YES, LORD, YES 348

Metrical Index of Tune Names

S.M. (6.6.8.6.)
BOYLSTON 346
DENNIS 387, 483
FESTAL SONG 504
FRANCONIA 498
SOUTHWELL 409
ST. THOMAS 482
TRENTHAM 292

S.M. with Refrain
MARION 657
REVIVAL HYMN 481

S.M.D.
DIADEMATA 175, 403
TERRA BEATA 31

C.M. (8.6.8.6.)
AMAZING GRACE 272
AMY 647
ARLINGTON 402, 477
AZMON 61, 170, 202, 277
CRIMOND 376, 468
DUNDEE 23
EVAN 442
MAITLAND 372
MARTYRDOM 38, 143, 494, 631
MESSIAH 171
MORNING SONG 189
SERENITY 135
ST. AGNES 228, 652
ST. ANNE 36
ST. PETER 223

C.M. with Refrain
BLESSED BE THE NAME 221
DUNCANNON 133
EL NATHAN 361
EXCELL 154
GOD CARES 42
HUDSON 138
LANDAS 564
MCAFEE 382
MINERVA 607
O HOW I LOVE JESUS 467
OTHELLO 562
PENTECOSTAL POWER 246
PROMISED LAND 426
SPRING HILL 386
THY HOLY SPIRIT 241

C.M. with Repeats
ANTIOCH 81
CHRISTMAS 92
CORONATION 163
DIADEM 165
ORTONVILLE 174

C.M.D.
ALL SAINTS, NEW 527
CAROL 102
ELLACOMBE 33, 476
KINGSFOLD 113
MATERNA 670

C.M.D. with Refrain
SANKEY 392

L.M. (8.8.8.8.)
ALLELUIA 236
CANONBURY 417, 509
DUKE STREET 555, 666
FAIRHILL 16
FEDERAL STREET 648
GIFT OF LOVE 451
HAMBURG 145
HURSLEY 431
LAMB OF GOD (abbrev.) 410
MARYTON 515, 644
O WALY WALY 326, 437
OLD HUNDREDTH 6, 69
OLIVE'S BROW 141, 142
PUER NOBIS 15
QUEBEC 224
RETREAT 444, 641
TRURO 130, 158
TRYGGARE KAN INGEN VARA 40
WALTHAM 99, 178
WOODWORTH 614

L.M. with Refrain
HAPPY DAY 591
HE LEADETH ME 43
HIGHER GROUND 330
LAMB OF GOD 150
LO, JESUS COMES 187
O LOVE DIVINE 460
SAVED BY GRACE 432
SHELTER 225
SOLID ROCK 339
ST. CATHERINE 394, 653
SWENEY 299
VENI EMMANUEL 73

L.M. with Alleluias
LASST UNS ERFREUEN 28, 79

L.M.D.
HOUR OF PRAYER 436

5.5.5.3.D.
BUNESSAN 105

5.4.5.4.D.
ADELAIDE 290

5.5.5.4.D.
BUNESSAN 32, 643

5.6.8.5.5.8
CRUSADERS' HYMN 213

6.4.6.4. with Refrain
NEED 334

6.4.6.4.D.
BREAD OF LIFE 490, 634

6.4.6.4.6.6.6.4.
BETHANY 434
CAMACHA 367

6.4.6.4.6.6.4.4.
MORE LOVE TO THEE 466

6.5.6.4. with Refrain
CHRIST AROSE 160

6.5.6.5
BEMERTON 622

6.5.6.5.D.
HOLINESS 438
HOLY IS THE LORD 19
WYE VALLEY (abridged) 196, 541

6.5.6.5.D. with Refrain
ARMAGEDDON 401
HIMSELF 303
ST. GERTRUDE 397
WYE VALLEY 304, 340

6.6.4.6.6.4.
WORTHY 235

6.6.4.6.6.6.4.
AMERICA 671
GOD SAVE THE QUEEN 673
ITALIAN HYMN 4, 523
OLIVET 279

6.6.6.4.4.
PAROUSIA 559

6.6.6.5.D. with Refrain
VICTORY 406

6.6.6.D.
LAUDES DOMINI 205

6.6.6.6.
O, THE BLOOD OF JESUS 259

6.6.6.6.4.4.8.
DARWALL 172, 199

6.6.6.6.D.
MADRID 204

6.6.6.6.8.8.8.
LENOX 177

6.6.6.6.12.12.
CHRISTMAS SONG 101

6.6.7.7. with Refrain
ALL TO CHRIST 568

6.6.8.4.D.
LEONI 59

6.6.8.6.6.8.6.6.6.
ARNSBERG 619

6.6.8.8.6.6. with Refrain
MARCHING TO ZION 375

6.6.9.D. with Refrain
I'M REDEEMED 571
TRUST AND OBEY 347

6.7.6.7.6.6.6.6.
NUN DANKET.............662

6.8.6.8.6.6.6.7. with Refrain
KINSMAN.....................268

7.4.7.4.D.
EASTER HYMN 155

7.4.7.4.4.4.7.4.
LIVING GOD................253

7.5.7.5. with Refrain
JESUS NEVER FAILS.............................349

7.5.7.6. with Refrain
DANIEL..........................396

7.6.7.6. with Refrain
NEAR THE CROSS.......139

7.6.7.6.6.7.6.
ES IST EIN ROS'...............78
LIU..................................98

7.6.7.6.7.6.7.4. with Refrain
SAFETY..........................581

7.6.7.6.D.
ANGEL'S STORY..........512
AURELIA.........473, 492, 602
LANCASHIRE.......127, 161, 404, 546
MUNICH 245, 302, 640
PASSION CHORALE....................132
RUTHERFORD 254
ST. THEODULPH.........126
WEBB.............................400

7.6.7.6.D. with Refrain
ARMS OF JESUS 428
HANKEY........................599

7.6.7.6.7.7.7.6.
JESUS SAVES.................528

7.6.8.6.8.6.8.6.
ST. CHRISTOPHER......140

7.7.7.4.D. with Refrain
HERE I AM, LORD........552

7.7.7.6.7.6.4.4.6.
DEEPER..........................331

7.7.7.7.
ALETTA..........................495
WEBER 255

7.7.7.7. with Refrain
COMING AGAIN 190
GLORIA............................95
JESUS LOVES ME.........459
LOWLINESS..................114
NEUMEISTER 601
TRUSTING JESUS.........343

7.7.7.7. with Repeat
HENDON.......................317

7.7.7.7.7.7.
DIX 30, 112, 206, 310
TOPLADY......................275

7.7.7.7.7.7. with Refrain
MY ANCHOR HOLDS.........................405

7.7.7.7.D.
ABERYSTWYTH 364
EVERLASTING LOVE 592
ST. GEORGE'S, WINDSOR............117, 663

7.7.7.7.D. with Refrain
MENDELSSOHN...........94

7.7.7.8.
MAN OF SORROWS....134

7.8.7.8. with Refrain
PLAINFIELD.................258

7.8.7.8.7.7.
GROSSER GOTT, WIR LOBEN DICH.........5

8.5.8.3.
BULLINGER..................360

8.5.8.5. with Refrain
PASS ME NOT..............608

8.5.8.5.D. with Refrain
NYACK 121, 122

8.6.6.8. with Repeats
LYNGHAM....................201

8.6.8. with Refrain
MILES LANE................166

8.6.8.5. with Refrain
JEWELS...........................645

8.6.8.6.6.6. with Refrain
WORDS OF LIFE..........496

8.6.8.6.6.6.8.6.
CLEANSING FOUNTAIN..................151

8.6.8.6.7.6.8.6.
ST. LOUIS........................97

8.6.8.6.8.6.
BROTHER JAMES' AIR.................................377

8.6.8.8.6.
REST (Maker)................284

8.6.9.6. with Refrain
PERFECT PEACE..........283

8.7.7.7.
LAST HOPE...................251

8.7.8.5.
ST. LEONARDS............333

8.7.8.5.D. with Refrain
TRANQUILITY.............306

8.7.8.7.
DOMINUS REGIT ME 450
GALILEE.........................324
RATHBUN 147
RENEWED.......................13
THE SERVANT SONG............................508
WELLESLEY 274

8.7.8.7. with Refrain
BENTON HARBOR......229
BLESSED QUIETNESS................237
BREATHE UPON US 248
CHANNELS 510, 533
FACE TO FACE 429
FILL ME NOW.............293
GREAT PHYSICIAN.....603
HARVESTTIME............538
HEAVEN 423
HYFRYDOL......265, 408, 560
I WILL PRAISE HIM......207
MY REDEEMER 569
MY SAVIOR'S LOVE ...152
PEARLY GATES 430
PRECIOUS NAME.........389
SATISFIED 572
SEND REFRESHING.............338
SHOWERS OF BLESSING....................596
STEP BY STEP 371
SURRENDER................312
TABERNACLE..............247
TRUST IN JESUS...........341
WONDROUS STORY 593

8.7.8.7.6.6.6.6.7.
EIN' FESTE BURG 35

8.7.8.7.6.6.8.7.
CLOSE TO THEE.........388

8.7.8.7.6.8.6.7.
GREENSLEEVES...........106

8.7.8.7.7.
COMMUNION 637

8.7.8.7.7.7.
IRBY 107

8.7.8.7.8.7.
ANDREWS.......................51
LAUDA ANIMA 474
PICARDY..........................74
REGENT SQUARE......1, 96

8.7.8.7.8.8.7.
CWM RHONDDA..........384, 385
DIVINUM MYSTERIUM.................77

8.7.8.7.D.
AUSTRIA..................475, 661
BEACH SPRING...........198, 503, 629
BEECHER 448, 500
BRADBURY 378
CONVERSE 439
CYMRAEG 453
EBENEZER....................458
ELLESDIE......................296
GLORY TO GOD.............9
HOLY MANNA.....308, 309
HYFRYDOL.....75, 162, 499, 519, 560
HYMN TO JOY 50, 159
IN BABILONE 240
NETTLETON 280, 307, 655

8.7.8.7.D. with Refrain
STORY OF JESUS 120

8.7.8.7.D. with Coda
HYMN TO JOY 543
KINGDOM PRAYER....261

8.7.8.7.8.8.7.7.
W ZLOBIE LEZY.............87

8.8.4.4.6. with Refrain
KINGS OF ORIENT......109

8.8.5.8.8.5.with Refrain
JERNIGAN 214

8.8.6.6. with Refrain
HEAVENLY DOVE 250

8.8.8.5.
ACCLAIM......................209

8.8.8.6. with Refrain
HEALING WINGS........412

8.8.8.7.
GREENWELL 574

8.8.8.7.D.
COME TO THE TABLE..........................630

8.8.8.8.6.
ST. MARGARET 449

8.8.8.8.8.8. or 8.8.8.D.
MELITA 667
ST. CATHERINE 653

8.8.8.8.8.8. with Refrain
SAGINA 266

8.8.8.9. with Refrain
NORRIS 374

9.4.9.4. with Refrain
I'LL FLY AWAY............422

9.6.9.6. with Refrain
MONTREAT 123

9.7.9.7. with Refrain
SWEETEST NAME........586

9.8.9.8.
EUCHARISTIC HYMN 633
SPIRITUS VITAE 480

9.8.9.8. with Refrain
LEMMEL 350
REDEEMED 567

9.8.9.12. with Refrain
RESURRECTION 582

9.9.6.6.6.4.
ALMOST PERSUADED 600

9.9.9.4. with Refrain
CALVARY 594

9.9.9.5. with Refrain
GLORY TO HIS NAME 579

9.9.9.9.
LIFT UP OUR EYES 531
USE ME TODAY 513

9.9.9.9. with Refrain
FREELY, FREELY 511
MOODY 271

9.10.9.9. with Refrain
ASSURANCE 344

9.10.9.10. with Repeat
MORRIS 356

10.6.10.6. with Refrain
ROTH 464

10.6.10.6.8.8.8.6.
ALL IS WELL 478

10.7.10.7. with Refrain
I AM THINE 329
SCHULER 507

10.8.8.7.7. with Refrain
MESSAGE 521

10.9.10.8. with Refrain
POWER IN THE BLOOD 595

10.9.10.9. with Refrain
BENNARD 549
DAVIS 550
ORWIGSBURG 440
RONDINELLA 314
SHOWALTER 357

10.10.8.6.8.6. with Refrain
O CANADA 672

10.10.9.8. with Refrain
ONCE FOR ALL 606

10.10.9.10.
SLANE 328

10.10.10.4.4.
SINE NOMINE 486

10.10.10.8.
ASSAM 570

10.10.10.10.
CRUCIFER 516
EVENTIDE 327, 435, 650
MORECAMBE 252
NATIONAL HYMN 530, 665

10.10.10.10. with Refrain
GLADNESS 465
GLORY SONG 427
WHITTLE 353

10.10.10.10.10.10.
FINLANDIA 363

10.10.11.11.
HANOVER 532
LYONS 48

10.11.11.11. with Refrain
JUDAS MACCABEUS 173

11.6.11.6. with Refrain
MCCABE 542

11.7.10.8. with Refrain
THE WAY OF THE CROSS 604

11.7.11.7. with Refrain
CARMICHAEL 611
THOMPSON 609

11.8.9.9. with Refrain
FILL MY CUP 589

11.8.11.8.
MEDITATION 362

11.8.11.8. with Refrain
KIRKPATRICK 575

11.8.11.9. with Refrain
VILLE DU HAVRE 352

11.9.11.9. with Refrain
WASHED IN THE BLOOD 605

11.10.11.10.
CONSOLATION 418
O PERFECT LOVE 39, 656
PEARCE 185

11.10.11.10. with Refrain
CHAPMAN 115
FAITHFULNESS 25
HINGHAM 355
O STORE GUD 66
RESCUE 597
RIDER 319
TIDINGS 525
WHIDDINGTON 294

11.10.11.10. with Coda
TORONTO 558
FINLANDIA 295

11.10.11.10.11.10.
FINLANDIA 654

11.10.11.10.11.10.11.12.
LONDONDERRY AIR 273

11.11. with Refrain
REVIVE US AGAIN 337

11.11.11.5.
FLEMMING 8
HERZLIEBSTER JESU 136

11.11.11.9. with Refrain
PROMISES 359

11.11.11.11.
AU CLAIR DE LA LUNE 649
AWAY IN A MANGER 85
CRADLE SONG 86
FOUNDATION 489
GORDON 472
I LOVE THEE 470
ST. DENIO 21

11.11.11.11. with Refrain
BLESSINGS 469
FISCHER 256
HIDING IN THEE 351
HUGG 232
TO GOD BE THE GLORY 44

11.11.11.12.11.
BOOTH 269

11.12.12.10.
NICAEA 2

12.8.12.8. with Refrain
MCDANIEL 587

12.9.12.9. with Refrain
WONDERFUL PEACE 282

12.9.12.9. with Coda
MILLER 638

12.9.12.12.9.
WONDROUS LOVE 452

12.10.13.10.
JANICE 111

12.11.12.11.
KREMSER 58, 664

12.11.12.11. with Refrain
HE GIVETH MORE GRACE 462
JOY OF THE LORD 287
REJOICE EVERMORE 288

12.11.12.11.D.
ASH GROVE 624, 659

12.12. with Refrain
PROMISED ONE 129

12.12.12.6. with Refrain
COMFORTER 238

12.12.12.12. with Refrain
HEALING IN JESUS 416

13.11.13.7. with Refrain
NUSBAUM 365

13.13.13.11. with Refrain
ACKLEY 583

14.11.14.11. with Refrain
I SHALL KNOW HIM 424

14.14.4.7.8.
LOBE DEN HERREN 47, 529

15.9.15.9. with Refrain
WALK WITH HIM 369

15.11.15.11. with Refrain
ROLL CALL 421

15.15.15.6. with Refrain
BATTLE HYMN 668

15.15.15.14. with Refrain
HARTFORD 580

Authors, Translators, Composers, Arrangers and Sources

A

Ackley, Alfred A. (1887-1960) 583
Ackley, Bentley D. (1872-1958) 386, 481
Adams, Sarah F. (1805-1848) 434
Adams, Stephen R. (b. 1943) 243
Adkins, Donna (b. 1940) 18
Adler, Dan (b. 1960) 261, 267, 298, 399, 416
African-American spiritual 41, 82, 137, 193, 373, 433, 585, 615, 635
Ahlwen, Elsie (1905-1986) 430
Ahnfelt, Oscar (1813-1882) 345
Alexander, Cecil F.H. (1818-1895) 107, 324
Alexander, James W. (1804-1859) 132
Alford, Henry (1810-1871) 663

Allen, Chester G. (1838-1878) 208
Allen, David (b. 1941) 447, 610
Allen, George N. (1812-1877)....................372
Allen, Tom (b. 1958) 629
Altrogge, Mark (b. 1950)....................455
Ambrose of Milan (339-397)....................15
American folk hymn....................426, 452
American melody, traditional....................151, 189, 198, 272, 280, 307, 489, 503, 668
Amsler, Vivian Kretz (20th c.) 283
Andrews, Mark (1875-1939)....................51
Anonymous....................4, 221, 370, 467, 470, 570, 648, 673
Arne, Thomas A. (1710-1778)....................402, 477
Atkinson, Frederick C. (1841-1897)....................252
Atkinson, Jennifer (20th c.) 311

B

Babcock, Maltbie D. (1858-1901) 31
Bach, J.S. (1685-1750) 132
Bacon, Leonard (1802-1881) 666
Bain, James L. (1840-1925) 377
Baker, Henry (1835-1910)....................224
Baker, Henry W. (1821-1877)....................77, 450
Baker, Theodore (1851-1934) 78, 664
Barham-Gould, Arthur C. (1891-1953)....................333
Baring-Gould, Sabine (1834-1924) 397
Barker, Brenda (b. 1959) 259
Barker, Ken (b. 1955)....................259, 647
Barnby, Joseph (1838-1896)....................205, 656
Barnett, John (20th c.)....................220
Barraclough, Henry (1891-1983) 123
Bartlett, Eugene M. (1885-1941) 580
Bateman, Christian H. (1813-1889) 204
Bates, Katherine L. (1859-1929) 670
Bathurst, William H. (1796-1877) 277
Baxter, Lydia (1809-1874) 389
Beaker (20th c.) 368
Beethoven, Ludwig van (1770-1827)....................50, 159, 543
Bennard, George (1873-1958) 549, 550, 573
Benson, Louis F. (1855-1930) 113, 637
Berg, Carolina V.S. (1832-1903) 40, 345
Bernard of Clairvaux (1091-1153) 132, 224, 228
Berry, Cindy (b.1949)....................180
Bevan, Emma F. (1827-1909)....................601
Bible, Ken (b. 1950)....................79, 111, 273
Bigley, Marlene (b. 1952)....................34
Bilhorn, Peter P. (1861-1936) 593
Bixler, Beatrice B. (b. 1916)....................551
Black, James M. (1856-1938)....................421
Blanchard, Richard (b. 1925) 589
Blandy, E.W. (19th c.) 374
Blankenship, Mark (b. 1943)....................83, 93, 373, 636
Bliss, Philip P. (1838-1876) 134, 265, 352, 396 465, 496, 569, 598, 600, 606
Blom, Frederick A. (1867-1927) 430
Bode, John E. (1816-1874) 512
Bonar, Horatius (1808-1889) 1, 254, 268
Bonhöffer, Dietrich (1906-1945) 39
Booth, William (1829-1912)....................269
Borthwick, Jane L. (1813-1897)....................363
Bottome, Frank (1823-1894) 238
Bourgeois, Louis (1510-1561) 6, 69
Bowring, John (1792-1872)....................147
Bradbury, William B. (1816-1868) 43, 141, 339, 378, 436, 459, 495, 614
Brazilian folk melody/song....................537
Breck, Carrie E. (1855-1934) 429
Bridgers, Luther B. (1884-1948)....................586
Bridges, Matthew (1800-1894)....................175
Bridges, Robert (1844-1930) 136
Brook, F. (19th c.) 327
Brooks, Phillips (1835-1893)....................97
Brown, Mary A. (19th c.)....................505
Brown, Scott Wesley (20th c.) 526, 531, 556
Brownlie, John (1859-1925)....................189
Brumley, Albert E. (1905-1977)....................422
Budry, Edmond L. (1854-1932) 173
Bullinger, Ethelbert W. (1837-1913)....................360
Burke, J.H. (19th c.)....................121, 122, 300, 301
Burton, John, Sr. (1773-1822)....................495
Butler, D.J. (20th c.)....................413
Byrne, Mary E. (1880-1931)....................328

C

Calkin, John B. (1827-1905)....................99, 178
Camp, Mabel J. (1871-1937) 118, 184
Campbell, Thomas (1777-1844) 266
Cantai ao Senhor....................537
Cantus Diversi, 1751....................100
Carlson, Nathaniel (1879-1957)....................430
Carlson, Richard K. (b. 1956) 13
Carmichael, Ralph R. (b. 1927) 611
Carrell and Clayton's *Virginia Harmony*, 1831 272
Carter, Russell K. (1849-1928)....................248, 359, 571
Cartford, Gerhard (b. 1923) 537
Caswall, Edward (1814-1878) 205, 228
Chambers, Brent (b. 1948)....................71
Chapman, J. Wilbur (1859-1918)....................115, 560
Chapman, Steven Curtis (b. 1962)....................414
Charles, Elizabeth R. (1828-1896)....................8
Charlesworth, Vernon J. (1839-1915) 225
Chatfield, Allen W. (1808-1896) 387
Chisholm, Thomas O. (1866-1960) 25, 314
Chisum, John (20th c.)....................553
Christensen, Chris (b. 1957)....................522
Christiansen, Avis M.B. (1895-1966)....................369, 584
Clark, William H. (19th c.) 221
Clarkson, Margaret (b. 1915) 199, 529, 558
Clemm, J.B.O. (19th c.) 538
Clephane, Elizabeth C. (1830-1869)....................140
Cloninger, Claire (b. 1942) 630, 647, 661
Cober, Kenneth L. (20th c.)....................478
Coffin, Henry S. (1877-1954)....................73
Coffman, Samuel F. (1872-1954) 641
Cogbill, K. Richard (b. 1956) 305
Conkey, Ithamar (1815-1867) 147
Converse, Charles C. (1832-1918) 439
Coomes, Tom (b. 1946)....................621
Cooper, W.G. (19th c.)....................282
Cornell, W.D. (19th c.)....................282
Cory, Julia Cady (1882-1963) 58
Cowper, William (1731-1800) 23, 151
Croft, William (1678-1727) 36, 532
Croly, George (1780-1860)....................252
Cropper, Margaret (1886-1980) 649
Crosby, Fanny J. (1820-1915) 11, 44, 120, 139, 208, 241, 329, 344, 388, 424, 428, 432, 567, 575, 597, 608

Crouch, Andraé (b. 1947) 191, 262, 566
Crüger, Johann (1598-1662) 136, 662
Cull, Bob (b. 1949) 447
Cummings, William H. (1831-1915) 94
Cushing, William O. (1823-1902) 351, 355, 645
Cutler, Henry S. (1824-1902) 527

D

Darwall, John (1731-1789) 172, 199
Davis, Katherine K. (1892-1980) 659
Davis, Michael B., Sr. (b. 1958) 550
Daw, Carl P., Jr. (b. 1944) 377
Dearman, Kirk (b. 1952) 616
Deck, James G. (1802-1884) 640
Dempsey, Larry (1946-1995) 233
DeShazo, Lynn (b. 1956) 218, 557
Dix, William C. (1837-1898) 106, 112, 162, 602
Doane, William H. (1832-1915) 44, 139, 329, 389, 428, 466, 597, 608
Doddridge, Philip (1702-1751) 591
Doerksen, Brian (b. 1965) 22, 291, 620
Draper, William H. (1855-1933) 28
Dudley-Smith, Timothy (b. 1926) 135
Duffield, George (1818-1888) 400
Dugan, Gertrude R. (1873-1948) 513
Dwight, Timothy (1752-1817) 482
Dykes, John B. (1823-1876) 2, 228, 450, 652, 667

E

Edmunds, Lidie H. (1851-1920) 564
Edson, Lewis (1748-1820) 177
Edwards, Robert L. (b. 1915) 499
Edwards, William (1848-1929) 453
Elliott, Charlotte (1789-1871) 614
Elliott, Emily E.S. (1836-1897) 108
Ellis, J. (19th c.) 269
Ellor, James (1819-1899) 165
Elvey, George J. (1816-1893) 117, 175, 403, 663
English carol, traditional 90
English melody 31, 113
English melody, traditional 106, 326, 437, 451
Espinosa, Eddie (b.1953) 257
Evans, David (1874-1948) 204, 643
Evans, David (b. 1957) 242
Excell, Edwin O. (1851-1921) 154, 272, 469, 562

F

Faber, Frederick W. (1814-1863) 274, 394, 468
Farjeon, Eleanor (1881-1965) 32
Farquharson, Walter (b. 1936) 655
Fasig, Bill (1929-2002) 637
Fawcett, John (1740-1817) 483, 494
Fay, Mike (20th c.) 621
Featherstone, William R. (1846-1873) 472
Ferguson, Greg (20th c.) 342
Ferguson, John (b. 1941) 129
Ferguson, Manie P. (1850-1932) 237
Fettke, Tom (b. 1941) 79, 111, 145, 522, 545
Filitz, Friedrich (1804-1876) 622
Filsinger, R.C. (b. 1950) 288
Fischer, William G. (1835-1912) 256, 599
Fishel, Donald (b. 1950) 215
Flemming, Friedrich F. (1778-1813) 8
Flint, Annie J. (1862-1932) 462
Fosdick, Harry E. (1878-1969) 385
Founds, Rick (b. 1954) 164
Francis, Samuel T. (1834-1925) 458
Franz, Ignace (1719-1790) 5
French carol, traditional 83, 93, 95
French melody 74, 649
Frey, Marvin V. (1918-1992) 230
From *Katholisches Gesangbuch*, Vienna, 1774 431
Fry, Charles W. (1837-1882) 577
Fry, Steven (b. 1954) 183, 502
Fullerton, William Y. (1857-1932) 273

G

Gabriel, Charles H. (1856-1932) 152, 246, 330, 427, 542, 587, 604
Gaelic melody, traditional 32, 105, 643
Gaither, Gloria (b. 1942) 64, 194, 227, 487, 582
Gaither, William J. (b. 1936) 194, 227, 487, 582, 588
Gardner, Daniel (b. 1956) 278
Garrett, Les (b. 1944) 618
Gauntlett, Henry J. (1805-1876) 107
Geistliche Kirchengesäng, 1599 78
Geistliche Kirchengesäng, 1623 ....28, 79
Geneva Psalter, 1551 ....6, 69
George, Bill (20th c.) 89
Gerhardt, Paul (1607-1676) 132
German 78, 205
German carol, traditional 91
German melody 88, 91, 209
Gesangbuch der Herzogl, Württemberg, 1784 ....33, 476
Giardini, Felice de (1716-1796) 4, 523
Gibbs, Ada R. (1865-1905) 510, 533
Gillard, Richard (b. 1953) 508
Gilman, Samuel (1791-1858) 648
Gilmore, Joseph H. (1834-1918) 43
Gilmour, Henry L. (1837-1920) 514
Gladden, Washington (1836-1918) 515
Gläser, Carl G. (1784-1829) 61, 170, 202, 277
Goodine, Elizabeth (b. 1962) 379
Goodine, Wayne (b. 1954) 379
Gordon, Adoniram J. (1836-1895) 472
Goss, John (1800-1880) 401, 474
Gottschalk, Louis M. (1829-1869) 251
Graham, David (b. 1948) 454
Grant, Amy (b. 1960) 491
Grant, David (1833-1893) 376, 468
Grant, Robert (1779-1838) 48
Grape, John T. (1835-1915) 568
Greatorex, Henry W. (1813-1858) 10
Greco, Eugene (b. 1960) 65
Greek hymn, ancient 189
Green, Fred Pratt (1903-2000) 39, 417
Greenelsh, Elizabeth (b. 1949) 203
Greenelsh, James (b. 1940) 203
Green-Sievright, Melody (b. 1946) 264
Greenwell, Dora (1821-1882) 574
Grotenhuis, Dale (b. 1931) 535
Groves, Alexander (1843-1909) 490
Grüber, Franz X. (1787-1863) 104
Gurney, Dorothy F.B. (1858-1932) 656
Gustafson, Gerrit (b. 1948) 65

H

Hahn, David (b. 1956) 250, 261, 267, 298, 305, 371, 399, 416, 460, 550
Hahn, Gelsie (b. 1958) 250

Hainsworth, Richard (1885-1959)....315
Hall, Elvina M. (1820-1889)....568
Hammond, Mary J. (1878-1964)....480
Hampton, David (20th c.)....556
Hanby, Benjamin R. (1833-1867)....114
Handel, G.F. (1685-1759)....81, 92, 171, 173
Hankey, Arabella C. (1834-1911)....599
Harkness, Robert (1880-1961)....75, 560
Harmonischer Liederschatz, 1738....498
Harrington, Karl P. (1861-1953)....101
Harris, Margaret J. (19th c.)....207
Hart, Barbara B. (b. 1916)....654
Harvill, Jamie (20th c.)....60
Hassler, Hans L. (1564-1612)....132
Hastings, Thomas (1784-1872)....174, 275, 418, 444, 641
Hatch, Edwin (1835-1889)....292
Hatton, John (ca. 1710-1793)....555, 666
Havergal, Frances R. (1836-1879)....310, 317, 340, 360, 401, 509
Havergal, William H. (1793-1870)....442, 498
Hawkins, Floyd W. (20th c.)....283
Hawks, Anna S. (1835-1918)....334
Haydn, Franz Joseph (1732-1809)....475, 661
Haydn, Johann M. (1737-1806)....48
Hayes, Mark (b. 1953)....32, 105
Hayford, Jack (b. 1934)....212, 623
Hays, William S. (1837-1907)....577
Head, Bessie P. (1850-1936)....480
Hearn, Naida (b. 1944)....76
Heber, Reginald (1783-1826)....2, 633
Hebrew melody....59
Hedge, Frederick H. (1805-1890)....35
Heermann, Johann (1585-1647)....136
Helmore, Thomas (1811-1890)....73
Hemy, Henri F. (1818-1888)....394, 653
Herbert, George (1593-1633)....524
Hewitt, Eliza E. (1851-1920)....299, 423
Hicks, Roy, Jr. (1943-1994)....226
Hillyer, J.O. (19th c.)....390
Hine, Stuart K. (1899-1989)....66
Hodges, Edward (1796-1867)....50, 159
Hodges, John S.B. (1830-1915)....633
Hoffman, Elisha A. (1839-1929)....229, 357, 440, 579, 605
Holden, Oliver (1765-1844)....163
Holland, Josiah G. (1819-1881)....101
Holst, Gustav T. (1874-1934)....103
Hopkins, John H., Jr. (1820-1891)....109
Hopson, Hal H. (b. 1933)....451, 536
Horn, Doris R. (b. 1918)....638
How, William W. (1823-1897)....486, 492, 498
Howe, Julia W. (1819-1910)....668
Hoyle, Richard B. (1875-1939)....173
Hoyt, May P. (19th c.)....634
Huber, Jane Parker (b. 1926)....245
Hudson, Ralph E. (1843-1901)....138, 221, 572
Hugg, George C. (1848-1907)....232
Hughes, John (1873-1932)....384, 385
Hull, Eleanor H. (1860-1935)....328
Hunt, Arthur B. (1890-1971)....338
Hunter, William (1811-1877)....603
Husband, John J. (1760-1825)....337
Hussey, Jennie E. (1874-1958)....133
Hustad, Donald P. (b. 1918)....445
Hymnal, 1933....363
Hymns for the Young, 1836....378
Hymns for Todays Church, 1982....117

I

Indian folk tune....570
Ingall's, Jeremiah, *Christian Harmony*, 1805....470
Irish hymn (ca. 8th c.)....328
Irish melody, traditional....273, 328
Irons, Herbert S. (1834-1905)....409
Irvine, Jessie S. (1836-1887)....376, 468
Isâis, Juan M. (b. 1926-2002)....535
Israeli folk song....129
Iverson, Daniel (1890-1977)....253

J

Jabusch, Willard F. (b. 1930)....129
Jackson, Robert (1842-1914)....292
Jacob, Gordon (1895-1984)....377
James, Mary D. (1810-1883)....302
Jarman, Thomas (1776-1861)....201
Jean de Fecamp (11th c.)....136
Jennings, Tom (b. 1966)....63
Jernigan, Dennis L. (b. 1959)....214
John of Damascus (ca. 700-754)....161
Johnson, Norman (b. 1928)....328
Johnston, Julia H. (1849-1919)....271
Jones, Lewis E. (1865-1936)....595
Jude, William H. (1852-1922)....324
Judson, Adoniram (1788-1850)....644
Jüngst, Hugo (1853-1923)....91

K

Kaiser, Kurt (b. 1934)....153
Katholisches Gesangbuch, Vienna, 1774....5, 431
Keble, John (1792-1866)....431
Keesecker, Lynn (b. 1953)....348
Kelly, Thomas (1769-1855)....170, 209
Ken, Thomas (1637-1711)....6, 16, 79
Kendrick, Graham (b. 1950)....124, 335, 463, 539, 547
Kentucky Harmony, Part Second, 1813....189
Kerr, Ed (20th c.)....557
Kethe, William (1510-1594)....69
Key, Francis Scott (1779-1843)....669
Kilpatrick, Bob (b. 1952)....506
Kirk, James M. (1854-1945)....237
Kirkland, Camp (b. 1946)....273
Kirkpatrick, William J. (1838-1921)....86, 133, 187, 221, 238, 241, 314, 341, 528, 564, 567, 574, 575
Kitchin, George W. (1827-1912)....516
Klein, Laurie (b. 1950)....471
Knapp, Phoebe Palmer (1839-1908)....187, 344, 563
Kocher, Conrad (1786-1872)....30, 112, 206, 310
Kremser, Edward (1838-1914)....58, 664

L

Lafferty, Karen (b. 1948)....383
Landsberg, Max (1845-1928)....59
Lathbury, Mary A. (1841-1913)....490
Latin....10, 73, 100, 474
Latin carol (14th c.)....88
Lavallée, Calixa (1842-1891)....672
Leavitt's, Joshua *The Christian Lyre*, 1831....296
Leech, Bryan Jeffery (b. 1931)....541, 632
Lehman, Frederick M. (1868-1953)....456
Lemmel, Helen H. (1864-1961)....350
Lewis, Freeman (1780-1859)....362

Lewis, Howell E. (1860-1953) 650
Lillenas, Haldor (1885-1959) 270, 369
Little Children's Book, 1885 ....85, 86
Liturgy of St. James, ca. 4th c. 74
Lloyd, Eva B. (b. 1912) 503
Lloyd, William F. (1791-1853) 346
Loes, Harry D. (1892-1965) 584
Longfellow, Henry W. (1807-1882) 99
Longstaff, William D. (1822-1894) 438
Lowry, Robert (1826-1899) 160, 258, 334, 375, 453
Luther, Arthur A. (1891-1960) 349
Luther, Martin (1483-1546) 35
Lutkin, Peter C. (1858-1931) 626
Lyon, Meyer (1751-1797) 59
Lyra Davidica, 1708 155
Lyte, Henry F. (1793-1847) 51, 296, 435

M

MacAlmon, Terry (b. 1955) 57
Macbean, Lachlan (1853-1931) 105
Macdonald, Mary (1789-1872) 105
Mackay, William P. (1839-1885) 337
MacMillan, J. Buchanan (1915-1983) 248
Main, Hubert P. (1839-1925) 296
Maker, Frederick C. (1844-1927) 140, 284
Malan, Henri A.C. (1787-1864) 317
Malotte, Albert Hay (1895-1964) 445
Mann, Arthur H. (1850-1929) 512
Mann, Newton (1836-1926) 59
March, Daniel (1816-1909) 519
Mark, Robin (20th c.) 311
Marsh, Charles H. (1886-1956) 115, 192
Marsh, Don (b. 1943) 122, 301
Marshall, W.S. (19th c.) 237
Martin, Civilla D. (1869-1948) 42
Martin, Greg (b. 1950) 98
Martin, W.C. (19th c.) 405
Martin, Walter S. (1862-1935) 42
Mason, Lowell (1792-1872) 61, 81, 145, 151, 170, 202, 277, 279, 346, 387, 434, 483
Matheson, George (1842-1906) 449
Matthews, Timothy R. (1826-1910) 108
Maxwell, Mary E. (1837-1915) 510
McAfee, Cleland B. (1866-1944) 382
McBride, Eldon (b. 1962) 182, 198, 295, 304, 308, 316, 321, 336, 408, 412, 543, 554
McCutchan, Robert G. (1877-1958) 524
McDaniel, Rufus H. (1850-1940) 587
McFarland, John T. (1851-1913) 85, 86
McGee, Bob (b. 1944) 80
McGranahan, James (1840-1907) 186, 268, 361, 569, 596, 601
McHugh, Phil (b. 1951) 64, 610
McIntosh, Rigdon M. (1836-1899) 426
McNeill, Edith (b. 1920) 24
Mendelssohn, Felix (1809-1847) 94, 245, 302, 640, 662
Mercer's *Cluster of Spiritual Songs*, 1817 489
Merrill, William P. (1867-1954) 504
Messiter, Arthur H. (1834-1916) 657
Metrical Psalter, 1855 431
Mieir, Audrey (1916-1996) 216
Miles, C. Austin (1868-1946) 590
Miller, Rhea F. (1894-1966) 578
Millhuff, Charles (b. 1938) 194
Mills, Pauline M. (1898-1995) 70
Milman, Henry H. (1791-1868) 130
Mitchell, Hubert (20th c.) 462
Moen, Don (b. 1950) 56, 65, 235, 411, 419
Mohr, Jon (b. 1955) 391
Mohr, Joseph (1792-1848) 104
Monk, William H. (1823-1889) 30, 112, 206, 310, 327, 435, 650
Monsell, John S.B. (1811-1875) 111, 546
Montgomery, James (1771-1854) 96, 442, 631
Moody, Dave (b. 1948) 176
Moody, May W. (1870-1963) 353
Moore, Thomas (1779-1852) 418
Moore, William (19th c.) 308, 309
Morley, Frederick B. (20th c.) 476
Morris, Lelia N. (1862-1929) 188, 322, 356
Mote, Edward (1797-1874) 339
Moultrie, Gerard (1829-1885) 74
Mountain, James (1844-1933) 196, 304, 306, 340, 541, 592
Mozart, Wolfgang A. (1756-1791) 296
Mullins, Rich (20th c.) 62
Münster Gesangbuch, 1677 213
Murray, James R. (1841-1905) 85
Murray, Robert (1832-1910) 500
Musseau, Craig (b. 1965) 27

N

Nägeli, Johann H.G. (1773-1836) 387, 483
Neale, John M. (1818-1866) 73, 77, 88, 126, 161, 178, 474
Neander, Joachim (1650-1680) 47, 619
Nehorai, Meir Ben Isaac (11th c.) 456
Nelson, Greg (b. 1948) 610
Netherlands folk melody (18th c.) 240
Netherlands folk song/hymn 58, 664
Neumeister, Erdmann (1671-1756) 601
Neuvermehrtes Gesangbuch, 1693 ....245, 302, 640
Newbolt, Michael R. (1874-1956) 516
Newell, William R. (1868-1956) 594
Newton, John (1725-1807) 154, 223, 272, 475
Nichol, Henry E. (1862-1928) 521
Nicholson, James L. (1828-1876) 256
Nicholson, Sydney H. (1875-1947) 516
Noel, Caroline M. (1817-1877) 196
Noland, Rory (20th c.) 342
Norris, John S. (1844-1907) 374
Norwegian folk melody 564
Nusbaum, Cyrus S. (1861-1937) 365
Nystrom, Martin J. (b. 1956) 323, 548, 630

O

Oakeley, Frederick (1802-1880) 100, 210
Oatman, Johnson, Jr. (1856-1926) 232, 330, 469
Oliver, Gary (b. 1956) 156
Oliver, Henry K. (1800-1885) 648
Olivers, Thomas (1725-1799) 59
Olson, Ernest W. (1870-1958) 40
Ortlund, Anne (b. 1923) 527
Osborn, Albert (1886-1967) 315
O'Shields, Michael (b. 1948) 68
Owens, Carol (b. 1931) 511
Owens, Jimmy (b. 1930) 14, 16
Owens, Priscilla J. (1829-1907) 528
Owens-Collins, Jamie (b. 1955) 398

P

Palmer, Phoebe Worrall (1807-1874) 563
Palmer, Ray (1808-1887) 224, 279
Paris, Twila (b. 1958) 49, 54, 150, 211, 410
Parker, Edwin P. (1836-1925) 251
Parry, Joseph (1841-1903) 364
Patten, A.B. (1871-1938) 653
Patty, Sandi (b. 1956) 64
Peace, Albert L. (1844-1912) 449
Pearce, Almeda J. (1893-1986) 185
Pennefather, William (1816-1873) 622
Perronet, Edward (1726-1792) 163, 165, 166
Perry, Jean (1865-1935) 118
Perry, Michael (1942-1996) 409
Peterson, John W. (b. 1921) 190, 558
Phillips, Keith (b. 1941) 635
Pierpoint, Folliott S. (1835-1917) 30
Pigott, Jean S. (1845-1882) 306
Plainsong 73, 77
Plumptre, Edward H. (1821-1891) 657
Polish carol/melody, traditional 87
Pollard, Adelaide A. (1862-1934) 290
Pounds, Jessie B. (1861-1921) 604
Praetorius, Michael (1571-1621) 15, 78
Prentiss, Elizabeth P. (1818-1878) 466
Prichard, Rowland H. (1811-1887) 75, 162, 265, 408, 499, 519, 560
Prince, Nolene (20th c.) 12
Prior, Charles E. (1856-1927) 505
Prudentius, Marcus Aurelius C. (348-413) 77

R

Rader, Paul (1879-1938) 247, 281
Ragsdale, Steve (20th c.) 3
Rambo, Dottie (b.1934) 148
Ramsey, Benjamin M. (1849-1923) 367
Rankin, Jeremiah (1828-1904) 627
Rebuck, Linda (20th c.) 545
Redner, Lewis H. (1831-1908) 97
Reed, Andrew (1787-1862) 251
Reed, Edith M.G. (1885-1933) 87
Rees, John P. (1828-1900) 272
Rees, Timothy (1874-1939) 240
Rees, William (1802-1883) 453
Reichardt, C. Luise (1780-1826) 401
Reinagle, Alexander R. (1799-1877) 223
Richards, Noel (20th c.) 517
Richards, Tricia (20th c.) 517
Rider, Lucy J. (1849-1922) 319
Rimbault, Edward F. (1816-1876) 254, 591
Rinkart, Martin (1586-1649) 662
Rippon, John (1751-1836) 163, 165, 166
Rippon's, John *Selection of Hymns*, 1787 489
Rivard, Gene (b. 1949) 182, 316, 321, 326, 336, 381, 408, 412, 446, 543, 554, 637
Roberts, Daniel C. (1841-1907) 665
Roberts', John *Canaidau y Cyssegr*, 1839 21
Robinson, George W. (1838-1877) 592
Robinson, Robert (1735-1790) 280
Root, George F. (1820-1895) 645
Rossetti, Christina (1830-1894) 103
Roth, Elton M. (1891-1951) 285, 464
Rounsefell, Carrie E. (1861-1930) 505
Rowe, James (1865-1933) 386, 581
Rowley, Francis H. (1854-1952) 593
Runyan, William M. (1870-1957) 25
Russell, Anna B. (1862-1954) 286

S

Sabolick, Joseph (b. 1958) 612
Sadler, Gary (b. 1954) 60, 548
Sammis, John H. (1846-1919) 347
Sanchez, Pete Jr. (b. 1948) 55
Sandys', William *Christmas Carols* 90
Sankey, Ira D. (1840-1908) 225, 343, 351, 355, 392
Sateren, Leland (b. 1913) 624
Saward, Michael (b. 1932) 643
Sawyer, Frank (b. 1946) 535
Schlesische Volkslieder, 1842 213
Scholtes, Peter (b. 1938) 485
Schrader, Jack (b. 1942) 537
Schubert, Franz (1797-1828) 19
Schuler, George S. (1882-1973) 507
Schumann, Robert A. (1810-1856) 417, 509
Schutte, Daniel L. (b. 1947) 552
Scott, Clara H. (1841-1897) 325
Scottish Psalter, 1615 23
Scottish Psalter, 1650 ....38, 69, 376
Scriven, Joseph M. (1819-1886) 439
Scruggs, Randy (20th c.) 318
Searcy, George (20th c.) 553
Sears, Edmund H. (1810-1876) 102
Seddon, James E. (1915-1983) 530
Seiss, Joseph A. (1823-1904) 213
Sellers, Ernest O. (1869-1952) 286
Shalley, Jerry (20th c.) 414
Shea, George Beverly (b. 1909) 578
Shepherd, Thomas (1665-1739) 372
Sheppard, Franklin L. (1852-1930) 31
Sherwin, William F. (1826-1888) 395, 490, 634
Showalter, Anthony J. (1858-1924) 357
Shrubsole, William (1760-1806) 166
Shuey, Tim (b. 1954) 288
Shurtleff, Ernest W. (1862-1917) 404
Sibelius, Jean (1865-1957) 295, 363, 654
Simpson, Albert B. (1843-1919) 121, 122, 182, 198, 250, 287, 288, 294, 297, 298, 300, 301, 303, 304, 305, 307, 308, 309, 316, 321, 336, 371, 406, 408, 410, 412, 416, 460, 518, 533, 543, 554, 559
Simpson, Margaret M. (1876-1958) 518
Simpson, Scott A. (b. 1966) 17, 41, 585
Sinclair, Jerry (1943-1993) 236
Siyahamba 536
Skoog, Andrew L. (1856-1934) 345
Sleeper, William T. (1819-1904) 613
Sloan, T. Lynn (b. 1966) 9
Smart, Henry T. (1813-1879) 1, 96, 127, 161, 404, 546
Smiley, Billy (20th c.) 89
Smith, Alfred B. (1916-2001) 11
Smith, Deborah D. (b. 1958) 53
Smith, Eddie (20th c.) 260
Smith, Henry (b. 1952) 660
Smith, Henry P. (1825-1898) 515, 644
Smith, Howard E. (1863-1918) 581
Smith, John Stafford (1750-1836) 669
Smith, Leonard E., Jr. (b. 1942) 534
Smith, Michael W. (b. 1957) 46, 53, 491
Smith, Oswald J. (1889-1986) 331, 481

Smith, Samuel F. (1808-1895) 671
Smith, Walter C. (1824-1908) 21
Snead, Alfred C. (1884-1961) 332
South African/melody 639
Spaeth, Harriet Krauth (1845-1925) 78
Spafford, Horatio G. (1828-1888) 352
Spanish folk melody 204
Spencer, Robert Nelson (1877-1961) 667
Sprunger, Ron (b. 1939) 437, 625
St. Francis of Assisi (1182-1226) 28
Stainer, John (1840-1901) 88, 90, 106
Stallings, John (b. 1938) 358
Stead, Louisa M.R. (1850-1917) 341
Stebbins, George C. (1846-1945) 290, 332, 432, 438, 513, 613
Stennett, Samuel (1727-1795) 174, 426
Stites, Edgar P. (1836-1921) 343
Stockton, John H. (1813-1877) 579, 603, 607
Stokes, Elwood H. (1815-1895) 293
Stone, Samuel J. (1839-1900) 473
Stowell, Hugh (1799-1865) 444
Stralsund Gesangbuch, 1665 ....47, 529
Sullivan, Arthur S. (1842-1900) 397
Swain, Joseph (1761-1796) 362
Swedish melody 40
Sweney, John R. (1837-1899) 120, 293, 299, 424
Synesius of Cyrene (375-430) 387

T

Talbot, John Michael (b. 1954) 415
Tappan, William B. (1794-1849) 141
Tate, Nahum (1652-1715) 92
Taylor, Mrs. Walter G. (20th c.) 561
Te Deum (4th c.) 5
Tersteegen, Gerhardt (1697-1769) 619
Teschner, Melchoir (1584-1635) 126
The Hymnal, 1933 363
The Sacred Harp, 1844 ....478, 503, 629
Theodulph of Orleans (ca. 760-821) 126
Thesaurus Musicus, ca. 1740 ....671, 673
Thompson, John (b. 1950) 318
Thompson, John O. (1782-1818) 538
Thompson, Will L. (1847-1909) 576, 609
Thomson, Mary A. (1834-1923) 525
Threlfall, Jennette (1821-1880) 127
Thring, Godfrey (1823-1903) 175
Thrupp, Dorothy A. (1779-1847) 378
Tomer, William G. (1833-1896) 627
Toplady, Augustus M. (1740-1778) 275
Tourjée, Lizzie S. (1858-1913) 274
Townend, Stuart (b. 1962) 144
Towner, Daniel B. (1850-1919) 271, 347, 405, 594
Traditional 259, 565
Trier manuscript (15th c.) 15
Tullar, Grant Colfax (1869-1950) 429
Turner, H.L. (19th c.) 186
Tuttle, Carl (b. 1953) 128

U

Urban, Chretien (1790-1845) 254
Utterbach, Clinton (20th c.) 169

V

Vail, Silas J. (1818-1884) 388
Van De Venter, Judson W. (1855-1939) 312
Van Dyke, Henry (1852-1933) 50
Vaughan Williams, Ralph (1872-1958) 28, 74, 113, 162, 486, 499
Von Brethorst, Leona (b. 1923) 617
von Schlegel, Katharina A.D. (18th c.) 363
von Weber, Carl M. (1786-1826) 255

W

Wade, John F. (1711-1786) 100, 210
Wade's, John F. *Cantus Diversi*, 1751 ....100, 210
Walch, James (1837-1901) 525
Walford, William W. (1772-1850) 436
Walker's, William, *Southern Harmony*, 1835 452
Wallace, William V. (1814-1865) 135
Walter, William H. (1825-1893) 504
Walton, James G. (1821-1905) 394, 653
Walworth, Clarence A. (1820-1900) 5
Ward, Samuel A. (1847-1903) 670
Ware, Henry, Jr. (1794-1843) 652
Warner, Anna B. (1820-1915) 459
Warren, George W. (1828-1902) 530, 665
Watts, Isaac (1674-1748) 33, 36, 81, 138, 143, 145, 375, 402, 555
Webb, George J. (1803-1887) 400
Webbe, Samuel, Sr. (1740-1816) 418
Weeden, Winfield S. (1847-1908) 312
Weir, R. Stanley (1856-1926) 672
Welsh folk tune/melody 21, 624, 659
Wesley, Charles (1707-1788) 61, 75, 94, 142, 155, 171, 172, 177, 201, 202, 206, 255, 266, 364, 403, 448, 532
Wesley, Samuel S. (1810-1876) 380, 473, 492, 602
Westendorf, Omer (1916-1998) 624
Weyman's *Melodia Sacra* (1815) 92
Whiddington, Ada A. (19th c.) 294, 295
Whitcomb, George W. (19th c.) 192
Whitfield, Frederick (1829-1904) 467
Whiting, William (1825-1878) 667
Whittier, John G. (1807-1892) 284
Whittle, Daniel W. (1840-1901) 338, 353, 361, 596
Wilbur, Richard (b. 1921) 98
Wilkinson, Kate B. (1859-1928) 333
Williams', Aaron *Psalmody*, 1770 482
Williams, Clara T. (1858-1937) 572
Williams, Peter (1722-1796) 384
Williams, Thomas J. (1869-1944) 458
Williams', Thomas *Psalmodia Evangelica*, 1789 ....130, 158
Williams, William (1717-1791) 384
Willis, Richard S. (1819-1900) 102, 213
Wilson, Emily D. (1865-1942) 423
Wilson, Hugh (1764-1824) 38, 143, 494, 631
Wilson, Ira B. (1880-1950) 507
Wimber, John (1934-1997) 219
Winkworth, Catherine (1827-1878) 47, 662
Wolcott, Samuel (1813-1886) 523
Wood, James H. (b. 1921) 503, 629
Wordsworth, Christopher (1807-1885) 117
Work, Frederick J. (1879-1942) 137, 615
Work, John W. (1872-1925) 82, 137, 615
Wren, Brian (b. 1936) 158, 159
Wyeth's, John *Repository of Sacred Music*, Part Second, 1813 ....280, 307, 655
Wyrtzen, Don (b. 1942) 234

Y

Yates, John H. (1837-1900) 392

Yigdal of Daniel ben Judah (ca. 1400)....59
York, Terry W. (b. 1949)....477
Young, John F. (1820-1885)....104

Z

Zelley, Henry J. (1859-1942)....514
Zschech, Darlene (b. 1965)....217
Zulu traditional song....536
Zundel, John (1815-1882)....448, 500

Scriptural Allusions

Genesis
1....32, 33
1:1....13
1:2....240
1:5....618
1:28....31
2:16....33
3:17-19....81
8:22....25
26:24....489
28:10-22....434
28:15....373
31:49....627
35:15....434
40:8....23

Exodus
3:14....59
13:21....384, 659
14:13....398
15:11....62
15:26....410, 411
16:7....32, 437
16:15....627
19:5....347
20:3....251, 324
20:11....33
25:17-22....444
33:22....275
34:6....22

Leviticus
11:44....317
20:7....321

Numbers
6:24-26....626
18:20....328

Deuteronomy
2:7....373
6:4....399
6:5....278
6:6-9....652
7:9....22
7:21....62
8:3....383
10:17....34, 62
11:13....504
31:6....39, 42, 48
32:3....532
32:10....482
33:25....345
33:27....357
34:1....436

Joshua
1:9....385
1:16....548
24:15....399, 401, 570, 652

1 Samuel
1:27-28....648
2:2....2
3:9....348, 509, 549, 550, 552
7:12....272, 280
15:22....347

2 Samuel
22:2....226
22:47....68

1 Kings
19:12-13....284, 478

2 Kings
2:11-12....433
4:3....322

1 Chronicles
16:9....593
16:29....10
21:13....274
28:9....513
29:11....17, 54, 212
29:13....662
29:14....498

2 Chronicles
5:13....565
7:14....260
15:15....308, 309
20:6....623
20:15....398, 401

Ezra
3:11....661
9:13....136

Nehemiah
1:5....62
8:10....287, 288
9:17....626

Esther
4:14....385

Job
1:21....40, 221, 352
12:10....41
12:23....669
19:25....68, 171
22:26....47
38:7....31, 97

Psalms
1....326
2:6....375
3:3....415
5:3....2, 32, 205, 368, 437, 585
5:8....380
7:17....209
8:1....46
8:3....30, 31, 66
9:1....61
13:5....48
16:2....39
16:11....362, 423
17:8....3
18:1....454, 468, 470, 471
18:2....35, 216, 226
18:2-3....68
18:46....68
18:49....57
19:1....13, 31, 50, 517, 665
19:6....659
21:13....11
22:4....665
23....376, 377, 450
23:1-3....43, 378
23:4....373
24:1....31
24:7-10....127, 129, 183
24:8....1, 665
24:10....114
25:4-5....360, 381, 509
25:7....387
26:8....482
27:1....357, 536
27:4....213
27:11....367
28:1....27
28:7....323, 415
29:2....44, 201, 202
29:11....626
31:3....509
31:15....346
31:21....452
32:7....286, 364
32:8....367
33:1....657
33:12....670, 671, 672
34:18....382
35:28....201, 202
37:5....284, 343
37:7....223
40:2....339
40:4....607
40:5....469
42:1....572
42:5....363
42:11....47, 323
43:3....542
44:8....210
45:4....130
45:8....123
46:1....35, 171
46:4....280
46:7-9....665
46:10....54, 242, 363
47:2....62
47:7....619
48:1....66
48:14....368, 369, 384, 662
50:23....207
51:2....409
51:7....256, 259, 271, 290, 387
51:10....257, 387
51:12....316
53:6....129
55:17....415
55:22....42
57:5, 9-11....54, 71
59:16....32
60:12....669
61:2-3....351, 486
62:2....27
63:1, 4....368
65:6....33
66:1-2....201, 202
66:4....524
66:16....599
67:4....666
69:13-16....581
72:11....555
72:19....56, 207
73:25....218
73:28....434
77:2....613
77:19....23
80:18....337
84:2....334, 442, 615
84:7....403
85:2....561
85:6....337, 478, 480
86:1....334
86:9....553
86:11....367
86:15....274
87:3....475
89:8....667
90:1-5....36
90:10....435
90:17....317
91:4....355, 364, 627
92:4....164
94:22....351
95:1....204, 208, 537
95:2....663
95:4....41
95:6....49, 100, 210, 620
96:1....524, 537
96:2-3....528
96:4....53, 57
96:8....532
97:9....54, 55, 71
98....81
98:1....398
98:4....217
98:6....10
99:5....5, 19, 220
100....69
100:2....620
100:4....503, 617, 661
100:5....456
103....1, 38
103:1-6....47
103:2....51, 499
103:3....411, 603
103:13....40
103:19....172
104....28, 48
104:1....212
104:2....21
107:2....567
107:9....224, 323, 572
107:22....616
107:25....33
108:1....537
108:4....255
110:3....623
113:2....64
115:1....579
115:12....664
116:12....566
117:2....668
118:8....341
118:9....672
118:24....617, 618

119:18 325
119:72 218
119:97 495
119:105 ....478, 491, 492, 494
119:130 492
119:133 356
121:7 415
126:3 660
127:3 647
130:2 553
133:1 624
136:1 ....27, 565
138:2 8
139:1 316
139:9-10 43
139:12 431
139:23 ....290, 316, 409
143:8 390
145:2 205
145:3 53
145:10 ....2, 28, 50
145:21 28
146 63
146:2 ....205, 344
148:3 30
148:5 28
149:2 ....211, 375
150:2 208
150:6 ....6, 16, 47, 79, 659

Proverbs
3:5 ....343, 358
4:18 ....206, 357, 659
14:34 671
18:10 ....64, 169
18:24 ....353, 576
25:4 291
29:25 428

Ecclesiastes
3:11 30
5:10 572

Song of Songs
2:1 ....78, 577
2:4 ....34, 659

Isaiah
1:18 ....259, 568
2:3 368
2:4 521
2:5 515
6:1-8 552
6:2 21
6:3 .....5, 12, 13, 19, 619
6:8 ....348, 379, 505, 549, 550, 552
7:14 ....73, 80
9:2 73
9:6 ....13, 46, 75, 216, 219, 286
9:7 555
11:1 ....73, 78
11:9 158
12:2 ....341, 360
12:5 566
24:14 212
25:1 562
25:4 .... 36, 364
25:8 178
26:3 ....283, 353
28:16 ....474, 477
29:19 228
30:18 611
32:2 ....140, 225
33:17 ....213, 219
33:20-21 475
35:1-2 78
35:3 507
35:10 375
40:3-4 429
40:5 273
40:9 ....53, 525
40:11 ....40, 208, 647
40:12 340
42:3 124
42:8 210
43:1-2 489
43:2 667
43:19 419
44:3 319
48:17 404
48:18 340
49:13 50
49:15 664
51:3 661
51:16 575
52:7 ....317, 534
52:10 528
53:2 78
53:3-4 ....120, 132, 134, 136, 138, 141, 143, 152, 208, 439
53:5 ....408, 412, 416
53:6 254
54:7-8 23
54:17 398
55:1 ....261, 614
57:15 480
61:1 613
61:10 266
62:2-4 413
63:1-4 668
63:16 58
64:6 258
64:8 ....257, 290
66:5 211
66:12 340

Jeremiah
6:16 306
18:6 ....257, 290
29:13 260
31:3 ....449, 456, 592
31:34 260

Lamentations
3:22-23 ....24, 25, 32, 39, 274

Ezekiel
11:19 568
34:26 596

Daniel
7:9, 13-14 ......21, 59, 60

Joel
2:1 187
3:10 660

Micah
5:2 97
5:5 99

Habakkuk
2:20 74
3:2 ....480, 481

Haggai
2:7 ....75, 96

Zechariah
8:13 507
9:9 130
12:10 145
13:1 ....151, 280, 563
13:9 291

Malachi
3:1 96
3:2-3 291
3:6 ....363, 435
3:17 645
4:2 ....206, 412

Matthew
1:18 90
1:18-23 77
1:21 118
1:23 ....79, 80, 94, 100, 176
2:1-12 ....90, 93, 96, 103, 106, 109, 112
2:5-6 97
2:11 ....89, 111
3:11 247
3:13 641
3:16 644
4:18-22 ....284, 324
4:23 129
4:24 114
5:6 ....261, 331, 615
5:8 ....161, 447
5:13-16 ....478, 522
5:16 ....394, 507, 541
6:6 438
6:9-13 ....445, 446
6:10 ....521, 522, 559, 637
6:15 409
6:33 ....383, 438
7:7 383
7:14 ....112, 357, 604
7:24-26 339
8:2 409
8:3 649
8:12 193
8:15 649
8:19 ....512, 570
8:20 108
8:23-27 113
9:29 649
9:36 541
9:37-38 ....519, 538, 545, 546
10:8 ....499, 507, 511
10:21 296
10:32 486
10:38 296
11:15 ....325, 447
11:28 ....75, 78, 358, 387, 439, 602, 609
12:18 539
12:21 539
13:36-43 663
13:45-46 214
14:19 551
16:18 ....473, 475
16:24 ....372, 570
16:27 196
17:8 ....300, 301, 328
18:3-5 459
19:13 650
19:14 459
21:8-9 ....64, 126, 127, 128, 183
22:37 535
24:14 521
24:29-31 117
24:35 349
24:42 361
25:1-13 ....187, 188, 190
25:35 541
26:26-29 ....262, 637
26:36-46 141
27:29-45 ....132, 135, 138
27:35-28:10 137
27:50-51 142
28:2 160
28:6 ....159, 582
28:9-10 161
28:18-20 ....9, 82, 162, 518, 522, 533, 543, 548

Mark
1:10 252
1:41 ....588, 649
4:26-29 663
6:34 610
7:33 649
8:36 527
8:38 402
9:23 281
9:24 277
9:29 523
10:14 459
10:16 647
10:28 ....312, 343
10:45 453
11:8-10 ....126, 130
12:30 252
13:26 429
13:37 ....139, 188
14:22-25 637
14:32-41 141
14:38 568
14:62 186
15:17-33 ....132, 135, 137
16:6 ....158, 159, 583
16:15 ....503, 523

Luke
1:14 88
1:46 9
1:47 88
1:53 261
1:70 83
1:78 73
2:6-20 ....81, 82, 83, 85, 86, 87, 88, 90, 91, 92, 93, 94, 95, 96, 98, 99, 100, 101, 104, 105, 106, 107, 108, 113, 120
2:25-38 96
2:30 668
2:51 113
2:52 107
4:2 120
4:18-19 ....220, 273, 523
4:40 129
7:34 560
9:11 416
9:12-17 490
9:23 133
9:57-62 ....512, 533
10:2 ....538, 543
10:27 504
11:1 442
11:2-4 ....445, 446
11:3 345
11:9 383
11:13 250
14:11 260
14:27 570
15:2 601
15:4-6 ....378, 593
15:15-17 588
17:5 277
18:15 647
18:22 312
19:9 ....591, 652
19:10 ....280, 564, 597
19:36-38 126
19:40 98
21:2-4 317

21:27 668
21:28 ....183, 187
21:36 ....190, 664
22:15-20................637
22:17 ....632, 634
22:19 ....631, 636
22:20 639
22:39-46 ....141, 152
23:33.......113, 115, 594
23:34 124
23:26-44................135
23:42 ....151, 387
23:44 98
23:53 133
24:2 477
24:5 159
24:6 ....156, 160
24:15 373
24:29 435
24:31 325
24:32 632
24:36 622
24:45 490
24:47 522
24:49-52................162

John

1:1 196
1:1-3.......................117
1:3 70
1:4.........206, 224, 267, 547, 602
1:9 15
1:11 ....108, 136
1:12 97
1:14...........77, 94, 107, 117, 127, 164, 206, 364, 490, 492
1:29........148, 150, 233, 254, 264, 279
2:9-10.....................117
3:3 94
3:13 337
3:16.........44, 144, 164, 264, 453, 463, 464, 521, 584
4:14 572
4:35........527, 531, 546, 610
4:42 229
5:23 213
5:24 265
5:39 490
6:1-13.....................490
6:33 ....384, 418
6:35-38 .....74, 224, 633
6:37........274, 602, 611, 612, 614
6:44 591
6:51-59 .... 630, 639
6:63............... 480, 496
6:68 496
7:37 572
8:12........15, 50, 74, 97, 213, 525, 547
8:32 325
8:36 394
9:5 547
9:25 272
10:10 613
10:11 208
10:14 ....216, 376, 377, 378
10:27 379
10:35 475
11:26 292
11:28 609
12:3 133
12:12-15 ....126, 130
12:21 447
12:26 512
12:28 18
12:32.......134, 504, 516
12:46 547
13:1 458
13:3-5.....................124
13:7 23
13:15 509
13:34-35 ....451, 485
14:1 341
14:2 423
14:3.........66, 107, 182, 185, 372, 512, 573
14:6.........44, 158, 199, 267, 442, 602, 607, 614
14:15 470
14:16.......237, 238, 240
14:19 582
14:23 ....652, 654
14:26 ....238, 252
15:4 307
15:7 438
15:8 558
15:9 364
15:10 347
15:12.......451, 463, 507
15:13.......153, 453, 458
15:15 ....439, 576
15:26 238
16:7 238
16:8 361
17:20-23 ....476, 629
17:26 463
19:25 139
19:30.......134, 142, 155
19:34 ....106, 151
20:11-18................590
20:19, 26 622
20:21 ....558, 624
20:22 ....248, 292
20:25-28 ....175, 216
20:29 424
21:17 470

Acts

1:8..........246, 312, 530
1:9 164
1:11.........182, 188, 196
1:14 ....245, 523
2:1-13 .....245, 246, 480
2:3 547
2:17-18 ....245, 246, 253
2:21 597
2:24........115, 155, 160
2:36 ....87, 230
2:38-39..................245
2:41 ....641, 643
2:42 635
3:1 436
4:12.........227, 467, 529
4:29 385
8:4 599
8:35 120
8:36 643
9:15 510
10:38 220
12:7.........201, 202, 266
13:47 556
14:17 500
15:11 270
16:23-32................266
17:25 21
17:28 ....199, 525
20:28 473
20:32 627
20:38 483
22:16 644
26:28 600
27:23 310

Romans

1:16 ....269, 526
3:23 529
5:1 282
5:6-8 ......115, 144, 266, 267, 564, 574
5:9 258
5:20 ....270, 271
6:3 640
6:4 643
6:19 332
6:23 597
8:10, 14 241
8:11 251
8:15 177
8:16 4
8:16-17 ....344, 487
8:22 81
8:28 23
8:29 ....314, 386
8:32 66
8:37 ....173, 403
8:38-39 .....40, 209, 592
10:9.........230, 614, 615
10:14 ....530, 545
10:17 361
11:33 331
12:1.......138, 143, 145, 311, 317, 332
12:1-2 ....347, 440, 503
12:9 656
12:15 508
13:1 673
14:8 574
14:11 ....553, 620
15:13 625

1 Corinthians

1:9 340
1:22-25..................573
1:30 265
2:2 133
2:7 574
2:9 ....228, 455
2:16 240
3:10-11..................477
3:11 ....339, 473, 474
4:2...........391, 423, 554
5:7-8..............161, 232
6:11 1
6:20 ....378, 510
7:31 435
9:22 527
10:13 334
10:16.........39, 632, 639
11:24-25 ....39, 631, 634, 636, 638
11:26-28 ....629, 635
12:3 216
12:13 253
12:25-26................508
13 451
13:1-3.....................451
13:12.......264, 429, 492
13:13 656
15:3-4 .....164, 215, 564
15:12-17................159
15:20 155
15:28 327
15:51-52.........115, 193
15:54 ....142, 170
15:55 ....155, 435
15:57 ....173, 215, 265, 406, 580
16:13.......396, 400, 402
16:23 514

2 Corinthians

1:20-21..................359
3:4 360
3:17 ....243, 253
3:18.........315, 386, 448
4:4 35
4:16 345
4:18 599
5:7 371
5:8 422
5:10 199
5:14 ....452, 527
5:17 ....448, 587
5:18 229
5:18-20..................529
6:2 ....612, 614
6:16 318
7:1 359
8:9..........108, 270, 271
9:7 500
9:8 272
10:5 311
12:7-10..................417
12:9-10 ....345, 414, 558, 560

Galatians

2:20 ....136, 152, 215, 290, 294, 295, 336, 583
3:13 265
3:28 ....483, 529
4:4-5..............103, 473
5:1 594
5:13 508
5:16 252
5:22 ....240, 656
5:25 ....252, 253
6:2 ....483, 508
6:14........139, 140, 145, 147, 268, 397, 573

Ephesians

1:6 209
1:7...........44, 177, 264, 566, 567, 571
1:13 643
1:23 ....293, 589
2:1 609
2:4 ....152, 153
2:6 566
2:8..........272, 432, 564
2:10 514
2:12 610
2:20-22..........474, 477
3:17 451
3:18-19..........274, 455
3:19 333
3:20 342
3:21 506
4:3 483
4:4 529
4:5-6.......................397
4:7 462
4:22-23..........308, 309
4:30 280
5:1 314
5:2 273
5:18 293
5:19 ....285, 586
5:25-26..................338
6:1-4.......................654
6:10 ....370, 395
6:10-18 ....398, 403, 404
6:12 558
6:13 401
6:14-17..................359
6:17 4
6:18 442

Philippians
1:6 ....342, 448
1:9 466
1:18 543
1:20 506
1:21 365
2:5 333
2:5-8 ....124, 266
2:5-11 ....87, 94, 98, 108, 124, 170, 266, 525, 593
2:9 ....76, 163, 165, 166, 213, 227
2:9-11 ....65, 77, 180, 182, 196, 230, 399, 553
3:7-10 ....145, 218, 328, 335
3:8 ....350, 576, 578, 585
3:10 ....583, 615
3:12 510
3:14 ....330, 423
4:4 ....591, 657
4:6 439
4:7 237
4:11 43
4:13 ....370, 560
4:19 ....42, 316, 360, 499, 576, 663

Colossians
1:12 486
1:14 595
1:16 70
1:17 199
1:20 138
1:27 ....297, 298
2:9 254
2:12 643
2:13 561
2:14 352
3:4 185
3:11 ....214, 303, 304, 305
3:14 448
3:15-16 ....333, 352
3:17 389

1 Thessalonians
4:16 ....66, 185, 188, 352, 372
4:17 ....172, 194, 361, 421, 422
5:10 209
5:16, 18 657
5:23 302

2 Thessalonians
2:8 189
2:9 35

1 Timothy
1:15 ....465, 574
1:17 21
2:3-4 521
2:5 177
3:16 ....105, 113, 114
4:10 ....229, 341
4:12 391
6:12 ....402, 404, 486
6:15 ....49, 176, 212

2 Timothy
1:5 653
1:6-7 391
1:12 ....273, 361, 564
2:2 509
2:3 ....397, 400, 402, 404
2:7 574
2:12 ....170, 400
2:19 ....474, 489
2:21 ....503, 510
3:15 654
4:7 ....403, 502
4:8 ....367, 404, 472, 573

Titus
2:12 312
2:13-14 ....265, 344, 569, 583
3:5 ....255, 258, 275
3:7 270

Hebrews
1:2 70
1:3 ....15, 172
1:3-7 100
1:4 223
2:9 ....100, 170, 172, 173, 174, 189
2:18 ....342, 440
4:7 620
4:9-11 75
4:14-16 ....124, 177
4:15 ....107, 158, 440
4:16 418
6:13 59
6:19 ....339, 405
7:19 434
7:25 ....162, 171, 177, 458, 528, 597, 605, 607
9:22 258
9:28 ....115, 188, 189, 190, 344, 473
10:10 606
10:22 ....139, 329, 344
10:23 359
10:25 621
11 397
11:16 426
11:35-38 394
12:1-3 391
12:2 ....170, 279, 350, 438, 573
12:3 133
12:14 438
13:5 ....205, 489, 560
13:7 673
13:8 ....121, 122, 209, 349, 458, 662
13:14 433
13:15 616

James
1:5 ....385, 499
1:12 472
1:17 ....25, 30, 499
4:8 ....329, 356, 382, 434
5:13 343
5:14 417

1 Peter
1:5 353
1:7 291
1:8 ....228, 467
1:15 321
1:18-19 229
1:19 ....150, 254, 271, 482
1:22 655
1:25 489
2:2 615
2:4-7 474
2:5 477
2:7 223
2:9 ....163, 165, 166, 475
2:21 ....368, 374
2:24 ....144, 154, 254, 417
2:25 593
4:1 403
5:4 ....192, 472
5:7 ....42, 370, 440, 565
5:8 35

2 Peter
1:3 300
1:4 359
1:19 206
3:8 36
3:9 525
3:18 299

1 John
1:7 ....151, 201, 202, 229, 258, 347, 369, 605
1:9 ....337, 418
2:6 388
2:15 401
3:1 ....143, 152, 153, 270, 452
3:2 ....44, 427, 613
3:16 120
3:18-21 325
4:12 656
4:18 581
4:19 ....467, 472, 565
5:4 392
5:6 275
5:7 1

Jude
1:3 394
1:14 194
1:24 ....40, 342, 360
1:25 ....126, 506

Revelation
1:5 591
1:6 1
1:8 10
1:18 ....156, 158, 172, 583
2:5 478
2:10 394
3:4 185
3:7 73
3:10 334
3:20 ....597, 611
4:8 ....12, 17, 74
4:8-11 ....2, 59, 205
4:10 ....190, 372, 448
4:11 ....53, 65, 70, 212, 214, 232, 234, 235, 236
5:9 ....163, 165, 166, 310, 516, 537, 555, 557
5:10 160
5:12 ....17, 53, 210, 232, 234, 337
5:13 ....203, 211, 233, 532
6:12-17 193
6:14 352
7:9-12 ....77, 162, 175, 185, 532, 557
7:14 ....259, 605
11:15 ....81, 555
13:8 148
14:3 571
14:13 486
15:3 4
15:4 ....14, 17, 539
17:14 ....87, 114, 211, 235
19:1-6 ....74, 532
19:4-6 ....204, 236
19:6-12 ....162, 175
19:12-13 227
19:15 668
19:16 ....49, 163, 165, 166, 176, 235
20:6 ....163, 165, 166
21:3-4 191
21:4 ....363, 423, 429
21:6 224
21:18 343
21:21 430
21:27 426
22:1 418
22:4 427
22:4-5 59
22:5 ....176, 426
22:7 496
22:12-13 ....77, 182
22:14 430
22:16 ....139, 176, 577
22:17 ....198, 598, 612
22:20 ....75, 189, 191, 198, 663

Topical Index

Abiding in Christ
Abiding and Confiding 307
Christ in Me (CHRIST IN ME) 297
Christ in Me (HOPE OF GLORY) 298
Hiding in Thee 351
Himself (EVERYTHING) 305
Himself (HIMSELF) 303
Himself (WYE VALLEY) 304
In the Garden 590
Jesus, I Am Resting, Resting 306
Jesus, Lover of My Soul 364
Moment by Moment 353
The King of Love My Shepherd Is 450
The Solid Rock 339
Under His Wings 355

Adoration
(see God, the Father—His Praise; God, the Son—His Praise)

Advent
(see God, the Son—His Advent)

Atonement
(see also Redemption and Salvation)
Alas, and Did My Savior Bleed.....143
At the Cross.....138
Blessed Be the Glorious Tidings...408
Hallelujah, What a Savior!.....134
He Died for Me.....154
Nothing But the Blood.....258
O, the Blood of Jesus.....259
There Is a Fountain.....151
What a Wonderful Savior.....229

Baptism
Baptized in Water.....643
Baptized into His Death.....640
Come, Holy Spirit, Dove Divine...644
We Bless the Name of Christ the Lord.....641

Blood of Christ
(see Atonement; God, the Son—His Sufferings and Death)

Celebration
(see God, the Father—His Praise; God, the Son—His Praise)

Children
(see Dedication of Children)

Christian Example
Channels Only.....510
I Would Be Like Jesus.....386
O Master, Let Me Walk with Thee.....515
Stand Up, Stand Up for Jesus.....400
We Give Thee but Thine Own.....498

Christian Workers
(see Ministry and Service)

Christmas
(see God, the Son—His Nativity)

Christ's Life on Earth
(see God, the Son—His Life and Ministry)

Church
A Revival Hymn.....481
Christ Is Made the Sure Foundation.....474
Glorious Things of Thee Are Spoken.....475
I Love Your Kingdom, Lord.....482
Living Stones.....477
O Breath of Life.....480
O Church of God, United.....476
Renew Your Church.....478
The Church's One Foundation.....473

Comfort and Encouragement
A Shelter in the Time of Storm.....225
Abide with Me.....435
Be Still, My Soul.....363
Children of the Heavenly Father.....40
Come Unto Me, Ye Weary.....602
Count Your Blessings.....469
He Leadeth Me.....43
I Am His, and He Is Mine.....592
Jesus, Lover of My Soul.....364
Just As I Am.....614
My Faith Looks Up to Thee.....279
Only Believe.....281
Safe in the Arms of Jesus.....428
Take the Name of Jesus with You.....389
Thy Word.....491
Wonderful Peace.....282
Yesterday, Today, Forever.....121
Yesterday, Today, Forever (arr.).....122

Commitment
(see also Sanctification, Consecration and the Deeper Life)
Beneath the Cross of Jesus.....140
Come, All Christians, Be Committed.....503
Fully Surrendered.....332
I Surrender All.....312
I Would Be Like Jesus.....386
Jesus, All for Jesus.....311
Jesus, I Would Faithful Be.....390
Lead Me to Calvary.....133
My Goal Is God Himself.....327
O, to Be Like Thee, Blessed Redeemer.....314
Rise Up, O Church of God.....504
Search Me, O God.....316
Stand Up, Stand Up for Jesus.....400
The Breaking of the Bread.....551

Communion
(see Lord's Supper)

Communion of Saints
(see Fellowship of Believers)

Confession and Repentance
(see also Forgiveness)
Change My Heart, O God.....257
Depth of Mercy! Can There Be.....255
Hide Me in Your Holiness.....3
I Lay My Sins on Jesus.....254
If My People.....260
Jesus, I Come.....613
Just As I Am.....614
Kingdom Prayer.....261
Nothing But the Blood.....258
O, the Blood of Jesus.....259
The Blood Will Never Lose Its Power.....262
Whiter Than Snow.....256

Creation
All Creatures of Our God and King.....28
For the Beauty of the Earth.....30
Glory Be to God, Creator.....13
How Great Thou Art.....66
I Sing the Mighty Power of God.....33
Let All Things Now Living.....659
Morning Has Broken.....32
This Is My Father's World.....31
Thou Art Worthy.....70

Cross
(see also God, the Son—His Sufferings and Death)
At Calvary.....594
At the Cross.....138
Beneath the Cross of Jesus.....140
Hallelujah for the Cross.....268
He Died for Me.....154
In the Cross of Christ I Glory.....147
Lead Me to Calvary.....133
Must Jesus Bear the Cross Alone?.....372
Near the Cross.....139
The Old Rugged Cross.....573
The Way of the Cross Leads Home.....604
When I Survey the Wondrous Cross.....145

Death, Resurrection and Life Everlasting
Abide with Me.....435
Come, Ye Disconsolate.....418
Face to Face.....429
For All the Saints.....486
Guide Me, O Thou Great Jehovah.....384
He Giveth More Grace.....462
He the Pearly Gates Will Open.....430
I'll Fly Away.....422
It Is Well with My Soul.....352
My Faith Looks Up to Thee.....279
My Savior First of All.....424
My Times Are in Thy Hand.....346
Nearer, My God, to Thee.....434
O, That Will Be Glory.....427
On Jordan's Stormy Banks.....426
Rock of Ages.....275
Safe in the Arms of Jesus.....428
Saved by Grace.....432
Sun of My Soul, Our Savior Dear.....431
Swing Low.....433
When the Roll Is Called Up Yonder.....421
When We All Get to Heaven.....423

Dedication of Children
Children of the Heavenly Father...40
Friend of the Home.....650
Good Shepherd, Take This Little Child.....647
Jesus' Hands Were Kind Hands.....649
Jesus Loves Even Me.....465
Jesus Loves Me.....459
This Child We Dedicate to Thee.....648
When He Cometh.....645

Dependence upon God
(see Trust)

Discipleship
Am I a Soldier of the Cross? 402
Hark, the Voice of Jesus Calling..........519
Jesus, I My Cross Have Taken 296
Jesus, Master, Whose I Am 310
My Spirit, Soul and Body..........302
O Master, Let Me Walk with Thee..........515
Take My Life, and Let It Be Consecrated 317

Divine Healing
Blessed Be the Glorious Tidings 408
Come, Ye Disconsolate..........418
God Will Make a Way 419
Good to Me 27
Heal Me, Hands of Jesus..........409
Healer of My Soul 415
Healing in His Wings 412
Healing in Jesus..........416
Himself (EVERYTHING) 305
Himself (HIMSELF) 303
Himself (WYE VALLEY) 304
His Strength Is Perfect..........414
I Am the God That Healeth Thee..........411
I Will Change Your Name 413
O Christ, the Healer 417
The Branch of Healing 410
Yesterday, Today, Forever 121
Yesterday, Today, Forever (arr.) 122

Doxologies
Doxology (FAIRHILL)..........16
Doxology (OLD HUNDREDTH)......6
Glory Be to God the Father (GLORY TO GOD) 9
Glory Be to the Father..........10
God Is with Us! Alleluia!..........79
Holy Is the Lord 19

Easter
(see God, the Son—His Resurrection and Exaltation)

Eternal Life
(see Death, Resurrection and Life Everlasting)

Evangelism and Invitation
Almost Persuaded..........600
Are You Washed in the Blood?.....605
Calvary Covers It All 561
Christ Receiveth Sinful Men 601
Come Just as You Are..........612
Come Unto Me, Ye Weary..........602
Fill My Cup, Lord..........589
I Have Decided to Follow Jesus 570
I Love to Tell the Story..........599
Jesus, I Come 613
Jesus Saves 528
Just As I Am..........614
Lord, I Want to Be a Christian 615
Only Trust Him 607
Pass Me Not 608
People Need the Lord 610
Rescue the Perishing 597
Softly and Tenderly 609
The Cleansing Wave..........563
The Great Physician 603
The Savior Is Waiting 611
The Way of the Cross Leads Home 604
There is Power in the Blood 595
There Shall Be Showers of Blessing..........596
This Is the Gospel of Christ 526
Whosoever Will May Come 598

Faith
A Mighty Fortress Is Our God 35
Come, Thou Fount..........280
Faith Is the Victory..........392
Faith of Our Fathers 394
Faith of Our Mothers 653
God Moves in a Mysterious Way 23
It Is Well with My Soul 352
My Anchor Holds 405
My Faith Looks Up to Thee..........279
O, for a Faith That Will Not Shrink..........277
Only Believe 281
'Tis So Sweet to Trust in Jesus 341

Faithfulness of God
Faithful One..........22
For All the Saints 486
Good to Me 27
Great Is Thy Faithfulness..........25
Ho, Everyone That Is Thirsty........319
How Firm a Foundation 489
O God, Our Help in Ages Past 36
Standing on the Promises..........359
The Lord My Shepherd Guards Me Well 377
The Lord's My Shepherd..........376
The Steadfast Love of the Lord 24

Family Life and Relationships
A Christian Home 654
Children of the Heavenly Father..........40
Faith of Our Mothers 653
Friend of the Home 650
Happy the Home When God Is There 652
O Perfect Love..........656
Would You Bless Our Homes and Families..........655

Fellowship of Believers
Blest Be the Tie That Binds..........483
For All the Saints 486
God Be with You till We Meet Again..........627
The Family of God 487
They'll Know We Are Christians 485

Forgiveness
(see also Confession and Repentance)
Amazing Grace..........272
And Can It Be That I Should Gain..........266
At Calvary 594
Christ Receiveth Sinful Men 601
Depth of Mercy! Can There Be.....255
Glory to His Name..........579
I Lay My Sins on Jesus 254
Once for All..........606
One Day! 115
Only Trust Him..........607
There's a Wideness in God's Mercy 274

Gathering and Dismissal
As We Gather..........621
Come, Now Is the Time to Worship 620
God Himself Is With Us 619
He Has Made Me Glad (I Will Enter His Gates) 617
Jesus, Stand Among Us 622
Now May the God of Hope 625
Sent Forth by God's Blessing 624
The Day of Thy Power 623
The Lord Bless You and Keep You 626
This Is the Day..........618
We Bring the Sacrifice of Praise....616

God and Country
America..........671
America, the Beautiful..........670
Battle Hymn of the Republic..........668
Eternal Father, Strong to Save 667
God of Our Fathers..........665
God Save the Queen 673
If My People..........260
O Canada! 672
O God, Beneath Thy Guiding Hand 666
The Star-Spangled Banner 669

God, the Father—His Nature
A Mighty Fortress Is Our God 35
Faithful One..........22
God Moves in a Mysterious Way 23
Good to Me 27
Great and Mighty..........34
Great Is Thy Faithfulness..........25
Guide Me, O Thou Great Jehovah..........384
He Is Able 342
I Sing the Mighty Power of God..........33
Immortal, Invisible, God Only Wise..........21
In the Name of the Lord 64
Mighty Is Our God 65

O God, Our Help in Ages Past.......36
O Worship the King.......48
Praise Ye the Triune God.......8
Psalm 146.......63
The Steadfast Love of the Lord.......24
There's a Wideness in God's Mercy.......274

God, the Father—His Praise

All Around Your Throne.......557
All Creatures of Our God and King.......28
All People That on Earth Do Dwell.......69
Alleluia.......236
Ancient of Days.......60
Awesome God.......62
Be Exalted, O God.......71
Bless the Lord, O My Soul.......38
Blessed Be the Name of the Lord.......56
Come, Thou Almighty King.......4
Come, Thou Fount.......280
Glory Be to God the Father (GLORY TO GOD).......9
Glory Be to God the Father (REGENT SQUARE).......1
Glory Be to God, Creator.......13
Glory Be to the Father.......10
Glory to His Name.......579
Great and Mighty.......34
Great Is the Lord.......53
He Is Exalted.......54
Holy, God Almighty.......17
Holy God, We Praise Your Name.......5
Holy, Holy.......14
Holy, Holy, Holy Is the Lord of Hosts.......12
Holy, Holy, Holy, Lord God Almighty.......2
Holy Is the Lord.......19
How Great Thou Art.......66
How Majestic Is Your Name.......46
I Exalt Thee.......55
I Sing Praises.......57
I Sing the Mighty Power of God.......33
I Will Call upon the Lord.......68
Immortal, Invisible, God Only Wise.......21
In the Name of the Lord.......64
Joyful, Joyful, We Adore Thee.......50
Let All Mortal Flesh Keep Silence.......74
Mighty Is Our God.......65
My Life Is in You, Lord.......278
O, for a Heart to Praise My God.......61
O, Sing to the Lord (Cantad al Señor).......537
O Splendor of God's Glory Bright.......15
O Thou, in Whose Presence.......362
O Worship the King
Praise, My Soul, the King of Heaven.......51
Praise to the Lord, the Almighty.......47
Praise Ye the Triune God.......8
Psalm 146.......63
Rejoice, the Lord Is King!.......172
The God of Abraham Praise.......59
Thine Is the Glory.......173
This Is My Father's World.......31
Thou Art Worthy.......70
To God Be the Glory.......44
We Are Singing, for the Lord Is Our Light (Siyahamba).......536
We Bow Down.......49
We Bring the Sacrifice of Praise.......616
We Praise You, O God, Our Redeemer.......58

God, the Son—His Advent

Come, Thou Long-Expected Jesus.......75
Emmanuel.......80
God Is with Us! Alleluia!.......79
Jesus, Name Above All Names.......76
Let All Mortal Flesh Keep Silence.......74
Lo, How a Rose E'er Blooming.......78
O Come, O Come, Emmanuel.......73
Of the Father's Love Begotten.......77

God, the Son—Nativity

A Christmas Hymn.......98
Angels, from the Realms of Glory.......96
Angels We Have Heard on High.......95
Away in a Manger (AWAY IN A MANGER).......85
Away in a Manger (CRADLE SONG).......86
Child in the Manger.......105
Go, Tell It on the Mountain.......82
Good Christian Friends, Rejoice.......88
Hark, the Herald Angels Sing.......94
He Is Born.......83
How Great Our Joy.......91
I Heard the Bells on Christmas Day.......99
In the Bleak Midwinter.......103
Infant Holy, Infant Lowly.......87
It Came upon the Midnight Clear.......102
Joy to the World!.......81
O Come, All Ye Faithful.......100
O Little Town of Bethlehem.......97
O, Sing a Song of Bethlehem.......113
Once in Royal David's City.......107
Silent Night! Holy Night!.......104
Sing We Now of Christmas.......93
The First Noel.......90
There's a Song in the Air.......101
Thou Didst Leave Thy Throne.......108
What Child Is This?.......106
While Shepherds Watched Their Flocks.......92
Who Is He in Yonder Stall?.......114
Worship the King.......89

God, the Son—His Epiphany

Adoration.......111
As with Gladness Men of Old.......112
We Three Kings.......109

God, the Son—His Life and Ministry

A Christmas Hymn.......98
Ivory Palaces.......123
Jesus' Hands Were Kind Hands.......649
Meekness and Majesty.......124
O, Sing a Song of Bethlehem.......113
One Day!.......115
Songs of Thankfulness and Praise.......117
Tell Me the Story of Jesus.......120
That Beautiful Name.......118
Who Is He in Yonder Stall?.......114
Yesterday, Today, Forever.......121
Yesterday, Today, Forever (arr.).......122

God, the Son—Palm Sunday

All Glory, Laud and Honor.......126
Hosanna.......128
Hosanna, Loud Hosanna.......127
Ride On, Ride On in Majesty.......130
The King of Glory Comes.......129

God, the Son—His Sufferings and Death

A Purple Robe.......135
Ah, Holy Jesus.......136
Alas, and Did My Savior Bleed.......143
At the Cross.......138
Behold the Lamb.......148
Beneath the Cross of Jesus.......140
Hallelujah, What a Savior!.......134
He Died for Me.......154
How Deep the Father's Love for Us.......144
In the Cross of Christ I Glory.......147
Lamb of God.......150
Lead Me to Calvary.......133
My Savior's Love.......152
Near the Cross.......139
O Sacred Head, Now Wounded.......132
O, How He Loves You and Me.......153
There Is a Fountain.......151
'Tis Finished! The Messiah Dies.......142
'Tis Midnight, and on Olive's Brow.......141
Were You There.......137
When I Survey the Wondrous Cross.......145

God, the Son—His Resurrection and Exaltation

All Hail, King Jesus.......176
All Hail the Power of Jesus' Name (CORONATION).......163

All Hail the Power of Jesus' Name (DIADEM)....165
All Hail the Power of Jesus' Name (MILES LANE)....166
Alleluia, Sing to Jesus....162
Arise, My Soul, Arise!....177
At the Name of Jesus (BERRY)....180
Be Thou Exalted....11
Because He Lives....582
Celebrate Jesus....156
Christ Arose....160
Christ Is Alive!....158
Christ Is Risen! Shout Hosanna!....159
Christ the Lord Is Risen Today....155
Crown Him with Many Crowns....175
He Lives....583
I Know That My Redeemer Lives....171
Lift Up, Lift Up Your Voices Now....178
Lord, I Lift Your Name on High....164
Majestic Sweetness Sits Enthroned....174
Rejoice, the Lord Is King!....172
The Day of Resurrection!....161
The Head That Once Was Crowned with Thorns....170
The Name of the Lord....169
Thine Is the Glory....173

God, the Son—His Coming in Glory

At the Name of Jesus (WYE VALLEY)....196
Christ Is Coming Back Again....182
Christ Returneth....186
Even So....198
He Is Coming Again....184
Is It the Crowning Day?....192
Ivory Palaces....123
Jesus Is Coming Again....190
Lift Up Your Heads....183
Lo, Jesus Comes!....187
My Lord, What a Morning....193
Soon and Very Soon....191
The King Is Coming....194
The King Shall Come....189
Thy Kingdom Come....559
What If It Were Today?....188
When He Cometh....645
When He Shall Come....185

God, the Son—His Praise

A Shelter in the Time of Storm....225
Adoration....111
All Glory, Laud and Honor....126
All Hail, King Jesus....176
All Hail the Power of Jesus' Name (CORONATION)....163
All Hail the Power of Jesus' Name (DIADEM)....165
All Hail the Power of Jesus' Name (MILES LANE)....166
All Heaven Declares....517
Alleluia....236
Alleluia, Alleluia! Give Thanks....215
Be Thou Exalted....11
Behold the Lamb....148
Blessed Assurance....344
Blessed Be the Name....221
Celebrate Jesus....156
Christ Is Made the Sure Foundation....474
Christ the Lord Is Risen Today....155
Christ, Whose Glory Fills the Skies....206
Come, Christians, Join to Sing....204
Come, Thou Fount....280
Crown Him with Many Crowns....175
Fairest Lord Jesus....213
Glory to His Name....579
Glory to the Lamb....233
Hallelujah for the Cross....268
Hallelujah, What a Savior!....134
He Is Lord....230
His Name Is Wonderful....216
Holy and Anointed One....220
How Sweet the Name of Jesus Sounds....223
I Will Praise Him....207
Isn't He?....219
Jesus, Name Above All Names....76
Jesus Only....300
Jesus Only (arr.)....301
Jesus Shall Reign....555
Jesus, the Very Thought of Thee....228
Jesus, Thou Joy of Loving Hearts....224
King of the Nations....539
Lamb of God....150
Let There Be Glory and Honor and Praises....203
Lord, I Lift Your Name on High....164
Majesty....212
More Precious Than Silver....218
O Come, Let Us Adore Him....210
O, for a Thousand Tongues (AZMON)....202
O, for a Thousand Tongues (LYNGHAM)....201
O Jesus, Jesus....468
O Word of God Incarnate....492
Of the Father's Love Begotten....77
Our Great Savior....560
Praise Him! Praise Him!....208
Praise the Name of Jesus....226
Praise the Savior, We Who Know Him....209
Shine, Jesus, Shine....547
Shout to the Lord....217
Tell Me the Story of Jesus....120
The Solid Rock....339
There's Something About That Name....227
To the Ends of the Earth....556
We Bless the Name of Christ the Lord....641
We Come, O Christ, to You....199
We Will Glorify....211
What a Wonderful Savior....229
When Morning Gilds the Skies....205
Worthy Is the Lamb (HUGG)....232
Worthy Is the Lamb (WORTHY IS THE LAMB)....234
Worthy, You Are Worthy....235
You Are My All in All....214

God, the Holy Spirit

Be Still, for the Spirit of the Lord....242
Blessed Quietness....237
Breathe on Me, Breath of God....292
Breathe Upon Us....248
Breathing Out and Breathing In....309
Breathing Out and Breathing In (arr.)....308
Bring Your Vessels, Not a Few....322
Come, Blessed Holy Spirit....250
Fill Me Now....293
Holy Spirit, Ever Dwelling....240
Holy Spirit, with Light Divine....251
Old Time Power....247
On Pentecost They Gathered....245
Pentecostal Power....246
Spirit of God, Descend upon My Heart....252
Spirit of the Living God....253
The Comforter Has Come....238
Thy Holy Spirit, Lord, Alone....241
Where the Spirit of the Lord Is....243

God, the Holy Trinity

Be Thou Exalted....11
Come, Thou Almighty King....4
Doxology (FAIRHILL)....16
Doxology (OLD HUNDREDTH)....6
Glorify Thy Name....18
Glory Be to God the Father (GLORY TO GOD)....9
Glory Be to God the Father (REGENT SQUARE)....1
Glory Be to God, Creator....13
Glory Be to the Father....10
Holy, God Almighty....17
Holy God, We Praise Your Name....5
Holy, Holy....14
Holy, Holy, Holy Is the Lord of Hosts....12
Holy, Holy, Holy, Lord God Almighty....2
Holy Is the Lord....19
O Splendor of God's Glory Bright....15
Praise Ye the Triune God....8

God's Love

He Giveth More Grace....462

Here Is Love....453
How Deep the Father's Love for Us....144
How Great Is Your Love....455
Jesus, Lover of My Soul....364
Jesus Loves Even Me....465
Jesus Loves Me....459
Love Divine, All Loves Excelling....448
Love Found a Way....584
Love Lifted Me....581
My Savior's Love....152
O, How He Loves You and Me....153
O Love Divine....460
O Love That Will Not Let Me Go....449
O, the Deep, Deep Love of Jesus....458
Such Love....463
The King of Love My Shepherd Is....450
The Love of God....456
The Steadfast Love of the Lord....24
What Wondrous Love Is This....452

Grace

Amazing Grace....272
Come, Thou Fount....280
Grace Greater Than Our Sin....271
He Giveth More Grace....462
Saved by Grace....432
Wonderful Grace of Jesus....270

Gratitude

And Can It Be That I Should Gain....266
Be Exalted, O God....71
Bless the Lord, O My Soul....38
Come, Ye Thankful People, Come....663
Count Your Blessings....469
For the Beauty of the Earth....30
Give Thanks....660
He Giveth More Grace....462
He Has Made Me Glad (I Will Enter His Gates)....617
In Thanksgiving, Let Us Praise Him....661
Let All Things Now Living....659
My Tribute....566
Now Thank We All Our God....662
Praise, My Soul, the King of Heaven....51
Rejoice, You Pure in Heart....657
There Is a Redeemer....264
We Bring the Sacrifice of Praise....616
We Gather Together....664

Guidance

(see also Providence)
Close to Thee....388
God of Grace and God of Glory....385
God Will Make a Way....419
Guide Me, O Thou Great Jehovah....384
He Leadeth Me....43
I'll Go Where You Want Me to Go....505
Lead Me, Lord (LEAD ME, LORD)....380
Lead Me, Lord (I Will Follow) (GOODINE)....379
Lead On, O King Eternal....404
Open My Eyes That I May See....325
Savior, Like a Shepherd, Lead Us....378
Show Me Your Ways, O Lord....381
Step By Step (BEAKER)....368
Step By Step (STEP BY STEP)....371
Take the Name of Jesus with You....389
Where He Leads Me....374

Healing

(see Divine Healing)

Heaven

(see Death, Resurrection and Life Everlasting)

Holiness

(see also Sanctification, Consecration and the Deeper Life)
Hide Me in Your Holiness....3
Himself (EVERYTHING)....305
Himself (HIMSELF)....303
Himself (WYE VALLEY)....304
I Lay My Sins on Jesus....254
I Want to Be Holy....321
May the Mind of Christ, My Savior....333
More About Jesus....299
My Goal Is God Himself....327
Not I, But Christ (FINLANDIA)....295
Not I, But Christ (WHIDDINGTON)....294
Search Me, O God....316
Take Time to Be Holy....438

Holy Week

(see God, the Son—Palm Sunday; God, the Son—His Sufferings and Death; God, the Son—His Resurrection and Exaltation)

Hope

Arise, My Soul, Arise!....177
Be Thou My Vision....328
Come Unto Me, Ye Weary....602
Come, Ye Disconsolate....418
For All the Saints....486
My Life Is in You, Lord....278
Only Believe....281
Take the Name of Jesus with You....389
The Solid Rock....339
Wonderful, Wonderful Jesus....286

Indwelling Christ

Christ in Me (CHRIST IN ME)....297
Christ in Me (HOPE OF GLORY)....298
Deeper and Deeper....331
Himself (EVERYTHING)....305
Himself (HIMSELF)....303
Himself (WYE VALLEY)....304
Jesus, I Am Resting, Resting....306
Jesus Is All the World to Me....576
Jesus, Lover of My Soul....364
May the Mind of Christ, My Savior....333

Intimacy with God

Be Still, My Soul....363
Breathe on Me, Breath of God....292
Close to Thee....388
Dear Lord and Father of Mankind....284
God Himself Is With Us....619
In the Garden....590
It Is Glory Just to Walk with Him....369
Jesus, Master, Whose I Am....310
Jesus, Stand Among Us....622
My Goal Is God Himself....327
Near to the Heart of God....382
O, for a Heart to Praise My God....61
O Thou, in Whose Presence....362
Step By Step (BEAKER)....368
Step By Step (STEP BY STEP)....371

Joy

Christ the Lord Is Risen Today....155
He Has Made Me Glad (I Will Enter His Gates)....617
He Keeps Me Singing....586
In My Heart There Rings a Melody....285
It Is Glory Just to Walk with Him....369
Jesus, Thou Joy of Loving Hearts....224
Joy to the World!....81
Joyful, Joyful, We Adore Thee....50
Rejoice, the Lord Is King!....172
Rejoice, You Pure in Heart....657
The Joy of the Lord (JOY OF THE LORD)....287
The Joy of the Lord (REJOICE EVERMORE)....288
This Is the Day....618
Wonderful, Wonderful Jesus....286

Kingdom of God

Glorious Things of Thee Are Spoken....475
I Love Your Kingdom, Lord....482
Thy Kingdom Come....559

Longing for God

(see also Intimacy with God)
Dear Lord and Father of Mankind....284
Draw Me Nearer....329
In the Garden....590
More About Jesus....299

My Goal Is God Himself 327
Nearer, Still Nearer 356
O Love Divine 460
O, for a Heart to Praise My God....61
O Thou, in Whose Presence 362
O, to Be Like Thee, Blessed Redeemer 314
Open Our Eyes, Lord 447
Pass Me Not 608

Lord's Supper
As We Gather Around the Table 636
Bread of the World 633
Come, Share the Lord 632
Come to the Table 630
For the Bread which You Have Broken 637
Hallelujah! We Sing Your Praises 639
Here, at Your Table, Lord 634
I Will Praise Him 207
I Will Remember Thee 631
In Remembrance of Thee 638
Jesus, at Your Holy Table 629
Let Us Break Bread Together 635

Love for God and Christ
Fairest Lord Jesus 213
How Can I Help but Love Him? 464
I Am His, and He Is Mine 592
I Love Thee, I Love Thee 470
I Love You, Lord 471
In Moments Like These 454
Jesus, the Very Thought of Thee 228
Jesus, Thou Joy of Loving Hearts 224
More Love to Thee 466
My Jesus, I Love Thee 472
O, for a Thousand Tongues (AZMON) 202
O, for a Thousand Tongues (LYNGHAM) 201
O, How I Love Jesus 467
O Jesus, Jesus 468

Love for Others
Blest Be the Tie That Binds 483
O Perfect Love 656
The Family of God 487
The Gift of Love 451
The Servant Song 508
They'll Know We Are Christians 485
Would You Bless Our Homes and Families 655

Ministry and Service
Channels Only 510
Come, All Christians, Be Committed 503
Freely, Freely 511
Go and Tell Them 533
God, Whose Giving Knows No Ending 499
Hark, the Voice of Jesus Calling 519
I'll Go Where You Want Me to Go 505
Let It Be Said of Us 502
Let Your Heart Be Broken 541
Lord, Be Glorified 506
Lord, Speak to Me, That I May Speak 509
Make Me a Blessing 507
Make Them a Blessing 514
Must Jesus Bear the Cross Alone? 372
O Jesus, I Have Promised 512
O Master, Let Me Walk with Thee 515
Onward, Christian Soldiers 397
Rescue the Perishing 597
Rise Up, O Church of God 504
So Send I You 558
Speak, My Lord (BENNARD) 549
Speak, My Lord (DAVIS) 550
The Servant Song 508
Use Me Today 513
We Give Thee but Thine Own 498
Who Is on the Lord's Side? 401

Missions
All Around Your Throne 557
All Heaven Declares 517
Christ for the World! We Sing 523
Go and Tell Them 533
Go Forth and Tell! 530
God Calls Us 545
Hark, the Voice of Jesus Calling 519
Heart for the Nations 548
Here I Am, Lord 552
I'll Go Where You Want Me to Go 505
I've Come to Tell 535
Jesus Saves 528
Jesus Shall Reign 555
Joy to the World! 81
King of the Nations 539
Let All the World in Every Corner Sing 524
Let Us Go 543
Let Your Heart Be Broken 541
Lift High the Cross 516
Lift Up Our Eyes 531
Lord of the Living Harvest 546
Macedonia 527
My Trust 554
O Zion, Haste 525
O, Sing to the Lord (Cantad al Señor) 537
One Race, One Gospel, One Task 529
Our God Reigns 534
Our Heart 553
Send the Light 542
Shine, Jesus, Shine 547
So Send I You 558
Song for the Nations 522
Speak, My Lord (BENNARD) 549
Speak, My Lord (DAVIS) 550
The Breaking of the Bread 551
The Call for Reapers 538
The Regions Beyond 518
This Is the Gospel of Christ 526
Thy Kingdom Come 559
To the Ends of the Earth 556
We Are Singing, for the Lord Is Our Light (Siyahamba) 536
We've a Story to Tell to the Nations 521
You Servants of God, Your Master Proclaim 532

Nation
(see God and Country)

Obedience
Come, All Christians, Be Committed 503
Fully Surrendered 332
I Have Decided to Follow Jesus 570
I'll Go Where You Want Me to Go 505
Kingdom Prayer 261
Take Time to Be Holy 438
Teach Me Thy Way, O Lord 367
Trust and Obey 347
We Choose to Bow 399
Where He Leads Me 374

Peace
Be Still, My Soul 363
Blessed Quietness 237
Dear Lord and Father of Mankind 284
God Will Take Care of You 42
It Is Well with My Soul 352
Like a River Glorious 340
Near to the Heart of God 382
Only Believe 281
The King of Love My Shepherd Is 450
The Lord My Shepherd Guards Me Well 377
Thou Wilt Keep Him in Perfect Peace 283
Where the Spirit of the Lord Is 243
Wonderful Peace 282

Perseverance
Am I a Soldier of the Cross? 402
Find Us Faithful 391
Higher Ground 330
Trusting Jesus 343
We Choose to Bow 399
Who Is on the Lord's Side? 401

Personal Communion with God
(see Intimacy with God; Prayer)

Pilgrimage
Close to Thee 388
Find Us Faithful 391
God of Grace and God of Glory 385
I Want Jesus to Walk with Me 373
I Would Be Like Jesus....386
It Is Glory Just to Walk with Him 369
Jesus, I Would Faithful Be 390
Just a Closer Walk with Thee....370
Lead Me, Lord (LEAD ME, LORD)....380
Lead Me, Lord (I Will Follow) (GOODINE)....379
Must Jesus Bear the Cross Alone?....372
Seek Ye First....383
Show Me Your Ways, O Lord....381
Step By Step (BEAKER)....368
Step By Step (STEP BY STEP) 371
Take the Name of Jesus with You 389
Teach Me Thy Way, O Lord....367
We're Marching to Zion....375
Where He Leads Me....374
Would You Live for Jesus? 365

Prayer
A New Day Dawns 437
From Every Stormy Wind That Blows....444
I Must Tell Jesus 440
Open Our Eyes, Lord....447
Our Father....446
Prayer Is the Soul's Sincere Desire 442
Sweet Hour of Prayer....436
Take Time to Be Holy....438
The Lord's Prayer 445
What a Friend We Have in Jesus....439

Protection
A Shelter in the Time of Storm 225
Children of the Heavenly Father....40
Close to Thee 388
Eternal Father, Strong to Save 667
Find Us Faithful 391
God of Grace and God of Glory 385
He Hideth My Soul....575
Healer of My Soul 415
Leaning on the Everlasting Arms....357
Lord Jesus, Think on Me....387
Moment by Moment 353
My Anchor Holds 405
Nearer, My God, to Thee....434
The Lord My Shepherd Guards Me Well 377
The Lord's My Shepherd....376
Under His Wings 355

Providence
A Mighty Fortress Is Our God 35
Bless the Lord, O My Soul....38
By Gracious Powers....39
Children of the Heavenly Father....40
Day by Day 345
Faithful One....22
God Moves in a Mysterious Way 23
God Will Make a Way 419
God Will Take Care of You 42
Great and Mighty....34
Great Is Thy Faithfulness....25
He Leadeth Me....43
He's Got the Whole World in His Hands....41
I Sing the Mighty Power of God 33
Like a River Glorious....340
My Times Are in Thy Hand 346
O God, Our Help in Ages Past 36
Praise to the Lord, the Almighty 47
To God Be the Glory....44

Psalms and Paraphrases of Scriptures
All Creatures of Our God and King (Psalm 148) 28
All People That on Earth Do Dwell (Psalm 100) 69
Bless the Lord, O My Soul (Psalm 103) 38
Holy Is the Lord (Isaiah 6:3)....19
How Blest Are They (Psalm 1) 326
Jesus Shall Reign (Psalm 72)....555
O God, Our Help in Ages Past (Psalm 90) 36
O Worship the King (Psalm 104) 48
Praise, My Soul, the King of Heaven (Psalm 103) 51
Psalm 146....63
The Gift of Love (1 Corinthians 13:1-3) 451
The King of Love My Shepherd Is (Psalm 23) 450
The Lord Bless You and Keep You (Numbers 6:24-26)....626
The Lord My Shepherd Guards Me Well (Psalm 23)....377
The Lord's My Shepherd (Psalm 23) 376
While Shepherds Watched Their Flocks (Luke 2:8-20) 92

Redemption and Salvation
Amazing Grace....272
And Can It Be That I Should Gain....266
Arise, My Soul, Arise! 177
Christ Receiveth Sinful Men 601
Grace Greater Than Our Sin 271
Hallelujah for the Cross 268
I Am Not Skilled to Understand....574
I Cannot Tell 273
I'm Redeemed 571
Jesus Paid It All....568
Jesus Saves 528
Joy to the World!....81
My Savior First of All....424
Nothing But the Blood....258
O Boundless Salvation 269
O Redeeming One....267
One Day! 115
Redeemed 567
Rock of Ages 275
Saved by Grace....432
Since I Have Been Redeemed 562
Since Jesus Came Into My Heart 587
The Cleansing Wave....563
The Way of the Cross Leads Home 604
There Is a Redeemer....264
There Is Power in the Blood....595
There's a Wideness in God's Mercy 274
Thou Didst Leave Thy Throne 108
Victory in Jesus....580
What a Wonderful Savior....229
Whosoever Will May Come 598
Wonderful Grace of Jesus....270

Rest
Be Still, My Soul 363
Blessed Quietness 237
Come Unto Me, Ye Weary....602
Deeper and Deeper 331
From Every Stormy Wind That Blows....444
God Will Take Care of You 42
He Hideth My Soul....575
Himself (EVERYTHING) 305
Himself (HIMSELF)....303
Himself (WYE VALLEY)....304
Jesus, I Am Resting, Resting....306
Like a River Glorious....340
Near the Cross....139
Near to the Heart of God....382
Softly and Tenderly....609

Revival and Renewal
A Revival Hymn....481
Macedonia....527
O Breath of Life....480
Renew Your Church....478
Revive Us Again....337
Send Refreshing....338
There Shall Be Showers of Blessing....596

Sanctification, Consecration and the Deeper Life
Abiding and Confiding....307
As the Deer....323
Baptized into His Death....640
Be Thou My Vision....328
Breathe on Me, Breath of God....292
Breathing Out and Breathing In....309

Breathing Out and Breathing In (arr.) 308
Bring Your Vessels, Not a Few 322
Christ in Me (CHRIST IN ME) 297
Christ in Me (HOPE OF GLORY) 298
Christ, Whose Glory Fills the Skies 206
Deeper and Deeper 331
Draw Me Nearer 329
Fill Me Now 293
Fully Surrendered 332
Have Thine Own Way, Lord! 290
Higher Ground 330
Himself (EVERYTHING) 305
Himself (HIMSELF) 303
Himself (WYE VALLEY) 304
Ho, Everyone That Is Thirsty 319
How Blest Are They 326
I Am Crucified with Christ 336
I Need Thee Every Hour 334
I Surrender All 312
I Want to Be Holy 321
Jesus Calls Us 324
Jesus Only 300
Jesus Only (arr.) 301
Jesus, All For Jesus 311
Jesus, I Am Resting, Resting 306
Jesus, I My Cross Have Taken 296
Jesus, Master, Whose I Am 310
Knowing You 335
Lead Me to Calvary 133
Let the Beauty of Jesus 315
Lord, I Want to Be a Christian 615
May the Mind of Christ, My Savior 333
More About Jesus 299
My Goal Is God Himself 327
My Spirit, Soul and Body 302
Not I, But Christ (FINLANDIA) 295
Not I, But Christ (WHIDDINGTON) 294
O Love Divine 460
O, to Be Like Thee, Blessed Redeemer 314
Open My Eyes That I May See 325
Refiner's Fire 291
Revive Us Again 337
Sanctuary 318
Search Me, O God 316
Send Refreshing 338
Take My Life, and Let It Be Consecrated 317
Take Time to Be Holy 438
We Give Thee but Thine Own 498

Second Coming of Christ

(see God, the Son—His Coming in Glory)

Spiritual Conflict and Victory

Am I a Soldier of the Cross? 402
Dare to Be a Daniel 396
Faith Is the Victory 392
Faith of Our Fathers 394
God of Grace and God of Glory 385
How Firm a Foundation 489
Jesus Giveth Us the Victory 406
Lead On, O King Eternal 404
Lord Jesus, Think on Me 387
My Anchor Holds 405
Onward, Christian Soldiers 397
Soldiers of Christ, Arise 403
Sound the Battle Cry! 395
Stand Up, Stand Up for Jesus 400
The Battle Belongs to the Lord 398
The Church's One Foundation 473
The Lord My Shepherd Guards Me Well 377
The Lord's My Shepherd 376
We Choose to Bow 399
Who Is on the Lord's Side? 401

Stewardship

Come, All Christians, Be Committed 503
Freely, Freely 511
God, Whose Giving Knows No Ending 499
Lord, You Love the Cheerful Giver 500
My Trust 554
We Give Thee but Thine Own 498

Submission to God

Beneath the Cross of Jesus 140
Fill My Cup, Lord 589
Fully Surrendered 332
God, Whose Giving Knows No Ending 499
Here I Am, Lord 552
I Surrender All 312
I'll Go Where You Want Me to Go 505
Jesus, All For Jesus 311
Jesus Calls Us 324
Jesus, I Would Faithful Be 390
Jesus, Master, Whose I Am 310
Lead Me, Lord (LEAD ME, LORD) 380
Lead Me, Lord (I Will Follow) (GOODINE) 379
Lord, Be Glorified 506
My Spirit, Soul and Body 302
Open My Eyes That I May See 325
Show Me Your Ways, O Lord 381
Speak, My Lord (Bennard) 549
Speak, My Lord (Davis) 550
Take My Life, and Let It Be Consecrated 317
Trust and Obey 347
We Give Thee but Thine Own 498
Where He Leads Me 374
Whosoever Will May Come 598
Would You Live for Jesus? 365
Yes, Lord, Yes 348

Testimony

And Can It Be That I Should Gain 266
At Calvary 594
Because He Lives 582
Calvary Covers It All 561
Fill My Cup, Lord 589
Give Me Jesus 585
Glory to His Name 579
God Is So Good 565
Good to Me 27
He Hideth My Soul 575
He Keeps Me Singing 586
He Lives 583
He Touched Me 588
I Am His and He Is Mine 592
I Am Not Skilled to Understand 574
I Have Decided to Follow Jesus 570
I Love to Tell the Story 599
I Will Sing of My Redeemer 265
I Will Sing the Wondrous Story 593
I'd Rather Have Jesus 578
I'm Redeemed 571
In My Heart There Rings a Melody 285
In the Garden 590
Jesus Is All the World to Me 576
Jesus Paid It All 568
Love Found a Way 584
Love Lifted Me 581
My Faith Has Found a Resting Place 564
My Redeemer 569
My Savior's Love 152
My Tribute 566
O Happy Day! 591
O Redeeming One 267
Our Great Savior 560
Redeemed 567
Satisfied 572
Saved by Grace 432
Since I Have Been Redeemed 562
Since Jesus Came Into My Heart 587
The Cleansing Wave 563
The Lily of the Valley 577
The Old Rugged Cross 573
Victory in Jesus 580
What a Wonderful Savior 229

Thankfulness

(see Gratitude)

Thanksgiving, Holiday

Come, Ye Thankful People, Come 663
Give Thanks 660
In Thanksgiving, Let Us Praise Him 661
Let All Things Now Living 659
Now Thank We All Our God 662
Rejoice, You Pure in Heart 657
We Gather Together 664

Trust

Be Still, My Soul 363
Blessed Assurance 344
Come Unto Me, Ye Weary 602

Come, Ye Disconsolate....418
Day by Day....345
Eternal Father, Strong to Save....667
God Will Take Care of You....42
Have Thine Own Way, Lord!....290
He Is Able....342
Hiding in Thee....351
I Am Trusting Thee, Lord Jesus....360
I Know Whom I Have Believed....361
I Need Thee Every Hour....334
It Is Well with My Soul....352
Jesus Never Fails....349
Jesus, Lover of My Soul....364
Leaning on the Everlasting Arms....357
Learning to Lean....358
Like a River Glorious....340
Moment by Moment....353
My Times Are in Thy Hand....346
Nearer, Still Nearer....356
O Thou, in Whose Presence....362
Only Believe....281
Only Trust Him....607
Standing on the Promises....359
The Solid Rock....339
'Tis So Sweet to Trust in Jesus....341
Trust and Obey....347
Trusting Jesus....343
Turn Your Eyes upon Jesus....350
Under His Wings....355

Victorious Life

Arise, My Soul, Arise!....177
Faith Is the Victory....392
Higher Ground....330
Jesus Giveth Us the Victory....406
Soldiers of Christ, Arise....403
The Joy of the Lord (JOY OF THE LORD)....287
The Joy of the Lord (REJOICE EVERMORE)....288
Victory in Jesus....580

Witnessing

(see also Evangelism and Invitation; Testimony)
Go and Tell Them....533
I Love to Tell the Story....599
I Will Sing of My Redeemer....265
You Servants of God, Your Master Proclaim....532

Word of God

Break Thou the Bread of Life....490
Holy Bible, Book Divine....495
How Firm a Foundation....489
How Precious Is the Book Divine....494
O Word of God Incarnate....492
Thy Word....491
Wonderful Words of Life....496

World Songs

Hallelujah! We Sing Your Praises....639
I've Come to Tell (Te Vengo a Decir)....535
O Redeeming One....267
O, Sing to the Lord (Cantad al Señor)....537
We Are Singing, for the Lord Is Our Light (Siyahamba)....536

Titles and First Lines

Titles in regular type; First lines in *italics*

A

A Christian Home (E♭)....654
A Christmas Hymn (e min.)....98
A Mighty Fortress Is Our God (C)....35
A New Day Dawns (G)....437
A Purple Robe (D)....135
A Revival Hymn (A♭)....481
A Shelter in the Time of Storm (E♭)....225
A stable lamp is lighted (e min.)....98
A wonderful Savior is Jesus, my Lord (D♭)....575
Abide with Me (E♭)....435
Abiding and Confiding (D)....307
According to Thy gracious Word (G)....631
Adoration (D)....111
Ah, Holy Jesus (A♭)....136
Alas! And did my Savior bleed (E♭)....138
Alas, and Did My Savior Bleed (G)....143
All Around Your Throne (E)....557
All Creatures of Our God and King (D)....28
All Glory, Laud and Honor (B♭)....126
All Hail, King Jesus (F)....176
All Hail the Power of Jesus' Name (CORONATION) (G)....163
All Hail the Power of Jesus' Name (DIADEM) (A♭)....165
All Hail the Power of Jesus' Name (MILES LANE) (G)....166
All Heaven Declares (A)....517
All I once held dear (C)....335
All my life long I had panted (D)....572
All People That on Earth Do Dwell (G)....69
All praise to Him who reigns above (A)....221
All to Jesus I surrender (C)....312
Alleluia (G)....236
Alleluia, Alleluia! Give Thanks (F)....215
Alleluia, Sing to Jesus (F)....162
Almost Persuaded (G)....600
Along the shores of Galilee (A♭)....551
Am I a Soldier of the Cross? (D)....402
Amazing Grace (G)....272
America (F)....671
America, the Beautiful (B♭)....670
Ancient of Days (D)....60
And Can It Be That I Should Gain (G)....266
Angels, from the Realms of Glory (B♭)....96
Angels We Have Heard on High (F)....95
Are you longing for the fullness (D)....322
Are You Washed in the Blood? (A)....605
Arise, My Soul, Arise! (A♭)....177
Around Your grave, Lord Jesus (D)....640
As the Deer (D)....323
As We Gather (D)....621
As We Gather Around the Table (D)....636
As with Gladness Men of Old (G)....112
At Calvary (C)....594
At the Cross (E♭)....138
At the Name of Jesus (BERRY) (B♭)....180
At the Name of Jesus (WYE VALLEY) (F)....196
Away in a Manger (AWAY IN A MANGER) (F)....85
Away in a Manger (CRADLE SONG) (F)....86
Awesome God (e min.)....62

B

Baptized in Water (C)....643
Baptized into His Death (D)....640
Battle Hymn of the Republic (B♭)....668
Be Exalted, O God (B♭)....71
Be Still, for the Spirit of the Lord (D)....242
Be Still, My Soul (F)....363
Be Thou Exalted (E♭)....11
Be Thou My Vision (E♭)....328
Because He Lives (A♭)....582

Because so many need to know (G) 545
Behold the Lamb (E♭) 148
Beneath the Cross of Jesus (D♭) 140
Bless the Lord, O My Soul (G) 38
Bless them, Lord, and make them a blessing (G) 514
Blessed Assurance (D) 344
Blessed Be the Glorious Tidings (F) 408
Blessed Be the Name (A) 221
Blessed be the name of the Lord (F) 169
Blessed Be the Name of the Lord (F) 56
Blessed Quietness (B♭) 237
Blessing and honor (D) 60
Blest Be the Tie That Binds (F) 483
Bread of the World (E♭) 633
Break Thou the Bread of Life (D) 490
Breathe on Me, Breath of God (E♭) 292
Breathe Upon Us (F) 248
Breathing Out and Breathing In (G) 309
Breathing Out and Breathing In (arr.) (F) 308
Bring Your Vessels, Not a Few (D) 322
Brother, sister, let me serve you (D) 508
By Gracious Powers 39

C

Calvary Covers It All (G) 561
Celebrate Jesus (F) 156
Change My Heart, O God (C) 257
Channels Only (A♭) 510
Child in the Manger (C) 105
Children of the Heavenly Father (D) 40
Christ Arose (B♭) 160
Christ for the World! We Sing (F) 523
Christ has for sin atonement made (D♭) 229
Christ in Me (CHRIST IN ME) (D) 297
Christ in Me (HOPE OF GLORY) (C) 298
Christ Is Alive! (C) 158
Christ Is Coming Back Again (C) 182
Christ Is Made the Sure Foundation (D) 474
Christ Is Risen! Shout Hosanna! (F) 159
Christ Receiveth Sinful Men (C) 601
Christ Returneth (C) 186
Christ the Lord Is Risen Today (C) 155
Christ, Whose Glory Fills the Skies (G) 206
Close to Thee (G) 388
Come, All Christians, Be Committed (F) 503
Come, Blessed Holy Spirit (E) 250
Come, Christians, Join to Sing (A♭) 204
Come, every soul by sin oppressed (G) 607
Come, Holy Spirit, Dove Divine (D) 644
Come, Holy Spirit, heavenly Dove (E) 250
Come Just as You Are (F) 612
Come, let us worship Jesus (F) 539
Come, Now Is the Time to Worship (D) 620
Come, Share the Lord (G) 632
Come, Thou Almighty King (F) 4
Come, Thou Fount (D) 280
Come, Thou Long-Expected Jesus (F) 75
Come to the Table (F) 630
Come Unto Me, Ye Weary (D) 602
Come, we that love the Lord (F) 375
Come, Ye Disconsolate (C) 418
Come, Ye Thankful People, Come (F) 663
Count Your Blessings (D) 469
Crown Him with Many Crowns (D) 175

D

Dare to Be a Daniel (G) 396
Day by Day (E♭) 345
Dear Lord and Father of Mankind (C) 284
Deeper and Deeper (C) 331
Depth of Mercy! Can There Be (F) 255
Down at the cross where my Savior died (G) 579
Down from His splendor in glory He came (B♭) 464
Doxology (FAIRHILL) (D) 16
Doxology (OLD HUNDREDTH) (G) 6
Draw Me Nearer (G) 329
Dying with Jesus, by death reckoned mine (F) 353

E

Earthly friends may prove untrue (G) 349
Earthly pleasures vainly call me (G) 386
Emmanuel (C) 80
Encamped along the hills of light (D) 392
Eternal Father, Strong to Save (C) 667
Even So (F) 198

F

Face to Face (A♭) 429
Fairest Lord Jesus (E♭) 213
Faith Is the Victory (D) 392
Faith of Our Fathers (G) 394
Faith of Our Mothers (G) 653
Faithful One (D) 22
Far and near the fields are teeming (G) 538
Far away in the depths of my spirit tonight (G) 282
Far dearer than all that the world (G) 561
Fear not, little flock (C) 281
Fill Me Now (F) 293
Fill My Cup, Lord (B♭) 589
Find Us Faithful (E♭) 391
For All the Saints (F) 486
For the Beauty of the Earth (G) 30
For the Bread which You Have Broken (D) 637
For Thou, O Lord, art high above (F) 55
Free from the law—O, happy condition (D) 606
Freely, Freely (E♭) 511
Friend of the Home (E♭) 650
From Every Stormy Wind That Blows (B♭) 444
Fully Surrendered (B♭) 332

G

Give Me Jesus (B♭) 585
Give Thanks (F) 660
Give us Your heart for the nations (A) 548
Glorify Thy Name (B♭) 18
Glorious Things of Thee Are Spoken (E♭) 475
Glory Be to God, Creator (C) 13
Glory Be to God the Father
(GLORY TO GOD) (E♭) 9
Glory Be to God the Father
(REGENT SQUARE) (B♭) 1
Glory Be to the Father (E♭) 10
Glory, glory, glory to the Lamb (C) 233
Glory to His Name (G) 579
Glory to the Lamb (C) 233
Go and Tell Them (G) 533
Go Forth and Tell! (E♭) 530
Go, Tell It on the Mountain (F) 82
God Be with You till We Meet Again (C) 627
God Calls Us (G) 545

God forgave my sin in Jesus' name (E♭)....511
God Himself Is With Us (F)....619
God Is So Good (D/E♭)....565
God Is with Us! Alleluia! (D)....79
God Moves in a Mysterious Way (E♭)....23
God of Grace and God of Glory (F)....385
God of Our Fathers (E♭)....665
God Save the Queen (F)....673
God sent His Son, they called Him Jesus (A♭)....582
God, Whose Giving Knows No Ending (F)....499
God Will Make a Way (G)....419
God Will Take Care of You (B♭)....42
Good Christian Friends, Rejoice (F)....88
Good Shepherd, Take This Little Child (C)....647
Good to Me (G)....27
Grace Greater Than Our Sin (G)....271
Great and Mighty (E♭)....34
Great Is the Lord (C)....53
Great Is Thy Faithfulness (E♭)....25
Guide Me, O Thou Great Jehovah (G)....384

H

Hallelujah for the Cross (B♭)....268
Hallelujah! We Sing Your Praises (G)....639
Hallelujah, What a Savior! (B♭)....134
Happy the Home When God Is There (F)....652
Hark, the Herald Angels Sing (F)....94
Hark, the Voice of Jesus Calling (F)....519
Have Thine Own Way, Lord! (E♭)....290
Have you been to Jesus for the cleansing (A)....605
He Died for Me (D)....154
He Giveth More Grace (E♭)....462
He Has Made Me Glad (I Will Enter His Gates) (E♭)....617
He Hideth My Soul (D♭)....575
He Is Able (C)....342
He Is Born (F)....83
He Is Coming Again (B♭)....184
He Is Exalted (F)....54
He Is Lord (F)....230
He Keeps Me Singing (G)....586
He Leadeth Me (C)....43
He Lives (A♭)....583
He the Pearly Gates Will Open (G)....430
He Touched Me (E♭)....588
Heal Me, Hands of Jesus (e min.)....409
Healer of My Soul (D)....415
Healing in His Wings (D)....412
Healing in Jesus (D)....416
Hear the Lord of harvest sweetly calling (G)....549
Hear the Lord of harvest sweetly calling (F)....550
Heart for the Nations (A)....548
Heavenly Father, we Your children (F)....338
Here I Am, Lord (G)....552
Here Is Love (G)....453
Here, at Your Table, Lord (E♭)....634
He's Got the Whole World in His Hands (C/D)....41
Hide Me in Your Holiness (E♭)....3
Hide me, Lord, in Your holiness (E♭)....3
Hiding in Thee (E♭)....351
Higher Ground (G)....330
Himself (EVERYTHING) (D)....305
Himself (HIMSELF) (F)....303
Himself (WYE VALLEY) (F)....304
His name is called Emmanuel (D)....79
His Name Is Wonderful (F)....216
His Strength Is Perfect (F)....414
Ho, Everyone That Is Thirsty (G)....319
Holy and Anointed One (G)....220
Holy Bible, Book Divine (F)....495
Holy, God Almighty (D)....17
Holy God, We Praise Your Name (F)....5
Holy, Holy (C)....14
Holy, Holy, Holy Is the Lord of Hosts (C)....12
Holy, holy, holy, holy is the Lord (E♭)....19
Holy, Holy, Holy, Lord God Almighty (D/E♭)....2
Holy Is the Lord (E♭)....19
Holy Spirit, Ever Dwelling (G)....240
Holy Spirit, with Light Divine (A)....251
Hosanna (G)....128
Hosanna, Loud Hosanna (C)....127
Hover o'er me, Holy Spirit (F)....293
How Blest Are They (F)....326
How Can I Help but Love Him? (B♭)....464
How can I say thanks (B♭)....566
How Deep the Father's Love for Us (E)....144
How Firm a Foundation (G)....489
How Great Is Your Love (G)....455
How Great Our Joy (B♭)....91
How Great Thou Art (B♭)....66
How I praise Thee, precious Savior (A♭)....510
How lovely on the mountains (B♭)....534
How Majestic Is Your Name (C)....46
How Precious Is the Book Divine (G)....494
How Sweet the Name of Jesus Sounds (D)....223

I

I Am Crucified with Christ (F)....336
I Am His, and He Is Mine (D)....592
I Am Not Skilled to Understand (D)....574
I am so glad that our Father in heaven (G)....465
I Am the God That Healeth Thee (D)....411
I am Thine, O Lord (G)....329
I Am Trusting Thee, Lord Jesus (A♭)....360
I can hear the Savior calling (F)....374
I can sing now the song (F)....571
I Cannot Tell (C)....273
I come to the garden alone (A♭)....590
I cry out for Your hand of mercy (G)....27
I Exalt Thee (F)....55
I have a song I love to sing (F)....562
I have a song that Jesus gave me (G)....285
I Have Decided to Follow Jesus (C)....570
I have found a friend in Jesus (F)....577
I have learned the wondrous secret (D)....307
I hear the Savior say (E♭)....568
I heard an old, old story (G)....580
I Heard the Bells on Christmas Day (E♭)....99
I know not why God's wondrous grace (D)....361
I know of a Name, a beautiful Name (G)....118
I Know That My Redeemer Lives (D)....171
I Know Whom I Have Believed (D)....361
I Lay My Sins on Jesus (F)....254
I Love Thee, I Love Thee (E♭)....470
I Love to Tell the Story (G)....599
I Love You, Lord (F)....471
I Love Your Kingdom, Lord (F)....482
I must needs go home by the way (G)....604

I Must Tell Jesus (D) 440
I Need Thee Every Hour (G)..334
I saw One hanging on a tree (D) 154
I serve a risen Savior (A♭) 583
I Sing Praises (G) 57
I Sing the Mighty Power of God (B♭) 33
I stand amazed in the presence (A♭)..152
I Surrender All (D) 312
I, the Lord of sea and sky (G)..552
I Want Jesus to Walk with Me (c min.)..373
I Want to Be Holy (D)..321
I was sinking deep in sin (B♭) 581
I Will Call upon the Lord (C) 68
I Will Change Your Name (G) 413
I will enter His gates (E♭)..617
I will give thanks to Thee (B♭)..71
I Will Praise Him (D) 207
I Will Remember Thee (G)..631
I will sing of my Redeemer (A♭) 569
I Will Sing of My Redeemer (F) 265
I will sing praise to the Lord (C) 63
I Will Sing the Wondrous Story (D)..593
I Would Be Like Jesus (G)..386
I'd Rather Have Jesus (C) 578
If My People (C) 260
I'll Fly Away (G) 422
I'll Go Where You Want Me to Go (F) 505
I'll say yes, Lord, yes (F)..348
I'm pressing on the upward way (G)..330
I'm Redeemed (F)..571
I'm so glad I'm a part of the family (F)..487
Immortal, Invisible, God Only Wise (A♭)..21
In heavenly armor we'll enter the land (e min.)..398
In Moments Like These (D)..454
In My Heart There Rings a Melody (G) 285
In my life, Lord, be glorified (C) 506
In Remembrance of Thee (C)..638
In Thanksgiving, Let Us Praise Him (E♭)..661
In the Bleak Midwinter (F) 103
In the Cross of Christ I Glory (C) 147
In the Garden (A♭) 590
In the morning when I rise (B♭) 585
In the Name of the Lord (A♭)..64
Infant Holy, Infant Lowly (G)..87
Into the heart of Jesus, deeper and deeper I go (C) 331
Is It the Crowning Day? (C) 192
Isn't He? (G)..219
It Came upon the Midnight Clear (B♭)..102
It Is Glory Just to Walk with Him (C) 369
It Is Well with My Soul (C) 352
It may be at morn, when the day is awaking (C)..186
It may not be on the mountain's height (F) 505
I've Come to Tell (Te Vengo a Decir) (G)..535
Ivory Palaces (E♭) 123

J

Jesus, All For Jesus (D) 311
Jesus, at Your Holy Table (F)..629
Jesus, breathe Thy Spirit on me (F) 308
Jesus, breathe Thy Spirit on me (G) 309
Jesus Calls Us (A♭)..324
Jesus Giveth Us the Victory (A♭) 406
Jesus' Hands Were Kind Hands (G) 649
Jesus, I Am Resting, Resting (G) 306
Jesus, I Come (G)..613
Jesus, I My Cross Have Taken (G)..296
Jesus, I Would Faithful Be (E♭) 390
Jesus Is All the World to Me (G) 576
Jesus Is Coming Again (B♭) 190
Jesus is coming to earth again (C) 188
Jesus, Jesus, Holy and Anointed One (G) 220
Jesus, Jesus, Jesus; There's just something (E♭)..227
Jesus, keep me near the cross (F)..139
Jesus, Lover of My Soul (e min.)..364
Jesus Loves Even Me (G) 465
Jesus Loves Me (C)..459
Jesus, Master, Whose I Am (G) 310
Jesus may come today, Glad day! (C) 192
Jesus, Name Above All Names (F)..76
Jesus Never Fails (G) 349
Jesus Only (G)..300
Jesus Only (arr.) (G)..301
Jesus Paid It All (E♭)..568
Jesus Saves (F) 528
Jesus Shall Reign (D) 555
Jesus, Stand Among Us (F) 622
Jesus, the Very Thought of Thee (G) 228
Jesus, Thou Joy of Loving Hearts (E♭)..224
Jesus, what a friend for sinners (F)..560
Jesus, You are Light in the darkest place (C)..267
Joy to the World! (D) 81
Joyful, Joyful, We Adore Thee (G) 50
Joys are flowing like a river (B♭)..237
Just a Closer Walk with Thee (B♭)..370
Just As I Am (C) 614

K

King of my life, I crown Thee now (D) 133
King of the Nations (F)..539
Kingdom Prayer (F)..261
Knowing You (C) 335

L

Lamb of God (C) 150
Lead Me, Lord (LEAD ME, LORD) (D)..380
Lead Me, Lord (I Will Follow) (GOODINE) (C) 379
Lead Me to Calvary (D) 133
Lead On, O King Eternal (C) 404
Leaning on the Everlasting Arms (A) 357
Learning to Lean (F)..358
Let All Mortal Flesh Keep Silence (d min.) 74
Let All the World in Every Corner Sing (D) 524
Let All Things Now Living (F) 659
Let It Be Said of Us (C) 502
Let the Beauty of Jesus (E♭)..315
Let There Be Glory and Honor and Praises (G)..203
Let Us Break Bread Together (E♭) 635
Let Us Go (F)..543
Let Your Heart Be Broken (E♭) 541
Lift High the Cross (C) 516
Lift Up, Lift Up Your Voices Now (E♭)..178
Lift Up Our Eyes (E♭) 531
Lift Up Your Heads (G)..183
Lift up your heads, pilgrims aweary (B♭)..184
Like a River Glorious (F) 340
Like the woman at the well (B♭) 589
Living Stones (E♭) 477
Lo, How a Rose E'er Blooming (F) 78

Lo, Jesus Comes! (C) 187
Lord, as of old at Pentecost (G) 246
Lord, Be Glorified (C) 506
Lord, I Lift Your Name on High (G) 164
Lord, I Want to Be a Christian (D) 615
Lord Jesus, I long to be perfectly whole (F) 256
Lord Jesus, Think on Me (F) 387
Lord of the Living Harvest (C) 546
Lord, prepare me to be a sanctuary (D) 318
Lord, Speak to Me, That I May Speak (G) 509
Lord, the light of Your love is shining (A) 547
Lord, we're broken, brokenhearted (F) 261
Lord, You are more precious than silver (F) 218
Lord, You have given me a trust (D) 554
Lord, You Love the Cheerful Giver (A♭) 500
Love Divine, All Loves Excelling (A♭) 448
Love divine, so great and wondrous (G) 430
Love Found a Way (A♭) 584
Love Lifted Me (B♭) 581
Loved with everlasting love (D) 592
Low in the grave He lay (B♭) 160

M

Macedonia (B♭) 527
Majestic Sweetness Sits Enthroned (G) 174
Majesty (B♭) 212
Make Me a Blessing (B♭) 507
Make Them a Blessing (G) 514
"Man of Sorrows," what a name (B♭) 134
Marvelous grace of our loving Lord (G) 271
Marvelous message we bring (B♭) 190
May I stand, O Lord (C) 623
May the Mind of Christ, My Savior (D) 333
May we be a shining light to the nations (A) 522
Meekness and Majesty (This Is Your God) (C) 124
Mighty Is Our God (B♭) 65
Mine eyes have seen the glory (B♭) 668
Moment by Moment (F) 353
More About Jesus (G) 299
More Love to Thee (G) 466
More Precious Than Silver (F) 218
Morning Has Broken (C) 32
Must Jesus Bear the Cross Alone? (G) 372
My Anchor Holds (B♭) 405
My Faith Has Found a Resting Place (G) 564
My Faith Looks Up to Thee (D) 279
My Goal Is God Himself (E♭) 327
My hope is built on nothing less (F) 339
My Jesus, I Love Thee (F) 472
My Jesus, my Savior, Lord, there is none (B♭) 217
My Life Is in You, Lord (G) 278
My Lord has garments so wondrous fine (E♭) 123
My Lord, What a Morning (D) 193
My Redeemer (A♭) 569
My Savior First of All (G) 424
My Savior's Love (A♭) 152
My Spirit, Soul and Body (E♭) 302
My Times Are in Thy Hand (C) 346
My Tribute (B♭) 566
My Trust (D) 554

N

Near the Cross (F) 139
Near to the Heart of God (D) 382
Nearer, My God, to Thee (F) 434
Nearer, Still Nearer (C) 356
No eye has seen and no ear has heard (G) 455
Not I, But Christ (FINLANDIA) (E♭) 295
Not I, But Christ (WHIDDINGTON) (E♭) 294
Nothing But the Blood (F) 258
Now May the God of Hope (C) 625
Now Thank We All Our God (E♭) 662

O

O beautiful for spacious skies (B♭) 670
O Boundless Salvation (A♭) 269
O Breath of Life (D) 480
O Canada! (E♭) 672
O Christ, my Lord and King (D) 559
O Christ, the Healer (G) 417
O Church of God, United (A) 476
O Come, All Ye Faithful (G) 100
O Come, Let Us Adore Him (F) 210
O Come, O Come, Emmanuel (e min.) 73
O, for a Faith That Will Not Shrink (G) 277
O, for a Heart to Praise My God (G) 61
O, for a Thousand Tongues (AZMON) (G) 202
O, for a Thousand Tongues (LYNGHAM) (G) 201
O, give us homes built firm upon the Savior (E♭) 654
O God, Beneath Thy Guiding Hand (D) 666
O God, Our Help in Ages Past (C) 36
O God, You are my God (G) 368
O Happy Day! (F) 591
O, How He Loves You and Me (A♭) 153
O, How I Love Jesus (G) 467
O, how sweet the glorious message (G) 121, 122
O, how sweet to walk with Jesus (D) 371
O Jesus, I Have Promised (F) 512
O Jesus, Jesus (E♭) 468
O Little Town of Bethlehem (G) 97
O Lord, my God! When I in awesome wonder (B♭) 66
O Lord, our Lord, how majestic is your name (C) 46
O Love Divine (F) 460
O love that give itself for me (F) 460
O Love That Will Not Let Me Go (G) 449
O Master, Let Me Walk with Thee (D) 515
O, may all who come behind us (E♭) 391
O, now I see the cleansing wave (D) 563
O Perfect Love (D) 656
O Redeeming One (C) 267
O Sacred Head, Now Wounded (C) 132
O, safe to the Rock that is higher than I (E♭) 351
O say, can you see (A♭) 669
O, Sing a Song of Bethlehem (e min.) 113
O, Sing to the Lord (Cantad al Señor) (e min.) 537
O soul, are you weary and troubled (F) 350
O souls that are seeking for pleasure (D) 321
O Splendor of God's Glory Bright (D) 15
O, spread the tidings 'round (B♭) 238
O, That Will Be Glory (G) 427
O, the Blood of Jesus (F/G) 259
O, the Deep, Deep Love of Jesus (e min.) 458
O Thou, in Whose Presence (D) 362
O thou my soul, bless God the Lord (G) 38
O, to Be Like Thee, Blessed Redeemer (D♭) 314
O Word of God Incarnate (D) 492
O Worship the King (G/A♭) 48
O Zion, Haste (B♭) 525
Of the Father's Love Begotten (E♭) 77

Old Time Power (B♭) 247
On a hill far away (B♭) 573
On Jordan's Stormy Banks (D) 426
On Pentecost They Gathered (D) 245
Once for All (D) 606
Once in Royal David's City (F) 107
Once it was the blessing (F) 303, 304
Once it was the blessing (D) 305
One Day! (C) 115
One is the race of mankind (F) 529
One Race, One Gospel, One Task (F) 529
Only Believe (C) 281
Only Trust Him (G) 607
Onward, Christian Soldiers (D) 397
Open My Eyes That I May See (A♭) 325
Open Our Eyes, Lord (D) 447
Our Father (F) 446
Our Father, which art in heaven (B♭) 445
Our God has built with living stones (E♭) 477
Our God is an awesome God (e min.) 62
Our God Reigns (B♭) 534
Our Great Savior (F) 560
Our Heart (B♭) 553
Out in the highways and byways of life (B♭) 507
Out of my bondage, sorrow and night (G) 613

P

Pass Me Not (G) 608
Pentecostal Power (G) 246
People Need the Lord (C) 610
Praise God from whom all blessings flow (G) 6
Praise God from whom all blessings flow (D) 16
Praise Him! Praise Him! (G) 208
Praise, My Soul, the King of Heaven (D) 51
Praise the Name of Jesus (E♭) 226
Praise the Savior, We Who Know Him (G) 209
Praise to the Lord, the Almighty (G) 47
Praise ye the Father for His loving (A♭) 8
Praise Ye the Triune God (A♭) 8
Prayer Is the Soul's Sincere Desire (A♭) 442
Psalm 146 (C) 63
Purify my heart (E) 291

R

Redeemed (A♭) 567
Redeemed—how I love to proclaim it (A♭) 567
Refiner's Fire (E) 291
Rejoice, the Lord Is King (C) 172
Rejoice, You Pure in Heart (F) 657
Renew Your Church (G) 478
Rescue the Perishing (B♭) 597
Revive Thy work, O Lord! (A♭) 481
Revive Us Again (F) 337
Ride On, Ride On in Majesty (C) 130
Rise Up, O Church of God (A) 504
Rock of Ages (B♭) 275

S

Safe in the Arms of Jesus (F) 428
Sanctuary (D) 318
Satisfied (D) 572
Saved by Grace (E♭) 432
Savior, Like a Shepherd, Lead Us (C) 378
Search Me, O God (C) 316
Seek Ye First (D) 383
Send Refreshing (F) 338
Send the gospel of salvation (G) 533
Send the Light (G) 542
Sent Forth by God's Blessing (F) 624
Shackled by a heavy burden (E♭) 588
Shine, Jesus, Shine (A) 547
Shout to the Lord (B♭) 217
Show Me Your Ways, O Lord (F) 381
Silent Night! Holy Night! (B♭) 104
Simply trusting every day (F) 343
Since I Have Been Redeemed (F) 562
Since Jesus Came Into My Heart (G) 587
Sing the wondrous love of Jesus (C) 423
Sing them over again to me (G) 496
Sing We Now of Christmas (e min.) 93
Sinners Jesus will receive (C) 601
So Send I You (F) 558
Softly and Tenderly (G) 609
Soldiers of Christ, Arise (D) 403
Some day the silver cord will break (E♭) 432
Some glad morning when this life is o'er (G) 422
Song for the Nations (A) 522
Songs of Thankfulness and Praise (F) 117
Soon and Very Soon (F) 191
Sound the Battle Cry! (A♭) 395
Speak, My Lord (BENNARD) (G) 549
Speak, My Lord (DAVIS) (F) 550
Spirit of God, Descend upon My Heart (B♭) 252
Spirit of the Living God (F) 253
Stand Up, Stand Up for Jesus (A♭) 400
Standing by a purpose true (G) 396
Standing on the Promises (A♭) 359
Star of hope for hearts forlorn (C) 182
Step by Step (BEAKER) (G) 368
Step by Step (STEP BY STEP) (D) 371
Such Love (E) 463
Sun of My Soul, Our Savior Dear (F) 431
Sweet Hour of Prayer (D) 436
Swing Low (F) 433

T

Take My Life, and Let It Be Consecrated (F) 317
Take the Name of Jesus with You (A♭) 389
Take Time to Be Holy (F) 438
Teach Me Thy Way, O Lord (E♭) 367
Tell Me the Story of Jesus (D) 120
That Beautiful Name (G) 118
The Battle Belongs to the Lord (e min.) 398
The blood that Jesus shed for me (A♭) 262
The Blood Will Never Lose Its Power (A♭) 262
The Branch of Healing (C) 410
The Breaking of the Bread (A♭) 551
The Call for Reapers (G) 538
The Church's One Foundation (D) 473
The Cleansing Wave (D) 563
The Comforter Has Come (B♭) 238
The cross is standing fast (B♭) 268
The Day of Resurrection! (C) 161
The Day of Thy Power (C) 623
The Family of God (F) 487
The First Noel (D) 90
The Gift of Love (G) 451
The God of Abraham Praise (e min.) 59
The Great Physician (D) 603

The Head That Once Was Crowned
with Thorns (A♭) 170
The Joy of the Lord (JOY OF THE LORD) (A♭) 287
The Joy of the Lord (REJOICE EVERMORE) (C) 288
The King Is Coming (A) 194
The King of Glory Comes (G) 129
The King of Love My Shepherd Is (G) 450
The King Shall Come (e min.) 189
The Lily of the Valley (F) 577
The Lord Bless You and Keep You (C) 626
The Lord My Shepherd Guards Me Well (C) 377
The Lord's My Shepherd (F) 376
The Lord's our rock, in Him we hide (E♭) 225
The Lord's Prayer (B♭) 445
The Love of God (D) 456
The Name of the Lord (F) 169
The Old Rugged Cross (B♭) 573
The Regions Beyond (B♭) 518
The Savior Is Waiting (F) 611
The Servant Song (D) 508
The Solid Rock (F) 339
The Star-Spangled Banner (A♭) 669
The Steadfast Love of the Lord (E♭) 24
The vision of a dying world (B♭) 527
The Way of the Cross Leads Home (G) 604
There Is a Fountain (B♭) 151
There is a healing branch that grows (C) 410
There is a name I love to hear (G) 467
There is a place of quiet rest (D) 382
There Is a Redeemer (E♭) 264
There is cleansing in Jesus (D) 416
There is never a day so dreary (G) 286
There Is Power in the Blood (A♭) 595
There Shall Be Showers of Blessing (B♭) 596
There's a battle raging in the heavenly (A♭) 406
There's a call comes ringing o'er (G) 542
There's a Song in the Air (G) 101
There's a sweet and sacred prayer (F) 198
There's a Wideness in God's Mercy (B♭) 274
There's Something About That Name (E♭) 227
There's within my heart a melody (G) 586
They'll Know We Are Christians (f min.) 485
Thine Is the Glory (E♭) 173
This Child We Dedicate to Thee (F) 648
This Is My Father's World (E♭) 31
This is my wonderful story (D) 297
This is my wonderful story (C) 298
This Is the Day (F) 618
This Is the Gospel of Christ (D) 526
Thou Art Worthy (A♭) 70
Thou Didst Leave Thy Throne (D) 108
Thou, my everlasting portion (G) 388
Thou Wilt Keep Him in Perfect Peace (C) 283
Though a million voices choose (f♯ min.) 399
Though I may speak with bravest fire (G) 451
Though the angry surges roll (B♭) 405
Thy Holy Spirit, Lord, Alone (F) 241
Thy Kingdom Come (D) 559
Thy Word (F) 491
'Tis Finished! The Messiah Dies 142
'Tis Midnight, and on Olive's Brow (A♭) 141
'Tis So Sweet to Trust in Jesus (G) 341
To destroy the works of the evil one (D) 526
To God Be the Glory (G) 44
To the Ends of the Earth (A) 556
To the regions beyond I must go (B♭) 518
To those who fear God's holy name (D) 412
Trust and Obey (F) 347
Trusting Jesus (F) 343
Turn Your Eyes upon Jesus (F) 350

U

Under His Wings (C) 355
Use Me Today (F) 513

V

Victory in Jesus (G) 580

W

Watch, ye saints, with eyelids waking (C) 187
We are gathered for Your blessing (B♭) 247
We are one in the Spirit (f min.) 485
We Are Singing, for the Lord Is
Our Light (Siyahamba) (G) 536
We Bless the Name of Christ the Lord (B♭) 641
We Bow Down (D♭) 49
We Bring the Sacrifice of Praise (D) 616
We Choose to Bow (f♯ min.) 399
We Come, O Christ, to You (C) 199
We gather here in Jesus' name (G) 632
We Gather Together (C) 664
We Give Thee but Thine Own (E♭) 498
We have heard the joyful sound (F) 528
We praise Thee, O God, for the Son of Thy love (F) 337
We Praise You, O God, Our Redeemer (C) 58
We Three Kings (e min./G) 109
We Will Glorify (E♭) 211
We're Marching to Zion (F) 375
Were You There (E♭) 137
We've a Story to Tell to the Nations (D) 521
What a fellowship, what a joy divine (A) 357
What a Friend We Have in Jesus (F) 439
What a wonderful change in my life (G) 587
What a Wonderful Savior (D♭) 229
What can wash away my sin (F) 258
What Child Is This? (e min.) 106
What If It Were Today? (C) 188
What Wondrous Love Is This (d min.) 452
When all my labors and trials are o'er (G) 427
When He Cometh (D) 645
When He Shall Come (C) 185
When I saw the cleansing fountain (D) 207
When I Survey the Wondrous Cross (F) 145
When Jesus died on Calvary (F) 336
When Morning Gilds the Skies (B♭) 205
When my life work is ended (G) 424
When peace like a river attendeth my way (C) 352
When the Roll Is Called Up Yonder (G) 421
When the trumpet of the Lord shall sound (G) 421
When upon life's billows you are tempest-tossed (D) 469
When We All Get to Heaven (C) 423
When we walk with the Lord (F) 347
Where He Leads Me (F) 374
Where the Spirit of the Lord Is (D) 243
While by the sheep we watched at night (B♭) 91
While Shepherds Watched Their Flocks (C) 92
Whiter Than Snow (F) 256
Who Is He in Yonder Stall? (A♭) 114

Who Is on the Lord's Side? (B♭) 401
"Whosoever heareth," shout, shout (C) 598
Whosoever Will May Come (C).......................................598
Wonderful Grace of Jesus (C) 270
Wonderful love that rescued me (A♭) 584
Wonderful Peace (G)..282
Wonderful Words of Life (G)...496
Wonderful, Wonderful Jesus (G) 286
Worship the King (B♭)..89
Worship the Lord in the beauty of holiness (D)......................111
Worthy Is the Lamb (HUGG) (D)......................................232
Worthy Is the Lamb (WORTHY IS THE LAMB) (B♭) 234
Worthy, You Are Worthy (E♭) 235
Would you be free from the burden (A♭) 595
Would You Bless Our Homes and Families (D) 655
Would You Live for Jesus? (G) 365

Y

Years I spent in vanity and pride (C)......................................594
Yes, Lord, Yes (F) 348
Yesterday, Today, Forever (G)...121
Yesterday, Today, Forever (arr.) (G)...................................122
You are Lord of creation (D♭)..49
You Are My All in All (F) 214
You are my strength when I am weak (F) 214
You Servants of God, Your Master Proclaim (G)...........532
Your only Son, no sin to hide (C)..150

ISBN 0-87509-981-5

9 780875 099811